Psychology and People: A tutorial text

Antony J. Chapman and
Anthony Gale

First published 1982 by THE BRITISH PSYCHOLOGICAL SOCIETY and THE MACMILLAN PRESS LTD.

Distributed by The Macmillan Press Ltd, London and Basingstoke. Associated companies and representatives throughout the world.

ISBN 0 333 33145 1 (hard cover)
ISBN 0 333 33147 8 (paper cover)

Printed in Great Britain by Wheatons of Exeter

Note: throughout these texts, the masculine pronouns have been used for succinctness and are intended to refer to both females and males.

The conclusions drawn and opinions expressed are those of the authors. They should not be taken to represent the views of the publishers.

Contents

List of contributors

M. Argyle Reader in Social Psychology, University of Oxford.

D. Bannister External scientific staff, Medical Research Council, High Royds Hospital, Ilkley.

H. R. Beech Professor of Clinical Psychology, Withington Hospital, Manchester.

A. T. Carr Principal Lecturer in Clinical Psychology, Plymouth Polytechnic.

A. J. Chapman Senior Lecturer in Applied Psychology, UWIST, Cardiff.

Peter G. Coleman Lecturer in Social Gerontology, University of Southampton.

Philip D. Evans Senior Lecturer in Psychology, North East London Polytechnic.

R. M. Farr Professor of Psychology, University of Glasgow.

D. Fontana Senior Lecturer in Educational Psychology, University College, Cardiff.

B. M. Foss Professor of Psychology, Bedford College, London.

N. Frude Lecturer in Psychology, University College Cardiff.

A. Gale Professor of Psychology, University of Southampton.

Barrie Hopson Director of Counselling and Career Development, University of Leeds.

D. Howitt Lecturer in Psychology, Loughborough University.

P. Kline Reader in Psychometrics, University of Exeter.

D. Legge Assistant Director, North Staffordshire Polytechnic.

Irene Martin Reader in Physiological Psychology, Institute of Psychiatry, London.

I. E. Morley Senior Lecturer in Psychology, University of Warwick, Coventry.

Jim Orford Senior Lecturer, University of Exeter, and Principal Psychologist, Exe Vale Hospital.

R. Payne MRC Senior Research Fellow, University of Sheffield.

W. P. Robinson Professor of Education, University of Bristol.

H. R. Schaffer Professor of Psychology, University of Strathclyde.

D. A. Shapiro MRC Clinical Psychologist, University of Sheffield.

Russell P. Wicks Senior Lecturer, University of Surrey, Guildford.

Preface

This book is designed to meet the needs of a broad spectrum of newcomers to psychology. It provides appropriate material for school pupils preparing for examinations at an advanced level, for first-year students at colleges, polytechnics and universities, and for students preparing for professional examinations in which psychology is part of the syllabus. It is called a 'tutorial text' because each chapter can stand on its own as a basis for group discussion.

As an introductory text the book is novel in conception. It does not profess to outline the full range of psychological enquiry. Instead the coverage is biassed towards topics and issues which hold direct and immediate significance within everyday life and personal experience. The contents were selected in consultation with various groups of people who apply psychology in the course of their work and/or who teach psychology to professional groups: teachers, managers and trade unionists, social workers, careers counsellors, physiotherapists, occupational therapists, speech therapists, doctors and nurses. Thus there are chapters on the family, ageing, the media, social skills and so forth. Within all chapters there is a corresponding bias towards applying existing knowledge in day-to-day living and work environments. Hence, for example, the chapter on learning draws more on human than animal studies, and similarly the chapter on the biological bases of behaviour concentrates on human existence and functioning.

Another distinguishing feature of the book is that at the end of each chapter there are suggestions for practical exercises. These are included because we believe that the applications and potential of psychology are appreciated best by those who themselves are disposed to engage in formal research. In attempting systematic enquiries of the sort formulated here the reader, through adopting the role of experimenter, should acquire a broader and more informed understanding of problems inherent in measuring behaviour and experience. Even when conducted on a small scale, systematic enquiry can help promote a fuller appreciation of psychological theory relating to the individual, to groups and to organizations; it can enable individuals to explore how psychology can be useful at a personal level, revealing, for example, aspects of the individual's aims and purposes

in life, as well as factors influencing that person's attitudes and treatment of other people; and it is an essential
part of psychological training. In the routine course of
their work most professional psychologists, whether 'researchers' or not, have to measure people in one way or
another (e.g. they assess personality, behaviour or experience), and they have to interpret their data in the context
of other evidence and theory. As a beginner in psychology,
it would be unwise for you to attempt any of the exercises
without having first digested the related chapter. Also it
is important to have read chapter 1 by Legge on scientific
method: this will help you understand psychological enquiry
and the ways of thinking inherent in other chapters.

Most readers will have conducted experiments before; for
instance, in biology, physics or chemistry. However, the
psychology experimenter has some special responsibilities
which do not apply in other laboratory-based sciences.
Chemists, for example, do not have to ask permission of
their chemicals before mixing them in a test tube and subjecting them to the flames of a bunsen burner. And when
they finish their experiments they need experience no pangs
of conscience when they cast aside the used chemicals. The
chemist's relationship with experimental material is that of
'I' to 'it'. But those of us who study human subjects must
sustain an 'I-you' relationship; for rules which routinely
apply to interpersonal relationships must still hold true
in our research and professional practice. Thus subjects of
psychological experiments should be asked their permission
to be studied; and they should feel free to withdraw as they
wish. As far as possible experimenters should explain the
purposes of their study to their subjects: this may not
always be practicable before an experiment, but is rarely
impracticable afterwards.

Some of the projects in this book call for subjects to
say things about themselves; for example, they might be
asked to say how they feel in one situation or another. We
must emphasize that the psychologist has no special right to
secure private and personal information from another person
without that person's consent. And even when such consent is
given people may subsequently worry about their responses to
questions and what is thought of them in the light of their
answers: they ask, 'Have I done well?', 'Am I normal?' or
questions which are yet more personal. These must all be
handled in a tactful and sensitive manner. Moreover, the
individual should feel that any information given is treated
with absolute discretion and confidentiality. Where we
believe that specific projects are particularly liable to
create ethical problems, we draw attention to it with a
standard caution, and at the end of the book we have added
the ethical guidelines of the British Psychological Society.
We believe that all students of psychology should familiar-
ize themselves with these guidelines before embarking on
research, because they increase the sensitivity of the
researcher to the need to treat other human beings with

dignity and respect. One reason people study psychology is that they wish to make life 'better' for others. It would be paradoxical if they were to make life difficult for some individuals who help them in the course of their training as psychologists.

We have encouraged our contributors, all of whom are experienced teachers and leading authorities in their respective fields, to break from convention and to restrict their use of references to a minimum. This is because, in their early days of study, students are only occasionally expected to consult a learned journal or specialist text, especially if other subjects are studied concurrently. For those wanting to read more, there are suggestions in annotated readings at the ends of chapters. There the authors draw attention to relatively accessible publications of appropriate levels of difficulty. They have also supplied review questions to help readers organize their material and prepare for examinations.

The companion volumes in this series 'Psychology for Professional Groups' (see p. ii) have been edited by fellow psychologists who have many years of involvement with particular professions. They have selected various combinations of topics from those in the present volume, and they have set those topics in the context of specific professional practice. The authors of chapters in the present volume have also produced more detailed analyses for the series. Elsewhere in the series, therefore, readers of the present volume can find fuller analyses of most topics herein, and they can also find supplementary accounts of how psychology is applied in practice. Further teaching materials, in the form of additional references and class notes, are contained in the tutor manuals prepared for each of the other volumes and available from the British Psychological Society.

The overriding aims of the series are to illustrate how psychology can be applied in professional contexts, how it can improve the skills of practitioners, and how it can increase the practitioners' and students' understanding of themselves.

In devising and developing the series we have had the good fortune to benefit from the advice and support of Dr Halla Beloff, Professor Philip Levy, Mr Allan Sakne and Mr John Winckler. A great burden has been borne by Mrs Gail Sheffield, who with skill, tact and courtesy has managed the production of the series: to her and her colleagues at the BPS headquarters and at the Macmillan Press, we express our thanks.

Antony J. Chapman
UWIST, Cardiff

Anthony Gale
University of Southampton

March 1982

Part one

Observing, Measuring and Understanding Human Behaviour

1

How do you know? Psychology and scientific method
D. Legge

How do you know?

Of all the lessons that one might learn at school, probably
the most important is how to find out. Systematic changes
in the school curriculum and in methods of teaching have
given pupils today arguably the soundest preparation they
have ever had and the best foundation for intellectual
independence.

There is a basic dilemma in education: on the one hand
there is the plethora of facts unearthed and polished by our
predecessors, and on the other is the need to prepare pupils
to find out for themselves and to develop sufficient confidence to question academic authority. It would be a denial
of the principal benefits of a literate culture to withhold
the hard-won knowledge received from earlier generations: we
have the advantage of standing on the shoulders of those who
have gone before. But too great a dependence on received
wisdom could over-emphasize the value of current knowledge,
hiding the real possibility that it is wrong, misunderstood
or out of its relevant context.

The introduction of discovery learning methods in
schools has tended to strike a better balance between these
two sources of knowledge than faced earlier generations of
pupils. In a previous time 'experiment' was used loosely as
a label to refer to a wide variety of practical demonstrations and enquiries. At the worst it was used about practical work that was designed to bring about a particular
specified outcome. If that outcome was not achieved the
'experiment' might even be said to have failed. This is a
travesty. An experiment cannot fail. It may give rise to
unexpected results, it may be poorly designed and the
desired experimental conditions may not be achieved, but it
cannot fail. In contrast, an attempt to demonstrate a
phenomenon can fail. The difference is that the experiment
is a special procedure for finding out. It gives rise to
knowledge. What the knowledge is about depends upon the
design of the experiment.

Discovery learning is a rather slow way of becoming
better informed. It would be many thousands of times quicker
to learn chemistry from textbooks than by repeating centuries of experimentation and building up the same body
of knowledge from one's own painstaking experimentation.
Didactic instruction is undoubtedly quicker, but knowledge

acquired from an authority may be received as if impressed on tablets of stone. It may be depended upon as if it were inviolable and unquestionably reliable. Few scientists have such a view about the original knowledge that they have personally discovered. Truth is a relative concept and the 'facts' of today may be exploded as myths tomorrow. It is important to be just a little sceptical of received wisdom lest it be elevated to the status of dogma. It is important to find out, and it is important to know how you know.

Making a mental model of the world

Few of our school experiences prepare us for a view of science that identifies a reality outside ourselves which we seek to describe by our scientific theories. That reality is not open to us. We have to build a model of it for ourselves, and that model is our scientific knowledge. In general, the model is simpler than reality, and it has the massive advantage that since we have built the model, we can understand it. Reality is a different order of problem. If the model is a sufficiently good one, it will behave like reality. It will give us a way of understanding reality because we understand our model.

For example, Newton developed his celebrated laws of motion. They describe how bodies move in space as a function of the forces bearing upon them. They are precisely formulated as mathematical equations and offer a basis for predicting the movements of physical bodies. They are not, however, correct under all circumstances. In particular they break down at extremes of velocity and distance. But on an earthly and human scale Newton's model is immensely valuable because it works. The model describes closely enough how certain aspects of the world work.

Acquiring knowledge

How do you know? The simplest way is by deduction from a set of assumptions or premises. Provided the assumptions are true and the logic is sound, knowledge flows unremittingly. This is knowledge that depends upon the existence of a developed model that is relevant to the issue. Sometimes such models relate to only part of the real world and we then extend them beyond their domain of relevance and validity at our peril. Scale models offer some assistance to design engineers but only as analogies. It could be disastrous to assume that the load-bearing characteristics of a model bridge would be reflected in comparable scale in the full-grown version.

Another way of finding out is to ask. Asking another person, or his writings, is a way of seeking human authority. The success of this approach depends upon the question being well phrased so that it is understood; and likewise the answer. It also depends upon the questioner choosing an authority who knows the answer! The main problem with this approach is that a critical evaluation of answers can only be attempted where several authorities can be approached. Several versions of the same basic authority should not mislead us into believing that such consensus guarantees truth. Reference to an authority does have one cardinal virtue, however, and that is its convenience and speed. No other way of getting answers can be accomplished so quickly.

Empirical enquiries

The best way of finding out about the real world, however, is to ask a question directly of that world rather than of its interpreters. If you have a question about the motion of moving bodies (like billiard balls) the best way of finding an answer is to study the motion of, say, billiard balls. It is more direct and less likely to be distorted than asking a snooker-player his opinion. It may even be better than asking a physicist. This reference of questions to the world to which they refer is the essence of empiricism. It is the foundation upon which all science is based. Science has as its principal aim the description of the world in sufficient detail that at least it will be possible to predict its behaviour.

The physical sciences were the first to break away from natural philosophy as a methodology developed that allowed these empirical questions to be posed. Chemistry and physics were born. Somewhat later biology established itself as well. At the same time it became clear that there were relatively good ways of asking empirical questions that led to unambiguous answers, and there were also less satisfactory ways.

Causal explanations

A prominent feature of the physical sciences was the success of explanations couched in causal terms. The concept was that a particular act or condition would unerringly be followed by another, much as a billiard ball will move predictably (by Newton's Laws more or less!) when struck by another. The causational concept is a very attractive one because it offers a very compact basis for description, but even more so because it provides an obvious basis for prediction. It also identifies strongly the sort of observation that should be made in order to test the prediction, and hence to test that particular model of the world.

Once a phenomenon of some kind has been identified an obvious first question is 'What causes it?' What set of conditions willl guarantee its occurrence? For example, what are the critical factors which determine photosynthesis? It is fairly obvious that one way of getting an answer to this sort of question is to vary conditions and observe what happens. It would quite quickly become clear that one of the main features of an efficient procedure is the unambiguous determination of the relation between the factor being manipulated (the independent variable) and the factor being observed (the dependent variable).

Attributing effects

Perhaps the strongest, and therefore most sought after, evidence in science is the kind that leads to 'unequivocal attribution of effect': in simpler language, 'we know what caused it'. It establishes that two variables should be considered and connected, perhaps by a causal chain. It may also establish the nature of that connection, perhaps in sufficient detail to admit a mathematical definition of the relationship.

The simplest way of achieving this desirable unequivocal attribution is to demonstrate that introduction of a factor is associated with the appearance of a phenomenon and removal of that factor with its disappearance. If no other factor affects the phenomenon, one would be likely to feel confident in asserting that the factor caused the phenomenon. An investigation in which a factor is carefully manipulated and the effects of such manipulation are carefully monitored is an experiment. The key feature of the experiment is the manipulation of some factor, which must not be left to vary by chance or by association with some other uncontrolled factor. Sometimes the term controlled experiment is used to stress the fact that close control of the conditions of observation is essential. The controlled experiment produces the best evidence there can be, leading to unequivocal attribution of effect.

The importance of the experiment as a method of finding out becomes more obvious when one compares it with other techniques that might be used instead. For example, let us consider the problem of isolating factors that lead to the development of lung cancer. A number of studies of the incidence of lung cancer (and also bronchitis and other chest diseases) revealed that cigarette smokers seemed to be more likely to develop lung cancer than non-smokers. The data were not absolute, of course, so that many smokers died of 'natural causes' without ever developing cancer and some lung cancer victims had never smoked. The next problem is to discover just what this statistical association between smoking and cancer means.

A number of substances are known to be carcinogenic. For example, certain coal tar compounds applied to the skin of mice have been shown to produce tumours. Though in much reduced concentrations, similar compounds are produced in burning tobacco, so the suggestion that tobacco smoke might produce tumours in the respiratory tract is not a far-fetched one. At least some of the intermediate links in a causal chain already exist. On the other hand, the fact that many smokers manage to avoid lung cancer shows that the story is not a very simple one. Smoking is clearly not the only factor and, indeed, it may very well not be the most significant one.

More sophisticated studies have contrasted the morbidity of smokers in rural and urban areas, of different ages and socio-economic groups. There have also been national comparisons. One of the most interesting findings is that smokers who give up the habit have a smaller chance of developing lung cancer than those who do not, though a higher chance than abstainers. This sort of study focusses on smoking and cancer rather than on the general problem of the aetiology of cancer. Decades of studies searching for a single cause have left researchers sceptical of finding such a solution and, instead, the prevailing expectation is that a cluster of factors will together determine the onset of the disease. At most, smoking could be identified as one of those causal factors. Its status might be a major factor, or subsidiary; it might have a primary or a contextual role to play. Either way, if causal, its influence would be relatively direct.

The principal limitation of the studies of associated incidence such as that described above is that one cannot be sure how whatever was observed happened. The effect cannot be unequivocally attributed to particular prior events and conditions. In the case of smoking and cancer the group of smokers differs from the group of non-smokers by more than just the breathing in of tobacco smoke. For instance, they comprise different individuals. This might not be a serious difficulty, provided that the people in one group do not share a common feature other than smoking. Unfortunately, they probably do. Why do the smokers smoke? Is it perhaps because they have some characteristic, no matter whether it be psychological (such as anxiety) or physiological (such as nicotine dependence)? If so, then smokers differ from non-smokers, not only in what they do (that is, smoke) but also in their constitution. Logically we are now incapable of separating two hypotheses about where the association between smoking and cancer comes from. On the one hand is the causal relationship, on the other the possibility that a tendency to smoke is due to some internal characteristic which is also a predetermining factor influencing the development of cancer.

One might argue that this confusion would be removed by observing that smokers who become abstainers have a reduced morbidity. Unfortunately, and this is borne out by the experiences of smokers who attempt to give up, some smokers find it relatively easy to give up, some difficult, and some try but never succeed. This variation between individuals could reflect a variation in the power of the internal factor. A weak factor would allow a smoker to give up easily but would also mean a relatively weak tendency to develop cancer. Studying the morbidity of smokers who become non-smokers voluntarily would tell nothing about the directness of the link between smoking and cancer. Smoking might still be no more than an index of an individual's morbidity.

The only way of settling this question is to gain control of the main variable that has hitherto been left uncontrolled: that is, the question of who smokes. If the experimenter chooses who smokes, instead of allowing the subjects to choose, the act of smoking can be effectively separated from the predilection to smoke. In practice this means either forcing non-smokers to smoke and smokers to stop smoking or both. The decision of who is treated in this way has to be unrelated to any other relevant factor and a random decision is usually found to be the best way of achieving this.

Ethical considerations make it unthinkable to carry out this experiment on human beings. Clearly it would be un-acceptable to force on people a treatment - smoking - that was thought might very well induce a fatal disease. Forcing people to give up a potentially dangerous habit is less of an ethical problem than a problem of practicability. It is doubtful whether sufficient control over other people's lives can be exerted outside a prison or similar institu-tion. Animals have, however, been subjected to enforced smoking and a sufficient proportion have developed tumours to lend very powerful weight to the hypothesis that tobacco smoking is a primary causative agent in the development of lung cancer. It is not a necessary cause, since non-smokers may also develop cancer. Nor is it a sufficient cause because by no means all smokers will succumb. It is, however, a very significant factor, and a very substantial improvement in health could be achieved if tobacco smoking were to become an extinct behaviour pattern.

When experiments may not be used

The logical preference for using experiments to ask ques-tions is, perhaps, an obvious one. The reasons for not using experiments are less obvious in the abstract, although when one is plunged into the actuality of doing research they become overwhelmingly real. We have mentioned one or two reasons in discussing the cancer example above. There are some things that it is generally agreed one should not do to one's fellow man. There are ethical constraints to our research. This difficulty is an intrinsic feature of social science or medical research, but it very seldom impinges upon research in the physical sciences. In general, we have little compunction about subjecting concrete beams to sufficient forces to destroy them, or stretching wires to the point that they cannot recover their previous form. Inanimate subject matter does not require much, if any, consideration. We see below that there are other advantages, too, that physical scientists enjoy and, perhaps, sometimes take for granted.

In the cancer example we saw how the ethical boundaries which would have prevented an experiment being carried out were circumvented by using animal subjects in place of the ethically unacceptable human ones. This is a partial solu-tion in some instances. The limiting circumstances are, first, that there are ethical reservations about using ani-mals (and there is increasing concern about the extent to which Man exploits sub-human species who have generally no way of lodging their objections) and, second, whether they really possess those essential characteristics which would permit the results of the experiment to be generalized to human beings. Animals may be invaluable in testing new drugs and pharmaceutical preparations that are intended for use with humans. The bulk of animal experiments are toxicity studies on new chemicals. It is reasonable to expect that substances which poison animals will probably poison Man, and vice versa. On the other hand, an experiment concerning feelings will inevitably have to be conducted on human subjects. Even if animals have feelings, they do not have the power to communicate them and this severely limits their usefulness. In consequence, it may be that no experiment could be done at all, in which case the only source of knowledge would be non-experimental.

In practice, surrendering the use of the experiment is seldom the result of ethical constraints. More often it is simply because the control necessary to do an experiment is not available. The resources required may exceed those that can be afforded. In some cases control is lacking on logical grounds. The missing resource may be knowledge rather than cash.

The classic example of resource limitations prohibiting experimentation is in astronomy. Observing the heavens from earth can lead to a plethora of hypotheses about the universe, its contents and how they relate to one another. Theories of planetary motion would be easiest to test if one could carry out experiments by, for example, moving planets about, extracting them from their orbits and so on. Failing the power to do that, astronomers have had to use other means of finding out. A considerable portion of social science research is like astronomy. The researcher lacks the power necessary to manipulate variables to the extent necessary to carry out an experiment.

The third main reason for not carrying out an experiment stems from the conclusions one would want to draw from its results. In order to effect the degree of control necessary to achieve experimental manipulations and make precise, preferably quantifiable, measurements, laboratory conditions are often preferred. In the physical sciences this is nothing but an advantage. It is of no concern to a concrete beam whether it is subjected to forces in a laboratory or in a tower block of flats. It is the forces, its composition and age, the prevailing temperature, humidity and to some extent, its past history that determines its behaviour.

Human subjects play a rather more active role in experiments than do concrete beams and they tend to be very well aware of the difference between the reality of their normal life and the unreality of the 'games' which they are invited to play in laboratories. Even without that awareness of context, it may be that the version of a task which is devised and enacted in the laboratory is critically different from the real-life situation it was designed to simulate. For example, one cannot be absolutely certain that the speed of reaction in a real-life emergency which arrives without warning will be accurately mimicked by a reaction-time experiment conducted in a laboratory where the 'unexpectedness' of the emergency is at best relative. The problem is to determine the 'ecological validity' of the simulation. It is really the old problem of what degree of generalization is permissible from the observations that have been made. Essentially the same questions have to be asked about the concrete beam. Its characteristics in a warm, dry laboratory might be radically different at the bottom of the North Sea. But it is generally true that there is more likely to be limited generalization in the social sciences.

This problem has led many researchers to maximize the reality value of their research situations and to minimize the use of laboratory-based research. They feel that the potentially misleading quality of laboratory research is so serious a problem that they prefer to make their observations in more realistic circumstances, accepting the severe restrictions placed on the manipulation and control of experimental variables. It is a dilemma. Should one conduct relatively well-controlled experiments (which allow quite precise attribution of experimental effects) but which have limited relevance to natural behaviour, or use real-life (ecologically valid) situations which frequently leave considerable uncertainty about what induced whatever was observed? There is likely to be room for both kinds of research, and there are probably persisting differences in preference between researchers. This underlines the importance of discovering the strengths and weaknesses of the non-experimental and quasi-experimental methods that have been devised as alternatives to experiments.

Alternatives to experimentation

One of the great advantages in doing experiments is that the conditions under which the observations are made are very carefully designed to provide information about particular questions. In other circumstances one has to make the most of whatever information is available. Returning for a moment to the example of astronomy, researchers only have available to them the options of looking in different directions at different times. Their difficulty is to relate the information gathered to their developing model of the universe. In these circumstances, since there is no way of knowing what particular aspects of what could be recorded might be relevant at some time and from some particular perspective, there is considerable pressure to record observations in as objective a way as possible. There is also a premium on precise description.

Non-experimental studies are usually either descriptive or correlational. In the former an attempt is made to record what is or what happens, without (necessarily) giving reasons or accounts of what causes what. Studies of this kind are potentially of immense value since they can define the general arena in which detailed accounts of what leads to what must be placed. They are also useful in relating the development of theoretical models to the reality of a life-situation. They are, however, very difficult to do because of the virtually infinite variety of things that could be relevant to record, so that even the most objective recorder would find it necessary to make some selection. The appropriateness of that selection is what makes the results of such a study valuable or worthless.

Correlational studies come in various forms, varying as to the restrictiveness of the set of variables that can be intercorrelated after the data have been collected. In essence, correlation is a statistical technique which measures the closeness of an association between two or more variables. Associations may vary from perfect correlation in which any change in one variable is reflected by a change in the other, to a much looser relationship marked by a mere tendency for changes in the two variables to go together. Correlational studies may involve selecting what to observe, and that is certainly the case when specialized instruments are used to make the observations (mental tests, for example), but they do not intervene in ways that are necessary in an experiment which depends upon manipulating and controlling variables, as well as accurate observation and recording. Studies of this kind can reveal what variables tend to change together, but they cannot reveal why. As we saw above, statistical studies of the incidence of lung cancer and smoking reveal that the disease is significantly correlated with the behaviour. They cannot lead to the inescapable conclusion that the one causes the other. If two variables are causally related there must be a correlation between them, but the reverse is not true.

One-subject studies

A particularly difficult set of problems surrounds asking questions about a particular individual. For example, if a young man visits a hypnotist before taking a driving test and subseqently passes it, what can be said about the effect of the hypnotist's treatment on his success? The answer is very little, with confidence. Clearly the hypnotist may have helped: there are several reports available of people believing that their test anxiety was reduced in this way. But our particular young man may not be exactly the same as other people so grouping him together with them may not be appropriate. One basic difficulty is that we cannot set up a control. We cannot discover how our examinee would have fared without hypnotism. Once he has taken the test and passed it, no fair comparison could be made by subsequently testing him again without a visit to his hypnotist. Though in some studies it makes sense to use a subject as his own control, in many others it does not. The subject is likely to be affected to a significant extent by one experience, so that he is not going to behave in a comparable manner if that experience is repeated. From the research point of view this raises almost insurmountable problems. There is no way in which one can achieve an unequivocal picture of what causes particular individuals to behave in particular ways, without either assuming that their individual behaviour patterns will be very similar to those of other people, or that they will be unaffected by their experiences. Neither assumption will ever be wholly true, and the advances that can be made in understanding those individuals will depend upon how true these assumptions are for particular aspects of their behaviour.

On theories and data

One of the reasons why it is important to be careful about collecting data in attempting to find out why something happens is that of the difficulty in spotting when an answer is a true one.

Many people have been taught that one of the most important aspects of science is that its theories are disciplined by data. They are kept in touch with the real world they seek to describe. If the theory says one thing and the data say something else, then the theory must change to accommodate the data.

Two schemes of investigation have been described as representing two distinct ideals. Inductive research involves making unselected observations of phenomena followed by ordering and categorizing them, from which a theoretical structure may emerge. Linnaeus' development of a taxonomy of plants is often held up as an example of inductive research. The alternative scheme is hypothetico-deductive research which progresses by a series of two-phase investigations. The first step involves establishing an hypothesis. Following that, a prediction is derived which can be tested directly against data collected for the purpose.

It is most unlikely that either of these schemes is actually used in its pure form. It is inconceivable that Linnaeus never developed any ideas about relevant dimensions of his taxonomy until all the observations had been made, and that his later observations were uninfluenced by his earlier ones. Likewise, the hypothetico-deductive method cannot be used unless there is a pre-existing theory, which is likely to have benefitted at some stage from random, if not comprehensive, unselected observations of phenomena under investigation.

This contrast focusses on the relative roles of theory and data. Ideally theory suggests relevant observations. Data indicate how satisfactory existing theories are and may point to how they should be modified to become more satisfactory. Having got an enquiry off the ground, progress ought to be orderly. In fact it very seldom is. The most basic problem is that human nature seems to abhor a theoretical vacuum. Almost any theory is better than none at all. Perhaps this explains why magical explanations are preferred to a simple state of ignorance. It is almost as if man needs to have the sense of power that 'knowing how it works' confers. Whatever the reason, however, an embarrassing piece of data is unlikely to result in the only available theory being jettisoned. If there are two or more competing theories, however, data appear to be more powerful and the relative credibility of different theories may very well be adjusted accordingly.

The unexpected weakness of data is not completely accounted for by the need to maintain at least one theory. No theory is likely to survive when faced with strong data that are incompatible with it. The problem is that many data are just not that strong. There is residual doubt about just what the observations from a particular study really mean for that particular theory.

This undesirable state of affairs can arise most easily if the theory has been only poorly defined and, especially, if the rules of correspondence between the elements of the theory and observable aspects of the real world have been omitted or only ambiguously specified. But even when the rules of correspondence are clear, the status of data can be diminished if the data collection scheme has been a rather haphazard one, and particularly if the attribution of any effects observed remains equivocal. A fair conclusion is that a poorly defined theory that seems to explain phenomena which otherwise defy explanation, and an area of enquiry that precludes, or makes very difficult, experimental research, has a very good chance of surviving for a long time irrespective of its actual validity.

Progress without experiment

Much of the foregoing might seem to be pointing in a rather unpromising direction. In order to establish unambiguously that a particular variable reliably produces a particular effect, the experiment is not merely the best available research design; it is irreplaceable. As the advertisements used to say, 'accept no imitations'. However, it would be wrong to conclude that experiments are inevitably effective, as our brief consideration of the relationship between theory and data reveals.

Research is basically a slow business in which researchers inch towards some better appreciation of the world they study. They develop their models, making them increasingly sophisticated as they make progress. The barriers to progress are many and varied including their own mental limitations and the pressures upon them from the prevailing intellectual atmosphere. Experiments can be done which shed no light at all on the question at issue. Many experiments promise more than they deliver once the post mortem has been completed. In this climate of imperfection the fact that experiment may be precluded is disappointing but not, relatively speaking, a disaster.

The development of models of the world is not as neat and tidy a process as, perhaps, we should wish. The prevailing model is the one that seems best able to cope with all that is known (or, better, all that we believe) to be true about the phenomenon we seek to understand. Provided that enough different snapshots from different vantage points can be correlated it is quite possible that ultimately the same model will arise as would have come from direct experimentation. It will almost certainly take longer, but the same end-point may well be reached. This optimism is supported by the progress made in astronomy where experimentation is virtually prohibited. Since the system under investigation is in motion, successive observations provided different but complementary information. As a result Man has managed to navigate unmanned space ships to the outer parts of the solar system and successfully explore the moon.

In many areas of social science, experimentation is either very difficult or unlikely to provide what is needed. In such circumstances correlational studies and descriptive studies of one kind or another are the only sources of information available. Perhaps this will mean slow progress, but there is little doubt that our curiosity about ourselves will be a sufficient motive for the questions to be pressed, and eventually useful answers will emerge. It matters not at all that they should emerge untidily, only that they turn out to be effective aids to our understanding.

Research and common sense

Doing research is essentially detective work, but often with an all-important difference. Police detectives cannot ask questions in the same way that the experimental scientist can. Instead they have to hope that the (probably incomplete) set of data which they collect will distinguish between the competing theories they hold about the crime under investigation. Some science is also like that, and social science especially. Maybe scientists have one major advantage in that their antagonist is nature, which may not be co-operative but is most unlikely deliberately to confuse and deceive.

Just as police detective work has a list of 'dos and don'ts' to guide it into a successful path, so there are good and bad ways of doing science. Most of this chapter is about using common sense in finding out. There are no magical methods and the main thing to remember is to avoid ambiguity. Before starting an investigation, be absolutely clear about what the question is. It will only get more confused later if it is not clear at the start. The study itself needs to yield data that can be interpreted. Ideally, any effect observed should be unequivocally attributable to a particular variable or set or variables. Whatever scheme seems likely to achieve these goals will be worth using. A scheme that will not may well not be worth the effort of putting into practice.

Unfortunately, while much of the physical sciences allow these guidelines to be followed closely, the social sciences are more difficult to tame. Unequivocal attribution is difficult to ensure, and easiest when dealing with laboratory behaviour: a version of behaviour which may not be identical with that in real life. Often compromise is necessary, and progress is painfully slow.

Statistics

There are relatively few special tools available to the researcher corresponding to the finger-print kit of the detective. One of the principal ones, however, is statistics, a branch of mathematics concerned with the determination of the likelihood of events occurring. It is a particularly useful tool in those areas of study which are not very clearly determinate. It was originally developed to help analyse various questions in agriculture which are made difficult by the fact that plant growth is affected by a vast number of factors, some intrinsic to the plant, some extrinsic. This situation is not unlike that in human behaviour and it is no surprise that psychologists have taken up statistics enthusiastically and developed specialized procedures for their own use.

The main advantages that statistics confer are schemes for summarizing data and making them easier to remember and communicate, schemes for measuring the relatedness of two or more variables (correlation) and schemes for aiding decision making. They are important for deciding whether any effects have been netted in the data, and that is a precondition for determining what caused them. In conjunction with experiments, statistics make it possible to face psychological research with some confidence. However, the techniques, though not particularly difficulty to use, are specialist and study in some depth is recommended before trying to use them. It is best to practise under the guidance of an expert first, before launching oneself into research.

Further study

It has only been possible to mention a few basic ideas in this brief introduction to psychological discovery. The interested reader will, we hope, feel an urge to plunge deeper into the jungle. There are an ever-increasing number of texts to guide the way. The next stage in that journey may be aided by three slim volumes out of the Essential Psychology series published by Methuen. They are:

Gardiner, J.M. and Kaminska, K. (1975)
First Experiments in Psychology. London: Methuen.
Legge, D. (1975)
An Introduction to Psychological Science. London: Methuen.
Miller, S.H. (1976)
Experimental Design and Statistics. London: Methuen.

Questions

1. Discuss different ways of determining the age of a horse. Consider analogues in psychology.
2. Write a short essay on the function of theory in psychological research.
3. What are the principal advantages of experimental enquiries? Are there any disadvantages?
4. 'One can never step into the same stream twice.' Discuss in relation to the problems of conducting psychological research.

5. Statistics developed in order to clarify the results of agricultural research. Why should they have been applied so enthusiastically to psychological research?
6. Discuss how theoretical generalizations might inform enquiries about a particular individual.
7. The two main methods of obtaining data about the development of processes and behaviour are longitudinal and cross-sectional. Discuss the advantages and disadvantages of each.
8. 'There are lies, damn lies and statistics.' Are there?
9. Some researchers argue that if the research method and the task for the subject have been properly designed, statistics are redundant. What does that say for the widespread use of statistics in psychology?
10. Discuss the limitations imposed on research by the exclusive use of correlational methods.
characteristics.

Annotated reading

Cook, T.D. and Campbell, D.T. (1979) Quasi-experimentation: Design and analysis issues for field settings. Chicago: Rand McNally.
  Describes techniques that may be available when experiments cannot be used.

Barber, T.X. (1977) Pitfalls in Human Research. Oxford: Pergamon Press.

Jung, J. (1971) The Experimenter's Dilemma. New York: Harper & Row.
  Some books have analysed the sources of difficulty in finding out; these are two useful ones.

Meddis, R. (1973) Elementary Analysis of Variance for the Behavioural Sciences. London: McGraw-Hill.
  The student can acquire more advanced treatments for complex experiments from this text.

Miller, S.H. (1976) Experimental Design and Statistics. London: Methuen.

Robson, C. (1973) Experiment, Design and Statistics in Psychology. Harmondsworth: Penguin.
  Two relatively simple and accessible paperback volumes which act as starter texts in psychological statistics.

Siegel, S. (1956) Nonparametric Statistics for the Behavioral Sciences. New York: McGraw-Hill.
  The 'bible' of the non-parametric techniques that has proved indispensable to psychologists.

Snodgrass, J.G. (1977) The Numbers Game: Statistics for psychology. London: Oxford University Press.
  The student who masters the first two may want to go

further. This should provide some help to that progress.

Acknowledgements

I am most grateful for the assistance received from Dr Hilary Klee who offered much constructive criticism and Ms Christine Harrison who painstakingly translated my early manuscript into a readable form.

Postscript

Each of the chapters which follows has a set of exercises for you to carry out. Before you tackle any of them read through David Legge's list of simulated research projects. Each project begins with a statement; David Legge then thinks aloud and shows how an experienced researcher considers different ways of handling a research problem. Can the assertion made in the statement be turned into a research project? Or is the problem it poses quite unmanageable?

Exercises

Although there is really no substitute for a good practical course in which various research techniques can be tried out, 'dry run' exercises can still be very valuable. In fact, real research programmes should be preceded by imaginary programmes in which the researcher thinks through the planned research. Real research can be very expensive, so it is a good idea to make extensive use of simulation. The analyses below are stimuli for such mental rather than operational research. Try to anticipate the results of an enquiry to clarify each of the ten following questions, issues and assertions:

A woman's place is in the home
What does this old saying mean? Is it a normative statement (about 'should' and 'ought') or is it an empirical statement guiding the searcher-after women to likely sites of discovery? Since psychology is an empirical science some version of the latter is preferable. The statement may be considered directly or it may be taken at one remove. The latter leads to an enquiry not about the assertion itself but, for example, about the people who believe or make it or its influence on people's beliefs and actions. Evidently many different studies could be undertaken as legitimate responses to this title, and equally clearly different studies will lead to different conclusions and inform different underlying questions. Perhaps the most obvious version to study is the direct assertion. This might mean several things. For example: (i) women are better suited to the domestic environment fulfilling domestic roles, in contrast, of course, with men who are granted wider scope including both home and non-home environments; (ii) women are better suited for the role of teacher of infants and children will develop quicker and more satisfactorily in a

home environment presided over by a 'full-time mother' (such an arrangement is jeopardized if women are invited or pressed to play major roles outside as well as inside the home); and (iii) women are incompetent in social, economic and political affairs and therefore need to be restricted to the home as an 'asylum' or place of safety.

The whole area of women's roles, rights and opportunities can be very emotionally provocative. It is easy for the issues to be equated to those surrounding the abolition of slavery and, of course, men are cast in the role of enslavers and slave-traders. If a dispassionate evaluation of the assertion is to be made it is essential for an objective perspective to be adopted. Failure to do so will encourage the development of polemic rather than science. (NB: perhaps one of the major problems in psychological discovery arises from the fact that human researchers all too easily identify with their human subjects. As in many disciplines getting too close to the problem may inhibit discovery because alternative viewpoints are not available and the total context is not visible.)

As an example let us take (i) above as a possible interpretation of the assertion and consider an enquiry that would throw light on it. One approach would be to carry out a study of men and women and contrast their performances of comparable tasks. A survey would immediately reveal that very few men are dedicated to a 'housewife' role, though many women are. Likewise very few men are acting as full-time child care-givers. Though a very considerable proportion of women are in paid employment, it is much lower than the proportion of men and more likely to be less than full-time. More working women seem to be discharging more multiple-role responsibilities (for example, bread-winner, lover, cook and mother, etc.) than are men. In general women seem to be less likely to be promoted into positions of management responsibility than men. This is most marked in mixed occupational groups in which promotion might make men subordinate.

Do these data help? It is not a bit newsworthy that training and practice improve skills. One needs opportunity for both and then a further opportunity to demonstrate one's skills. Society may have effectively stifled certain kinds of development and have channelled and restricted others. In general men are poor performers in the kitchen, at least in terms of the creative and productive activities like cooking. Yet most top chefs are men, which at least shows that possession of a Y-chromosome does not ensure that one's soufflés fail! It may be changing now but today's adults were mainly socialized into a world that practised many varieties of divisions of labour. There were men's and women's jobs and one did not infringe the demarcation boundaries.

A study of what men and women are actually doing bears witness to just that; it does not say why these patterns might be found, and that is probably the main underlying question we should wish to answer. The problem is that equality of performance could be lacking because of lack of equality of opportunity. However, it might also be because there are genuine sex differences.

It is clear that no simple survey will establish one hypothesis without question. It would, however, throw up sufficient unconventional cases to show that while there could be genuine sex differences of an average kind, no hard cut-off between the sexes exists. Some women are as 'successful' as the 'best' men, and some men have been very successful in the 'mothering' role traditionally made the exclusive province of women.

Because this is a real question, it cannot be made easier to solve by restating it in a simpler form. It should not be overlooked that real questions may have to go unanswered if we are not yet ready to answer them.

The child is father to the man
Like many sayings this one gets its impact from its essentially counter-intuitive nature. Everyone knows that the man has to be the father to the child: the facts of life say so! So how can the reverse be true?

Fathers have up to three relationships with children: predecessor, determiner, and protector. The child precedes the man temporally. The child is rarely in a position to act as a protector of the man by virtue of relative size, vigour and potency. The question of determination is not so clear cut. The reproduction cycle ensures that fathers precede sons but the growth cycle demands that men shall previously have been children. In the sense of precedence, then, the saying is true, and not particularly illuminating.

The determination question is the one that should engage psychologists. In some ways the question is trivial and the answer self-evident. For example, we are aware that most of our current skills and knowledge are the products of past experience and training. We may possess some inherited characteristics but they are likely to be in the form of potential for development as soon as one considers attributes more complex than shapes of noses and 'wired in' behaviour patterns like facial expression and walking. This means that, a priori, one would expect to find relatively few manifest characteristics which are unaffected by earlier experience.

These considerations can be turned round, however, to ask about the immunity of our potential from the effects of experience. Is our personality essentially determined by the particular chromosomal structure we inherited through the genetic lottery of reproduction? Or, to take the opposite posture, are we the product of the myriad forces and influences that bombard us from the moment of conception onwards? Initially the dominant influence is the non-nuclear part of the ovum that has been fertilized by our father's sperm. Later the intra-uterine environment provided by our mother assumes the dominant role. After birth, influences multiply initially in the family but soon through inter-action with a wider world. It would be no surprise to find that such a plethora of influences should have lasting effects. The more precise question is what influences produce which effects.

The initial saying can be accepted as true, at least in particular circumstances. From it grow more interesting questions that are phrased more precisely and are aimed at disentangling the relative influences of heredity and en-vironment on a range of psychological attributes that is so large it may seem to be limitless.

This question, sometimes called the 'nature-nurture' question, has engaged psychologists for many decades. This may be partly because of an intrinsic motive to discover the answers to unanswered questions. It may also be because ac-tion could follow from discovering an unequivocal answer. For example, if it is found that intellectual capacity is unaffected by educational opportunity and environmental enrichment, it would be unnecessary to bother too much about the educational system provided that it produces a few 'high-flyers'. Conversely, if single parenting is shown to produce maladjusted adults it would be desirable to make available to single-parent families some kind of surrogate parent system to remedy the deprivation that has been identified.

Setting up an enquiry in this area clearly requires that a precise question be posed before any empirical work can be carried out. The main point is to define the psychological attribute in question and, preferably at the same time, how it is manifested and observed or measured.

The first problem will be to define unambiguously the subject of the enquiry: just what psychological attribute is to be studied? The second problem follows hard upon its heels and may not be solved just by evolving a clear defini-tion. There needs to be an explicit statement about how the attribute will be recorded. This is really an operational definition of that attribute. One of the main reasons for being very careful at this stage is that the relationship between the behaviour that is recorded and the attribute of interest may not be direct and obvious. Instead the rela-tionship may depend upon a number of assumptions that could themselves be challenged and made the subject of independent enquiries. If the attribute in question is, for example, emotional maturity, there must be a statement of the ob-servable conditions which are deemed to be evidence of emotional maturity (or its absence).

The next problem would be to discover a way of relating adult emotional maturity to pre-adult circumstances. Unless the question is refined it is unanswerable in a research project of realistic proportions. There need to be at least some hypotheses about what to look out for. Let us simplify the question by asserting one; for example, that single parenting delays the development of emotional maturity. This step is a very important one because it narrows down the range of influences that are to be considered. It does not,

however, focus very precisely because it fails to identify
the particular aspect of single-parenting that might be
influential. On the other hand, the question is narrow
enough to ask in a sensible way.

Several schemes could be considered as ways of collecting relevant data. At one extreme one could ask the opinion
of a number of judges, at the other one could design an
empirical study that would seek to quantify the relationship
between single parenting and emotional maturity. The former
mode of enquiry is obviously vulnerable to the prejudice of
the judges and there is no obvious way of correcting for it.
The latter scheme would be more attractive but it highlights
the dependence of the study on the assessment of emotional
maturity. It is clearly important that a scheme as objective
as possible be devised to avoid the possibility that the
investigator may influence the assessment and so influence
the relationship with the early care variable.

Clearly the study will not be an experimental one. It
would be unacceptable to subject children to planned deprivation in order to test an hypothesis about its effects.
Observing the association between naturally occurring deprivation and adult characteristics is free from such ethical
constraints and would offer useful information. It will be
necessary to decide whether the study is to concentrate on
deprivation and relate emotional maturity to it, or vice
versa, selecting more or less mature individuals and then
seeking to discover the conditions in which they were
raised. The former enquiry could be done as a longitudinal
study, waiting to see how children turn out as adults. Such
studies are unpopular for several reasons but particularly
because of the immensely long time they take to complete.

However the study is finally done, and even assuming
that there are no major snags in assessing degrees of
emotional maturity (and there will be!) or determining the
nature of the home conditions, the conclusions that the
study will allow must be limited. The essential nature of
a correlational study like this precludes logically the
conclusion that deprivation causes reduced, delayed or
retarded emotional maturity. It may be that it does but the
best this kind of study can do is to raise one's confidence
in the truth of the hypothesis. If it is a very extensive
study perhaps the rise in confidence will be very considerable.

Spare the rod and spoil the child

A pithy saying that purports to justify the use of corporal
punishment on children. The crucial word to define before
getting down to seeing how to test the validity of the
saying is 'spoil'.

'Spoil' is probably used here to mean to alter in an
undesirable way, probably irreversibly. The usage is then
similar to that in other contexts such as 'the concrete was
spoilt by adding too much aggregate', or 'the cake was
spoilt by using eggs that were not fresh'.

However, this simplistic interpretation rapidly leads to a highly contentious deduction. Beating children is intrinsically good for them regardless of their behaviour. There may be a view that suffering, and particularly physical suffering, is an important precondition to growing up. It might be justified, for example, by arguing that it is only through physical pain that one comes to learn certain characteristics of oneself and maturity cannot arrive in advance of extensive self-knowledge.

An alternative, and more sophisticated interpretation, is that physical punishment for misdemeanours is 'good' for the development of children rather than physical suffering per se. A hard-line version of this would be to distinguish physical punishment from other forms of punishment such as restriction of liberties, fines and additional duties. A softer interpretation would distinguish between punishment (the application of events and experiences normally avoided and escaped from) and the withholding of rewards such as the withdrawal of privileges, absence of praise, and so on.

Designing an appropriate study will obviously be dependent upon which particular interpretation of the saying is adopted. We will assume that it is physical punishment that is supposed to be critical for optimal development of children.

Having arrived at an interpretation of the meaning of 'spare the rod', it is now necessary to discover an operational definition of 'spoil the child'. Do spoilt children have recognizable characteristics? If so, what are they? Can one positively identify an unspoilt child? The first problem is to find out what people mean by this term. It cannot be discovered simply by analysis. Once a moderate size sample of people are invited to say what they mean by 'spoil' when applied to children, it will probably be found that there is not a consensus which will justify one particular meaning. Equivocality here must make the basic study very much more difficult to undertake.

Supposing that a particular meaning has been selected, there is now the problem of assessing and recording the 'spoiling', preferably in terms of its degree. One must be realistic and anticipate that whatever instrument is chosen or devised to do this will be imperfect and substantially less than perfectly reliable.

Naturally it is not ethically acceptable to carry out a longitudinal experimental study in which randomly chosen children are subjected to physical punishment and non-physical punishment regimes respectively. Instead the researcher will have to make use of data that arise simply because both regimes are still used. It is a serious problem that the communities and social groups which use physical punishment differ in many ways from those which do not. It will be very difficult to pin down the actual factors that were responsible for any differences between the psychological properties of the two groups of subjects.

One may wonder whether this may be a profitable question to ask.

Yellow is clearly a mixture of green and blue
This assertion recalls the debate that sometimes bordered on
the acrimonious around the turn of the century and sought to
determine the nature of sensation.

Some hues seem to be fundamental in nature and provide
the basis for making other, derived colours. For example,
there are those primary colours which painters can use to
make any other colours they want simply by varying the
proportions in the mixture.

This question is made more complex by the fact that the
rules governing the mixing of lights are different from
those governing the mixing of paints. This is not surprising
perhaps when one remembers that the light reflected by a
paint is, say, red because the paint absorbs all other light
wavelengths. A judicious mixture of coloured lights will
produce white (or grey if the amount of light energy is not
too high); this is the result of adding lights together
until all the wavelengths in the visible spectrum are
represented in their (approximately) correct proportions.
However, putting paints together will tend to reduce the
range of reflected light, not increase it, and the tendency
will be to produce a a mixture that will be nearer black
than white.

The essence of the question concerns the nature of yellow. Is it a fundamental, primary colour or is it a mixture
of, for example, green and blue? But the question is not one
about physics; it concerns how we react to coloured light
stimuli and how they appear to us.

Early enquiries based on the use of introspection sought
to discover the nature of sensation by internal interrogation of consciousness. In this case one can imagine exploring how one feels the sensation yellow. Not, perhaps, a very
rewarding exercise. Later, more indirect methods were
developed.

It is the case that exploring the sensitivity of the
retina (the back of the eyeball) to small coloured stimuli
presented to controlled positions on the retina reveals some
very interesting and surprising data. For example, the area
of the retina which is sensitive to colour is confined to
the central region and is very much smaller than the area
that responds to black and white stimulation. Furthermore,
the area sensitive to red is not coterminous with that
sensitive to green, although both are appreciably smaller
than that sensitive to blue. The yellow-sensitive area is
intermediate.

Another relevant observation is the phenomenon of
successive contrast. Staring at a red square for a little
while and then transferring one's gaze to a grey screen
produces the illusion of seeing a green square. Likewise
yellow and blue are complementary and a yellow square will
appear after staring at a blue one.

These kinds of observations reveal that there are
complex relationships between stimuli of different wavelengths and that mixtures of them give rise to some unexpected sensations. The relationships between, in this

case, yellow, blue and green are not simple ones, and even
if the assertion above is wrong there are many questions to
answer about them.

'I don't know anything about art but I knows what I likes'

This spoof question is used to imply that an artistically
untutored person can still make valid and reliable aesthetic
judgements based, perhaps wholly, on some kind of hedonic
dimension.

There are, of course, ways in which the statement can
be both true and false. It is probably bordering on the
impossible to be completely ignorant of art. Painting and
sculpture are the two most common visual arts, music the
aural art. Theatre, opera and cinema involve mixtures of
visual, aural and linguistic art forms.

Our environment is packed with 'artistic' impact.
Language is an all pervading experience and, at least for
sighted people, both natural and built environments assail
us continually. Musical stimuli are commonly experienced
and, in some sub-cultures, are an essential if not life-
dependent part of one's aural environment. It is exceedingly
unlikely that an adult could become so without having experienced a massive range of artistic stimulation. In that
sense no one can be ignorant. However, the person's knowledge may very well not be codified in the way that it is
for a trained painter or musician.

Nevertheless, there is a question about whether people
do know what they like. For this to be true one would expect
people to be consistent in making aesthetic judgements; and
for the whole statement to be true one must assert that
consistent judgements can be made without prior experience
or training. This seems to be unlikely. The phenomenon of
fashion indicates that aesthetic judgements are unstable and
subject to manipulation. The concept of an 'acquired taste',
be it for beer or Bach, indicates that aesthetic appreciation can be tutored.

A starting point in submitting this question to empirical enquiry might be to investigate subjects' abilities to
discriminate and make judgements about stimuli of varying
degrees of unfamiliarity. Clearly a basic problem to overcome is that of defining sufficient unfamiliar stimuli. It
may be sensible to use aural stimuli since we seem to have
adopted a rather less elaborate musical environment than,
say, oriental traditions. One may show that practice aug-
ments ability to make auditory discriminations and therefore
make judgements more reliable.

More sophisticated questions hinge on social variables
perhaps, rather more than neutral experience. It is arguable
whether people would develop a taste for beer were it not
for the social significance of beer-drinking. Berg and
Stockhausen are composers with a solid following but their
fans may have had to work at developing their appreciation.
However, change does take place either semi-spontaneously,
as in the cyclic variation of fashion, or deliberately

following a prolonged course of study. There are many interesting questions that could be framed.

Actually carrying out relevant studies is not easy in this area. Basic studies depend upon assessing whether people can make reliable judgements; and their degree of reliability has to be assessed quantitatively. The effects of neutral experience could be examined in an experiment. Studying fashion and the other more complex relationships is more difficult and it would not normally be practicable to mount an experiment. Instead it would be necessary to make a series of careful observations, sampling opinions and carrying out carefully prepared interviews. This will not allow unequivocal conclusions to be reached quickly but it will allow some light to be shed on a fascinating topic.

Discovery learning methods have resulted in our children becoming more intelligent

The first issue in addressing this assertion is to determine exactly what is meant by 'intelligent'. The other key concept is 'discovery learning'. Once these two have been sorted out conceptually and adequate definitions agreed it is an empirical question to discover whether the one has affected the other.

Speaking generally, we use 'intelligent' as an adjective describing behaviour to mean effective, successful, with minimum fuss and use of energy and with reasonable speed. When applied to individual people the word is usually used to convey a view about their capacities. It then tends to mean not only capable of acting intelligently; it also means relatively quick to learn and knowledgeable.

Psychologists have for more than half a century developed special tests of intelligence designed to assess a person's capacity and potential quantitatively. Intelligence tests, though far from perfect, are amongst the most sophisticated and reliable sorts of psychological test. Several different kinds are available, many dependent upon the use of words, but some non-verbal intelligence tests have also been developed. The existence of instruments for quantifying intelligence is clearly a major asset in determining whether any change has taken place, regardless of its cause.

The form of the question makes it necessary to mount a retrospective study. This is always much more difficult than setting up an investigation to be carried out in the future. For example, when one has control over the project one can choose what tests to do, when, where and on how many subjects. A retrospective study only permits a choice of tests to apply now: there is no opportunity of choosing how to assess the subjects before they had experienced particular educational processes.

Suppose Test A was routinely used to assess children in a particular education authority. Over the years primary education has changed so that teachers have become less didactic in style and children have been encouraged to find ways of finding out for themselves. One approach to the question would be to compare the test scores achieved by children of the same chronological age nowadays with scores attained 30 years ago (assuming that such a date precedes the introduction of discovery learning methods). The assertion we are testing would be supported by data showing that test scores are higher now than they used to be. Unfortunately such a result does not logically lead to that exclusive conclusion. Other extraneous factors might affect scores on Test A. For example, the test might assume that particular knowledge was so rare that only very intelligent people acquired it in 1950. Thirty years later, however, it might turn out that previously arcane and obscure facts have become commonplace. There is cultural and technological evolution that might be manifested through their effects on test scores.

A fairer test would be to search for schools that introduced discovery learning methods in a given period and others which did not. It might then be possible to contrast the change in test scores in one group of schools with the change in the other. This would go some way to dealing with the problem of confusing a change attributable to a specific educational practice with one due to a general trend independent of the educational system. Unfortunately there could be a number of other difficulties that would make an unambiguous interpretation difficult. For example, there might be differences between the children living in different education authorities, at least with respect to their performance on Test A. Or the introduction (or lack of it) of the new procedures might cause families to move into or out of the area. These relocations would play havoc with the data and make it very difficult indeed to be certain what caused any differences observed.

However, though interpretational difficulties may abound, the first step is to discover whether there is anything to explain. If no differences in test score can be discovered there will be nothing to give an account of, and whether it should be in terms of educational practice, cultural change or population shift is an irrelevant issue. If a difference can be substantiated it then becomes a priority matter to attribute it to a defined independent variable.

The difficulties of reaching unequivocal conclusions from a retrospective study may well lead to the proposal to set up a current study, and to devote at least five and preferably ten years to it. The advantages are very great since the investigator can now make all the relevant choices except which child experiences which educational system. That remains an essential weakness, but larger samples of children and several different local education authorities will go a long way towards making up for that deficiency.

There may be many ways of training the mind but study of the classics is one of the best

The school curriculum has changed a great deal during this century. It varied anyway between different sectors of education. Public (private) schools stressed games and particular forms of socialization as an essential part of building what was called 'character'. Grammar schools insisted upon the study of classical languages (Latin and Greek) and often justified this not in terms of an entrance to classical literature and culture but rather in terms of a generalized training of the mind. Those who were subjected to this experience may be interested to discover whether there is any reason to suppose that sweating over Latin unseens conferred any benefits at all. The logically prior question, however, is what meant by 'training the mind' and whether there are any ways of doing it successfully.

The concept of a trained mind, in contrast with actually possessing a particular skill such as speaking a foreign language, is the key to this question. It is an empirical question just what people who refer to a trained mind mean by it. A survey of people's views on this issue might reveal that a trained mind is expected to be orderly, able to communicate, capable of reasoning effectively and literate. The trained mind is expected to be efficient in acquiring new knowledge, evaluating and judgement. These are generally the attributes that are supposed to distinguish the educated person. They also, perhaps, correlate with the unusual dependence of British government on the gifted amateur, both in Parliament and the permanent civil service. This practical consideration points up the question as to whether the trained mind actually possesses the manifold properties attributed to it.

The first step must be to list the attributes of a trained mind and to establish an operational definition of each so that it is clear how one discovers whether a particular individual possesses that desirable feature. It has to be a possibility that the concept is, in fact, a myth and that nobody exists with one. In that case, there would be no point in seeking the conditions that produce a trained mind: like the unicorn it would be simply a product of the imagination. However, assuming that it proves possible to assemble a credible scheme for detecting 'trained minds' and that a significant number of people can be found to possess such an attribute, the way ahead is clear to investigate from whence it came.

Although the classical study hypothesis presumes that the trained mind is, in fact, the result of 'training', it must not be assumed that such a presumption is valid. It is possible that what we identify and label as a trained mind is no more than an intelligent person with general experience, the detailed components of which could be largely interchangeable. Intelligence could be mainly determined by the genetic lottery preceding one's birth and so training might be a minor or even, at the extreme, irrelevant factor in the determination of a trained mind. This consideration widens the range of permissible attributions that have to be entertained.

Having made this much progress the next step is to formulate a series of testable hypotheses to prevent the whole enquiry getting out of hand. The long history of attempts to determine the proportions of general intelligence that should be considered to be determined by heredity (as opposed to environmental factors) does not give one much confidence in expecting either a quick or a clean answer to the same kind of question as applied to the genesis of a trained mind. It might be better to consider instead comparisons amongst different environmental conditions and, so far as possible, to limit comparisons to those between classical studies, education and other curricula including, for example, expressive arts and science.

Even this more limited goal is not going to be easy to achieve. The main problem will always be that the investigator cannot carry out an experiment, except on such a minor scale with adult subjects as to be too low in credibility to be worth bothering about. The choice about who receives what kind of education will have been made by other people including, in large measure, those actually receiving it. This must contaminate the data that would be collected, because it might be the case that people who have the potential to develop trained minds selectively choose to undertake particular forms of education and training. If that were to be the case, discovering that a higher proportion of trained minds had studied the classics rather than science, for example, would not necessarily indicate the greater potential of classical studies for producing trained minds.

Even admitting these problems it could be useful to carry out a study which associated the possession, in whatever degree, of a trained mind with prior educational curriculum. For example, it might be the case that no difference was found between different curricula, which would make it very unlikely indeed that the superior claims for a classical education should be given credence.

A word means what I choose it to mean
Children in school are taught that words have particular meanings. There are classes or words called synonyms that share the same meanings and there are books of reference, dictionaries, which act as umpires resolving disputes about the meanings of particular words. Our schooling all points to language as based on a set of words with rigidly defined, dependable meanings. it also has a well-defined structure or grammar which imposes discipline upon how meaning-words may be deployed, presumably to avoid utterances, which are designed to communicate, actually increasing confusion. Unfortunately, perhaps, the real world is not like that. It is replete with confusing messages. Words do not have a universal currency amongst speakers of that language. Even grammatical rules vary with geography, even if the full richness of a dialect is not entered.

Instead of the neat and tidy model from school, real language is far more approximate. Meanings of words change and, instead of definitive meanings, usage is the only reliable guide to why people use particular words in particular circumstances. Very dramatic variations in meaning can be found by contrasting British and American English. A 'flat' is either a puncture or an apartment. 'Suspenders' prevent either stockings or trousers from descending. 'Pants' always adorn the lower half of the body but whether they are creased or Y-fronted depends on where you are. It is interesting to consider whether these variations in usage are essentially the same as polysemy. Many words in English have several meanings and which is intended can only be discovered by the context or by subsequent interrogation. In many cases the two or more meanings are related but this is not always so and some words have several meanings that seem to be totally unrelated to each other. 'Train' may be used perfectly properly in connection with journeys, weddings and race-horses. Is he 'lying' on his back or in his teeth? Some 'sentences' are distinguished by main verbs, others by restricted liberty. The situation can sometimes become even more ambiguous by adding extra words. Aristocrats, bureaucrats, pedagogues and coaches all mean something different by 'good form'.

A different source of variation from the 'standard' definition is when new words are coined and naturally take on a meaning along with their use, or when old words are forced into new roles and contexts. Scientific jargon is an example of the choice of a verbal label to allow a new concept to be communicated. This sometimes involves taking words that are already used and giving them a precise new meaning. Psychology is particularly confusing when it tends to mislead lay-persons into thinking they understand what is being said; terms borrowed from the vernacular are used in a special sense. Chemistry may involve learning a whole new language but that avoids one thinking one has mastered a subject of which one is ignorant.

In the last 20 years a number of new words have entered the language and others have acquired new meanings and usages. For example, grotesque has given rise to its familiar diminutive 'grotty'. However, the original meaning has not persisted and when eventually the Oxford English Dictionary catalogues grotty it is likely to stress its shoddy, unpleasant and uncomfortable characteristics rather than something to do with lack of visual attractiveness. At about the same time 'fancy' made the transition from noun to verb, and its meaning shifted very significantly from general preference to a specific statement about sexual attraction.

These considerations reveal that the speaker's intentions not only influence the choice of words to utter, but the words themselves may not be an adequate indication of what the intended meaning was. Polysemous words (those with several meanings) in an utterance have to be placed in a context in order to remove their essential ambiguity. However, the evolution of meaning of words implies that a fashionable usage can develop and eventually a new meaning can overtake the old. Currently 'pathetic' is coming to mean 'of poor standard', which is a significant deviation from the dictionary definition 'deserving of pity; contemptible'.

The fashionable meaning develops because users want the word to convey a particular meaning, and by repetition the new meaning is conferred upon it. There is a tacit agreement that the new meaning should be accepted rather than rejected as being 'not what it means'. In this sense a word can be said to mean what its utterer intends it to mean.

This question is fundamental to understanding about language but exceedingly difficult to explore. Clearly the meaning of words is not stable, though it would give rise to communicational chaos if the meaning of words altered very quickly. It would be like talking in a code which was always changing according to complex and unpredictable, or even random, principles. It would negate the whole purpose of communication if speakers redefined the words they used without regard to the conventions accepted by the listener. There has to be only a limited degree to which such idiosyncratic re-definition could be introduced without destroying the purpose of the utterance.

The first question, then, is to formulate an enquiry which is tractable. For example, it would be interesting to discover ways of determining what a speaker means. Or one might seek to discover how far speakers typically deviate from dictionary definitions: an investigation that would depend on a considerable amount of prior study of the ways of knowing what people mean when they speak. Another question would be to experiment with using words in atypical or even illegitimate ways in order to discover how messages are vulnerable to linguistic distortions and rule-breaking.

As an area of investigation, progress would depend very much on creative approaches to setting answers to these sorts of questions and on being sceptical of neat answers. No tidy methodology exists to make studies in this area easy.

A batsman's dressing ritual is usually idiosyncratic and superstitious: why should it work for him?

Many sportsmen have a ritual that they adopt in preparation for a game, especially ones in which they invest great importance. Cricketers and footballers may always put one particular boot on first. Batsmen may have a ritual of dressing in a particular order, practising in a particular way, even rehearsing particular thoughts before they are summoned to take their turn at the crease.

Since it seems impossible that which pad he dons first could actually affect the balls bowled to him or anything else except possibly his own belief about himself and his 'luck', the nature of the question is in the realm of superstition. There is a wealth of literature on superstitious behaviour to call upon, some of it in sub-human species. A ready account of the development of superstitious behaviour can be couched in terms of reinforcement theory, and 'superstitious' behaviour has been deliberately developed in pigeons using random reinforcement schedules which make it impossible for the pigeon to solve the problem of 'what to do to win'.

This is probably the clue to development of superstitious behaviour in the sporting context. Success in competitive sports depends upon each one of many different factors being exactly right, and just a slight inaccuracy in one of them will preclude it. It is a feature of sports that they are not open to articulate verbal analysis, nor are they governable by verbally precise instructions. One cannnot define and then impart a fool-proof recipe for success. Naturally the sportsman who manages to get all the contributing factors together to the right degree at the same level is likely to rise to champion status and will achieve generally better performance than one who does not. But at any level no player can positively guarantee a perfect or even good performance (as opposed to trying hard).

From one occasion to another, therefore, performance will vary and only rarely will there be a clear reason why. Other fluctuations will be near-random and as uncontrollable as the seasons. However, it is uncomfortable to accept that one's performance is out of one's control, and certainly the highly motivated performer is unlikely to accept such an idea unless there is no alternative. This is a custom-made situation for the development of beliefs about what promotes good performance which bears no relation at all to the actual causes of variation. In fact, since success happens in a near-random fashion, the batsman and the randomly-reinforced pigeon are in very similar circumstances.

The pigeon tends to repeat whatever behaviour preceded the delivery of the reinforcement. The batsman will persist with some act which 'he believes' preceded a good performance, or which actually did. The fact that reinforcement of this kind is intermittent also explains why superstitious behaviour has such an enormous resistance to extinction. The batsman is 'hooked' on his ritual like the gambler is hooked on the one-armed bandit. A long period without any success may be necessary to break the behavioural dependence.

The question posed here is why such a ritual should work. The logically prior question should be to discover whether it does work, or whether it is simply a belief that the batsman has that it works. A number of enquiries could be considered. It would be interesting to plot the incidence of this kind of behaviour both in terms of frequency and how far they are widespread across different sports. That would establish a measure of the relative importance of the topic. Then a study of the beliefs of individual ritual-using sportsmen would provide insight into the phenomenological perspective of this sort of behaviour. Intervention studies could be undertaken to explore the effects of interfering with the ritual. Finally, it might be possible to design an observational study aimed at observing the development of a superstitious ritual.

There are important psychological factors which affect sporting performance: are there?

Some years ago the directors of Ajax football club in Amsterdam appointed a team psychologist, presumably to improve the team's performance on the field. However, the team manager was so concerned that his players should not be upset that he forbade the psychologist to have any direct contact with the players. His role degenerated to that of being an adviser to the manager and the trainer/coach. This example points to a number of ways in which psychological factors may relate to sporting performance.

At the outset it would be sensible to distinguish between psychological mechanisms which directly subserve motor co-ordination and skilled performance, and other factors such as motivation, conscious belief and so on. Clearly the former have to be involved or there would be no performance at all. Any question about their involvement must have a self-evident answer. It is presumably the second category of psychological factors which this question addresses.

The whole relationship between conscious verbal processes and motor skills is complex and obscure. At one extreme is the view that there is no functional connection at all, since motor performance is essentially non-verbal. Any apparent connection forged during a post-performance verbal analysis is delusory. The alternative view is that non-skill processes, including conscious verbal processes, might affect performance although the way in which this influence is mediated may often be obscure. For example, by realizing the critical status of the game, the importance of a particular event may be heightened and the performers' level of arousal thereby increased. The consequence of this might be to raise his level of performance, or to reduce it through the destructive effects of over-arousal. Alternatively, he might attend more closely and make better use of the available information, or be distracted by the thought of the consequences of failure.

This question is potentially a very big one indeed since it could quickly lead to needing to explain the fluctuations which occur in sportsmen's performances. The second phase of the enquiry could then go on to investigate the extent to which these fluctuations can be brought under control. In recent years many professional sportsmen have enlisted the aid of hypnotists in an attempt to eradicate 'bad days' from their record. They are hoping always to be on top form, and at least some claim that post-hypnotic suggestions have made a significant contribution to that goal.

The literature includes a considerable amount of information about the effects of motivation and emotion on various types of performances but very little on sporting performance that is characterized by a very high degree of motivation and a very high level of skill. The results of experiments carried out on poorly trained, moderately motivated undergraduates may be of little help in predicting the performance of a top-class professional golfer or tennis player. The most important aspect of this question is to realize that the subjects are probably quite different from those from whom most of our knowledge of human psychology has been obtained. It would, therefore, be a mistake to approach the enquiry as if the answers were already known.

In such circumstances it would be as well to begin using naive observation in order to develop some initial hypotheses. These might lead on to depth interview enquiries, or experimental studies, or controlled observations of particular events under specified conditions. In the study somewhere there needs to be an opportunity to examine the utility of procedures such as hypnosis that are claimed to influence performance.

Most performers believe that there is a strong relationship between confidence and performance. Perhaps that offers one tractable question that, if negated, would raise questions about the likelihood of any significant progress being made on this issue.

2

Personality and individual assessment
P. Kline

In this chapter we examine individual differences among human beings, how such differences are measured, and the psychological implications of such differences for understanding personality and behaviour. First of all we discuss psychological tests and testing techniques, for it is by the application of these measures that individual differences have been discovered.

Characteristics of good psychological tests and how these may be achieved

Efficient testing devices must be (i) reliable, (ii) valid and (iii) discriminating.

Reliability
Reliability has two meanings: first, self-consistency. Tests must be self-consistent; each item should measure the same variable. An instrument, for example, which measured in part pressure as well as temperature would not give a reliable measurement of either of these. The second meaning is consistency over time: that is, test-retest reliability. If a test is administered a second time to a person then, unless a real change has taken place, the score on the two occasions should be the same. Reliability is measured by the correlation coefficient, an index of agreement running from +1 (perfect agreement) to -1 (perfect disagreement). A correlation of 0 shows random agreement. Good tests should have a reliability coefficient of at least 0.7 which represents 49 per cent agreement (square the coefficient).

1. FACTORS INFLUENCING RELIABILITY

*   Test length: it can be shown that reliability increases with the length of a test. The typical university essay exam has only four items (four essays) and is thus not highly reliable. To increase reliability, most psychological tests have a large number of items. Twenty items are about the minimum necessary for reliability.
*   Objective scoring: scores should be objective: that is, there should be no personal judgement required of the scorer. Where judgement is required, as in essays, differences arise, often large, between different markers and with the same markers if they rescore the

test. A good test has items that are objectively scored.

If a test is reliable then it can be valid. Notice the 'can'. It is possible to devise a highly reliable test that measures virtually nothing. A test for measuring the length of people's noses would be easy to devise and would be highly reliable, but it is unlikely to be a valid test of intelligence or personality. On the other hand, an unreliable, inconsistent test which gives different scores on different occasions cannot possibly be valid.

Validity
A test is said to be valid if it measures what it claims to measure. This may sound obvious but many tests are quite invalid. For example, essay-type tests of scientific subjects are highly unlikely to be valid since essay writing demands verbal ability, and ability in physics is somewhat different from this. The term validity is used in psychological testing (psychometrics) in several ways.

1. FACE VALIDITY: this refers to the appearance of a test which is said to be face valid if it looks as if it measures what it claims to measure. This is important in testing adults who may balk at doing tests which look absurd. They may simply refuse to co-operate or even treat the test as a bit of a joke. Children, however, are used to overlooking such niceties. Face validity is not usually related to true validity.

2. CONCURRENT VALIDITY: this refers to studies of the validity of a test made on one occasion. For example, the concurrent validity of a new test of intelligence would be assessed by its correlation with well-established intelligence tests; does the new test give a similar score to the score on an existing test? Concurrent validity studies are beset by problems of criteria: what tests or other measurement should be used in establishing the concurrent validity of a test? If other similar tests are used, and the correlation is very high, the question arises as to what value the new test has since it is measuring the same variable as the old.

3. PREDICTIVE VALIDITY: this refers to the capacity of a test to correlate with some future criterion measure. This can be the most powerful evidence for the validity of a test. Some examples will clarify this point. A good test of anxiety should be able to predict future attendance at the psychiatric clinic, and a good test of intelligence given at 11 years of age should correlate with future academic performance in GCE examinations and subsequently. Thus the test predicts events external to itself.

4. CONSTRUCT VALIDITY: the construct validity of a test

is defined by taking a large set of results obtained with the test and seeing how well they fit in with our notion of the psychological nature of the variable which the test claims to measure. Thus it embraces concurrent and predictive validity. In effect, we set up a series of hypotheses concerning the test results and put these to the test. For example, if our test was a valid measure of intelligence we might expect:

* high-level professional groups would score more highly than lower-level professionals;
* children rated highly intelligent by teachers would score more highly than others;
* scores would correlate positively with level of education;
* scores would correlate highly with scores in public examinations;
* scores would correlate highly with scores on other intelligence tests;
* scores would not correlate with scores on tests not claiming to measure intelligence.

If all these hypotheses were supported then the construct validity of our test would be demonstrated. It is deserving of note that it is always useful to show (as in the final point above) what tests do not measure, a technique used by Socrates in his examination of the meaning of words.

Unlike reliability, for which there can be clear unequivocal evidence, the validity of a test is to some extent subjective. Nevertheless, most well-known tests, especially of ability, have now accumulated so much evidence relating to validity that there is no dispute about them. It is more difficult to demonstrate the validity of personality tests but, as we see later, it can be done. Many psychological tests have little support for their validity and a large number are clearly invalid.

Discriminatory power

Good psychological tests should be discriminating: that is, they should produce a wide distribution of scores. For example, if we test 10 children and all score 15 we have made no discriminations at all. If four score 13, three score 12 and three score 14 then we have made only three discriminations. If, on the other hand, each child scores a different score, then the distribution of scores is wide. The scatter of scores in a distribution is known as the variance and the standard deviation is the usual measurement. A good test has a large standard deviation.

With reliable, valid and discriminating tests it is possible to investigate the nature of individual differences in human beings. In fact, this has been going on since the turn of the century when Binet began the assessment of the educability of Parisian children.

Types of tests and categories of individual differences

Individual differences among human beings fall into relatively independent categories for which different types of tests have been developed.

Intelligence and ability tests

The most important ability as studied by psychometrists is general intelligence, the ability to educe correlates; a general reasoning ability which underlies much problem-solving ability. Modern studies of this general reasoning factor (e.g. Cattell, 1971) tend to reveal two aspects: (i) fluid ability which is close to inherited reasoning ability; and (ii) crystallized ability, which is fluid ability as it is evinced in a culture. The old-fashioned 11+ intelligence tests were largely concerned with crystallized ability. More will be said later about intelligence.

Other typical abilities are: verbal ability, V; numerical ability, N; and spatial ability, K. Performance on various tasks will depend upon our status on these variables. For example, a writer and an engineer may both score much the same on general intelligence, but on verbal ability the writer should be higher, whereas on numerical and spatial ability the engineer should be superior. Intelligence can be thought of as a general factor, while verbal and numerical ability are group factors. Intelligence plays its part in almost all skills, while verbal ability is involved only in certain groups. Some factors are more narrow than this; auditory pitch discrimination would be an example.

Aptitude tests

Aptitude tests comprise a group of tests related to tests of ability. Aptitude tests tend to be of two different kinds. One type may be identical with the group tests discussed above. Thus it would be difficult to distinguish between verbal ability and verbal aptitude. However, computer aptitude tests are clearly different; they should test the collection of traits (perhaps more than just abilities) necessary for this particular job. In some instances, such as clerical aptitude, the necessary skills are quite disparate and unrelated to each other. Generally, aptitude tests measure the separate abilities demonstrated to be important for a particular job or class of jobs.

Personality tests

Personality tests can be divided into tests of temperament, mood and dynamics. Temperament tests measure how we do what we do. Temperamental traits, such as dominance and anxiety, are usually thought of as enduring and stable. Dynamic traits are concerned with motives; why we do what we do. These attempt to measure drives such as sexuality or pugnacity. Moods refer to those fluctuating states that we all experience in our lives: for example, anger, fatigue and fear.

Temperament tests

The most used type of temperament test is the personality questionnaire. These consist of lists of items concerned with the subject's behaviour. Typical items are: do you enjoy watching boxing? Do you hesitate before spending a large sum of money? Items come in various formats. Those above would usually require subjects to respond 'Yes' or 'No'; or 'Yes', 'Uncertain' or 'No'. Sometimes items are of the forced choice variety; for example, 'Do you prefer: (i) watching boxing; (ii) going to a musical; or (iii) sitting quietly at home reading?'

The disadvantages of questionnaires are considerable, yet in spite of them many valid and highly useful personality questionnaires have been constructed. These disadvantages are outlined below.

* They are easy to fake: that is, subjects may not tell the truth for one reason or another. This makes them difficult to use in selection, although for vocational guidance or psychiatric help, where subjects have no reason to fake, this is not too serious.
* They require a degree of self-knowledge and some subjects, while attempting to be honest, may respond quite unrealistically.
* They are subject to response sets. An important set is social desirability, the tendency to endorse the socially desirable response. People like to present themselves in the best possible light. For example, to the item 'Do you have a good sense of humour?', the response 'Yes' would be given by about 95 per cent of subjects. The other serious response set is that of acquiescence; the tendency to put 'Yes' or 'Agree' to an answer, regardless of content. Balanced scales, with some responses keyed 'No', obviate this to some extent.

OBJECTIVE TESTS: these, defined by Cattell (cf. Cattell and Kline, 1977) as tests of which the purpose is hidden from the subject and which can be objectively scored (see the section on reliability), have been developed to overcome the disadvantages of questionnaires. Ironically, because their purpose is hidden from subjects, considerable research is necessary to establish their validity and as yet most are still in an experimental form. These tests will probably take over from questionnaires when the necessary research has been done. The following examples indicate their nature.

* Balloon blowing: subjects are required to inflate a balloon as much as they can. Measures taken are the size of the balloon, time taken in blowing it up, whether they burst it, and delay in beginning the task. This test may be related to timidity and inhibition.
* The slow-line drawing test: subjects are required to draw a line as slowly as possible. The measure is the length of line over a fixed time.

In fact more than 800 such tests have been listed and more can easily be developed, depending upon the ingenuity of the researcher. The technique is to administer a large battery of such tests and to determine experimentally by so-called validity studies what each of them measures.

PROJECTIVE TESTS: these essentially consist of ambiguous stimuli to which the subjects have to respond. These are some of the oldest personality tests and one, the Rorschach test (the inkblot test), has achieved a fame beyond psychology. The rationale of projective tests is intuitively brilliant: if a stimulus is so vague that it warrants no particular description, then any description of it must depend on what is projected on to it by the subject. Projective testers believe that projective tests measure the inner needs and fantasies of their subjects.

A serious problem with projective tests lies in their unreliability. Responses have to be interpreted by scorers and often considerable training, experience and expertise is necessary. Inter-marker reliability is low. Generally, too, it is difficult to demonstrate test validity. However, the present writer has experimented with entirely objective forms of scoring these tests and some evidence has now accrued that this is a useful procedure.

PROJECTIVE TEST STIMULI: although any ambiguous stimulus could be used as a test, the choice of stimulus is generally determined by the particular theory of personality which the test constructor follows. For example, a psychoanalytically-orientated psychologist would select stimuli relevant to that theory, such as vague figures who could be mother and son (the Oedipus complex) or figures with knives or scissors (the castration complex). The TAT (Thematic Apperception Test) developed by Murray uses pictures which, it is hoped, tap the inner needs held by Murray to be paramount in human behaviour.

Mood and motivation tests
Mood and motivation tests are essentially similar to temperament tests, but relatively little work has been done with these and their validity is not so widely attested as that of temperament tests.

Mood tests generally use items that concentrate, as might be expected, on present feelings rather than on usual ones. With these, high test-retest reliability is not to be expected. However, fluctuations in scores should not be random but should be related to external conditions. Thus experiments can be conducted in which the tests, if they are valid, can be retaken. If the experimental manipulations are good and the tests valid, the relevant scores should change in response to these changes in mood.

The results of motivation tests should be similarly fluctuating, according to whether drives are satisfied or frustrated. In one study the scores of a single subject over a 28-day period were related to a diary recording all that

happened to her and everything she felt or thought (Kline
and Grindley, 1974). In fact, the relation of scores to
diary events was close. For example, the fear drive rose
each weekend when the subject went touring in a dangerous
car. The career drive was flat except on the day when the
subject was interviewed for a course in teacher-training,
and so on.

Motivation tests can be of the questionnaire variety,
although objective and projective tests are more frequently
used. For moods, questionnaire tests are more usually employed though they suffer, of course, from the same response
sets as bedevil questionnaire measures of temperamental
traits.

Interest tests

The tests of motivation described above are very general:
that is, they measure variables thought to account for a
wide variety of human behaviour. Vocational and industrial
psychologists, however, have long felt the need for more
specific measures of motivation, assessing the variables
which seemed of immediate relevance to them: for instance,
interests. We all know of motoring enthusiasts who seem to
have an all-embracing interest in cars, which seems to
account for much of their behaviour and conversation.

A number of interest tests have been developed which
attempt to assess the major interests such as outdoor,
mechanical, or interest in people. In some tests, the
scoring of items is in terms of occupational groups. The
performance of particular occupational groups on the tests
is known and if, for example, foresters score high on a
particular item then this item contributes to the 'interest
in forestry' score. In other tests, the scoring involves
little more than subjects having to rank jobs. In other
words, interest tests of this type are like formalized
interviews.

Generally, the correlations of interest test scores with
success in a job relevant to those interests are modest and
little better than the correlation obtained between job
success and the subject's response to the question of
whether the job would be enjoyable or not.

Attitude tests

Social psychologists have attempted to measure attitudes for
many years now. Usually, the attitudes tested apply to important aspects of an individual's life: for example, attitudes to war, or to coloured people (in white populations)
or to religion. Obviously, if efficient measures of such
attitudes are possible then progress can be made in understanding how such attitudes arise or are maintained; important knowledge, it is thought, in a complex multi-racial
society. There are three kinds of attitude test, differing
in their mode of construction.

1. THE THURSTONE SCALES: in these tests items are given

to the judges to rank 1-11 (favourable-unfavourable) in respect of an attitude. Items on which there is good agreement among the judges are then retained. The subject then
taking the test is given the highest judged rank score of
the items with which that subject agrees. The reason for
this is clear if we consider a few examples. (1) 'War is
totally evil' would probably be ranked high as unfavourable
to war. (2) 'Wars sometimes have to be fought if there is no
alternative': this is clearly against war, but not strongly.
(3) 'Wars are not always wrong': this is yet further down
the scale, while the item (4) 'Wars are good: they select
the finest nations' is favourable. Thus a subject who agreed
with (1) would not agree with (2), (3) or (4). Similarly, a
subject agreeing with (3) would not agree with (4). These
tests are difficult to construct because much depends on
obtaining a good cross-section of judges. A more simple
alternative is the Likert scale.

2. LIKERT SCALES: in the Likert scales statements relevant
to the attitude being measured are presented to the subject
who has to state on a five-point scale the extent of his
agreement. Thus a 'Hitler' would score 100 on a 20-item
attitude to war scale. A 'Ghandi' would score zero, one
presumes. To make the scale less obvious, items are so
written that to agree with items represents both poles of
the attitude.

3. THE GUTTMAN SCALE: this is a scale constructed so
that if the items are ranked for positive attitude, then any
subject who endorses item 10 will also endorse items 1-9
below it. While this tends to happen by nature of its construction with the Thurstone scale, such perfect ordering of
items can usually only be achieved by leaving huge gaps
between the items (in terms of attitude) which means few
items and rather coarse measurement.

Such, then, are the main types of psychological tests with
which individual differences are measured in psychology.
Needless to say, these are not the only kinds of test. In
the remainder of this chapter we briefly describe some intelligence tests, discuss some of the substantive findings
that have emerged from these tests and examine their
application in practical psychology.

Intelligence tests

Intelligence has been most widely studied of all test variables and, since it is a topic of considerable importance in
applied psychology and education, let us examine in detail
some intelligence tests to help us to understand the nature
of intelligence as conceptualized by psychologists.

**Individual intelligence
tests**

Some intelligence tests are given to subjects individually.
This enables the tester to measure not only the intelligence

of the subject but also to see whether a child panics at difficulties or goes on and on obsessionally even when it is obvious that no solution will result. Similarly, it can be seen whether an individual is easily distracted, and all this is valuable in attempting to understand any educational difficulties which may arise.

The WISC

The Wechsler Intelligence Scale, WISC (Wechsler, 1938), consists of the following sub-tests which fall into two groups: verbal tests and non-verbal tests. A total IQ score is obtainable, as are a verbal IQ and a performance IQ. Large differences between these two sub-scores are of some psychological interest and call for further study. Some of our examples are taken from Kline (1976).

1. THE VERBAL TESTS

*   Vocabulary: a straightforward vocabulary test. Vocabulary is highly related to intelligence although social class differences in reading habits do, obviously, affect this particular sub-test. Nevertheless, if forced to make a selection of intelligent children or adults as quickly as possible, the vocabulary sub-test would be about the best measure obtainable.
*   Information: a test of general knowledge.
*   Arithmetic: an ordinary arithmetic test.

These three tests are heavily affected by school learning and social class. They therefore reflect what Cattell called crystallized intelligence, or the result of cultural influences upon innate ability.

*   Comprehension: this is an interesting test because it presents problems which are dependent upon how much the child is capable of making sensible decisions on its own initiative. One example (which is not in the test) might be a question like 'What would you do if you saw a burglar in the house next door?' Two points would be scored by a response such as 'Phone the police - dial 999'; one point by the response 'Run and tell Mummy', and no points by 'Shoot him with my bow and arrow' or 'Push his car over'. At the higher level this sub-test requires abstract analytical reasoning on such questions as 'Why is there a Hippocratic oath?'
*   Similarities: a common form of intelligence test item, simple to write and easy to vary the level of difficulty. For example, 'What is similar about peaches and prunes?' The correct response requires that the essential similarity (fruit) is recognized.
*   Digit span (forward and reverse): digits are read out and the subjects repeat them immediately. Seven or eight digits is the usual span for bright adults.

In the majority of cases most psychologists give five of the six tests, the last two of which in part measure fluid ability.

2. THE NON-VERBAL TESTS: these are generally quite novel to most subjects, so they are more a measure of fluid (inherited) ability than are the verbal tests. Large disparities between the verbal and performance score are often found in middle-class children whose upbringing is highly verbal. The performance sub-tests are as follows.

* Block design: patterns are presented to the child in a booklet and they must be copied by arranging building blocks such that the top surfaces represent the pattern. This test can be made of varying difficulty. It is also one which indicates well how a child tackles a strange problem.
* Picture arrangement: here series of strip cartoons tell stories. Each series is presented in jumbled order and the child must put them in their correct sequence: a neat way of testing a child's ability to work out the relationships involved.
* Object assembly: this is a timed jigsaw-like task of arranging broken patterns.
* Mazes: the child is required to trace the way through pencil and paper mazes.
* Coding: here the key to a simple cipher system is given. The child then completes as many examples as possible (presented in random order) in a fixed time.
* Picture completion: pictures with a missing element, often only a small detail, are shown to the subject who is required to spot this.

This, then, is the Wechsler Intelligence Scale, one of the standard individual intelligence tests. The verbal and performance IQ scores are highly reliable, as is the total score: all around 0.9 or beyond.

The WISC is an individual test. It is obviously not suitable for group administration. Let us now look at some item types used in group intelligence tests (rather than examine any one test in detail) since these are widely used in applied psychology.

Group intelligence tests Items can be verbal or non-verbal, testing largely fluid or crystallized ability.

1. ANALOGIES

Easy: a is to c as g is to ...
            sparrow is to bird as mouse is to ...

Difficult: Samson Agonistes is to Comus as the
            Bacchae are to ...

With analogy items all kinds of relationships may be tested, as in the examples where we find sequence, classification, double classification (by author and type of play, for example), and opposites. Analogy is thus a useful form for encapsulating a wide variety of relationships. We can use shapes for this type of item, as distinct from verbal forms.

Thus   is to

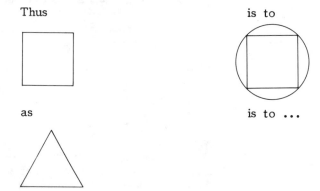

as   is to ...

Here we would supply possible answers in multiple choice form, for example:

2. ODD-MEN-OUT

Odd-men-out items also allow us to test wide varieties of relationships in many materials. Some examples are given below.

* carrot, turnip, swede, beetroot, cabbage
* valley, coomb, hillock, gorge, chasm
* early, greasy, messy, swiftly, furry

For these three examples some knowledge is required of vegetables, geography and grammar, but this alone is not enough.

3. SIMILARITIES

These are essentially the same item form (where the common relationship must be worked out), but are more difficult to write for a group test, because the multiple choice answer will give the game away. Non-verbal odd-men-out items are simple to produce; see the following examples.

4. SEQUENCES AND MATRICES

Numbers, of course, offer easy ways of creating complex relationships without needing any special knowledge of mathematics and hence sequences are a useful item form. For example, 20, 40, 60, 80 ... is entirely unequivocal. Sequences allow also for the development of highly complex or multiple relationships. A matrix involving several sequences might be of the following form:

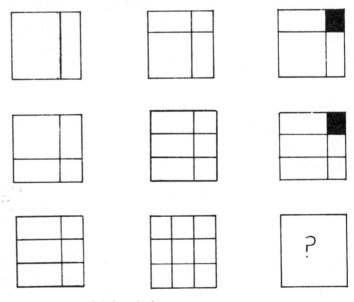

followed by a multiple choice

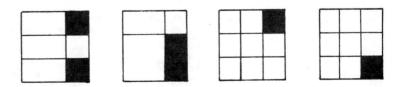

Raven's Matrices is an example of a test composed entirely of such sets of non-verbal items. Many forms have been produced and it is capable of extending the intelligence of subjects from about five years upwards to the limits. It is one of the best single measures of fluid ability. Despite its non-verbal appearance, however, it is related to some extent to verbal ability, presumably because verbalization improves performance.

These, then, are typical items in tests of intelligence. From our description of these and of the WISC scale, it should be possible to get an insight into what it is that intelligence tests measure.

We have concentrated on intelligence tests in our more detailed study of tests because they have been at the centre of so much controversy, both in respect of their use as selection devices for secondary school education and more recently in respect of the heritability of success in these tests. It is to this latter topic, which is of great social importance and intellectual interest, that we now turn, a further reason for ensuring that the nature of such tests is fully appreciated.

The heritability of intelligence test scores

This is so large and complex a subject that inevitably our summary must be somewhat assertive and dogmatic. To make it even more difficult, well-known writers reviewing the same evidence come to opposite conclusions. For example, Cattell (1971) and Eysenck (1971) conclude that about 80 per cent of the variance in intelligence test scores is heritable, at least in the west. Kamin (1974), reviewing the same evidence, comes to the conclusion that there are no sound data to reject the hypothesis that differences in test scores are determined by different life experiences.

To make our discussion of this matter comprehensible rather than comprehensive let us first establish a number of important points.

* All results of heritability studies refer only to the population from which the sample was drawn. Thus results in Great Britain are not applicable in other cultures. If culture has any effect, then in a country with a diverse cultural background (such as India) the heritability index would be smaller than in a more homogeneous culture.
* All workers in the field argue that there is an interaction between genetic and environmental determinants of intelligence test scores. Where there is disagreement is in the matter of how large is the influence of each factor.
* In principle, an ideal method of studying the topic is to investigate the differences in intelligence test scores of monozygotic twins (i.e. twins with the same genetic endowment) reared apart. All differences in test scores within such pairs must be environmentally

determined (ignoring differential effects of placental deprivations, etc., in such pairs which would exaggerate any differences).

Critics of this approach argue that it is vitiated by the fact that twins are, by definition, a different population from singleton children. Furthermore, there is a tendency for identical twins to be placed in foster homes similar to each other, thus making their scores similar.

* Burt carried out the most extensive twin studies. His data, however, must be ignored. It appears, alas, that he doctored the figures.
* However, other twin studies show the same results, namely that in America and Great Britain there is a substantial hereditary component in the determination of test scores, the critical finding being that identical twins reared apart show less differences in intelligence test scores than do non-identical twins reared together.
* Kamin's (1974) arguments attempting to refute these results are statistically weak, as has been fully exposed by Fulker (1975).
* More sophisticated methods of statistical analyses known as biometric genetic methods, which have been demonstrated as powerful in animal work, have been employed in the study of human intelligence test scores. These can assess the kind of gene action and the mating system in the population by analysing within and between family differences and their interactions. The results of these methods are difficult to impugn and it appears from such studies that: (i) around 70 per cent of the variance in IQ score is heritable in Great Britain and the USA; (ii) there is a polygenic dominance for IQ and that assortative mating is an important influence.
* Such biometric methods can be applied to any variable to reveal its heritability. The major personality variables such as extraversion, neuroticism and psychoticism, are also similarly highly genetically determined.

The factorial description of personality

Factor analysis is a statistical technique for simplifying correlations: this is extremely useful in the study of personality by questionnaires, of which there are very large numbers. Factor analysis reveals dimensions which can mathematically account for the observed correlations. For example, almost all tests of ability are highly correlated together. Factor analysis reveals that this is largely due to the operation of two related factors: fluid and crystallized ability.

Personality questionnaires have been subjected, over the years, to factor analyses in the hope of discovering what are the basic temperamental dimensions. The main researchers in this area have been Cattell (working in Illinois) and Eysenck (in London), both students of Burt, and Guilford (in

California). Although superficially each has produced what looks like a separate set of factors, recent research in this field has enabled some sort of consensus to be arrived at (see Cattell and Kline, 1977, or Kline, 1979, for a full discussion of this work). In effect, the study of individual differences has led to the establishment of the main dimensions of personality. These dimensions are therefore those that demand study. They are outlined below.

Extraversion
The high-scoring extravert is sociable, cheerful, talkative and does not like to be alone. Extraverts enjoy excitement, take risks and are generally impulsive: they are outgoing optimists, active and lively. Introverts are the opposite of this: cold, retiring and aloof. This dimension has been related by Eysenck to the arousability of the central nervous system. Scores on tests of this factor have a large genetic component.

Neuroticism (or anxiety)
Highly anxious subjects worry a lot, are moody and often depressed. They are highly emotional and take a long time to calm down. They tend to sleep poorly and to suffer from psychosomatic disorders. This variable is claimed to be related to the lability of the autonomic nervous system. These variables are both measured by the Cattell 16PF test and Eysenck's EPQ. If we know an individual's status on these two factors, then already we know a good deal about that person's temperament.

Psychoticism
This variable has not been as extensively studied as extraversion and anxiety and only recently (1975) has it appeared in a published questionnaire: the EPQ. Nevertheless, the nature of psychoticism is clear. High scorers on this dimension are solitary, uncaring of people, troublesome, lacking in human feeling and empathy, thick skinned and insensitive. They are cruel, inhumane, hostile and aggressive, reckless to danger, and aggressive even to their own family. Naturally enough, most normals score low on P but many criminals score high. This factor has been related by Eysenck to masculinity, and to be related to levels of male sex hormones.

It is to be noted that these three factors have not only been clearly identified from the factor analysis of questionnaires: there is also a considerable mass of experimental data supporting their identification and nature.

These are the three second-order factors claimed by Eysenck to be the most important in accounting for temperamental differences. (Second-order factors are factors arising from the correlations among first-order factors; i.e. the factors accounting for the original correlations.) The first-order or primary factors are more problematic than the second-orders but, as the work of Cattell has shown, can be of considerable power in applied psychometrics.

In brief, the factorial analysis of personality has revealed three basic dimensions, each tied to the basic physiology of Man and hence largely heritable.

The application of findings in applied psychology

The study of individual differences, described in this chapter, has implicit within it a model of Man which might be called the psychometric model. Explanation of this model, which is remarkably simple, will make the application of results obvious.

The implicit psychometric model

This model states that any given piece of behaviour is related to that individual's status on the main factors in the sphere of ability, temperament, motivation and mood. This model does not ignore past experience because this itself affects status on these variables. The psychometric model is therefore a variant of a trait model of behaviour. Thus, for example, performance on GCE examinations depends upon intelligence, verbal and numerical ability, extraversion, anxiety, psychoticism, mood at the time of taking the exam and the various motivation variables discussed above (to take the main variables). Obviously, for different behaviours (e.g. exam passing and serving well behind a bar) different weights for each of the factors is required.

How important each factor is - that is, what its weight is - has to be determined empirically. In fact, the statistical technique of multiple correlation or regression does this precisely. Thus, the argument runs, we put all the test variables into a multiple correlation with the criterion and these are then weighted to achieve the highest possible correlation. These weights (beta weights) indicate the relative importance of the variable for the behaviour in question. Cattell and Butcher (1968) have done exactly this with academic success both in America and Great Britain and found multiple correlations around 0.7.

Thus in educational guidance and selection we find the beta weights of the variables and select and guide children accordingly. If X, Y and Z have the highest weights for academic success, then we select and encourage children high on these variables. In industrial psychology, we can choose and guide people to various jobs according to their scores on the highest weighted variables. In clinical psychology, too, we can find the tests most related to psychiatric breakdown or diagnose into clinical groups. Then we know who in the population is at risk and can avoid putting them into stressful conditions.

References

Cattell, R.B. (1971)
Abilities: Their structure, growth and action. New York: Houghton-Mifflin.

Cattell, R.B. and Butcher, H.J. (1968)
The Prediction of Achievement and Creativity. New York: Bobbs Merrill.

Cattell, R.B. and Kline, P. (1977)
   The Scientific Analysis of Personality and Motivation.
   London: Academic Press.
Eysenck, H.J. (1971)
   Race, Intelligence and Education. London: Temple-
   Smith.
Fulker, D. (1975)
   The science and politics of IQ. American Journal of
   Psychology, 88, 505-537.
Kamin, L.J. (1974)
   The Science and Politics of IQ. Harmondsworth: Penguin.
Kline, P. (1976)
   Psychological Testing. London: Malaby Press.
Kline, P. (1979)
   Psychometrics and Psychology. London: Academic Press.
Kline, P. and Grindley, J. (1974)
   A 28-day case study with the MAT. Journal of
   Multivariate Clinical Experimental Psychology, 1, 13-32.
Wechsler, D. (1938)
   The Wechsler Intelligence Scale for Children. New York:
   Psychological Corporation.

Questions

1. What is meant by test reliability, and why should psychological tests be reliable?
2. What is the meaning of test validity?
3. What factors contribute to the efficiency of psychological tests?
4. What are the main types of psychological test? Give a brief description of them.
5. Compare projective and questionnaire personality tests.
6. Discuss the main types of attitude tests.
7. Outline the main arguments concerning the heritability of intelligence.
8. Discuss the concept of intelligence as factorially defined.
9. What are the main factors of personality?
10. If individuals are unique, how can they be measured by tests of universal dimensions?

Annotated reading

Cattell, R.B. and Kline, P. (1977) The Scientific Analysis
of Personality and Motivation. London: Academic Press.
   A full account of the factor analysis of personality
   where the results are related to clinical theories.

Cronbach, L. (1976) Essentials of Psychological Testing.
Chicago: Harper & Row.
   A clear comprehensive discussion of psychological
   testing and tests.

Hall, G.S. and Lindzey, G. (1973) Theories of Personality.
New York: Wiley.
   A good summary of a variety of personality theories.

Vernon, P.E. (1979) Intelligence, Heredity and Environment. San Francisco: Freeman.

> Vernon is well-known for his balanced account of issues relating to intelligence, its measurement, and social significance. This is one of the most recent reviews of topics in the field and is written in a lucid style.

Exercises

1. Measure your own IQ

Obtain a copy of H. J. Eysenck's book 'Test your own IQ', and complete a verbal and non-verbal test. Make sure you have read all that Eysenck suggests you read before taking the test and that you observe the testing conditions which he prescribes. One of the main purposes of this exercise is not that you should measure your own IQ but that you should reflect upon the processes involved in completing the test. One strategy is to tape-record your thoughts aloud while you complete a non-verbal test. Do you have a personal strategy for solving the items? Is it a strategy which is heavily saturated with verbal reasoning, even if the test is called a non-verbal test? When you think of friends you know, would they have tackled the items in the same way? If friends are willing, ask them if they would talk through their attempts at some of the items. To what extent do the processes involved reflect other problem-solving work you have to do? From your results, do you think you could construct a 'culture free' test; that is, one which did not draw upon different educational experience or specialized knowledge? If you know something about computer programming, could you devise a programme which would be able to solve some of the problems set in the tests?

2. Extraversion-introversion

This is an exercise which can be done among friends or members of a class. The first step involves rating the whole group on extraversion. This is done by asking yourself which member of the group is most extraverted, second most extraverted and so on, until you have rated the whole group, including yourself. These ratings should be done independently and without group discussion. When this part is complete each of you should have a list with everyone's name on it. You can then combine all the lists by setting out a matrix with everyone's name on both axes. Then insert the rank number for each person for each judge. The ranks for each person can then be added up, so that if someone is generally agreed to be very extraverted then they will end up with a very low-ranking score (in the extreme case rank '1'), and if they are very introverted they will have a high-summed rank score. If you have access to the Eysenck Personality Inventory (which is not a 'closed test' and therefore can be purchased by members of the general public and which appears in some of Eysenck's popular texts) you can interrupt the process immediately following the initial rankings and ask everyone to complete the inventory for themselves.

Pooling of the ranking data would then follow this stage. You will now have an interesting set of data. First, you will be able to see how well the judges agree and whether some judges are more near the average as a judge than others. If someone's rankings are very different from every-one else's, invite that person to comment. This could lead to an interesting discussion about the nature of extraversion and the situations in which the trait is exhibited. Among the rankings there may be individuals who induce a wide range of judgements among the group; that is, someone who is placed high by some people and low by others. Again, this should lead to an interesting discussion. Finally, one can compare people's self-rating (as measured by the Personality Inventory) with the group view. This enables one to ask if one's judgements of oneself are correlated with the ways other people see oneself. Again, we must emphasize that there is no right or wrong answer to items on a personality inventory. People differ, and it is such differences which the inventory sets out to measure. There is no way in which a psychologist can move from the statement, 'This is John's score' to statements of the sort, 'John should (or should not) be like that'. Indeed it would be a very tedious and boring world if we were all alike!

3. Keeping a record of your dreams

Keep a record over a short period of time of some of your dreams (three or four should be enough). It may help to tell yourself as you are nodding off to sleep that you will remember your dreams upon awakening. Keep a notebook and a pencil by your bed or, if you find it easier, a tape-recorder. Write down or record your dreams as soon as you wake up. Once you have sufficient material you must ask yourself whether it forms the basis for psychological study. Is it the case that they are recurring themes, and if so, what are they? Was Freud correct to suggest that dreams are the 'royal road to the unconscious'? Can you make sense of your dreams in a straightforward way or do you need to construct elaborate explanations? To what extent does your dream content reflect happenings and concerns which occurred during the previous day? One possible way of seeing whether there might be a 'deep meaning' in your dream is to free associate (i.e. say anything which comes into your head) in response to some of the content. There are two very different views about dreams. The psychoanalytic view is that dreams are the expression of desires which reveal basic personality traits, personal fears and suppressed wishes. The other view is that dreams reflect the storage of information relating to events which occurred during the day and that, for example, dreams relating to the past are analogous to opening a file to put new material into it.

4. Defence mechanisms

Observe yourself and your friends in conversation and look out for the presence of defence mechanisms (e.g. projection, rationalization, reaction formation, denial and so on). When you blame other people for doing unacceptable things or when you claim that you do not have certain beliefs or attitudes, are there grounds for believing that you are indulging in defence mechanisms? Are there in fact areas of your life which you do not wish to talk about? We are not suggesting that you talk about everything to anyone, but rather that the things you do not wish to talk about may actually influence some of the things you say or do. Because of the processes of socialization, so essential for the orderly running of society, we all have had to learn that some behaviours are acceptable and some are not. That does not mean to say that there are not things which we would really like to do!

5. Some creativity tests
The majority of the intelligence tests referred to by Kline are convergent tests; that is to say, they call for the correct answer to each item. Many creativity tests are said to be divergent because they invite the individual to produce a variety of answers and break away from the notion of a standard answer. Below are some creativity-type tests for you to do on your own. If you have done Exercise 1 you will be able to contrast the experience of performing two very different types of test.

USES OF OBJECTS TEST. Think of an everyday object like a house brick, a paperclip, a frying pan or a pencil. Write down as many uses as you can. For example, a brick could be used as a bookend, as a counterweight, or to throw through a jeweller's window! Try the exercise a week later and see if it is easier the second time.

MEANINGS OF WORDS TEST. Take a word like 'iron', 'carpet', 'rule' or 'bolt' and try to write down as many meanings as you can for each.

CONSEQUENCES. Something unusual happens, for example, someone locks a car with the keys inside or you come home and find a burglar ransacking your bedroom. Try to think of as many things as possible which could follow each event.

A CIRCLES OR SQUARES TEST. Cover a sheet of paper with circles or squares or both; then see how many different things you can draw by starting with these simple shapes.

6. Constructing a test
Choose a variable within the field of personality; for example, sociability, tolerance, friendliness, political involvement, sensation seeking, etc. Construct a short inventory designed to test people. One way of identifying items is to read the psychological literature on the topic in question to see what the authorities think are the main attributes of a trait similar to the one you are interested

in. Try to avoid existing tests and use your own ingenuity.
Assemble about 20 items and then discuss them with your
friends. Please note that such a test, constructed in this
fashion, cannot be treated as a genuine psychometric instrument. As Kline makes absolutely clear, a test must be developed in very clearly defined ways before its reliability
and validity are established. The point of this exercise is
to enable you to experience the difficulties and processes
involved in developing a test.

Part two

The Life Span

powered by physiological urges, and others that it arises
from the way life events are perceived and interpreted. It
has also been proposed that human social organizations
represent a new stage of evolution, a viewpoint which has
been vigorously attacked by those who object to the 'bio-
logizing' of human society because of ethical and political
implications.

It is useful for a biologically-based psychology to make
assumptions about the working organization of the brain, and
a typical classification refers to: (i) an input sensory
system which provides information about the world through
eyes, ears, touch, taste, smell; (ii) a central processing
unit which stores, codes and interprets the input; and (iii)
an output muscular system through which we move and act in
the world. It is also a useful assumption that an organism
cannot survive unless it has an innate mechanism that tells
it when it is favourably correlated with its environment.
This carries the implication that there must be some form of
subjective awareness of welfare and comfort, including the
machinery for not liking to be uncomfortable.

A welfare system

Detection of the positive and negative in the world is an
innate feature of all forms of life. A plant turns towards
the sun and light; it absorbs water and minerals as
required. For animals, positive or negative evaluations are
accompanied by a pattern of physiological changes organized
towards approach or withdrawal. Most animals move towards
those events which are good and promote welfare, and move
away from those which are dangerous and destructive of
life.

These positive and negative evaluations and perceptions
of beneficial and harmful factors can be generalized to
other environmental events through processes of conditioning, and in this way many likes and dislikes can be
acquired. Experiments with humans have shown that if neutral
stimuli are paired closely in time with a pleasant event
such as a good lunch or with unpleasant putrid odours, the
neutral stimuli will subsequently be rated as more pleasant
or more unpleasant.

It is a common experience that tastes which were once
pleasant become disagreeable or even revolting when they
have been associated with discomfort or nausea. In this way
new evaluations allow the anticipation of favourable or
unfavourable events, thus diminishing harmful effects and
enabling the organism to ensure a better adjustment to its
environment.

Concepts of behaviour

There are a number of concepts which link the study of
behaviour and the brain and these include arousal, emotion,
motivation, learning and memory. One of the most striking
and easily observable features of human activity is the
shift along a dimension of arousal, from deep sleep to
intense wakefulness. Another is the episodic occurrence of

emotion, especially love, fear and anger; and, of course, those motivated states relating to hunger, thirst and sex.

Arousal

Humans, in line with many animals, show phases of sleep, wakefulness and high energy output. At high levels of arousal, many cognitive functions such as speed of reaction, memorizing, learning, etc., improve. The spur of high arousal when writing examination papers must be a common experience; extreme agitation, on the other hand, can exert an unpleasant handicapping effect. It seems that up to a certain optimal point arousal acts as a spur to do well, but when it becomes too intense and spills over into anxiety behaviour is disorganized and people are unable to perform efficiently. Although the concept of general arousal was initially described from observation of behaviour, its status has been made more plausible by the discovery of a structure within the brain, the reticular formation, which seems to serve as a general arousal system for the cortex.

Emotion

Many observations indicate that emotionality is related to the activity of the autonomic nervous system, and internal bodily upheaval is one of the surest signs we have that we are emotionally disturbed. This physiological disturbance is believed to have a biological utility in the preparation for action. Under emotional arousal the heart beats faster, hormones are released, and blood is diverted to the brain and skeletal muscles to mobilize the body for prompt and efficient fight or flight.

Action in the jungle often means escape from predators. Man is a highly socialized and domesticated animal, whose emotionality is more likely to be triggered by social factors such as evaluation by other people, threat of failure, meeting strangers and so on. In adult humans, social interactions at work and in the family, and the means of smoothing social relationships, assume great importance.

In all these situations extensive psychophysiological changes occur, although largely below conscious awareness. Many people do not judge their internal states very precisely, even with physiological events which might seem obvious, like an increased heart rate or high level of muscle tension. The evidence suggests rather that perception of bodily activity and actual bodily activity are not very highly related.

The significance of concepts of arousal and motivation lies not only in their linkage with the brain and nervous system but also in relation to stress, health and well-being. Man no longer lives in a jungle, but the 'emergency' services he has inherited still act as though he did; the signs of danger are not from predators but become conditioned to stimuli, events and people in the course of everyday interaction with the environment. These events can trigger excessive physiological arousal which may be felt as behaviour. Not all of them relate to the brain and nervous system, but in this section we concentrate on those theories which relate personality to arousal and emotion systems of the brain.

Eysenck, for example, postulates that individuals range along a continuum of arousal, extraverts having a chronically lower level of cortical arousal than introverts, who have a relatively high level. Because of this, introverts have a reduced need for external stimulation to attain their optimal levels of arousal. Thus a high level of internal arousal accounts for the introvert's relative aversion to stimulating activities, exciting events and social contacts. By contrast, the extravert's low level of internal arousal leads to a search for external stimuli - noise, excitement, new experiences and many social contacts - in order to achieve an optimum level of arousal. If prevented from seeking these kinds of varied stimuli the extravert may become bored and readily distractable.

Eysenck's scheme also includes the dimension of neuroticism. This has been related to excessive activity of the autonomic nervous system; people who are high on the neuroticism dimension are described as having strong and labile emotions, while those at the other end experience less strong and more stable emotions. Taken together, the two dimensions of extraversion-introversion and neuroticism form four quadrants: those people who are both introverted and unstable tend to be moody, anxious, reserved, unsociable; those both introverted and stable tend to be calm, even-tempered, careful and thoughtful. People who are both extraverted and unstable tend to be touchy, restless, aggressive, excitable and impulsive; those who are both extraverted and stable are lively, easy-going, outgoing, carefree people. Further descriptions refer to the introvert as reacting to low levels of sensory stimuli, and as being sensitive and reactive to frustration.

Other personality scales measure such traits as impulsiveness (e.g. the tendency to act on the spur of the moment without planning), and sensation-seeking, which refers to unusual activities such as sky-diving, speed-racing, taking drugs, etc. Attempts have been made by many investigators to relate personality measures derived from such questionnaires to general autonomic reactivity, cortical excitability, adrenalin/noradrenaline output, and, more recently, to a number of biochemical variables.

Intelligence is another source of variation between individuals which is believed to have a biological/genetic basis. Conventional tests of intelligence (IQ) usually measure cognitive tasks similar to those involved in scholastic examinations, and might give disadvantageous results for members of minority groups from different cultural and educational backgrounds. This has stimulated a search for alternatives to the usual IQ test and in recent years measurements of small electrical changes obtained from surface scalp electrodes have been made as indices of 'neural efficiency', the hypothesis being that when a stimulus occurs, neurones which are fast and efficient generate characteristic waves of evoked potential.

Several studies have reported correlations between these measures and intelligence, but it is too early to say whether this approach will have any practical value in the intelligence issue.

**Environmental
stressors**

Conditions on which life and health depend are found both within and without the living organism. Inside there is the whole complex machinery which regulates the internal 'environment'; that is, the circulating organic liquid which surrounds and bathes all of the body tissues. Outside are all the changing features of the environment which require powers of adaptation and learning to cope with change.

Most animals are innately equipped to deal with the specific changes of importance they are likely to encounter; most, too, learn to react more efficiently as a result of experience. One important mechanism, for example, is that of habituation; learning not to respond when a response is no longer necessary. Thus animals once alarmed by the irregular rattle of passing trains soon learn that they can safely graze in adjacent fields without generating endless fear responses.

There are several theories of stress which involve the concept of individuals being driven beyond their powers of coping or adaptation, such that equilibrium is not easily restored.

The psychobiological use of the term 'stress' has its origins in the work of Selye in Canada, who sees stress as the state of the organism following failure of the normal mechanisms of adaptation. If stressor agents (Selye's work was mainly with rats and involved such stressors as intense heat, cold, virus infections, intoxicants, haemorrhage, muscular exercise, drugs, injury and surgical trauma) are applied intensely or long enough, they produce certain general systemic changes which represent the animal's attempt to cope with the situation. These common changes constitute the response pattern of systemic stress. They include autonomic excitability, adrenalin discharge, and such symptoms as an increased heart rate, decreased body temperature and muscle tone, blood sugar changes and gastro intestinal ulcerations. These changes occur in an initial reaction to the stressor agent, which Selye labelled the alarm reaction. If noxious stimulation continues but is not too severe, a second phase occurs, which he labelled the stage of resistance, and in which the adaptive powers of the body act to counteract the stressor. If noxious stimulation persists, this stage gives way to the final stage of exhaustion, which may ultimately lead to death.

It is important to know whether psychological stimuli can also induce a systemic stress syndrome, with similar physiological response patterns occurring in similar stages. Men in stressful situations such as paratroopers,

submariners, pilots and combat infantrymen, have demonstrated that life-threat and social-status-threat situations
can induce symptoms of systemic stress, the degree of stress
depending on the type, intensity and duration of the threat
and on certain pre-stress sensitizing factors such as personality and previous conditioning experiences. However, the
attempt to extend Selye's idea of general systemic stress to
include psychological aspects has met with many problems.
Psychological stress factors are less easy to define,
measurements of the physiological changes are less easy to
make and there are obvious ethical limitations on laboratory
research with human volunteers.

Certain issues in psychological stress are amenable to
laboratory-type investigations with both human and animal
subjects, and one theme relates to general 'coping behaviour', particularly with reference to the control which individuals feel they have over frustrating situations. These
studies indicate that stress reactions to unavoidable and
uncontrollable aversive stimuli are much more severe than
those resulting from exposure to situations over which the
individual can develop control. It seems to be not only the
exposure to, say, painful and unpleasant stimuli which leads
to distress, but the knowledge of not being 'in control' of
them which leads to feelings of helplessness in susceptible
individuals. Contemporary life provides many frustrating
situations over which we have little or no control, for
example, bureaucratic decisions, cancellation of scheduled
trains, being treated rudely when no retaliation is possible, traffic disruptions, and so on: situations in which
there may be few successful methods of coping. One specu-
lation is that persistent exposure to such conditions can
generate feelings of hopelessness and helplessness, which
may contribute towards lack of motivation and possibly even
to depression.

Relations between physiology and behaviour

A fundamental assumption is that the unique character of
human beings, their ability to think, feel, learn and
remember, lies in the brain and in the pattern and chemistry
of inter-connections between neurones. Exactly how information is received about the world, how it is processed,
interpreted, learnt and stored are questions being pursued
with an enormous range of sophisticated techniques.

Brain research
Under this heading come those studies which use brain imp-
lantation techniques, that is, the placing of electrical or
chemical stimulation devices in the brain, and these have
provided many illustrations of how brain stimulation affects
motivational and emotional behaviour. In some experiments,
animals have been provided with a lever which triggers
electrical stimulation of their own brains and when electrodes are placed in parts of the limbic system (a phylo-
genetically old part of the brain, the functions of which

are obscure but believed to relate to emotionality) these animals press the lever almost continuously, as if there were something very positive about this experience. This work often refers to the 'pleasure' areas of the brain.

Dramatic effects have also been produced through destroying localized regions of the brain: wild, unmanageable animals have been transformed into gentle creatures that could be fed by hand, while other procedures have produced a state of violent rage even in very tame laboratory rats.

As a result of the development of surgical techniques and the powerful effects of brain intervention observed on behaviour, it has been thought that brain surgery might alleviate severe and intractable behaviour problems such as hyperexcitability and violent, destructive and uncontrollably aggressive behaviour, and some exploratory attempts have been made in this direction. It is not easy to evaluate the results of these operations: on the whole, there is always a cost-benefit factor in neurosurgery. No miraculous recovery is ever accomplished with the kinds of very severe behavioural problems which have been referred, and although relief from disabling symptoms may be obtained, there is always the chance that it will create other difficulties.

There are also ethical problems associated with brain surgery. Some people have argued that violent prisoners, for example, should be treated by surgical means rather than spend a lifetime in prison. Others feel that because the brain is the reservoir of creativity and individuality it should never be disturbed unless it is clearly diseased or injured.

Many brain-behaviour studies arise from accidental brain lesions, following which a variety of disorders have been noted in speech, motor behaviour, memory and perception. These vary in extent and quality as a function of the nature and place of injury, and detailed mapping of the disability will hopefully lead to a better understanding of how speech, memory, etc., are organized within the brain. Assessment of this type of deficit can be assisted by the use of appropriate psychological tests; in the case of emotional deficits, however, no tests are available and assessment is more difficult. As a result, much less is known about the effects of brain and central nervous system damage on normal human feelings. Reports on the emotional life of those suffering from accidental spinal lesions suggest a reduction in the intensity of feeling, and an awareness of a more 'mental' kind of emotional response than of a powerful physiological drive.

Recent work has highlighted the psychological importance of brain chemistry, which seems to be involved in processes such as attention and sensitivity to pain, mood and emotionality. One theory, for example, is that certain chemicals in the brain determine mood shifts as seen in mania and depression, from which it might follow that corrections for chemical imbalance could be achieved by drug administration.

There are, however, many complications when human beings are involved in treatment of this kind, for as well as direct pharmacological effects, psychological factors such as expectancies of both the therapist and patient, and aspects of the therapeutic setting, also play a part. A related observation is that some patients claim satisfactory pain relief from placebos (i.e. completely inactive, 'dummy' tablets) for many kinds of symptoms, and attempts have been made, so far without clear resolution, to identify who these people are and what the mechanism is by which the effect is produced.

Physiological psychology

Topics frequently studied under this heading include motivation, memory and learning, and this kind of research usually involves animal subjects. A traditional method of study is to lesion specific regions of the brain to examine the effect on behaviour. Another approach is to correlate electrical events within the brain with the course of learning and performance.

A major unresolved question is whether there is a single anatomical site or physiological process responsible for memory, learning, and motivated behaviour. Several theories concentrate on the synaptic connections between the neurones of the brain, long thought to relate to learning and memory. In recent years there has been an interest in the role of the hippocampus in learning and the storage of short-term memories. This is a structure tucked within the very old part of the cerebral cortex. In humans, bilateral lesions associated with this area have been shown to cause a severe and lasting memory deficit characterized by the inability to learn new information. Patients with such lesions appear to have undiminished powers of perception but they are largely incapable of incorporating new information into their long-term store.

A topic of profound importance is how we register and record the events of the world about us. Research in the past decade has revealed the existence of cells within the brain which appear to react quite specifically to different aspects of a sensory stimulus. They have been termed 'feature detectors' in that some cells will fire at the onset of a stimulus, others to its colour, others again to its duration, intensity and localization in space. Some neurones are specially tuned to respond to complex stimuli, to time characteristics and to novelty. Thus incoming stimuli leave traces of their characteristics within the nervous system. These traces or 'neuronal models' preserve information about the intensity, quality, duration, etc., of past stimuli and it is against these stored models that new events are compared. Several theorists have proposed that there is an analysing mechanism within the brain which assesses the novelty and significance of incoming events in such terms as: is this event new or has it happened before? Is it significant or irrelevant? It then activates the appropriate response or damps down responding (as in habituation) if the event has occurred many times before and is unimportant. In this way we build up an internal picture of the external world, and act on that information.

The brain appears to have two halves (hemispheres) which were once assumed to be similar in function, as are the two kidneys and two lungs. Actually, there are some specialized functions which are found only in one or other of the two sides. The best example is that of language: damage to a particular region of the cortex on the left side of the brain leads to aphasia; damage to the corresponding area on the right side leaves the faculty of speech intact. This asymmetry is also reflected in memory defects arising from damage to the temporal region of the brain. Injury to the left side can impair the ability to retain verbal material but leave intact the ability to remember spatial locations, faces, melodies and abstract visual patterns.

One of the most interesting recent findings is that different emotional reactions follow damage to the right and left sides of the brain. Comprehension of the affective components of speech is impaired with right but not with left lesions, and the comprehension of humorous material is different in patients with left and right hemisphere lesions. While this specialization of the hemispheres should not be over-exaggerated, it does suggest a unique kind of specialization within the human brain.

Psychosomatic medicine
One of the most striking features of psychosomatic illness is the marked individual difference in susceptibility to illness, and in the patterning of symptoms. Why one patient should develop gastric ulcers while another develops high blood pressure is a question that has often been asked and not yet satisfactorily answered.

There is reasonably general agreement that prolonged emotional disturbance associated with deleterious physiological effects can arise from conflict, stress and certain life changes and that these may lead to tissue change and organic disease.

There have been many theories concerning the psychophysiological specificity, or patterning of response, which is a feature of psychosomatic disorders. One possibility is a genetic component which determines the organ system involved, another that this combines with a learning process such as classical conditioning. Conditioned visceral responses can occur to all sorts of stimuli and can be remarkably persistent over time. They are of particular interest in that while visceral organs have cortical representation, the activity of visceral organs is not easily discriminated and is generally below normal conscious awareness. This suggests that an individual might become conditioned to respond to inappropriate internal or external stimuli over long periods of time during which there would be self-knowledge of the progressive disturbance of function.

As just mentioned, it is believed that the recent occurrence of conflict, emotional upheaval or environmental stress is implicated in the precipitation of symptoms. Several researchers have attempted to assess the recent changes in individuals' lives prior to illness onset, and an association between them has been repeatedly documented. However, even the highest of these correlations is relatively modest, suggesting that recent life changes alone do not exert a strong primary effect on illness onset. What effect they do exert seems to be influenced by the way in which an individual perceives them, as well as by the individual's coping capabilities and illness behaviour characteristics.

Investigations into coronary heart disease both in the USA and Europe have reported a constellation of personality traits, attitudes and life styles alleged to characterize this illness. A 'Type A' behaviour pattern comprising ambitious, driving and competitive work behaviour with a sense of urgency towards deadlines and associated with more intense cardio-vascular reactions has been compared with the more placid, less reactive 'Type B' individual who is less inclined to develop coronary heart disease. However, no clear-cut method of dividing people into 'Type A' or 'Type B' categories is available, and correlations between behaviour patterns and illness are still at a preliminary stage.

A fully satisfactory explanation of psychosomatic illness must account for the continuity, chronicity and specificity of symptoms, and explanations are likely to be multifactorial in nature. Undoubtedly progress will follow better diagnosis. Psychosomatic disorders traditionally include asthma, gastric ulcers, some cardio-vascular disorders, hypertension, and tension headaches. These are very globally defined illness categories, within each of which specific subforms of the illness can probably be delineated.

Psychophysiology

Attention, interest, thinking and feelings are accompanied by generalized changes throughout the brain and nervous system. Against this background, specific excitation occurs in the performance of specific tasks: looking at a picture entails a complex mosaic of eye movements, playing tennis involves the patterning of muscle action potentials and attending to a speaker requires the inhibition of other inputs.

How the psychological constructs of attention, thinking, and feeling interact with physiological changes, and what the nature of their interaction is, remains a complex and fascinating research problem. The direction of causality is uncertain: is it the perception of a threatening situation which arouses the physiological concomitants of anxiety, or does the physiological arousal come first and determine the nature of the perception?

Psychophysiology is an area of study which concentrates on human behaviour, and tries to analyse the cognitive, verbal and psychological aspects of behaviour in relation to the physiological. The term physiological in this context refers to those variables which can be recorded by means of small disk electrodes which can be attached to the surface of the skin. The range of variables which can be recorded in this way is very wide and includes heart rate, palmar skin resistance (attributable to palmar sweating), skin temperature, blood flow, respiration, and cortical potentials recorded from the surface of the brain.

Most of these variables show constant on-going activity: the heart, lungs and cortical potentials show rhythmic changes and also quite striking changes in response to simple stimuli such as lights and tones. More complex situations - verbal instructions, conversation, calling the individual by name, mental arithmetic tasks, and so on - can produce larger changes of long duration.

When the individual is left quietly to relax this activity shows a steady decline. If now an unexpected stimulus is given, a startle or orientating ('what is it?') response occurs. When the same stimulus is repeated, the response becomes smaller on each subsequent occasion until it no longer occurs: that is, it has habituated. Among psychophysiologists there is substantial interest in the physiological changes which occur in habituation, in conditioned autonomic responses, and in the patterning of reactivity to mild stressors which occurs in different individuals.

Useful information concerning the neurophysiology of cognitive processes in humans can be obtained from recording cortical potentials in response to stimuli. The combined electrical activity of millions of neurones in the brain is recorded in electro-encephalographic recordings. There is evidence that certain components of the cortical response are related to the physical attributes of the stimulus (its sensory modality, intensity), while other components reflect the individual's evaluation of the significance or meaning of the stimulus. Selective attention to one stimulus and not to another can be demonstrated in that components of the cortical response to the monitored stimulus are enhanced, as compared with those to an irrelevant stimulus.

Psychophysiological responsivity has often been considered in relation to clinical anxiety. Anxious patients frequently report trembling, sweating, shortness of breath, palpitations and muscular tension, and these have been recorded in situations where the patient is at rest, trying to relax, and also in response to different stimuli. There are several reports of anxious people typically responding more readily, habituating more slowly, and taking longer to recover from stimulation.

Psychophysiological measures can provide useful indicators of autonomic and cortical reactivity in different situations. They are helpful in their demonstration of individuals' idiosyncratic response profiles, in the study of habituation, relationship to task performance, processing of information, and in their indication of the variety of changes which occur along the sleep-wakefulness continuum. Perhaps the future may also see further links between psychophysiological research and the problems of psychosomatic medicine and psychiatry.

Concluding comments

If the aim of psychology is to clarify Man's behaviour in this world it must accord a central position to biology, since this of all disciplines is the most directly linked to the understanding of living beings. The biological basis of behaviour refers to evolutionary, genetic, physiological and brain-behaviour mechanisms, and more recently has been extended to human social behaviour. Such an approach does not deny the importance of environmental factors or their capacity to modify the organism's behaviour; indeed, it strives towards methods of studying and assessing their contribution.

The biological approach has gained in impetus from the massive technological and theoretical advances of recent decades. The discovery within molecular biology of deoxyribonucleic acid (DNA) and the theory of the genetic code tell us how the information is coded which determines that a new life will inherit the characteristics of its parents. Other developments make it possible to record electrical events from single neurones within the brain, and to measure minute traces of brain chemicals. Studies by ethologists have made us all familiar with the behavioural repertoire of animals in their natural habitat.

Yet there remain many challenges to the understanding of human nature. The work which psychologists have to do centres on the analysis of behaviour into useful segments, and the derivation of meaningful concepts such as attention and arousal, emotion, memory and stress. It must contend with individual variation, possibly along dimensions such as extraversion, neuroticism and impulsiveness, and elucidate the psychophysiology of neurosis and stress reactions. The goal which lies ahead in the biological context is the fitting together of these psychological concepts with the mechanisms of bodily activity which underlie human individuality and welfare.

Questions

1. What explanations would you offer of the fact that some people are more anxious than others?
2. Some stressful life events may have an effect on health. Describe some of the bodily symptoms which are believed to be related to stress.
3. What cues enable you to judge the kind of emotion a person is experiencing? Discuss the relative importance of the different cues which you use.
4. Describe the method of classical conditioning.

5. Why do you suppose that it is generally ineffective to 'tell' someone not to be afraid or not to be angry?
6. What is meant by 'habituation'? What is its practical usefulness?
7. What are the symptoms likely to be mentioned by people who feel anxious?
8. Suggest some ways in which individuals could be taught to reduce excessively high autonomic and muscular tension.
9. What is meant by the nature/nurture controversy?
10. There is controversy about the extent to which intelligence is inherited. What do you think are the social implications of this controversy?

Annotated reading

Boddy, J. (1978) Brain Systems and Psychological Concepts. Chichester: Wiley.

The chapter on adapting to the environment is a simple introduction to such themes as adaptation, innate behaviour patterns, information storage and behavioural flexibility. The chapter on the need for stimulation deals with themes of optimal arousal, the need for sensory input, effects of enriched and impoverished environments, and related topics. Other chapters in this useful book deal at a more advanced level with the subject matter of the biological bases chapter.

Eysenck, H.J. (1976) Psychology as a bio-social science. In H.J. Eysenck and G.D. Wilson (eds), A Textbook of Human Psychology. Lancaster: MTP.

An introduction to psychology as the study of behaviour with special reference to the interaction of social and biological factors.

Gale, A. and Edwards, J. (eds) (in press) Physiological Correlates of Human Behaviour. London: Academic Press.

An undergraduate text which approaches physiological processes from the human point of view. There are basic chapters which include a philosophical chapter on the logical bases of physiological psychology and special sections on the correlates of personality and mental illness.

Martin, I. (1976) Emotions. In H.J. Eysenck and G.D. Wilson (eds), A Textbook of Human Psychology. Lancaster: MTP.

Strongman, K.T. (1978) The Psychology of Emotion (2nd edn). Chichester: Wiley.

The above two references discuss a number of facets concerning the study of emotion.

Van Toller, C. (1979) The Nervous Body: An introduction to the autonomic nervous system and behaviour. Chichester: Wiley.

The chapter on psychosomatic disease, and the ways in which genetic and social factors cause it, is a useful outline of the different approaches to psychosomatic complaints.

Exercises

1. Correlates of emotion

Prepare a list of six or so words which describe emotional states (e.g. anger, fear, excitement). Then interview your friends, asking them to describe the physiological concomitants which they experience in these states. Now compare the different lists. Is there evidence of a common response to a particular emotion? Do your respondents vary in the ease with which they are able to report the physiological changes? If so, why?

2. Facial expression and body posture

Taking your list of emotions again, ask different friends to simulate them. If you have a video camera you can record the expressions and postures made for each emotion. Ask another set of friends to act as judges; can they clarify the emotions accurately, without knowing the label in advance? Interview your actors. Can they tell you what they do to achieve the simulated emotion?

3. The meaning of emotional words

Interview a group of children and ask them what they mean by such words as fear, anger, jealousy, love and so on. How do they describe these feelings? Repeat the exercise with another group of a different age. What comparisons can be made?

4. Circadian rhythms

For this exercise you will need to keep a diary for a week. Prepare separate sheets of paper, each with a seven-point scale marked 'alert' and 'sleepy' at either end. Leave space to write the day of the week and the time. Every two hours, rate how you feel and then put the paper in a box, so that you cannot refer to it until the exercise is finished. At the end of the week, plot all the data on a graph. Are there consistent times each day when your alertness varies in a systematic fashion?

5. Arousal and pulse rate

It is quite easy to learn to take your own pulse. A 15-second sample will be sufficient; multiply the number of beats by four to give your heart rate (beats per minute: b.p.m.). Now try a variety of situations, gathering a few samples of each. They could include: standing, lying down, waiting for an aeroplane to take off, meeting someone you are very fond of, just before an important interview, after climbing the stairs, and so on. As far as possible obtain an average for each type of event. Then rank the events for b.p.m. Do the heart rate changes match your expectations?

List the situations on a sheet of paper. Ask friends to rate each situation on a seven-point scale for 'relaxed' to 'highly aroused'. Do their judgements correlate with your heart-rate data?

6. Manwatching
Prepare a coding sheet and observe people in different situations. (i) Watch people in two sorts of queue, say, outside a cinema or waiting for a bus. Are there differences in the two situations, and why? (ii) Observe people in a park on a sunny day or in a library. How do they arrange themselves in terms of the space they leave between them and the opportunities for eye-contact or verbal communication? Within these situations, do you observe differences between people? For example, are some people closer in proximity? What reasons might there be, and how could you test your hunches?

7. Cues to emotion
Conduct an informal survey of several person-to-person situations; for example, two people in conversation in a restaurant or bus. What evidence of physiological arousal do you observe in the interchange, and how could the evidence be used to infer what the individuals are experiencing?

4

Social development in early childhood
H. R. Schaffer

Psychologists study children for two main reasons. First, they want to find out how a helpless, naïve and totally dependent baby manages in due course to become a competent, knowledgeable adult. They are interested therefore in studying the process of development. The second reason stems from the many social problems associated with childhood. Should we protect children from viewing violence on television? Are children of mothers who go out to work more likely to become delinquent? Does hospitalization in the early years produce later difficulties? How can one mitigate the effects of divorce on children? Why do some parents become baby batterers? Increasingly the psychologist is asked to examine such problems and produce answers useful to society. It is primarily to this aspect of child psychology that we pay attention here.

The child's socialization

How children develop depends very much on the people around them. From them the child learns the skills and values needed for social living, from the use of knives and forks to knowing the difference between right and wrong. Other people are always around the child, being of influence by means of example and command, and none more so at first than the members of the immediate family. On them depend the initial stages of socialization.

Disadvantaged children and their families
It is, of course, only too apparent that not every family carries out its socializing task with equal effectiveness. By way of illustration, let us look at the way in which intellectual development is shaped by the child's social environment.

At one time it was thought that intelligence is entirely determined by an individual's inborn endowment. There are few who now believe this: it seems rather that the environment in which a child is reared can have a powerful effect on development.

The issue has been much debated in relation to the poor educational achievement of 'disadvantaged' children. These are children who come from the economically and socially most deprived sectors of the community and who so often appear to be at a severe disadvantage when first starting school, because (as it has been put) 'they have learnt not to learn'. Their failure in the education system, in other words, is ascribed not so much to some genetic inferiority as to factors operating in the home, which result in an inability to make use of whatever intellectual capacities they have.

A great many schemes have been launched to counter this situation, especially in the USA. Some of the earlier efforts, designed to give children some extra training in basic cognitive skills before school entry, were clearly inadequate and produced no lasting benefits. This is partly because the schemes were too brief, partly because they came too late in the child's life, but partly also because they left untouched the home situation. Given a conflict of values about education between home and school it is highly likely that the home will always win. It is there that the child has already lived and learnt for several years before ever starting school, and it is therefore significant that more recent efforts have attempted to involve the parents as well as the child or even to work solely through the parents.

There is now little doubt that parents can enhance or suppress the child's educational potential. One way in which they apparently do this is by the extent to which they foster the development of language: a function so necessary for the expression of intelligence. There are pronounced social class differences in the style of language mothers use to communicate with their children; in addition, however, it has also been shown that mothers from disadvantaged homes engage in face-to-face talking with their infants less frequently than middle-class mothers. The poorer child often lives in much noisier surroundings than the middle-class child in a quiet suburban home, but to profit from stimulation the young child must be exposed to it under the personalized conditions that only the to-and-fro reciprocity of a face-to-face situation provides. It is in this respect that many lower-class 'socially deprived children' are at a disadvantage.

Child effects on adults

Let us not now jump to the conclusion that children's development is totally a matter of what parents do to them. A child is never just a passive being that one can mould into whatever shape the adult desires. Even the youngest babies can already exert an influence on their caretakers and so help to determine how they behave towards them.

Take an obvious example: babies cry and thereby draw attention to themselves. It is a sound that can have a most compelling effect on the adult: we have all heard of the mother who can sleep through a thunderstorm, but is immediately awoken by her child's whimper in the next room. Babies, by this powerful signal, can initiate the interaction: they can thereby influence both the amount and the timing of attention which others provide.

Babies come into the world as individuals. Some are active and restless, others quiet and content; some are highly sensitive, others are emotionally robust and easy-going. The kind of care provided for one is therefore inappropriate for another, and any sensitive mother will therefore find herself compelled to adopt practices suitable for her individual child. A good example is provided by babies' differences in 'cuddliness'. Not all babies love being held and cuddled: some positively hate it and resist such contact by struggling and, unless released, by crying. It has been found that these 'non-cuddlers' tend to be more active and restless generally, and to be intolerant of all types of physical restraint (as seen when they are being dressed or tucked into bed). Mothers are accordingly forced to treat these children in a manner that takes into account their 'peculiarity': when frightened or unwell these children cannot be comforted by being held close but have to be offered other forms of stimulation such as bottles, biscuits or soothing voices. Each mother must therefore show considerable flexibility in adjusting to the specific requirements of her child.

There is one further, and perhaps unexpected, example one can quote of the way in which parents are influenced by their children. It concerns the phenomenon of baby battering, which has attracted so much attention in recent years. It is by no means a new phenomenon; historically speaking, it is probably as old as the family itself. What is new is public concern that such a thing can happen, and this in turn has given rise to the need for research into such cases. As a result of various investigations it is now widely agreed that violence results from a combination of several factors: the presence of financial, occupational and housing problems facing the family; the parents' emotional immaturity which makes it difficult for them to deal with such problems; their social isolation from potential sources of help such as relatives and neighbours; and, finally, some characteristic of the battered child which singles out that child as a likely victim.

It is the last factor that is particularly relevant to us, for it illustrates once again that the way in which parents treat their children is influenced by the children themselves. There is evidence that children most likely to be battered are 'difficult': they are more likely to be sickly, or to have been born prematurely, or to have feeding and sleeping problems. Being more difficult to rear, they make extra demands that the parents are just not able to meet. The child's condition acts on the parent's inadequacy, and so the child, unwittingly, contributes to its own fate.

Mother–child mutuality
It is apparent that children do not start life as psychological nonentities. From the beginning they already have an individuality that influences the adults around them. Thus a mother's initial task is not to create something out of

nothing; it is rather to dovetail her behaviour to that of the child.

Such dovetailing takes many forms. Take our previous example of the non-cuddlers. If the mother herself has a preference for close physical contact which the baby rejects, some mutual readjustment will need to take place. Fortunately, most mothers quickly adjust and find other ways of relating to the child. It is only when they are too inflexible, or interpret the baby's behaviour as rejection, that trouble can arise from a mismatch.

Mutual adjustment is the hallmark of all interpersonal behaviour; it can be found in even the earliest social interactions. The feeding situation provides a good example. Should babies be fed by demand or by a rigid, predetermined schedule? Advice by doctors and nurses has swung fashion-wise, sometimes stressing the importance of exerting discipline from the very beginning and of not 'giving in', at other times pointing to the free and easy methods of primitive tribes as the 'natural way'. In actual fact each mother and baby, however they may start off, sooner or late work out a pattern which satisfies both partners. On the one hand, there are few mothers who can bear to listen for long to a bawling infant unable as yet to tell the time; on the other hand, one should not under-estimate the ability of even very young babies to adjust to the demands of their environment. An example is provided by an experiment, carried out many years ago, in which two groups of babies were fed during the first ten days of life according to a three-hour and four-hour schedule respectively. Within just a few days after birth each baby had already developed a peak of restlessness just before the accustomed feeding time, and this became particularly obvious when the three-hour group was shifted to a four-hour schedule and so had to wait an extra hour for their feed. In time, however, these babies too became accustomed to the new timetable and showed the restlessness peak at four-hourly intervals. We can see here a form of adaptation to social demands that must represent one of the earliest forms of learning.

Not surprisingly, the major responsibility for mutual adjustment lies initially with the adult. The degree of flexibility one can expect from very young children is limited. Yet the very fact that they are involved in social interactions from the very beginning of life means that they have the opportunity of gradually acquiring the skills necessary to become full partners in such exchanges. Observations of give-and-take games with babies at the end of the first year have made this point. Initially babies know only how to take: they have not learnt that their behaviour is just one part of a sequence, that they need to take turns with others, and that the roles of two participants are interchangeable (one being a giver, the other a taker). Such, and other, rules of behaviour they will learn in time; rules form the basis for much of social intercourse, and it is through social intercourse that children acquire them in the first place.

Socialization is sometimes portrayed as a long drawn-out battle, as a confrontation between wilful young children and irritated parents that must at all cost be resolved in favour of the latter. Goodness knows such battles occur, yet they are far from telling us everything about the process of socialization. There is a basic mutuality between parent and child without which interaction would not be possible. The sight of the mother's face automatically elicits a smile from the baby; that produces a feeling of delight in the mother and causes her in turn to smile back and to talk or tickle or pick up, in this way calling forth further responses from the baby. A whole chain of interaction is thus started, not infrequently initiated by the baby. Mother and child learn about each other in the course of these interactions, and more often than not mutual adjustment is brought about by a kind of negotiation process in which both partners show some degree of flexibility. On the mother's part, this calls for sensitivity to the particular needs and requirements of her child, an ingredient of parenthood that we return to subsequently; on the child's part, it refers to one of the most essential aspects of social living that must be accepted early on.

Some conditions that foster development

If we are to promote the mental health and social integration of children, it is necessary to identify the factors that further, or on the contrary hinder, such an aim. We all have our favourite theories as to why some children do not develop in what we regard as a desirable manner: not enough parental discipline, too much violence on television, the declining influence of religion, the social isolation of today's family, and so on. It is much more difficult, however, to substantiate through objective research that any one factor does play a part. Nevertheless, there are some conclusions to which we can point.

The blood-bond: myth or reality?

Is it essential, or at least desirable, that children should be brought up by their natural parents? Is a woman who conceived and bore a child by that very fact more fitted to care for this child than an unrelated individual?

This is no academic question. Children have been removed by courts of law from the foster parents with whom they had lived nearly all their lives and to whom they had formed deep attachments, in order to restore them to their biological mother from whom they may have been apart since the early days of life, and all because of the 'blood-bond'. Yet such a thing is a complete myth. There is nothing at all to suggest that firm attachments cannot grow between children and unrelated adults who have taken over the parental role. The notion that the biological mother, by virtue of being the biological mother, is uniquely capable of caring for her child is without foundation.

Were it otherwise, the whole institution of adoption would be in jeopardy. Yet there is nothing to suggest that adoptive parents are in any way inferior to natural parents. In a study by Barbara Tizard (to which we refer again), children who had been in care throughout their early years were followed up on leaving care. One group of children was adopted, another returned to their own families. It was found that the latter did less well than the adopted children, both in the initial stages of settling in and in their subsequent progress. The reason lay primarily in the attitudes of the two sets of parents: the adoptive group worked harder at being parents, possibly just because the child was not their own. There have been a good many studies which have examined the effects of adoption, and virtually all stress the high proportion of successful cases to be found. And this despite the difficulties such children may have had to face, such as problems in the pre-adoption phase and the knowledge gained later on of the fact of their adoption. Successful parenting is a matter of particular personality characteristics that need to be identified, not of 'blood'.

Fathers as parents: more myths?
Do children have to be cared for primarily by women? Is there something about females that makes them more suitable for this task than males? What part should fathers play in the child's upbringing?

The answer is simple. There is no 'should' or 'should not'. It is a matter of what each society and each family decides about the division of roles between the parents. There have in fact been marked changes over the last few decades in the extent to which fathers participate in child care. They now do so to a far greater extent than they used to, and this trend is continuing. For instance, with increasing unemployment it is no longer uncommon to find families in which a complete role reversal has taken place: mother, having found a job, goes out to work, leaving her unemployed husband in charge of home and children. Fortunately, there is no evidence to indicate that the biological make-up of men makes them unfit for this task or even necessarily inferior to women in this respect. Parenting is unisex; the reasons for the traditional division of labour (such as the need to breast-feed the child and the importance of using men's greater physical strength for hunting and tilling the fields) are no longer applicable.

Children brought up without a father are more likely to encounter difficulties than those in a complete family. There are various reasons for this. One is that in any single-parent family the remaining parent must cope with a great multiplicity of stresses - financial, occupational, or emotional - and the strain felt by him or (more often) her is very likely to have repercussions for the child too. Again, a fatherless boy has no model to imitate, and the developmental tasks of acquiring sex-appropriate behaviour may be more difficult. And, finally, children isolated with the mother and caught up in one all-encompassing relationship do not have the same chance of learning from the beginning about some of the complexities of the social world: having two parents helps them to learn at once that not all people are alike and that they must adapt their own behaviour according to the parents' different characteristics and different demands.

Parenthood: full-time or part-time?

Until fairly recently there was a widespread belief among parents and professional workers that children in the pre-school period required full-time mothering, and that it was the duty of mothers to stay with the child night and day, 24 hours on end. Otherwise, it was feared, children's mental health would suffer.

We can look at this situation from both the mother's and the child's point of view. As far as mothers are concerned, a crucial consideration is the recent finding of an extremely high incidence of depression among house-bound women. With no outlet such as a job, tied to the house by the presence of several dependant children, a large proportion of mothers (especially among the working class) become isolated and hence depressed. Mothers, on the other hand, who do go out to work are far less likely to suffer from depression, anxiety and feelings of low self-esteem.

As far as the children are concerned, comparisons of those with mothers at work and those with mothers at home have not found any differences between them. Far from being adversely affected, the former may even stand to gain both intellectually and socially. The intellectual effects stem from the extra stimulation and extra provision of play materials that most children in day-care obtain: a point of particular significance for those from disadvantaged backgrounds. And, socially, not only is there no evidence that the child's attachment to the mother is in some way 'diluted' by a daily period of being apart, but also the child in day-care has the enormous advantage of coming into contact with other children. The benefit of such experience for social development has until quite recently been overlooked; yet other children, even in the early years, can exercise a considerable socializing influence, and in addition may further the child's diversification of social behaviour. After all, the more children are encouraged to adapt to a variety of other individuals the more their repertoires of social skills will grow.

Thus a daily period away from mother may produce good rather than harm. There is, however, one important proviso, and this concerns the quality of the substitute care which the child receives. For one thing, there is a need for consistency: a young child continually being left with different people is likely to become bewildered and upset. And for another, we have the enormous problem of illegal child-minders, looking after an estimated 100,000 children in Britain. According to recent findings, the quality of care provided by such childminders is only too frequently of an unsatisfactory nature, being marked by ignorance and neglect that in some cases can be quite appalling. It is only in the

officially provided facilities, such as nursery schools,
that the care given by trained staff is such that the social
and intellectual benefits can be felt.

Sensitive and insensitive parents

Child development does not take place in a vacuum; it occurs
because the people responsible for the care of children
carefully and sensitively provide them with the kinds of
environment that will foster their growth. They do so not
only by such conscious decisions as what toys to buy for
Christmas or which nursery school to choose, but also quite
unconsciously by the manner in which they relate to the
individual child.

Take the language which adults use in talking to a
child. This is in many ways strikingly different from the
language used to address another adult: it has a much more
restricted vocabulary, a considerably simplified grammar,
and a great deal of repetition. In addition, it is characterized by a slowing down in the rate of speech, a high
pitch of voice, and the use of special intonation patterns.
Not only mothers but most adults will quite unconsciously
adopt this style when confronted by a young child. What is
more, the younger the child the more marked is the simpli-
fication, repetition, slowing down and all the other characteristics listed. It is as though the adult is making allowance for the child's limited ability to absorb whatever is
said, thereby showing sensitivity to the abilities and requirements of that particular child.

Such examples of (usually quite unconscious) sensitivity
in relating to children are numerous. Watch how a mother
hands her baby a rattle to grasp: how carefully she adjusts
the manner and speed with which she offers the toy to the
still uncertain reaching skills of the child. She shows
thereby that she is able to see things from the child's
point of view, that she is aware of the child's requirements
and can respond to these appropriately. Sensitivity is an
essential part of helping a child to develop. Children
brought up in institutions, in which they are all treated
the same and where care is never personalized, become deve-
lopmentally retarded. While most adults show sensitivity to
children quite naturally, some parents are unfortunately
devoid of this vital part of parenting. Why this is so we
still do not know for certain; it does seem, however, that
parents who themselves had a deprived childhood and did not
themselves experience sensitive care are more likely to show
the same attitude to their own children.

**Are the early years
special?**

There is a widespread belief that experience in childhood,
and particularly so in the earliest years, has a crucial
formulative influence on later personality. Thus the early
years are said to be the most important, and special care
therefore needs to be taken to protect children during this
period against harmful experiences that might mark them for
life. Let us look at the evidence for this belief.

The influence of child-rearing practices

According to Freud, a child's development is marked by a series of phases (oral, anal, genital) during which the child is especially sensitive to certain kinds of experience. During the oral phase, for example, the baby is mainly concerned with activities like sucking, chewing, swallowing and biting, and the experiences that matter most thus include the manner of feeding (breast or bottle), the timing of feeding (schedule or demand), the age of weaning, and so on. When these experiences are congenial the child passes to the next developmental phase without difficulty; when they are frustrating and stressful, however, the child remains 'fixated' at this stage in the sense that, even as an adult, the individual continues to show personality characteristics such as dependence and passivity that distinguish babies at the oral stage. In this way Freud's theory suggests that there are definite links between particular kinds of infantile experiences on the one hand, and adult personality characteristics on the other.

However, this theory has not been borne out. A large number of investigations have compared breast-feeding with bottle-feeding, self-demand with rigidly scheduled regimes, early with later weaning, and other aspects of the child's early experience that could be expected to produce lasting after-effects. No such effects have been found. The sum total of these investigations adds up to the conclusion that specific infant care practices do not produce unvarying traces that may unfailingly be picked up in later life. Whatever their impact at the time, there is no reason to believe that these early experiences mark children for good or ill for the rest of their lives.

And just as well! Were it otherwise we would all be at the mercy of some single event, some specific parental aberration, that we happened to have experienced at some long-distant point in our past. Freud's theory made little allowance for the ameliorating influence of later experience, yet the more we study human development the more apparent it becomes that children, given the opportunity, are able to recuperate from many an early misfortune. Let us consider some other examples that make this point.

Maternal deprivation

In 1951 a report was published by John Bowlby, a British child psychiatrist, pointing to the psychological ill-effects of being deprived of maternal care during the early years. The evidence, Bowlby believed, indicated that children must be with their mothers during the crucial period of the first two or three years if they are to develop the ability to form relationships with other people. Deprived of a relationship with a permanent mother-figure at that time, such an ability will never develop. Thus children in institutions and long-term hospitals, where they are deprived of this necessity, become 'affectionless characters': that is, they are unable ever to form a deep, emotionally meaningful relationship with another person. Having missed out on a vital experience, namely being mothered, the child is mentally crippled for life. And that experience has to happen at a particular time, namely in the first years. No amount of good mothering subsequently can remedy the situation.

There is no doubt about the tremendous influence on the practice of caring for childen that Bowlby's ideas have had. And no wonder, for so many children are thereby implicated. Many thousands of children every year are taken into the care of local authorities; many thousands are admitted to hospital. Anything that can be done to improve the lot of so many children is therefore worth considering, and there is no doubt that in the last two decades a great deal has been done in the UK. Children's institutions have become less impersonal with the introduction of family group systems; there is greater emphasis on fostering children with ordinary families and, most important, far more stress is placed on prevention and keeping children with their own parents. Similarly, the psychological care of children in hospitals has improved greatly during this period. Visiting by parents is nowhere near as restricted as it was at one time; mother-baby units make it possible for parents to stay with their children; and again the emphasis on prevention means that rather more thought is now given to the need to admit the child in the first place.

Anyone who has ever seen young children separated from their mothers and admitted, say, to a strange hospital ward, where they are looked after by strangers and may be subjected to unpleasant procedures like injections, knows the extreme distress that one then finds. It is perhaps difficult for an adult to appreciate the depth of panic accompanying the 'loss' of a child's mother: a panic that may continue for days and only be succeeded by a depressive-like picture when the child withdraws from a too painful world. Parents also know only too well about the insecurity which children show subsequently on return home, even after quite brief absences, when they dare not let the mother out of sight. There is no doubt about these dramatic short-term effects, and for their sake alone the steps taken to humanize procedures have been well worth while.

Far more problematic, however, is the question of long-term effects: that is, the suggestion that periods of prolonged maternal deprivation in the early years impair the child's capacity to form interpersonal relationships. What evidence we have here suggests that things are not as cut and dried as Bowlby indicated, and to make this point we can do no better than to turn to the report by Barbara Tizard to which we have already referred.

Tizard examined adopted children who had spent all their early lives in institutions, with no opportunity to form any stable attachments to any adult during that period. One might have expected them to be so marked by this experience as to be incapable of forming any emotional relationship to their adoptive parents and to show all the signs of the affectionless character. Yet this proved not to be the case.

Nearly all these children developed deep attachments to their adoptive parents, and this included even a child placed as late as seven years of age. They did show some deviant symptoms, such as poor concentration and over-friendliness to strangers, but there was no indication that the inevitable outcome of their earlier upbringing was the 'affectionless character'. We must conclude that children's recuperative powers should not be under-estimated: given a new environment in which they receive very much improved treatment, the outlook can be good. There is no reason to believe that they will be marked for life by earlier misfortunes, just because these occurred early on.

Birth abnormalities and social class

When misfortune takes a 'physical' form, such as some abnormality of the birth process, the outcome is again not necessarily a poor one. Once more, it all depends on the child's subsequent experience.

Take such birth complications as anoxia (the severe shortage of oxygen in the brain) or prematurity. Follow-up studies of children who arrive in the world in such a precarious condition show that, on the basis of condition at birth, it is impossible to predict subsequent development. Two children coming into the world with the identical kind of pathology may develop along quite different lines. In one case, the child's condition at birth may give rise to a whole sequence of problems that continue and even mount up throughout life; in the other, the difficulty is surmounted and the child functions normally.

The answer to this paradox lies in the different kinds of social environment in which the children develop. Where these are favourable the effects of the initial handicap may be minimized and in due course be overcome altogether. Where they are unfavourable the deficits remain and may even be amplified. The outcome depends not so much on the adverse circumstances of the child's birth as on the way in which the family then copes with the problem. And this, it has been found, is very much related to the social class to which the family belongs.

Social class is in many respects a nebulous concept. Nevertheless, it does refer to a set of factors (concerned with education, housing, health and so forth) that usually exert a continuing influence throughout the child's formative years, and it is therefore not surprising that social and economic status turn out to have a much stronger influence on the course of development than some specific event at birth.

Thus even organic damage, just as the other aspects of a child's early experience, cannot in and of itself account for the particular course which that child's development takes. The irreversible effects of early experience have no doubt been greatly overrated. To believe in such effects is indeed dangerous for two reasons: first, because of the suggestion that during the first few years children are so vulnerable that they are beyond help if they do encounter some unfortunate experience; second, because it leads one to conclude that the latter years of childhood are not as important as the earlier years. All the evidence indicates that neither proposition is true: the effects of early experiences are reversible if need be, and older children may be just as affected by unfortunate circumstances (though possibly different ones) as younger children.

Conclusions

A child's development always occurs in a social context. Right from the beginning individual children are members of a particular society, and the hopes and beliefs and expectations of those around them will have a crucial bearing on their psychological growth.

There is still a tremendous amount to be learnt about the nature of the child's development and the way that it is affected by particular features of the environment. But in the meantime we can at least make one negative statement with some very positive implications: development can never be explained in terms of single causes. Thus we have seen that isolated events, however traumatic at the time, do not preclude later influences; that the one relationship with the mother does not account for everything. For that matter, development is not simply a matter of the environment acting on the child, for children too can act on their environment. Not surprisingly, when confronted with a specific problem such as child abuse, we invariably find that a combination of circumstances needs to be considered if one is to explain it. Simple-minded explanations of the kind, 'juvenile delinquency is due to poverty (or heredity or lack of discipline)' never do justice to such a complex process as a child's development. And, similarly, action taken to prevent or treat which focusses on only single factors is most unlikely to succeed.

Questions

1. What are the principal controversial issues that have been raised by the study of maternal deprivation?
2. In what way can the intellectual development of a child be affected by social experience?
3. What advice would you give to the mother of a three year old who is considering taking up employment?
4. What is known about the reasons for baby battering? What effects on the child would you expect such treatment to have?
5. What is the role of the father in the family?
6. The parent-child relationship is said to be 'reciprocal'. Explain what is meant and provide examples.
7. What principles ought to guide a child's adoption?
8. Should education begin during the pre-school years? Explain what is meant by 'education' and discuss the settings in which it could take place.

9. How do relationships with other children affect development during the pre-school years?
10. What psychological principles should be taken into account in looking after children in residential care?

Annotated reading

Booth, T. (1975) Growing up in Society. London: Methuen (Essential Psychology Series).

A general account of the influences that determine the way in which people grow up together. It takes into account not only the contribution of psychology but of such other social sciences as sociology, anthropology and social history. Its main value lies in the way child development is seen as occurring within the social context of each particular culture.

Bowlby, J. (1965) Child Care and the Growth of Love. Harmondsworth: Penguin.

A more widely available version of Bowlby's classic report, first published in 1951, concerning the link between maternal deprivation and mental pathology. It should be read in conjunction with Rutter's book (see below).

Clarke, A.M. and Clarke, A.D.B. (1976) Early Experience: Myth and evidence. London: Open Books.

A collection of contributions by different authors, all concerned with the question of whether early experience exerts a disproportionate influence on later development. A wide range of research studies are reviewed, and the consensus is against seeing the early years as in some sense more important than later stages of development.

Dunn, J. (1977) Distress and Comfort. London: Fontana/Open Books.

Discusses some of the issues that concern parents during the early stages of the child's life, with particular reference to the causes and alleviation of distress, but places these issues in the wider context of the parent-child relationship and its cultural significance.

Kempe, R.S. and Kempe, H. (1978) Child Abuse. London: Fontana/Open Books.

An account by the foremost experts on child abuse of the state of knowledge regarding all aspects of this vexed area: causation, treatment and prevention.

Lewin, R. (1975) Child Alive. London: Temple-Smith.

Various researchers summarize in brief and popularized form what we have learnt about child development in recent years. Most contributions deal with young children, and the book as a whole emphasizes how babies are already psychologically sophisticated.

Rutter, M. (1972) Maternal Deprivation Reassessed. Harmondsworth: Penguin.

> A systematic review of the evidence on this controversial topic that has accumulated since Bowlby highlighted its importance. Discusses the various studies that have been carried out on the effects, both short- and long-term, of early deprivation of maternal care.

Schaffer, H.R. (1971) The Growth of Sociability. Harmondsworth: Penguin.

> A description of work on the earliest stages of social development. It shows how sociability in the early years has been studied, and reviews what we have learnt about the way in which a child's first social relationships are formed.

Schaffer, H.R. (1977) Mothering. London: Fontana/Open Books.

> An account of what is involved in being a parent. Brings together the evidence from recent studies of the mother-child relationship, and examines different conceptions of the parent's task. Gives special emphasis to the theme of mutuality in the relationship.

Tizard, B. (1977) Adoption: A second chance. London: Open Books.

> An account of an important research study on children in residential care who were subsequently adopted. Raises some crucial issues regarding the effects of early experience and the public care of young children.

Exercises

1. Mothers' talk

It has been suggested that the way in which mothers talk to children differs according to the child's age; the younger the child the simpler the mother's sentences, the more restricted her vocabulary, the slower her speech, and the more emphatic her gestures and facial expressions. See if this difference can be captured by observing mothers of children of different ages. Observe a mother talking to a baby, a toddler, and a school-age child. Concentrate on how the mothers talk; for example, the pitch of voice (high or low), the length of sentences, the rate of speech (fast or slow), the length of pauses between phrases, and so on. Do you get the impression of a definite 'style' of talking different from that found between adults? Are there differences according to the age of the child? Ideally one and the same mother should be used; ideally, also, a tape-recorder (or better still a video-camera) would be employed to record the session. But even if these aids are not available, you can still describe at a more impressionistic level how the mother behaves. No more than a ten-minute sample is require in each case.

2. Fathers' talk
The above exercise can be carried out using fathers.

3. Children's reactions to strangers
One of the earliest achievements of social development is
that children learn to differentiate people, in particular
familiar from unfamiliar individuals. Observe how children
of different ages respond to a stranger. Start with a baby
less that six months of age and work upwards. How do these
children compare in 'friendliness'? What can one learn from
their behaviour about the way in which the child's ability
to discriminate people changes with age? From about eight or
nine months on children often become rather cautious with
strangers, sometimes showing outright fear. Approach a child
in a fairly standardized manner which you can repeat with
other children. Cover an age range of, say, four months to
three years. Observe carefully how the child reacts in each
case; decide if there are any marked age changes. A Child
Welfare Clinic is a useful place for getting access to
children for this purpose.

4. Child–child relationships
It used to be said that children cannot relate to each other
for the first two years or so, and that even then one sees
only 'parallel play' and not true interaction. Is this so?
It is much better if you have a room to which you can invite
pairs of children of the same age with their mothers. Otherwise a day nursery may provide access. This situation, more
than any of the other exercises mentioned here, will bring
up the problem of how one observes: what one looks out for,
what one notes down, whether one looks at only one child at
a time or not, whether one keeps a running record or only
notes what is happening (say) every minute or so, and so on.
A problem to focus upon is how children of different ages
behave towards each other. For simplicity's sake observe
just two children of the same age at the same time, starting
with one year olds and going up to five. Do they play together? How?

5. Mother's attention to the child
Watch a mother with a young child on her knee in some public
place (a bus, a train. a doctor's waiting room, etc.). To
what extent is she 'tuned in' to the child's interests in
the environment? Does she look where the child is looking?
What does she do when she has identified what the child is
interested in - point to it, name it, talk about it? Does
she spend more of her time following the child's spontaneous
interests in this way, or does she attempt to direct the
child's attention. A mother's sensitivity to her child takes
many forms. One of these involves her knowing what it is the
child is interested in: that is, what things in the environment are being attended to. She can then share the child's
interest by talking about it or (if it is out of reach)
bringing it closer or (if it is an undesirable object)

removing it. A waiting room in a Child Welfare Clinic is a particularly good place to observe in. You should concentrate on mothers with children in the age range of about five months to two years; especially children sitting in their mother's knee should be chosen. Observe whether the mother follows the direction of the child's gaze, and whether she then uses this shared focus of attention to talk about the object, point to it, name it, and so on.

6. Mother with several children

Talk to a mother with several children. Ask her to compare the children: to what extent are they alike and to what extent are they different? How soon did she notice the differences - from the very early weeks on or later? Ask about her 'theory' regarding these differences: does she think they were there from the beginning; or did they arise because she treated the children differently? The aim is to draw attention to the fact that children may differ because they are different individuals from birth, not just because they have been brought up in different ways. The same mother should therefore be asked to compare her children as they were at the same age, say in the early months of life. This involves interviewing skills and is a good opportunity to consider or discuss the problems involved in getting reliable information, what sort of things you should ask about: the more concrete and specific your questions the better. What are the comparative advantages of a standardized interview (i.e. asking everyone the same set of questions) and an unstructured interview (more like a conversation)?

5

Abilities and behaviour in childhood and adolescence
B. M. Foss

Early development

Even at birth the differences between infants are very great, and the range of abilities and behaviour which can be called normal is large at all ages.

Apart from sleeping (80 per cent of the time), newborns seem to spend most of their time eating, excreting or crying. There are several kinds of cry which most mothers can distinguish from each other and which can be analysed using spectographs (which break up the sound into its frequency components). The birth cry appears to be unique. Then there is a basic cry, sometimes called a hunger cry, which is the common pattern. The pain cry, which may be elicited on the first day (for instance, when a blood sample is taken), is characterized by an initial yell followed by several seconds of silence during which the baby maintains expiration and which finally gives way to a gasp and loud sobbing, which in its turn reverts to a basic cry. There is also a frustration cry which is rather like a diminished version of the pain cry. Many mothers have also recognized a different kind of cry which starts at, say, the fourth week. It seems to be a sham cry in the sense that it is caused by no specific need, but seems simply to be a way of calling for attention. Presumably this kind of cry develops into the distress which older children show when separated from their mothers.

What things does the infant attend to? Can it recognize its mother's face and voice, or are these learnt gradually over a period of time? Until recently it was believed that recognition of faces and voices did not occur until the infant was several months old, but it now looks as though infants become competent in this way very much earlier, as many mothers already suspected. At least, what they can do is distinguish between different voices and faces probably as early as the third week of life, and it is likely that they can tell difference in smell between different people as early as the second week of life, and there is some evidence that even at this age infants are particularly attracted to representations of the human face. This is a topic on which there is a conflict of evidence. What is clear, though, is that most babies have a great deal of opportunity to get to know faces, in that mothers play face-to-face games with their babies from the very first days of life;

indeed, where they are allowed to be with the baby from birth they will tend to play these games immediately. By the time the baby is three weeks old it gets 'turned off' if, when face to face with an adult, the adult fails to react to the baby's changes in facial expression.

Perception

What seems vital for later perceptual learning is some kind of interaction between the child and the environment. In describing what happens it is useful to think in terms of perceptual categories. Probably from birth, infants are able to categorize movements and discriminate them from lack of movement and also to categorize various colours; so they probably have a category for 'red moving objects'. If later in life an infant reaches out to touch such objects, a red moving object which is a flame may be encountered, and as a result of touching it the infant's behaviour will have an outcome which is different from that when other kinds of objects are touched. In such a way the infant learns to discriminate a special sub-category of red moving objects. Movements of all kinds - eye movements, head movements, and body movements, and all kinds of interaction with the environment - seem to be important for the development of new perceptions, and this leads to the possibility that perceptual development will be affected by the child's interests (in the wider sense; that is, matters of concern): the child is more likely to attend to and interact with those aspects of the environment which are relevant to those interests. One can see evidence for this kind of effect in the many cross-cultural studies that show, for instance, that Eskimos have many categories for snow. Similarly, small boys may have many categories for motor cars. It will be seen that the psychological idea of a percept is not very different from a concept. One's perception of a dog is not only affected by the sight of the dog, but also knowing what it sounds like, or what it feels like to be patted, or to be bitten by, and what it smells like; and if one happens to be a dog fancier one's perception of the dog will involve very much finer discriminations than those made by other people. Perception, then, is affected not only by the present state of affairs - the stimuli from the environment, and the perceiver's attention, and motivation and emotional state - but also by the perceiver's whole previous history, and this leads to the possibility that different kinds of people have rather different perceptions. The members of a gang will perceive that gang's symbols (haircut and clothing, favourite music, favourite drink, etc.) quite differently from the way they would be perceived by a member of an opposing gang.

Skills

It is only about halfway through the first year of life that children begin to show good evidence for integrating their movements with their perceptions by being able to get hold

of objects in an obviously intentional way. The gradual
development from these early stages through walking and
various kinds of play activity to complex skills involved in
sports, for instance, are well documented. It may be useful to have a model of the way in which such skills are
acquired, and one such model is to regard the skill as built
up of a hierarchy of lower-order habits. For instance, a
child learning to write must have first learnt to hold a
pencil (there is an innate grasping reflex but the child
will have to relinquish this method of grasping for one
using finger and thumb opposition), will have had to learn
to move the pencil across the paper hard enough to leave a
mark but not break the paper, will have had to learn to
match shapes, to move from left to right across the page,
to distinguish between mirror image letters, and so on.
Many of these habits can be learnt only in a fairly definite
sequence because each one will depend on the acquisition
of previous habits. Eventually the child will have a whole
hierarchy of writing and drawing habits, and at some stage
these will have to be integrated with other hierarchies of
talking and hearing habits if the child is to become an
ordinary literate person. The establishment of these hierarchies depends obviously on having the necessary sensory
and motor abilities. They also depend on practice (one
cannot learn to drive a car just by reading a book), the
knowledge of results (otherwise movements will not become
perfected) and on having the motivation to continue learning. One of the characteristics of these skill hierarchies
is that the lower-order habits become automatic, and the
skilled person does not have to think about them at all but
can concentrate on the 'higher' aspects of what is being
done. Such a model helps to throw light on some of the
reasons why children may fail to develop skills necessary
for everyday life. For instance, some sensory or motor
abilities may be deficient, an essential lower-order habit
may be missing, there may have been difficulty in integrating one or more hierarchies, or there may have been
inadequate motivation.

Solving problems
Investigation of problem-solving has been one of the main
ways in which psychologists have studied thinking. A main
impetus in the study of the development of this kind of
ability was the work of the Swiss psychologist Jean Piaget.
He based an elaborate theory on the way in which children
develop concepts of number, space, relationships, etc., and
claimed that the thinking of a child develops through a
series of definite stages, rather as in the development of a
skill hierarchy. His results and his theory have been called
into question, and although many psychologists do not agree
with his theoretical formulation, many of his empirical
results have been replicated in a variety of cultures. There
has, though, been a tendency to show that some of the problems which Piaget posed can be solved by children at a

slightly earlier age given a different method of presenting the problem, and it turns out that sometimes the child fails to solve a problem for reasons other than those given by Piaget. For instance, the child's short-term memory may be inadequate for the storage of information necessary to solve the problem. One of the most interesting class of problems used by Piaget is concerned with what he called conservation. For instance, in testing a child's ability to show conservation of volume, the child is faced with two identical beakers filled with equal amounts of, say, lemonade. If the child agrees that there is an equal amount in each beaker the lemonade from one is then poured into a tall thin glass. The child who has not acquired the concept of conservation will choose the lemonade in the tall thin glass in preference because it will appear greater in quantity. According to Piaget, it is only in middle childhood that children acquire conservation concepts, and it is only when they are, say, 11 or 12 that full logical thinking is possible.

One major concern of psychologists has been to determine how important language is in the development of a child's thinking abilities. Perhaps it is because educationists themselves are rather verbal people that many believe language to be the most important single thing. However, there is some contrary evidence. For instance, deaf mutes who have very little vocabulary or syntax may nevertheless be rather competent in dealing with a whole range of problems varying from those found in ordinary intelligence tests to complicated problems in logic. Of all the tests which have been tried, it happens to be that conservation problems are those which seem most affected by lack of adequate language. In dealing with questions of this kind it is important to realize that there are several kinds of thinking and of intelligence. For instance, when a very broad range of intelligence tests are analysed by a technique such as a factor analysis (which is essentially a way of classifying tests), it usually turns out that there are two broad groups of tests: those involving language and those which do not, but may depend more, for instance, on being able to manipulate space and pattern. There are also large individual differences between people in this matter. Some seem to use language very much more in ordinary thinking, and there is some evidence across cultures that on the whole girls are better at language skills and boys are better at spatial skills. There is one kind of problem whose solution seems to depend on developmental stages and which may hold the key to some of the changes which occur with age. If young children are given a series of objects varying in colour, size and shape, and asked to sort them, they may do so by their colour or their shape or their size, but having sorted by one method they will be unable to see that there is a second or third method of sorting them, and it is only when they are considerably older that they can see from the start that there is an ambiguity about how sorting should be done.

Play

Play in animals and humans is usually easy to recognize but not so easy to define. Most play does have the property of appearing to be 'not for real', but there are difficult borderline cases. For instance, when children are playing together with toys there may be frequent episodes where there is competition for toys or for territory, and this may involve aggression which certainly appears real. Play at first tends to be solitary even when other children are there. There may be 'parallel play' in which children pursue the same tasks though with no obvious co-operation. Fully co-operative play is not seen much before children are three or four years old. In most cultures it seems that there are sex differences in typical play. Boys tend to play more with boys and girls with girls, and boys show much more of what has come to be called 'rough and tumble play'. This is the sort of play where there is a lot of wrestling and tumbling about and rolling over, sometimes with open-handed arm beating, often without contact, and rapid jumping up and down sometimes with arm slapping, and the whole thing is often accompanied by laughter. Where there is a largish group of children, one variant is that there is a great deal of group running, usually in a circle and often occurring with a lot of laughter. Chasing is another very common variant. Another sex difference is observed when children play with their mothers, in that girls tend to have closer proximity to the mother than boys do, at least on the average. When play is solitary, dolls and other playthings and pets are sometimes made to stand for parents and for children. Such play is often taken to reveal a child's preoccupations, and play therapy is based on the notion that emotional preoccupations can be acted out. In older children a lot of play becomes competitive. The dominance fighting to establish a 'pecking order', which can be seen in all social animals, is very evident in children. Some of it may be symbolic and indirect, especially in girls, where dominance fighting is more likely to be verbal than physical.

Arguments about the functions of play are centuries old, and the theories are on the whole untestable (as are most functional theories). However, there is now a certain amount of evidence from animals and from children regarding the effects of deprivation of play. Harlow's experiments at Wisconsin on the effects of various kinds of upbringing on later behaviour in rhesus monkeys have shown that if small monkeys are deprived of play, especially rough and tumble play, they may become maladroit later at both sexual and social behaviour. It is possible that play has this kind of functional importance for humans also. A more popular theory is that play in humans is essential for cognitive development. Many educationists believe this, and they get theoretical support from Piaget's notion that the growth of understanding depends heavily on a child's actions with respect to the environment. An intervention programme has been reported in which children who appeared to be intellectually backward as a result of malnutrition were given regular structured play sessions with toys, and as a result showed considerable development compared with children not given such a programme.

Reinforcement

This is the notion that behaviour is controlled by its consequences. In the sense in which 'reinforcement' is used by B. F. Skinner, a reinforcing state of affairs is one which, when it follows a response of an animal or human, will reinforce that response so that the probability of that response occurring in similar circumstances in the future will increase. Much of the fundamental work on reinforcement has been done on rats and pigeons but also on a very wide variety of other animals and on humans too, and it is the basis for many of the techniques used in behaviour modification. In a typical experiment a rat learns to press a lever which results in the delivery of a food pellet, and this is reinforcing to the hungry rat. Using such a simple set-up it is possible to investigate the effects of a wide variety of variables on the rate of learning. When the animal has learnt that food is no longer delivered when the lever is pressed (extinction trials) it will go on pressing for a while and then cease; but there may be spontaneous recovery. If the animal has been put on a schedule of reinforcement, in which reinforcement is not given for every response but only now and again, either regularly or irregularly and unpredictably, then the animal tends to be much more persistent in pressing the lever and will go on doing so for much longer when food is no longer delivered at all. In other words, after a schedule of reinforcement, especially if the reinforcement has been irregular, the behaviour is much more 'resistant to extinction'. A rat can also be put very much under the control of the environment, in that if a light is always on during reinforced trials but never on during unreinforced trials the animal will learn quite rapidly to press the lever only when the light is on. The light is then described as a 'discriminative stimulus'. A wide variety of things may act as reinforcers. For instance, isolated monkeys will press a lever for a view of the monkey colony or for a tape-recording of other monkeys, and these stimuli act as reinforcers. These kinds of experimental results have to be applied to humans with a good deal of caution. It is not clear how human behaviour is modified if individuals know that they are being subjected to a patterning of reinforcement; nor is it clear what the effects are of having language and being able to conceptualize the set-up.

Apart from behaviour modification techniques as used by therapists, the following are some applications which may be made. There is one kind of crying, which was mentioned earlier, whose function seems to be to get attention even though there is nothing physically wrong with the child. Such attention-getting crying may be very persistent, and attempts have been made to extinguish it by not attending to children when they produce this kind of cry. There are several published papers indicating that this kind of procedure is effective. Getting attention, presumably benign attention, is an important reinforcer for many children. There are reports, for instance, of a child who spent most of his time in a horizontal position and crawling, and as a result obtained a lot of attention which presumably reinforced his crawling behaviour. The teachers were trained to attend to the child only when he approximated standing up and not to attend to him when he was crawling, and as a result the child learnt to produce more normal behaviour. One well-known experiment controlled the smiling of babies by reinforcing them with smiles and pleasant noises whenever they smiled. A comparison was made of babies who had been reinforced at every smile, and those who had been put on a schedule, that is, they had been reinforced only at every fourth smile. As predicted, the babies on the schedule smiled more and the smiling was more resistant to extinction. It is not known, though, how long this kind of learning persisted. One prediction of the theory would be that if a child produced a certain kind of behaviour to obtain affection, then that behaviour would be more persistent if the affection were given capriciously and, for the child, unpredictably. As Skinner himself pointed out, in everyday life most reinforcers are irregular rather than regular. This is particularly true in gambling and it is quite likely that one of the mechanisms at work in the persistent gambler is the direct result of unpredictable reinforcement. Bearing in mind the way in which an animal's behaviour can be controlled by a discriminative stimulus in the environment, one could argue that it would be much easier for a child to learn appropriate behaviour if it were made quite clear in the environment when that behaviour was appropriate and when not. To caricature the situation, if a father wore a tie whenever the child was expected to behave in a fairly orderly fashion, but not to wear a tie during playtime, then it should be much easier for the child to discriminate between those two situations. It must be very difficult for young children to know what is appropriate behaviour in a typical supermarket when everyone else is taking goods off the shelves but they themselves are not allowed to do so.

Imitation

There is some evidence that infants will imitate facial expressions when they are only a few weeks old. For instance, they will put out their tongue apparently imitatively at two or three weeks. However, it may not be true imitation since they will also put out their tongues at a pencil pointed at them at the same age. In the second half of the first year, though, a great deal of facial imitation does go on. Detailed analysis of videotape shows that in most cases it is the mother imitating the infant and not the other way around. A lot of this imitative play seems to be a precursor of language and conversation but it is not yet known how important it is. In the second and third year and later, there is a great deal of imitation, much of it important for 'sex typing'. For instance, a three-year-old girl will spend a great deal of time imitating her mother's activities about the house. There have now been many studies of the extent to which imitation or copying occurs in middle childhood from adults or television. Boys in particular tend to copy aggressive movement, especially if the person they are imitating is a man and more especially if the man appears to be rewarded for what he is doing. It is still very unclear to what extent this sort of behaviour persists as a result of such imitation. It is still also not known in general which people children imitate most.

Freud

Many present-day theories of child development are more or less based on classical psychoanalytic theory, and many people would consider that Freud's main contribution was to focus attention on the first five years of life as being of paramount importance in determining later personality. For Freud the central concept in child development is identification, and he believed that imitation was one of the best behavioural signs that identification existed. He believed that identification with the mother figure occurred very early in life and that later, at about the time the super-ego develops, identification with the aggressor (the aggressive aspects of either mother or father figure) took place. Freud also suggested that the child passes through stages related to the way in which the libido (instinctual energy) operates. The first stage is the oral stage, in which the child's erotic life (in Freud's rather special meaning) centres on the mouth; this is followed by the anal stage, when life centres on excretion; then the phallic stage in which sexual (but of course pre-pubertal) interests centre on the genitals and the body surface as a whole. There then follows a latent period during which there is little development until the genital period is reached at adolescence. Mental illness in later life was seen as originating from traumatic experiences occurring during these periods. The situation is complicated for boys by the Oedipus situation in which the five year old sees himself as competing with his father for the love of the mother. Some of these ideas were elaborated by other psychoanalysts by devising personality typologies which were based on infantile experience. For instance, an orally-accepting type of person would be a lover of food and drink, a smoker, fond of words; the phallic type might be a lover of the body beautiful, perhaps an exhibitionist or an admirer of sculpture. Needless to say, it is extremely difficult to test the validity of such speculations.

Adolescence

In the first half of this century adolescence was treated as a period of 'storm and stress', of rebellion, of altruism, and searching for an identity. Some of these characteristics of adolescence now seem to be specific to the cultures in which the originators of the ideas lived, and this is particularly true for the notion that adolescence is a period of storm and stress. From anthropological and other studies, it is clear that in some cultures such a period does not exist. The last few decades have seen major changes occurring in the adolescent world so that many of the old generalizations no longer apply. A few decades ago the situation could be stated in fairly black and white terms: young adolescents were economically dependent; they were sexually capable but not expected to have, or were even legally forbidden from having, intercourse; and their social roles were essentially non-adult. In the course of a decade they were expected to go through a fairly clear series of transitional stages until they inevitably reached the desired position in an adult society in which their economic, sexual and social roles would all have changed utterly. At the present day sexual intercourse is often practised soon after the onset of puberty; many children, including working-class children, have considerably more spending money than their parents had at the same age; and there are now so many sub-cultures all the way from pre-adolescence to adulthood that at any age children can find themselves fully accepted within a culture, as a full member of society.

Biological factors
It is now generally accepted that the onset of puberty occurs earlier as time passes. The results of the onset of puberty on individual children seem to depend very much on what they and their peers expect those effects to be. For instance, there are large differences in the extent of menstrual pain, and those differences vary somewhat between cultures and seem to reflect the expectations within those cultures. Some studies suggest that menarche affects performance at school, whereas there are other studies giving contrary evidence. Here again much may depend on expectations. It is likely that if an individual reaches puberty long before or long after other children in the peer group, this may have considerable effect on behaviour and attitudes. It may be that ignorance of biological factors is detrimental in individual cases, but no one has yet shown what is the best way to carry out sex education, or indeed yet shown that sex education is a good thing (and it would be extremely difficult to show, since the investigator would have the problem of deciding what sex education is good for).

Social factors
Not many generations ago a person was unlikely to survive if not attached physically to a group of people. The need to belong to a group is still as great, though little is known about the psychological mechanisms involved. Avoidance of loneliness is one powerful drive. In modern Man this need may be satisfied by simply identifying with the group and

not necessarily belonging to it physically. A century ago a person's choice of group was limited usually to the family, the immediate neighbourhood, work, church, and perhaps hobbies and sport. Now, especially in cities or where people are mobile, groups are based more on common interests. It is very easy these days for a person to find other people who want to behave in the same way or have common goals. There is a tendency for members of a group to come to look alike, talk alike, make the same choices in food, music, beliefs, etc.; and these tendencies are often seen in an exaggerated form in adolescent groups, especially where the identification with the group is so complete that members see themselves as belonging to that group only and to no other. One very noticeable thing about human groups of all kinds (and this applies to groups at all levels of sophistication) is that they are not only bound together by common likes but also by common dislikes. All groups are against something. Anything which lessens old group allegiances will also make new groupings easier so that one would expect gangs to be especially prevalent in new high-rise housing estates, or with people who have just left school. One idea about adolescence, which seems not to have changed over the centuries, is that there is something called 'adolescent revolt'. It has been observed in many cultures (though not in all) that soon after puberty there tends to be a reaction against the parental ways of life. The idea that there is something primitive and possibly biological about this has been reinforced by many observations of primate societies which show that young males tend to form breakaway groups and also start fighting for dominance within the old group.

Dominance fighting is well accepted as an explanatory concept applied to social animals of all kinds, and some biologists and psychologists see it as a main source of competitiveness in human behaviour. Besides the pressures to belong to a group and to conform to it, there are still these largely competitive tendencies which may take the form of wanting to be unique, and to have a role of one's own within the group. Very often such a role involves being best at something. Being best may involve owning things, being most daring, or beautiful, or cleverest. With small boys, competitiveness may show itself in actual dominance fighting. Psychologists of various kinds have talked a lot about the adolescent need for having an identity. It is possible that that need may be partly and perhaps completely satisfied once the person finds a role within a group, especially if the role and the group are of high esteem.

Attitudes and beliefs

Sociologists and social psychologists use the concept 'reference group'. Market researchers may want to know how to advertise a certain kind of cosmetic product. If it is intended to be attractive to adolescent girls, they may well use the technique of finding out which reference group is relevant. For instance, they may, using questionnaire techniques, ask questions of the kind designed to find out with whom adolescent girls identify when buying cosmetics. In general, one's reference group is the group of people with whom one identifies with respect to one's attitudes, beliefs and values. Developmental studies show that for young children the home provides the main reference group, but in middle childhood there is already a tendency to adopt values of heroes from stories or from television and this becomes very marked in pre-adolescence. In adolescence there may be a complete change of reference groups as has already been suggested, and if this change is very radical then it may be a source of conflict. The way in which the conflict expresses itself will, of course, vary between individuals, and any of the usual clinical manifestations are possible, such as anxiety, depression, hysterical reactions, aggression, and in some cases an attempt at a rational solution of the conflict. Attitudes towards choice of work will be affected by group pressures in just the same way as all other attitudes. The situation is affected by the fact that in many adolescent sub-cultures all the heroes and heroines are roughly of the same age as members of the sub-culture, and there is no need to look ahead to what is going to happen when one belongs to an older age group. In such cases attitudes towards work are likely to be unrealistic in terms of planning ahead.

Questions

1. Write short notes on: crying; the development of perception and attention; the development of movement.
2. How do skills develop? Illustrate with examples of your own choosing from early and later childhood.
3. What is reinforcement? How may it operate in controlling behaviour?
4. In what ways does a child's ability to solve problems vary with age?
5. How would you classify different kinds of play? What functions may they have?
6. What are the main developmental stages a child passes through according to (i) Piaget, (ii) Freud?
7. Discuss the extent to which development during adolescence is determined by social factors.
8. How do attitudes and beliefs change during childhood and adolescence?
9. How do children learn to categorize things and people in their environment?
10. What part may imitation play in the development of personality?

Annotated reading

Hadfield, J.A. (1979) Childhood and Adolescence. Harmondsworth: Penguin.

Sandstrom, C.I. (1968) Psychology of Childhood and Adolescence. Harmondsworth: Penguin.

These cover both childhood and adolescence. The book by Hadfield is particularly useful for parents. The one by Sandstrom is a little dated though there is a revised edition from 1979.

Bower, T. (1977) Perceptual World of the Child. London: Fontana.

Garvey, C. (1977) Play. London: Fontana.

Donaldson, M. (1978) Children's Minds. London: Fontana.
These belong to a series of short books on children called 'The Developing Child' and edited by Jerome Bruner, Michael Cole and Barbara Lloyd. The last of these three references is particularly good on cognitive growth and its relevance to education.

Turner, J. (1975) Cognitive Development. London: Methuen.

Green, J. (1974) Thinking and Language. London: Methuen.
These are part of a series called 'Essential Psychology' and are particularly relevant.

Watson, R.I. and Lindgren, H.C. (1979) Psychology of the Child and the Adolescent (4th edn). New York: Collier Macmillan.
This is an American book, but covers the non-American work well, and is slightly more advanced than the other suggested readings.

Exercises

1. Conservation of volume
For this demonstration four glasses are required; two average sized tumblers, one tall, thin vessel and one short, wide vessel. A liquid (for instance, orangeade which the child may drink at the end of the demonstration) is poured into the two tumblers in equal amounts and the child has to agree that they are equal; it is of no consequence to the child which of the two is offered for drinking. The liquid from one is then poured into the tall vessel and from the other into the short vessel. The child is then invited to choose one of them. This should be tried on children of say, six, seven and eight years of age and possibly older. A transition to being able to conserve volume occurs on average at about eight. Are there any ways in which the child's judgement can be altered? For instance, what happens if a little of the liquid being poured into the taller glass is accidentally spilt? Whether or not a child shows conservation of volume depends a good deal on the way in which the test is actually given to the child.

2. Sorting
For this, blocks or other materials are required which vary along various dimensions, for instance, in colour, in height or in shape. They might be of four shapes, four colours and

tall and short, and wide and thin. The children are required to sort the objects. Having done that, they are then asked to sort them in a different way. Can they do that? Are they able to see from the start that various methods of sorting are possible? In younger children it is characteristic that one aspect of the stimuli, for instance colour or form, is most salient and tends to dominate the way in which the child does the sorting. It is only when very much older that they are able to see from the start that many different kinds of sorting are possible.

3. To what do children attend?
This kind of observational study can be done with infants and children of any age (and with adults too). Over intervals of, say, 30 seconds (preferably randomly chosen) note to what things and people in the environment the child attends. Attempt an explanation of why some objects and people attract attention more than others. In older children, are there any important individual differences in this kind of selective attention and do these differences have consequences for later development? This kind of observational study can well be done in public places. It is a good chance to learn to be as objective as possible in observation and to introduce yourself to the use of check-lists and time-sampling.

4. Observation of play
After observing children of a given age at play, design a check-list to compare the play of two or more children (for instance, a girl and a boy, or an older and a younger child). The check-list might include items like solitary, parallel or co-operative play; rough and tumble; playing with objects or toys (what kind?). To make the observations study more objective, use time-sampling. Here again check-lists and time-sampling should be used. This kind of study can either be done out of doors in playgrounds or parks, or indoors in nursery or other settings. Ideally, of course, the behaviours would be video-recorded and analysed later.

5. Individual differences
Some studies show that girls on the whole are better on verbal tests and boys better at spatial ones. For one particular age level, design your own vocabulary test (meaning of words) and your own spatial test (for instance, being able to recognize shapes in different orientations) and give these tests to a selection of boys and girls. Are there any sex differences? If you have tested enough children, say five of each sex, it will be possible to analyse your results satisfactorily by applying, for instance, the Mann-Whitney U Test. This kind of study can be done at various levels of sophistication. You will enjoy designing your own kits, but it is of course a complicated matter to construct tests which are reliable and valid and appropriate for the age level at which one is working.

6. Adolescent tastes

Design a short questionnaire to sample the tastes of as
random a sample as possible of adolescents. This might
include items such as preferred music, drink, clothing,
games and sports, catch-phrases, television programmes, and
so on. From these choices is it possible to decide what
group or groups the person is identifying with (the 'reference group')? What are the main influences which have determined these choices? Identify the social pressures which
exist for the adolescent.

6

The family
Neil Frude

Psychology and the family

The psychologist may regard the family as a background against which to view the individual, asking perhaps how the parents influence the development of a child or how families of alcoholics may help the individual to overcome his or her difficulties, or alternatively the family itself may be the unit of study. The family is a small group and we can observe the patterns of communication within it, the process of mutual decision making, and so forth. It is a system, with individuals as sub-units or elements within. Typically, psychologists have focussed their interests on the biological and social nature of the individual, but they are now becoming increasingly concerned not only with individuals or even 'individuals in relationships' but with the relationships themselves.

Clinical and educational psychologists, for example, are increasingly working within the family context and some problems which were initially identified as 'belonging' to the individual adult or child are now seen, more appropriately, as problems of the 'family system'. Also, psychologists working, for example, with handicapped children have come to recognize that the powerful influence and involvement of the parents means that they can be harnessed as highly potent sources of training, and such clinicians are increasingly using these strategies to establish a far more effective educational programme than they themselves could possibly provide. But the needs of parents, and the stresses which such a high level of involvement may place upon them, are also recognized and so the psychologists may well regard themselves as involved with the problems of the family as a whole.

So there are vital problems in the area and there are some impressive results. Let us look at some of these, choosing some of those areas which relate to major social problems and some innovations which suggest methods for their alleviation.

Family planning

Current surveys of the plans of young married couples for families have shown a high level of conscious control and active planning, a reflection of the wide availability of highly effective contraceptive techniques. The number and spacing of children are controlled with varying degrees of skill and success. The number of couples who opt for voluntary childlessness seems to be increasing. In about half of such cases the couple have planned from the start not to have children, while the other half postpone pregnancy and eventually decide to remain childless.

Contraceptive use varies greatly. Despite the numerous methods available, none is perfect, for various reasons. Some men and women find that the sheath reduces pleasurable sensation; the pill may have side effects on health or mood; and a number of women find methods such as the cap bothersome and distasteful. The coil may involve a painful initial fitting and an extensive gynaecological involvement which some find embarrassing and disturbing. Sterilization or vasectomy may be advisable for the older and highly stable couple, but a number of people who have undergone such surgery later change their partners. They may then request reversal surgery and in many cases successful reversal will not be possible. The solution to the contraception problem is thus by no means always simple and family planning counselling, and the tailoring of recommendations to the particular needs and life stage of the couple, is a task requiring considerable skill and insight as well as knowledge of the technical features of the particular methods.

Different couples have different 'ideal family structures', often specifying not only the number of children but also their spacing and sex. There is still some preference, overall, for boys, and current research makes it likely that in the near future couples will be able, with some accuracy, to determine the sex of their baby. Many will prefer to 'leave it to nature' but others will choose one option or the other. This is likely to result in a relative excess of boys, with longer-term social results which can only be guessed.

Reactions to pregnancy range from unqualified delight to profound despair. The option of abortion is now increasingly available. Reactions to this also vary from relief to regret and while, overall, the evidence is that there are rarely long-term negative consequences for the women, several studies have suggested the need for pre- and for post-termination counselling. A number of women miscarry, some repeatedly, and again this can be a very stressful experience requiring skilled intervention.

Birth and early interaction

The process of birth is biological, but the importance of social variables is also apparent. The pregnant woman may anticipate the sex and looks of her baby, but initial acceptance is by no means inevitable. Premature babies, for example, may look very unlike the baby-food advertisements which may have conditioned the mothers' expectations.

Fathers are now often present at the delivery and there is evidence that this helps the woman in the birth process itself and also helps the couple to feel that the baby is part of both of them. The demands which the baby makes may not have been fully anticipated and the initial period with the infant may call for a difficult process of adaptation and adjustment, just as the first period of the couple living together calls for give and take and the setting-up of new norms of interaction.

Not all babies are the same: they differ in their activity level, their crying and their patterns of sleep and wakefulness. Some are not easy to care for, and may be unresponsive and difficult to soothe. Baby-care makes great demands and the mother may be totally unprepared for the energy and level of skill required. Surveys show that many of them find the period of early childhood highly stressful. They may be tired and feel inadequate and, at times, very angry. If mothers fail to understand and control their babies, their treatment of them may be poor and sometimes harsh.

The level of medical care in pregnancy and around the time of the birth may be high, but many mothers then feel isolated with the baby, unsure about such matters as feeding, toileting and weaning.

In assuming that a 'mother's instinct' will aid her in these tasks we may have seriously under-estimated the extent to which, in earlier times, the informal training opportunities offered to the young girl by larger family units and the close neighbourhood community helped her in her own parenting.

The developing child

In the early years interactions with parents form the major social background for the child. There is a good deal of informal teaching and the child learns by example. Guidance and discipline help the infant to establish a set of internal rules and encouragement and praise help to develop skills and intellectual abilities. Overhearing conversations between adults enables the child to learn about the structure of language and conversation and the rules of social interaction. Watching the parents' interactions and reactions enables children to develop their own emotional repertoire and social skills, and they will experiment and consciously imitate the behaviour of their parents. The child may identify strongly with a particular parent. Games of pretence enable youngsters to practise complex tasks and build a repertoire of interactive styles, and in collaboration with other young children they may rehearse a number of roles. In both competitive and co-operative play social interaction patterns are devised and perfected, children learn about rule-following and discover their strengths and weaknesses relative to their peers.

Different parents treat their children differently, and there are many styles of parenting. Some parents are warm and affectionate, others are more distant, and some are openly hostile. Some give the child a lot of freedom and exercise little control while others are very restrictive.

Not surprisingly, the children reared in such atmospheres develop somewhat differently. The children of highly restrictive parents tend to be well-mannered but lack independence, the children of warm parents come to have a confident high regard for themselves, and the children of hostile parents tend to be aggressive. There are various ways in which such findings can be explained. Do the aggressive children of hostile parents, for example, behave in that way because they are reacting against the pressures which their parents put on them, are they simply imitating the behaviour of the adults around them and picking up their interactive styles, or is there perhaps some hereditary biological component which makes both parents and children hostile?

Probably, as in so many cases of such overall correlations, there is a combination of such factors. It is also possible, of course, that hostility originating in the children themselves causes a parental reaction. We must be wary of the conclusion that children simply respond to the atmosphere of their home. They also help to create that atmosphere and the relationship between parents' behaviour and the child's behaviour is a fully interactive one. Children are not shapeless psychological forms capable of being moulded totally in response to their social environment, but have dispositions and levels of potential of their own which they bring into the family.

Children have certain psychological needs which the family should be able to provide. They need a certain stability, they need guidance and a set of rules to follow and the feeling needs to be conveyed to them that they are 'prized' by their parents. In the traditional system with two parents there may be a certain safeguard for the constant provision of these needs by one or other of the parents, and for the prevention of total lack of interest or of rejection. But if the natural family with two parents is ideal in many ways as an arrangement in which to provide for the child's development, this is not to say that the child's best interests cannot also be met in alternative contexts. Most children in single-parent households fare well and develop happily. For the child living apart from the natural parents adoption seems a better option than does fostering (though long-term fostering seems to share many of the positive features of adoption) and fostering seems to be better for the child than a continued stay in an institution. Even this context, however, can provide reasonably well for the child's needs if there is stability, a high level of staffing, high intimacy between staff and children and the provision of high levels of verbal and other types of stimulation.

The family and stress

Just as the family is a principal source of a person's happiness and well-being, it can also be the most powerful source of stress. Research has now been done to try to establish inventories of the life stresses which people experience and in even a cursory glance through such a list it is difficult not to be struck by the extent to which the relationships within the family are bound up with personal change. Some of these events, like the birth of a handicapped child or the death of a child, happen to only a few people, but others, such as the older child leaving home, marital conflict, sexual problems, and the death of a parent happen to many or most. Stress precipitated by such life events has been shown to have a marked effect on both physical and mental health, and if illness is the result then this in turn will provide added hardship.

It is not only particular events which cause stress. The constant presence of ill-health, handicap or marital conflict can similarly take its toll over the years. On the other hand, the stability and comfort of the family setting and the constant presence of others seems to provide much that is beneficial. Marriage reduces the risk of alcoholism, suicide and many forms of psychological ill-health, and interviews with separated and widowed people reveal the elements which they feel they are now missing in their lives, and which in turn may help to explain why living in relative isolation tends to be associated with a greater risk of experiencing psychological problems. As well as providing the opportunity to discuss problems and providing stability, the presence of a spouse reduces loneliness. It also facilitates discussion of a variety of issues and so enables the partners to forge a consensus view of the world: it provides extra interest and social contact, the opportunity to give love and express concern, and provides constant feedback to the individuals about themselves, their value and their role. Practical tasks may be shared and the person may be aware of being prized by the other. This then fosters the sense of self-worth which has been found to be very important for overall well-being.

Of course, not all marital relationships are good and some may lead to far greater problems than those of living in isolation. Certainly recent family changes and conflict seem, in many cases, to be a trigger factor leading to subsequent admission to a psychiatric hospital. Overall, however, it seems that the emotional impact of an intimate relationship, in adult life as in childhood, is likely to involve many more gains for the individual than losses, that people value the protection which such relationships provide and that they often suffer when such support ends.

Schizophrenia, depression and the family

There is a popular notion that schizophrenic illness originates in family relationships, and that certain forms of family communication, in particular, may cause an adolescent or young adult to become schizophrenic. A considerable number of studies have now been carried out to establish whether or not there is a firm evidential basis for such an assumption and, at this point, it looks as if the decided lack of positive evidence should lead us to abandon the hypothesis that such relationship problems constitute the major cause of the illness. While no strong data have been forthcoming to support the family interaction claim, a great deal of evidence implicating the role of genetics in schizophrenia has been found and it now looks as if a predominantly biological explanation may eventually be given. But while there is no good evidence that family relationships are formative in schizophrenia, there is strong support for the notion that family interaction markedly influences the course of a schizophrenic illness and the pattern of relapses and remission from symptoms over the years. It seems that the emotional climate in the home and particular family crisis events often trigger renewed episodes of schizophrenic breakdown.

On the other hand, it seems that depression often has its origin in severe life events and difficulties and that the family context provides many of these. In a recent study conducted in London, Brown and Harris (1978) found that depression was more common in those women in the communi who had recently experienced a severe event or difficulty. Many of the events involved loss. Women with several young children were more vulnerable than others, as were the widowed, divorced and separated. Social contact seemed to provide a protective function against the effects of severe life events and the rate of depression was lower in those women who had a close intimate relationship with their husbands. Women without employment outside the home were found to be more vulnerable and the loss of a mother in childhood also seemed to have a similar effect. Brown and Harris suggest that such early loss through the death of a parent may change the way in which the person comes to view the world and attempts to cope with the problems that arise. The study provides clear evidence that family relationship factors may make a person more or less susceptible to clinical depression, and again illustrates how the contribution of family life to personal problems is two-sided. The family may be the source of much stress, but a close supportive marital relationship will enable the individual to cope with many problems without succumbing to the threat of clinical depression.

Sexual behaviour and sexual problems

Married couples vary greatly in the frequency of their sexual contact and in the style and variety of their sexual interaction. The rate of intercourse does not seem to be related to overall satisfaction with the marriage, except that where a marriage is failing for other reasons sexual contact may be low or absent. If there is a marked discrepancy, however, between the expectations or needs of the partners then this may lead to conflict and dissatisfaction. Sex is also one of the factors which can cause problems in the early stages of adjustment to marriage.

Although several medical men and women wrote 'marriage manuals' during the nineteenth century and in the early part of this century, our knowledge of human sexuality was very limited before the studies of people such as Kinsey and Masters and Johnson. Using interviews, and later observational and physiological techniques, researchers have now provided us with extensive information about sexual practices. Masters and Johnson (1966, 1970), in particular, have supplied a thorough and detailed account of human sexual behaviour, and they have also provided insights into such questions as sexuality in the older person and sexual behaviour during pregnancy.

It has become clear that problems of sexual dysfunction affect a great many people at some stage in their marriage. Masters and Johnson have produced a range of therapies which has been shown to be highly effective, and many of these have now been adopted by other psychologists, psychiatrists and marriage counsellors. The couple, rather than the individual man or woman, is considered to be the most appropriate treatment unit, and discussion and detailed advice are followed up with 'homework assignments' which the partners carry out in the home. Anxiety about sexual performance can have a serious effect on behaviour and a vicious circle can easily form, for example, between anxiety and failure to achieve erection. Awareness of the female orgasm has increased considerably in recent years and it appears that the pattern of problems for which advice is sought has changed. Whereas the majority of sexual problems encountered by counsellors some decades ago involved a mismatch of sexual appetites, with the woman complaining about her husband's excessive demands, a dominant problem now seems to be that of the woman's dissatisfaction with her husband's ability to bring her to orgasm.

Opinions differ about how much the 'couple unit' is always the appropriate focus for treatment and how far deep-seated relationship difficulties, rather than specific sexual skills and attitudes, underlie the problems presented. It does appear that in about half of the cases seen there are other serious marital difficulties in addition to the sexual dysfunction being treated by sex therapy which is aimed at improving other aspects of the relationship.

Family conflict and violence

There is open conflict at times in most families. Sometimes the focus of disagreements is easily apparent; it may centre, for example, on matters concerning money, sex or the handling of children; but at other times the row seems to reflect underlying resentments and difficulties in the relationship. Studies have been made of how arguments start, how they escalate and how they are resolved, and some research in this area has been successful in identifying patterns of conflict which seem to predict later marital breakdown. It appears that there are right ways and wrong ways to fight with other family members. In some marriages there may be constant conflict which, however, is successfully worked through and which does not endanger the basic relationship.

Inter-generational conflict is also common. In the early years the parents have the power and may use discipline to settle matters of disagreement. Again, the way in which this is done is important and it seems that parents should not use their power in such a way that the child feels rejected. Children should be made to feel that their behaviour, rather than their whole personality, is the target of the parents' disapproval. In the adolescent years, the child's struggle for power and independence is often the focus of conflict. Adolescence is frequently a period of stress and young people may have doubts about their status and future. It is also a time when peer-influence may conflict with that of the parents.

Marital conflict sometimes leads to physical assault and a number of wives have to receive medical attention for injuries inflicted by their husbands. Many such wives choose to return to the home after such an incident although some seek the haven of a women's refuge. Even where there is repeated violence, the wife often feels that her husband is not likely to treat her badly in the future; she may feel that drinking or stress triggered the assault, and such wives often report that the man is generally caring and responsible and that his violent outbursts are out of character. Jealousy and sexual failure or refusal are also associated with attacks on the wife, though it is also true that for some couples physical assault or restraint represents a modal response in conflict situations, and that in some marriages (and indeed in some sub-cultures) there are few inhibitions against the couple hitting one another.

Violence against children also occurs with alarming frequency in families, and it is estimated that about two children die each week in England and Wales as a result of injuries inflicted by their parents. The children involved are often very young, and it does not take much physical strength to seriously injure a small child or baby. Only a small proportion of the parents involved in these attacks have a known psychiatric history and, contrary to one popular image, they often provide well for the general needs of their children. Sadistic premeditated cases do occur but they are relatively rare. Generally the attack occurs when a child is crying or screaming or has committed some 'crime' in the eyes of the parent. The mother or father involved is often under considerable stress, and there are frequently severe marital difficulties. The parents involved are often young and may have little idea of how to cope with the crying child, and there is evidence that many abused children are themselves difficult to handle. They may be disturbed, over-active or unresponsive although, of course, many such problems may themselves be the result of longer-term difficulties in the family.

Family therapy

There has recently been a considerable growth of interest in 'family therapy'. This is practised in a variety of ways and with a number of alternative theoretical underpinnings but it claims, in all its forms, that when there is a psychological disturbance it is useful to work with the 'family system' rather than with the individual identified client. The view is often expressed that the symptom should properly be seen as an attribute not of the individual but of the family as a whole. By focussing on the structure of the group, on the emotional climate and on the pattern of relationships and communication, an attempt is made to bring about a fundamental change which will result in a well-functioning family and an alteration in the circumstances which have maintained the symptom.

Thus a child who is truanting from school may be presented as the only problem by a family who, in fact, have a number of difficulties. By focussing on or scapegoating the child in this way, the family system may preserve itself from serious conflict between other members or between the family group and another part of the wider social system. The child's problem with school is therefore in some way 'useful' to the family and any direct attempt to deal with the truanting may be directed at reducing the underlying conflict or at changing a disordered style of communication which has led to the family 'needing' the child's symptom.

In the therapeutic sessions family members are seen together. The focus is largely on the group processes operating and involves the observations of such interactional elements as coalitions, stratagems and avoidances. As these are further analysed, they may be revealed to the family or they may be simply 'corrected' by the direct authoritative action of the therapist. The periods intervening between treatment sessions are seen as being of primary importance for the family, who may then revert to original dysfunctional patterns or may continue in the direction of therapeutic change.

The role of the therapist is varied. Some therapists regard themselves primarily as analysts and concentrate on making the family aware of its interactional style, whereas some regard themselves as mediators or referees or may take sides with one or more family members to provide a necessary balance of power. If two or more therapists work as a team then they may present their own relationship as a model of open communication and in this way try, for example, to illustrate the constructive potential of conflict.

The professional background of family therapists is highly varied and their original training may be in psychology, social work or psychiatry. The theoretical concepts used similarly cover a wide range including psychoanalysis, communications theory and behavioural analysis. Concepts have also been borrowed freely from general systems theory, which is predominantly a mathematical theory with applications in cybernetics and biology. In behavioural family therapy the focus is on the manipulation of the family consequences of individual behaviour and the attempt is made to analyse and modify social reinforcement patterns and observational learning.

Because family therapy involves a varied and often subtle set of procedures, it is very difficult to carry out satisfactory studies to measure its effectiveness. Many of the variables said to be involved are rather intangible and the processes underlying changes in social systems are highly complex. Preliminary evidence suggests that it is often useful but this can also be said of many other forms of therapy, and the 'cost-effectiveness' considerations which play a part in treatment choice sometimes make it difficult to support a strong case for the use of family therapy. Many critics would return a general verdict of 'not proven', but the level of interest by professionals is undoubtedly high and growing. One special difficulty has been the failure of those working in this area to provide an adequate means of identifying the cases which may be most appropriately treated in this way. Any attempt to treat all conditions with a uniform approach is unlikely to return a high overall rate of effectiveness. With a more limited set of identified problems this mode of treatment may in future prove to be the optimal means of effective intervention for a range of cases. At present, family therapy reflects just one aspect of the increasing awareness of the importance of understanding the social context when dealing with a pre-sented psychological symptom.

The effects of marital breakdown

Divorce statistics represent a very conservative estimate of marital failure and a still more conservative estimate of marital unhappiness and disharmony, but the rates are high and increasing. There are various estimates of the likely divorce rate of currently made marriages but one in four is a frequently encountered figure. There are certain known predictors of marital breakdown. It is more frequent, for example, when the couple married at an early age, when they have few friends, when they have had relatively little education and when their life style is unconventional. The marital success or failure of their own parents also bears a direct statistical relationship to the couple's chances of breakdown.

Psychological studies have shown that certain measures of personality and social style are also predictors of failure. If the wife rates her husband as being emotionally immature, if the husband's self-image is lacking in coherence and stability, or if either of the partners is emotionally unstable then marital breakdown is more likely than if the reverse holds. Good communication, a high level of emotional support and the constructive handling of conflict situations are, not surprisingly, features of relationships which are associated with high levels of marital happiness and low rates of breakdown. In many of these studies it is, of course, difficult to disentangle cause and effect.

The process of adjustment to a marriage may be a long and difficult one, and some marriages never successfully 'take'. The highest rates of breakdown therefore occur in the first years, but many relationships are stable and satisfactory for a while and are then beset with difficulties at a later stage. Divorce is usually preceded by months or years of intense conflict and may eventually come as a relief, but the evidence suggests that generally the whole process is a very painful one for many members of the family involved, both adults and children.

Research with divorcees has revealed a high degree of stress and unhappiness which may last for a very long time. On the whole, it appears that the experiences of women in this situation result in rather more disturbance than those of men, but for both sexes the status of divorce is associated with higher risk of clinical depression, alcoholism and attempted suicide. The psychological effects of a marriage breakdown may stem largely from lack of social support, the absence of an intimate relationship and a loss of self-esteem, but there are often additional pressures relating to the loss of contact with the children or of having to bring them up alone. There is a high rate of remarriage among the divorced; and divorce itself, for all the apparent risks which it brings, is still often preferable to continuing in a marriage which has failed.

The 'broken home' is associated with increased aggressiveness and delinquency in children, but there seems to be only a weak association with neurotic and other psychiatric problems of childhood. While the rate of conduct problems in the children of divorce is considerably higher than that for children of stable marriages, there is apparently little increase in such antisocial behaviour for children whose homes have been broken by the death of a parent. This suggests that it is the discord in the home which produces the effect rather than the mere absence of one parent. This is supported by the finding that conduct problems also occur with increased frequency in homes with continual discord, even when there is no separation or divorce.

ingle-parent families

Children are raised in single-parent families when the mother has not married, when there has been a divorce or separation, or when one parent has died. 'Illegitimacy' is a somewhat outmoded term and an increasing number of single women now feel that they want to rear their child on their own. Social attitudes against illegitimacy and single parenthood have softened over the years and this has encouraged more mothers to keep the baby rather than have it adopted.

Single parenthood appears to be more stressful for the remaining parent than sharing the responsibilities with a partner. Lack of emotional support and of adult company are some of the reasons for this but there are also likely to be increased financial hardships, and the homes of single parents have been shown to be overcrowded and often lack both luxuries and basic amenities. During times of parental illness there may be few additional social resources to call upon, and the single parent is less likely to be able to organize a social life for herself (about 90 per cent of single parents are women). A number of self-help organizations have now been formed to fulfil some of the special needs of the single parent.

One-parent families are viable alternatives to the more traditional nuclear families, and most of the children raised in such circumstances do not appear to show any signs of disturbance or impaired development. There have been suggestions that the boy without a father might tend to be more effeminate but it has been found that most boys brought up by their mothers are as masculine as the rest. If anything, they tend to make fewer sex-identity based assumptions about tasks and roles. We could say that they seem to be less 'sexist' than other boys. Similarly, the girl brought up with the father alone does not seem to lack feminine identity. These findings reflect a more general conclusion that children seem to base their own stereotypes on the wider world around them rather than on the conditions prevailing in their own immediate family.

The family life of old people

Old age is marked by declining health and mobility and by a process of disengagement from several life enterprises, notably employment. There may be low income and financial difficulties, contemporaries are likely to die, and the old person may find it difficult to replace such contacts with the result that they live in a shrinking social world. The high emphasis which some old people place on privacy may reduce the uptake of potential neighbourhood and community resources.

The major exception made to such concern with privacy is with the immediate family. Typically, contacts with children and grandchildren are highly prized and may be a major focus of interest in their lives. While there is likely to be an increase in dependency, however, this is often recognized by the old and they often respect the independence of the younger family and feel a crushing sense of obligation if they are forced through circumstance to accept aid from them. In some families there is an informal 'exchange of services' between generations with the older person, for example, looking after the grandchildren while parents are working or having a short holiday.

Recent social change has resulted in fewer three-generation households, but with increasing age and decreasing health, and perhaps the death of one of the parents, the younger couple may want to offer the surviving partner a place in their home. There may be doubts about how well this will work out and conflict may be initiated between the marital partners over how far feelings of duty should lead to changes which might disrupt the family. As the children become older the pressure on space may build up, and with

increasing health difficulties the burden of the older
person may become too great. Deafness may become an
irritation, there may be restricted mobility and the elderly
parent may become incontinent.

The increased strain on the family may lead to harsh
feelings or even violence towards the old person as well as
to a detrimental effect on the health of other members of
the family. Eventually the pressure may become unmanageable
and the old person may be forced to enter an institution.
For many elderly people, living with a child is a halfway
stage between having a home of their own and living in an
old people's home. Both moves may involve their giving up
possessions and pets. The quality of institutions varies
greatly, but a frequent reaction is one of withdrawal, depression and depersonalization. Despite having many people
around the old person may suffer from a deep sense of
loneliness and isolation.

While it seems inevitable that old age will always bring
unhappiness to some people, for many it is a time of
contentment and fulfilment and in a number of cases the
positive aspects centre on activities and memories of
relationships within the family. Older women, for example,
may play a major role in organizing family get-togethers and
may act as a social secretary for members of the extended
family, and grandmothers and grandfathers may gain great
satisfaction from their relationships with their grandchildren. Many of the recent social changes in housing
organization and mobility, it is true, militate against a
high level of interaction between the generations, and there
seems as yet little awareness by policy-makers of the social
costs which such changes entail.

The future of intimate life styles

Contact with intimates in the family group seems to provide
the individual, overall, with considerable benefits. Significant relationships are highly potent and there may be
dangers, but generally the benefits far outweigh the costs.
A variety of psychological needs are very well fulfilled in
the traditional family setting. The child growing in the
caring and stable family setting can generally develop
skills and abilities and achieve a potential for happiness
better than in any other setting, and the adult can fulfil
with the marital partner the needs of emotional support,
freedom from loneliness, sex, stability, and the building
of a mutually comfortable 'social reality'. When the basic
family pattern is disturbed there can be grave consequences
for each of the people involved.

There is no uniform change in western society to a
single alternative life style arrangement but there is
rather an increasing diversity. There are now fewer children
in families, more single-parent families, more divorces and
separations, and there is a high incidence of transitory
relationships and less contact between generations. Several
lines of evidence suggest that children are valued less than
in the recent past; that women, in particular, are looking

more outside the family for their role-orientation and their life satisfactions; that there is now less 'family feeling'; and that family duties and responsibilities impinge upon individual decision making less than was the case some decades ago.

We may expect this variety to increase further as ideas regarding the roles of men and women evolve, as changes in biological and 'hard' technology take place and as patterns of employment and leisure alter. It would be premature to forecast, at this stage, what effects such changes will bring to interpersonal relationships and personal life styles. What does seem certain, however, is that there will be important effects. To some extent these can be affected by direct social intervention and some undesirable effects may be prevented.

Family life, then, is a key variable in society and adverse changes may inflict an enormous social bill. For this reason the effects on individuals must be carefully monitored. Psychologists are just one of the groups which will be involved in this vitally important enterprise.

References

Brown, G.W. and Harris, T. (1978)
Social Origins of Depression. London: Tavistock Publications.

Masters, W. and Johnson, V. (1966)
Human Sexual Response. Boston: Little, Brown.

Masters, W. and Johnson, V. (1970)
Human Sexual Inadequacy. London: Churchill.

Questions

1. Consider some of the factors which might lead a couple to decide to remain childless.
2. Many mothers find looking after a young baby a difficult and stressful experience. Why is this?
3. Hospital births may be medically the safest, but are there likely to be psychological dangers in treating birth more as a biological than as a social and family process?
4. Some people have maintained that schizophrenia arises as a result of problems within the family. Critically assess the evidence relating to this issue.
5. Write an essay on alcoholism in the context of the family.
6. The family seems to be the context for a good deal of violence, particularly towards children and wives. Why should this be so?
7. Consider the special problems of the single-parent family.
8. 'The natural social setting for old people is with their younger family.' How true is this statement? Consider the problems which may arise in a three-generation household.

9. Are there 'experts' in child-rearing? Is this process too important to be left to parents?
10. Some authors have claimed that the family is oppressive and that people should be liberated from the limits that it places on them. How far do you share this view? Give reasons.

Annotated reading

Belliveau, F. and Richter, L. (1971) Understanding Human Sexual Inadequacy. London: Hodder & Stoughton.
Non-technical report of the work of Masters and Johnson on sexual behaviour and sexual problems, including details of treatment methods.

Herbert, M. (1975) Problems of Childhood. London: Pan.
A comprehensive account of the problems of the early years, their treatment and prevention.

Kellmer Pringle, M. (1980) The Needs of Children (2nd edn). London: Hutchinson.
Important review of children's needs and how they may be met both inside and outside the family. Readable and authoritative book with important implications for social policy.

Kempe, R. and Kempe, E. (1978) Child Abuse. London: Fontana/Open Books.
The nature of treatment of violence and sexual assault on children in the family, with an account of methods of treatment and prevention.

Rutter, M. (1976) Helping Troubled Children. Harmondsworth: Penguin.
Leading British child psychiatrist examines the nature of the more severe problems of childhood. Provides good coverage of the importance of family factors and related methods of treatment.

Exercises

1. Defining the family

Attempt to define the term 'family' and then, thinking about your own relationships, draw up a list of the members of your family with clearly formulated criteria for including any others who may be close to you from the 'family group'. Write down your criteria.

The definition of the term 'family' is notoriously difficult but there are several elements which need consideration. How important, for example, is the criterion of 'household', of people living together? How important are legal and blood ties? Those people who are psychologically important to the individual need not be the same as those who are living with the person or who are tied legally to the person.

Do your criteria provide a satisfactory means of separating 'family' from 'non-family' friends? The function of this project is not to enable you to derive criteria which would be universally acceptable, for that would seem to be an impossible task, but rather to stimulate thinking about the relevant issues.

2. Stresses during pregnancy

Interview a couple with whom you are acquainted to find out how they were affected by pregnancy. Before preparing your interview, study the chapters on interviewing. You could also look at medical and 'baby-care' books before deciding which issues you wish to explore. It is often useful to divide pregnancy into three three-month 'trimesters' and to consider the particular features of each. A woman's reaction to discovering that she is pregnant may range from utter delight to profound despair. There are biological changes (including negative ones such as those leading to feelings of nausea or tiredness), direct psychological changes (derived from anticipation of the baby and of the mother role), and changes in social relationships (including those with the husband, if there is one, and with the wider family). All of these may be expected to lead to changes in the woman's psychological state. She may be anxious about the birth process itself or about the possibility of giving birth to a handicapped child; she may feel ambivalent about the 'costs' involved in a change of life style, for example as a result of having to give up her job. Pregnancy will often bring a couple closer together, but if it is experienced as a 'crisis' then it can have the opposite effect. The father-to-be may feel that the child is likely to be a rival for the wife's attention and affection. Pregnancy will also affect the couple's sex-life, their economic position and their relationship with in-laws and the wider community.

3. Written reconstruction of an incident of child-abuse

The aim of this exercise is to write a dramatized account of an incident involving child abuse. Case-histories of child abuse show a wide variation, and there appear to be no universal features of the abusing parent or the abused child. Before writing your narrative collect newspaper accounts so that you can integrate these with analyses from textbooks. First of all set the scene by describing the background to the family, leading to the circumstances in which it finds itself on that day. Then write a dialogue which reveals how the family members are feeling and thinking, and how they react to events which occur and to each other. Continue writing up to the point where physical abuse occurs. Then move to the day following and write accounts from the perspectives of each of the family members involved, together with those, say, of a police officer, social worker and neighbour who have been called in.

4. Patterns of interaction in the family

The aim of this exercise is to reveal the structure of your own family in psychological terms. Begin by making a list of interpersonal behaviours which characterize family life in general; for example, showing affection towards, becoming angry with, seeking comfort from, making decisions, going out together, giving orders and so on. It may help in compiling your list to read the chapter by Michael Argyle and in particular the section on communication. The next step is to draw circles on a piece of paper, writing the name of each family member in a circle. For one of the interpersonal behaviours (e.g. showing affection towards) draw arrows between the circles for appropriate family members. To indicate the strength or frequency of behaviours you can attach numbers (e.g. one to five) to the arrows. Repeat this step for each of the other interpersonal behaviours. No two families are the same. See if a friend is willing to do this exercise so that you can compare a second family with your own. Imagine that you are someone else in your family. How might these diagrams be different? Would that relative's perceptions be similar to yours?

5. Drawing a geneogram

Find an elderly relative who is willing to reminisce about the family. The aim is to reconstruct a 'family tree'. (You will need a large sheet of paper, and you are well-advised to start in the middle of the page.) Adopt standard symbols; for example, a square for a male and a circle for a female. You will need to indicate date of birth, death, marriage, divorce, and so on. You should also indicate each person's occupation. As the story unfolds, you may observe repeated patterns across generations. More will be known (or said) about some people than others: why should this be? Particular events in family life are more charged with emotion than are others. Remember that you are likely to touch on very sensitive areas and that tact and caution may therefore be important. Refer to Barrie Hopson's chapter on transitions, and in particular the discussion of stressful life events.

7

Transition: understanding and managing personal change
Barrie Hopson

> In the ongoing flux of life, (the person) undergoes many changes. Arriving, departing, growing, declining, achieving, failing - every change involves a loss and a gain. The old environment must be given up, the new accepted. People come and go; one job is lost, another begun; territory and possessions are acquired or sold; new skills are learnt, old abandoned; expectations are fulfilled or hopes dashed - in all these situations the individual is faced with the need to give up one mode of life and accept another (Parkes, 1972).

Today, more than at any other time in our history, people have to cope with an often bewildering variety of transitions: from home to school; from school to work; from being single to being married and - increasingly - divorced; from job to job; from job to loss of employment; retraining and re-education; from place to place and friend to friend; to parenthood and then to children leaving home; and finally to bereavements and death. Alongside these and other major life events people are having to learn to cope with the passage from one stage of personal development to another: adolescence, early adulthood, stabilization, mid-life transition and restabilization.

What is a transition?
We define a transition as a discontinuity in a person's life space (Adams, Hayes and Hopson, 1976). Sometimes the discontinuity is defined by social consensus as to what constitutes a discontinuity within the culture. Holmes and Rahe (1967) provide evidence to show the extent of cultural similarity in perceptions of what are important discontinuities, in the research they conducted to produce their social readjustment rating scale. The life changes represented here (see table 1), along with their weighted scores, were found to be remarkably consistent from culture to culture: Japan, Hawaii, Central America, Peru, Spain, France, Belgium, Switzerland and Scandinavia. For example, death of a spouse requires about twice as much change in adjustment worldwide as marriage, and ten times as much as a traffic violation. The correlation between the items ranged from 0.65 to 0.98 across all the cultures.

Another way of defining a discontinuity is not by general consensus but by the person's own perception. These two may not always coincide: for example, adolescence is considered to be an important time of transition in most western cultures, whereas in other cultures like Samoa it is not considered to be a time of stressful identity crisis. Also, in a common culture some children experience adolescence as a transition while others do not. Consequently it cannot be assumed that everyone experiences a transitional event (e.g. a change of job) in the same way.

Table 1

The Holmes and Rahe social readjustment rating scale

LIFE EVENT	Mean value
1. Death of a spouse	100
2. Divorce	73
3. Marital separation from mate	65
4. Detention in jail or other institution	63
5. Death of a close family member	63
6. Major personal injury or illness	53
7. Marriage	50
8. Being fired at work	47
9. Marital reconciliation with mate	45
10. Retirement from work	45
11. Major change in the health or behaviour of a family member	44
12. Pregnancy	40
13. Sexual difficulties	39
14. Gaining a new family member (e.g. through birth, adoption, oldster moving in, etc.)	39
15. Major business readjustment (e.g. merger, reorganization, bankruptcy, etc.)	39
16. Major change in financial state (e.g. a lot worse off or a lot better off than usual)	38
17. Death of a close friend	37
18. Changing to a different line of work	36
19. Major changes in the number of arguments with spouse (e.g. either a lot more or a lot less than usual regarding childbearing, personal habits, etc.)	35
20. Taking on a mortgage greater than $10,000 (e.g. purchasing a home, business, etc.)	31
21. Foreclosure on a mortgage or loan	30
22. Major change in responsibilities at work (e.g. promotion, demotion, lateral transfer)	29

23. Son or daughter leaving home (e.g. marriage, attending college, etc.)	29
24. In-law troubles	29
25. Outstanding personal achievement	28
26. Wife beginning or ceasing work outside the home	26
27. Beginning or ceasing formal schooling	26
28. Major change in living conditions (e.g. building a new home, remodelling, deterioration of home or neighborhood)	25
29. Revision of personal habits (dress, manners, associations, etc.)	24
30. Trouble with the boss	23
31. Major change in working hours or conditions	20
32. Change in residence	20
33. Changing to a new school	20
34. Major change in usual type and/or amount of recreation	19
35. Major change in church activities (e.g. a lot more or a lot less than usual)	19
36. Major change in social activities (e.g. clubs, dancing, movies, visiting, etc.)	18
37. Taking on a mortgage or loan less than $10,000 (e.g. purchasing a car, TV, freezer, etc.)	17
38. Major change in sleeping habits (a lot more or a lot less sleep, or change in part of day when asleep)	16
39. Major change in number of family get-togethers (e.g. a lot more or a lot less than usual)	15
40. Major change in eating habits (a lot more or a lot less food intake, or very different meal hours or surroundings)	15
41. Vacation	13
42. Christmas	12
43. Minor violations of the law (e.g. traffic tickets, jaywalking, disturbing the peace, etc.)	11

For an experience to be classed as transitional there should be:

* personal awareness of a discontinuity in one's life space;
* new behavioural responses required because the situation is new, or the required behaviours are novel, or both.

A person can sometimes undergo a transitional experience without being aware of the extent of the discontinuity or that new behavioural responses are required. This at some point will probably cause the person or others adaptation problems. For example, following the death of her husband, the widow may not be experiencing strain - she might even be pleased that he is dead - but suddenly she becomes aware that no house repairs have been done, and a new dimension or loss becomes evident along with the awareness of new behavioural responses required.

Why is an understanding of transitional experience important?

Life in post-industrial society is likely to bring more and more transitions for people in all arenas of living. Any transition will result in people being subjected to some degree of stress and strain. They will be more or less aware of this depending upon the novelty of the event and the demands it makes upon their behavioural repertoires. Thus, there is likely to be a rise in the number of people experiencing an increased amount of stress and strain in the course of their daily lives.

Many practitioners in the helping professions are dealing directly with clients who are in transition. It is vital for them to understand how people are likely to react during transition, and to recognize the symptoms of transitional stress. Professionals also need helping techniques to ensure that individuals cope more effectively with their transitions, and to make organizations and social groups more aware of what they can do to help people in transition.

Is there a general model of transitions?

As we began to discover other work on different transitions, a general picture increasingly began to emerge. It appeared that irrespective of the nature of the transition, an overall pattern seemed to exist. There were differences, of course, especially between those transitions that were usually experienced as being positive (e.g. marriage and desired promotion) and those usually experienced negatively (e.g. bereavement and divorce). But these differences appeared to reflect differences of emphasis rather than require a totally different model.

The major point to be made in understanding transitions is that whether a change in one's daily routine is an intentional change, a sudden surprise that gets thrust upon one, or a growing awareness that one is moving into a life stage characterized by increasing or decreasing stability, it will trigger a cycle of reactions and feelings that is predictable. The cycle has seven phases, and the identification of these seven phases has come about through content analysis of reports from over 100 people who have attended transition workshops for the purpose of understanding and learning to cope more effectively with transitions they were experiencing and through extending the findings reported above.

Immobilization

The first phase is a kind of immobilization or a sense of being overwhelmed; of being unable to make plans, unable to reason, and unable to understand. In other words, the initial phase of a transition is experienced by many people as a feeling of being frozen up. It appears that the intensity with which people experience this first phase is a function of the unfamiliarity of the transition state and of the negative expectations one holds. If the transition is not high in novelty and if the person holds positive expectations, the immobilization is felt less intensely or perhaps not at all. Marriage can be a good example of the latter.

Minimization

The way of getting out of this immobilization, essentially, is by movement to the second phase of the cycle, which is characterized by minimization of the change or disruption, even to trivialize it. Very often, the person will deny that the change even exists. Sometimes, too, the person projects a euphoric feeling. Those readers who recall seeing Alfred Hitchcock's film 'Psycho' will remember that Tony Perkins spent considerable time shrieking at his mother in the house on the hill. It is not until the end of the film that one learns the mother has been dead for some time, and it is her semi-mummified body with which he has been carrying on his 'dialogue'. That is an extreme example of denying or minimizing the reality of a major change in one's life. Denial can have a positive function. It is more often a necessary phase in the process of adjustment. 'Denial is a normal and necessary human reaction to a crisis which is too immediately overwhelming to face head-on. Denial provides time for a temporary retreat from reality while our internal forces regroup and regain the strength to comprehend the new life our loss has forced upon us' (Krantzler, 1973).

Depression

Eventually, for most people - though not for Tony Perkins in 'Psycho' - the realities of the change and of the resulting stresses begin to become apparent. As people become aware that they must make some changes in the way they are living, as they become aware of the realities involved, they sometimes begin to get depressed: the third phase of the transition cycle. Depression is usually the consequence of feelings of powerlessness, of aspects of life out of one's control. This is often made worse by the fear of loss of control over one's own emotions. The depression stage has occasional high energy periods often characterized by anger, before sliding back into a feeling of hopelessness. They become depressed because they are just beginning to face up to the fact that there has been a change. Even if they have voluntarily created this change themselves, there is likely to be this dip in feelings. They become frustrated because it becomes difficult to know how best to cope with the new life requirements, the ways of being, the new relationships that have been established or whatever other changes may be necessary.

Letting go

As people move further into becoming aware of reality, they can move into the fourth phase, which is accepting reality for what it is. Through the first three phases, there has been a kind of attachment, whether it has been conscious or not, to the past (pre-transition) situation. To move from phase three to phase four involves a process of unhooking from the past and of saying 'Well, here I am now; here is what I have; I know I can survive; I may not be sure of what I want yet but I will be OK; there is life out there waiting for me.' As this is accepted as the new reality, the person's feelings begin to rise once more, and optimism becomes possible. A clear 'letting go' is necessary.

Testing

This provides a bridge to phase five, where people become much more active and start testing themselves vis-a-vis the new situation, trying out new behaviours, new life styles, and new ways of coping with the transition. There is a tendency also at this point for people to stereotype, to have categories and classifications of the ways things and people should or should not be relative to the new situation. There is much personal energy available during this phase and, as they begin to deal with the new reality, it is not unlikely that those in transition will easily become angry and irritable.

Search for meaning

Following this burst of activity and self-testing, there is a more gradual shifting towards becoming concerned with understanding and for seeking meanings for how things are different and why they are different. This sixth phase is a cognitive process in which people try to understand what all of the activity, anger, stereotyping and so on have meant. It is not until people can get out of the activity and withdraw somewhat from it that they can begin to understand deeply the meaning of the change in their lives.

Internalization

This conceptualizing, in turn, allows people to move into the final phase of internalizing these meanings and incorporating them into their behaviour. Overall, the seven transition phases represent a cycle of experiencing a disruption, gradually acknowledging its reality, testing oneself, understanding oneself, and incorporating changes in one's behaviour. The level of one's morale varies across these phases and appears to follow a predictable path. Identifying the seven phases along such a morale curve often gives one a better understanding of the nature of the transition cycle. This is shown in figure 1.

Figure 1

Self–esteem changes during transitions

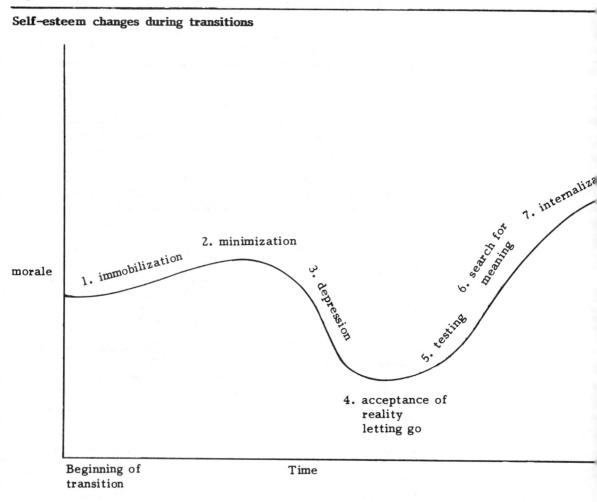

Interestingly, the Menninger Foundation's research on Peace Corps volunteers' reactions to entering and experiencing training (a transition for each person) produced a very similar curve. More recently, Kubler–Ross and those who joined her death and dying seminars have also charted a very similar curve of the reaction cycle people go through upon learning they are terminally ill, which is the ultimate transition.

Before proceeding, it is necessary to make it clear that seldom, if ever, does a person move neatly from one phase to another as has been described above. It can help someone in distress, however, to be made aware that what they are experiencing is not uncommon, that it will pass, and that they have a great deal they can do in determining how quickly it will pass.

It is also important to point out that each person's experience is unique and that any given individual's progressions and regressions are unique to their unique circumstances. For example, one person may never get beyond denial or minimization. Another may end it all during depression. Yet another might experience a major failure just as things begin to look up, and slip back to a less active, more withdrawn posture.

What is important is the potential for growth arising from any major disruption or calamity. One realizes this potential and moves toward it when one lets go and fully accepts the situation for what it is; one dies a 'little death' to become larger.

What effects do transitions have on people?

It is important to note here that all transitions involve some stress, including those considered by society to be positive changes, such as being left large sums of money, parenthood or marriage (Holmes and Rahe, 1967). Our own studies investigating this relationship show the following results:

* transitions are most stressful if they are unpredictable, involuntary, unfamiliar, of high magnitude (degree of change), and high intensity (rate of change);
* the incidence of illness is positively correlated with the amount of life change one undergoes;
* lack of feedback on the success of attempts to cope with strain-inducing events causes more severe stress-related diseases than when relevant feedback is present;
* interpersonal warmth and support during stressful periods seems to reduce the impact of the stress;
* viruses alone do not cause illnesses. The incidence of bad emotional experiences seems to upset the body and allow the viruses to take over;
* hypertension occurs more often in environments characterized by high stressors and few ways of responding to those stressors;
* the more major the life changes the higher the risk of coronary heart disease.

Every transition contains 'opportunity value' for the mover

However undesirable a particular transition may be for the mover, there is always opportunity for personal growth and development contained within it. If one takes a severe example such as death of a spouse, for the majority of those bereaved nothing will compensate for that loss. On the other hand, given that the loss is out of their control, what is under their control is what they decide to do with their lives from there on. There are opportunities for new relationships, travel, career change, new interests, etc. Obviously, during the grief process - which is essential - the opportunities are difficult and often obnoxious to contemplate but part of the 'letting go' stage involves doing exactly that. The Chinese have two symbols for the concept of 'crisis': one means 'danger' while the other signifies 'opportunity'.

What are the coping tasks relevant to all transitional events?

We believe that there are common elements in any transition which enable us to talk generally about transitional behaviour. We also assert that in dealing with any transitional event a person has two tasks to perform as he moves through the phases of the model:

* MANAGEMENT OF STRAIN: to manage the degree of strain generated by the stress in such a way that the individual can engage with the external problems caused by the transition.
* COGNITIVE COPING TASKS: a transition will always necessitate adjustment. Any adjustment requires decisions to be made about the appropriateness of new and old behaviour patterns. The individual will be asking questions such as: (i) how can I accept this situation?; (ii) what behaviour is expected of me?; and (iii) what do I want from this situation?

How successfully these two tasks are managed determines the speed with which the transition is completed.

What are the coping skills relevant to transitions?

At the Counselling and Career Development Unit at Leeds University we have been working for a number of years on developing training programmes to help adults in transition and to teach transition coping skills to young people in schools and colleges.

We have developed a questionnaire to be used to help people identify the transition coping skills they already possess and which simultaneously highlights the deficits in their coping repertory. Table 2 reproduces the questionnaire designed for use with adults. People are asked to answer 'yes' or 'no' to all the questions. Each time they reply 'no', it suggests an area where they are lacking in some theoretical understanding of the nature of transitions, or deficient in cognitive or behavioural skills. Each of the items is dealt with briefly below, along with some teaching points we make to participants. In a workshop, this learning would take place experientially and participants would have an opportunity to develop and practise their skills. The language used is written to convey the flavour of the workshop approach. The text which follows should be read in conjunction with the questionnaire below.

Table 2
_____

Coping skills questionnaire

1. KNOW YOURSELF
a. Would I have chosen for this to have happened?
b. Am I proactive in new situations: do I take initiatives,
   have a purpose as opposed to sitting back and waiting on
   events?
c. Do I know what I want from this new situation?
d. Do I know what I don't want from this new situation?
e. If I feel under stress do I know what I can do to help
   myself?
f. Do I know how to use my feelings as indicators of where
   I am?

2. KNOW YOUR NEW SITUATION
a. Can I describe the transition?
b. Do I know how I'm expected to behave?
c. Can I try out the new situation in advance?

3. KNOW OTHER PEOPLE WHO CAN HELP: do I have other
   people:
a. To depend on in a crisis?
b. To discuss concerns?
c. To feel close to - a friend?
d. Who can make me feel competent and valued?
e. Who can give me important information?
f. Who will challenge me to sit up and take a good look at
   myself?
g. With whom I can share good news and good feelings?
h. Who will give me constructive feedback?

4. LEARN FROM THE PAST
a. Is there anything similar that has happened to me?
b. Can I identify what I did which helped me get through
   that experience?
c. Can I identify what I would have done differently?

5. LOOK AFTER YOURSELF
a. Do I know how to use supportive self-talk?
b. Do I get regular exercise or have a personal fitness
   programme?
c. Am I eating regularly and wisely?
d. Do I know how to relax?
e. Am I keeping to a regular schedule?
f. Do I know my 'personal anchor points'?
g. Do I give myself 'treats' when under stress?
h. Do I have other people who will take care of me?
i. Can I survive?
j. Do I know when my low points are likely to be?

6. LET GO OF THE PAST
a. Do I easily let go of old situations?

b. Do I continually feel that this should not happen to me?
c. Do I know how to vent my anger constructively?

7. SET GOALS AND MAKE ACTION PLANS
a. Do I know how to set goals?
b. Do I know what my goals are for this transition and for my life generally?
c. Do I know how to make and implement action plans?
d. Do I know how to set priorities?
e. Do I know how to make effective decisions?
f. Do I know how to generate alternatives, because there is always an alternative?

8. LOOK FOR THE GAINS YOU HAVE MADE
a. Can I find one thing which is positive about this experience?
b. Can I list a variety of new opportunities that did not exist before or that I would not have thought of previously?
c. Have I learnt something new about myself?

Know yourself
1. WOULD I HAVE CHOSEN FOR THIS TO HAVE HAPPENED? You may not have chosen this situation. This could make it more difficult for you to accept the transition. But it has happened. You now have three options:

(A) accept it and put up with it
(B) refuse to accept
(C) accept it and try to benefit from it

(A) will help you to survive. (B) will bring you nothing but bad feelings and worse; you will be less able to cope with the tasks facing you in the new situation. (C) will help you to grow in addition to merely surviving.

Given the inevitable, ask yourself the key question: 'What is the worst thing that could happen?' Having identified it, ask yourself if you can cope. Is it really so terrible?

It is essential to remember that problematic situations constitute a normal aspect of living. It is also useful to recall the variety of transitions that you have encountered and survived up until now. Through having survived you will probably have developed some skills. If, on looking back, you feel dissatisfied with how you managed a transition, it is important to ask yourself whether you had all the skills needed to deal effectively with that situation. More than likely you did not. Do not berate yourself for not having these skills. Instead be glad that you have identified the need for additional skills, for that in itself is the first stage of skill development.

2. AM I PROACTIVE IN NEW SITUATIONS: DO I TAKE INITIATIVES, HAVE A PURPOSE, AS OPPOSED TO SITTING BACK AND WAITING ON EVENTS? To be proactive involves a certain sequence of behaviour:

* knowing what you want;
* knowing alternative ways of achieving this;
* choosing one alternative;
* evaluating the results against your original objective.

The essence of proactive behaviour is that there is a reason for it, even if the end result involves no action. The reason, however, must stem from what Maslow (1968) calls a 'growth' need as opposed to a 'deficiency' need. Deciding not to give a public talk (objective), and knowing various ways of avoiding this (knowing alternatives), choosing one, and thereby achieving the objective at first glance seems to fit the description of 'proactive behaviour'. However, if the reason is based on fear of making a fool of oneself, this would not be classed as proactive. If it were due to over-commitment, or the feeling that you are not the best equipped person to do it, that would be proactive.

3. DO I KNOW WHAT I WANT FROM THIS NEW SITUATION?

4. DO I KNOW WHAT I DO NOT WANT FROM THIS NEW SITUATION? If you are unclear as to what you want or do not want from a new situation this usually signifies a lack of knowledge about your own values or about what the new situation has to offer. There is an entire educational technology designed to help young people and adults to crystallize their needs and values. It has been developed in the USA and is known generically as 'values clarification' (Simon, Howe and Kirschenbaum, 1972; Simon, 1974; Howe and Howe, 1975; Kirschenbaum, 1977). Obtaining more information about the new situation is dealt with in the next section.

5. IF I FEEL UNDER STRESS DO I KNOW WHAT I CAN DO TO HELP MYSELF? Avoid situations where you might over-react. If you have recently separated from your spouse and it is still painful, do not accept an invitation to an event where you know you will encounter your spouse again. Make as few decisions as possible as you will not be thinking clearly enough. Do not make more than one transition at a time. It is amazing how often people choose one transition to be the stimulus for a host of others. If you have changed your job, do not change your spouse, residence and/or life style all at the same time. A new broom can sometimes sweep you over!

Look after yourself (see below).

Do not waste time blaming yourself (see below).

Remember that time itself will not eliminate the stress or heal you, it is what you do with that time. There are a variety of cognitive shielding techniques that you can use

to minimize the strain. These all involve controlling the
amount of stimulation in the environment. Some examples are

* time management: making priorities;
* making lists;
* queuing: delaying decisions during a difficult period
  by queuing them up, dealing with them one at a time,
  and not thinking about future decisions until the time
  to make them arrives. Writing down a decision in a diary
  to be made at a future date is a good way of queuing.
* temporary drop-out: refusing to resolve decisions until
  after a recuperation period. This can appear initially
  as reactive; however, it is correctly termed proactive
  as the mover is deliberately opting out of the situation
  temporarily as part of a strategy to move in later and
  thereby more effectively.

There are now some excellent resources available for
techniques of preventing and managing stress (e.g. Lamott,
1975; Sharpe and Lewis, 1977; Forbes, 1979).

6. DO I KNOW HOW TO USE MY FEELINGS AS INDICATOR
OF WHERE I AM? Many people, especially men, as a result
of their upbringing are emotionally illiterate: that is,
they have not developed the skills of 'reading' their own
emotions. One's 'gut' feelings are the surest indicator of
how one is coping at any particular time. The skill is in
learning to recognize the changes in feelings when they
occur and then having an emotional vocabulary to be able
to label them correctly. Often when people are asked what
they are feeling they will answer you in terms of only
what they are thinking (see Johnson, 1972; Hopson and
Scally, 1980a).

Know your new situation
1. CAN I DESCRIBE THE TRANSITION? An essential
prerequisite to successful transition coping is to know that
you are in one. It is essential to be aware of when the
transition began, where you are in relation to it and what
are all the variables involved. For example, considering
changing your job might involve geographical change,
relationship changes, financial implications, holiday plans
for this year, and so on.

2. DO I KNOW HOW I AM EXPECTED TO BEHAVE? Transitions are naturally accompanied by stress even if they are
desired. Anxiety certainly increases the less information
you have about your new situation. Collect as much data as
you can about what others expect of you, what society ex-
pects and how you are to behave. You may decide not to live
up to or down to those expectations, but again you need the
initial data before you can make that decision. You also
need to know the consequences of any decision before you
make it.

You can ask people who have made a similar transition or indeed are presently going through the same transition. A variety of self-help and special interest groups have developed in recent years to provide mutual support and information to people undergoing similar transitions: ante-natal classes, induction courses, orientation programmes, women's and men's 'rap' groups for people redefining their sex roles, widows' clubs, singles' clubs, one-parent family groups, and so on.

It is important to remember that other people often forget, or in some cases are not even aware, that this is a new situation for you. They may need reminding. For example, one new day at the end of your first week at a new job con-stitutes 20 per cent of the time you have worked there. For people who have been here for five years, one new day rep-resents less than 0.4 per cent of the time they have been there. Consequently, their feelings about that day are like-ly to be quite different from your feelings about the same day.

3. CAN I TRY OUT THE NEW SITUATION IN ADVANCE?
Some transitions can be 'sampled' in advance, for example, starting a new job, moving to another country; even a divorce or death can sometimes be anticipated. Reading books about anticipated transitions can be valuable, as can talk-ing to others who have experienced it, while remembering that no one will experience it just like you. Where appro-priate you can visit places, meet people, watch films, etc., prior to your transition.

Knowing other people who can help
There is now considerable evidence to show the beneficial effects on stress reduction of talking problems through with people: friends, colleagues, even strangers.

We often make the mistake of expecting too few people, typically a spouse and children, to satisfy too great a proportion of our needs. Check the list in the question-naire. How many categories of person do you have available to you in your life? Are there any gaps? How many different people make up your 'support' group? How dependent are you on one or two?

We are also better at developing some forms of support at the expense of others. For example, people are often better at developing friendships than relationships with people who challenge us. The challengers in most people's support systems are about as abrasive as a marshmallow. Yet sometimes challengers are exactly what we require to shift us out of stereotyped thinking. Who are the challengers in your support systems? Remember, you may not even like them.

Learn from the past
Our past is an important part of our present. Our past is the history of our successes and our failures and is thereby a record of our learning. As such, we can continue to learn

from our past experiences. 'Mistakes' are another way of labelling 'opportunities for learning'. If we can identify times in the past when we have had similar feelings or experienced similar transitions, we have an opportunity to monitor those chapters of our history and evaluate our performances against the criteria of our own choosing. What did we do that really did not help the situation? What would we avoid if we were to have that experience again? Can we learn from that experience and generalize it to the new transition? A sense of one's own history is a prerequisite to a fully functioning present and a portent for one's range of possible futures.

Look after yourself

1. DO I KNOW HOW TO USE SUPPORTIVE SELF-TALK? Many of the problems we create for ourselves and much of the support that we give ourselves derives from the same source: our internal dialogue with ourselves. This dialogue continues throughout most of our waking hours. These 'cognitions' are vital to our survival and growth. They enable us to adapt to new situations, to learn, to feel and to enact cognitively a variety of scenarios without having to perform any of them. Ellis, with his Rational-Emotive Therapy, for years has claimed that the way we think determines what we feel, with the corollary that if we can change how we think we can also change how we feel (Ellis and Harper, 1975). His therapeutic method involves re-training people to talk internally to themselves to minimize the negative emotions which they otherwise would create. Ellis claims that most people carry a variety of 'irrational beliefs' in their heads unfounded in reality, but which result in their creating bad feelings for themselves as a result of 'shoulds' and 'oughts' which they believe are infallible. These beliefs usually belong to one of three categories, which Ellis calls the 'Irrational Trinity' on the road to 'mustabation':

*   A belief that I should be a certain sort of person, or a success, or perfect, or loved by everyone, and if I'm not, I'm a failure and worthless;
*   a belief that you, or other people, should do as I want them to do: love me, work for me, understand me, etc. and if they do not, it is terrible, and I deserve to be miserable or they should be made to suffer;
*   a belief that things should be different; there should not be racial hatred, this organization should run better, our parents should not have to die, etc., and if things are not as I want them to be it is awful and either I cannot cope and deserve to be miserable, or I have every right to be furious.

Since it takes years to develop our patterns of self-talk, changing them involves practice. There are a variety of programmes now available for helping people to restructure their self-talk into more supportive statements. Mahoney and Mahoney (1976) call this process 'cognitive ecology': cleaning up what you say to yourself.

2. DO I GET REGULAR EXERCISE OR HAVE A PERSONAL FITNESS PROGRAMME? Physical fitness is related to one's ability to cope with stress. It has also been shown to be related to the ability to create effective interpersonal relationships (Aspy and Roebuck, 1977) which in turn is related to stress reduction.

You need to be fit to cope effectively with transitions. Yet, of course, it is often when we are most in need of fitness that we are often least inclined to make time for it. There are a number of well-researched fitness programmes available (Health Education Council, 1976; Carruthers and Murray, 1977; Cooper, 1977; Royal Canadian Air Force, 1978).

3. AM I EATING REGULARLY AND WISELY? Now is not the time for a crash diet. Your body needs all the help it can get. People in transition often have neither the time nor inclination to eat wisely. There is sometimes a reliance on quick junk foods, take-away meals or eating out. Remember to eat something every day from the four major food groups: meat, fish, poultry; dairy products; fruits and vegetables; bread and cereals.

Do not replace food with alcohol or smoking. Obviously there may be times when alcohol will help you get through a lonely evening. You need a holiday from self-work as much as from any other kind of work. The danger signs are when alcohol or a cigarette is used as a substitute for meals.

Be wary of developing a dependence on drugs at this time. Sleeping tablets can sometimes be helpful during a crisis, but get off them quickly. They can serve to prevent you from developing healthier coping strategies.

It is a good idea to acquire an easy to read book on diet but one that is critical of food fads. The Health Education Council's booklet, 'Look After Yourself' (1976), contains a simple introduction to good nutrition, and Breckon's 'You Are What You Eat' (1976) is a fascinating survey of dietary facts and fiction, arguing strongly against overdosing oneself with vitamins and dealing in a balanced way with the hysteria over additives.

4. DO I KNOW HOW TO RELAX? There are two ways of reducing stress. One is to organize your life to minimize the number of stressors working on you. The other concerns how to reduce the effect of stress when it hits you. The latter is typically the biggest problem when coping with a transition. Unfortunately, the very people who are most prone to stress illnesses often exacerbate the problem by packing their lives with transitions.

There are numerous relaxation methods, each of which have their advocates. A brief guide follows.

* Learn a relaxation technique. Progressive relaxation is simple and easy to learn. It is described in Hopson and Hough (1973) as a classroom exercise. Transcendental meditation is now well researched and strong claims are made for it as a technique which directly affects the body's physiology. Most cities have a TM centre. You could also read Russel (1977). For those who do not enjoy the ritual cliquishness that accompanies TM, read Benson (1977).

* Direct body work to encourage relaxation: massage. The basics can be learnt quickly on a course. If there is a Personal Growth centre near you, make contact as they might run courses. Read Downing (1972). You will need keep an open mind regarding some of the sweeping generalizations made on behalf of some of these techniques.

5. AM I KEEPING TO A REGULAR SCHEDULE? If your internal world is in crisis, keep your external world in order. Keeping irregular hours, eating at strange times, going to lots of new places, meeting new people; all these can be disorientating.

6. DO I KNOW MY 'PERSONAL ANCHOR POINTS'? Toffler (1970) described this concept as one antidote to 'future shock'. When all around us things are changing we need an anchor point to hold on to. For some people it is their home, for others a relationship, children, a job, a daily routine, a favourite place or a hobby. Anchor points are plentiful, and it is vital to have at least one. In the midst of instability a stable base offers confirmation of identity, disengagement from the problem, and maybe even relaxation.

7. DO I GIVE MYSELF 'TREATS' WHEN UNDER STRESS? This list of tips has been packed with work. But play is vital too. If you are feeling low, or under stress, how about simply giving yourself a treat? It might even be a reward for accomplishing a difficult test or situation, but it does not have to be.

Draw up a list of treats. Try to become an expert on self-indulgence: a theatre trip, a massage, a book, see friends, make love, have a disgustingly 'bad for you' meal, take a holiday, or pamper yourself.

The only warning about treats is: do not spend so much time treating yourself that you use these as a diversion from coping directly with the transition.

8. DO I HAVE OTHER PEOPLE WHO WILL TAKE CARE OF ME? It is all right to be taken care of sometimes. Allow a friend, lover or colleague to look after you. If they do not offer, be proactive, ask them. Be brave enough to accept help from others. Recall what you feel when others close to you ask for help. There are pay-offs for helpers as well as those who receive help.

9. CAN I SURVIVE? Of course you can. You may doubt it at the moment. Perhaps it will help to remind yourself that what you are feeling now is normal for someone having experienced what you are experiencing. It is also necessary before you can move on to the next stage of finding out more about you and what this transition can do for you instead of to you.

Do not worry about feelings of suicide. Sometimes survival does not seem like such a good idea. If these feelings really seem to be getting out of hand see a counsellor, ring a Samaritan, or consult a doctor; you will probably get more librium than counselling, but that can take off the pressure until you have regrouped your resources.

The feeling will pass. Talk to people, keep a regular routine, treat yourself; at the end of each day recall one good experience, then you can match it with a bad one, then another good experience followed by a bad one, etc., or contract with a friend to call you at certain times.

10. DO I KNOW WHEN MY LOW POINTS ARE LIKELY TO BE? These can usually be predicted quite easily; after a phone call to your children (in the case of a divorced parent), seeing your ex-spouse with a new partner, just seeing your ex-spouse, discovering a personal belonging of your dead spouse, seeing an old workmate (redundancy, retirement), and so on.

Keep a diary or a journal. This will help you to clarify your thoughts and feelings as well as to identify times, places and people to avoid. If you are experiencing the loss of a love it is usually advisable to fill your Sundays, bank holidays and Saturday nights!

Let go of the past
1. DO I EASILY LET GO OF OLD SITUATIONS? Sometimes people cannot let go because they try too hard to hold on. It is permissible to grieve. Grief shows that you are alive. Think about what you are missing, feel it. Ask people if you can talk to them about it. They will often be too embarrassed to mention it or worry that it will 'upset' you. Cry, rage, scream, recognize the loss, do not deny the pain. Wounds hurt when you dress them, but you know that is the first stage of the wound getting better. It is permissible to feel anger too.

2. DO I CONTINUALLY FEEL THAT THIS SHOULD NOT HAPPEN TO ME? Then you are guilty of making yourself unhappy by hitting yourself over the head with 'shoulds' and 'oughts'. You need to look again at the section on supportive self-talk.

3. DO I KNOW HOW TO VENT MY ANGER CONSTRUCTIVELY? Allow yourself to feel the anger. If it is kept inside it will only hurt you. Feel angry at the person who

left you, at the person who took something from you, at the
world that let you down or at friends who cannot be trusted.
Hit a pillow, scream aloud (in a closed car this is very
effective; just like an echo chamber) or play a hectic
sport. Do not hurt anyone, including yourself.

Anger is only a feeling. It cannot hurt anyone. Only
behaviour hurts. Once the anger is cleared away, you are
then freer to begin to evaluate, make plans and decide.

Set goals and make action plans
1. DO I KNOW HOW TO SET GOALS? Some people fail to
manage their transitions effectively because they have not
identified a desirable outcome. 'If you don't know where
you're going, you'll probably end up somewhere else'
(Campbell, 1974).

It is essential to identify what you want to achieve in
terms which are as behaviourally specific as possible, such
as 'I want a new job worth £8,000 per annum where I have
overall responsibility for financial operations of a medium-
scale department.' 'In six months I want to be able to go
out on my own, to visit friends by myself, and to have
developed one new interest' (this was an objective of a
recent widow in one of my workshops).

2. DO I KNOW WHAT MY GOALS ARE FOR THIS TRANS-
ITION AND FOR MY LIFE GENERALLY? This requires the
specific skill of knowing how to set, define, and refine
objectives.

3. DO I KNOW HOW TO MAKE AND IMPLEMENT ACTION
PLANS? Once the objectives are clear the action steps follow
next. There are a variety of resources available with
guidelines on making effective action plans. Carkhuff's two
books (1974a, b) are useful. An action plan needs to be
behaviourally specific: 'I will make an appointment to see
the solicitor tomorrow morning'. It needs to be in terms of
'what I will do now', not in terms of 'what I will do
sometime', or 'what we will do eventually'. An action plan
should read like a computer programme, with each step so
clearly defined that someone else would know how to carry it
out.

4. DO I KNOW HOW TO SET PRIORITIES? Having a variety
of goals is one thing, having the time to achieve them all
is another. Skills of time management are required along
with a systematic way of measuring the desirability of one
goal with another.

5. DO I KNOW HOW TO MAKE EFFECTIVE DECISIONS?
Katz (1968) has talked about the importance, not so much
of making wise decisions but of making decisions wisely.
There are a variety of teaching programmes now available to
help people become more proficient at making choices (Hopson
and Hough, 1973; Watts and Elsom, 1975).

6. DO I KNOW HOW TO GENERATE ALTERNATIVES,
BECAUSE THERE IS ALWAYS AN ALTERNATIVE? Often
people do not make as good a decision as they might have
simply because they have not generated enough alternatives.
The techniques of 'brainstorming', 'morphological forced
connections' and 'synectics' (all described in Adams, 1974)
are ways of doing this. The key quite often, however, is the
belief that no matter now hopeless the situation, how constrained one feels, there is always an alternative, no matter how unpalatable it may initially appear, and that you
can choose. This is the central concept in the model of the
'self empowered person' described by Hopson and Scally
(1980b).

Look for the gains you have made
If gains are not immediately apparent, review the section
again under 'Know yourself'. Have you had to cope with
something with which you have not had to cope before? If so,
this will have shed light on a new facet of your personality. What is it? Do you like it? Can you use it to any
advantage in the future?

Quick check-list on
client's transition
coping skills

1. DOES HE KNOW WHAT HE WANTS FROM THE NEW
SITUATION? If not, you must help him to define what he
wants; getting him to be as specific as possible. He may not
be used to thinking in terms of objectives. You will have to
teach him. Write down options on a blackboard, flip chart,
or a note-book. Help him to evaluate the costs and benefits
of different alternatives. Give him homework on this to be
discussed at a future session.

2. DOES HE TEND TO BE PROACTIVE IN NEW SITUATIONS
OR TO SIT BACK AND WAIT FOR THINGS TO HAPPEN? If
he appears to be proactive, check out that it really is
proactivity and not just acting to minimize anxiety, for
instance jumping into something to alleviate ambiguity. If
he is reactive you will need to point out that this will
minimize his chances of getting what he wants and you will
need to give him a task which is small enough for him to
complete successfully (e.g. doing some homework) in order
to develop his confidence in the ability to make things
happen. Give him a suitable book to read (see the section
on self-help books) which is simultaneously instructive and
a task to be completed.

3. DOES HE HAVE OTHER PEOPLE HE CAN RELY ON
FOR HELP? Get him to specify who and what they can do
for him. If he is deficient in help, steer him towards an
appropriate self-help group.

4. HAS ANYTHING LIKE THIS HAPPENED TO HIM
BEFORE? Look for links with previous experiences. Help him
to discover what he did then which helped, and what in
retrospect he would now choose to do differently.

5. HOW WELL CAN HE LOOK AFTER HIMSELF? Is he physically fit and eating sensibly? If not, advise him of the importance of this. Similarly, help him to discover the 'anchor points' in his life and persuade him to keep to a regular schedule. Encourage him to give himself a treat from time to time. Help him to identify when the low points are likely to be and to plan to minimize the impact of these: for example, always have something planned for Sunday when you are newly divorced.

6. CAN HE LET GO OF THE PAST? If not, encourage him to experience the grief and the anger as a way of discharging it and accepting that these feelings are normal and acceptable. They only become a problem if we can never let go of them.

7. CAN HE SET GOALS AND MAKE ACTION PLANS? Persuade him to begin thinking about specific goals as outlined under point 1. Help him define priorities, generate alternatives, and weigh them up.

8. CAN HE SEE POSSIBLE GAINS FROM HIS NEW SITUATION? Gently pressure him to begin to look for gains. The timing of this is vital. If he has not sufficiently let go of the past your intervention can appear heartless. Empathy is essential, but also you are trying to get him to see that however much he may not have chosen for an event to happen, that there will be something to gain.

Is it possible to train people to cope more effectively with transitions?

This has had to be empirically tested. Our general hypothesis is that people experiencing transitions will have similar tasks to cope with, namely, managing strain and dealing with cognitive tasks presented by the transition. We are assuming that to a considerable extent people's reactions to being in transition are learnt as opposed to being inherited. To the extent that individuals' reactions are learnt, we should be able to develop preventive, educative and re-educative strategies to help them manage their affairs and relationships more effectively at lower psychological costs, and derive greater benefits from the opportunity values embedded in every major transition.

This means that training programmes could be generated to help develop more effective coping styles for a number of people either (i) experiencing different transitional events, or who are anticipating transitional events, or (ii) as general training for any presently unknown future transitions.

We have already conducted a variety of transitions workshops in the UK, the USA and Scandinavia with populations including managers, trade unionists, counsellors, organization development specialists, social workers, case workers, teachers and youth workers. These have been primarily designed for participants who in turn will have to deal with individuals in transition. We believe that it is only possible to do such work when one has a clear understanding not just of a theoretical orientation, a collection of coping skills and teaching techniques, but also of one's own transitional experiences, skills and deficits, joys, confusion and sadness.

The final question is always 'why'? Why spend the energy, use the time, deplete the resources, all of which could be directed to something else?

We can only give our answer. A transition simultaneously carries the seeds of our yesterdays, the hopes and fears of our futures, and the pressing sensations of the present which is our confirmation of being alive. There is danger and opportunity, ecstasy and despair, development and stagnation, but above all there is movement. Nothing and no one stays the same. Nature abhors vacuums and stability. A stable state is merely a stopping point on a journey from one place to another. Stop too long and your journey is ended. Stay and enjoy but with the realization that more is to come. You may not be able to stop the journey, but you can fly the plane.

References

Adams, J.L. (1974)
Conceptual Blockbusting. San Francisco: Freeman.
Adams, J.D., Hayes, J. and Hopson, B. (1976)
Transition: Understanding and managing personal change. London: Martin Robertson.
Aspy, D.N. and Roebuck, F.N. (1977)
Kids Don't Learn From People They Don't Like. Amherst, Mass.: Human Resource Development Press.
Benson, H. (1977)
The Relaxation Response. London: Fountain Well Press.
Breckon, W. (1976)
You Are What You Eat. London: BBC Publications.
Campbell, D. (1974)
If You Don't Know Where You're Going You'll Probably End Up Somewhere Else. Hoddesdon, Herts.: Argus Publications.
Carkhuff, R.R. (1974a)
The Art of Problem Solving. Amherst, Mass.: Human Resource Development Press.
Carkhuff, R.R. (1974b)
How To Help Yourself. Amherst, Mass.: Human Resource Development Press.
Carruthers, M. and Murray, A. (1977)
F/40: Fitness on forty minutes a week. London: Futura.
Cooper, K. (1977)
The New Aerobics. New York: Bantam.
Downing, G. (1972)
The Massage Book. New York: Random House.
Ellis, A. and Harper, R. (1975)
A New Guide to Rational Living. Hollywood, Ca: Wilshire Books.

Forbes, R. (1979)
Life Stress. New York: Doubleday.
Health Education Council (1976)
Look After Yourself. London: Health Education Council.
Holmes, T.H. and Rahe, R.H. (1967)
The social readjustment rating scale. Journal of
Psychosomatic Research, 11, 213-218.
Hopson, B. and Hough, P. (1973)
Exercises in Personal and Career Development. Cambridge
Hobsons Press.
Hopson, B. and Scally, M. (1980a)
How to cope with and gain from life transitions. In B.
Hopson and M. Scally, Lifeskills Teaching Programmes
No. 1. Leeds: Lifeskills Associates.
Hopson, B. and Scally, M. (1980b)
Lifeskills Teaching: Education for self-empowerment.
London: McGraw-Hill.
Howe, L.W. and Howe, M.M. (1975)
Personalizing Education: Values clarification and
beyond. New York: Hart.
Johnson. D.W. (1972)
Reaching Out. Englewood Cliffs, NJ: Prentice-Hall.
Katz, M.R. (1968)
Can computers make guidance decisions for students?
College Board Review, No. 72.
Kirschenbaum, H. (1977)
Advanced Value Clarification. La Jolla, Ca: University
Associates.
Krantzler, M. (1973)
Creative Divorce. New York: M. Evans.
Lamott, K. (1975)
Escape from Stress. New York: Berkley.
Mahoney, M.J. and Mahoney, J. (1976)
Permanent Weight Control. New York: W.W. Norton.
Maslow, A. (1968)
Towards a Psychology of Being (2nd edn). New York: Van
Nostrand.
Parkes, C. M. (1972)
Bereavement: Studies of grief in adult life. London:
Tavistock.
Royal Canadian Air Force (1978)
Physical Fitness. Harmondsworth: Penguin.
Russel, P. (1977)
The Transcendental Meditation Technique. London:
Routledge & Kegan Paul.
Sharpe, R. and Lewis, D. (1977)
Thrive on Stress. London: Souvenir Press.
Simon, S. (1974)
Meeting Yourself Halfway. Hoddesdon, Herts.: Argus
Publications.
Simon, S., Howe, L.W. and Kirschenbaum, H. (1972)
Value Clarification. New York: Hart.
Toffler, A. (1970)
Future Shock. London: Bodley Head.

Watts, A.G. and Elsom, D. (1975)
Deciding. Cambridge: Hobsons Press.

Questions

1. Why is an understanding of the psychological processes associated with transitions important in your life?
2. What are the major types of transition and how are they related?
3. How would you set about rating the impact of life events on people?
4. Critically evaluate the Hopson-Adams model of transitions.
5. What effects do transitions have on people?
6. What are the coping tasks relevant to all transitions?
7. Describe the coping skills which are relevant to transitions.
8. Which will be the most important influence in ensuring a successful transition and why? Is it the coping skills of the mover or the structure and practices of the organization, institution or social norms?
9. Describe a life transition in terms of the stages the person might go through and what that person could do to maximize the chances of coping with it effectively and gaining from the experience.
10. How effectively can we train people to improve their transition coping skills?

Annotated reading

Adams, J.D., Hayes, J. and Hopson, B. (1976) Transition: Understanding and managing personal change. London: Martin Robertson.
> This is the first attempt to provide a conceptual framework to describe the psychological sequence of a transition. It is primarily a theoretical book, although some guidelines for the practitioner are available.

Hopson, B. and Scally, M. (1980) How to cope with and gain from life transitions. In B. Hopson and M. Scally, Lifeskills Teaching Programmes No. 1. Leeds: Lifeskills Associates.
> This is for a classroom teacher of young people and consists of a series of carefully described group exercises to teach young people about transitions and how to cope more effectively with them.

Parkes, C. M. (1975) Bereavement: Studies of grief in adult life. Harmondsworth: Penguin.
> This book is about more than bereavement, although this topic is discussed at great length. Parkes generalizes from bereavement to other aspects of separation and loss in people's lives.

Exercises

1. Examining a transition
Draw a line to represent a transition you are experiencing

or have recently experienced. On the line, indicate the
point you entered with (1), the time you have spent up until
now with (2), and so on. Then, for each point on the line,
consider the issues raised in the following list:

1. ENTRY. What were your feelings at the time of the
transition? What was your behaviour around the entry point?
Did you cope? If so, how? (By 'coping' we mean managing
feelings and not being overwhelmed by them, producing
effective behaviours required by new situations, and utilizing the opportunity value contained in the new situation
for personal growth.) The way you felt and the way you
behaved: are they typical for you?

2. UP UNTIL NOW. Describe the high/low points entering
the transition. What have been the critical learning events
relative to this transition and what has been the impact on
you?

3. NOW. How do you now feel about yourself relative to the
transition? How are your feelings affecting your behaviour
now? Do you have any ways of checking this out? Is there
anything you feel now that you have learnt from what has
happened and the way you dealt with it? What is your
strategy for coping with the transition?

4. WHAT DO YOU ANTICIPATE WILL BE THE HIGH/LOW
POINTS IN THE NEAR FUTURE? Does this correspond with
your hopes? What do you anticipate/hope will be critical
learning events relative to this transition?

5. HOW MIGHT YOU BENEFIT OR NOT BENEFIT FROM
THE TRANSITION? Ideally, what would your feelings be in
coping with this transition? How would this relate to other
transitions that you have had or may be experiencing? What
does the way you manage this transition say about you as a
person?

2. A transition interview

In this exercise you and a partner will take turns to interview each other. This partner should be someone with whom
you can share confidences and speak frankly. Decide who is
going to be interviewed first.

QUESTIONS. Think about the first big change you can remem
in your life. What was it? How old were you? Did you know i
was going to happen or was it a surprise to you? How did you
feel when it happened? (If your interviewee finds this difficult, you can prompt: 'Did you feel happy, sad, curious,
angry, anxious, afraid or nothing in particular?') Did you
do anything that made the change easier? Did anyone else do
anything that made things easier for you? Did you expect the
change to be good for you or not good for you? How did it
turn out for you? Looking back, could you have done anything
more to have got more out of it?

Now change places: the interviewer becomes the interviewee. Repeat the above. Then swap around again. The next set of questions is to help you find out for yourself how you normally cope with major changes or transitions in your life.

* Some people look forward to life changes with excitement; others dread them; some have mixed feelings. How do you tend to feel?
* When you know that a big life change is about to happen do you (i) talk it over with friends; (ii) keep it to yourself but think a lot about it; (iii) think or talk very little about it?
* Some people feel that they can do very little to change what is going to happen to them; others feel they can do a great deal. What do you feel?

Now change places. The interviewer becomes the interviewee. Repeat this part of the exercise.

3. Your transition coping skills
Go back to the transition coping skill questionnaire. Ask yourself about one item at a time. Do you have that skill, or is it one you do not have or that needs developing? Remember the optimistic message of the chapter which is that we can learn and grow as the result of any transition and that new skills can be developed. According to Barrie Hopson every transition carries gains with it in the long run.

8

Ageing and social problems
Peter G. Coleman

What is it to be old?

The study of ageing and problems associated with it are now recognized as important. This is not surprising, for older people have become the major clients of the health and social services. They also have a lot of free time at their disposal. If there is to be an expansion in adult education and opportunities for creative leisure activities, the benefits should go especially to retired people.

What is surprising is that it has taken so long for the social sciences to pay attention to ageing and old age. So many young professionals are called on to devote their attention to the needs of people at the other end of the life span, yet they are likely to have received little in the way of stimulating material about the distinctive psychological features of old age.

Professional people do nevertheless have to be introduced to the subject of ageing, and it is interesting to note how that introduction has come to take on certain standard forms over the last ten years. There are two very popular ways, almost obligatory it seems, to begin talking or writing about ageing. The first way is to present the demographic data about the increasing numbers of elderly people in the population; the second way is to discuss the negative attitudes people have about working with the elderly.

The common introduction to ageing

In important respects old age as we know it today is a relatively modern phenomenon. Though there may have been individual societies in the past where a comparably large part of the population was old, it is clear that there has been a dramatic change in developed countries since the turn of the century. At that time in Britain those over the age of 65 constituted one in 20 of the population; today they constitute one in seven.

In recent years much more use is being made of the statistic 'over the age of 75', since it has become clear that this is the group in the population which makes the largest demands on the health and social services. This has highlighted the worrying news for service planners in a time of economic constraints that, while the total number of those over 65 will not increase very much in the coming years, the population of those over 75 has already passed 5 per cent of the total population and will reach 6 per cent by the end of the 1980s.

However, expressing concern simply at the number of elderly people in the population is misleading. Why after all should it be a problem that 15 per cent rather than, say, 10 per cent or 5 per cent of the population is over the age of 65, or that 6 per cent rather than 4 per cent or 2 per cent is over the age of 75? A lot of the issues have to do with economics. The State must find the means to continue paying adequate and perhaps even improved pensions, and to provide welfare services to larger numbers of people.

Yet perhaps the more fundamental issues are the availability and willingness of people, whether relatives, neighbours, professionals or volunteers, to give assistance to large numbers of disabled people in the population. For ageing, as any introduction to the subject makes abundantly clear, is associated with an increasing likelihood of developing chronic disability.

Global estimates of disability in daily living (in getting around the house and providing for oneself) indicate that the need for assistance is present in 15-20 per cent of the age group 65-74, rising to 35-40 per cent in the 75-84 age group and to over 60 per cent in those above 85. If one adds on the number of people living in institutions (hospitals and old people's homes), which is about 4-5 per cent of the total elderly population, one can conclude that about 30 per cent, or nearly one in three, of all people over the age of 65 are disabled and in need of help.

A typical introduction to ageing then goes on to present further numerical data on the social position of the elderly. Almost one-third of people over 65 have been found to live alone and large numbers are lonely. Many live in poor housing, lack basic amenities and so on.

The need for a life-span perspective

Large numbers of elderly people, large numbers of disabled elderly people, and large numbers of elderly people living in deprived circumstances; such is a typical introduction to old age. But there are vitally important perspectives missing. No wonder indeed that we should be concerned with attitudes, with finding enough people prepared to work with the elderly, enough geriatricians, enough nurses, enough social workers and so on, when the only image we present of old age is a negative one. If the only perspective we emphasize is one of endless problems, often insoluble because of irremediable physical and mental deterioration, we cannot expect many people to have the courage to become involved.

Old people are people like the rest of us. What is special about them is not that they may be mentally deteriorated, disabled or isolated. The majority, after all, is none of these things and many people reach the end of their lives without suffering any disadvantages. What is special about old people is that they have lived a long time. They have had all the kinds of experience we have had and many, many more. They are moving towards the end of life it is true, but it is every bit as important how one ends one's life as how one begins it.

The perspective on ageing that is needed is one which takes into account the whole life span. The discovery any student of old age has to make is not only that old people have a long life history behind them but that their present lives, their needs and wishes, cannot be understood without an appreciation of that life history.

If we really talk to old people all this will become evident. But how often do we do this? A most eloquent testimony of our neglect is a poem (88 lines long) that was found in the hospital locker of a geriatric patient. (It can be found in full, quoted in the preface of the Open University Text, Carver, V. and Liddiard, P., 1978, 'An Ageing Population', Hodder & Stoughton.)

> What do you see nurses
>   What do you see?
> Are you thinking
>   When you are looking at me
> A crabbit old woman
>   Not very wise,
> Uncertain of habit
>   With far-away eyes
> ....
> Then open your eyes nurse,
>   You're not looking at me.

The writer emphasizes the continuity between her identity as an old person and her identities at previous stages in the life cycle. She is still the small child of ten with a large family around her, still the 16 year old full of hopes and expectations, still the bride she was at 20 and the young woman of 30 with her children growing up fast. At 40 her children are leaving home, and she and her husband are on their own again. But then there are grandchildren for her to take an interest in. Years pass and she has lost her husband and must learn to live alone. She is all of these people. But the nurse does not see them.

Psychological changes with age

It is only proper to admit at the outset that the main activity of psychologists interested in ageing, with some exceptions, has not been of a life span perspective. Their work has mainly been concerned with trying to establish what psychological changes, usually changes of deterioration, occur with advancing age, with understanding the bases of such changes and finding ways of compensating for them. These are obviously important questions.

Cognitive deterioration
It would be wishful thinking to deny that there is any

deterioration with age. Physical ageing is a fact which is easy to observe, though it may occur at different rates in different people. Performance in everyday tasks in which we have to use our cognitive ability to register things we see or hear, remember them and think about them also deteriorates. Absent-mindedness is one of the most common complaints of older people in everyday life.

In more recent cross-sectional studies of the performance of different age groups on experimental tasks, psychologists have tried their best to control for obvious factors which might produce differences in their own right, like education, illness, sensory impairment and willingness to carry out the tasks in question. Of course, certain question marks remain over differences in attitude and perceived role: for instance, whether older people see the purpose of such tasks in the same way as younger people. Nevertheless, certain conclusions can be drawn about the abilities which seem to change the most as one grows older. In the first place, older people take much longer to carry out tasks and this is not only because their limb movements are slower. In tasks in which they have to divide their attention ('try to do two things at once'), decline with age is very marked and is already evident in those over 30. Ability to remember things we have seen or heard declines, as does the ability to hold associations in mind.

However, in some older people decline is not evident at all. Particular experiences, for example particular occupational backgrounds, may develop certain abilities in an individual to such an extent that they remain well developed throughout old age. Retired telephone operators who have no difficulty in dividing attention between a number of messages are a case in point. The prominence of so many older people in public life where they reap the fruit of years of experience in political dealings is also an obvious illustration. Moreover, it seems to be true that in some old people deterioration does not, in fact, occur. There are studies which indicate that the cognitive ability of a sizeable minority of elderly people, perhaps as many as one in ten, cannot be distinguished from that of younger people.

This, then, is evidence that age itself is not the important thing. Indeed it seems better to view age simply as a vector along which to measure the things that happen to people. Some things that happen with age are universal. They occur at different times, but they are unavoidable. These things we can, if we like, describe as 'age' changes. But a lot of the things we associate with old age are not due to ageing processes and are not universal. There is a great variation in the extent to which people are hit by physical and social losses as they grow old. Some people are fortunate, some people are unfortunate.

From the point of view of cognitive ability, the most unlucky are those people who suffer from the various forms of dementia or brain diseases which lead to a progressive deterioration in mental functioning. But health is by no means the only extrinsic factor influencing mental state in old age. A lot of research has been done recently on the psychological effects of such brain-washing treatments as isolation and sensory deprivation. Disorientation and confusion are common results. Yet we are often slow to recognize that old people may be living in circumstances where by any ordinary standards they are extremely isolated and deprived of stimulation. No one calls to see them, to engage them, to remind them of their names, roles and relationships. Disorientation in time and space, and confusion about identity and relationship with others, can be a natural result. From our own experience we know how time can lose meaning after one has been ill in bed for a day or two, away from the normal daily routine.

Other social and psychological factors play a role too. Motivation to recover or maintain abilities is obviously a crucial factor, and a number of studies have shown that amount of education remains one of the major factors in cognitive ability and performance throughout life.

Personality and life style

Scientific work on personality and style of life in old age does not match the amount that has been done on cognitive functioning. The evidence we do have, however, relates both to change and stability.

One clear finding from research is that introversion or interiority increases with age. This means that as people grow old they become more preoccupied with their own selve their own thoughts and feelings and less with the outside world. This change is only relative, of course, but it is evident both from responses to questionnaires and also from projective tests, where people are asked to describe or react to stimuli they are presented with, such as pictures of family and social situations.

The term disengagement has been used to describe such a change in orientation; a decreased concern with interacting with others and being involved in the outside world and an increased satisfaction with one's own world of memories and immediate surroundings. However, critics have been quick to point out the dangers of exaggerating the extent to which disengagement is a 'natural' development in old age. Most of the decreased interaction and involvement of older people is forced upon them by undesired physical and social changes: disability, bereavement, loss of occupational roles and so on. Moreover, there is also clear evidence that old people are happier when there is a good deal of continuity between their past and present activities.

Indeed, in contrast to any change in personality that may occur, the stability that people show in their characteristics and style of life over a period of time is far more striking. Longitudinal studies show that people continue to enjoy the same interests and activities. When striking negative changes occur in a person's interests or familiar mode of activities, or ways of coping with life in old age, for no obvious reason, this is often a sign of psychiatric illness, especially depression.

Some of the most valuable studies on personality in old age are, in fact, those which have shown how important it is to take into reckoning a person's life style, for instance in explaining why people react differently to changes and losses such as retirement, bereavement and living alone, or a move to a residential home. Any research finding about old people usually has to be qualified by reference to life style. This is mentioned again when talking about adjustment to relocation.

Growth and development

Though deterioration has been the main perspective of psychological research on ageing up to now, it is not the only one. Certainly in literature old age has been treated much more generously. The works of Nobel prize winners, such as Patrick White ('The Eye of the Storm', 1973), Saul Bellow ('Mr Sammler's Planet', 1969) and Ernest Hemingway ('The Old Man and the Sea', 1952), present vivid and compelling pictures of old age that, like King Lear, have to do with deterioration and change but also with growth in understanding and the values of existence.

Indeed, a characteristic theme in literature is of old age as a time of questioning; of one's own achievements, of the meaning of one's life, of the values one lived by and of what is of lasting value. It is as if an old person, freed from the strait-jacket of society, suffering losses in his ability to function and in his social position - perhaps indeed precisely because of them - is, somehow, let free to question life. Psychologists have only begun tentatively to approach these issues, but have devoted considerable attention to the meaning of life.

Adaptation to loss in old age

From what has already been said it should be clear that old age is a time of great inequality. It is a time when losses occur, loss of physical and mental abilities, loss of people who were close to one, loss of roles and loss of activities. These losses are not inevitable; they do not occur in the same degree to everyone; but adapting to loss is a characteristic feature of old age.

Attitudes to health and well-being

Severe disability is one of the major losses of old age and its central importance in shaping the rest of an individual's life is one of the most common findings to emerge from investigations on social aspects of ageing. People who are disabled have more problems in maintaining their desired styles of life and are more dissatisfied than people who are not disabled. This is not surprising.

What is more surprising, or at least not logically to be expected, is the fact that, in general, levels of well-being do not decline with age. This is despite the fact that the incidence and severity of disability tend to increase with age and have a great influence on well-being. The key to understanding this comes from studies on subjective health.

The clear evidence from both longitudinal and cross-sectional studies is that whereas objective health and physical functioning of elderly people tend to deteriorate with age, the same is not true in regard to how they feel about their health. The most likely explanation has to do with expectations. People expect to become somewhat more disabled with old age. If they do, they accept it. But if their physical functioning remains stable they may in fact experience this as a bonus and feel better as a result. Only if their health deteriorates beyond the expected norm are they likely to feel badly about it.

This argument applies strictly only to feeling well, but it has a wider implication for well-being generally and for reactions to other losses in old age. Expectation is a very important aspect of reaction to loss. It is what people expect and what people find normal that determines how they react to things and how satisfied they feel with their situation. This kind of consideration also leads one to reflect how different things could be if old people's expectations changed. This is in fact not so unlikely. Future generations of elderly people may be far less accepting of lower standards of health and also, for instance, of income. They may expect things to be a good deal better for them. And if things are not going to be better they are going to be less happy as a result.

Adjustment to relocation

Another misfortune often following from disability is that people can find themselves being obliged to move, sometimes quite unexpectedly and against their will, to different environments, particularly institutional settings, where they often have to remain for the rest of their lives. Though this is usually done to them 'for their own good' (they are judged incapable of looking after themselves in their own homes), the end result may be much worse than leaving them alone: for instance, further deterioration and loss of interest in life.

There has been growing realization of the extent to which environmental changes can contribute to physical illness and psychiatric disorders. Even where it is voluntarily undertaken and has otherwise favourable effects, there are indications that rehousing can undermine a person's health. There is also a great deal of variation between individuals in their reactions, so it is important to discover which factors might predict the ability to adjust easily to new surroundings.

Among psychological factors cognitive ability is clearly crucial. There appear to be two major reasons why cognitively impaired old people react worse to relocation. In the first place, their lack of ability to anticipate and prepare means that they experience more stress on making the move.

Second, because of their poor short-term memory and orientation abilities it may take them a long while to understand their new surroundings.

Personality is important too. We are not sufficiently sensitive to the fact that the institutional environments we provide may be fine for one kind of elderly person but not for another. American studies have shown the importance, for instance, of rebellious and aggressive traits, as opposed to passive and compliant ones, in predicting survival and lack of deterioration after relocation to institutional settings. Vital as well, of course, are attitudinal factors concerned with what a move means to the persons concerned, whether they want to go, and how they see their own future in a new setting.

Self-esteem and its sources: the lynchpin of adjustment?

Disability and environmental change have been picked out for consideration as two of the negative changes associated with old age. There are others, of course. Bereavement requires a major adjustment which seems to follow certain definite stages. Grieving is a normal, healthy part of the process, and the support and understanding of those around in allowing bereaved people to express themselves may be very important to it. Loss of occupational role with retirement is another big change. Indeed, adjustment to it is often thought of in the same terms as adjustment to the old age role itself. Most people make good adaptations, but not all, and retirement can be a major precipitating factor in the onset of late life depression.

Then again, a very significant loss for many people as they grow older is that of income: they must adapt to making do with less. There has been almost no psychological investigation of this kind of adaptation. From what one can see it would seem that a lot of old people positively take pride in stretching their money. This, of course, may also have a lot to do with their experience of deprivation in the past.

Naturally, in all these adaptations much depends on the characteristics of the individual person involved, and one is led to ask whether there are any general ways in which one can conceptualize how a person adapts to the various losses and changes that occur with old age. Some authors talk in terms of the individual possessing particular qualities: for instance, 'coping ability'. But the most valuable index of adjustment in old age is that of self-esteem.

Maintenance of positive attitudes to oneself seems to be one of the key issues in old age. An especially important component of self-image is a sense of being in control of one's own life. Development in childhood and adulthood is associated with an increasing sense of effectiveness and of impact on the external world. In old age this sense may well be taken away.

Intrinsic to this conception of self-identity is the notion that it must have roots outside itself. Therefore, if individuals are to maintain self-esteem they have a continuing need of sources from which they can define acceptable self-images. For some people these sources can exist in past relationships and achievements or in an inner conviction about the kind of person one is, but in the main they depend on the present external circumstances of their lives; their roles in the family, in relation to other people, in work and in other activities.

When these circumstances change, as they often do in old age, individuals may have to find alternative sources to maintain positive views of themselves. Here again it is vital to understand a person's life history. A person whose sense of self has been based on one particular kind of source, for instance relationships with close family members, is going to suffer especially if such family contacts are lost through death.

One way to investigate sources of self-esteem is to ask people directly what makes them say that they feel useful or feel useless, for instance. Not surprisingly, lack of infirmity and contact with other people including the family emerge as the major sources of self-esteem. Especially in disabled people, being able to do things for oneself, and in particular to get around, appear to be key factors; also being a source of help and encouragement to others is very important.

In this context it is worth putting in a good word for residential care and other types of grouped housing schemes. In a previous part of this section it was noted that a move to an institutional setting can be damaging for certain types of individual, but a good institutional setting can also be of great benefit to certain people. This is possible when sources of self-esteem are likely to be strengthened rather than weakened by the move.

For instance, some people could be said to be 'living independently in the community'. But in reality they may be extremely isolated and totally dependent on the services being brought to them. Once they have moved to a genuine communal setting the burden of infirmity and consciousness of being alone can be diminished. Precisely because they are better able to cope for themselves in the new environment and to be of importance to others, they may gain a new lease of life.

Helping old people

Not all the loss and trauma of old age can be countered from an individual's own resources. The modern welfare state provides a range of services for the elderly; housing, health and social services. These are, of course, limited, subject to decisions about what level of services the country can 'afford'. We do not know what a perfect service for the elderly would be like, but we certainly do know that what we provide at present falls a long way short of it.

However, the achievement of the present level of services needs to be respected if we are to develop further, and it is important that people in the various caring professions who carry out these services remember their responsiblities. One of the real dangers is taking the operation of a service for granted and applying it automatically or mindlessly. The people on the receiving end then cease to be considered as individuals.

A key element in any work with elderly people is the individual assessment, and it is here that the psychological perspective has a vital role. We need a good assessment not only of people's physical condition and capabilities and of their social situations, but also of their individual needs, their abilities and interests, which should include a good picture of how they used to be.

Besides helping in assessment, psychology can also play a role in the actual provision of therapeutic interventions both to old people themselves and to those around them. Applied psychology should be able to show the best way: for example, to help recover abilities that seem to be lost or to mend social relationships that have become tense.

Maintenance of interests, activities and functioning

One of the most tragic images we have of old age is that of an old person with shoulders sunk, sitting collapsed in a chair, totally uninvolved in the world around. In a previous section the question of 'disengagement' in old age was raised, and let us repeat the point made there that, although some decline in activity may be an intrinsic part of growing old, most of such decline is the result of physical disability and environmental trauma.

When there is a dramatic decline in a person's activities for no obvious reason, we need to alert ourselves to the possibility that the person may be depressed. Loss of well-established habits and activities and lack of interest or anxiety about trying to regain them may be symptoms of the kind of depression which will respond to treatment, even though the person may not admit to having depressed feelings. But, of course, there also has to be some activity and interests for the person to go back to. Particularly if someone is disabled there may be few possibilities available, and the person is then likely to decline again. It is also quite clear that prolonged inactivity has deleterious effects both on physical and psychological functioning. Skills that are not exercised tend to atrophy.

In recent years a lot of new initiatives have been taken in geriatric hospitals in providing opportunities for patients to engage in different types of activity, arts and crafts, music discussion and so on. Generally, staff report improvements in elderly people who do take part in such activities, which can be seen in their personal appearance, in their physical and mental functioning and in their contact with others.

An even greater challenge is offered by people who are mentally deteriorated. In the first place it is very important to distinguish elderly people who really have irretrievable brain disease from those who only appear to have because they are depressed. Indeed, it may be symptomatic of someone's depression that he thinks his brain is rotting. It may be no easy matter to distinguish this, because it is difficult to motivate someone who is depressed actually to demonstrate his abilities. With the right treatment and support depressed people can be encouraged to regain their old abilities.

However, elderly people who clearly are deteriorating mentally should not be abandoned to their fate. Tests have shown that such people, given encouragement and help, can still acquire and retain new information and maintain skills. But the effort needed from outside is great. A good example is the use of so-called 'reality orientation', where people around the elderly person, either informally through-out the day or in concentrated formal classes, systemati-cally try to help remind the person of time, place and season, of names of people, of objects, and of activities and so on.

Psychologists have a lot to do applying findings from the study of learning and memory to help old people. The trouble at present is that such people are often left alone, and this only exacerbates their condition. Dementia is a progressive illness, but what happens between its onset and death is important. If in the future we find medical means of slowing down its progress, it will become an even more urgent matter to find means as well to allow people to maintain their optimum potentialities in the time that remains left to them.

Family relationships

Another vital issue is the relationship between disabled elderly people and their families. Many more of such people are supported by their families than live in institutions for the elderly. For instance, in the case of severe demen-tia, there are four to five times as many suffering from such a condition living in the community as live in resi-dential homes or hospitals. Yet often families who are doing the caring get pitifully little in the way of support services.

If they become overburdened by the stress of their involvement, both they and their elderly relatives suffer. The old person's mental condition may well be aggravated by tired and irritable relatives, and if there is a breakdown in care and there is no alternative but to take the old person into an institution, the family members are likely to suffer greatly from feelings of guilt. They often want to care for a relative until that person dies, but need help in carrying it out.

It is an important principle to accept that work with families is an integral part of work with elderly people. Family ties after all usually form a substantial part of an individual's identity. If those ties are damaged, so is the person's identity. The physical and mental deterioration that affects many people as they grow older and their ensuing state of dependency can put a strain on many relationships. Men, for instance, usually do not expect to outlive their wives. They can encounter great problems if they find instead that they have to spend their old age looking after a physically or mentally deteriorated wife, especially if in the past it was their wives who ran the household. Children too often find difficulty in taking over responsibility for ailing parents.

The actual symptoms, particularly of mental disturbance in old age, can be very disturbing. In some forms of dementia (probably dependent on the part of the brain that has been affected) the behavioural changes that can occur, caricaturing the person's old personality, increasing aggression or leading to a loss in standards of cleanliness, can be very painful for relatives to bear. It may be difficult for them to accept that the patient is not simply being difficult or unreasonable.

Families need counselling about the nature of the illness and, in the case of dementia, of its progressive nature, and preferably, too, promise of continued practical support. Group meetings held for relatives of different patients by doctors, social workers or other professionals can also be useful in allowing relatives to share common experiences and problems. Groups for the bereaved, particularly husbands or wives, can also play their part. The last years of their lives may have revolved around the care of a sick spouse and they must now find new meaning in life.

The future

In discussing ageing and social problems it may seem strange to end with a note about the future. But from what has been said it should be obvious that great improvements need to take place, both in society's provision for the elderly and in the attitudes of each and every one of us to the elderly people we live among.

For most people old age is not a particularly unhappy time, though for some it is. In part that may be, as we have suggested, because old people have low expectations. They quietly accept a society that treats them meanly and as somehow less important. In the future that may all change. We may see new generations of elderly people, foreshadowed in today's Grey Panthers in America, who will mobilize their potential power as a numerically important part of the electorate and pressurize society to give them a better deal.

On the other hand, old people may continue to remain on the sidelines. They may refuse to see their own material and other interests as being of central importance to society, in which case the rest of the population must see they are not forgotten.

The most important changes indeed are the attitudinal ones. We must recognize that old people are ourselves. They are our future selves. There is a continuity in life both between their past and present and between our present and future.

Old people remain the same people they were. Indeed, if we really want to know about a person's needs and wants and how they could be satisfied, the best introduction would be to let them tell us about their life history. Whatever new steps are taken in the future must follow on from this and make sense in relation to it.

Better provision would follow from such a recognition. If we really respected people's individuality we would provide them with choice about the circumstances and activities with which they end their days, not just enforce certain standard solutions. In short, we must allow people to grow old in ways that suit them, perhaps to explore new avenues of development in order to make the most of the years that remain. Also, when we consider those who need our help, who suffer in old age and perhaps are dependent upon us, we should not forget these wider perspectives.

Bibliography

Birren, J.E. and Schaie, K.W. (eds) (1977)
Handbook of the Psychology of Ageing. London: Van Nostrand Reinhold.

Brearley, C.P. (1975)
Social Work, Ageing and Society. London: Routledge & Kegan Paul.

Bromley, D.B. (1974)
The Psychology of Human Ageing (2nd edn). Harmondswo Penguin.

Carver, V. and Liddiard, P. (eds) (1978)
An Ageing Population (Open University text). Sevenoaks: Hodder & Stoughton.

Chown, S.M. (ed.) (1972)
Human Ageing. Harmondsworth: Penguin.

Dibner, A.S. (1975)
The psychology of normal aging. In M.G. Spencer and C.J. Dorr (eds), Understanding Aging: A multidisciplinary approach. New York: Appleton-Century-Crofts.

Gray, B. and Isaacs, B. (1979)
Care of the Elderly Mentally Infirm. London: Tavistock.

Kastenbaum, R. (1979)
Growing Old - Years of Fulfilment. London: Harper & Row.

Kimmel, D.C. (1974)
Adulthood and Ageing. An interdisciplinary developmental view. Chichester: Wiley.

Miller, E. (1977)
Abnormal Ageing. The psychology of senile and presenile dementia. Chichester: Wiley.

Neugarten, B.L. and associates (1964)
Personality in Middle and Later Life. New York: Atherton Press.

uestions

1. Discuss the view that old people do not differ from young people except in the number of years they have lived.
2. What factors influence mental performance in old age? What evidence do we have on their relative importance?
3. How important is a knowledge of life style or personality type to understanding how people react to change and stress in old age?
4. Are the changes we observe in old people's behaviour related more to the physical and social losses they incur or more to intrinsic processes of ageing?
5. Do old people show genuine developmental changes as well as changes of deterioration?
6. Analyse the relationship between well-being and health in old age with particular regard to increasing occurrence of disease and disability.
7. Discuss the role of 'expectations' in adaptation to loss in old age.
8. What behavioural and other psychological techniques are there available to help people to recover interests and customary activities that they may have lost in old age?
9. Social and psychological factors are more responsible for mental deterioration in old age than are physical disorders of the brain. Discuss.
10. 'Too many of our views on the psychology of ageing are restricted by the limits of our own society.' Discuss the value of a cross-cultural approach to the psychology of ageing.

mnotated reading

Brearley, C.P. (1975) Social Work, Ageing and Society. London: Routledge & Kegan Paul.
    A book written for social workers, bringing together a wide range of material from medicine, psychology and sociology.

Bromley, D.B. (1974) The Psychology of Human Ageing (2nd edn). Harmondsworth: Penguin.
    Written by a British psychologist, it gives a very thorough coverage of subjects such as changes in performance and cognitive skills with age, and is good on the methodological issues involved in doing research on ageing.

Carver, V. and Liddiard, P. (eds) (1978) An Ageing Population (Open University Text). Sevenoaks: Hodder & Stoughton.
    A collection of readings for the Open University course. The papers have been drawn from a variety of sources to provide a multidisciplinary perspective on the needs and circumstances of the elderly.

Gray, B. and Isaacs, B. (1979) Care of the Elderly Mentally Infirm. London: Tavistock.
A specialized book on the elderly mentally infirm also intended for social workers, written jointly by a geriatrician and a social worker.

Kastenbaum, R. (1979) Growing Old - Years of Fulfilment. London: Harper & Row.
A short introduction to the subject written by an American psychologist. He presents a balanced approach to old age, giving due weight to positive perspectives. The book is also attractively illustrated.

Exercises

1. Influence of past experience

Talk to elderly people you already know and try to get to know some you have not spoken to before. Elderly people living in residential homes or sheltered housing schemes may enjoy a visit, and an officer in charge or warden may be able to introduce you to suitable people. As you talk to them, begin considering the lives they have had, the particular experiences they grew up with and the events that have shaped their lives.

What was the impact of great upheavals like the First World War and the economic depression of the 1930s? What were living conditions like when they were young adults, and when they were in middle age? What kind of experience of family life have they had? What kind of education did they get? What were their opportunities for employment? Find out too about the special events in their lives, perhaps unique to them as individuals.

Then try and reach some conclusions about how these experiences affected their expectations in life; for example, in regard to the things for which it would be worth striving. How did they develop their ideals and values and their view of themselves? And how do all these things relate to their current view of themselves?

If they are in particular difficulties at present, consider to what extent their reactions to them and the needs they express are influenced by these past events. Do professional people who try to help them, like doctors and social workers, take note of them? Have these people grasped the really important things about their patients' and clients' lives?

Too little of the research that has been done into the needs of elderly people has looked sufficiently at individuals and their past histories. Researchers have been too keen to reach generalizations about 'the elderly', too little interested in elderly people as individuals and in the context of their whole life history. A human life is one story and old age is an integral part of it. Old age cannot be considered in isolation from what has gone before.

2. Personality, life style and reaction to growing old

Differing life experiences make people different from one

another. By the time people reach old age they have had many experiences. Old people are therefore especially 'unique'. And yet at the same time there is sense in looking for similarities between people in personality and style of life. Individuals are not only passive victims of fate; they seek out certain experiences and impose structure on their own lives. The resulting life style may equip the person well or badly in dealing with the various stresses of ageing.

A number of studies have tried to look at 'types' of people in old age. One of the most fruitful ways of categorizing people is to look not so much at personality traits but at the areas of major interest or investment. Some people's lives may have revolved around work, others around the family; others may have managed to give both family and work equal importance. Among those with close involvement with their families some may have concentrated this in one or two people, such as spouse or children, whereas others may have been concerned with a larger number of members of an 'extended' family. For those whose work connections were all-important, some may have made close commitments to an organization and individual people within it. Others may have been very much 'loners' without close involvement with anyone.

For each different type the problems in old age are likely to be different, as are also the prerequisites for maintaining their particular kind of life style. Adjustment to events like retirement or moving into an old people's home is going to depend a lot on life style, and we need to consider life style much more when preparing old people for changes and helping then to adapt to them.

One exercise worth trying is to ask elderly people you know about their sources of self-identity. What are the things that make them feel as they want to feel? Bi-polar self-esteem items of the following type are useful in eliciting information of this kind.

*	I feel useful	-	I feel useless
*	I get little enjoyment out of life	-	I get much enjoyment out of life
*	I am still capable of doing quite a lot	-	I am quite helpless
*	I have no aims left in life	-	I have a clear aim in my life
*	I am of importance to others	-	I don't count any more

Put the sentences on cards and ask people if they agree more with one side than the other. If people choose the positive side, ask them to give an illustration of why they feel that way about themselves. Do the same for choices on the negative side. Try and find ways of categorizing the answers. For example, to what extent is self-esteem based on a person's relationship with the marriage partner, with other members of the family, or with other people; or is it based

more on work, on activities and interests or on particular
everyday tasks the person is able to carry out? Perhaps
self-esteem is based more on a person's environment, on the
circumstances of life, or maybe instead on deeper personal
convictions.

Once you have built up a picture of an individual's
source of self-esteem, consider how that individual might
react to changes in life, to changes like disability, relocation, bereavement or other loss of roles. Do you think
the individual would be able to compensate for losses to
personal 'roots' of self-identity? Where could the individual get alternative sources upon which to base a sense
of self?

3. Comparison with your own experience

The object of each of these exercises is to help you gain a
better appreciation of what it feels like to be old. Too
often, of course, we make the mistake of thinking of old
people as a race apart. But old people are continuations of
the person they always were. Old people should remember wh
it was like to be children, to be young or to be in the
middle of life. The differences they experience in feeling
old are of a subtle rather than gross nature.

It is also a mistake to exaggerate the separateness of
the problems people face in old age, like retirement, disability, bereavement and re-location. Old age is usually a
time when we have to come to terms with loss more often, I
most people have already encountered experience of loss
earlier in life, sometimes in a severe way.

Try and find as many parallels and similarities as you
can from earlier life for the common problems of being old.
Think of examples such as the following:

* the effects of being immobile or ill in bed for a day or
  two. Consider how this affects one's sense of orientation in time and of the relative importance of activities like going out to work as compared with watching
  television.

* the stress involved in moving house to a new neighbourhood, or going to a new school. Remember what it was
  like the first days and how strange the new environment
  appeared. How long did it take to settle in and what
  were the things that helped the process?

* making decisions for the future. How did you make you
  decisions about where to go to university or college,
  where to apply for a job or where to live? What considerations did you bear in mind? Whom did you consult?

Once you have seen the similarities between the situation of
younger and older people, try to consider what the differences may be. How, for example, are we affected differentl
by the loss of a spouse in old age from the loss of parents
in middle age? What circumstances make life particularly
difficult for some elderly people? Consider, too, the importance of sensory deficits like poor hearing or eyesight or

deficits in mobility. (In one foreign university the students were encouraged to empathize with such conditions by wearing special 'glasses', hearing muffs and constricting clothing for a short while. The experience was valuable. However, it is not advisable to try it for too long!) Last and not least, find some accounts of being old which old people have written themselves and some written by sensitive observers as well.

Part three

The Self, Adaptation and Learning

9

Knowledge of self
D. Bannister

Definition is a social undertaking. As a community we
negotiate the meaning of words. This makes 'self' a
peculiarly difficult term to define, since much of the
meaning we attach to it derives from essentially private
experiences of a kind which are difficult to communicate
about and agree upon. Nevertheless, we can try to abstract
from our private experience of self qualities which can
constitute a working definition. Such an attempt was made
by Bannister and Fransella (1980) in the following terms.

**Each of us entertains a notion of our own separateness from
others and relies on the essential privacy of our own
consciousness**
Consider differences between the way in which you communicate with yourself and the way in which you communicate with
others. To communicate with others involves externalizing
(and thereby blurring) your experience into forms of speech,
arm waving, gift giving, sulking, writing and so on. Yet
communicating with yourself is so easy that it seems not to
merit the word communication: it is more like instant recognition. Additionally, communicating with specific others
involves the risk of being overheard, spied upon or having
your messages intercepted and this contrasts with our
internal communications which are secret and safeguarded.
Most importantly, we experience our internal communications
as the origin and starting point of things. We believe that
it is out of them that we construct communications with
others. We know this when we tell a lie because we are aware
of the difference between our experienced internal communication and the special distortions given it before transmission.

**We entertain a notion of the integrity and completeness of
our own experience in that we believe all parts of it to be
relatable because we are, in some vital sense, the
experience itself**
We extend the notion of me into the notion of my world. We
think of events as more or less relevant to us. We distinguish between what concerns and what does not concern us.
In this way we can use the phrase 'my situation' to indicate
the boundaries of our important experience and the ways in

which the various parts of it relate to make up a personal world.

We entertain the notion of our own continuity over time; we possess our biography and we live in relation to it

We live along a time line. We believe that we are essentially the 'same' person now that we were five minutes ago or five years ago. We accept that our circumstances may have changed in this or that respect, but we have a feeling of continuity, we possess a 'life'. We extend this to imagine a continuing future life. We can see our history in a variety of ways, but how we see it, the way in which we interpret it, is a central part of our character.

We entertain a notion of ourselves as causes; we have purposes, we intend, we accept a partial responsibility for the consequences of our actions

Just as we believe that we possess our life, so we think of ourselves as making 'choices' and as being identified by our choices. Even those psychologists who (in their professional writing) describe humankind as wholly determined, and persons as entirely the products of their environments, talk personally in terms of their own intentions and purposive acts and are prepared to accept responsibility, when challenged, for the choices they have made.

We work towards a notion of other persons by analogy with ourselves; we assume a comparability of subjective experience

If we accept for the moment the personal construct theory argument (Kelly, 1955, 1969) and think not simply of 'self' but of the bipolar construct of self versus others, then this draws our attention to the way in which we can only define self by distinguishing it from and comparing it to others. Yet this distinction between self and others also implies that others can be seen in the same terms, as 'persons' or as 'selves'. Our working assumption is that the rest of humankind have experiences which are somehow comparable with, although not the same as, our own and thereby we reasonably assume that they experience themselves as 'selves'.

We reflect, we are conscious, we are aware of self

Everything that has been said so far is by way of reflecting, standing back and viewing self. We both experience and reflect upon our experience, summarize it, comment on it and analyse it. This capacity to reflect is both the source of our commentary on self and a central part of the experience of being a 'self'. Psychologists sometimes, rather quaintly, talk of 'consciousness' as a problem. They see consciousness as a mystery which might best be dealt with by ignoring it and regarding people as mechanisms without awareness. This seems curious when we reflect that, were it not for this problematical consciousness, there would be no psychology to have problems to argue about. Psychology itself is a direct expression of consciousness. Mead (1925) elaborated this point in terms of the difference between 'I' and 'me', referring to the 'I' who acts and the 'me' who reflects upon the action and can go on to reflect upon the 'me' reflecting on the action.

Do we or do we not know ourselves?

The question 'do you know yourself?' seems to call forth a categorical 'yes' by way of answer. We know, in complete and sometimes painful detail, what has happened to us, what we have to contend with and what our thoughts and feelings are. We can reasonably claim to sit inside ourselves and know what is going on.

Yet we all have kinds of experience which cast doubt on the idea that we completely know ourselves. A basic test (in science and personal life) of whether you understand someone is your ability to predict accurately what they will do in a given situation. Yet most of us come across situations where we fail to predict our own behaviour; we find ourselves surprised by it and see ourselves behaving in a way we would not have expected to behave if we were the sort of person we thought we were.

We also sense that not all aspects of ourselves are equally accessible to us. There is nothing very mysterious in the notion of a hidden storehouse. We can confirm it very simply by reference to what we can readily draw from it. If I ask you to think about what kind of clothes you wore when you were around 14 years old you can probably bring some kind of image to mind. That raises the obvious question: where was that knowledge of yourself a minute ago, before I asked you the question? We are accustomed to having a vast knowledge of ourselves which is not consciously in front of us all the time. It is stored. It is not a great step to add to that picture the possibility that some parts of the 'store' of your past may not be so easily brought to the surface. We can then go one stage further and argue that although parts of your past are not easily brought to the surface they may nevertheless influence the present ways in which you feel and behave.

The best known picture of this kind of process is the Freudian portrait of the unconscious. Freud portrayed the self as divided. He saw it as made up of an id, the source of our primitive sexual and aggressive drives; a super-ego, our learnt morality, our inhibitions; and an ego, our conscious self, struggling to maintain some kind of balance between the driving force of the id and the controlling force of the super-ego. Freud argued that the id is entirely unconscious and a great deal of the super-ego is also unconscious, and that only very special strategies such as those used in psychoanalytic therapy can give access to the contents of these unconscious areas of self. We do not have to accept Freud's particular thesis in order to accept the idea of different levels of awareness, but it may well be that the enormous popularity of Freudian theory is due to the fact that it depicts what most of us feel is a 'probable' state of affairs; namely, that we have much more going on in us than we can readily be aware of or name.

Indeed, if we examine our everyday experience then we may well conclude that we are continually becoming aware of aspects of ourselves previously hidden from us.

A great deal of psychotherapy, education and personal and interpersonal soul-searching is dedicated to bringing to the surface hitherto unrecognized consistencies in our lives.

How do we know ourselves?

There is evidence that getting to know ourselves is a developmental process: it is something we learn in the same way that we learn to walk, talk and relate to others. In one study (Bannister and Agnew, 1977), groups of children were tape-recorded answering a variety of questions about their school, home, favourite games and so forth. These tape-recordings were transcribed and re-recorded in different voices so as to exclude circumstantial clues (names, occupations of parents and so forth) as to the identity of the children. Four months after the original recording the same children were asked to identify their own statements, to point out which statements were definitely not theirs and to give reasons for their choice. The children's ability to recognize their own statements increased steadily with age, and the strategies they used to pick out their own answers changed and became more complex. Thus, at the age of five children relied heavily on their (often inaccurate) memory or used simple clues such as whether they themselves undertook the kinds of activity mentioned in the statement; 'That boy says he plays football and I play football so I must have said that'. By the age of nine, they were using more psychologically complex methods to identify which statements they had made and which statements they had not made. For example, one boy picked out the statement 'I want to be a soldier when I grow up' as definitely not his because 'I don't think I could ever kill a human being so I wouldn't say I wanted to be a soldier'. This is clearly a psychological inference of a fairly elaborate kind.

Underlying our notions about ourselves and other people are personal psychological theories which roughly parallel those put forward in formal psychology. A common kind of theory is what would be called in formal psychology a 'trait theory'. Trait theories hinge on the argument that there are, in each of us, enduring characteristics which differentiate us from others, who have more or less of these characteristics. The notion that we are, or someone else is 'bad-tempered' is closely akin to the notion in formal psychology that some people are constitutionally 'introverted' or 'authoritarian' and so forth. The problem with trait descriptions is that they are not explanatory. They are a kind of tautology which says that a person behaves in a bad-tempered way because he is a bad-tempered kind of person. Such approaches tend to distract our attention from what is going on between us and other people by firmly lodging 'causes' in either us or the other person. If I say that I am angry with you because I am 'a bad-tempered person' that relieves me of the need to understand what is going on specifically between you and me that is making me angry.

Environmental and learning theories in psychology have their equivalents in our everyday arguments about our own nature. The fundamental assertion of stimulus-response psychology, that a person can be seen as reacting to his environment in terms of previously learnt patterns of response, is mirrored in our own talk when we offer as grounds for our actions that it is all 'due to the way I was brought up' or 'there was nothing else I could do in the circumstances'. Those theories and approaches in formal psychology which treat the person as a mechanism echo the kinds of explanation which we offer for our own behaviour when we are most eager to excuse it, to deny our responsibility for it and to argue that we cannot be expected to change.

Any theory or attempt to explain how we come to be what we are and how we change involves us in the question of what kind of evidence we use. Kelly (1955) argued that we derive our picture of ourselves through the picture which we have of other people's picture of us. He was arguing here that the central evidence we use in understanding ourselves is other people's reactions to us, both what they say of us and the implications of their behaviour towards us. He was not saying that we simply take other people's views of us as gospel. Obviously this would be impossible because people have very varying and often very disparate reactions to us. He argued that we filter others' views of us through our view of them. If someone you consider excessively rash and impulsive says that you are a conventional mouse, you might be inclined to dismiss their estimate on the grounds that they see everyone who is not perpetually swinging from the chandelier as being a conventional mouse. However, if someone you consider very docile and timid says that you are a conventional mouse, then this has quite different implications. You do not come to understand yourself simply by contemplating your own navel or even by analysing your own history. You build up a continuous and changing picture of yourself out of your interaction with other people.

Do we change ourselves?   That we change in small ways seems obvious enough. Looking at ourselves or others we readily notice changes in preferred style of dress, taste in films or food, changes in interests and hobbies, the gaining of new skills and the rusting of old and so forth.

Whether we change in large ways as well as small involves us in the question of how we define 'large' and 'small' change. Kelly (1955) hypothesized that each of us has a 'theory' about ourselves, about other people, and about the nature of the world, a theory which he referred to as our personal construct system. Constructs are our way of discriminating our world. For many of them we have over labels such as nice-nasty, ugly-beautiful, cheap-expensive, north-south, trustworthy-untrustworthy and so forth. He also distinguished between superordinate and subordinate constructs. Superordinate constructs are those which govern large areas of our life and which refer to matters of central concern to us, while subordinate constructs govern the minor detail of our lives.

If we take constructs about 'change in dress' at a subordinate level then we refer simply to our tendency to switch from sober to bright colours, from wide lapels to narrow lapels and so forth. If we look at such changes superordinately then we can make more far-reaching distinctions. For example, we might see ourselves as having made many subordinate changes in dress while not changing superordinately because we have always 'followed fashion'. Thus at this level of abstraction there is no change because the multitude of our minor changes are always governed and controlled by our refusal to make a major change: that is, to dress independently of fashion.

Psychologists differ greatly in their view of how much change takes place in people and how it takes place. Trait psychologists tend to set up the notion of fixed personality characteristics which remain with people all their lives, which are measurable and which will predict their behaviour to a fair degree in any given situation. The evidence for this view has been much attacked (e.g. Mischel, 1968). Direct examination of personal experience suggests that Kelly (1955) may have been right in referring to 'man as a form of motion and not a static object that is occasionally kicked into movement'.

Psychological measurement, to date, suggests that people change their character, if only slowly, and have complex natures so that behaviour is not easily predictable from one situation to another. Psychologists have also tended to argue that where change takes place it is often unconscious and unchosen by the person. The issue of whether we choose change or whether change is something that happens to us is clearly complex. One way of viewing it might be to argue that we can and do choose to change ourselves, but that often we are less aware of the direction which chosen change may eventually take.

A person in a semi-skilled job may decide to go to night school classes or undertake other forms of training in order to qualify themselves for what they regard as more challenging kinds of work. They might be successful in gaining qualifications and entering a new field. Up to this point they can reasonably claim to have chosen their direction of personal change and to have carried through that change in terms of their original proposal. However, the long-term effect may be that they acquire new kinds of responsibility, contacts with different kinds of people, new values and a life style which, in total, will involve personal changes not clearly envisaged at the time they went to their first evening class.

On the issue of how we go about changing ourselves, Radley (1974) speculated that change, particularly self-chosen change, may have three stages to it. Initially, if we are going to change, we must be able to envisage some goal; we must have a kind of picture of what we will be like when we have changed. He argued that if we have only a vague picture or no picture at all then we cannot change; we need to be able to 'see' the changed us in the distance. He went on to argue that when we have the picture then we can enact the role of a person like that. That is to say, we do not at heart believe that we are such a person but we can behave as if we were such a person, rather like an actor playing a role on stage or someone trying out a new style. (This may relate to the old adage that adolescence is the time when we 'try out' personalities to see which is a good fit.) He argued that if we enact in a committed and vigorous way for long enough then, at some mysterious point, we become what we are enacting and it is much more true to say that we are that person than that we are our former selves. This is very much a psychological explanation, in that it is about what is psychologically true, rather than what is formally and officially true. Thus the student who qualifies and becomes a teacher may officially, in terms of pay packet and title, be 'a teacher'. Yet, in Radley's terms, the person may still psychologically be 'a student' who is enacting the role of teacher, who is putting on a teaching style and carrying out the duties of a teacher but who still, in his heart of hearts, sees himself as a student. Later, there may come a point at which he becomes, in the psychological sense, a teacher.

However, we are also aware that there is much that is problematic and threatening about change. The set expectations of others about us may have an imprisoning effect and restrict our capacity to change. People have a picture of us and may attempt to enforce that picture. They may resist change in us because it seems to them unnatural, and it would make us less predictable. Phrases such as 'you are acting out of character', or 'that is not the true you', or 'those are not really your ideas' all reflect the difficulty people find and the resistance they manifest to change in us. Often the pressure of others' expectations is so great that we can only achieve change by keeping it secret until the change has gone so far that we can confront the dismay of others.

This is not to argue that we are simply moulded and brainwashed by our society and our family so that we are merely puppets dancing to tunes played by others. We are clearly influenced by others and everything, the language we speak, the clothes we wear, our values, ideas and feelings, is derived from and elaborated in terms of our relationships with other people and our society. But the more conscious we become of how this happens, the more likely we are to become critical of and the less likely automatically to accept what we are taught (formally and informally), and the more we may independently explore what we wish to ma[ ] of ourselves as persons.

Equally, when we attempt to change we may find the process personally threatening. We may lose sight of the fact that change is inevitably a form of evolution: that is to say, we change from something to something and thereby there is continuity as well as change. If we lose faith in our own continuity we may be overwhelmed by a fear of som[ ] kind of catastrophic break, a fear of becoming something unpredictable to ourselves, of falling into chaos. Whether or not we are entirely happy with ourselves, at least we are something we are familiar with, and quite often we stay as we are because we would sooner suffer the devil we know than the unknown devil of a changed us. Fransella (1972) explored the way in which stutterers who seem to be on the verge of being cured of their stutter often suddenly relapse. She argued that stutterers know full well how to live as 'stutterers'; they understand how people react and relate to them as 'stutterers'. Nearing cure they are overwhelmed with the fear of the unknown, the strangeness of being 'a fluent speaker'.

Monitoring of self

One of the marked features of our culture is that it does not demand (or even suggest) that we formally monitor our lives or that we record our personal history in the way in which a society records its history. True, a few keep diaries, and practices such as re-reading old letters from other people give us glimpses into our past attitudes and feelings. For the most part, our understanding of our past is based on our often erratic memory of it. Moreover, our memory is likely to be erratic, not just because we forget past incidents and ideas but because we may actively 're-write' our history so as to emphasize our consistency and make our past compatible with our present.

Psychologists have tended to ignore the importance of personal history. The vast majority of psychological tests designed to assess the person cut in at a given point in time; they are essentially cross-sectional and pay little heed to the evolution of the person. It would be a very unusual psychology course that used biography or autobiography as material for its students to ponder. There are exceptions to this here-and-now preoccupation. In child psychology great emphasis is laid on the notion of 'development' and a great deal of the research and argument in child psychology is about how children acquire skills over a period, how they are gradually influenced by social customs and how life within the family, over a period of years, affects a child's self-value. Additionally, clinical psychologists involved in psychotherapy and counselling very often find themselves engaged in a joint search with their clients through the immediate and distant past in order to understand present problems and concerns. This does not necessarily argue that a person is simply the end product of their past. We need to understand and acknowledge our past, not in order to repeat it but in order either to use it or to be free of it. As Kelly (1969) put it, 'you are not the victim of your autobiography but you may become the victim of the way you interpret your autobiography'.

Obstacles to self-knowledge and self-change

To try and understand oneself is not simply an interesting pastime, it is a necessity of life. In order to plan our future and to make choices we have to be able to anticipate our behaviour in future situations. This makes self-knowledge a practical guide, not a self-indulgence. Sometimes the situations with which we are confronted are of a defined and clear kind so that we can anticipate and predict our behaviour with reasonable certainty. If someone asks you if you can undertake task X (keep a set of accounts, drive a car, translate a letter from German and so forth) then it is not difficult to assess your skills and experience and work out whether you can undertake the task or not. Often the choice or the undertaking is of a more complex and less defined nature. Can you stand up in conflict with a powerful authority figure? Can you make a success of your marriage to this or that person? Can you live by yourself when you have been used to living with a family? The stranger the country we are entering the more threatening the prospect becomes; the more we realize that some degree of self-change may be involved, the more we must rely upon our understanding of our own character and potential.

In such circumstances we are acutely aware of the dangers of change and may take refuge in a rigid and inflexible notion of what we are. Kelly (1955, 1969) referred to this tendency as 'hostility'. He defined hostility as 'the continued effort to extort validational evidence in favor of a type of social prediction which has already been recognized as a failure'. We cannot lightly abandon our theory of what we are, since the abandonment of such a theory may plunge us into chaos. Thus we see someone destroy a close relationship in order to 'prove' that they are independent or we see teachers 'proving' that their pupils are stupid in order to verify that they themselves are clever.

Closely connected to this definition of hostility is Kelly's definition of guilt as 'the awareness of dislodgement of self from one's core role structure'. Core constructs are those which govern a person's maintenance processes; they are those constructs in terms of which identity is established and the self is pictured and understood. Your core role structure is what you understand yourself to be.

It is in a situation in which you fail to anticipate your own behaviour that you experience guilt. Defined in this way guilt comes not from a violation of some social code but from a violation of your own personal picture of what you are.

There are traditional ways of exploring the issue of 'what am I like?' We can meditate upon ourselves, ask others how they see us, or review our history. Psychologists have devised numerous tests for assessing 'personality', though in so far as these are of any use they seem to be designed to give the psychologist ideas about the other person rather than to give the people ideas about themselves. Two relatively recent attempts to provide people with ways of exploring their own 'personality' are offered by McFall (in Bannister and Fransella, 1980) and Mair (1970).

McFall offers a simple elaboration on the idea of talking to oneself. His work indicated that if people associate freely into a tape-recorder and listen to their own free flow then, given that they erase it afterwards so that there is no possible audience other than themselves at that time, they may learn something of the themes, conflict and issues that concern them; themes that are 'edited out' of most conversation and which are only fleetingly glimpsed in our thinking. Mair experimented with formalized, written conversation. Chosen partners wrote psychological descriptions of each other (and predictions of the other's description) and then compared and discussed the meaning and the evidence underlying their written impressions.

Although we have formal ways of exploring how we see and how we are seen by others (the encounter group), and informal ways (the party), it can be argued that there is something of a taboo in our society on direct expression of our views of each other. It may be that we fear to criticize lest we be criticized, or it may be that we are embarrassed by the whole idea of the kind of confrontation involved in telling each other about impressions which are being created. Certainly if you contemplate how much you know about the way you are seen by others, you may be struck by the limitations of your knowledge, even on quite simple issues. How clear are you as to how your voice tone is experienced by other people? How often do you try and convey to someone your feelings and thoughts about them in such an oblique and roundabout way that there is a fair chance that they will not grasp the import of what you are saying?

Psychologists are only very slowly seeing it as any part of their task to offer ways to people in which they may explore themselves and explore the effect they have on others.

Role and person

Social psychologists have made much use of the concept of 'role'. Just as an actor plays a particular role in a drama it can be argued that each of us has a number of roles in our family, in work groups, in our society. We have consistent ways of speaking, dressing and behaving which reflect our response to the expectations of the group around us. Thus within a family or small social group we may have inherited and developed the role of 'clown' or 'hardheaded practical person' or 'sympathizer'. Jobs often carry implicit role specifications with them so that we perceive different psychological requirements in the role of teacher from the role of student or the role of manager from the role of worker. We are surprised by the randy parson, the sensitive soldier, the shy showbusiness person. Society also prescribes very broad and pervasive roles for us as men or women, young or old, working-class or middle-class and so forth. It is not that every word of our scripts is pre-written for us, but the broad boundaries and characteristics of behaviour appropriate to each role are fairly well understood. These social roles can and do conflict with personal inclinations and one way of defining maturity would be to look on it as the process whereby we give increasing expression to what we personally are, even where this conflicts with standard social expectations.

Kelly chose to define role in a more strictly personal sense in his sociality corollary which reads: 'to the extent that one person construes the construction processes of another he may play a role in a social process involving the other person'. He is here emphasizing the degree to which, when we relate to another person, we relate in terms of our picture of the other person's picture of us. Role then becomes not a life style worked out by our culture and waiting for us to step into, but the on-going process whereby we try to imagine and understand how other people see the world and continuously to relate our own conception to theirs.

The paradox of self-knowing

We reasonably assume that our knowledge of something does not alter the 'thing' itself. If I come to know that Guatemala produces zinc or that the angle of incidence of a light ray equals its angle of reflection, then this new knowledge of mine does not, of itself, affect Guatemala or light. However, it alters me in that I have become 'knowing' and not 'ignorant' of these things. More pointedly, if I come to know something of myself then I am changed, to a greater or lesser degree, by that knowledge. Any realization by a person of the motives and attitudes underlying their behaviour has the potential to alter that behaviour.

Put another way, a person is the sum of their understanding of their world and themselves. Changes in what we know of ourselves and the way in which we come to know it are changes in the kind of person we are.

This paradox of self-knowledge presents a perpetual problem to psychologists. An experimental psychologist may condition a person to blink their eye when a buzzer is pressed, simply by pairing the buzzer sound with a puff of air to the person's eyelid until the blink becomes a response to the sound of the buzzer on its own. But if the person becomes aware of the nature of the conditioning process and resents being its 'victim' then conditioning may cease, or at least take much longer. Knowledge of what is going on within that person and between the person and the psychologist has altered the person and invalidated the psychologist's predictions. Experimental psychologists seek to evade the consequences of this state of affairs by striving to keep the subject in ignorance of the nature of the experimental process or by using what they assume to be naturally ignorant subjects: for example, rats. But relying on a precariously maintained ignorance in the experimental subject creates only a mythical certainty in science. Psychotherapists, on the other hand, generally work on the basis that the more the person (subject, patient, client) comes to know of themselves, the nearer they will come to solving, at least in part, their personal problems.

This self-changing property of self-knowledge may be a pitfall for a simple-minded science of psychology. It may also be the very basis of living, for us as persons.

References

Bannister, D. and Agnew, J. (1977)
The Child's Construing of Self. In A.W. Landfield (ed.), Nebraska Symposium on Motivation 1976. Nebraska: University of Nebraska Press.
Bannister, D. and Fransella, F. (1980)
Inquiring Man (2nd edn). Harmondsworth: Penguin.
Fransella, F. (1972)
Personal Change and Reconstruction. London: Academic Press.
Kelly, G.A. (1955)
The Psychology of Personal Constructs, Volumes I and II. New York: Norton.
Kelly, G.A. (1969)
Clinical Psychology and Personality: The selected papers of George Kelly (ed. B.A. Maher). New York: Wiley.
Mair, J.M.M. (1970)
Experimenting with individuals. British Journal of Medical Psychology, 43, 245-256.
Mead, G.H. (1925)
The genesis of the self and social control. International Journal of Ethics, 35, 251-273.
Mischel, W. (1968)
Personality and Assessment. New York: Wiley.
Radley, A.R. (1974)
The effect of role enactment on construct alternatives. British Journal of Medical Psychology, 47, 313-320.

Questions

1. Examine the way in which a person's idea of 'self' is affected by the nature of their work.
2. Discuss the nature of sex differences in ideas about 'self'.
3. Describe some way in which you have increased your knowledge of yourself.

4. How do parents influence their children's ideas about 'self'?
5. To what extent is our picture of our self influenced by our physical state and appearance?
6. We come to understand ourselves through our relationship with others. Discuss.
7. Examine the way in which social customs inhibit our revealing of 'self'.
8. People are born with a fixed character which they cannot alter. Discuss.
9. 'He is not himself today.' What triggers off this kind of comment, and does it say more about the speaker than the person of whom it is said?
10. Your job enables you to express yourself. Your job prevents you being yourself. Discuss.

notated reading

Axline, V.M. (1971) Dibs: In search of self. Harmondsworth: Penguin.
> A finely written description of a withdrawn and disturbed child who in the process of psychotherapy comes vividly to life. It casts light on our early struggles to achieve the idea of being a 'self'.

Bannister, D. and Fransella, F. (1980) Inquiring Man: The psychology of personal constructs. Harmondsworth: Penguin.
> The second edition of a book which sets out the way Kelly sees each of us as developing a complex personal view of our world. The book describes two decades of psychological research based on the theory and relates it to problems such as psychological breakdown, prejudice, child development and personal relationships.

Bott, M. and Bowskill, D. (1980) The Do-It-Yourself Mind Book. London: Wildwood House.
> A lightly written but shrewd book on the ways in which we can tackle serious personal and emotional problems without recourse to formal psychiatry.

Fransella, F. (1975) Need to Change? London: Methuen.
> A brief description of the formal and informal ways in which 'self' is explored and change attempted.

Rogers, C.R. (1961) On Becoming a Person. Boston: Houghton-Mifflin.
> Sets out the idea of 'self-actualization' and describes the ways in which we might avoid either limiting ourselves or being socially limited, and come to be what Rogers calls a fully functioning person.

xercises

An important caution for the reader
Many of the projects in this book involve obtaining information from individuals. People have a right to protect

personal information, and as we, as Editors, have emphasize
in our Preface to the book, such a right must be treated as
sacrosanct by the psychologist. The projects which follow
involve a great deal of self-revelation and discovery.
Because they are personal they can arouse anxiety, so they
should only be attempted on a voluntary basis. If you have a
friend with whom you can share some aspects of the exercis
then you will benefit from a sharing of experience. Again,
however, we must emphasize that there is no self-evident
right which allows a person access to another person's
thoughts and feelings. This principle must be borne in mind
so that people can stop participating at any time they
choose and should not feel subject to group pressure.

1. Self-characterization

This is a mode of self-exploration originally outlined by
Kelly and further discussed in Bannister and Fransella
(1980). You have 20 minutes or so to write a self-portrait.
This is to be a sketch of your own character written in the
third person, beginning with your name and the word 'is';
thus 'Bill Smith is ...'. These self-portraits are written
in the third person to give writers a little 'distance' from
themselves, and it is to be written as if it were penned by
a sympathetic friend. Obviously this is a friend who knows
much more about you than any friend normally does, but
writing in this mode allows for criticism while discouraging
excessive modesty.

Self-characterizations can be analysed by the writers
themselves or they can be exchanged between members of a
class and each person can be working on the analysis of
someone else's self-characterization. As a classroom project, the group procedure should be explained to students in
advance of the exercise. There should be free choice as to
whether individuals wish to work on the analysis of their
own self-characterization or whether they would like someon
else to work on it. There is no standard 'scoring system'
for a self-characterization but a group of students can be
taken through the self-characterizations by answering certain questions and making notes. Some possible questions
are:

1. What is the main theme of the self-characterization?
   What is the characteristic problem or issue around which
   the person's self-portrait seems to pivot?
2. Does the self-characterization make reference to
   history? Is it in any sense biographical with references
   to past events and times or is it written entirely in
   the 'here-and-now'? If it does refer to the person's
   past what kind of 'cause and effect' relationship is
   implied?
3. Are there any apparent contradictions in the self-
   characterization? Are there, for example, two sentences
   which you could pull out from different parts of the
   self-characterization and which, if you put them side by
   side, seem to be saying somewhat different and rather

conflicting things? It should be noted that the contradiction may only be apparent and that the writer of the self-characterization may have some way of integrating the two ideas.

4. Does the self-characterization refer to the views of others about the person who wrote it? If there are any references (direct or implied) to the impression that other people have about the subject, does the subject see these impressions as fair or as based on some kind of misunderstanding?

5. How sympathetic was the 'friend' who wrote the characterization?

6. Does the self-characterization imply change? Does it suggest (directly or indirectly) that the person has changed in the past or may change in the future or does it imply that the person has a fairly fixed character?

7. If you are training for a particular line of work then the self-characterization can be examined to see what personal assets and liabilities (or characteristics which are both an asset and a liability) you have for the job for which you are training.

After the self-characterizations have been read and analysed you can discuss them in pairs if you wish to and then discuss, as a class, what has been learnt from the exercise.

2. Conversational model techniques

These were proposed by Mair (1970). He argued that our most frequently used technique for finding out about each other is conversation and went on to examine the possibilities of constructing 'formal' conversations so that we could examine and interrogate what we learn about the other person. The following is a description of a fairly elaborate form of conversational technique which takes up quite a time and which depends upon there being several or more of you. It can be shortened by missing out any of the descriptions of the other, with the exception of the basic public description.

1. You should divide your group into pairs and members of each pair should write a brief character description of their partner which they are prepared to let the partner read. Thus A writes a 'public' portrait of B and B writes a 'public' portrait of A (the writing taking, say, 20 minutes). The aim of each partner giving impressions of the other is to be helpful. That is not to say that the portrait cannot be critical, but you should be aware that you ought to write in such a way that the other person is able to benefit from, and gain insight from, what is written. The portrait should be sympathetic.

2. Person A now writes a private portrait of B, and B writes a private portrait of A. That is to say, these

portraits are to remain in the possession of the writer and not to be shown to the other person.

3. Person A now writes a prediction of what might be found in B's public portrait of A and B similarly writes a prediction of the points that might be made in A's public portrait of B.

4. The pair now exchange and read through the public portraits. They can now begin to discuss the portraits. They discuss any points that strike them as significant, but there are at least two kinds of enquiry into what the other person has written that may be useful. The first is enquiry into the meaning of the terms used in the description. What is meant if the other person says that you are 'sensitive': are you artistic and under-standing, or are you timid and fearful and so forth? Second, the pair can discuss the question of evidence for the statements made in the sketches. What kinds of behaviour and/or talk have given the person the psycho-logical impression recorded in the sketch?

The predictions about what the other person might write can be discussed between members of the pair if you wish, with each partner noting omissions of anticipated comments which come as a surprise. The private portrait is obviously not discussed but again, as a member of a pair you can re-examine your private portrait of the other in relation to their public portrait and consider what the differences between the two imply. It could be argued that the differ-ence between the two sketches, public and private, is an indication of the nature of the relationship between the two. If possible, conclude with a general group discussion of the exercise: what it meant for everyone, and what it brings to mind about the problem of being understood by someone else.

3. Introspection

There is a widespread myth in academic psychology which claims that introspection, as a psychological tool, has been shown to be useless. If the history of psychology is examined, what this turns out to mean is that one particular way of introspecting, designed largely by Wundt and the Wurzburg school, was discredited. There are many other ways of introspecting which may be useful as a source of self-knowledge. This is an exercise which lends itself to class discussion.

You should prepare yourself with several sheets of blank paper and pens and be ready to associate freely about a given theme. The theme can be chosen by the teacher or the class and can be literally anything. If the class is consi-dering the problem of self-knowledge, it may be as well to choose themes which particularly relate to that. Themes such as secrecy, personal relationships, families, loneliness, and so forth, clearly offer themselves in this area. You have 15 minutes or so to jot down in a free, fast flowing and uncritical way any thoughts, ideas, or fragments of thoughts or ideas that come to mind when you simply gaze at the words representing the theme. It should be stressed that you are not being asked to write any kind of essay, only spontaneous jottings. You are not being asked to offer those logical ideas which you would be prepared to defend or explain; you are being asked to react to the theme with outpourings of any odd notions that go through your mind, however confused or strange these may seem. These jottings must not be read out or seen by anyone else, so that they do not have to be censored or edited in any way.

When you have had time to pile up your free associations to the theme, and not before, you are asked to read on and to undertake the second part of the task. You go back over your jottings, looking at them, and trying to draw from them any propositions which seem to be implied by the material in front of you. These are to be written down as logical propositions taking the form of assertions about the nature of the psychological area covered by the theme title. Thus, if the theme were, say, 'family relationships' then you might find that an implication of several of your individual jottings, when combined, was the proposition that 'families make you hide what you are so that all can survive as a family', or 'you spend your entire adult life trying to escape from your family', or 'the time you live with your family is the only time in your life when you are really secure' and so forth. You should not worry for the moment about defending or explaining or even believing your propositions; you are simply trying to look over the free associations you have made and crystallize them into the form of simple propositions. (It is important that you did not know that you would be asked to make propositions out of your spontaneous associations before the free scribbling period was finished.) When you have managed to find the 'hidden assertions', the one or more propositions implicit in your introspective material, these propositions are read out to others and freely discussed. The essential quality of the discussion is that it should not be about whether the propositions are right or wrong, or whether you are being clever or stupid, or whether the propositions are popularly believed or not. The discussion should be about the echoes which are aroused in others by the propositions, the thoughts they stimulate, the extent to which even though they are not literally true they tell those others something about their own experience. A class can look for common themes in the various propositions and, if members wish, they can try and build even larger propositions about secrecy or personal relationships or whatever the theme was, by combining several propositions together. They can examine the way in which some propositions apparently contradict each other and enquire into the nature of the contradiction.

10

Creating change
H. R. Beech

Politicians and kings have perhaps made the most distinctive and historically interesting attempts to change the behaviour of those they seek to control. Sometimes this has involved extreme measures, such as torture and execution, sometimes more subtle legal approaches to behaviour control, but these attempts perversely - and to the bafflement of the controller - have often failed to produce the desired outcome. Somehow, it seems, human nature appears to be resistant to change.

Psychologists are disposed to argue that such failures are mainly attributable to two causes. First, until recently, there was an obvious lack of the technology to effect changes with any degree of reliability: the methods which had been used before were both crude and unsystematically applied. Second, sometimes the attempts to effect change involved very fundamental aspects of human functioning and it might not be within the capacity of the species to accomplish them. Indeed, the contention of the behavioural psychologist these days might be that substantial changes can be wrought in carefully selected behaviours where the appropriate techniques can be freely applied. This is not to say, of course, that some psychologists fail to perceive in these strategies a means of acquiring very substantial or near complete control over human nature or, indeed, the means by which the very fabric of society could be altered. Of course, it would be unwise to allow psychologists (even if their techniques did permit such achievements) also to determine the types of change to be brought about. Psychologists are in no better position to decide what kind of society we should live in than is any other group.

For the most part, however, the aims and aspirations of psychologists are generally less ambitious and merely involve the deployment of strategies for change to areas where help is needed and requested. But to understand the origin of these strategies it is first useful to describe the influence exerted by Freud and Pavlov.

Freud's theories (Munroe, 1955) were important because they gave an entirely new interpretation to 'bad', 'wrong' or 'unacceptable' behaviour. Rather than seeing these behaviours as the reflection of something defective in the very substance of Man, Freud argued that such conduct arose out of environmental experiences. Indeed, Freud is often thought of as a thoroughgoing psychic determinist, believing that all behaviour is determined by prior experience and, in a very real sense, is programmed to be just the way it is, free will and choice being merely illusory. In short, enormous importance is attached to the influence of the environment as a determinant of what we are.

Pavlov (1927) was also interested in how behaviour became modified (although primarily concerned with how the physiological systems of animals worked) and devised the method of classical conditioning to assist in this endeavour. The definitive experiment carried out in his laboratory was to show that, after training, the sound of a bell could produce salivation in dogs. Clearly the dog does not start life with this capacity and needs to learn this reaction, and it is the process by which such learning takes place that is called 'classical conditioning'. Briefly, the process involves presenting the new stimulus (bell) before the old stimulus (food) to the response (salivation). Repetitions of this arrangement, with only a brief (say half a second) interval between the sound of the bell and presentation of food leads to the new association being formed. Instead of requiring food before salivating, the dog now has come to salivate at the sound of the bell alone.

Perhaps not of itself a particularly compelling piece of learning, but to many psychologists this type of association appeared as one of the fundamental building blocks of learning; such learning could be seen as underpinning all human behaviour.

An early enthusiast of Pavlov's work, Watson, was said to have been so impressed by such demonstrations of conditioning that he declared that any American child might be turned into the President using these methods. Whether or not Watson accorded such power to classical conditioning, he was certainly enthusiastic to use it and has achieved an important place in psychological history through his Little Albert experiment (Watson and Rayner, 1920).

In this study Watson's aim was to investigate the acquisition of emotional responses, arguing that they are probably learnt by the associative process called conditioning. For this demonstration he chose an 11-month-old boy called Albert and set out to create a learnt emotional reaction in this child. Watson had observed Albert's fondness for a tame white rat and chose to reverse this feeling by arranging for a loud noise to be made (by crashing two metal plates together behind Albert's head) whenever the child reached out for this pet. After just a few trials of this kind, Albert's fear, occasioned by the sudden loud noise, was transferred to the white rat so that every time this animal appeared Little Albert would whimper and crawl away. Furthermore, it was noted that the new fear reaction had transferred to other objects with some similarity to the rat (e.g. a ball of cotton wool) and it appeared to be enduring over the period of observation.

This latter observation led Watson to speculate upon the fate of a more mature Albert, lying on the psychoanalyst's couch, and vainly trying to understand how he came to worry about white fluffy objects! But the conditioning process might well be the basis for all our irrational (neurotic) fears.

It is important to point out, however, that the environment is not the only contributing factor to learning since, from Pavlov on, it has been observed that not all learning opportunities are realized or, if they are, there are individual differences in the character of the learning which is affected.

The earliest experimental observations of such limitations of a purely environmentalist approach were made by Pavlov. He is said to have first formed this conclusion as a result of flood waters entering his laboratories in Leningrad, finding that this had made some of the animals very disturbed while others appeared to treat the matter with indifference. Later, experiments showed more conclusively that some animals appeared to be susceptible to disturbance and others more phlegmatic, these two types being labelled 'weak' and 'strong' nervous systems respectively. This differentiation has been repeatedly confirmed in the experimental work of other investigators and clearly shows that an opportunity to learn is not all that is involved: a major influence is the basic temperament of the organism which is doing the learning.

Another study which points to this conclusion was conducted by Rachman (1966). The problem posed by the investigator here was that of whether or not fetishistic behaviour (sexual arousal to unusual stimuli) could be acquired by a simple associative process. Briefly, three male volunteers were exposed to conditions in which pictures of boots were linked with pictures of an erotic nature to see if bonding occurred in such a way that the sight of boots alone would produce sexual excitement. Such was in fact found to be the case and establishes that fetishes can come about through associations of this kind. However, the point to be made here is that the subjects took varying numbers of trials to lose such reactions; in short, the disposition of the individual seems to be very much implicated in what we learn and how well such learning is preserved.

Generally these results are thought to reflect some permanent characteristics of the individuals concerned, but it is important to add that even temporary states of the organism can affect learning, a point which has been made by Beech and others (see Vila and Beech, 1978).

Clinical experience would tend to indicate that symptoms of distress (e.g. inability to go out of the house or to meet others socially without feeling anxious) often appear to be preceded by a period of general tension and emotional upset; it is as if such states prepare the ground for certain kinds of learning to take place: as if they put the organism on a defensive footing, ready to react adversely to relatively minor provocation. The kind of disturbance referred to here is quite commonly experienced by women in the few days prior to menstruation and has been given the name of pre-menstrual tension. If this condition is a good parallel to the situation in which abnormal fears can arise, then it should be possible to show a propensity for 'defensive' or adverse learning in pre-menstrual days which is not present at other times in the cycle. This is, in fact, what has been found. The evidence indicates that the state of the organism at the time when some noxious event is present not only determines the speed at which learning takes place but also any tendency for the learning to be preserved over time. One might be tempted to argue that this 'natural' disposition to acquire neurotic symptoms could explain why disproportionately large numbers of women complain of neurotic symptoms.

Another influence to be taken into account as limiting the scope of a purely environmentalist view of human behaviour is that of biological potential for learning. The argument here has been cogently presented by Seligman and Hager (1972), who conclude that all organisms appear to show a great readiness to acquire certain associations while other connections will be made only with difficulty or even not at all. Among the examples cited by Seligman and Hager is that of the dog which can very quickly associate the operation of a latch with its paw to escape from a box, but seems quite unable to learn to effect escape by wagging its tail. It is not that tail-wagging is a difficult action for the dog to perform or even that it is an uncommon reaction; rather it seems that the problem lies in making the connection itself. It is argued that the species has no biological propensity to make such a connection; the evolutionary history of the dog did not prepare the animal for this kind of learning.

It is not yet known to what extent humans are affected by preparedness, although it is obvious that certain connections appear to be 'natural' and made quite easily, while others are not. It has been suggested that a good example of preparedness is to be found in the prevalence of spider and snake phobia found in populations not at all at risk from these creatures. A more purely environmentalist approach might argue that one would need to be bitten by a spider or snake before a phobic reaction could be developed yet, obviously, there seems to be a great readiness in many people to display a wariness about spiders in a country such as England, while no such widespread fear is evoked by horses or hamsters. Somewhere in our evolutionary history, it can be argued, the species has acquired a readiness to respond with fear to potential dangers, including spiders and snakes. Perhaps this is why open spaces present a problem for many people; such 'exposure' was to be avoided in the interests of survival and this potential for acquiring a fear of open spaces is easily tapped.

The thoroughgoing environmentalist would want to argue that Man is virtually a blank sheet, a complicated learning machine and, given the appropriate incentives and opportunities, can be moulded to any desired pattern. In the light of the limitations to learning which have been mentioned it is obviously appropriate to take a more moderate view and regard Man as a creature highly susceptible to modification through learning, but far from infinitely so. As yet, we do not know quite how far the capacity to learn can take us. Can it, for example, so change human nature that one becomes entirely altruistic, and greed, selfishness and other 'human failings' become totally alien? There are those, like Dawkins (1978) who would not think this possible but, on the other hand, Skinner (1953) and many others see almost limitless possibilities to behaviour modification with the psycho-technology currently available even now.

For Skinnerians the basic principle of change can be stated quite simply; the consequences of any piece of behaviour affects the future of that behaviour. If the consequence is rewarding then the behaviour is strengthened (i.e. rendered more likely to occur again); if it is punishing, then the same response tends to be weakened. Using this basic proposition, it is argued, far-reaching changes can be made to occur.

Of course, such a view is as profoundly hedonistic as Pavlov's or Freud's, the basic contention being that Man is simply a pleasure-maximizing, pain-minimizing organism; this is as much part and parcel of his make-up as any other creature. Changing behaviour, according to this view, depends upon the nature, timing and other attributes of rewards and punishments rather than upon appeals to reason or religious precepts.

There is, understandably, considerable resistance to accepting such a stark view of Man's nature; it appears to accord no place at all to free will and choice, nor does it allow Man any special place in biological or other terms. Hedonism is the key mechanism in what we are; Man can (and does) learn to do and to be anything, providing that the rewards and punishments are there to chart the way.

What we can now do is to examine the achievements to date; to see how far Pavlovian and Skinnerian principles of learning have been effective in producing change. It is anyone's guess how much further it is possible to go.

Aversive learning

Most of us subscribe to the validity of the adages that 'the burnt child dreads the fire' or 'once bitten, twice shy'. These sayings simply embody the importance of pain avoidance in our biological make-up. Clearly, deprived of such protection the species could hardly be expected to survive; we learn pretty quickly and thoroughly if the consequences of some actions are painful. Yet there appear to be some notable exceptions to such a compelling principle; martyrs and heroes often seem to subject themselves to avoidable pain while hard-bitten criminals may appear unaffected by the punishment society metes out to them. Obviously the problem is more complex than at first sight appears. Perhaps one should not be overly influenced by these exceptions, since the rule does seem to hold in general, but it is just as well to begin by recognizing that the results of punishment are unpredictable. For that matter, the outcome of rewarding behaviours shows much the same variability and such findings make fools of those who argue for simple solutions. For example, on the one hand there are those who want to create a better society by wreaking extreme retribution upon all who infringe rules while, on the other, the 'progressives' appear to think that the solution to crime is to remove all sources of discomfort and irritation. Both views, obviously, are patently absurd; crime has persisted in spite of great harshness in past years and, as is now well documented, the rate has risen dramatically as the number of social workers, leisure centres and social welfare has increased.

There are several arguments advanced to explain why punishment fails to achieve good effects in the context under discussion. In the first place it is said that its application is seldom timely: it works very well if immediate, but poorly or not at all if the crime and later court sentence are separated by lengthy intervals of time. Second, it is said that the rate of successful to unsuccessful crime is unfavourable to learning to resist temptation: numerous crimes may be rewarded before one act leads to punishment. A third argument is that the rate of criminal behaviour is inversely related to the strength of punishment, and that deterrents are not nearly strong enough to be effective. Yet another reason is said to be the temperament of the habitual criminal who, it is alleged, does not generate the kind of anxiety which most of us experience when 'wrong doing'. This last point refers to evidence that the nervous systems of individuals appear to extend over a range from the excessive 'jumpiness' of the chronically anxious at one end of the spectrum to those who appear to be 'psychopathically' resistant to showing disturbance to even strong stimulation.

There is probably something to be said for each of these points and, at least, all serve to indicate the complexities which may underlie the application of punishments.

To some extent it is possible to avoid a number of these problems when aversive consequences are part of a treatment programme; here, more of what takes place is under the control of the therapist or experimenter. Perhaps the best-known example of this is to be found in the treatment of alcoholism. With this, an attempt is made to ensure that drinking (and stimulus situations related to it) leads to aversive consequences; a convenient means of achieving this in practice has been to administer an emetic drug and, when this is beginning to take effect, the individual is permitted to sip the alcohol to which he is addicted. Unpleasant feelings of nausea and vomiting will, in this way, become associated with the particular sight, smell and taste involved (Voegtlin and Lemere, 1942).

Of course, it can be argued that simply punishing the 'wrong' response is hardly likely to lead to the adoption of a socially-acceptable reaction. What, for example, can the homosexual do with the sexual impulses he experiences after the usual way in which these are expended have been denied to him by punishment? Accordingly, more sophisticated attempts to help have included not only punishment but also opportunities to escape from punishment. In the context of treating homosexuals, for instance, the individual concerned has been allowed access to slides depicting homosexual activity only at the cost of receiving strong electric shocks, while the rejection of such slides and their substitution by heterosexual material can lead to the avoidance of punishment altogether.

A perennial problem of aversive training has been that of securing appropriate levels of co-operation and motivation and, no doubt, many failures are attributable to this difficulty. A simple example of this clarifies the point in practical terms. The investigation here was of a young boy whose habit of thumb-sucking was to be dealt with by capitalizing upon his enjoyment of cartoons. The therapist arranged for the boy to sit through protracted showings of cartoon films but these showings ceased abruptly if thumbsucking occurred, and the film would only be continued when this behaviour stopped. It took a relatively short time for the boy to control his bad habit during the film shows but it was noted that the training had no effect upon what happened outside that situation! Indeed, one might reasonably argue that, in this case, the boy had learnt how to control the behaviour of the psychologist, rather than the opposite!

Since aversion therapy is given only to those voluntarily submitting themselves to this form of training, one should be able to assume a reasonable level of motivation to change. However, as we all recognize from personal experience, our commitment to change can be quite ephemeral and today's resolution to give up smoking (or whatever) can disappear completely tomorrow. Perhaps this is only another way of saying that the aversive condition has not been applied sufficiently vigorously or intensively to inhibit the temptation: the associative bond between aversive feelings and the 'unwanted' action is insufficiently strongly made. Nevertheless, it is apparent that this problem is a major obstacle to the success of punishment as a means of control.

Systematic desensitization

Few doubt the power of anxiety to alter and disrupt ordinary behaviour patterns; anxiety can handicap our attempts to cope with a whole range of life's problems, it may prevent anything approaching an adjustment to quite ordinary events and it may totally ruin our enjoyment of relationships and circumstances which should be pleasurable. The capacity to deal with and eliminate anxiety can be regarded as of major importance to the effective control of our behaviour since, essentially, anxiety is a disruptive influence which erodes our capacity to control our own thought and action. In short, changing behaviour often seems to involve removing anxiety.

The behavioural strategy to resolve this problem appears to be surprisingly direct and simple. All that is needed is a gradual, step-by-step approach to the feared object or situation together with some means of inhibiting anxiety at each of these stages. The technique for accomplishing this was developed and refined by Wolpe (1969). More than 30 years earlier Mary Cover Jones (1924) had described essentially the same method in successfully eliminating the children's fears and, in a sense, there seems to be nothing particularly remarkable or novel in the method. Nevertheless, Wolpe's standardization of an effective technique for the analysis of anxiety and the application of a treatment strategy was enormously important from both practical and theoretical points of view.

The basic argument is that fear (or anxiety) has inadvertently, through a process of association, become a learnt reaction to the presence of certain cues. For example, fear may be triggered by the presence of several people because, at some time in the past, the individual has been made anxious in a social setting; or anxiety is aroused by the sound of quarrelling voices because, at some time, the individual was threatened by the belligerence of others. The task of treatment, therefore, is to sever this connection: to detach anxiety from the innocuous cue.

Some years ago the author was asked for help in removing an extreme fear of spiders in a lady so incapacitated by this anxiety that she was unable to perform household chores. Any article of furniture moved or corner dusted might dislodge one of these alarming creatures and so occasion acute anxiety. Being outdoors clearly also presented problems to this lady, although she recognized that her fear was actually groundless in the sense that none of the spiders she encountered, indoors or out, could actually harm her.

Questioning revealed that the fear she experienced could be broken down into a number of separate components which, in various combinations, could evoke either more or less anxiety. Size, for example, was an important variable: the larger the spider the more fear would be experienced. Similarly, blackness, hairiness, degree of activity, and proximity all affected the amount of fear experienced. It was possible, therefore, to describe 'spider situations' which would produce little by way of upset, and others which would create a good deal. A small, light-coloured, apparently hairless spider, quite dead and at some distance away, would cause only mild apprehension, while an active, large, black and hairy spider, galloping across her body, would produce a sense of panic.

One must begin, in desensitization treatment, with the least anxiety-provoking situation and as each of these ceases to produce anxiety, so one moves on to the next step in the hierarchy. In the spider phobic case quoted, one can obviously begin with exhibiting a small, dead, pale-coloured, hairless spider in one corner of the room, while the patient sits in the opposite corner. When this condition ceases to produce anxiety, then the insect can be moved a little closer or, alternatively, some characteristic can be changed (e.g. substitution of a slightly larger specimen) so that we have moved one notch up the fear hierarchy.

What is notable here is that each step in the hierarchy appears to produce a smaller reaction than was anticipated before treatment; it is as if accomplishing each step has resulted in some small but discernible loss in the total anxiety now experienced. This kind of psychological arithmetic applies with every step taken, so that the total amount of anxiety to be eliminated becomes less and less.

So far so good, but systematic desensitization involves some means of inhibiting anxiety at each stage, for only in this way can the anxiety connection be broken. Each hierarchical step, therefore, must be capable of producing some amount of fear, but this must be sufficiently small to be extinguished by some other feeling state, and the most convenient means of achieving this is to train the individual in muscle relaxation.

It is argued that muscle relaxation is in fact an ideal counter to anxiety feelings, since it is both easy to learn and very effective. In short, there is good evidence that one cannot be anxious and completely relaxed at the same time; relaxation effectively inhibits the experience of fear. Accordingly, such training precedes the hierarchical presentation of fear stimuli; the individual is instructed to remain as relaxed as possible each time the fear-stimulus is presented so that the experience of anxiety is controlled. In this way a new type of association is being learnt: that in the presence of certain cues which previously occasioned fear, no such feelings are present.

Understandably, while this method may work quite well it is not one which is easily put into practice in all cases. The various spider specimens needed to form the hierarchy may be easily secured, but in the case of, say, a fear of flying, there are serious practical problems. One could not, for example, easily arrange that the aeroplane merely completes the dash down the runway (as one item on the hierarchy) without actually taking off (which may occupy a very different hierarchical level). The necessary control over the situation here, and in numerous other cases, simply could not be achieved.

This problem is solved by presenting such situations as imagined scenes instead of as real-life experiences. This obviously makes it very much easier to arrange for events to accord precisely with treatment requirements and allows all the refined control over circumstances that one would wish to have. The only question to ask about this solution is that of whether or not dealing with an imagined situation is as beneficial as dealing with the real one. The evidence indicates that it is, although all therapists like to include experience of the real event (the real spider, lift, aeroplane, etc.) as a way of consolidating and affirming the new found absence of fear. Merely learning not to experience anxiety in imagined examples of fear aspects or situations, using the little-by-little approach and suppressing any worry by preserving muscle relaxation, can produce important changes in behaviour.

This approach is widely used in the treatment of major and incapacitating phobias with considerable success, but it is worth pointing out that less extreme conditions, including those commonly found in young children, respond very well to sympathetic handling along these lines. Fear of school, of being left by mother, of playing with strange children, of insects, of the car, and many others respond well to the graduated approach described and, of course, the benefit to behaviour generally of shedding such fears makes the effort well worth while.

•gnitive learning

It will be apparent from the description of the behavioural approaches given so far that they seem to depend upon a rather mechanical conception of learning. Insight, explanation, logic and other ways in which we come to modify or correct our view of things appear to count for nothing: the assumption is that we simply cannot talk anyone out of being alcoholic or experiencing acute anxiety; they must be taught to do so by a painstaking and carefully conceived programme of training which avoids any appeal to the 'mind'. Yet we are aware that cognitive learning does occur since we can behave differently as a result of being told that this or that is the case, or by receiving instructions to do something in a particular way. Indeed, if everything about our behaviour had to be acquired by trial and error or successive approximations, then learning would be tedious, slow and in many cases inefficient.

The charge often levelled at the behavioural approach is that it ignores the conceptual thinking that is so peculiarly and importantly human. But this is to misunderstand the situation since it is apparent that the kind of learning process required to effect change appears to depend upon what it is about our behaviour that we are trying to modify. Furthermore, it has been argued that mental events (cognitions, thoughts) are also behaviours and amenable to the same laws and, to an extent, the same training methods.

A good example is the technique called 'thought stopping'. Essentially this represents the attempt to produce the disruption or inhibition of a mental process in much the same way as some more overt activity might be stopped. It is usual to begin (see Wolpe, 1969) with a demonstration by the therapist that a sudden, unexpected and loud noise (banging the table, for example) can interrupt a particular focus of attention. In the same way, it is pointed out, an unpleasant and persistent idea can be interrupted and, with practice, might become permanently inhibited. By stages, t control of the interruptive signal is transferrred from therapist to patient and then from an external signal (banging on the table) to an internal one (saying 'stop' to oneself).

It is readily apparent that this strategy is direct, simple, and treats ideas or cognitions in much the same way as any reflex or motor action. There is, in the application of this technique, nothing special about mental events: they are simply regarded as internal behaviours.

A rather less rigorous behaviour approach is to be found in Rational Emotive Therapy; indeed, many hard-nosed behaviourists would reject any claim that RET derives from learning or conditioning theories and deny that there is any identifiable trace of the behavioural tradition in RET. Nevertheless, this cognitive approach has features which are 'behavioural' in character; for example, the emphasis upon the here-and-now rather than the influence of early life experiences, the parsimonious theoretical formulations, the implicit and explicit dependence upon reinforcing experiences and the directness of attack upon a clearly-identified source of malfunctioning. The main thrust of the technique (Ellis, 1962) derives from the assumption that faulty thinking is revealed in what people say to themselves; such 'self-talk' influences overt behaviours, so changing the cognitions can influence the way we act and feel.

Part of the immediate appeal of this technique lies in the very obviousness that 'self-talk' is a major preoccupation of us all when we are beset by difficulties. As a simple example, when girl informs boy that their relationship is ended a positive torrent of internal conversations is likely to be triggered: 'I am in a terrible mess ... I can't believe it ... there's no hope ... what can I do, nothing matters any more ...' etc. Such self-talk is likely to be accompanied by observable behaviour such as weeping, not eating or sleeping, refusing to socialize, failing to deal adequately with work assignments, and so on.

RET concentrates attention upon those things which are objectively true (e.g. 'she no longer loves me') and those which are not ('no one cares ... life is over ... there'll never be anyone else for me ...'). It is contended that when one is forced to examine the illogicality of deducing certain conclusions from the premise 'she doesn't love me', then shifts toward more positive emotions and behaviours have to occur. Attention is, of course, directed to all faulty ideas which serve as props for disappointment and disillusion: many of these quite commonplace errors of thinking which we are better rid of. For example, that one must always appear competent and without sign of weakness that one must always have evidence that one is loved, needed and approved of, or that any adverse comment mean that no one is to be trusted.

There is no doubt that this kind of counselling approach can help us to gain a perspective on life's bumps and abrasions and so prevent exaggerated and damaging emotional reactions. Yet there are obviously important limitations to an approach which depends so heavily upon exposing the illogicality of much self-talk; the point about such states of mind, as about prejudices of all kinds, is that they tend to be rather resistant to a logical approach. There is, it often seems, a strong desire to bring ideas into line with the feelings being experienced.

Furthermore, a cognitive strategy tends to pay little attention to the internal alterations of state which can often prompt the appearance of faulty ideas. Anyone with experience of depression will recognize that talking someone out of such a state is not just a tall order but pretty well impossible. No doubt where the pattern of gloomy thoughts and ideas arise out of what may be a purely environmental circumstance - a lost job, a failed exam, a lost love - a logical analysis of thoughts and feelings can be beneficial, but perhaps such circumstances are less common than one might at first suppose. Perhaps in part these environmental traumas are not random events but, to a degree, are visited upon those of us who are already vulnerable to an extent.

A cognitive technique which translates rather better from the traditional areas of behavioural concern to mental events is covert sensitization (Cautela, 1966). Basically, this method represents the application of aversive control to thoughts (as opposed to 'actions' such as drinking alcohol or operating a fruit machine) and involves imagined scenes of the unwanted behaviour followed by imagined noxious consequences. For example, the overweight gluttonous lady may be asked to conjure up images of a table groaning under the weight of delicious food, stuffing herself to bursting with cream cake and other goodies and then to create the mental picture of being sick: vomit spilling out over the table, over her dress, on to the food, and so on. In short, it is hoped to create the cognitive equivalent of real events with the consequences of overeating being highly unpleasant and embarrassing.

Another example comes from Foa (1976), whose male client derived sexual gratification from dressing in woman's clothing. This had brought him to the courts, where he was then referred for treatment. Covert sensitization took the form of requiring the patient to imagine that he was driving along in his car when he saw a clothes line on which desirable articles of clothing were hanging; he stops, gets out and attempts to take these clothes, but as he does so, he is overcome by intense feelings of nausea. He was then required to imagine throwing the clothes away and feeling very much better.

It is worth pointing out that in this case, as in other examples of aversive training, the unwanted habit returned again following an initially successful outcome. Generally, the therapist takes account of the need to deal with this problem by arranging 'booster' courses of treatment as and when the need arises.

Operant training

It is apparent from the accounts given that the behavioural approach to change is strongly hedonistic; organisms learn when rewarded and 'unlearn' when punished. Perhaps more th in any other technique of learning, operant training exemplifies this dependence upon the manipulation of the consequences of behaviour: a consequence which is rewarding (positively reinforcing) will strengthen some reaction or response, whilst one which is punishing will weaken and discourage further behaviour of the same kind.

It was not until B. F. Skinner's 1953 publication that there was any systematic account of the circumstances unde which rewards and punishments work best. Experimenting wi small animals, often rats, Skinner was able to demonstrate convincingly that if some observable piece of behaviour (response) was followed consistently by reward, the chances of the same behaviour occurring in a similar situation on subsequent occasions would increase. Similarly, if a response was punished, it would become less likely to occur. Three very important aspects of the apparently simple relationship between response and consequences arose from these animal studies. First, it is imperative that the reinforcement applied to the subject really is rewarding or punishing for them. A puff at a cigarette is obviously pleasant and rewarding to some humans but would probably prove aversive to most rats, whereas the dry food pellets enjoyed by rats would be of little interest to most humans. The second point was that, at least initially, the reinforcement (reward or punishment) must follow immediatel after the target response is performed. If we wish to increase the frequency with which a rat presses a lever, it is no use providing the reward half-an-hour after the response has occurred; the necessary association between lever-pressing and, say, food reward would simply not be made. Third, as well as being immediate, the reinforcemen must be applied consistently. Under all but very extreme circumstances, the rat does not learn to press a lever as a result of a single reward for doing so but needs numerous rewarded trials until lever-pressing is acquired. It is best to reward every trial initially, for although learning can take place if rewards (or punishments) are more spread out, it is very much slower. However, once learnt, a response may be maintained by occasional reinforcement.

Many psychologists have been attracted by Skinnerian research and have applied the rules to the modification of human behaviour. The degree of success which has been achieved has been surprising in view of the frequent criticisms of Skinner's approach as essentially simplistic and mechanistic. Perhaps the greatest changes that have be made in order to accommodate Skinner's system to work wit humans have been in response to the obvious superiority of their thinking, memory and reasoning as well as their capacity to use and to understand language. These skills have had most effect on the second aspect of reinforcement described above. As long as individual persons realize that reinforcement will be contingent upon their behaviour within a reasonable time, it may not be necessary for the reinforcement to be immediate. An individual will be able to think about or anticipate the delayed outcome. When working with children, however, some tangible reminder may be given of the reinforcement to come, such as a gold star immediately on completion of some school work as a token representing, say, extra playtime during the day.

The types of problems to which reinforcement procedures may be applied range from minor irritating habits to major disorders which threaten the well-being or even life of the sufferer. Many examples from the field of child-management may be cited to illustrate the least severe end of this scale.

Many young children go through 'phases' which are both worrying and irritating to their parents but usually not harmful in themselves. An example of this would be the temper tantrums fairly frequently observed in toddlers. In nearly all cases such episodes last a few weeks or at most months and then disappear of their own accord. In a few cases they persist much longer, or with greater severity, and perhaps begin to disrupt family life. Providing the cause is not due to some physical illness, one may attempt to modify the behaviour by applying appropriate reinforcements. Very often it is found that a great deal of attention is given when a child has a tantrum, usually because it is alarming and upsetting to the parents. On the other hand, when the child is occupied and behaving well, the parents, sighing with relief, turn their attention to other things, effectively ignoring good behaviour. Evidently the child is being rewarded for having a tantrum but is punished (as being ignored can be aversive) for being well behaved. With these contingencies it is no wonder that such behaviour becomes more frequent and good behaviour becomes rarer. Tantrums may be modified simply by reversing reward and punishment; parents leave children to their own devices when they have a tantrum but take great care to play with them and talk to them when they are being good. Applied systematically, such a straightforward alteration of reinforcements can have amazingly rapid and beneficial effects.

Even relatively minor behaviour problems in children may have more serious effects on their eventual welfare. One form of difficulty that has been tackled fairly often in this way is disruptive classroom behaviour. Children who are frequently out of their seats, moving around and making a noise, usually benefit less from their schooling than their more appropriately behaved peers and are likely to fall behind with their work. In addition they may become unpopular with their companions as they upset the others' work and interfere with their games. In busy classrooms, such children are often reprimanded by teachers when they are a nuisance but receive very little attention for being 'good' since this occurs infrequently and they rarely produce work of a high enough standard to merit praise. Relatively mild chastisements from the teacher may be more rewarding for child (being preferred to no attention at all) so the child is rewarded for being disruptive and ignored for practically everything else. As with the younger child, the task is to reverse the contingencies. In this case it may not be possible for the teacher to ignore the bad behaviour entirely but, usually, the amount of time and effort spent in the reprimand can be reduced significantly so that the child receives a minimum of attention for each disruptive act. At the same time reward is given for appropriate behaviour and an acceptable (although possibly lower than average) standard of work. If possible, the reward is given immediately with attention and praise but may be supplemented by the use of stars or marks for good conduct, and these tokens can be exchanged for privileges at the end of the day. Usually the co-operation of not only the teacher and pupil but also of the entire class is required to make this procedure fully effective.

The much-publicized condition of anorexia nervosa is an example of a life-threatening state which may sometimes be ameliorated by the use of reinforcement procedures. Patients suffering from this disorder are most commonly girls in their mid- to late-teens who have begun to diet excessively, and now refuse to eat and sabotage attempts to feed them by hiding the food or vomiting. Many lose so much weight that they must be confined to bed. The main management problem is to reinstate eating.

There is no single acceptable account of why a girl begins to become anorexic but there is commonly evidence of considerable social reinforcement for not eating once serious dieting is under way, since serious weight loss causes friends and relatives to become increasingly concerned and respond to refusals to eat by attention and attempts to coax and persuade, and this attention contributes to the maintenance of not eating. Attempts have been made to make positive reinforcement contingent upon eating rather than not eating and, to do this, the patient has been socially isolated and denied pleasures such as radio and television in order to maximize the rewarding effect of social contact. It has been arranged that a friendly therapist will eat each meal with the patient and converse with her when, and only when, she eats a mouthful of food. Once eating a meal has been established, the reward is made less immediate by allowing the patient to earn time with the therapist or friends after the meal has been eaten. She is also allowed access to television, etc., in the same way. This kind of procedure has been found to produce important weight gain in a number of patients. When described in outline it may appear that the patient is the passive recipient of reinforcement, unaware of the contingencies that have been planned, but this is far from the case, as most patients become involved with the preparation of their programmes, the negotiation of weight targets, amounts to be eaten, planning rewards and agreeing to contingencies.

It is clear that reinforcement contingencies can be applied effectively to a wide range of behaviour problems in humans. As long as the contingencies are appropriately rewarding or punishing, and the consequences fairly immediate and consistent, the reinforcements are likely to be effective, but the chances of success will be increased if the individuals with the problems are involved in the construction and discussion of their own management programmes.

conclusion

Behavioural approaches to change tend to lack appeal when compared to other methods. We would prefer, for example, to think that we are amenable to logic and reason and that if only the facts are made available to us we could change to be in accord with them. Or, in other contexts, we may find the dramatic aspects of psychoanalysis more compelling, with the eccentricities of human behaviour being explained as the result of mysterious and excitingly interesting forces. Certainly, behavioural approaches stand in sharp contrast and seem to inspire all the excitement of Latin conjugations!

On the other hand, while the techniques admittedly tend to apply about as well to animals as to Man, their clarity and simplicity arises from sound experimental work and scientific thought, qualities which in any other context would be thought commendable. It is worth while to offer the example of bedwetting as a means of showing how such thinking offers distinct advantages over a more tortuous and complex account.

Psychoanalysts are inclined to regard bedwetting as merely the external sign of some inner turmoil. It has been regarded, for example, as a substitute for sexual gratification or a means by which a child can express aggression and resentment toward others. The behavioural formulation is starkly simple; individuals learn to be dry at night and some fail to acquire this skill. If the former view is correct, then simply removing the behaviour (bedwetting) would not cure the inner discontent; if the behavioural view is correct, however, then getting rid of the symptom would be a very useful thing.

Mowrer's simple device to unlearn bedwetting (Mowrer and Mowrer, 1938) was in fact highly successful and is very widely used today. It deals directly with the symptom and in most cases bedwetting is eliminated. The process of urination is remarkably complex from a neurophysiological viewpoint, but the essential feature from a treatment point of view is that urination occurs in spurts. If the saline content of an initial spurt is used to close a circuit which rings a bell and wakes the child, urination is inhibited and the child is able to go to the toilet. Initial success is, of course, rewarding and a cumulative process ensues which eliminates bedwetting altogether. No evidence exists of any underlying pathological process of the kind postulated by the psychoanalyst.

Naturally one example of a greater claim to effectiveness does not establish the general superiority of the behavioural approach, yet it does seem that such examples ca[n] be multiplied many times over. This is, in fact, what one would expect from a model constructed from painstaking laboratory experimental work and scientific formulations.

It is not, of course, that the approach or the techniques deriving from it, some of which have been briefly reviewed here, are either wildly successful or beyond criticism. There are, indeed, numerous difficulties and shortcomings and, as indicated earlier, one of the most serious of these is the partiality of the purely environmentalist viewpoint and the almost complete neglect of genetic/constitutional influences. Nevertheless, behavioural strategies now occupy a position of high importance for psychologists, and the influence of these strategies in many and diverse areas of application is still growing.

References

Cautela, J.B. (1966)
Treatment of compulsive behavior by covert sensitization. The Psychological Record, 16, 33–41.
Dawkins, R. (1978)
The Selfish Gene. Oxford: Oxford University Press.
Ellis, A. (1962)
Reason and Emotion in Psychotherapy. New York: Kyle Stewart.
Foa, E.B. (1976)
Multiple behaviour techniques in the treatment of transvestism. In H.J. Eysenck, Case Studies in Behaviou[r] Therapy. London: Routledge & Kegan Paul.
Jones, M.C. (1924)
The elimination of children's fears. Journal of Experimental Psychology, 7, 383–90.
Mowrer, O.H. and Mowrer, W. (1938)
Enuresis: a method for its study and treatment. America[n] Journal of Orthopsychiatry, 8, 436–59.
Munroe, R.L. (1955)
School of Psychoanalytic Thought. New York: Dryden Press.
Pavlov, I.P. (1927)
Conditioned Reflexes (Transl. Anrep). London: Oxford University Press.
Rachman, S. (1966)
Sexual fetishism: an experimental analogue. The Psychological Record, 16, 293–296.
Seligman, M.E.P. and Hager, J.L. (1972)
Biological Boundaries of Learning. New York: Appleton-Century-Crofts.
Skinner, B.F. (1953)
Science and Human Behavior. New York: Macmillan.
Vila, J. and Beech, H.R. (1978)
Vulnerability and defensive reactions in relation to the human menstrual cycle. British Journal of Social and Clinical Psychology, 17, 93–100.

Voegtlin, W.L. and Lemere, E. (1942)
The treatment of alcohol addiction. Quarterly Journal of Studies on Alcohol, 2, 717-803.

Watson, J.B. and Rayner, R. (1920)
Conditioned emotional reactions. Journal of Experimental Psychology, 3, 1-14.

Wolpe, J. (1969)
The Practice of Behavior Therapy. New York: Pergamon Press.

Questions

1. Describe the theoretical underpinnings of systematic desensitization as a treatment strategy to eliminate fear.
2. Drawing upon your personal experience, describe and discuss the incapacitating effect of anxiety on coping with a life problem you have had to face. Outline the behavioural strategies that might be useful in overcoming it.
3. Describe the process of classical conditioning and how this process can account for the development of abnormal fears.
4. What are the implications of classical and operant conditioning for a crime prevention policy?
5. Describe the limitations of using aversive therapy as a means of changing behaviour.
6. What are the basic differences between 'cognitive' and behavioural strategies where behaviour change is concerned?
7. In what sense can the behavioural approach be said to be hedonistic?
8. Responses and consequences are the two basic elements of operant training. What are the basic requirements in providing reinforcement in order to secure effective behaviour change?
9. To what extent do you think that we are affected in real life situations by the operation of reinforcement principles?
10. How could one apply an operant approach in a classroom to deal with disruptive class behaviour?

Annotated reading

Griffiths, D. (1981) Psychology and Medicine. London: Macmillan and the British Psychological Society.
This is primarily intended for GPs and students to enable the medical profession to acquire concepts relevant to their work so as to facilitate professional skill and expertise. Many of the topics covered will be of interest to the occupational therapist.

Kanfer, F.H. and Goldstein, A.P. (1975) Helping People Change: A textbook of methods. Oxford: Pergamon Press.
An account of practical behavioural approaches to change.

Oakley, D. and Platkin, H. (1979) Brain, Behaviour and Evolution. London: Methuen.
> Undergraduate level synthesis of disciplines relevant to psychology. How the evolutionary perspective can help our understanding of psychological questions.

Rachman, S. (1971) The Effects of Psychotherapy. Oxford: Pergamon Press.
> An account of the problems associated with psychotherapy and the way in which the behavioural approach deals with issues of treatment and training.

Walker, S. (1976) Learning and Reinforcement. London: Methuen.
> Introductory text on key concepts to understanding behavioural approaches to change.

Exercises

1. Changing verbal responses by positive and negative reinforcement

What we say, and the words we use, can depend upon the rewards and punishments afforded. This experiment examines the effects of reward (positive reinforcement) upon the use of a chosen verbalization. You will need to collect data carefully from a number of subjects in this project.

THE TASK: 100 cards (filing or index cards) are prepared by writing on each one of them the same five names, say George, Robert, Philip, Gordon, James. The names should appear in random order on these cards (i.e. the order in which they appear is varied).

Every subject is told that this is a test involving constructing sentences, each of which must begin with one or other of the names appearing on the card and should make use of the verb printed below those names. For example, a card like this:

Joan   Mary   Janice   Lucy   Vicki

LOST

might produce the sentence 'Janice lost her handbag on her way to work'. Each subsequent card shown, of course, bears the same five names (in random sequence) but a different verb for each card.

PROCEDURE. At the outset you will choose one name to re-inforce positively (say, Gordon) and set out to increase the use of this name. In short, your reinforcement is aimed at producing a change in the subject's verbal behaviour.

The reinforcement should be given when the 'correct' name is given, this being in the form of the word 'good', 'fine', a confident and encouraging 'yes', and so on. The use of any other name by the subject is not accompanied by any remark from you at all.

RESULTS. We should find that increasing use is made of the positively reinforced name. In order to determine this, leave the first 20 trials without any comment at all and only begin to introduce the reinforcements on trial 21 (or whenever the reinforceable name is used thereafter). Stop after 50 or so trials are completed.

The use of each name can be plotted for each of the subjects used in your project. All subjects can be combined together in one graph to show an 'overall effect' of reinforcement on the name chosen.

The same experimental method can be used to study changes in verbalizations in a number of contexts. Think of other ways in which you can test the influences of this kind of reward on verbal behaviour, perhaps in 'free' conversation.

This type of experiment illustrates the power of what are called 'social reinforcers' (as opposed to the tangible ones we often think about as rewards, such as money). Although relatively unobtrusive, social reinforcements affect our behaviour to a considerable extent, and this type of exercise will help you to become more aware of their presence and effectiveness.

COMMENT. Obviously what is being investigated represents only a rather restricted aspect of the general point and the 'test' itself appears somewhat artificial. Indeed, it may well be that a person asked to take the 'sentence construction test' will easily spot the contingency (i.e. approval quickly follows the use of one particular name). This does not matter too much since the exercise is only intended to give practical form to the systematic application of positive reinforcement. The points to bear in mind are:

1. Care in preparing the material. Here two things are important:

* the names appear in 'mixed-up' order. In this way we are trying to ensure that the choice of name will depend upon the reward given for using it, rather than upon any other factor;
* that the index cards are well prepared, clear and legible, and a good selection of common verbs is employed.

2. The administration of the social reinforcement is difficult, but crucial. The general idea is to make some utterance (even 'um hum' will do) which signifies approval ('um hum's can, of course, be approving or the opposite, depending on how they are uttered).

3. The social reinforcer should be given as closely as possible after the 'correct' name has been used. If a long rambling sentence is given, using the reinforcer at the end of the sentence gives a reduced opportunity to connect any name with the pleasant consequences.

4. Try to administer the reinforcement as naturally as possible. The increase in the use of the reinforced name is quite compelling if the subject has remained 'unaware' of what is happening, and a stylized application of the reinforcement is sure to alert the subject.

5. Make sure 'hits' and 'misses' are recorded. A simple code of recording when a reinforcement has been given will do very well.

6. Prepare a graph of the results, using 'blocks' of, say, ten trials to record the information.

7. Consider the means by which any increase in the use of a particular name can be discouraged (how can the new response level be subjected to extinction?).

2. The effects of relaxation training on psychological discomfort

You will recall that relaxation is an important part of desensitization treatment. It is also quite beneficial in its own right and often used by people to calm themselves when faced by examinations or interviews, and so on. The skill can be acquired to an extent by following the instructions given. It would be useful to check on the value of relaxation in connection with some slightly upsetting task you may need to perform, for example, talking to someone w usually manages to rub you up the wrong way, or making a visit to the dentist. The sequence involved in this project is:

1. Identify a situation such as those depicted and which you will be encountering about two weeks hence.

2. Rate how upset you expect to become on a scale such as

Not at all   Slightly   Moderately   Very   Extremely
I------------I------------I------------I-----------I

3. Practise relaxation training, say, once each day for about two weeks.

4. Relax as much as possible, drawing upon your training, when in the upsetting situation.

5. Check the degree of upset you actually experienced and compare this rating with the pre-relaxation training level.

3. Relaxation training

Here are a few simple exercises to try.

GENERAL

Choose a quiet place to train, where you can be quiet, comfortable and warm. Lying on a bed or couch is preferable.

Loosen tight clothing. Do not strain muscles in the exercises. Consult your doctor if you are in doubt about any relevant medical condition.

SPECIFIC

1. Make a fist and hold right arm out, straight and stiff. Keep these muscles 'tight' for a few seconds, then let go and allow your arm to rest by your side. Let all tension out of this arm.

2. Repeat with left arm. Relax.

3. Repeat first with right and then with left leg, raising each leg about nine to twelve inches above the bed to perform the 'stiff leg' exercise. Relax.

4. Take a deep breath, hold this for ten seconds, and concentrate on the sensations of tension in chest walls. Let this breath out slowly. Allow breathing to become shallow and effortless.

5. Brace stomach muscles (as if you were preparing to receive a blow to the stomach). Hold this tension for ten seconds. Let go and relax.

6. Bring your shoulders across your body toward the midline of your chest. Hold the tension created for a few seconds, then let go; relax your muscles completely.

7. Clench your teeth tightly, feeling the large muscles 'bulge' at each side of your jaw. Hold for a few seconds, then let go and relax these muscles completely.

8. Wrinkle your nose, purse your lips, and screw up your eyes; activate all the muscles of the face in this way, hold for a few seconds, then allow these muscles to relax completely.

9. Raise your eyebrows as far as possible toward your hairline. Hold the tension for several seconds, then relax completely.

These exercises should each be repeated two or three times in each practice session. When tensing muscles, concentrate on that tension; when relaxing focus upon the alteration in your muscle state. Try to become vigilant in detecting undue and unwanted tension; for example, when driving, cleaning teeth, vacuuming, and so on.

11

Motivation
Philip D. Evans

Poetically speaking, motivation may be considered to be about the 'springs of action'. More prosaically, motivation theorists ask themselves why any bit of behaviour occurs: what are the necessary and sufficient conditions which make any organism, human or animal, in the ever-flowing stream that constitutes behaviour give up one activity and take up another?

In everyday life, people answer essentially motivational questions by giving 'reasons' or 'intentions' for their actions, but these are often given after the event and cannot be said to 'explain' behaviour in any scientific fashion. The psychologist is more interested in specifying conditions beforehand which, if they pertain, inevitably lead to a prediction that some behaviour probably will (or will not) occur. Where do we find these all-important conditions? Traditional wisdom, in the case of human behaviour, has until this century always taught us that the answer to questions about why we behave lies inaccessibly in the mind, whatever that may be. The mind wills the body, and since the will is supposedly free, we might as well give up any attempt to predict human behaviour! Fortunately the work of Charles Darwin changed all that and all animal behaviour, including human behaviour, became fair game for systematic and scientific enquiry. Like other areas of psychology, then, empirical research in the field of motivation has been largely a twentieth-century endeavour. First of all, let us briefly sketch in the historical aspects of our subject matter.

Historical perspective

When Ivan Pavlov (1849-1936) discovered the phenomenon of the 'conditioned reflex', the scene appeared to be set for explaining all behaviour as the sum of responses and conditioned responses, which in turn could be traced inexorably back to their controlling stimuli. The answer to the question 'What motivated that particular response?' would simply be: 'that particular stimulus'. This was the revolutionary behaviourism preached in the 1920s by the American psychologist, John B. Watson.

In the 1930s, this strident behaviourism was somewhat moderated by the ideas of Clark Hull, perhaps the most

influential theorist of motivation and behaviour right up to
the 1950s. Like Watson, Hull believed that all behaviour
could be seen as stimulus-response chains. However, he was
also influenced by the work of an earlier psychologist,
Thorndike, who had shown how animals can learn to solve
certain problems by 'trial and error' if successful responses were reliably followed by important consequences
such as food for a hungry animal or escape for a confined
one. Hull believed that such consequences 'reinforced' a
connection between a stimulus and a response and built it
into a habit. In trying to define the nature of reinforcement of this kind, Hull committed himself to a belief in
internal mediators of behaviour, hidden sources of motivation. Briefly, he believed that physiological needs
resulting from deprivation of food, water, etc., brought
about a general motivational state within the organism
called 'drive' which goaded it into activity. When such
activity finally resulted in the animal finding a source of
satisfying the need, drive reduction would take place. It
was this drive reduction which Hull identified as the basis
of reinforcement. Thus, for Hull, the performance of any act
was the result of two basic types of variables: the strength
of the habit being considered and the motivation, resulting
from drive, to perform the habit. The two variables were
assumed to act multiplicatively; thus if drive is zero,
the animal will not perform the response however well it
'knows' how to perform it: that is, however great the habit
strength. Conversely, the animal will not perform the response however great its motivational drive if it does not
know how to perform: that is, if habit strength equals
zero.

This theoretical approach may seem over-simplified and
applicable more to laboratory rats in simple mazes than
human beings in more complex situations, but Hull assumed
that more complex motives could be acquired by association
with more primary ones, through conditioning procedures of
a Pavlovian kind.

One of the major embarrassments to Hull's early theory
came from findings which suggested that, even in the case of
simple animals in mazes, sources of motivation could not be
confined to the internal drive variable. It appeared that
the reinforcer itself seemed to have incentive properties,
which acted to 'pull' the animal towards a goal, as much as
the assumed drive force was taken to 'push' it there. An
animal's running speed to a goal would reflect, for example,
the quantity and quality of the reinforcement given. Hull
did not like the mentalistic notion that animals could be
motivated by expectations of some future event in the goal
box, but he was forced to admit a new motivational term into
his theoretical model to account for such incentive motivational effects. The fact that he phrased such incentive
effects in mechanistic stimulus-response language reflects
only a bias of vocabulary.

The modern era

Hull's intention had been to build up a complex and general model of all motivated behaviour, human and animal. Despite increasing complexity the endeavour failed. Prediction on such a grand scale was impossible. The modern trend within psychology as a whole has been to develop mini-theories which can tell us something useful about more limited areas of behaviour, and particularly human behaviour. Whereas Hull had been content to speculate that human motives could be ultimately traced back to biological imperatives shared by all organisms, that formidable task of tracing the development of motives has lost ground to theories which simply assume motives, arising perhaps out of particular human needs, demonstrate that the strength of the motive can be effectively measured, and then propose predictions about how such specified motives interact with an environmental context to produce behaviour related to that motive. The approach is still vaguely Hullian, but by being more narrow in its scope offers greater opportunity for useful application. There are two areas of research which illustrate this. First, work on achievement motivation, that is, striving behaviour in human beings: this is described immediately after a general theory of human needs is outlined. Second, research in the field of anxiety as a motive is examined. The research in both areas has been done with human beings and has scope for application. Lastly, we return to the animal laboratory to show that results from that quarter can themselves be very illuminating when discussed in the context of human problems.

Maslow's theory of human needs

Maslow, like Hull, believed that actions spring from needs but, unlike Hull, was not interested in the derivation of all needs and motives from a few primary biological survival needs. Rather he put forward the interesting idea that the major human needs could be put into a hierarchical order. Having done this, he postulated a theoretical prediction that needs higher up the 'ladder' would only produce striving for fulfilment when those lower down the ladder were satisfied. His category order from lowest to highest was:

* biological survival needs: for example, need for food, water, oxygen, etc.;
* safety needs: for example, need to avoid danger, need for security;
* affiliation needs: for example, love, friendship, acceptance by others;
* self-esteem needs: for example, self-acceptance, success in life;
* self-actualization needs: for example, achievement of one's full potential.

Although Maslow's ideas were not earth shattering, they were put forward at a time (just after the Second World War) when people were becoming receptive. Particularly ready to receive them were the growing number of management training establishments. Managers of industry were of necessity becoming interested in the question of what motivated people to work in modern society where it had to be taken for granted that survival needs would be taken care of by at least a token Welfare State. Nineteenth-century notions of keeping a person at work by keeping the wolf of hunger at the door were no longer practically or ethically possible. Maslow's theory was soon taken up by business schools particularly in the USA, and was used to generate ideas about how work conditions could be arranged to satisfy higher-level needs, rather than just provide a pay-packet at the end of the week. Applied researchers were stimulated to ask whether a particular job allowed affiliative needs to be satisfied; alternatively, did another job foster a sense of personal responsibility which could satisfy self-esteem needs?

Although Maslow's theory could not be said to be predictive of behaviour (it is too general for that), it was generative of much piecemeal research which paid dividends in terms of productivity and job satisfaction. It was also a reference point for later, more specific, theories of work motivation which related performance to an interaction between non-monetary need variables and monetary incentive variables (see Murrell, 1976).

Maslow's views of human motivation have also been taken up in the field of psychotherapy. Traditionally, psychotherapy has been concerned with resolving, in Maslow's terms, problems with affiliative and self-esteem needs. Maslow's theory, however, hints that people who are reasonably well satisfied with respect to these needs will inevitably turn their attention to satisfying self-actualization needs: that is, fulfilment of full potential. The idea that so-called 'normal' people may seek 'therapy' to help themselves along the road to full growth is no more than a necessary corollary of Maslow's theory. It is less than surprising, therefore, that the human 'growth' movement, with its encounter groups and sensitivity training groups and so on, should have grown up particularly in the rich state of California, where lower-level needs may have been satisfied to a point of boredom!

Achievement motivation

If Maslow's theory of needs lacks predictive power and is instead a useful and productive way of looking at human behaviour, the same is not true of the next motivational theory, which does generate quite specific predictions about how different people react in different situations. In many areas of life one could point to standards which define excellence, achievement, success. A person's motivation to achieve these standards has been called 'need achievement motivation' or nAch for short. One of the pioneers of research in this area, McClelland, was the first to demonstrate that a person's hidden reserves of nAch could reliably be measured by looking at their fantasy life in certain controlled conditions. By using a 'personality test', in which the person invented stories around certain pictures on cards, McClelland found that he could score these stories for the number of achievement-related themes in them. The scores which resulted were reliable enough to differentiate low nAch people and high nAch people. More importantly the scores also had validity: that is, they would to an important degree predict real differences in 'striving' behaviour in real contexts of an achievement kind. In the laboratory, for example, high nAch subjects could be shown to persist longer at some task or other than low nAch subjects. Outside the laboratory, studies have shown that high nAch subjects are more likely to be 'up-wardly socially mobile' in terms of changing socio-economic status, while low nAch subjects are more likely to stay still, or even move down the scale.

However, it became clear to the early researchers that achievement-related behaviour was powerfully affected by more than just the nAch motive. In particular, certain subjects seemed to behave in such striving situations as if their primary motivation was to avoid failure rather than simply succeed. By using a questionnaire to measure this 'fear of failure' trait, it was possible to make predictions about real achievement behaviour in a more exact fashion. Atkinson, one of the foremost of modern motivation theorists, proposed a modified theory of achievement behaviour, incorporating two major motives, nAch and fear of failure, together with certain contextual variables, notably the perceived probability of success (or failure), and the incentive (or 'negative incentive': 'shame' if you like) associated with success (or failure). The probability variables are related in a complementary way to their respective incentive variables. This is common sense in a way, since if a task is very easy (i.e. the probability of success is very large), then the incentive attached to succeeding is not very high. Conversely, if the task is very difficult (i.e. the probability of success is low) the incentive, or kudos, attached to succeeding is correspondingly high. Now if we look at how the theory works in principle we find that it gives rise to some quite specific predictions. Consider first those individuals whose need to achieve (nAch) is dominant over their fear of failure. Their tendency to approach a task or strive at it is going to be maximized when the probability of success multiplies with the incentive value to give the highest overall result. If, as we have said, probability of success and incentive are intrinsically related and therefore:

$$\text{Incentive value} = (1) - (\text{probability of success})$$

then it is clear that the multiplicative product of the two variables is at its greatest when probability of success is 0.5 and the incentive is also therefore 0.5 (i.e. 1 - 0.5).

All that really needs to be understood is that high nAch subjects, relatively speaking, are predicted to show a real preference for tasks of middling difficulty. Now let us consider the person whose dominating motive is to avoid failure. Where the probability of success is 0.5, so obviously is the probability of failure. Also, if the probability of failure is 0.5, the negative incentive or shame of failing is 0.5 (i.e. 1 minus the probability of failure). Thus the person's avoidance tendency is maximally aroused in exactly the same situation as that which attracted the more nAch-orientated person. Once again, regardless of the mathematics, the prediction is that people whose fear of failure is stronger than their level of nAch will show a preference for either very easy tasks or very difficult ones, but definitely avoid ones of middling difficulty. If the prediction that such a person may seek out very difficult tasks seems to you paradoxical, then just remember that in such tasks the negative incentive or shame of failing is very low; such a person may be considered to have a 'get-out' clause which allows people to say, 'He didn't succeed, but it was very difficult and at least he tried.'

So much for the theory. Are its predictions borne out? In the laboratory, a simple test is to ask subjects to play a hoop-la game of throwing a ring over a peg. In such a situation, the probability of success is clearly largely influenced by how closely one stands to the peg. When given a free choice, dominant nAch subjects showed a much greater propensity to stand a middling distance from the peg than did dominant fear-of-failure subjects. However, Atkinson's theory stands up to examination not just in the laboratory but in the world outside.

Achievement motivation in classroom and college
One of the perennial discussions in education is whether to 'stream' or not. Is mixed ability teaching to be recommended or not? Well, it is not our intention here to give any full answer to the question but it can be shown that Atkinson's theory is of relevance. Let us assume that a child very reasonably gauges the probability of success in academic matters by reference to classroom peers. This means that a child who is in a class of corresponding ability range is more likely to put the probability of success (and probability of failure) not far from 0.5. Our theory predicts that this is ideally motivating for a child whose motivation towards achievement is greater than any fear of failure, but is the worst situation for a child whose two compelling motivations are balanced the other way. In fact, O'Connor tested out the theoretical predictions and largely verified them, both with respect to interest in school work and measures in academic improvement. It should be said that motivational effects of the type of classroom situation are not the only variables which may be important when this controversy is debated; however, anyone's performance is a mixture of ability and motivation, so such motivational factors deserve attention.

Atkinson's theory has also been applied in higher education. Researchers have examined the choice of options that students take in college. Options were first of all classed as easy, middling, or difficult. Students were then measured both in terms of nAch and fear of failure motivation. Once again the predictions were upheld. Students who were relatively high in nAch tended to go for options of middling difficulty, whilst this tendency was not pronounced in the students who were relatively strong on fear-of-failure motivation.

Lastly, some research has been done into how achieveme[nt] motivation and fear-of-failure motivation influence career choice. Mahone has shown that students whose dominant motivation is nAch are more realistic in their career choices, whilst those students higher in fear-of-failure tend to be unrealistic by going for too easy and unchalleng-ing careers or, alternatively, aiming too high for their abilities.

Can we talk of achieving societies?

The originator of nAch research, McClelland, has tried to investigate this question by examining the literature of different societies and societies at different times with a view to measuring the amount of achievement themes shown, just as for an individual his fantasy stories are examined. Some fascinating results have been reported. Measures of nAch taken from literary sources do predict economic per-formance. For example, nAch themes in English literature from 1500 to 1800 correspond in their ups and downs very well with economic performance as measured by coal imports into the port of London. In the USA, nAch between 1810 and 1950 rose and fell in tune with the number of patents issued per million of population. Even non-literate societies have been measured for nAch by analysing achievement themes in vase paintings and orally-transmitted folk tales!

The really interesting finding to come out of this work is that changes in nAch typically occur some years before the subsequent change in economic performance. Hence it is possible to make some predictions for the future. According to nAch measures the USA, for example, peaked in nAch around 1945, so the outlook is pretty gloomy for subsequent economic performance! However, all this work is extremely tenuous. The studies are all correlational in nature and difficult to interpret without a degree of arbitrariness. They are crucially dependent on measurement which is diffi-cult to assess in terms of its reliability. And yet it must be said that McClelland's recent work is stimulating, and his claim that scientists should turn away from 'an ex-clusive concern with the external events of history to the internal psychological concerns that in the long run determine what happens in history' is worthy of consider-ation.

nxiety as a motive

We all know individuals who claim to act better when goaded with a bit of 'adrenalin', as the saying goes. Actors claim to give their peak performances when anxiety is there to give them a helping hand. Equally there are many (students taking exams, for example) who claim that anxiety is responsible for poor performance. What then is the truth? To predict the effects of anxiety we have to specify more variables. First, we obviously must take into account the level of anxiety experienced. Second, we must expect that the type of task being considered is important as a variable. Third, whatever the level of anxiety likely in the situation, we should expect some difference in the level experienced by different people: that is, it is to be expected that people have different capacities for being aroused in an anxious way by identical situations.

Let us deal with the simple relationship first between level of anxiety and performance. If we think back to Hull's notion of drive, it is clear that we can consider anxiety a source of drive or, some might say, general arousal of the organism. Now there is a long-standing law in psychology which relates drive to performance by a so-called 'inverted-U function'. This is simply illustrated in figure 1.

Figure 1

The inverted-U function relating drive to performance

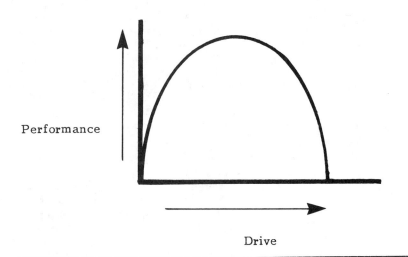

Performance

Drive

The predictions that this law makes are equally simple. Other things being equal, performance will be enhanced by increasing drive, but only up to a certain point. Beyond this, further increases in drive will lead to poorer and poorer performance. We can assume anxiety, then, acts broadly in this fashion. However, we should still like to know a bit more. When, for example, is the peak of the inverted U likely to be met? This is where it is important to consider our other factors, such as the nature of the task and the nature of the person. One of the major ways tasks differ is in their difficulty. Spence and Taylor, two psychologists who may be described as latter-day Hullians, did a series of experiments to shed light on how high-anxiety and low-anxiety persons were differentially affected by tasks which were either easy or difficult. Without going into too much theoretical detail, let us say something more about drive. Drive is taken to be a non-directive general pushing force and hence is taken to energize incorrect performance as much as correct performance. The prediction was made, therefore, that in an easy task, where incorrect responses are not much in evidence, high anxiety serves mainly to energize just the correct responses. Therefore Spence and Taylor predicted that high-anxiety subjects would perform such tasks better than low-anxiety subjects. In the case of a difficult task we can assume that incorrect responses are constantly competing with correct ones and that high levels of drive are counter-productive in the sense that they serve only to energize further such incorrect responses. The prediction, therefore, was that low-anxiety subjects would outperform high-anxiety subjects in such tasks. These predictions were in fact upheld in the laboratory tests. Moving outside the laboratory, then, we may speculate that actors may thrive on anxiety because they are performing presumably well-rehearsed material; our exam-taking student is, on the contrary, having to create novel and creative essays by integrating knowledge on the spot, and anxiety here is likely to be disruptive.

Recent trends in 'trait' motive research

Most of the work so far described could be classified as 'trait' motive research. In other words, psychologists have adopted the approach of measuring some assumed stable characteristic of personality, a trait which has motivational properties, such as nAch or anxiety. Within this tradition a large amount of integration is now under way. The work of Spence and Taylor, for example, is considered within the same framework of theory as that of Atkinson. New motives are being measured and entered into ever more complex equations to predict performance with more accuracy, often with the aid of computers.

There is another aspect to the modern trend, however, which needs to be mentioned, and that is the questioning of the unity of these assumed motives. Nowhere is this more in evidence than in the case of 'fear' or 'anxiety' as assumed single entity motives. Motives are usually felt (it is no accident that motivation and emotion share the same Latin root!) and it is when we try to measure that felt emotion or motive at the individual level that we run into difficulties. Clinical psychologists, for example, have learnt a lot recently about phobic reactions and their treatment; and yet, as they find out more, they have increasingly come to question the traditional view that the motive of fear motivates the avoidance behaviour which is the essence of a clinical phobia. The point is that fear is not a 'lump' (see Rachman, 1978); it is divisible. Some people show fear by reporting that they feel afraid, but show no fear in their behaviour. Others show fear by their physiological reactions, such as a pounding heart and clammy hands, but report that they are not feeling fear. There is, in other words, often a non-correspondence between the different measures that we have traditionally conceived as indicating fear. The message, in the case of individuals at any rate, is that the measurement of an assumed single unitary motivational trait is full of pitfalls. This is to some extent, then, a limitation of the type of research strategy that we have been describing so far. Note, however, that we say limitation rather than criticism. To be capable of reasonable prediction of the behaviour of broad types of people in a reasonable variety of situations is no mean achievement. The work described so far has demonstrated that such prediction is possible.

The reinforcement view of motivation: no hidden motives

We promised at the beginning to return to the animal laboratory for an assessment of the relevance of that work to motivational questions. We mentioned then that one of the embarrassing findings for Hull's early theory was that the incentive or reinforcement which followed a response had motivational properties in its own right. The way in which different patterns of responding in an organism can be motivated and maintained by different patterns of reinforcement has been of central interest to that body of researchers who, broadly speaking, have followed in the footsteps of the celebrated psychologist B. F. Skinner. The literature which has accumulated is so vast that we can here do no more than give one or two examples and refer interested readers elsewhere, if they like the flavour of what they read.

Let us dive straight in with an example of a problem which might be faced by any marketing man. You have a product called 'Superchoc' which you want to promote. You devise a traditional promotion campaign which requires your young consumers to collect 20 wrappers, send them in, and be reinforced by the gift of a Superchoc plastic space-ship. Can this basic strategy be improved upon? Let us look at the animal laboratory. Your technique so far resembles that in which a rat is trained to press a bar 20 times for one sugar-pellet reward. The ratio of responses to reinforcement is fixed at 20 to 1; that is, in psychologists' terms, the

rat is on a fixed-ratio 20 schedule of reinforcement. Now w
know that all organisms respond in the same sort of way on
fixed-ratio schedule. The pattern of cumulative responding
is given below in figure 2.

Figure 2

**The typical scalloped record of cumulative responding
obtained on a fixed-ratio schedule.** The schedule is FR20,
and instances of reinforcement are shown by slashes.

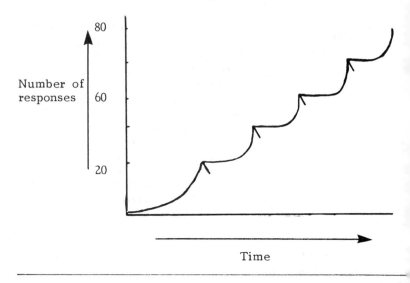

Note that after each reinforcement the organism takes
a break; there is a lull in responding shown by a scallop on
the graph. In terms of your marketing problem, these
scallops represent unprofitable periods which you could do
without. Now there are easy ways of removing scallops by
making the reinforcement come after a varying amount of
responses, but this method is not applicable in this case,
nor would it motivate more vigorous (buying) behaviour
overall. Let us then adopt a different method. Let us
redefine the problem by considering it in terms of two
schedules, one superimposed on the other. First we say that
one response is going to be made up of five of our previous
responses, and that the organism has to make four of these
larger unit responses in order to get the reinforcement. In
terms of the rat in the laboratory, what we do is to give it
some sort of signal, perhaps a tone or a light, after each
five bar-presses which signals that it has made one composite response; when it has made four composite responses it
gets its food pellet. In the case of the marketing problem,
we say that five wrappers get a certificate and that four
certificates earn a space-ship. Well, you might say, nothing
has really been changed: the same number of wrappers are
finally exchanged for the same amount of reinforcement. Th

may be so, but the two methods of going about the exercise motivate very different patterns of performance and in the case of the second method, the lull that we talked about is shortened and performance as a whole is more vigorous; a worth-while thing to know in applied contexts.

Note that this area of research is not concerned with 'hidden motives'. It is solely interested in how behaviour patterns can be predicted from a knowledge of the way behaviour is externally reinforced. It must be said that individual differences are largely ignored, which is the very opposite of the 'trait' motive research that we have previously dealt with. On the other hand, when one is interested in motivating behaviour of large numbers of people, on the average so to speak, it is perfectly possible to ignore individual differences in the certain knowledge that one's reinforcement contingencies will by and large have the predicted results.

The reader who wishes to explore further this entire area, known as the experimental analysis of behaviour, should consult any major text such as Rachlin (1976).

Conclusions

Let us try now to pull together some theoretical strands. Motivation is a potentially vast and wide-ranging area of psychology. Traditionally it has been about the causes of action. There are two traditions which have defined the major approaches to the study of motivation. One sees action as a result of an interaction between current environmental variables - the context of the act, if you like - and a motivational tendency within the organism. Such a tendency may be considered a convenient fiction since no one supposes that motives are real things like tables and chairs; to talk of a motive is to use a kind of shorthand for referring to a relatively stable propensity for engaging in certain acts.

The other broad tradition is the Skinnerian approach mentioned latterly and perforce briefly since it takes motivation into almost a new field altogether. If we think of behaviour as output, the Skinnerian would have us believe that all output can in principle be predicted from a knowledge of input in terms of environmental observables, with no necessity to ask what goes on inside the organism. Motivation as traditionally conceived is rather redundant. Motivation becomes at once everything and nothing.

The former approach which does allow for the term 'motive' stems directly from the Hullian tradition. Note how similar Atkinson's theory is to Hull's. Probability of success is like habit strength and both reflect the capability of the organism; nAch is like drive and reflects the motivational push to perform; finally, both admit an incentive variable which also motivates the organism towards a goal. All three variables interact in both systems in a broadly multiplicative fashion.

Both approaches have proven to be useful and lastly we should perhaps point out that in certain areas, notably choice of behaviour where an organism has a choice of activities, it is becoming evident that their predictions are essentially the same (see Atkinson and Birch, 1979). Perhaps, like so many differences of approach and theory, eventually our two traditions described here will be seen to differ solely in their vocabulary, terms, and ways of putting the argument.

References

Atkinson, J.W. and Birch, D. (1979)
An Introduction to Motivation. Princeton, NJ: Van Nostrand.
Murrell, H. (1976)
Motivation at Work. London: Methuen.
Rachlin, H. (1976)
Introduction to Modern Behaviorism. San Francisco: Freeman.
Rachman, S.J. (1978)
Fear and Courage. San Francisco: Freeman.

Questions

1. What do you understand by the term 'drive' as used by psychologists? Discuss its merits and demerits.
2. We have to 'interpret' a stimulus before we react to it as that particular stimulus. Do we have to interpret our motives before we act on the basis of that particular motive?
3. How do nAch and fear of failure work together in determining the extent to which different people approach achievement-orientated situations?
4. Write an essay on the motivational properties of reinforcers and 'secondary' reinforcers.
5. What can psychologists working in the animal behaviour laboratory tell us about motivating changes in behaviour patterns in individuals and groups of individuals by the operation of reinforcement principles?
6. Are some societies more 'motivated' to achieve than others?
7. Examine the proposition that motives can be measured by looking at fantasy themes.
8. Why might anxiety give the edge to one person's performance and take the edge off another's?
9. What human needs underlie the motivation of human behaviour?
10. Is fear a unitary motive?

Annotated reading

Atkinson, J.W. and Birch, D. (1979) Introduction to Motivation. Princeton, NJ: Van Nostrand.
This book covers the area of human motivation well from the point of view of internal trait motives interacting with environmental contingencies. It fills in the details of recent research in achievement motivation and allied topics. At times the mathematical statements of theory might be too much for certain arts-biassed

students, but the essential logic - all that is needed for an introductory appreciation - is clear.

Evans, P. (1975) Motivation. London: Methuen.
This is a short book which should not present the reader with any difficulty. It is very much a theoretical-cum-historical overview of approaches to the study of motivation, leaving it to other texts, such as the one above, to fill in details of particular approaches. It also has chapters on instinct and on biologically based motivations such as hunger, thirst, sex, and sleep. This might interest a student who wishes to extend the chapter's coverage at a still introductory level.

Rachlin, H. (1976) Introduction to Modern Behaviorism. San Francisco: Freeman.
The best introductory book for the student who is interested in following up the idea mentioned in the chapter that 'Motivation = Reinforcement'. In line with that view, it is no surprise that the word 'motivation' does not occur in the index! (Reinforcement, however, does.)

xercises

1. Thematic apperception

From colour supplements or other magazines select pictures which represent work or study themes. Paste the pictures on separate backgrounds. You will need either a tape-recorder to tape your conversation with subjects, or a response sheet on which the subject can write. Tell your subject that you want a story made up about the characters depicted in the picture. You then guide the story by asking a series of questions: 'Who are these people?'; 'What are they doing?'; 'What has happened just before the picture was taken?'; 'What is X (one of the characters) thinking?'; 'What is Y (etc.) thinking?' and so on. Encourage your subjects to talk freely and let their imagination reign. Intersperse supplementary questions among the main questions. Many subjects will become absorbed in story-telling very quickly; others will need some encouragement. Be careful what feedback you give. Do not forget the rationale for this technique: it is supposed to enable individuals to project their innermost thoughts on to the material, so subjects may well ask for reassurance that they have 'done well', or that their story is 'normal' and so on. The good experimenter will reply that the purpose of the exercise is to get different stories from different people and that there is no right or wrong answer.

Once you have collected, say, six stories on the same material, you will need to find two independent judges to rate the thematic content. From what has been said in this chapter you should be able to rate each sentence in the subject's replies on, say, a three-point scale: highly achievement-orientated (2), moderately achievement-orientated (1), or neutral (0). Because subjects will have produced material of differing lengths you will not be able simply to add up the total achievement motive score. One approach could be to express the number of non-neutral and achievement-motivated responses as a percentage of the total number of responses for each subject. If you have two judges and six sets of materials you will then be in a position to examine the reliability of the judges. This is done by comparing either the order in which they rank each subject's material, or even in terms of the absolute or percentage scores assigned to each set of material. You can plot the correlation between judges on a scattergram (Judge 1 on the ordinate, Judge 2 on the abscissa). Note that the two scores may correlate well but may be out of line with each other in a consistent way. That will be because on of the judges has a consistent bias to overrate or underrate the material. If the judges have a reasonable degree of agreement, you can then ask questions about the performance of the original subjects; for example, is there great variation in achievement-related content? Knowing the subjects (if you do) can you account for this variation? If subjects were a mixture of males and females, were there any consistent sex differences?

2. The hoops test

Place a stick vertically in the ground and mark the ground at, say, one, two and three metres from the stick. Give each subject, say, six hoops. Then set up a reward/loss table in which you vary the possible gains or losses associated with successfully throwing the hoop on to the upright stick. For example, succeeding from a metre away will be easier, but could gain only a small reward for success. The furthest distance will have the lowest chance of success but a reward which exceeds the total possible for six close-up throws with perhaps only one successful throw. You can, of course, vary the possibilities of success and reward in a variety of ways, including loss of reward from an initial bonus. After subjects have finished their attempt with the six hoops, ask them to explain their choices. How did people balance the promise of reward against the fear of failure? Can you calculate the probabilities involved? If you know the individuals well, how does their performance on the hoop test relate to their strategies in other contexts: for example, on the sports field or when playing games of chance?

3. Job motivation

Take a piece of paper and divide it vertically down the middle. Head one column 'Things I would like about a job' and the other column 'Things I wouldn't like about a job'. Then compile the two lists. Sometimes it is useful to treat likes and dislikes as bipolar constructs; for example, 'working with machines/not working with machines' may allow an entry in both columns; other entries may not have an opposite which comes to mind immediately. You can either compile the lists separately or simultaneously. Once the list is complete, you will have to face the hardest part of the task. One rarely gets everything one wants in life and every job will have some perceived disadvantages. You now have to rank each positive and negative feature in order of importance; that is, 'the aspect I would like most/second best' and so on, and 'the aspect I would dislike most/second best' and so on. The exercise should tell you a great deal about yourself. One thing you might try doing is to see what combination of favourable and unfavourable characteristics would suit you. For example, what is there on the list of dislikes which you would accept, given a very large salary; under what conditions would you be willing to work unsociable hours; would you be willing to make sacrifices in terms of salary early on for a job which brought rewards after a very long period of training, and so on?

4. Becoming aware of basic needs

Maslow's theory tells us that lower-order needs have to be satisfied before we can move on to higher-order needs. If you live in a society where basic needs are typically satisfied without an exceptional struggle, then there must have been very few occasions on which you did not have at least one square meal a day. The aim of this project is to sensitize you to what it might feel like if you were unable to expect a proper level of food intake. If you are fit and healthy and have no medical disorder affecting diet, try to go without food for a whole day. After a few hours of fasting you will find that you think about food in new ways. Pass by a baker's shop or a greengrocer's. Does the food look very different to you? Has there been a change in the things you think about during the day? Do thoughts of food intrude into other thoughts, about work, leisure, and social relationships? Some charitable organizations invite their members to eat only limited amounts of food on one day in the week, so that they can experience the hunger felt in underdeveloped countries. In his chapter Evans suggests that it was no coincidence that Maslow's theory became popular in California, where salaries and access to life's essentials allow for the satisfaction of lower-order needs. To what extent does your experience during your day of fasting lead you to agree with Evans' views?

5. An analysis of moral themes in children's readers

Take a children's reader series and analyse it for moral content. You will find that your local library will have early reading material, either in the form of a series which increases the order of reading difficulty, starting with very young children and ending with, say, 10 year olds, or a set of related story books or short stories. According to McClelland, the content of these books will not be neutral. You should be able to find models of behaviour which are seen as desirable and undesirable. There may be evidence of sex stereotyping; that is, what are the sorts of things which little boys and girls are expected to enjoy helping

Mummy and Daddy do? What sorts of games do children play
Are characters depicted as 'good' or 'bad', and if so, in
what ways? Are there unstated rules for the ways in which
people should relate to each other? Are certain goals in
life seen to be more worth achieving than others? According
to McClelland, the content of children's readers reflects
the moral temperature of the times. If at all possible, try
to obtain readers written, say, 50 years ago. Your elderly
relatives may have kept books from their own childhood. Are
there detectable differences in their content? You might
also try reading a story to a young child and then asking
about some of the themes in the story: for example, 'Why
did no one like the giant?'; 'Was the witch very naughty?
Why?'; 'Why does Sally like helping Mummy in the kitchen?';
'Why does Johnny help Daddy to clean his motor car?'; or
'Why were the robbers put in prison?' When you interview the
child try to detect whether the norms implied in the story
are seen as universal and given. Think about other sources
of influence on the child's beliefs and attitudes.

12

Learning and teaching
David Fontana

Learning can be defined as a relatively persistent change in an individual's possible behaviour due to experience. It is thus clearly distinguished from those changes in behaviour which come about as a consequence of maturation (i.e. as a consequence of the individual's physical growth and development). Learning can take place either as a result of informal circumstances (e.g. parent-child relationships, interaction with friends and with the mass media), or as a result of the formal efforts of society to educate its members through schools and academic institutions. Though both are important our main concern is with the latter: that is, with the ways in which the teacher or the tutor can best monitor and assist learning within the class or lecture room.

Bruner (1973) considers that in dealing with learning activities the teacher must take account of three important variables, namely the nature of the learner, the nature of the knowledge to be learnt and the nature of the learning process. Accordingly we adopt this threefold division as a way of structuring the present chapter, taking each of the variables in turn and examining the major factors associated with them.

The nature of the learner

There are a number of factors within individual learners that influence their ability to learn. Best known of these are cognitive factors such as intelligence and creativity, but there are many others of equal relevance. These include affective factors, motivation, age and sex, study habits and, above all perhaps, memory.

Affective factors
Psychologists take the term 'affective' to cover all aspects of personality. One of these aspects which has particular importance for learning is anxiety. From general experience the teacher soon discovers that a mild degree of anxiety in a pupil can be a useful aid to learning, but that too much anxiety has an inhibiting effect (particularly if the learning task is a complex one). We see this particularly in a student preparing for an important examination, or in a student fearful of the anger or ridicule that failure in a particular task may invite from unsympathetic tutors or

classmates. The anxiety consequent upon these stressful situations interferes with both learning and performance, and results are produced way below the individual's potential. Closely linked to anxiety as an affective factor is the individual's self-esteem. Research studies show that individuals with low self-esteem (i.e. with a low regard for their personal worth and abilities) consistently set themselves artificially depressed learning and attainment goals, and consistently perform less well than individuals of similar intelligence and background who enjoy high levels of self-esteem. It appears that low self-esteem subjects are so fearful of further blows to their self-regard that they set themselves low goals in order to avoid the chances of failure.

High and low self-esteem can be referred to as a dimension of personality. Another such dimension that has implications for learning is that of extraversion-introversion. Typically the extravert is an individual who enjoys change and variety and is orientated towards the external world of people and experiences, while the introvert is more concerned with stability and the inner world of thoughts and feelings. All of us find our place at some point on this dimension, and the evidence suggests that those who incline towards the two extremes learn best in different kinds of learning environments. The extravert tends to favour groups and social activities, with plenty of variety and fresh stimuli, while the introvert generally prefers more ordered individual activity. Thus a particular learning failure may be due less to any lack of ability on the part of the learner than to the fact that the working environment is not really suited to relevant aspects of that learner's personality. On occasions teachers or tutors may also tend to favour pupils whose personalities approximate to their own, with the extravert complaining that an introverted pupil is too quiet, and the introvert complaining that an extraverted pupil is too noisy.

Motivation
Satisfactory learning is unlikely to take place in the absence of sufficient motivation to learn. We have already mentioned one possible source of motivation, namely a degree of anxiety, but there are many others. For convenience we can divide these into intrinsic forms of motivation, which come from within the individual, and extrinsic which are imposed by the environment. Taking intrinsic first, it is axiomatic that people work generally harder at learning tasks that interest them than at those that do not. If we had to say why a particular thing captures a person's interest we would probably argue that it has some direct relevance to the individual's daily life. It either diverts or amuses in some way (and thus makes the person feel better) or it enables him to cope more effectively with the problems and achieve the ambitions in his daily life. No matter what the subject, however, there is often the danger that learners are asked to tackle theoretical issues whose

practical application escapes them, or to work towards goals that are too remote or not of their own choosing. Whilst of course students cannot be the arbiters of what they should or should not learn, it is important that tutors who wish to appeal to intrinsic motivation should be fully aware of the concerns and aspirations of their students, and should demonstrate clearly the way in which the proposed learning relates to them.

Nevertheless, however stimulating the teacher, there will always be occasions when intrinsic motivation is insufficient and recourse has to be made to motivation of an extrinsic kind. Such motivation usually consists of marks, grades, examinations, and of course tutor praise and approval. Success in these areas builds up prestige in the student's own eyes and standing is enhanced in the eyes of others. Students find that success is rewarding. It builds up expectations which they have to work harder and more purposefully to fulfil. Thus extrinsic motivation can be highly effective, but it raises a number of important considerations (quite apart from the obvious fear that it may raise anxiety to an inhibiting level).

*   Instead of success, some individuals experience only failure. This tends to produce either the low self-esteem to which we have already made reference, or a rejection of everything to do with the formal learning tasks offered through educational institutions. Such rejection is a defensive attempt to protect self-esteem by insisting that it is these tasks that are at fault rather than the individuals themselves (i.e. it is a way of saying 'I could do it if it was worth doing'). To combat the harmful effects of consistent failure the wise tutor provides students with opportunities for success at however low a level. Through such opportunities students gradually build up new self-images and new attitudes to work, and are encouraged progressively to set their sights higher.
*   Sometimes motivation suffers because students are not supplied with prompt knowledge of results. The longer the gap between performance and the provision of this knowledge, the greater the chance that students will lose interest in the whole exercise.
*   Competition between students is a useful extrinsic motivator provided they are all of a similar level of ability and can all experience a fair degree of success. Co-operation, where students adopt group norms and work together to achieve them, can be of even more benefit.
*   Wherever the pressures of extrinsic motivation are too strong students may resort to strategies like feigned illness (or even cheating) to avoid the consequences of failure.

Age and sex
The ability to tackle complex learning tasks increases throughout childhood. Both Piaget (cf. Inhelder and Piaget,

1958) and Bruner (1966) have demonstrated that children appear to go through a number of stages in the development of their powers of thinking, and that unless learning tasks are presented to them in the form appropriate to their particular stage they may be unable to understand what is required of them. For example, before children reach what Piaget calls the stage of formal operations (usually at approximately age 12) they are strictly limited in their ability to engage in abstract thinking, and can only handle concepts when they have experienced them in some practical sense (e.g. they can deal with weight and number, which can be practically experienced, but not with density and volume, which require to be defined more theoretically). On the basis of this kind of evidence it seems that the individual's powers of thinking reach maturity during adolescence, and we know that measured intelligence and memorizing abilities also appear to have reached their peak by the end of this period. Much less is known about the subsequent decline of these powers and therefore of the ability to learn. There certainly appears to be a general slowing of the rate at which the individual can learn many mental and physical skills throughout adult life, and this decline may have reached significant proportions in people not involved in academic work by the mid- and late-twenties. In those constantly using academic skills, however, the decline may be more gradual, and may be amply offset by greater self-discipline, higher motivation, and the increased ability to organize learning that comes through experience.

Just as the ability to learn is influenced by age variables, so is it influenced by sex. Girls are generally more verbal than boys at school age, and have fewer reading, speech, and general behaviour problems (Davie, Butler and Goldsmith, 1972), while boys are more advanced in number skills. These differences tend to disappear by the age of 16, however, and boys between five and ten years of age appear twice as likely to show an increase in measured intelligence as girls (Kagan, Sontag, Baker and Nelson, 1958). Throughout school life, however, girls tend to be better all-rounders, while boys are better at the subjects they enjoy and spurn those they do not. These sex-related differences could be in part genetic and in part related to the home (where girls are generally taught to be more dependent and more concerned for adult approval), but recent research in the USA suggests that they could also be due to the fact that most early school teaching is done by women, and boys therefore come to associate school with feminine values. Where such teaching is done by men, the higher rate of backwardness and school rejection shown by boys tends to disappear. Sadly, at all ages, girls tend to show lower self-esteem than boys, and may artificially depress their level of performance in conformity with an outmoded and unfortunate social conception of the inferiority of the female role.

Memory

Clearly, learning depends intimately on memory. At the
practical level psychologists recognize the existence of two
main kinds of memory, short-term and long-term. All information received by the senses and to which we pay attention
seems to enter short-term memory, but it can be held there
briefly and is either then forgotten (as when we look up a
telephone number and forget it the moment we have dialled
it) or translated to long-term memory where it can be held
more permanently (though it is still, of course, subject to
forgetting). Obviously this transfer is vital for effective
learning. Available evidence suggests it involves some form
of consolidation, typically a short pause during which the
information is held consciously in the mind. Even after an
interesting lesson or lecture students often remember
little, probably because each piece of information is so
quickly followed by the next that there is no time for
consolidation. However, a number of strategies exist for
helping consolidation and for increasing the efficiency of
long-term memory generally.

* By pausing, repeating and questioning, the lecturer can
  prompt students to dwell sufficiently upon material for
  transfer from short- to long-term to take place.
* By putting material to immediate practical use consolidation is also greatly helped. Material that is interesting, and that is properly understood, is also more
  likely to be remembered than is material which is
  perceived as dull or irrelevant.
* By practising overlearning, material is made particularly resistant to forgetting. Overlearning implies
  the continued revision of a learning task even after it
  appears to have been perfected, and is particularly
  valuable where the material has to be remembered in a
  stressful situation (e.g. in the examination room or on
  the concert platform).
* By associating new material with something that is
  already familiar, or with something that is particularly
  striking or novel in itself, the chances of its being
  remembered are greatly improved. Through the association
  with something that is already familiar the material is
  placed within context, and can be recalled readily when
  cued in by this material in future; through the association with something striking the material tends to be
  remembered when this striking stimulus is called to
  mind. This is particularly true if the stimulus is a
  visual one: hence the importance of visual aids. Such
  aids need not necessarily be closely linked in terms of
  meaning with the material to be learnt (witness the
  highly successful advertisements on commercial television), but they must be presented concurrently with
  this material so that a strong association is built up.

In discussing memory, it is important to stress that there

appears to be a functional difference between recognition (where we spot as familiar some stimulus physically presented to us) and recall (where we have to retrieve some word or fact from memory itself). Recognition appears to come more readily than recall (e.g. it is easier to recognize a face than to recall a name, to recognize a work in a foreign language than to recall it from memory), and in consequence, unless we are deliberately setting out to test recall, it is of value to provide appropriate cues that bring recognition to the aid of recall.

So much for the factors that aid long-term memory. Now for those that appear to interfere with it. One of these, anxiety, has already been touched upon. Material that can readily be recalled in a relaxed state may prove elusive when one is under stress. Two others of importance are known as retroactive and proactive interference respectively. Retroactive interference occurs when recently learnt material appears to inhibit the recall of that learnt earlier. The phenomenon appears to take place at all levels of learning, and is apparent, for example, in students who cram for an examination and find that the facts they learnt the night before keep coming back when attempts are made to recall those studied earlier in the week. Proactive interference, on the other hand, occurs when earlier learning seems to block the recall of later, as when students start learning a second foreign language and find themselves unable to remember the word they want because the equivalent in the first language keeps coming to mind. We discuss ways of minimizing retroactive inhibition when we deal with study habits below, but proactive inhibition is only likely to be a problem when the two subjects being studied share certain similarities, and it tends to disappear as the new material becomes more familiar and overlearning takes place.

Finally, we come to the subject of memory training. It is often assumed that the memory can be trained, like a muscle, if we exercise it (e.g. by learning large chunks of poetry). There is no evidence, however, that this assumption is correct. The memory is improved by learning how to memorize rather than by the simple act of memorizing itself. We have already listed some of the skills relevant to this task, and reference is made to others in the next section, but we should perhaps mention here the value of mnemonic devices. These are devices created specifically to aid recall, and range from simple tricks like tying a knot in a handkerchief and short jingles like 'thirty days hath September ...' to the elaborate devices used by stage 'memory men'. One such device is the so-called peg-word system, where the digits 1-10 (or more) are each associated with a rhyming word (e.g. 1 is bun, 2 is shoe, 3 is a tree, etc.). These simple associations are learnt, and then the facts to be memorized are associated with them in turn, preferably using visual imagery. Thus, for example, if we wished to learn the agricultural produce exported by New Zealand we could visualize first butter spread on a bun, second a lamb wearing shoes and so on. Such devices are remarkably effective in the learning of long lists of facts, though their use beyond this is limited.

Study habits

Much of the effectiveness of learning depends upon good study habits, particularly in older students who have to take more responsiblity for their own work. Some of these habits, like working in an environment free from distraction, are obvious while others, like overlearning, have already been covered. We can summarize the remainder as outlined below.

* REALISTIC WORK TARGETS. Realistic work targets, which the student plans in detail, are far more effective than impossibly ambitious or vague commitments. Ideally these targets should be expressed publicly (so that prestige is at stake if the student fails to stick to them!).

* REWARDS. Small rewards, built into the student's work schedule, can be very effective in helping sustain effort. These can take the form of a cup of coffee, for example, or a five-minute break at the end of each hour of solid work, with the purchase perhaps of an inexpensive though coveted treat each time weekly or monthly targets are met.

* PUNCTUALITY. Work should be started promptly at the appointed hour. This forestalls the elaborate (and plausible) strategies we each develop to delay actually sitting down at our desks and getting on with it.

* WHOLE AND PART LEARNING. A new learning task should be read through first in its entirety to get the general drift of it before being broken down into small units and learnt methodically.

* ORGANIZING MATERIAL. Often textbooks (and lectures) do not present material in a way which accords best with the learner's own experience and understanding. Time spent reorganizing the material into notes that render it generally more comprehensible and assimilable is time well spent.

* REVISION. A programme of phased revision throughout the duration of a course is of far more value than an attempt to cram everything in during the final weeks before an exam. Retroactive inhibition (and increased anxiety) are the almost inevitable consequences of such cramming. Phased revision, however, leads to a growing mastery of the whole course as students work their way through it, with each new piece of knowledge being placed in its proper context. When it comes to final examination preparation the student is therefore looking back over material that has already been overlearnt. Revision is best done before material has actually been forgotten. This is known as maintenance revison.

The nature of knowledge to be learnt

Obviously in any learning activity we have to consider not only the abilities of the learner but the nature of the new material. Equally obviously, this material must be organized in such a way that learning is facilitated, and in such a way that we can assess afterwards whether the desired learning has taken place or not. In considering such matters we have first of all to decide the level at which we wish learning to take place. Do we want the learner simply to learn facts, or do we want him to operate at higher levels and understand these facts, and be able to put them to use? Bloom (1956) has presented us with a comprehensive list of the various levels at which learning can take place, and this list is an indispensable aid in all matters relating to the planning and assessment of learning. The list arranges the various levels in hierarchical order, from the simplest to the most complex. Each of the higher levels subsumes those inferior to it (e.g. learning at level 3 involves learning at level 1 and 2 as well), and we can summarize them in ascending order. It will be noted that this taxonomy, as it is called, relates only to thinking skills (or skills in the cognitive domain). Other taxonomies exist which cover aspects of personality (the affective domain: see Krathwohl, 1964) and physical skills (the psychomotor domain: see Simpson, 1972), but these are of less immediate relevance for our purpose.

Levels of learning in the cognitive domain (after Bloom et al, 1956)

* Knowledge (i.e. simple knowledge of facts, of terms, of theories, etc.).
* Comprehension (i.e. an understanding of the meaning of this knowledge).
* Application (i.e. the ability to apply this knowledge and comprehension in new and concrete situations).
* Analysis (i.e. the ability to break material down into its constituent parts and to see the relationship between them).
* Synthesis (i.e. the ability to re-assemble these parts into a new and meaningful relationship, thus forming a new whole).
* Evaluation (i.e. the ability to judge the value of material using explicit and coherent criteria, either of one's own devising or derived from the work of others).

Having decided the level at which we intend to work, the next step (both for the tutor and for the student planning his own study programme) is to define the precise outcomes (or objectives) that our learning is intended to achieve. This is often one of the hardest parts of the exercise. Frequently learning objectives make the mistake of simply outlining what is to be done rather than concentrating upon why it is done. The best way to avoid this error is to remember that a learning objective should state the behaviour expected from a student as the result of a lesson. Thus, for example, we would not write that our objective is 'to demonstrate a particular skill (whatever it may happen to be) to the class', but rather that at the end of the lesson the students should be able to do one or more of the following (depending upon the level at which we intend learning to take place):

* to recognize and identify the elements involved in the skill (these elements would then be specified - this is an objective at the knowledge level);
* to define these elements and to know the part they play in the skill (an objective at the comprehension level);
* to practise the skill itself (an objective at the application level);
* to describe what is happening - and why - during this practice (an objective at the analysis level);
* to utilize elements of this skill in solving a particular novel problem (an objective at the synthesis level);
* to assess the degree of success achieved in this solution and to propose improvements (an objective at the evaluation level).

It can be readily appreciated that, once a clear objective (or objectives) has (or have) been stated at the beginning of the lesson plan, the tutor is in a much better position to determine the lesson content and to keep it practical and relevant. It is also easier to assess whether learning has taken place or not at the end of the lesson, since it is specified in advance that student behaviour will provide evidence of that learning. An assessment is a major topic in itself, as we now turn to it in more detail.

Assessment

Much assessment takes place simply observing student behaviours, or by directing questions at students, but often the tutor wishes to provide a class with specially devised opportunities to demonstrate whether their behaviour has changed in the desired direction or not. The tutor's choice of which opportunities to offer (i.e. of which assessment techniques to use) will be influenced by the level (in terms of the taxonomy discussed above) at which it is intended learning should take place. All too frequently, particularly in arts and social science subjects, assessment simply takes the form of a written essay, which may be appropriate for gauging progress at the more complex cognitive levels but which samples only a very limited range of knowledge and comprehension. The main alternative to the essay is the so-called objective test, each of whose items carries only a single right answer. Such items are usually of the multiple choice variety, with the student being asked which of a range of possible answers is the correct one: for example, 'The Theory of Association was first advanced by; Herbart/ William James/Francis Galton/none of these'. It will be noted that multiple choice questions test recognition; if it was desired to test recall, the question would be allowed to stand on its own without the addition of the possible answers.

It is often claimed that objective tests take the tutor longer to construct than tests of the essay type. There is no gainsaying this, but on the other hand they are quicker to mark, and teachers are left with the satisfaction of knowing that they have adequately tested the knowledge that they set out to test. Further, students are motivated to acquire this knowledge since they know that it is to be comprehensively tested, rather than fractionally sampled as in an essay. They are also left with the reassurance that good marks really do mean that they know the field and are equipped with the basic grammar of the subject.

The nature of the learning process

Having looked at the learner and at the knowledge to be learnt we now come to the last major variable, namely the process (or methods or techniques) by means of which learning actually takes place. Gagné (1974) suggests that the learning act involves a chain of eight events, some internal to the learner and others external. These events are, in their usual order of occurrence:

* motivation (or expectancy);
* apprehending (the subject perceives the material and distinguishes it from the other stimuli competing for his attention);
* acquisition (the subject codes the knowledge - i.e. makes sense of it, relates it to what is already known);
* retention (the subject stores the knowledge in short- or long-term memory);
* recall (the subject retrieves the material from memory);
* generalization (the material is transferred to new situations, thus allowing the subject to develop strategies for dealing with them);
* performance (these strategies are put into practice);
* feedback (the subject obtains knowledge of results).

Where there is a failure to learn, Gagné argues, it will take place at one of these eight levels, and it is thus the task of tutors to ascertain which. It may be that the learning has failed to capture the pupils' attention, or it makes no sense to them, or they have failed to transfer it to long-term memory, or they are unable to recall it from their memory. Analysing learning failure in this way renders tutors much better able to help the pupil since it enables them to concentrate upon the specific point at which the pupil appears to be going wrong. Frequently, too, they may discover that the fault lies not simply with the pupil but with the way in which the learning task has been presented - and explained - to the pupil.

The manner in which this presentation should be effected depends again upon the level (in terms of Bloom's taxonomy) at which we intend learning to take place. Where we are concerned with levels 1-3 (knowledge, comprehension, and application) then the strategy derived from the experimental findings of Skinner (e.g. Skinner, 1969) is of most help. Skinner's work indicates that factual knowledge and its comprehension and application is normally absorbed most efficiently if it is presented to the learner in small steps, each of them within his competence; if he is then required to demonstrate this learning in some way; and if he is given immediate knowledge of results on whether his demonstration was correct or not. In the event of failure, the whole procedure is repeated. This strategy cannot only be put to efficient use by teachers in their direct deal-ings with pupils, it also lies at the heart of what has come to be known as programmed learning. Programmed learning uses either specially written textbooks or rolls of paper mounted in simple learning devices to present each unit of learning in turn to individual learners, to question them on it, and to inform them whether or not their answers to questions are correct. An example of an item from a programme on electrical wiring illustrates this clearly.

Stage 1 (information): In wiring a 13 amp plug the brown
    wire is connected to the live terminal.
Stage 2 (question): Which colour wire is connected to the
    live terminal of a 13 amp plug?
Stage 3 (answer): A. the blue; B. the brown; C. the green
    and yellow.
Stage 4 (results): The brown wire is connected to the live
    terminal of a 13 amp plug.

This example tests recognition in Stage 3 by offering the three possible right answers, but of course these could be omitted if we wished to test recall.

    This learning procedure involves what Skinner calls operant conditioning in that at each point it involves, after the presentation of the information to be learnt, a stimulus (the question), an item of behaviour (the student's answer), and a reward or reinforcement (the knowledge of results). This operant conditioning (or S-B-R) model lies behind all learning, claims Skinner, and where there is learning failure this is normally because we have omitted to present the appropriate stimulus or, more frequently, the appropriate reinforcement. For many pupils immediate and accurate knowledge of successful results (remember that Skinner advocates presenting material to pupils in small steps, each one within their competence) is sufficient reinforcement, but for others teacher approval, good marks and grades, and even small physical rewards (e.g. where the child is retarded or handicapped and cannot understand the significance of marks and grades) may have to be used. Similarly, where incorrect learning has taken place, Skinner claims this can also be due to misapplied reinforcement. The parents or teachers, for example, fail to realize that the very fact of their attention (whether angry or not) is a powerful reinforcement for some children. Thus the more scolding the adult directs at the child's misbehaviour the more persistent it may tend to become. The correct procedure would be to ignore children when they produce this behaviour and reward them with attention when they show behaviour of the opposite, desirable kind. This approach is part of a range of strategies based upon conditioning theories (and known collectively as behaviour modification techniques) which are attracting increasing attention in educational and clinical circles.

Many psychologists, however, though granting the effectiveness of Skinner's approach at the first three levels in Bloom's taxonomy, consider it an inadequate basis for prompting learning at the higher levels. Learning at these levels involves more than a mere knowledge of the facts and formulae produced by other people (the so-called middle language of the subject); it involves the ability to discover the fundamental logic underlying the subject. Bruner (1966) argues that to help students achieve such discovery we must present them with problems and challenges, with questions that contain an element of controversy and contradiction. Such questions, known as springboard questions, introduce material which does not quite fit in with the student's accepted knowledge and beliefs. A 'level 1' question, such as 'What is the population of Britain?' or 'What is the formula for water?' demands nothing from the student beyond a single answer delivered in the form in which it was first heard. A springboard question, on the other hand, such as 'The poles are equidistant from the equator, yet the south is colder than the north; why?' or 'Christianity teaches you that you should love your enemies, yet men have committed terrible massacres in its name; why?' prompts students to reflect on the subtle ways in which their subject works, on the relationship between cause and effect, on methods of procedure and enquiry. The same is true of simulation exercises, which present learners with imaginary problems designed to mimic those faced in real life by social workers, nurses and economists, for example, and ask them to produce solutions. These solutions are then compared with genuine case histories, and comparisons and contrasts are drawn which promote debate, understanding, and the efficient workings of memory.

References

Bloom, B.S. (1956)
Taxonomy of Educational Objectives. Handbook 1: The cognitive domain. London: Longmans Green.
Bruner, J.S. (1966)
Towards a Theory of Instruction. Cambridge, Mass.: Harvard University Press.
Bruner, J.S. (1973)
The Relevance of Education. New York: Norton.
Davie, R., Butler, N. and Goldsmith, H. (1972)
From Birth to Seven. London: Longmans.

Gagné, R.M. (1974)
Essentials of Learning for Instruction. Hinsdale, Ill.:
Dryden Press.

Inhelder, B. and Piaget, J. (1958)
The Growth of Logical Thinking from Childhood to
Adolescence. London: Routledge & Kegan Paul.

Kagan, J., Sontag, L., Baker, C. and Nelson, V. (1958)
Personality and IQ change. Journal of Abnormal and
Social Psychology, 56, 261-266.

Krathwohl, D.R. (1964)
Taxonomy of Educational Objectives. Handbook II: The
affective domain. New York: David McKay.

Simpson, E.J. (1972)
The classification of educational objectives in the
psychomotor domain. The Psychomotor Domain, Volume III.
Washington: Gryphon House.

Skinner, B.F. (1969)
Contingencies of Reinforcement: A theoretical analysis.
New York: Appleton-Century-Crofts.

Questions

1. Sometimes anxiety is an aid to learning and sometimes the reverse. Why is this? Do we think we are ever right to encourage even mild anxiety?

2. Outline the kinds of learning environment likely to appeal to the marked extravert. How does this environment differ from that suitable for the marked introvert?

3. Make lists of the intrinsic and extrinsic motivators which have respectively been of most importance to you in your own learning experiences.

4. Why is it that the experience of consistent failure is so damaging to a person's readiness to learn?

5. List some of the factors both in the home and in the school which you feel may influence the respective rates at which boys and girls learn.

6. Define short- and long-term memory respectively. What are some of the strategies that aid transfer from one to the other?

7. Write down as many examples as you can of well-known mnemonics. Construct a mnemonic for aiding memory in an important area of your own subject.

8. Construct a simple multiple-choice test designed to establish whether a student has correctly learnt the principles and/or the facts behind one or more of the following: (i) propagating plants by means of softwood cuttings; (ii) starting a motor car and drawing safely away from the kerb; (iii) swimming the crawl; (iv) the symbols on a map (or on a weather map).

9. What are the eight events in a learning chain according to Gagné?

10. Construct a simulation designed to help students face common problems in their practical work. Suggest ways of evaluating their responses.

Annotated reading

Bigge, L. (1976) Learning Theories for Teachers (3rd edn).
New York: Harper & Row.
  One of the best and most comprehensive surveys of
  learning theories and their application to teaching.

Fontana, D. (1977) Personality and Education. London: Ope
Books.
  A more general discussion, with an examination of the
  implications for the teacher.

Gagné, R.M. (1975) Essentials of Learning for Instruction.
Hinsdale, Illinois: Dryden Press.

Gagné, R. M. (1977) The Conditions of Learning (3rd edn).
London: Holt, Rinehart & Winston.
  Good introductions to Gagné's work.

Gronlund, N.E. (1978). Stating Objectives of Classroom
Instruction (2nd edn). London: Collier Macmillan.
  One of the best short books on the writing of educational objectives. It also has something useful to say
  on the construction of objective tests.

Hintzman, L. (1978) The Psychology of Learning and
Memory. San Francisco: Freeman.
  A good choice for those who want to take their study
  of learning theories rather further, and examine their
  relationship to memory.

Hunter, I.M.L. (1964) Memory (rev. edn). Harmondsworth:
Pelican.
  Difficult to beat as an examination of all aspects of
  memory.

Jones, R.M. (1972) Fantasy and Feeling in Education.
Harmondsworth: Penguin.
  A good discussion of Bruner's ideas within the practical
  classroom context.

Klatsky, R.L. (1975) Human Memory. San Francisco: Freem
  Gives a more up-to-date picture than Hunter's book.

Marjoribanks, K. (1979) Families and Their Learning
Environments. London: Routledge & Kegan Paul.
  A thorough and scholarly survey of the research into the
  relationship between intelligence, personality, family
  variables and learning.

Rowntree, D. (1974) Educational Technology in Curriculum
Development. London: Harper & Row.
  The best approach to programmed learning and the whole
  field of educational technology.

Rowntree, D. (1976) Learn How to Study. Harmondsworth:
Pelican.

Mace, C.A. (1968) The Psychology of Study (rev. edn).
London: MacDonald.
> Both of these are among the good books currently
> available on study habits, and are highly recommended.

Taylor, J.L. and Walford, R. (1972) Simulation in the
Classroom. Harmondsworth: Penguin.
> Simulation exercises are comprehensively explained, with
> examples.

Vernon, P.E. (1964) An Introduction to Objective-type
Examinations. London: Schools Council Examinations Bulletin
No. 4.
> One of the most valuable short introductions to the
> subject.

xercises

1. The nature of the learner
Make a list of fellow students whom you knew in your last
class at school. Try to rank the group for each of the following characteristics taken separately: anxiety, extraversion, self-esteem, fear of failure, persistence. Try to
recall incidents which illustrated individual differences
in learning ability: that is, people who appeared to have
little difficulty or those who seemed to struggle. How do
the individuals concerned appear in the rankings of personality characteristics? In the case of individuals who
experienced difficulties in learning, what procedures could
be successful in helping them to overcome their problems?

2. Experiments in memory
Memory research is one of the most vigorous areas of psychological experimentation. We therefore hesitate to suggest
particular projects, since in the space available we could
provide only a limited sample. The books listed among the
annotated readings contain accounts of many interesting
experiments which you can replicate or extend.

3. Study habits
Keep a diary for a week in which you record your pattern of
study. Prepare a check-list based on the list of habits
given in the chapter. Note examples of your failures to work
according to plan, as well as your successes. What circumstances were associated with successful and unsuccessful
work? In the light of your experiences prepare an interview
schedule and interview a sample of other students. In what
ways do study habits vary? What factors outside the students' control influence their patterns of working? Is there
any evidence from your survey that individuals with different personalities prefer to work in different ways? Focus in
particular on the activities people engage in which seem to
distract them from or act as a substitute for their work.
Could you suggest alternative work habit strategies to
increase success in working?

4. A learning programme for an adult with a history of learning problems

The aim of this project is to devise a practical curriculum for an adult male illiterate who is otherwise of normal intelligence. Once you have devised the curriculum in theory, you will be able to devote some time to helping someone wh has this very real problem. There are many adults seeking help with reading skills. Preparation of the curriculum will require a great deal of thought and will involve virtually all the issues discussed in David Fontana's chapter.

Start with the problem of defining curriculum objectives. These will not consist of simple statements like 'Mr X will be able to read'! What skills are involved in reading? What range of materials exist which have to be read in a normal life? In what range of situations must reading occur fluently and without hesitation? What is the distinction between reading and comprehension? How do reading skills transfer to writing skills? Apart from the skill aspects, what about personal effects of illiteracy; how do they undermine confidence and self-esteem? All these questions, and many more, will influence the list of objectives you create.

You will then have to provide a specification for learning experiences and materials appropriate for learning. The schedule of learning to be followed will need to reflect the fact that your student has a long history of experienced failure at a basic skill. The reading materials used will call for careful selection. Early reader material is typically designed for very young minds, not adults with fully developed interests and responsibilities. You will need to visit your local library and seek out special adult literacy materials.

What sort of assessment will be appropriate and what ar its purposes?

In considering these problems you will soon realize how very personal and anxiety-inducing it is even to confess to illiteracy, never mind facing the challenge of trying late in life to learn a set of skills which most children take in their stride. With a friend, role-play the part of the adult illiterate. Try and recapture the individual's past history. What was it like to sit through lessons in school without being able to participate fully? Did the inability to read affect other behaviour? How does one reveal to a boyfriend or a girlfriend that one cannot read? How does one pluck up enough courage to ask for help? What is one's past experience of help which was well intentioned, but unguided and in its turn led to a further cycle of despair and self-defeat?

Finally, you may wish to role-play as yourself. There are likely to be areas of learning where you have experienced anxiety and failures of confidence. Are you now sufficiently distant from such incidents to face them squarely and objectively? You may even discover that some of the things you have chosen to do reflect more a desire to avoid other things, than to make a positive choice!

13

Language development in young children
W. P. Robinson

For over 15 years now a steady river of books about language
development in children has flowed on to the market, while
the journals have been flooded by research on the same
topic. Much of this work has been clever and ingenious; not
all of it has been sensible in its point of departure. It is
encouraging that the more recent productions (see de
Villiers and de Villiers, 1979) have begun at the starting
point that common sense would have recommended; Halliday
(1975) expresses the contrast between the earlier and some
of the later work in terms of the questions asked by
psycholinguists and sociolinguists. The former have tended
to focus upon the child mastering the syntax of language
(rules for combining words) at the expense of the other
components of language: phonology (sounds), lexis (words),
semantics (meaning), and pragmatics (significance for action). They have asked: how does the child combine units
into structures (combinations of units), particularly words
into sentences? What do a child's errors, in terms of what
is acceptable in the adult language, tell us about the
system the brain uses for generating sentences? Are these
errors universal, common to all children learning all
languages? Are there fixed sequences of syntactic development within and across all languages? What are the characteristics of the language acquisition device that all
children are born with? With the possible exception of the
last, all these questions are proper in that evidence could
be and has been collected to answer them.

Flow charts have been drawn up setting out stages in the
development of negation and question formation, and these
have been 'explained' by writing out rules that the child's
mind appears to be following in producing these forms. The
grammatical errors of children learning different languages
have been examined for similarities and differences, and
explanations have been offered for the patterns observed.

However, this emphasis upon syntactic structure and
a corresponding neglect of function is alien to the socio-
linguistic stance. From that perspective the questions are
liable to be asked in terms of the ways in which units and
structures develop to serve functions. Function is primary:
children talk to communicate. Introductory questions would
be: why do children talk, and what kinds of meanings do they
encode to what ends? We can proceed to ask how they code

meanings: that is, what units and structures they use. How do the functions and their associated structures change in development and why?

The main reason for preferring the functional/structural to the purely structural approach might be summarized by stating that young children issue commands rather than utter imperative forms ('Stand up!'); they make requests and ask questions rather than form interrogatives; they comment about themselves, about others and about the world rather than utter declarative sentence forms; they achieve purposes by communicating meanings rather than construct linguistic structures. In addition and crucially, a functional/structural approach obliges us to ask questions about the nature of children and their learning as well as about the language they are mastering.

That being so, if we wish to find out which units and structures are learnt when and how, we have to turn to examine ways in which children can be encouraged to exercise functions requiring such units and structures. If we are to be able to specify what children can learn, what they do learn, and how, we have to look closely and attentively at theories of development, learning and instruction.

Three approaches have dominated thinking about the learning of children: associative principles, ideas of modelling, and the cognitive developmental. The first stresses that events occurring close to each other in terms of time and space are likely to become associated: the fact of their co-occurrence is likely to be learnt. The work of Pavlov showed that new artificial stimuli could be substituted for the original stimuli to elicit responses already in the animal's repertoire, under certain conditions (classical conditioning). Thorndike, and latterly Skinner, have shown that new responses to stimuli can be learnt if these are followed quickly by rewards or punishments (operant conditioning). What roles can classical conditioning and operant conditioning play for which aspects of language development? Have rewards and punishment and the contingent use a significant part which they can and do play?

What determines when and how imitation can be important? Children can and do learn through observation as well as action; how might observational learning fit into the picture? Piaget offered a portrait of the child as an active organizer of experience, building up schemes for action through processes of assimilation and accommodation. These schemes grow in number. They become co-ordinated and differentiated. They become organized so as to afford symbolic as well as physical solutions to problems. The symbolic systems themselves become qualitatively more powerful with growth, which is promoted through different interaction with a challenging environment. How is language development to be integrated into this approach and how do these developments relate to language mastery? The existence of each of these kinds of learning is thoroughly established. What we have yet to determine is whether they are relevant to language learning, and if so, how and under what conditions. Sadly, even recent texts are relatively reticent about these issues, but less so than those of earlier writers.

After closely observing the development of language, particularly the syntax, in three children over a number of years, Brown (1973) concluded: 'What impels the child to "improve" his speech at all remains something of a mystery'. At least two weaknesses in his reasoning might be offered to explain this pessimism. First, the actual tests made of the possible relevance of principles of reinforcement (rewards and punishments), and confirmation/correction, or of observational learning examined only very few linguistic features in very few children. We have, however, no reason to expect that identical processes will be of equal significance for all aspects of language learning in all children. Brown is not enthusiastic about common sense, but common sense easily observes that children learn the language and dialect of their caretakers rather than one of the several thousand other languages in the world. That being so, modelling must have some potential role to play in part of the learning process, even if we cannot as yet be precise in saying how and when it occurs. While imitation and reinforcement principles of learning and performance may not be able to explain some features of language mastery - for example, how adults become capable of generating an infinite number of novel sentences - it does not follow logically that these principles are irrelevant to everything else that is involved in learning to use language.

The second weakness in Brown's approach is revealed by the stripped-down characteristics of the data examined. Child speech was analysed as transcripted sequences of words. Prosodic features of intonation, pitch, and stress were not included. The caretaker's utterances and the non-verbal context in which utterances were made were generally but not entirely ignored. But the child's speech is only one component of the co-operative action involving conversation, and conversations are not about nothing. Imagine trying to describe and explain the learning of a trapeze artist's skills without mentioning the behaviour of his partner or of the trapeze! How can one expect to examine the role of the child's caretakers in the development of speech if their possible contribution to the interaction is not included in full measure? And how can one expect to study either without reference to the contextually embedded actions and interactions to which speech is directed? And if you have no theories of learning to test, then none will prove to be helpful in explaining the data.

The perspective adopted here recognizes that the growing child is an active self-organizing subject capable of building up action schemes, symbolic schemes, and sign systems through interaction with events, things and people (following Piaget), but we recognize that the child is at the same time an object whose behaviour can be shaped and

developed through the contingent use of rewards and punishments (following Pavlov and Skinner). We also need to accept
the idea that to produce and understand speech is to manifest a set of at least semi-automated skills (see Claim 7
below) whose mastery will need repeated and varied practice
in situations where others in the environment offer corrective feedback. Accepting this eclectic view of a child as a
growing person who is both agent and victim allows us to
conceive of that child as inventing functions as well as
units and structures to realize these skills, and as discovering them to be already available in the speech of
others. We can also conceive of children as being responsive
to direct instruction and training, both for learning new
features and for deploying these fluently in action.

What follows is a list of claims about children's mastery of language and the role of their caretakers in this
endless task. The claims may need amendment or partial
abandonment in the light of advances in knowledge, but in
1981 they represent what is intended to be a balanced
assessment of the evidence to hand.

**Claims about language
development**

**Claim 1: the use of language develops out of already
established non-verbal means of communication**
From birth children interact with their caretakers; child
and caretaker act upon and react to each other. This
reciprocity involves an exchange of signals each to the
other. The child responds differentially (e.g. with smiles
or cries) to different maternal actions, such as different
facial expressions (Bruner, 1975). For example, the caretakers endeavour to decode distress signals and cease to
search for further solutions when their actions result in
signals of satisfaction from the child. It is out of this
interchange of communication through body movements,
gestures, facial expressions, and vocalizations that
verbal communication emerges; it does not arise suddenly
with a first 'word'.

**Claim 2: initial functions of language are social-
interactional**
If we distinguish broadly between language uses which
attempt to comment upon the nature of things, for example,
making statements which are either true or false, and those
which appear to be attempts to regulate the states or
behaviour of self and others or to define role relationships
(see Robinson, 1978), then in Halliday's child, Nigel, the
former began to appear over nine months after the first
socially relevant language units had emerged. Halliday found
that instrumental (getting things for self), regulatory
(making others do things), interactional (encounter-
regulation), and personal (reactions to events or states)
units were the first to appear. Among these were nã̃ (give
me that), bø (give me my bird), ə̃ (do that again), do (nice
to see you), ñ̃ŋ (that tastes nice). (See glossary under

Phonology.) This child began to talk, it seems, because verbal interaction with others was pleasurable; it was not because he was hungry or in pain. The design of the baby includes an impetus to interact with people, an impetus to interact with other features of the environment, and an impetus to develop the schemes of interaction. If one wishes to say that the reasons why babies begin to talk are bio-logical, then they are socio-biological: joint action with caretakers. That being so, the promotion of co-ordinated joint action may be one form of inducement to develop communicative skills.

As Halliday illustrates, Nigel later expanded his func-tional range to include the heuristic (finding out) and imaginative (let's pretend) functions, and he increased the number of communicative acts associated with each of these until by the age of one-and-a-half he had over 50 in his repertoire. This 50 is a misleading figure because from the outset the child had both general and specific variants of each function, for example, nã (give me that - general), bø (give me my bird - specific). The general form may be an important growth point as well as having general utility, in that it affords the caretaker an opportunity to respond non-verbally with the appropriate action, verbally to label the unspecified object, and to continue the conversation, all at the same time. The opportunity to learn a specific referent for the particular 'that' can be fitted into the sequence of activity, without this constituting a major diversion.

About the time Nigel reached his 50 meanings he also ceased to rely solely upon inventing his own units (mainly un-English in form and actually heavily reliant on tone). Two important changes occurred.

First, Nigel interpolated a third level of linguistic structure, the lexico-grammatical, between soundings and meanings. Individual sounds ceased to be expressive of individual meanings. Combinations of sounds were used to form 'words', and words and tones were sequenced to create 'meanings'. Thus the tri-stratal essence of language became established. (At some later point in time the child has also to learn to distinguish between the semantic and pragmatic levels; different forms can serve the same general functions and the same form can serve different functions, the appro-priate choice requiring knowledge of the cultural norms of the society.)

Claim 3: the child makes deliberate efforts to learn language

Second, Nigel's speech began to distinguish between using language and learning language. He deliberately solicited from his caretakers 'names' of objects, attributes and actions and he practised combinations and alterations both in monologue and dialogue. Whether all children do this we do not yet know. How do caretakers respond to these enquiries about words (and structures)? On the principles of any associative theory of learning (see de Cecco, 1968), supplying the requested items emphatically, clearly and with some measure of repetition and extension should increase the chances of the child learning the language feature and its use. It should also encourage him in the process of finding out more. Not supplying the requested information or supplying it in a form that the child cannot assimilate in the short run forgoes an opportunity for learning about the specific matter in hand, and in the long run should result in the child ceasing to make enquiries.

Claim 4: units and structures are accumulated piecemeal but inexorably

An extreme position might argue that units are mastered one at a time, always being linked to some unit or structure already in the child's repertoire. They may be learnt and lost again. The cycle may be repeated until the unit disappears or becomes established. The units which become finally established and relatively stable will be those in the speech of the child's circle of interactants, particularly of those with whom the child is most frequently in a learning and interactive relationship.

By 'unit' is meant any feature of the language at any level, such as phonemes, morphemes, words, groups, clauses sentences, utterances, rules of explicitness, rules of politeness or rules of differential social status. It should be remembered that a unit at one level can be a structure at another, for example, a sequence of particular pitches can form an intonation pattern, but this pattern serves as a unit if it forms an interrogative; a principle or rule can therefore become a unit when treated as such.

A new unit will be more likely to enter and remain in the repertoire of the child who is intellectually capable of grasping some aspect of its approximate meaning or significance. Capability is not the only factor; a unit is more likely to be mastered if its meaning and significance is relevant to something the child wishes to communicate or comprehend. Reasons for a unit not entering would be that the child may already be using available capacity and energies to develop other units or structures of verbal or non-verbal behaviour. The child may also be performing and living rather than learning; there is more to life than learning. A unit will only become stabilized in use if it is encouraged to do so by others (see Claim 6).

Claim 5: the new is often first learnt in terms of the old

An ancient Greek paradox points to the impossibility of change, and this principle is sometimes invoked as a reason why children cannot learn language! If understanding a word must precede the learning of that word, how can it be learnt? If learning must precede understanding how can the child come to understand something that has no meaning? And yet children clearly do learn. One of several lines of escape from the paradox is to argue that the child can express new meanings 'badly' with old, already available units and structures, and that caretakers can reformulate the child's meaning with the new units and structures which the child may then be able to assimilate to the meaning intended. Evidence is consistent with the idea that the child learning to associate the various kinds of negation in English with the appropriate adult lexical and syntactic structures can rely on adults continuing to supply the new forms upon the occasions of the child's using those already known and assimilated.

Since syntactic systems such as interrogation and negation are compound and complicated, it may follow that the developing child will only master them piecemeal, generating transitional forms, if Claim 4 is valid. The evidence pointing to the many transitional forms of syntactic construction (e.g. 'Why it is raining?'; see Brown, 1973) is probably consistent with the idea that these variants are best left to correct themselves unless particular examples of them appear to have stabilized over many months. If a child cannot learn quickly from a correction there is probably little point and may be harm in pursuing it.

Claim 6: caretakers control the probability of new features being learnt and remaining in the child's repertoire

Montessori is responsible for the last observation made in Claim 5, and a second injunction of hers may be used to introduce Claim 6. Her 'cycle of three' for teaching was: This is an X - Show me the/an X - What is this? (pointing to X). The first labels the activity, event, object or attribute, the second checks the child's capacity for recognition, and the third encourages the child to produce the label. She adds that repeated failures to elicit appropriate reactions from the child are best taken as suggestions for dropping the matter and returning to it later. This model can easily be abused if taken too literally, but it has considerable value if used as a framework to bear in mind when combining instruction with conversation.

How is a child to find out the conventional linguistic means of expressing meanings but from caretakers? Why should they leave children to extract features as best they can from the discourse of adults? Why not structure learning opportunities as clearly as possible leaving the child to accept or reject them? (Many mothers object to viewing themselves or being viewed as teachers. Whether or not they are to be seen as teaching is contingent only upon the definition of 'teach'. If the provision of opportunities for learning is enough to be called 'teaching' then all people interacting with children are teachers. If this provision has to be intended to help learning, then fewer people are teachers of children, but presumably there are some things all mothers intend that their children should learn. My own view is that mothers should accept that there is much they can teach their children and that they can enjoy this role to the benefit of all concerned.)

Two studies can be quoted to illustrate the power of caretakers at the relatively early period of language development when the child's utterances are on average between one-and-a-half and three words (mean length of utterance: MLU). At this stage of development the number of morphems is closely related to the number of words.

Ellis and Wells (1980) contrasted the maternal inter-action characteristics of slow language developers (12 months to move from MLU 1.5 to MLU 3.5) with those of early fast developers (less than 6 months to make this change and achieved before 21 months old). At the outset mothers of the two groups differed, the latter talking generally more during routine household activities, issuing more instructions and commands, being more likely to acknowledge their child's utterances, and more likely to repeat or correct these. By the time the children had reached 3.5 MLU, maternal differences were still present, but they were different in type, the early fast children's mothers using more statements and questions, particularly teaching-type questions, to which the mother already knew the answers. Cross (1978) found in a contrast between faster and slower developers that different maternal speech vari-ables discriminated at different ages. The implications of these two studies are several. Optimal facilitation of deve-lopment may require the employment of different tactics at different points in development and may also require the application of different principles.

More basic general principles are also relevant. Mothers whose speech is more unintelligible, in that it is mumbled and incoherent with no clear breaks and stresses at custo-mary points, are likely to have children whose speech is developing more slowly.

In a study of the mother-child interaction among six year olds (see Robinson, in press) it was found that child-ren who asked more questions, more complex questions, and revealed more verbally mediated knowledge about an assort-ment of objects, games, and toys, had mothers who were me likely to:

* set any remark in a previously shared context;
* answer any question with a relevant, accurate reply that extended somewhat beyond the question posed;
* confirm children's utterances which were true and well-formed and to point out or correct errors;
* maintain themes over several utterances.

These findings probably need qualification and supplemen-tation. Pointing out and correcting errors is likely to be productive only if individual children can learn from this, and provided they do not become afraid to make mistakes. O feature of maternal behaviour that was unrelated to child-ren's performance was the mother's questioning of the child; it seemed that at least in this context questioning may have been intended to re-focus the interest of children who were already actively attending to something else and were unwil-ling to be distracted. Hess and Shipman (1965), for example, treated questioning as motivating and found it to be posi-tively associated with more advanced performance, but perhaps in their case the questioning was creating and achieving concentration rather than trying to re-direct attention. Questioning which encourages extension of interest may have different consequences from questions which are failed attempts to direct the child. (These two may be distinguishable in terms of quality of voice and intonation.)

If two words were to be used to sum up the contrast they would be 'push' versus 'pull'. Pushing did not work, pulling did: adults could set up the context of the situation in which activity took place, but beyond that the children decided what interested them. Adults can set the scene, offer suggestions, and tempt children, but the latter direct the form and content of their scripts. The 'push' is already there; it is a design characteristic of human children. By their reactive behaviour adults can encourage and develop both this intrinsic motivation and the learning which results from its activity. They may also be able to treat it in ways which may slow down, check, deflect, distort, prevent or otherwise impede development.

Providing, tempting and modelling appear to be the main activities caretakers can offer to facilitate language (and general) development. How far the success of these actions depends upon the caretaker's genuine concern with the child and his behaviour remains unknown. One would have to say, as an act of faith, that caring in action, realized as an expression of a sincere liking and cheerful interest in what children find important, is certainly desirable, if not essential. Entering both intellectually and emotionally into the spirit and perspective of children's orientation to their world must make the processes easier to achieve.

Claim 7: coming to 'know that' reorganizes the possibilities of developing 'know how'

Halliday (1975) noted that, at an early age, young Nigel discriminated between using the language and learning the language. Some children of four already 'know that' there are rules governing how things are to be said and can say something about their nature. We can also ask how children come to realize that speech can be ambiguous: that a speaker may send messages too vague for correct comprehension and appropriate action. At an early stage children do not realize a message should refer uniquely to its referents if it is to be acted upon appropriately. In a situation where speaker and listener have identical sets of cards, each set depicting stick-men holding flowers differing in size and colour, they will pick up a card in response to 'A man with a flower' without necessarily asking for more information. If their choice turns out to be wrong they will state that the speaker had said enough (told properly) and that it was their fault that the mismatch had occurred (phase 1 below). When older they will be more likely to demand more information by asking questions, and if a mismatch does still occur they can blame the inadequacy of the message and the speaker for the failure. They 'know that' messages can be inadequate. They can reflect upon and analyse the efficiency and precision of their own speech and that of others (phase 2 below).

At present we can only speculate about the general significance of this work, but the possible implications are considerable and can be represented roughly in a three-phase model that could apply to many aspects of language development. For illustrative purposes let X be a truth, principle or fact about language.

* PHASE 1: children are mainly victims of X. Their capacities for being agents with control over X are limited by their ignorance of the character of X and how it functions in the language in communication. However, they achieve a measure of mastery of X in use (know ho as a result of associative learning both in its classical and instrumental conditioning guises, and they may also learn about X in use through observation. Additionally, they are agents and can purposefully use X, relying on corrective feedback from others for the development of context-bound rules of use. These various processes acting separately and in combination may lead to a child using X successfully much of the time. However, limitations of intellectual capacity and an absence of opportunitites and/or capacities for reflecting upon the workings of X will be manifested when their rules for using X fail. They will not be able to diagnose the reasons for failure and will not be able to formulate a diagnosis and act effectively upon it.

* PHASE 2: either through their own reflective efforts or as a result of a competent other teaching and telling them about the workings of X, they will come to realize how (and perhaps why) X works as it does. As a result reflective analysis, in particular new situations or through a consideration of past events, or through imaginative rehearsing of situations involving X, they will consciously develop and organize their knowledge about X. We might expect an associated period of learning-practice in which the use of X is tried out with care and awareness. Children (or adults) become reflecting agents in respect of X organizing their 'knowing that', and perhaps temporarily less efficient in their 'know how'.

* PHASE 3: the use of X will become reduced to an automated skill except for situations where for various reasons it might be important not to make mistakes with X and for situations where trouble in using X occurs. In the face of trouble the problem can be raised to a conscious reflective analysis, diagnoses made and corrective action taken, other things being equal. The 'know how' is greater than at the transition from phase 1 to phase 2 and is in a potential dialectic relation to a 'knowing that' of understanding.

We are thinking in this fashion only about the child's control of ambiguity in verbal referential communication, but see a range of possible applications to a whole variety of behaviours within the orbit of language in communication: learning the meanings of words, rules of spelling in the written language, rules of pronunciation in the oral, rules of grammar, rules for varying forcefulness and politeness of requests, rules of etiquette more generally, rules for taking the listener into account and rules for telling jokes well.

Perhaps one important set of reasons why schoolchildren have difficulty in learning to use language more competently is that we ourselves cannot formulate the rules for them. Instead we leave them to continue to operate at a particular and concrete level, learning many instances rather than fewer principles and rules. And when we do find out the rules and principles we do not necessarily set up conditions of learning and practice that carry the child's competence through to the phase of out-of-awareness efficient use with reflective facilities for analysis when trouble occurs or is anticipated. It is worth comparing the relative ease of learning a game like chess or tennis with and without the help of information about rules. To learn how to play will require observation, practice and correction, but knowing the rules renders these easier. Discovering them for yourself could be simply a frustrating waste of time and effort.

Erroneous beliefs

The most fundamental, and possibly the most common, false assumption is that the rate and extent of younger and older children's learning how to use language is not affected by the behaviour of their caretakers; that some innate features of the child's brain or temperament determine what emerges. (We have avoided mentioning ages of children at points where readers might have preferred them to be specified. The arguments in the section on backwardness, below, offer some reasons why it is misleading and dangerous to hold firm expectations as to what individual children ought to have achieved at particular ages. The educational problems with children are to advance their knowledge, understanding, values and motivation; not to categorize them.) While systematic investigations of parents' and teachers' beliefs about language development have yet to be made, it is quite clear that within some cultures, some parents believe that the child will become what it will become regardless of what they do. The empirical evidence is that these beliefs do not correspond to reality; while many facts about relations between caretaker behaviour and language development have yet to be discovered, the positive results already established are too numerous and theoretically plausible to be discounted.

Unfortunately, academic thinking about these matters is still dominated by a simplicity that is naive. One common assumption in research seems to be that if a certain kind of caretaker behaviour can be shown to be beneficial then the more of it the better: that its efficacy will hold true for all children at all phases of language development regardless of the context of operation and the state of relationship between caretaker and child. Neither the basic assumption nor its presumed generality is likely to be true.

For example, it is likely that caretakers can talk too much with children as well as too little. And they can overteach particular features. Developmental social psychologists have been slow to appreciate that many relations between variables are likely to be curvilinear rather than monotonic. 'The more the better' may have a limit beyond which 'more' may mean 'worse' or 'nothing' and not 'better'.

Just as caretakers may talk too much as well as too little, they can talk at or past children instead of with them. They can initiate and control without responding. Som adults seem anxious to hurry their replies without having listened first; they act, but do not react or interact. One of the first lessons to be learnt in dealing with young children is not to impose oneself too quickly upon them, and this applies to continuing as well as initial encounters. While children have to learn how and when to listen, they need to be listened to as well. It has been argued that mothers listen attentively to children, trying to decipher the meanings of their cries, but one can be sceptical about the continuing and pervading applicability of such parental commitment to all children as they grow older. Brown (1973) showed that 40 per cent of his children's questions were met with replies that were unrelated to the sense of the question: one therefore wonders how many caretakers make serio efforts to listen to children, encourage them to talk about their activities, and maintain interest and cohesion in such conversations. Those caretakers who are concerned to promo development may push too hard or pull too hard. On the evidence to date, 'pushing' is not productive; 'pulling', pitched at the right level with not too high or low a frequency, is an important facilitator of development, however. Caretakers can pitch their initiations and reactions to children at too low a level or too high a one. Too low may be generally uncommon, but certainly some mentall retarded children appear to be kept at a lower standard of performance by adults unwilling to extend their conversation with them. But how are caretakers to judge what is too muc too often, or too hard?

Caretakers can solve these problems only in context. A monitoring of the child's actions and reactions in combination with an appraisal of the verbal interaction itself should suffice to indicate whether the child is attentively involved. Adults should be able to appraise whether or not their remarks are understood by children both from their non-verbal reactions and from their succeeding remarks. Adults should be able to judge whether they themselves are understanding and reacting appropriately to a child's utterances. Does the child have great difficulty constructing replies? Are there many disfluencies and intervening silences? Are themes maintained over a succession of utterances? In short, does the conversation have an orderly structure? Does the talk relate to the contextual features of the situation in which it is occurring? If it does, and if the adult is injecting new information about the world and about language at such a rate that the child can take up and use some of the features being introduced, the worst mistakes are being avoided.

This capacity to adjust speech to a developing child is itself a skill that has to be learnt. Child-rearing manuals (Leach, 1978) or pre-school teachers' advice (Tough, 1977) offer much constructive (and some wrong!) advice on such matters. Perhaps both under-estimate the value of two activities: conversation as such, and the appropriate injection of small doses of teaching about language during conversations.

Finally, the conversation has to be anchored to the outside world of actions and events and/or the inner personal world of wishes, intentions, feelings and ideas. The talk has to be more than wording. Experiences have to be arranged and/or exploited. Topics have to be selected. If they are not, children are in danger of separating rhetoric from reality (or fantasy). They can come to believe that they have to accommodate to a world of words and another world of things and fail to realize that the two ought to be in a dialectical and corresponding relation to each other.

Special problems

Backwardness

Backwardness is not an absolute concept but a relative one. Backwardness can exist only after a norm is defined. For various reasons our society has selected biological age from birth as a reference point. For many aspects of growth and development we have devised ways of measuring characteristics of children that give a spread of scores about an average norm of some kind for children of a particular age. Then we use our tests to obtain scores for individual children. However, to expect then that each individual child should score close to the average is importantly irrational: such an expectation is logically and empirically inconsistent with the spreading procedures adopted to construct the test.

This is not to say that it is foolish to ask why a child or group of children is below (or above) average. Answers to such questions may enable us to take constructive action to facilitate the development of particular children who are unnecessarily and undesirably backward in certain respects.

Many people in our society may also adopt a moral position that special efforts should be made to promote more rapid development in some sub-sample of the population defined as 'backward'; say, the lowest ten per cent. That is defensible. However, it is not logically or empirically possible to eliminate a bottom ten per cent. We can take action to raise the absolute performance or characteristics of children; what we cannot do is use norm-referenced tests and eliminate the variation about the norm.

We must also accept the fact that, at any moment in a society, there are limits both to what can be done and what the members of society think it is important to do. There are biological, sociological-historical and economic limits to what can be done. There are moral limits as to what we might consider it proper or fair to do.

We can also observe that there are wrong ways of conceptualizing these problems. Over the last 20 years and before, questions have been asked about why children fail at school. Some have blamed the biology and psychology of failing children. Others have blamed bad homes. Bad teaching and bad schools have been cited, as have curricula. The government and the social structure of the society have not escaped blame. In reality, the reason why n per cent of children fail CSE, O level or A level is that the examiners have set a fail rate of n per cent: and that is the sole reason. We can sensibly proceed to ask why children from certain identifiable groupings are particularly at risk of failure.

We ought also to note that explanations for such failure have generally made appeals to deficiency models of some kind, deficiency in language being a frequently cited factor. Oddly, we have only resorted to this kind of explanation within age groups, particularly for social categories such as social class, rurality, cultural minorities and psychological categories such as the mentally retarded or the maladjusted. We do not see nfant school children as language-deficient adults who need to be brought up to a state of adult competence forthwith. Education is normally seen as promoting and facilitating development and not in terms of removing deficiencies. And yet, within a particular age cohort, we have tended to apply the deficiency model to the backward, even for 'normal' children. Whether a glass of water is seen as half full or half empty is a fact about the observer, not the water. The fate of water may not be affected by that perception. However, when children are seen as more empty (or filled with the wrong stuff) than they ought to be, there are likely to be consequences for themselves, their families, their teachers and ultimately the society of which they are to become citizens.

However, need we consider the language of a developing child normatively, and if so, against which norms? If we are to make special educational or other provision for those defined as being in special need then testing individuals against norms is essential as a diagnostic means of some objectivity. Age-based norms may constitute the single most efficient screening frame of reference for operation. Once the presenting characteristics are defined by reference to test scores, the hard work of explanation and decision making starts. Are the scores deviant enough from the age per norm to warrant further enquiry? Are the scores deviant enough from what might be expected from this individual to warrant further enquiry? If either is true, are the scores themselves what are important or are they symptoms of something else? If the scores are judged to be indicators of problems rather than problems in themselves, are these best treated by being left to remedy themselves with subsequent monitoring? Or should we intervene? Where intervention is judged as desirable, the norm-referenced tests are likely to have played a crucial role in detection and perhaps in diagnosis, but not in the explanation or specification of treatment as such.

Dialects and accents

'Standard English' (SE) can be usefully thought of as that dialect of British English whose rules of prosody, grammar, lexis, semantics and pragmatics have become institutionalized as the variety of English towards whose mastery the educational endeavour aspires. 'Received Pronunciation' (RP) refers to the accent that defines the corresponding phonology. The components of SE which are stressed most frequently are its grammar and lexis; it is usually in respect of those characteristics that SE is contrasted with other regional and social dialects. When a variety is accorded the status of a dialect is not closely defined. Dialectologists have mapped out the distribution of regional dialects in Britain, particularly rural ones. Socially-stratified dialects have not been well investigated. And for both we have yet to learn what their similarities and differences are. Are dialects more alike than they are different in each of their components? The number of differences in grammatical rules is probably few in relation to the total in the language.

Those responsible for educating children need to distinguish between features in their speech that indicate ignorance of language and its workings and those which mark social identity, through the dialect of the child's home. If teachers denigrate the local dialect while teaching SE, they are denigrating the people who speak that dialect and may eventually force children to choose between SE and the local dialect. Are they to equip themselves for upward social mobility at the cost of social separation from their families and local community? But why create conditions where a choice has to be made?

One false belief is that people can master only one dialect. Where the need for mastery of two different languages exists, children learn two, often without the benefit of schools to teach them. The factors that operate to prevent children mastering several dialects are mainly socio-cultural and not biological-cognitive.

If education is to open up opportunities rather than to close them down, that system has to facilitate the development of control of the dialects and languages of greatest potential significance to the child, of which the two most important are the local social/regional dialect or language and SE, so that the child may be able to use each as and when appropriate.

Similarly, arguments can be advanced for the educationa[l] support of more than one accent. It is now well documented that people do not always utter the same sound in the same way; it is a matter of proportion. And the proportions vary: this has been shown most frequently through manipulations of the formality-casualness of the situation.

Moreover, we also converge towards and diverge away from the speech of our fellow conversationalists (Giles and Powesland, 1975), such movements being interpreted as indicative of goodwill and separateness respectively. Giles and Powesland review studies which show how accents are evaluated in Britain. Evaluation can be along more than one dimension, and in this case two emerge that may be most simply summarized as expertness and trustworthiness. Unfortunately these are not independent, RP speakers being seen as untrustworthy experts and broadly-accented countryfolk as trustworthy but ignorant. But children as well as adults are judged by their accents, and it must be incumbent upon the expert caretakers to increase their knowledge and understanding about these matters.

In sum, we need to extend and disseminate our knowledge about the way language functions in our community. We need to develop and act upon policies that enable children to master in sufficient measure those varieties of language which will both promote their learning and enable them to retain or gain access to membership of those social groups in and through which their identity is realized.

Conclusions

One common complaint made by members of the public, their elected representatives and their paid servants is that academics address problems rather than solve them; they spend too much time posing questions and too little answering them. At least in language development we have now moved to a position where the types of question being asked begin to embrace a comprehensive functional-structural framework. We have begun to ask how children learn units and structures to communicate meanings which have significance for action. We are confronting language as a four-component system (language in its pragmatic, semantic, lexico-grammatical and phonological aspects), just as developing children themselves confront, cope with and learn to use all four interdependently. We have appreciated that, although function may be a useful primary focus, we have to note that children who can distinguish between 'knowing how to' and 'knowing that' are in a strong position to hold and develop both structures and functions in a dynamic interactive relation to each other, and that such capacity in fact predates the conscious onset of this discrimination. The questions being posed now are more likely to lead to progress than some of those narrower and stranger questions of 20 years ago.

Furthermore, we have begun to answer quite a number of questions. The claims made here are a distillation focussing on processes and mechanisms of development rather than

content. What is now known about the content and sequence
of language development is considerable, especially in young
children. The claims made are couched in a form at as low
a level of abstraction as appears to be compatible with the
evidence. To be more specific would require the prior specification of more details of the particular children, caretakers, context of situation, and learning problems under
consideration; the claims are principles that may guide
practice but cannot prescribe its concrete characteristics.
They also mark a departure from what might be called the
'one-answer-only' mentality. Psychologists have tried to
look for the process that converts all substances to gold,
or in this case all pre-linguistic babies into verbally competent toddlers. We have seen the invalid logic that takes
the form of arguing that, because process X may not be
invariably necessary for mastering Y, it has no relevance.
It is likely that all learning processes are relevant or can
be made relevant to some aspects of language development
in some children. Once we ask whether, when, and how a
process can be used to facilitate development, our answers
may become more positive and useful.

But are the claims made here any improvement on common
sense? They are, in two ways. Unfortunately, a particular
form of sense is not common to all people, as can be speed-
ily demonstrated by revealing the extent of individual sub-
cultural and cultural differences as to what it is sensible
to believe. At present we know next to nothing about parents' (or even teachers') beliefs about language development, but we do know they differ. Some are wrong. This is
not to insult them. We are all wrong in some of our beliefs,
and none of us is omniscient. Appeals to common sense will
not yield the truth. At present, too, the experts continue
to disagree among themselves as to ways and means likely to
facilitate language development. If we mean by 'common
sense' the accumulated wisdom of experienced caretakers,
then experts would surely be well advised to solicit their
opinions; if they have learnt through observing the consequences of their teaching methods then they are a prime
population for ideas. But the convictions that have derived
from their private experience have then to be checked in
the publicly demonstrable contexts of systematic investigation. While the evidence obtained through scientific procedures is prone to errors of various kinds, investigators
are trained to try to avoid these. Hence the evidence and
the interpretations they offer should be less prone to
error, especially when empirical studies conducted in a
variety of settings yield results which can be shown to be
consistent. The claims put forward have been subject to
systematic scrutinizing activity, and that is why they,
rather than others, are presented.

Accommodation
A Piagetian term referring to the development of new schemes

arising out of the failure of current schemes to regulate action. Hence sensori-motor schemes for sucking will not enable an infant to drink from a cup: new schemes have to be constructed.

Adaptation
In Piagetian development, adaptation is the combination of the processes of assimilation and accommodation.

Assimilation
The application of currently available schemes to inter-action with the environment. If a baby has a sucking scheme used for breast feeding, it may readily assimilate the sucking of a bottle teat to this scheme. The sucking scheme will also be applied to fingers and toys but this transfer will not, in the long run, be adaptive. New schemes will be required to accommodate to the use of toys.

Intonation
Patterns of variation in pitch and stress that distinguish (i) between what is believed to be accepted already by conversation partners and what is new, and (ii) the charac-ter of utterances as questions, statements, commands, etc.

Lexico-grammar
The rules governing what is generally acceptable within a language system. Grammar is said to have two components: morphology and syntax. Rules in morphology define changes to words themselves as their functions in sentences change; for example, 'he' is subject, 'him' is the form for object. Syntax defines the possible sequences, substitutions and co-occurrences of words, phrases and clauses permitted in the construction of sentences.

About 150 special words in English (conjunctions, pre-positions, pronouns, etc.) are sometimes seen as having predominantly grammatical/semantic significance. The remaining half-million or so are lexical items. Both are listed in dictionaries.

Morpheme
The smallest unit of meaning in language.

Norm
In its descriptive sense, norm refers to the typical or most common behaviour of members of a group. It is also used evaluatively to assert what is to be expected of such members. The failure to separate the two can lead to the idea that everyone has to be average, which is self-contradictory.

Phonology
The study of sound systems of languages. Within a language, which sounds make a significant difference to meaning? What are the rules which define which combinations of sounds can occur? To aid these descriptions, linguists have devised an

International Phonetic Alphabet that attempts to write down sounds so that their pronunciation is defined. This does not yet include conventions that represent stress or pitch.

Pragmatics
See semantics. Pragmatics is concerned with the significance for action of utterances. To use language effectively, people have to be able to interpret the speech of others and to know how their own utterances are likely to be interpreted. This requires a knowledge of rules of the culture and not just the semantics.

Psycholinguistics
The study of the psychological processes that underlie speech performance. The main focus in child development has been upon the encoding and decoding of syntax, but a comprehensive study would include comparable analyses of sounds and written symbols and meanings. Some people would also include pragmatics.

Scheme
The procedures that regulate an action or set of actions. Hence if infants have a sucking scheme, their brains must contain a set of instructions for action that result in a co-ordinated sequence of movements that relate the body, mouth and hands to nipples. Not all schemes relate to sensori-motor skills: they can also relate to intellectual products.

Semantics
Units at and above the level of morpheme have meanings. A cat is not a dog; 'on' does not mean the same as 'in'. It is through their combinations, in accordance with lexico-grammatical rules, that sequences of sounds come to have meaning. Some people have difficulty in grasping the distinction between semantics and pragmatics; pragmatics is concerned with action. 'The door is open', uttered by a teacher in a classroom means what it says. The semantics declares a state of affairs to be true. The pragmatic significance could be 'The last child to have come in should get up and shut the door'. Unfortunately, we can use the question 'What did he mean?' to refer to both the semantics and the pragmatics. 'Meaning' is ambiguous.

Sociolinguistics
Traditionally the study of language variation in relation to variations in the nature of the setting, participants, ends, aesthetics, key, modality, norms, and genre, within a speech community. The focus is upon pragmatics and how functions relate to the forms used. Sociolinguistics and psycholinguistics overlap.

Syntax
The rules for combining words into phrases, clauses and sentences.

References

Brown, R. (1973)
A First Language: The early stages. London: Allen & Unwin.

Bruner, J.S. (1975)
The ontogenesis of speech acts. Journal of Child Language, 2, 1-19.

Cross, T.G. (1978)
Mother's speech and its association with role of linguistic development in the young child. In N. Waterson and C. Snow (eds), The Development of Communication. Chichester: Wiley.

De Cecco, J.P. (1968)
The Psychology of Learning and Instruction. Englewood Cliffs, NJ: Prentice-Hall.

De Villiers, R.A. and De Villiers, J. (1979)
Early Language. Glasgow: Fontana/Open Books.

Ellis, R. and Wells, C.G. (1980)
Enabling factors in adult-child discourse. First Language, 1, 46-62.

Giles, H. and Powesland, P.F. (1975)
Speech Style and Social Evaluation. London: Academic Press.

Halliday, M.A.K. (1975)
Learning How to Mean. London: Arnold.

Hess, R.D. and Shipman, V. (1965)
Early experience and the socialization of cognitive modes in children. Child Development, 36, 860-886.

Leach, P. (1978)
Baby and Child. London: Michael Joseph.

Robinson, W.P. (1978)
Language Management in Education. Sydney: Allen & Unwin.

Robinson, W.P. (ed.) (in press)
Communication in Child Development. London: Academic Press.

Tough, J. (1977)
Talking and Learning. London: Ward Lock.

Questions

1. What can adults do to facilitate language development in young children?
2. Write a government leaflet giving advice to young mothers about language development in their children.
3. If mothers wish to facilitate language development in their children, which is it more important for them to know: details about the nature of language, or rules of interaction?
4. Is it the ignorance of parents and teachers rather than the incapacity of children that delays their development?
5. Describe and comment upon the child's development of syntax.
6. What learning processes underlie which aspects of language development?

7. What roles can imitation play in language development?
8. Why do children stretch familiar units to cope with new meanings?
9. Why encourage language development in children?
10. What should be done in infant schools about the dialects of children?

Annotated reading

Ausubel, D.P. (1978) Theory and Problems of Child Development (2nd edn). New York: Grune & Stratton.
A general textbook about child development from an educational perspective.

Coulthard, C.M. (1977) An Introduction to Discourse Analysis. London: Longmans.
What are the relations between linguistic form and the discourse functions of speech? Coulthard offers some suggestions.

De Stefano, J.S. (ed.) (1973) Language, Society and Education. Worthington, Ohio: Charles Jones.
A collection that brings life to varieties of American English and discusses learning simply and clearly. No comparable book on British English, alas.

De Stefano, J.S. (1978) Language, the Learner and the School. New York: Wiley.
Introductory books about language are still liable to concentrate upon syntax and ignore language in use. This is a welcome exception. Examples of language varieties are mainly American.

De Villiers, J.G. and de Villiers, P.A. (1978) Language Acquisition. Cambridge, Mass.: Harvard University Press.
The most balanced, comprehensive, clear, introduction to language acquisition. Cognitive rather than social emphasis.

De Villiers, J.G. and de Villiers, P.A. (1979) Early Language. London: Fontana/Open Books.
A simplified and highly readable version of the authors' more substantial text. Compulsory reading.

Moerk, E.L. (1977) Pragmatic and Semantic Aspects of Early Language Development. Baltimore: University Park Press.
The emphasis on pragmatics is compatible with contemporary concerns.

Waterson, N. and Snow, C. (eds) (1978) The Development of Communication. Chichester: Wiley.
A collection of papers illustrating the kinds of questions being posed and answers being offered in respect of the communicative development in young children.

Exercises

Practical exercises to inform about the language development in young children cannot be like recipes in cookery books: 'take a three-year-old child and ...'. Neither age nor any other easily chosen index will define states of development with precision; individual differences among children are too great. The investigations recommended below should be instructive if carried out with children between the ages of three and six or with mothers of such children. It may be useful to have a graded series of tasks in the carrier bag (or in mind) so that something which is not too difficult can be selected fairly quickly after warm-up conversation. For example, if studying the range and kind of meanings children ascribe to words then an extended series like 'daddy, cow, animal, why, cause, time' is one where the later words look difficult for the average three year old. Similarly the techniques for checking understanding would differ; whereas younger children might be asked 'Is this an X?' when shown an object, older ones might be able to cope with 'What does X mean?' Finding out what procedures elicit what kind of reaction is itself informative about the child's understanding of language.

1. Mothers' beliefs about language development in young children

Find out whether the mother has a policy about language development and what principles guide her actions. Talk with the mother about children learning language. How does she think children develop mastery? Does she think her behaviour can help? If so, what does she think she can do? Does she arrange for conversations with her child about activities, past, present and future? When she arranges activities or buys games and toys does she think about development as wel as enjoyment? Does she talk with her child at meal-times, bed-times, and so on? Record the interview. Can the mother state a policy or not? If so, on what principles is it based, in terms of claims made in the chapter? What variety exists? Can mothers be classified into groups and, if so, of what kind?

2. Mothers' reports about how they answer questions or use language to mediate control

By devising an interview schedule and a coding procedure you can expose variation in mothers' use of language for communication and/or control (for children aged five or six). In preparing your interview questions make sure you read the appropriate sections of this chapter.

3. Observation of mothers interacting with children

To examine relations between maternal tactics and child's mastery, select a series of materials suitable for child and mother to play with and let them work through the items, replacing items as interest in each wanes. Tell mothers the object is to see how they play with their children. You can then compare what does happen with what the mother believe

4. Observation of mothers teaching their children

Mothers vary in their effectiveness as teachers. Using a simple game, appropriate to the child's age, observe how the mother teaches the child a new game. Try to classify the behaviours involved so as to draw comparisions between two or three mothers.

5. Introduction to the nature of young children's mastery of language

To gain some experience of the strengths and limitations of tests of language development, select and administer a language test to a child of appropriate age: for example, (i) Reynell Developmental Language Scales (Slough: National Foundation for Educational Research). This is appropriate for children aged between six months and six years; (ii) Illinois Test of Psycholinguistic Ability, Urbana, Illinois (this is appropriate for children between two and nine years). Have a conversation with the child about some objects: for example, a catalogue from a discount store. Ask whether the score seemed to be a reliable and valid measure of the child's command of language? Did the conversation and test present a consistent picture? Were the test instructions and material suitable for the children?

6. Range of meaning associated with a word

Find out how the young child categorizes the word with its verbal labels. After establishing some suitable words, probably nouns referring to visible objects, use picture materials to ascertain (i) the borders of a category and (ii) the subordinate and superordinate categories, if any. The basic question would probably take the form 'Is this an X?' Hence sweets, pets or socks might be a target word. What counts as a sweet? Chocolate, cake, ice-cream? Is a sweet food? Is a Smartie a sweet?

7. Beliefs about grammar

Find out what grammatical rules young children apply to units and structures. To examine tolerance of word order variations, the child can be presented with short sentences and either asked 'Can you say ...?' or requested to imitate: for example, 'The cat is sitting. Cat the is sitting', and so on. To examine beliefs about morphology, adaptation of Berko's technique can be used. This relies on nonsense words. Here is a wing. Now there are two. Here are two ...? This bird is flibbing down the pole. Now he has finished. He has ... down the pole. Many morphological systems can be explored in this way.

8. The teachability of children

See whether children can be taught syntax readily and, if so, how. Choose young children (say, three years of age), check for mastery of some structure such as question formation, relying on ability to repeat back the form as an index of mastery. Try teaching a more advanced form by modelling, elicited imitations, or some other technique. Was the teaching successful? If so, how? If not, why not?

Part four

Social Influences

14

Social behaviour
Michael Argyle

We start by presenting the social skill model of social behaviour, and an account of sequences of social interaction. This model is relevant to our later discussion of social skills and how these can be trained. The chapter then goes on to discuss the elements of social behaviour, both verbal and non-verbal, and emphasizes the importance and different functions of non-verbal signals. The receivers of these signals have to decode them, and do so in terms of emotions and impressions of personality; we discuss some of the processes and some of the main errors of person perception. Senders can manipulate the impressions they create by means of 'self-presentation'. The processes of social behaviour, and the skills involved, are quite different in different social situations, and we discuss recent attempts to analyse these situations in terms of their main features, such as rules and goals.

We move on to a number of specific social skills. Research on the processes leading to friendship and love makes it possible to train and advise people who have difficulty with these relationships. Research on persuasion shows how people can be trained to be more assertive. And research on small social groups and leadership of these groups makes it possible to give an account of the most successful skills for handling social groups.

Social competence is defined in terms of the successful attainment of goals, and it can be assessed by a variety of techniques such as self-rating and observation of role-played performance. The most successful method of improving social skills is role-playing, combined with modelling, coaching, videotape-recorder (VTR) playback, and 'homework'. Results of follow-up studies with a variety of populations show that this form of social skills training (SST) is very successful.

Harré and Secord (1972) have argued persuasively that much human social behaviour is the result of conscious planning, often in words, with full regard for the complex meanings of behaviour and the rules of the situations. This is an important correction to earlier social psychological views, which often failed to recognize the complexity of individual planning and the different meanings which may be given to stimuli, for example in laboratory experiments.

However, it must be recognized that much social behaviour is not planned in this way: the smaller elements of behaviour and longer automatic sequences are outside conscious awareness, though it is possible to attend, for example, to patterns of gaze, shifts of orientation, or the latent meanings of utterances. The social skills model, in emphasizing the hierarchical structure of social performance, can incorporate both kinds of behaviour.

The social skills model also emphasizes feedback processes. A person driving a car sees at once when it is going in the wrong direction, and takes corrective action with the steering wheel. Social interactors do likewise; if another person is talking too much they interrupt, ask closed questions or no questions, and look less interested in what is being said. Feedback requires perception, looking at and listening to the other person. Skilled performance requires the ability to take the appropriate corrective action referred to as 'translation' in the model: not everyone knows that open-ended questions make people talk more and closed questions make them talk less. And it depends on a number of two-step sequences of social behaviour whereby certain social acts have reliable effects on another. Let us look at social behaviour as a skilled performance similar to motor skills like driving a car (see figure 1).

Figure 1

The motor skill model (from Argyle, 1969)

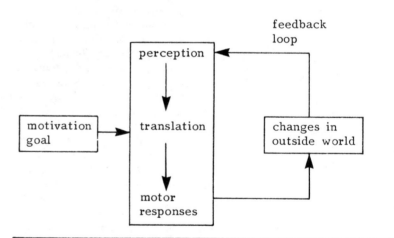

In each case the performer is pursuing certain goals, makes continuous response to feedback, and emits hierarchically-organized motor responses. This model has been heuristically very useful in drawing attention to the importance of feedback, and hence to gaze; it also suggests a number of different ways in which social performances can fail, and suggests the training procedures that may be effective, through analogy with motor skills training (Argyle and Kendon, 1967; Argyle, 1969).

The model emphasizes the motivation, goals and plans of interactors. It is postulated that every interactor is trying to achieve some goal, whether or not there is awareness of that. These goals may be, for example, to be liked by another person, to obtain or convey information, to modify the other's emotional state, and so on. Such goals may be linked to more basic motivational systems. Goals have subgoals; for example, doctors must diagnose patients before they can be treated. Patterns of response are directed towards goals and sub-goals, and have a hierarchical structure: large units of behaviour are composed of smaller ones, and at the lowest levels these are habitual and automatic.

The role of reinforcement

This is one of the key processes in social skills sequences. When interactor A does what B wants done, B is pleased and sends immediate and spontaneous reinforcements: smile, gaze, approving noises, and so on, and modifies A's behaviour, probably by operant conditioning; for example, modifying the content of subsequent utterances. At the same time A is modifying B's behaviour in exactly the same way. These effects appear to be mainly outside the focus of conscious attention, and take place very rapidly. It follows that anyone who gives strong rewards and punishments in the course of interaction will be able to modify the behaviour of others in the desired direction. In addition, the stronger the rewards that A issues, the more strongly other people will be attracted to A.

The role of gaze in social skills

The social skills model suggests that the monitoring of another's reactions is an essential part of social performance. The other's verbal signals are mainly heard, but non-verbal signals are mainly seen; the exceptions being the non-verbal aspects of speech and touch. It was this implication of the social skills model which directed us towards the study of gaze in social interaction. In dyadic interaction each person looks about 50 per cent of the time, mutual gaze occupies 25 per cent of the time, looking while listening is about twice the level of looking while talking, glances are about three seconds, and mutual glances about one second, with wide variations due to distance, sex combination, and personality (Argyle and Cook, 1976). However, there are several important differences between social behaviour and motor skills.

* Rules: the moves which interactors may make are governed by rules; they must respond properly to what has gone before. Similarly, rules govern the other's responses and can be used to influence behaviour; for example, questions lead to answers.
* Taking the role of the other: it is important to

perceive accurately the reactions of others. It is also necessary to perceive the perceptions of others; that is, to take account of their points of view. This appears to be a cognitive ability which develops with age (Flavell, 1968), but which may fail to develop properly. Those who are able to do this have been found to be more effective at a number of social tasks, and more altruistic. Meldman (1967) found that psychiatric patients are more egocentric (i.e. talked about themselves more than controls), and it has been our experience that socially unskilled patients have great difficulty in taking the role of the other.

* The independent initiative of the other sequences of interaction: social situations inevitably contain at least one other person, who will be pursuing personal goals and using social skills. How can we analyse the resulting sequences of behaviour? For a sequence to constitute an acceptable piece of social behaviour, the moves must fit together in order. Social psychologists have by no means discovered all the principles or 'grammar' underlying these sequences, but some of the principles are known, and can explain common forms of interaction failure.

Verbal and non-verbal communication

Verbal communication

There are several different kinds of verbal utterance.

* Egocentric speech: this is directed to the self, is found in infants and has the effect of directing behaviour.
* Orders, instructions: these are used to influence the behaviour of others; they can be gently persuasive or authoritarian.
* Questions: these are intended to elicit verbal information; they can be open-ended or closed, personal or impersonal.
* Information: may be given in response to a question, or as part of a lecture or during problem-solving discussion.

(The last three points are the basic classes of utterance.)

* Informal speech: consists of casual chat, jokes, gossip, and contains little information, but helps to establish and sustain social relationships.
* Expression of emotions and interpersonal attitudes: this is a special kind of information; however, this information is usually conveyed, and is conveyed more effectively, non-verbally.
* Performative utterances: these include 'illocutions' where saying the utterance performs something (voting, judging, naming, etc.), and 'perlocutions', where a goal

is intended but may not be achieved (persuading, intimidating, etc.).
* Social routines: these include standard sequences like thanking, apologizing, greeting, and so on.
* Latent messages: in these, the more important meaning is made subordinate ('As I was saying to the Prime Minister ...').

There are many category schemes for reducing utterances to a limited number of classes of social acts. One of the best known is that of Bales (1950), who introduced the 12 classes shown in figure 2.

Non-verbal signals accompanying speech
Non-verbal signals play an important part in speech and conversation. They have three main roles:

* completing and elaborating on verbal utterances: utterances are accompanied by vocal emphasis, gestures and facial expressions, which add to the meaning and indicate whether it is a question, intended to be serious or funny, and so on;
* managing synchronizing: this is achieved by head-nods, gaze-shifts, and other signals. For example, to keep the floor a speaker does not look up at the end of an utterance, keeps a hand in mid-gesture, and increases the volume of his speech if the other interrupts;
* sending feedback signals: listeners keep up a continuous, and mainly unwitting, commentary on the speaker's utterances, showing by mouth and eyebrow positions whether they agree, understand, are surprised, and so on (Argyle, 1975).

Other functions of non-verbal communication (NVC)
NVC consists of facial expression, tone of voice, gaze, gestures, postures, physical proximity and appearance. We have already described how NVC is linked with speech; it also functions in several other ways, especially in the communication of emotions and attitudes to other people.

A sender is in a certain state, or possesses some information; this is encoded into a message which is then decoded by a receiver.

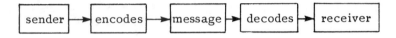

Encoding research is done by putting subjects into some state and studying the non-verbal messages which are emitted. For example Mehrabian (1972), in a role-playing experiment, asked subjects to address a hat-stand, imagining it to be a person. Men who liked the hat-stand looked at it more, did not have hands on hips and stood closer.

Figure 2

The Bales categories (from Bales, 1950)

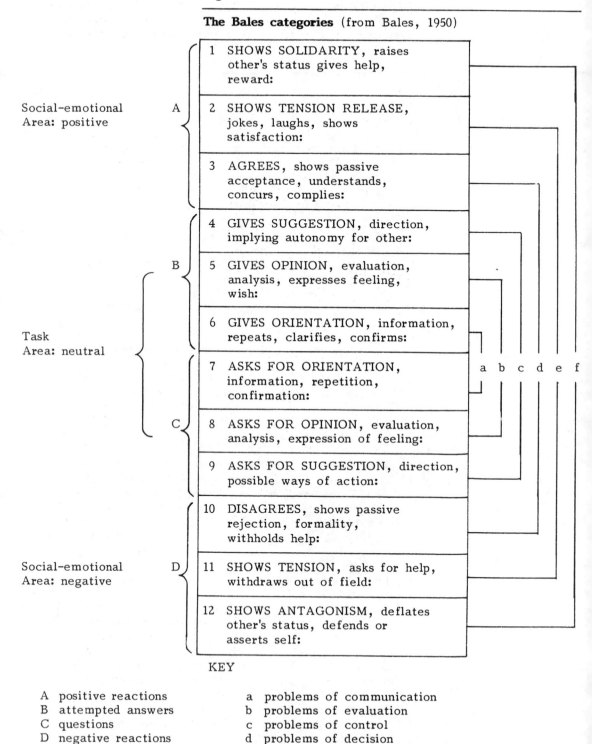

Social-emotional
Area: positive   A

Task
Area: neutral

Social-emotional
Area: negative   D

KEY

A positive reactions   a problems of communication
B attempted answers   b problems of evaluation
C questions   c problems of control
D negative reactions   d problems of decision
                                           e problems of tension reduction
                                           f problems of reintegration

Non-verbal signals are often 'unconscious': that is, they are outside the focus of attention. A few signals are unconsciously sent and received, like dilated pupils, signifying sexual attraction, but there are a number of other possibilities as shown in table 1.

Table 1
___

Awareness of non-verbal signals

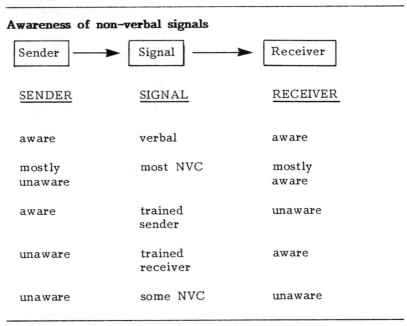

SENDER	SIGNAL	RECEIVER
aware	verbal	aware
mostly unaware	most NVC	mostly aware
aware	trained sender	unaware
unaware	trained receiver	aware
unaware	some NVC	unaware

___

Strictly speaking pupil dilation is not communication at all, but only a physiological response. 'Communication' is usually taken to imply some intention to affect another; one criterion of successful communication is that it makes a difference whether the other person is present and in a position to receive the signal; another is that the signal is repeated, varied or amplified if it has no immediate effect. These criteria are independent of conscious intention to communicate, which is often absent.

* Interpersonal attitudes: interactors indicate how much they like or dislike one another, and whether they think they are more or less important, mainly non-verbally. We have compared verbal and non-verbal signals and found that non-verbal cues like facial expression and tone of voice have far more impact than verbal ones (Argyle, Salter, Nicholson, Williams and Burgess, 1970).
* Emotional states: anger, depression, anxiety, joy, surprise, fear and disgust/contempt, are also communicated more clearly by non-verbal signals, such as facial expression, tone of voice, posture, gestures and gaze. Interactors may try to conceal their true emotions, but these are often revealed by 'leakage' via cues which are difficult to control.

Person perception

In order to respond effectively to the behaviour of others it is necessary to perceive them correctly. The social skills model emphasizes the importance of perception and feedback; to drive a car one must watch the traffic outside and the instruments inside. Such perception involves selecting certain cues, and being able to interpret them correctly. There is evidence of poor person perception in mental patients and other socially unskilled individuals, while professional social skills performers need to be sensitive to special aspects of other people and their behaviour. For selection interviewers and clinical psychologists the appraisal of others is a central part of the job.

We form impressions of other people all the time, mainly in order to predict their future behaviour, and so that we can deal with them effectively. We categorize others in terms of our favourite cognitive constructs, of which the most widely used are:

* extraversion, sociability;
* agreeableness, likeability;
* emotional stability;
* intelligence;
* assertiveness.

There are, however, wide individual differences in the constructs used, and 'complex' people use a larger number of such dimensions. We have found that the constructs used vary greatly with the situation: for example, work-related constructs are not used in purely social situations. We also found that the constructs used vary with the target group, such as children versus psychologists (Argyle, Furnham and Graham, 1981).

A number of widespread errors are made in forming impressions of others which should be particularly avoided by those whose job it is to assess people:

* assuming that a person's behaviour is mainly a product of personality, whereas it may be more a function of situation: at a noisy party, in church, and so on;
* assuming that behaviour is due to the person rather than the person's role; for example, as a hospital nurse, as a patient or as a visitor;
* attaching too much importance to physical cues, like beards, clothes, and physical attractiveness;
* being affected by stereotypes about the characteristics of members of certain races, social classes, etc.

During social interaction it is also necessary to perceive the emotional states of others: for example, to tell if they are depressed or angry. There are wide individual differences in the ability to judge emotions correctly (Davitz, 1964). As we have seen, emotions are mainly conveyed by non-verbal signals, especially by facial expression and tone of voice. The interpretation of emotions is also based on perception of the situation the other person is in. Lalljee at Oxford found that smiles are not necessarily decoded as happy, whereas unhappy faces are usually regarded as authentic.

Similar considerations apply to the perception of interpersonal attitudes, for instance who likes whom, which is also mainly based on non-verbal signals, such as proximity, gaze and facial expression. Again use is made of context to decode these signals: a glance at a stranger may be interpreted as a threat, an appeal for help or a friendly invitation. There are some interesting errors due to pressures towards cognitive consistency: if A likes B, then A thinks that B likes A more than B on average actually does: if A likes both B and C, A assumes that they both like each other more than, on average, they do.

It is necessary to perceive the on-going flow of interaction in order to know what is happening and to participate in it effectively. People seem to agree on the main episodes and sub-episodes of an encounter, but they may produce rather different accounts of why those present behaved as they did. One source of variation, and indeed error, is that people attribute the causes of others' behaviour to their personality ('He fell over because he is clumsy'), but their own behaviour to the situation ('I fell over because it was slippery'), whereas both factors operate in each case (Jones and Nisbett, 1972). Interpretations also depend on the ideas and knowledge an individual possesses: just as an expert on cars could understand better why a car was behaving in a peculiar way, so also can an expert on social behaviour understand why patterns of social behaviour occur.

Situations, their roles and other features

We know that people behave very differently in different situations; in order to predict behaviour, or to advise people on social skills in specific situations, it is necessary to analyse the situations in question. This can be done in terms of a number of fundamental features.

Goals
In all situations there are certain goals which are commonly obtainable. It is often fairly obvious what these are, but socially inadequate people may simply not know what parties are for, for example, or may think that the purpose of a selection interview is vocational guidance.

We have studied the main goals in a number of common situations, by asking samples of people to rate the importance of various goals, and then carrying out factor analysis. The main goals are usually:

* social acceptance, etc.;
* food, drink and other bodily needs;
* task goals specific to the situation.

We have also studied the relations between goals, within and between persons, in terms of conflict and instrumentality.

This makes it possible to study the 'goal structure' of situations (cf. Argyle et al, 1981).

Rules
All situations have rules about what may or may not be done in them. Socially inexperienced people are often ignorant or mistaken about the rules. It would obviously be impossible to play a game without knowing the rules and the same applies to social situations.

We have studied the rules of a number of everyday situations. There appear to be several universal rules; to be polite, friendly, and not embarrass people. There are also rules which are specific to situations, or groups of situations, and these can be interpreted as functional, since they enable situational goals to be met. For example, when seeing the doctor one should be clean and tell the truth; when going to a party one should dress smartly and keep to cheerful topics of conversation.

Special skills
Many social situations require special social skills, as in the case of various kinds of public speaking and interviewing, but also such everyday situations as dates and parties. A person with little experience of a particular situation may find that he lacks the special skills needed for it (cf. Argyle et al, 1981).

Repertoire of elements
Every situation defines certain moves as relevant. For example, at a seminar it is relevant to show slides, make long speeches, draw on the blackboard, etc. If moves appropriate to a cricket match or a Scottish ball were made, they would be ignored or regarded as totally bizarre. We have found 65-90 main elements used in several situations, like going to the doctor. We have also found that the semiotic structure varies between situations: we found that questions about work and about private life were sharply contrasted in an office situation, but not on a date.

Roles
Every situation has a limited number of roles: for example, a classroom has the roles of teacher, pupil, janitor, and school inspector. These roles carry different degrees of power, and the occupant has goals peculiar to that role.

Cognitive structure
We found that the members of a research group classified each other in terms of the concepts extraverted and enjoyable companion for social occasions, but in terms of dominant, creative and supportive for seminars. There are also concepts related to the task, such as 'amendment', 'straw vote' and 'nem con', for committee meetings.

Environmental setting and pieces
Most situations involve special environmental settings and

props. Cricket needs bat, ball, stumps, and so on; a seminar requires a blackboard, slide projector and lecture notes.

How do persons fit into situations, conceived in this way? To begin with, there are certain pervasive aspects of persons, corresponding to the 20 per cent or so of person variance found in P x S (personality and situation) studies. This consists of scores on general dimensions like intelligence, extraversion, neuroticism and so on. In addition, persons have dispositions to behave in certain ways in classes of situations; this corresponds to the 50 per cent or so of the P x S variance in relation to dimensions of situations like formal–informal, and friendly–hostile. Third, there are more specific reactions to particular situations; for example, behaviour in social psychology seminars depends partly on knowledge of social psychology, and attitudes to different schools of thought in it. Taken together these three factors may predict performance in, and also avoidance of, certain situations - because of lack of skill, anxiety, etc. - and this will be the main expectation in such cases.

Friendship

This is one of the most important social relationships: failure in it is a source of great distress, and so it is one of the main areas of social skills training. The conditions under which people come to like one another have been the object of extensive research, and are now well understood.

There are several stages of friendship: (i) coming into contact with the other, through proximity at work or elsewhere; (ii) increasing attachment as a result of reinforcement and discovery of similarity; (iii) increasing self-disclosure and commitment; and, sometimes, (iv) dissolution of the relationship. Friendship is the dominant relationship for adolescents and the unmarried; friends engage in characteristic activities, such as talking, eating, drinking, joint leisure, but not, usually, working.

Frequency of interaction
The more two people meet, the more polarized their attitudes to one another become, but usually they like one another more. Frequent interaction can come about from living in adjacent rooms or houses, working in the same office, belonging to the same club, and so on. So interaction leads to liking, and liking leads to more interaction. Only certain kinds of interaction lead to liking. In particular, people should be of similar status. Belonging to a co-operative group, especially under crisis conditions, is particularly effective, as Sherif's robbers' cave experiment (Sherif, Harvey, White, Hood and Sherif, 1961) and research on inter-racial attitudes have shown.

Reinforcement
The next general principle governing liking is the extent to which one person satisfies the needs of another. This was

shown in a study by Jennings of 400 girls in a reformatory (1950). She found that the popular girls helped and pro-tected others, encouraged, cheered them up, made them feel accepted and wanted, controlled their own moods so as not to inflict anxiety or depression on others, were able to establish rapport quickly, won the confidence of a wide variety of other personalities, and were concerned with the feelings and needs of others. The unpopular girls on the other hand were dominating, aggressive, boastful, demanded attention, and tried to get others to do things for them. This pattern has been generally interpreted in terms of the popular girls providing rewards and minimizing costs, while the unpopular girls tried to get rewards for themselves, and incurred costs for others. It is not necessary for the other person to be the actual source of rewards: Lott and Lott (1960) found that children who were given model cars by the experimenter liked the other children in the experiment more, and several studies have shown that people are liked more in a pleasant environmental setting.

Being liked is a powerful reward, so if A likes B, B will usually like A. This is particularly important for those who have a great need to be liked, such as individuals with low self-esteem. It is signalled, as discussed above, primarily by non-verbal signals.

Similarity
People like others who are similar to themselves, in certain respects. They like those with similar attitudes, beliefs and values, who have a similar regional and social class background, who have similar jobs or leisure interests, but they need not have similar personalities. Again there is a cyclical process, since similarity leads to liking and lik-ing leads to similarity, but effects of similarity on liking have been shown experimentally.

Physical attractiveness
Physical attractiveness (p.a.) is an important source of both same-sex and opposite sex liking, especially in the early stages. Walster, Aronson, Abrahams and Rottmann (19 arranged a 'computer dance' at which couples were paired at random: the best prediction of how much each person liked their partner was the latter's p.a. as rated by the experi-menter. Part of the explanation lies in the 'p.a. stereo-type'. Dion, Berscheid and Walster (1972) found that attrac-tive people were believed to have desirable characteristics of many other kinds. However, people do not seek out the most attractive friends and mates, but compromise by seekir those similar to themselves in attractiveness.

Self-disclosure
This is a signal for intimacy, like bodily contact, because it indicates trust in the other. Self-disclosure can be measured on a scale (1-5) with items like:

What are your favourite forms of erotic play and sexual lovemaking? (scale value 2.56)

What are the circumstances under which you become depressed and when your feelings are hurt? (3.51)

What are your hobbies, how do you best like to spend your spare time? (4.98) (Jourard, 1971).

As people get to know each other better, self-disclosure slowly increases, and is reciprocated, up to a limit.

Commitment
This is a state of mind, an intention to stay in a relationship, and abandon others. This involves a degree of dependence on the other person and trusting them not to leave the relationship. The less committed has the more power.

Social skills training
The most common complaint of those who seek SST is difficulty in making friends. Some of them say they have never had a friend in their lives. What advice can we offer, on the basis of research on friendship?

* As we showed earlier, social relations are negotiated mainly by non-verbal signals. Clients for SST who cannot make friends are usually found to be very inexpressive, in face and voice.
* Rewardingness is most important. The same clients usually appear to be very unrewarding, and are not really interested in other people.
* Frequent interaction with those of similar interests and attitudes can be found in clubs for professional or leisure activities, in political and religious groups, and so on.
* Physical attractiveness is easier to change than is social behaviour.
* Certain social skills may need to be acquired, such as inviting others to suitable social events, and engaging in self-disclosure at the right speed.

The meaning and assessment of social competence

By social competence we mean the ability, the possession of the necessary skills, to produce the desired effects on other people in social situations. These desired effects may be to persuade the others to buy, to learn, to recover from neurosis, to like or admire the actor, and so on. These results are not necessarily in the public interest: skills may be used for social or antisocial purposes. And there is no evidence that social competence is a general factor: a person may be better at one task than another, for example, parties or committees. SST for students and other more or less normal populations has been directed to the skills of dating, making friends and being assertive. SST for mental patients has been aimed at correcting failures of social competence, and also at relieving subjective distress, such as social anxiety.

To find out who needs training, and in what areas, a detailed descriptive assessment is needed. We want to know, for example, which situations individual trainees find difficult (formal situations, conflicts, meeting strangers, etc.), and which situations they are inadequate in, even though they do not report them as difficult. And we want to find out what individuals are doing wrong: failure to produce the right non-verbal signals, low rewardingness, lack of certain social skills, and so on.

Social competence is easier to define and agree upon in the case of professional social skills: an effective thera- pist cures more patients, an effective teacher teaches better, an effective salesperson sells more. When we look more closely, it is not quite so simple: examination marks may be one index of a teacher's effectiveness, but usually more is meant than just this. Salespersons should not simply sell a lot of goods, they should make the customers feel they would like to go to that shop again. So a combination of different skills is required and an overall assessment of effectiveness may involve the combination of a number of different measures or ratings. The range of competence is quite large: the best salesmen and saleswomen regularly sell four times as much as some others behind the same counter; some supervisors of working groups produce twice as much output as others, or have 20-25 per cent of the labour turnover and absenteeism rates (Argyle, 1972).

For everyday social skills it is more difficult to give the criteria of success; lack of competence is easier to spot: failure to make friends, or opposite sex friends, quarrelling and failing to sustain co-operative relation- ships, finding a number of situations difficult or a source of anxiety, and so on.

Methods of SST training

Role-playing with coaching
This is now the most widely-used method of SST. There are four stages:

* instruction;
* role-playing with other trainees or other role partners for five to eight minutes;
* feedback and coaching, in the form of oral comments from the trainer;
* repeated role-playing.

A typical laboratory set-up is shown in figure 3. This also shows the use of an ear-microphone for instruction while role-playing is taking place. In the case of patients, mere practice does no good: there must be coaching as well.

For an individual or group of patients or other trainees a series of topics, skills or situations is chosen, and introduced by means of short scenarios. Role partners who can be briefed to present carefully graded degrees of difficulty are used.

It is usual for trainers to be generally encouraging, and also rewarding for specific aspects of behaviour, though there is little experimental evidence for the value of such reinforcement. It is common to combine role-playing with modelling and video-playback, both of which are discussed below. Follow-up studies have found that role-playing combined with coaching is successful with many kinds of mental patients, and that it is one of the most successful forms of SST for these groups.

Role-playing usually starts with 'modelling', in which a film is shown or a demonstration given of how to perform the skill being taught. The feedback session usually includes videotape-playback and most studies have found that this is advantageous (Bailey and Sowder, 1970). While it often makes trainees self-conscious at first, this wears off after the second session. Skills acquired in the laboratory or class must be transferred to the outside world. This is usually achieved by 'homework': trainees are encouraged to try out the new skills several times before the next session. Most

igure 3

social skills training laboratory

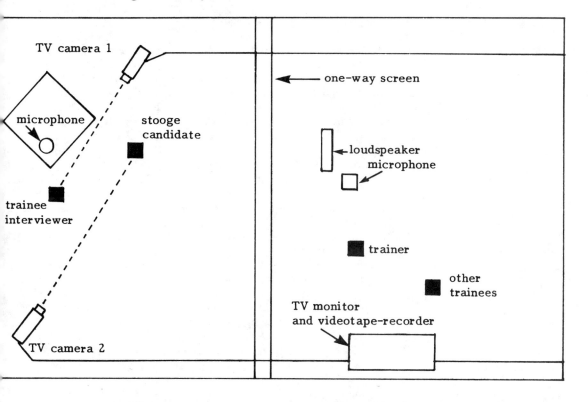

trainers take people in groups which provides a source of role partners, but patients may need individual sessions as well for individual problems.

Other methods of training

*   Training on the job: this is a widely used traditional method. Some people improve through experience but others do not, and some learn the wrong things. The situation can be improved if there is a trainer who regularly sees the trainee in action, and is able to hold feedback sessions at which errors are pointed out and better skills suggested. In practice this method does not appear to work very well, for example with trainee teachers (see Argyle, 1969).
*   Group methods: these, especially T-groups (T standing for training), are intended to enhance sensitivity and social skills. Follow-up studies have consistently found that 30-40 per cent of trainees are improved by group m thods, but up to 10 per cent are worse, sometimes needing psychological assistance (e.g. Lieberman, Yalom and Miles, 1973). It has been argued that group methods are useful for those who are resistant to being trained.
*   Educational methods: these, such as lectures and films, can increase knowledge, but to master social skills it is necessary to try them out, as is the case with motor skills. Educational methods can be a useful supplement to role-playing methods.

Areas of application of SST

*   Neurotic patients: role-playing and the more specialized methods described above have been found to be slightly more effective than psychotherapy, desensitization, or other alternative treatments, but not much (Trower, Bryant and Argyle, 1978). Only one study so far has found really substantial differences: Maxwell (1976), in a study of adults reporting social difficulties and seeking treatment for them, in New Zealand, insisted on homework between training sessions. However, SST does produce more improvement in social skills and reduction of social anxiety. A few patients can be cured by SST alone, but most have other problems as well, and may require other forms of treatment in addition.
*   Psychotic patients: these have been treated in the USA by assertiveness training and other forms of role-playing. Follow-up studies have shown greater improvement in social behaviour than from alternative treatments. The most striking results have been obtained with intensive clinical studies of one to four patients, using a 'multiple baseline' design: one symptom is worked on at a time over a total of 20-30 sessions. It is not clear from these follow-up studies to what extent the general condition of patients has been improved, or

how well they have been able to function outside the hospital (Hersen and Bellack, 1976). It has been argued by one practitioner that SST is more suitable than psychotherapy for working-class patients in view of their poor verbal skills (Goldstein, 1973).

Other therapeutic uses of SST

*   Alcoholics: alcoholics have been given SST to improve their assertiveness, for example in refusing drinks, and to enable them to deal better with situations which they find stressful and make them drink. Similar treatment has been given to drug addicts. In both cases treatment has been fairly successful, though the effects have not always been long-lasting; SST is often included in more comprehensive packages.
*   Delinquents and prisoners: these have often been given SST with some success, especially in the case of aggressive and sex offenders. SST can also increase their degree of internal control.
*   Teachers, managers, doctors, etc.: SST is increasingly being included in the training of those whose work involves dealing with people. The most extensive application so far has been in the training of teachers by 'micro-teaching'. They are instructed in one of the component skills of teaching, such as the use of different kinds of question, explanation or the use of examples; they then teach five or six children for 10-15 minutes, followed by a feedback session and 're-teaching'. Follow-up studies show that this is far more effective than a similar amount of teaching practice, and it is much more effective in eradicating bad habits (Brown, 1975). In addition to role-playing, more elaborate forms of simulation are used, for example to train people for administrative positions. Training on the job is a valuable addition or alternative, provided that trainers really do their job.
*   Normal adults: students have received a certain amount of SST, especially in North American universities, and follow-up studies have shown that they can be successfully trained in assertiveness (Rich and Schroeder, 1976), dating behaviour (Curran, 1977), and to reduce anxiety at performing in public (Paul, 1966). Although many normal adults apart from students have social behaviour difficulties, very little training is available unless they seek psychiatric help. It would be very desirable for SST to be more widely available, for example in community centres.
*   Schoolchildren: a number of attempts have been made to introduce SST into schools, though there are no follow-up studies on its effectiveness. However, there have been a number of successful follow-up studies of training schemes for children who are withdrawn and unpopular or aggressive, using the usual role-playing methods (Rinn and Markle, 1979).

Conclusion

In this chapter we have given an account of those aspects of social psychology which are most relevant to the work of teachers, social workers and others, both in understanding the behaviour of their clients and also in helping them with their own performance. We have used various models of social behaviour, such as the social skills model and the model of social behaviour as a game. Some of the phenomena described cannot be fully accounted for in terms of these models: for example, the design of sequences of interaction. A number of practical implications have been described; in particular, discussion of the skills which have been demonstrated to be the most effective in a number of situations, and the methods of SST which have been found to have most impact. should be emphasized that much of this research is quite new and it is expected that a great deal more will be found out on these topics in the years to come.

References

Argyle, M. (1969)
   Social Interaction. London: Methuen.
Argyle, M. (1972)
   The Social Psychology of Work. London: Allen Lane and Penguin Books.
Argyle, M. (1975)
   Bodily Communication. London: Methuen.
Argyle, M. and Cook, M. (1976)
   Gaze and Mutual Gaze. London: Cambridge University Press.
Argyle, M., Furnham, A. and Graham, J.A. (1981)
   Social situations. London: Cambridge University Press.
Argyle, M. and Kendon, A. (1967)
   The experimental analysis of social performance. In L. Berkowitz (ed.), Advances in Experimental Social Psychology, Volume 3. New York: Academic Press.
Argyle, M., Salter V., Nicholson, H., Williams, M. and Burgess, P. (1970)
   The communication of inferior and superior attitudes by verbal and non-verbal signals. British Journal of Social and Clinical Psychology, 9, 221-231.
Bailey, K.G. and Sowder, W.T. (1970)
   Audiotape and videotape self-confrontation in psychotherapy. Psychological Bulletin, 74, 127-137.
Bales, R.F. (1950)
   Interaction Process Analysis. Cambridge, Mass.: Addison-Wesley.
Brown, G.A. (1975)
   Microteaching. London: Methuen.
Curran, J.P. (1977)
   Skills training as an approach to the treatment of heterosexual-social anxiety. Psychological Bulletin, 84, 140-157.
Davitz, J.R. (1964)
   The Communication of Emotional Meaning. New York: McGraw-Hill.

Dion, K., Berscheid, E. and Walster, E. (1972)
What is beautiful is good. Journal of Personality and
Social Psychology, 24, 285-290.

Flavell, J.H. (1968)
The Development of Role-taking and Communication Skills
in Children. New York: Wiley.

Goldstein, A.J. (1973)
Structured Learning Therapy: Toward a psychotherapy for
the poor. New York: Academic Press.

Harré, R. and Secord, P. (1972)
The Explanation of Social Behaviour. Oxford: Blackwell.

Hersen, M. and Bellack, A.S. (1976)
Social skills training for chronic psychiatric patients:
rationale, research findings, and future directions.
Comprehensive Psychiatry, 17, 559-580.

Jennings, H.H. (1950)
Leadership and Isolation. New York: Longmans Green.

Jones, E.E. and Nisbett, R.E. (1972)
The actor and the observer: divergent perceptions of the
causes of behavior. In E.E. Jones, D. Kanouse, H.
Kelley, R.E. Nisbett, S. Valins and B. Weiner (eds),
Attribution: Perceiving the causes of behavior.
Morristown, NJ: General Learning Press.

Jourard, S.M. (1971)
Self Disclosure. New York: Wiley Interscience.

Lieberman, M.A., Yalom, I.D. and Miles, M.R. (1973)
Encounter Groups: First facts. New York: Basic Books.

Lott, A.J. and Lott, B.E. (1960)
The formation of positive attitudes towards group
members. Journal of Abnormal and Social Psychology, 61,
297-300.

Maxwell, G.M. (1976)
An evolution of social skills training. (Unpublished,
University of Otago, Dunedin, New Zealand.)

Mehrabian, A. (1972)
Nonverbal Communication. New York: Aldine-Atherton.

Meldman, M.J. (1967)
Verbal behaviour analysis of self-hyperattentionism.
Diseases of the Nervous System, 28, 469-473.

Paul, G.L. (1966)
Insight v. Desensitization in Psychotherapy. Stanford,
Ca: Stanford University Press.

Rich, A.R. and Schroeder, H.E. (1976)
Research issues in assertiveness training. Psychological
Bulletin, 83, 1081-1096.

Rimn, R.C. and Markle, A. (1979)
Modification of social skill deficits in children. In
A.S. Bellack and M. Hersen (eds), Research and Practice
in Social Skills Training. New York: Plenum.

**Sherif, M., Harvey, O.J., White, B.J., Hood, W.R. and
Sherif, C.** (1961)
Intergroup Conflict and Cooperation: The Robbers' Cave
experiment. Norman, Oklahoma: The University of Oklahoma
Book Exchange.

Trower, P., Bryant, B. and Argyle, M. (1978)
Social Skills and Mental Health. London: Methuen.
Walster, E., Aronson, E., Abrahams, D. and Rottmann, L.
(1966)
Importance of physical attractiveness in dating
behavior. Journal of Personality and Social Psychology,
5, 508-516.

Questions

1. Is it useful to look at social behaviour as a kind of
   skill?
2. What do bad conversationalists do wrong?
3. What information is conveyed by non-verbal communication, and in what ways do non-verbal signals supplement
   verbal ones?
4. How is the perception of other people different from the
   perception of other physical objects?
5. What information about a social situation would a
   newcomer to it need to know?
6. Do we like other people primarily because they are
   rewarding?
7. Why do some people have difficulty in making friends?
8. What criticisms have been made of experiments in social
   psychology? What other methods are available?
9. Does social behaviour take the same form in other
   cultures?
10. Are there fundamental differences between social
    behaviour in families, work-groups and groups of
    friends?

Annotated reading

Argyle, M. (1978) The Psychology of Interpersonal Behaviour
(3rd edn). Harmondsworth: Penguin.
Covers the field of the chapter, and related topics at
Penguin level.

Argyle, M. and Trower, P. (1979). Person to Person. Londo
Harper & Row.
A more popular account of the area covered by the
chapter, with numerous coloured illustrations.

Argyle, M. (1975). Bodily Communication. London: Methuen.
Covers the field of non-verbal communication in more
detail, with some illustrations.

Berscheid, E. and Walster, E.H. (1978). Interpersonal
Attraction (2nd edn). Reading, Mass.: Addison-Wesley.
A very readable account of research in this area.

Bower, S.A. and Bower, G.H. (1976). Asserting Yourself.
Reading, Mass.: Addison-Wesley.
An interesting and practical book about assertiveness,
with examples and exercises.

Cook, M. (1979). Perceiving Others. London: Methuen.
A clear account of basic processes in person perception.

Goffman, E. (1956). The Presentation of Self in Everyday Life. Edinburgh: Edinburgh University Press.
A famous and highly entertaining account of self-presentation.

Trower, P., Bryant, B. and Argyle, M. (1978). Social Skills and Mental Health. London: Methuen.
An account of social skills training with neurotics, with full details of procedures.

xercises

1. Participant observation of formal and informal interactions

Compare and contrast behaviour in two small groups, one more formal than the other: for instance, in a tutorial group and in a cafeteria with friends or contemporaries. Consider the ways in which non-verbal behaviours as well as language are used to convey information and express emotions. For example, look for social routines, performative utterances, social reinforcement, latent messages, different types of questioning, status effects, use of humour and sex differences (e.g. in eye contact and interpersonal distance).

Self-assessment of social competence profile

Use a list of 40-50 common social situations, rating yourself on how difficult you find each situation on a five-point scale of difficulty. Group the situations according to perceived similarity, and find what is in common to the situations which you find difficult. Research on these difficult situations is reported in Argyle et al (1981).

1. Walking down the street
2. Going into shops
3. Going on public transport
4. Going to parties
5. Mixing with people at work
6. Making friends of your own age
7. Going out with an opposite-sex partner
8. Being with same age/sex group
9. Being with same age/mixed sex group
10. Being with opposite sex group
11. Entertaining people in your own house
12. Going into restaurants/cafés
13. Going to dances/discos
14. Being with older people
15. Being with younger people
16. Going into a room full of people
17. Meeting strangers
18. Being with people you don't know

19. Being with friends
20. Approaching others
21. Making decisions affecting others
22. Being with one person rather than group
23. Getting to know people in depth
24. Taking initiative in conversation
25. Looking people in the eye
26. Disagreeing and being assertive
27. People standing/sitting very close
28. Talking about yourself/self-disclosure
29. People looking at you
30. Introducing two people
31. Attending a formal dinner
32. Complaining about satisfactory service
33. Seeing a doctor/bank manager
34. Being the leader of a small group
35. Dealing with people of higher status
36. Reprimanding a subordinate
37. Complaining to a neighbour whom you know well about constant noisy disturbances
38. Taking a person of the opposite sex out for the first time for an evening
39. Going for a job interview
40. Going to a close relative's funeral
41. Going round to cheer up a depressed friend who asked you to call
42. Being a host or hostess at a large party (e.g. twenty-first birthday)
43. Give a short formal speech to a group of about 50 people that you don't know
44. Taking an unsatisfactory article back to a shop where you purchased it
45. Going across to introduce yourself to new neighbours
46. Dealing with a difficult and disobedient child
47. Going to a function with many people from a different culture
48. Playing a party game after dinner (charades, musical chairs)
49. Attending a distant relative's wedding ceremony when you know few people
50. Apologizing to a superior for forgetting an important errand

15

Interviewing: the social psychology of the inter-view
Robert Farr

Interviewing is an everyday social phenomenon as well as being a widely used technique for gathering data both in professional practice and in social research. It is essentially a technique or method for establishing or discovering that there are perspectives or viewpoints on events other than those of the person initiating the interview. Those who work professionally in the media are accustomed to conducting interviews in the course of a day's work. Many thousands more listen to, view, or read about these self-same interviews. The interview is thus a common event, though many participate only vicariously in such encounters.

An interview is a social encounter between two or more individuals with words as the main medium of exchange. It is, in short, a peculiar form of conversation in which the ritual of turn-taking is more formalized than in the commoner and more informal encounters of everyday life. A conversation or interview is a co-operative venture. Despite the common assumptions that make conversations or talks possible, the interface between the individuals involved is always potentially present. When talks break down or conversation proves difficult this highlights the interface which is always potentially present within the inter-view. Conversations are embryonic interviews even though the participants might not so conceive of them. This general approach is compatible with the viewpoint adopted by Gorden (1975): 'I consider as an interviewer any person who uses conversation as a means of obtaining information from another person.'

The distinctive approach of this chapter

This chapter is intended to be an introduction to the social psychology of the inter-view. As such, it is a modest contribution to the development of a theory appropriate to the practice and conduct of interviews. There is, at present, no adequate theory in psychology of direct relevance to the practice of interviewing. This may surprise the reader. There is much advice offered and many guides are to be found in the literature as to how best to conduct interviews. There is also much research relevant to certain aspects of the interview, such as research in cognitive psychology on how we perceive persons (inspired by Heider's seminal work) and purely behavioural research on various aspects of non-verbal communication, etc. There is, however, no overall framework within which these theoretically opposed areas of research could be integrated with one another and made relevant to the practice of interviewing. We need theory in order to understand what goes on in the interview situation.

Any purely psychological theory is likely to be inadequate as the interview is so obviously a social encounter. Any adequate social psychology of the interview must enable us to account for the actions and experience both of the person being interviewed and of the person conducting the interview. Any theory of the interview which was not also at one and the same time a theory of the human self would be inadequate to the task in hand. Any theory which failed to account for states of awareness or consciousness in the parties to the interaction would similarly be inappropriate. We have sought to keep salient the inherently social nature of the interview by the simple expedient of using a hyphen: that is, by talking about inter-views rather than interviews, and similarly, inter-face and inter-action.

In devising an appropriate theory for the understanding of the interview we have drawn on Heider's psychology of interpersonal relations; on Goffman's work in sociology on the presentation of self in everyday life; on the work of Freud, in psychiatry, in devising a psychology based on listening rather than one based exclusively on visual observation; and on the philosophy of George Herbert Mead. While the influences derive from a number of disciplines the theory is an explicitly social psychological one. We have also found it convenient to adopt and adapt the divergence in perspective between actors and observers first noted by Jones and Nisbett in 1971. We have been impressed by the advantages which Becker and Geer (1957) claim for participant observation as a methodology over an exclusive reliance upon the interview alone. We have sought to include in this approach to the inter-view some of the advantages which Becker and Geer claim for participant observation. In our approach to the inter-view we are, therefore, influenced by the experience of social anthropologists and of sociologists.

The psychology of inter-personal relations

There is much that psychologists can learn from a study of the social psychology of everyday life. This is the viewpoint taken by the psychologist Fritz Heider (1958). He was particularly interested in how we perceive other persons and the evidence we use when we make inferences as to what is going on in the minds of those with whom we inter-act. He referred to the perceiver as P and the person whom he observes as O (i.e. the 'other'). The man-in-the-street does not hesitate to infer the attitudes, hopes, fears, motives, opinions, intentions, etc., of those with whom he inter-acts. Indeed, he is only intermittently aware that most of what he 'knows' about others is highly conjectural. The professional psychologist, however, is more acutely aware of the extent to which our knowledge of the minds of others involves our going beyond the information available; that is, it is based on inference rather than strictly on observation. We cannot directly 'observe' another's motives, intentions, aspirations, attitudes, and so on.

Heider's psychology of inter-personal relations is highly relevant to the inter-view situation. While Man is seldom aware that most of his knowledge of others is based on conjecture, he is sometimes acutely aware that what others know about him is highly conjectural. This is particularly true in the inter-view situation. The persons being interviewed (i.e. the interviewees) are only too well aware that the other (i.e. the interviewer) is likely to be making inferences concerning their motives, intentions, etc., on the basis of what they say and do in the interview.

Heider was primarily concerned with how P perceives O. In common with many other psychologists Heider's primary interest was in what we can learn about others by observing them from the outside. O, however, need not remain silent in the presence of P. O can talk about, or 'reveal', opinions, attitudes, aspirations, motives, hopes, fears and so on. The interview is the technique par excellence for eliciting such self-reports. When O speaks, a perspective other than that of P is revealed. P and O engage in conversation while the unique perspective of each is retained. This difference in perspective between them helps to produce an inter-view in the literal sense of that term.

An interview is also a form of social encounter between persons. Heider set out to devise a psychology of inter-personal relations. It is worth reflecting briefly on what we understand by the word 'person'. The philosopher Strawson considered it to be a characteristic of persons that they can monitor their own actions and give an 'account' of them (see Harré and Secord, 1972). We are accustomed in everyday life to accounting for our actions. Persons have names. When we know people's names we can address them as individuals rather than needing to hail them as strangers. They are 'accountable' and normally 'respond' when others address them. In the technical literature relating to the interview as a research tool in social science, the person being interviewed is normally referred to as the 'respondent'. Persons readily respond to being inter viewed because it is a constituent part of their everyday social experience. It is not an alien or obtrusive mode of investigation.

The divergence in perspective between actors and observers

Heider introduced us to the perspective of P, the observer or perceiver. An actor is any person whose behaviour is currently the focus of attention. In the language of drama which suffuses the writing of Goffman, the actor is the person who is currently 'on stage'. Jones and Nisbett (1971) note an important divergence in perspective between actors and observers: 'There is a pervasive tendency for actors to attribute their actions to situational requirements, whereas observers tend to attribute the same actions to stable personal dispositions' (Jones and Nisbett, 1971). Actors are more likely to consider their actions to be situationally appropriate whilst observers are more likely to make inferences about the sort of person an actor is on the basis of observable actions.

The awareness of actors that they are objects in the social worlds of others leads them to become 'apprehensive' as to how those others might evaluate them. The actors are here clearly aware of the divergence in perspective between themselves and the observing others. Too acute an awareness of this may cause an inter-viewee to perform poorly. For th chronically shy this is likely to be a particular problem. A certain measure of self-confidence is necessary if a person is to create a favourable impression in the inter-view situation. In his description of the art of impression management, Goffman (1959) makes telling use of the metaphor of the theatre. In his everyday presentation of himself, Man as an actor is putting on a 'performance' for a particular audience. The audience may be the 'other' with whom he is inter-acting. This obviously is the case in the typical inter-view. Goffman describes action in terms of its relation to the observing and listening other: that is, his conception of the audience is critical to his portrayal of action. This is why he is so much more genuinely socio-psychological in his approach than any mere psychologist could be. This is an important contribution to an understanding of the dynamics of the inter-view.

Goffman notes that the mirror is one of the most useful devices to be found backstage in any theatre. The mirror enables an actor to become an object to himself before he goes 'on stage' and becomes an object to others. In preparing for inter-views candidates often find mirrors to be similarly useful. The work of Goffman beautifully illustrates why a theory of the human self is necessary in order to understand what occurs in the inter-view. We also believe that an adequate analysis of the nature of human consciousness is an essential ingredient in any theory which purports to shed significant light on what occurs in the course of an inter-view. Mead's theory of action provides us with the necessary theory both of human consciousness and of the human self.

We have drawn on the work of Goffman for an account human action and for his portrayal of Man as agent or actor and on the work of Heider for his delineation of the perspective of Man as an observer of others. We are indebted to Jones and Nisbett for suggesting that these two perspectives might be different. It is worth considering how we might apply their distinction to accounting for differing views of the same actions. In a series of experimental studies, Milgram (1974) obtained high levels of obedience to an experimental request to administer what the subject believed to be high levels of electric shock to a fellow subject. Those who complied with the experimental request regarded their actions as being entirely appropriate in the particular experimental setting in which they occurred. This is the perspective of Jones and Nisbett's 'actor'.

The majority of subjects in Milgram's experiment would reject the inference which any who observed their acts of obedience might have made about them as persons on the basis of their actions. That this is so is revealed in an interesting variation on his main theme which Milgram later introduced. He described his experiment to a number of subjects whom he then invited to respond by saying how they would act in this situation. This is more akin to the hypothetical questions which persons being inter-viewed are often invited to consider. Indeed, this particular study was an inter-view rather than being an experiment in any strict sense of the term. The actual task in the original experiment involved increasing the level of shock administered, by way of punishment, to a subject in a learning task each time he made a mistake. Few subjects in this hypothetical situation saw themselves as advancing much beyond the earlier low levels of shock on the generator. It was almost as if there were different 'selves' for each button on the shock generator. In considering how they would act, subjects were able to reject the selves corresponding to the buttons at the 'high shock' end of the generator. They were thus able to consider what they would think of themselves if they were to press each of these buttons. This 'pause for reflection' enabled subjects to adopt the perspective of being an observer of their own hypothetical actions. They were thus able to inter-act with themselves. This is a process which the philosopher, G. H. Mead, called thinking.

In the analysis of Jones and Nisbett, actor and observer are two different persons. The actual face-to-face encounter of the inter-view, however, produces social states of awareness which are infinitely more complex and subtle than those envisaged by Jones and Nisbett. These more complex states of awareness arise because each of the interactants in an inter-view is both an actor and an observer and each is capable of alternating between these two perspectives.

demise of the
rview as a way of
ssing persons and the
of the psychological
: a brief historical
:

Humans are liable to 'react' to the knowledge that their actions are being observed. If the very act of investigating behaviour alters what is there to be observed, then the techniques of investigation used can be described as 'reactive' (Webb, Campbell, Schwartz and Sechrest, 1966). The interview is clearly a highly 'reactive' way of appraising people. The inter-view, as proposed in this chapter, is even more explicitly 'reactive' than the commoner and more conventional varieties of the same species. Psychologists, early in the history of their discipline, rejected the interview as a valid way of assessing either the intelligence of children or the suitability of adults for jobs. At the time this rejection was hailed as an important scientific advance. It is worth briefly considering why this was so.

The amount of information potentially present in the face-to-face encounter of an interview is liable to overwhelm even the most experienced of interviewers. Different interviewers sample from the available evidence differently. They use and combine the information they do select in highly impressionistic or subjective ways. Psychologists were quick to prove their worth by reducing the amount of 'noise' (i.e. irrelevant information) present in the appraisal setting. Rather than ranging over the whole gamut of information potentially available they instead preferred to 'tune in' to information transmitted on much narrower wavebands. This information could be collected under quite rigorously controlled conditions. The psychological test yielded much more precise information and this information could be combined objectively in ways which research had demonstrated to be valid. This is how the psychological test - or rather a battery of such tests - came to supersede the interview as the preferred way of assessing persons.

It is worth briefly noting certain aspects of this early critique of the interview. The origins of the doubts which still linger on in the minds of psychologists concerning the validity of the interview can be found in the very success of this early critique. This is one reason why psychologists so far have done so little to improve the interview as a method of investigation. Eysenck (1953) presents a convenient account:

> One of the earliest investigations of the interview is reported by Binet, the creator of modern intelligence tests. Three teachers interviewed the same children and estimated the intelligence of each. These estimates were based on the results of an interview conducted by each teacher as he saw fit. Binet reports two outcomes of this experiment which have since been verified over and over again. Each interviewer was confident that his judgement was right. Each interviewer disagreed almost completely with the judgement of the other interviewers

This was the kind of evidence which highlighted, at an early stage, the unreliability of the interview as an appraisal device. The failure amongst interviewers to agree in their judgements led to the development of standardized tests. Here psychologists were quite consciously adopting a scientific perspective: that of being the detached observer of others. In commenting on the significance of Binet's first conclusion concerning the confidence with which each interviewer held his judgement, Eysenck notes that this 'explains why, in spite of all the factual information regarding its inadequacy, the interview has remained the firm favourite of most people who have to select personnel for industrial and other purposes' (Eysenck, 1953). Here interviewers are behaving like Jones and Nisbett's 'actors':

that is, they see their actions as being situationally appropriate. Eysenck neatly captures the difference in perspective noted above between the 'actor' (i.e. the interviewer as agent) and the 'observer' (i.e. the scientist who 'validates' the predictive accuracy of the interviewer's judgements).

Interviewers, naturally, feel that their actions are justifiable and so seek to maintain their autonomy even in the face of scientific evidence:

> Time and time again does one encounter the individual who admits all the evidence about the inadequacy of the interview but stoutly maintains that he or she is the one outstanding exception to this general rule, and that his or her opinions are almost invariably correct. (Needless to say, experimental studies of such individuals fail to disclose any greater ability to forecast success and failure among them than is found among other people) (Eysenck, 1953).

This very human tendency to consider oneself to be an exception may derive from the unique perspective of the 'actor'. Kay (1971) has noted a similar tendency with respect to the occurrence of accidents. Individuals find it difficult to conceive of themselves as having an accident. However, scientists, as observers of others, can afford from the greater distance of their own quite different perspectives to be more sceptical. From this perspective, accidents do not just 'happen': they are caused.

The early pioneers of psychological tests who so readily dismissed the interview as a valid way of assessing people were bewitched by the magic of measurement. Their perspective was that of being a scientific observer of others. Their basic strategy was to standardize the conditions under which they made their observations and then to attribute all of the variance in observed performance to the existence of individual differences. In so doing, they unwittingly adopted the perspective of Jones and Nisbett's 'observer': that is, on the basis of test scores they inferred the existence of 'traits', 'abilities', 'attitudes', etc., as relatively permanent dispositions in those whom they observed or tested.

The social antecedents of mind and self: the philosophy of G. H. Mead

Our sense of our own 'selfhood' has its origin in the experience of interacting with others within the framework of a shared culture and of a common language. This was the viewpoint of the American philosopher, G. H. Mead, who developed a form of social behaviourism at Chicago in the opening decades of the present century (Mead, 1934). Mead understood the symbolic nature of language and its key role in the development and creation of 'mind' in Man.

The model of Man which emerges from the writings of Mead is one of Man as being both speaker and listener. The social

behaviourism of Mead is thus more directly relevant to an
understanding of the dynamics of inter-viewing than are any
of the forms of behaviourism which developed within psycho
logy. Our own approach in this chapter to the dynamics of
inter-viewing is much influenced by the work of Mead. Man
according to Mead, is self-reflexive; that is, he is self-
aware as distinct from being merely conscious. Consciousnes
is something which Man shares with other species. Self-
consciousness is a distinctly human state of mind. Man is
unique as a species in that he can act towards himself as ar
object. He can do so because he is an object in the social
world of those others with whom he interacts. By 'assuming
the role of the other' (Mead) with respect to himself, he
becomes an 'other' to himself. Man can thus engage himself
in inter-action. When he does so we refer to this activity
as thinking. Thinking, for Mead, was a kind of internalized
dialogue between 'I' and various 'me's. We have already
noted above how some of the subjects in Milgram's experime
engaged in such internalized dialogues.

A theory of the human self is needed if we are to unde
stand the dynamics of the inter-view. The meaning of an ac
for Mead was to be found in the response which it elicits
from observing others. Man not only acts but also re-acts t
his own actions. He reacts to his own behaviour on the basi
of the actual or anticipated reactions of others.

These processes of action and of reaction are highly
characteristic of what happens in the course of an interview. Individuals will often anticipate in imagination a
formal interview, in the outcome of which they have a
personal stake. They may rehearse what they intend to say
and do and they may anticipate likely questions which might
be asked. After the event they are also likely to 're-enact'
what actually occurred in the course of the interview. Some
times these re-enactments are purely 'private' ones which
they carry out solely for their own benefit. Sometimes they
are more explicitly social in that they are 'accounts' which
the individual provides for others as to what occurred in
the course of the interview. Without an adequate theory of
the human self the psychologist could not possibly give a
coherent account of these important mental events which bo
precede and follow the interview proper. These fairly familiar experiences can be accounted for, given a theory of the
inherently social nature of the mind of Man. Mead provides
just such a theory.

Mead developed a purely behavioural account of the
origins of mind in Man: a theory of the human self. He also
shed important new light on the social nature of 'perspectives'. As children develop, according to Mead, they learn
to 'assume the role of the other' with respect to themselves. These social skills are first acquired in role-
playing and are then further developed in the playing of
games. Commercial transactions, such as those which were
interest to Adam Smith, depend for their success on the
reciprocal ability of buyer and seller to assume each

other's role. Those who excel in interviewing, either as interviewers or as interviewees, are adept at assuming each other's role in the interview situation.

In his later writings, Mead was much influenced by Einstein. He preferred to talk of 'assuming the perspective' of the other instead of his earlier preference for 'assuming the role' of the other. For Mead these 'perspectives' were objectively real: that is, they represented points in space/ time from which one could view events. It was, therefore, entirely possible to change one's perspective by the simple expedient of changing one's position in space/time. It is thus possible both literally and metaphorically to 'turn the tables' and for interviewers and interviewees to 'exchange places'. Successful interviewees already do this mentally in preparing themselves for an interview. Poor interviewers may experience much difficulty in imagining such an exchange of roles or places. Role-playing exercises and the techniques of self-confrontation (e.g. where interviewers watch a videotape of themselves actually conducting an interview) are now increasingly used in the training of interviewers. If the theoretical approach developed in the present chapter is a sound one then such training devices are well-founded.

Observing, questioning and listening: interpreting what we see and hear

Goffman belonged to that important tradition of social psychological thought at Chicago which drew at least some of its inspiration from the work of Mead. In referring to the social interactions of everyday life, Goffman had this to say: 'Many crucial facts lie beyond the time and place of interaction, or lie concealed within it' (1959). This is particularly true of the interview. One fails to grasp the significance of what is happening in an interview if one's attention is confined, in the interest of science, only to what can be directly observed from the outside.

Psychologists, when they accepted behaviourism, came to value what they could see and measure over what they could hear. It was only too easy to overlook the significance of something as invisible to the human eye as speech. In their attempts to make psychology a branch of natural science, the early pioneers stressed the physical rather than the symbolic nature of stimuli. Speech was thought of in terms of sound waves: as changes in the patterns of energy impinging on the human ear. The outcome of collaboration between psychologists and telecommunications engineers was the development within psychology of information theory as a specialism. To reduce language to 'information' as the human engineer uses that term is to destroy something distinctly human. In order properly to appreciate the significance of speech in human development it would first have been necessary to understand the symbolic nature of language. Only a philosopher like Mead would be likely to ask such a preliminary question.

If, instead of observing the actions of others one listens to them talking, one arrives at a totally different type of psychology. Freud established a whole new psychology based entirely upon listening. It is called psychoanalysis. As a theory about human behaviour, psychoanalysis was born and developed within the context of the clinical interview. Rather than visually exploring the natural world as a research physiologist, which was Freud's early training, he became instead, reluctantly, a practising clinician. He spent hours listening to his clients talking about themselves and their problems.

The difference in perspective between speaker and listener in Freud's consulting room gave birth to a psychology of the unconsciousness. There were aspects of the analysand's 'account' of his own actions which were more apparent to the listener than to the speaker. Listener and speaker were here two separate persons. Speakers are less likely to be aware of the non-verbal aspects of their own accounts than listeners. 'Actors' generally are unaware of their own non-verbal behaviour. Non-verbal cues are more salient to the observers/listeners than they are to the actors themselves. The study of non-verbal behaviour is a significant contribution to an understanding of the interview which flows from the perspective of the behaviourist as an observer of others. Behaviourists tend to note or record this behaviour rather than to 'interpret' it. It is worth quoting Freud (1905) on this issue:

> When I set myself the task of bringing to light what human beings keep hidden within them, not by the compelling power of hypnosis, but by observing what the say and what they show I thought the task was a harder one than it really is. He that has eyes to see and ears to hear may convince himself that no mortal can keep a secret. If the lips are silent, he chatters with his finger tips; betrayal oozes out of him at every pore. And thus the task of making conscious the most hidden recesses of the mind is one which it is quite possible to accomplish.

The difference in perspective between analyst and analysand (i.e. the person undergoing analysis) may have important therapeutic implications. It corresponds to the difference in perspective between actors and observers previously noted. In seeking therapy the analysand might consider himself to be the victim of circumstances; for instance, as being, like King Lear, 'more sinned against than sinning'. The therapist, however, may not accept this 'account'. Therapists usually make the opposite attributional assumption: that is, they see the analysand as being the cause of their own problems. It is possible to consider psychoanalysis as a protracted negotiation of the analysand's original account by two persons who initially make opposite attributional assumptions.

Psychoanalysis, however, is not held in high esteem within scientific circles. As a science based on listening rather than one founded on observation, it is highly marginal within the context of natural science. It is, at one and the same time, both an odd kind of psychology and an odd kind of medicine. Its oddity in both respects may reflect, in part, a strong preference for vision over hearing as the preferred modality of research in both psychology and medicine.

Within psychology, behaviourists sought to make their discipline a branch of natural science by concentrating on what they could observe rather than by striving to understand what they could hear. Watson and Skinner typify this general strategy while Freud remains a striking, but solitary, example of someone who chose the latter alternative. There could scarcely be a more marked contrast than the one between behaviourism and psychoanalysis. This contrast is further mirrored in the differences between behaviour therapy and psychotherapy. In the former one 'treats' people, whilst in the latter one interviews them. In the former one removes 'symptoms', whilst in the latter one 'interprets' them.

The question of interpretation is an important one for the professional interviewer. Freud, in his early clinical interviews, listened to his clients relating how, as young girls, they had been seduced by their own fathers. He was inclined, at first, to believe in the truth of these accounts. When the number of such incidents, of which he had heard tell, came to greatly exceed his own prior expectations concerning the likelihood of such events occurring in Viennese society, he dramatically changed his interpretation of these 'accounts'. His decision to interpret these accounts as fantasy rather than as reflecting reality had dramatic consequences for the subsequent development of psychoanalysis. He was forced to distinguish between fantasy and reality and to oppose the pleasure to the reality principle. This was how he resolved his obligations as an interviewer to indicate the level of reality to which his observations referred.

There are two opposing dangers which threaten to ensnare the unwary social scientist. The first is to believe that he does not need to ask questions in order to establish the veracity of what he can observe for himself. The asking of questions helps to establish the existence of perspectives other than that of the investigator who has initiated the study. This leads to the establishment of an inter-view. There are a number of professional groups whose work directly involves them in observing and recording behaviour, yet who only rarely conduct interviews in the conventional sense of the term, such as nurses and classroom teachers. The written reports of these professional groups, summarizing their observations of behaviour on the wards or in the classroom, are often included as background information on the basis of which others, elsewhere in the organization, conduct clinical or educational interviews. However, persons in the higher reaches of these professions (nursing and teaching) almost certainly spend a great deal of their time interviewing in the more conventional sense of the term. This is probably true of almost anyone in a position of managerial responsibility. When a nurse on the ward, or a teacher in the classroom, asks questions in order to clarify or to verify what they observe, they are engaging in the process of inter-viewing as that term is used in this chapter. This is also true of the manager or supervisor in industry. The process of inter-viewing as outlined here is just such a process of checking on the veracity of one's observations. It is, therefore, a wider process of research than the interview as conventionally conceived. Failure to supplement and verify what one can observe by the asking of questions results in one type of error: that is, the limitations and biasses inherent in one's perspective as an observer are not subject to any process of cross-checking and hence one remains blind to them. A different sort of error arises if one accepts at face value the 'accounts' one elicits. In relation to the work of Herzlich on people's conceptions of health and illness (Herzlich, 1973) and of Herzberg on the nature of work motivation, Farr has identified some of the consequences that can flow from a too uncritical acceptance of what people say in the course of an unstructured or semi-structured research interview (Farr, 1977a,b).

Harré and Secord (1972) advocate the collection of 'accounts' as a brave new methodology for research in psychology. They base their case on Strawson's criterion of a person as being someone who can monitor his own behaviour and give an account of it. Collecting 'accounts' is thus equivalent to treating people as people. 'In order to be able to treat people as if they were human beings it must be possible to accept their commentaries upon their actions as authentic, though revisable, reports of phenomena, subject to empirical criticism' (Harré and Secord, 1972). If their plea were heeded then the interview would become the privileged mode of research in psychology, much as the experiment has been in the past and is still currently. The inter-view, as outlined here, might be more defensible from a scientific point of view, as it highlights the fact that the perspectives of researcher and informant are different and so sensitizes one to the possibility that important consequences might flow from this divergence in perspective.

Harré and Secord's proposal is not a particularly revolutionary one. Social psychologists traditionally have relied upon the collection of just such self-reports. This reflects the influence of Gestalt psychologists on the historical development of social psychology. Gestalt psychologists were interested in the study of perception. In order to explain a person's behaviour it was first necessary, in the opinion of Gestalt psychologists, to understand how that person perceived the world. The best way of finding out about a person's unique perspective, of course, is to invite him to tell you about it. You can best establish that his perspective is different from your own by means of an inter-view. Behaviourists, by directly relating aspects of the physical environment to observable responses, had completely by-passed perception as an important field of study.

In the study of attitudes the 'view of the world' approach which stems from Gestalt psychology came to prevail over the 'consistency of response' approach associated with behaviourism (see Campbell, 1963). To date, in the history of psychology, either the one or the other of these two perspectives has prevailed. How to inter-relate two such contrasting perspectives is perhaps the most interesting single problem which psychologists now face. By studying attitudes, social psychologists had hoped to avoid the laborious task of noting consistencies in a person's res-ponse to his social environment. The relationships between what people say and what they do turn out to be rather tenuous. These findings continue to pose problems for the social psychologist (see Deutscher, 1973). They also pose problems for the professional interviewer. Can one accept at face value what people say? Or does one have to 'interpret' what they tell you? Can one accept oral accounts obtained in interviews as a basis for predicting behaviour in con-texts other that that of the interview? Can a knowledge of a person's 'attitudes' help us to predict his behaviour?

Harré and Secord contend that one does not have to accept 'accounts' at face value. They can be 'negotiated'. Here the inter-face within the inter-view enables one to question the face validity of any particular account. The co-existence of more than one perspective helps to ensure that work gets done in the course of the inter-view. The perspec-tive of the interviewer is always different from that of the interviewee. This divergence in perspective is an adequate basis on which to negotiate. Work on inter-views needs to be integrated with work on inter-actions. We have noted above, more than once, how rarely an actor's view of his own actions corresponds to an observer's view of those same actions. Individuals may remain blissfully unaware of all that they communicate in the course of an interview. Goffman observed that impressions are 'given off' as well as 'man-aged'. One could view psychoanalytic theory as an elaborate set of rules for 'interpreting' the significance of a per-son's words and actions, especially those which occur in the course of therapy. Whilst most interviewers would agree with the truth of Goffman's observation, quoted earlier, that 'many crucial facts lie beyond the time and place of interaction, or lie concealed within it', few have need to draw on 'depth' psychologies such as psychoanalysis in order to interpret what they hear and observe. Good interviewers, however, listen not only to what persons choose to talk about but also to what they may not want to talk about or cannot say without help.

The recent explosion of research on non-verbal behaviour is of considerable relevance to the practice of interviewing (e.g. Weitz, 1974; Argyle, 1975; Ekman and Friesen, 1975).

It accurately reflects the perspective of the outside observer on the behaviour of others. Much of the classic literature on interviewing is highly 'cognitive' in tone and is now rather dated (Cannell and Kahn, 1968). It tends to reflect the perspective of the interviewer as 'actor': that is, presenting the rationale for conducting interviews in particular ways. Having to sample, in the writing of this chapter, from two such separate, but unrelated, literatures has not been an easy task. The fact that the two literatures are unrelated testifies to the absence of a relevant theory on the basis of which they might be integrated. Much recent research of a purely behavioural nature (e.g. on non-verbal aspects of social interaction), while highly relevant to the practice of interviewing, has not yet been satisfactorily integrated into the literature on interviewing. We would claim that this failure in integration reflects the absence of an appropriate theory of the interview. It is highly artificial, in practice, to distinguish between inter-views and inter-actions. For the theory and practice of inter-viewing it is necessary to understand both: hence the priority we accord in this chapter to the development of suitable theory. My approach to theory is a very Lewinian one; there is nothing so practical as a good theory.

The model of the observer favoured in psychological circles is that of the detached and objective scientist. The role of psychologists in relation to selection is often of this nature: they are usually to be found at several removes from the face-to-face encounter between assessors and candidates at the point of selection. There are, of course, important exceptions such as Civil Service Selection Boards, where psychologists are actively involved in conducting interviews. The model of the observer which prevails more widely in social science is a more active one; the researcher is often a participant observer. Becker and Geer (1957), in what is now a classic paper, argue that participant observation is a more complete method of research than the interview used alone: 'Participant observation can thus provide us with a yardstick against which to measure the completeness of data gathered in other ways, a model which can serve to let us know what orders of information escape us when we use other methods' (Becker and Geer, 1957).

By participant observation Becker and Geer mean 'that method in which the observer participates in the daily life of the people under study, either openly in the role of researcher or covertly in some disguised role, observing things that happen, listening to what is said, and questioning people, over some length of time'. Inter-viewing as outlined in this chapter is virtually synonymous with Becker and Geer's characterization of participant observation.

This wider conception of the inter-view enables us to encompass professional groups who rarely interview in the conventional sense: for instance, classroom teachers, nurses, supervisors in industry, etc. The skills involved in participant observation are akin to those which a social anthropologist might employ. The seminal work of Goffman, which is highly relevant to an understanding of the dynamics of inter-viewing, is largely based on participant observation; for example, his studies of the under-life of mental institutions (Goffman, 1961) or his study of life in the Hebrides (Goffman, 1959). One can observe and ask questions about what one has observed. One can test out that one has correctly learnt the native language by trying it out in the presence of skilled users of that language. This is synonymous with the process of inter-viewing as outlined here.

We have previously noted the distinction which Jones and Nisbett make between the perspective of the actor and the perspective of the observer. Participant observation preserves both perspectives within the one methodology, as does inter-viewing. The observer is an actor in so far as he is also a participant in the scene he observes. In inter-viewing the participants alternate between the roles of actor and of observer, of speaker and of listener. Observers and inter-viewers, if they are to be effective, need to be conscious of their own actions and of the effects of these on those whom they are observing or interviewing. This awareness of being an 'object' in the social world of the 'other' is enhanced by the face-to-face nature of the inter-view situation. The mechanisms of gaze and mutual gaze help to maintain this duality of awareness in being both observer and observed (Argyle and Cook, 1976). This social psychology of the inter-view applies equally well both to inter-viewers and to inter-viewees.

It is easy to be aware of one's 'other-ness' when the person whom one is observing or inter-viewing comes from a different culture from one's own. This is the typical experience of the social anthropologist. Becker and Geer trenchantly note that persons within the one culture often inhabit different social worlds but that this is not always recognized. There is much merit, in their eyes, in approaching the social worlds of others in much the same way as a social anthropologist approaches a strange culture.

> In interviewing members of groups other than our own, then, we are in somewhat the same position as the anthropologist who must learn a primitive language, with the important difference that, as Ichheiser has put it, we often do not understand that we do not understand and are thus likely to make errors in interpreting what is said to us (Becker and Geer, 1957).

This inter-face is more explicitly recognized in the literature on participant observation than it is in the literature on interviewing. We have tried to introduce into the literature on interviewing some of the advantages of participant observation by choosing, on occasion, to distinguish between inter-viewing and interviewing.

Becker and Geer are critical of the interview 'when it is used as a source of information about events that have occurred elsewhere and are described to us by informants'. We noted above the problems Freud faced in regard to estimating the likely incidence of incest in Viennese society. Becker and Geer continue:

> In working with interviews, we must necessarily infer a great many things we could have observed had we only been in a position to do so. We add to the accuracy of our data when we substitute observable fact for inference. More important, we open the way for the discovery of new hypotheses for the fact we observe may not be the fact we expected to observe.

It may be that it is only through the process of interviewing that Man develops an awareness of the social world of others. It is only through Piaget's brilliant use of the inter-view that we are today as aware of just how different the world of the child is from the world of the adult (Farr, 1982). Adults often falsely assume, because they were children once themselves, that they therefore understand the world of a child. By the simple device of inter-viewing Piaget made quite explicit the many different ways in which the world of the child and the world of the adult failed to coincide. Thanks to Piaget, many teachers-in-training become sensitive to such differences before they encounter children face-to-face in the classroom.

Postscript on industrial psychology

A good deal is known in industrial psychology about the behaviour of candidates in selection contexts and the experience of assessors, for example, advice concerning how best to conduct interviews, etc. Here again, there is the same dichotomy between the perspective of the observer and the perspective of the 'actor'. The time is now ripe to redress this imbalance in our current knowledge by studying the behaviour of assessors and sampling the experience of candidates within selection contexts. Such additional information could significantly contribute to the emergence of a social psychology of selection which would be highly compatible with the dynamics of inter-viewing as outlined in this chapter. The recognition of the existence of more than one viewpoint or perspective is quite explicit in the notion of the inter-view. At present we know very little about the perspective of candidates within selection contexts.

The classic approach in selection is to collect standardized data about candidates by means of psychological tests, the results of which are then entered into a decision formula based on a regression analysis. The outcome is an 'institutional' decision. The candidate either is or is not offered a job. Such 'objective' test data could, however, be analysed in relation to the candidate's own response to the system either at the time of selection or subsequently on receiving a job offer. Are the inferences that candidates might make about their suitability for a particular job radically different from those which the organization might make concerning their suitability? This is a question which only research can resolve. We have presented evidence elsewhere on the possible use of self-appraisal within a selection context (Downs, Farr and Colebeck, 1978).

References

Argyle, M. (1975)
Bodily Communications. London: Methuen.
Argyle, M. and Cook, M. (1976)
Gaze and Mutual Gaze. Cambridge: Cambridge University Press.
Becker, H.S. and Geer, B. (1957)
Participant observation and interviewing: a comparison. Human Organization, 16, 28-32. Reprinted in G. McCall and J. Simmons (eds), Issues in Participant Observation: A text and readings. Reading, Mass.: Addison-Wesley.
Campbell, D.T. (1963)
Social attitudes and other acquired behavioral dispositions. In S. Koch (ed.), Psychology: A study of a science, Vol. 6. New York: McGraw-Hill.
Cannell, C.F. and Kahn, R.L. (1968)
Interviewing. In G. Lindzey and E. Aronson (eds), Handbook of Social Psychology (2nd edn), Vol. 2. Reading, Mass: Addison-Wesley.
Deutscher, I. (1973)
What we say/What we do: Sentiments and acts. Glenview, Illinois: Scott, Foresman & Co.
Downs, S., Farr, R.M. and Colebeck, L. (1978)
Self-appraisal: A convergence of selection and guidance. Journal of Occupational Psychology, 51, 271-278.
Ekman, P. and Friesen, W.V. (1975)
Unmasking the Face: A guide to recognizing emotions from facial clues. Englewood Cliffs, NJ: Prentice-Hall.
Eysenck, H.J. (1953)
Uses and Abuses of Psychology. Harmondsworth: Penguin.
Farr, R.M. (1977a)
Heider, Harré and Herzlich on health and illness: some observations on the structure of 'représentations collectives'. European Journal of Social Psychology, 7, 491-504.
Farr, R.M. (1977b)
On the nature of attributional artifacts in qualitative research: Herzberg's two-factor theory of work motivation. Journal of Occupational Psychology, 50, 3-14.
Farr, R.M. (1982)
Social worlds of childhood. In V. Greaney (ed.), The Rights of Children. New York: Irvington Publications.
Freud, S. (1905)
Fragments of an analysis of a case of hysteria. In The Standard Edition of the Complete Psychological Works of Sigmund Freud (1953), Volume 7. London: Hogarth Press.

Goffman, E. (1959)
The Presentation of Self in Everyday Life. New York: Doubleday.

Goffman. E. (1961)
Asylums: Essays on the social situations of mental patients and other inmates. New York: Anchor Books.

Gorden, R.L. (1975)
Interviewing: Strategy, techniques and tactics (revised edition). Homewood, Ill.: The Dorsey Press.

Harré, R. and Secord, P.F. (1972)
The Explanation of Social Behaviour. Oxford: Blackwell.

Heider, F. (1958)
The Psychology of Interpersonal Relations. New York: Wiley.

Herzlich, C. (1973)
Health and Illness: A social-psychological analysis. European Monographs in Social Psychology, No. 5. Londo Academic Press.

Jones, E.E. and Nisbett, R.E. (1971)
The actor and the observer: divergent perspectives of the causes of behaviour. In E.E. Jones, D.E. Kanouse, H.H. Kelly, R.E. Nisbett, S. Valins and B. Weiner (eds), Attribution: Perceiving the causes of behaviour. Morristown, NJ: General Learning Press.

Kay, H. (1971)
Accidents: some facts and theories. In P.B. Warr (ed.), Psychology at Work. Harmondsworth: Penguin.

Mead, G.H. (1934)
Mind, Self and Society: From the standpoint of a social behaviorist. Edited and introduced by C.W. Morris. Chicago, Ill.: University of Chicago Press.

Milgram, S. (1974)
Obedience to Authority: An experimental view. London: Tavistock.

Weitz, S. (ed.) (1974)
Non-verbal Communication: Readings with commentary. N York: Oxford University Press.

Webb, E.J., Campbell, D.T.M, Schwartz, R.D. and Sechres L. (1966)
Unobtrusive Measures. Nonreactive research in the social sciences. Chicago: Rand McNally.

Questions

1. Why might a theory of the human self be a necessary prerequisite to understanding the social psychology of the interview?
2. What are the dangers of relying exclusively on the interview as a source of information in social research?
3. What were the inadequacies of the interview as a way of appraising a person's fitness for a particular job?
4. Discuss the similarities and differences between interviewing and participant observation as techniques of research in social science.

5. 'Many crucial facts lie beyond the time and place of interaction, or lie concealed within it' (Goffman). Discuss with reference to the interview.
6. Can one accept at face value what people say in an interview or does one have to 'interpret' what one hears? If you advocate the first strategy, are there any qualifications to your acceptance? If you advocate the latter strategy, suggest the guidelines you might use in making your interpretations.
7. What are the problems of inter-relating what one hears in an interview with what one observes?
8. Compare and contrast interviews with conversations.
9. 'It is crucial to an understanding of the interview situation to appreciate that more than one perspective is involved'. Discuss.
10. Discuss the strengths and weaknesses of behavioural approaches to the study of interviews.

annotated reading

Argyle, M. (1975) Bodily Communication. London: Methuen. A popular account of different aspects of non-verbal behaviour. Compare and contrast this approach with Goffman. Goffman is much more 'cognitive', whilst Argyle is more 'behavioural'. Is there scope for both approaches?

Goffman, E. (1959) The Presentation of Self in Everyday Life. Harmondsworth: Penguin. Based on astute observations of everyday life. It is essentially a theory of action in relation to the observing and listening other (i.e. his conception of the audience is critical to his portrayal of action). Consider the relevance of this book to the problems faced by the interviewee as he prepares for an interview.

Kahn, R.L. and Cannell, C.F. (1957) The Dynamics of Interviewing: Theory, technique and cases. New York: Wiley. Available in paperback. This has been the standard work for over 20 years. Presents a group dynamic approach to the interview. Concerned with the events of feedback as a way of improving interviewing skills, for example, such self-confrontation devices as tape-recorders. Needs to be up-dated to include video-feedback. Basically very sound.

exercises

Exercises on interviewing are given on pp. 319-322 following chapter 16 by Wicks.

16

Interviewing: practical aspects
Russell P. Wicks

If there is one universally applied technique to be found
in behavioural research it is 'interviewing'. If there is
one technique basic to all professional practice it is the
interaction between people that is called 'interviewing'. It
is the nature of this interaction between people which is
the concern of this chapter. It is to be hoped that what
is said can be applied not simply to 'the interview' in
'an interview situation' but to all purposive contacts
between individuals; the critical feature, it is claimed,
being the purposive nature of the encounter. The participants bring hopes, fears, expectations, misconceptions and
many other cognitions to the situation, most times in the
hope that their wishes will be met, fears reduced and so on.
Customarily this view is found in the characterization of an
interview as a 'conversation with a purpose'. So it is, but
all those participating in an interview have their purposes
and not simply, for example, the interviewer. In the comple
transactions of getting and giving information we observe
effort aimed at achieving purposes. Thus the psychologist
testing a client by means of, say, the Wechsler Adult
Intelligence Scale is conducting an interview as defined.
The purpose from one point of view is to help the client in
some way, from the other to be helped. In the exchange of
information each has purposes and expectations that they
hope will be met. Each may be optimizing their strategies
towards fulfilling these purposes. Roles will be assumed
constraining and shaping behaviour. If participants in
interviews can become more skilful and aware of the processes involved there is some hope of raising levels of
satisfaction. It is, therefore, the aim of this chapter to
examine such interview processes with this goal in mind. For
this purpose a simple model of an interview is described
(see figure 1) and for illustrative purposes reference made
to three particular interview situations; occupational
counselling, job interviews and research interviewing.

Initiation

The view that it is the purposive nature of the interview that is crucial leads us to consider the motives of
the participants. An individual approaching a counselling
situation may be motivated by a complex of needs, and

306

Figure 1

Model of an interview

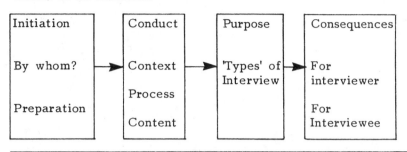

voluntary or compulsory attendance may be crucial in structuring these needs. Whether these needs are shared and
whether they can be fulfilled is another matter. It may well
be the case that some frequently voiced criticisms of interviews arise, in part, from a failure to make explicit the
needs and expectations of the parties involved. Nowhere is
this more important than in those situations with a high
level of emotional involvement. Two people may look back on
an interview as a total failure because each had different
expectations which unfortunately were not fulfilled. We all,
interviewers and interviewees, bring hopes and fears to the
task. Just as Orne (1962) draws our attention to the 'demand
characteristics' of the experimental situation as a result
of which subjects perform as they believe they are expected
so to do, so participants in interviews will seek a role
that they perceive as being appropriate. Not always,
unfortunately, do they choose correctly.

In analysing an interview it follows, therefore, that
attention to preliminaries and preparation is vital. Many
writers on interviewing stress the physical preparations
needed, literally setting the scene. Here, 'cognitive' scene
setting is judged to be more important; for example, in
employment interviewing paying attention to providing
information about the organization, or providing an adequate
job description. Considering the contribution of application
forms and references, together with other 'scene setting'
activities, will go a long way towards minimizing the cognitive gap that may occur. Furthermore, such preparations
are in fact part of the information exchange that lies at
the heart of an interview. In general, preparation from the
interviewer's point of view means careful planning of all
aspects of the situation. Briefing oneself, rehearsing the
interview, anticipating needs; all contribute to an
efficiently managed, worth-while encounter.

Recently, increasing attention has been given to preparation on the part of the interviewee, especially for
those about to be interviewed for a job. For example, a
great deal of work stemming from careers work with young
people has resulted in programmes aimed at developing 'life
skills'. There is clear evidence that all can profit from

paying attention to the activities and skills involved in job seeking. The material included in such programmes varies widely but may cover:

* where to get job information;
* work experience;
* how to reply to advertisements;
* how to become more self-aware;
* how to be interviewed.

The techniques employed range from self-instructional material to the use of video-recording of role-play situations. In general, however, the emphasis is on providing guidelines, improving social skills, self-presentation and making people more aware of the processes of social interaction.

Conduct

Context

What effect on the behaviour of the participants in an interview might the following environments have: a police station; a doctor's surgery; a street corner; a psychology laboratory? Clearly the effect can be dramatic. We have the clearest evidence here for the importance of the frame of reference, role expectations and construal of the situation upon behaviour in an interview. Indeed, the subtlety of the rules of the 'games' played out in different contexts is such that we spend our lives refining and editing our private rule books. Within each context there may be a range of indicators signalling to us how to behave, how to address people, what to say and what not to say, an obvious example being dress, particularly a uniform which may be anything from a pin-stripe suit to a white coat. What is the experience of people who customarily wear a 'uniform' when they discard it? What might people say to a priest in mufti that they would not say if he donned his clerical garb? Thus our perception of the interview context is an essential part of the scene setting previously discussed. Most interviewers, being aware of this, go to some trouble to ensure that the physical setting signals what they wish it to: they dress in a particular style, arrange the seats appropriately, adjust the lighting, ensure that interruptions do or do not occur. They try to ensure that the interview is conducted in a 'good mannered' way.

A further aspect is that participants bring substantial resources to the task: their background knowledge, and skills expectations. Whilst these resources may bring benefits to an interview, they sometimes create problems. Such difficulties have been extensively investigated by Rosenthal and his co-workers (e.g. Rosenthal and Rosnow, 1969) in studies of the characteristics of 'volunteers' in research and studies of the expectations of subjects in experiments, as well as the experimenters. Avoiding bias and error arising from these factors is a major concern of investigators; thus one should be aware that volunteers for survey research tend to be better educated; if male, they score higher on IQ tests; and they are better adjusted than non-volunteers. Such factors should be taken into account in evaluating data. Similarly, the survey interviewer asked to find a sample of five people, even though certain characteristics of the sample are specified, may unwittingly choose those they feel it would be 'nice' to interview.

Process

A great deal of what we know about interpersonal communication has been learnt by systematic study of interviews, especially the face-to-face two-person encounter. What is offered here, however, is a general communication model which may be used to analyse an interview (see figure 2). The utility of this model as a tool for examining interpersonal behaviour rests upon the conceptualization of communication as a system; the model is dynamic because it has independent parts with provision for feedback.

Figure 2

A communication model

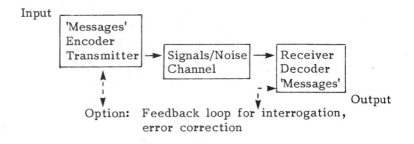

Input

'Messages' Encoder Transmitter → Signals/Noise Channel → Receiver Decoder 'Messages'

Output

Option: Feedback loop for interrogation, error correction

Such a model could stand for many communication systems: radio or television transmission; a nervous system; or, in this case, an interview. A useful procedure arising from the 'system' model is that we can examine its integrity. In other words, we can see what happens when one part of the system is distorted or eliminated.

In this model, 'message' is taken to stand for that which we wish to transmit. Embedded in this is the difficult problem of meaning, and an obvious use of the model is to compare inputs and outputs according to some criterion of meaningfulness. Such a comparison is the basis of an often hilarious game in which the distortion occurring when a 'message' is passed along a line of people by word of mouth is examined. Bartlett (1972) showed in his method of serial reproduction the simplifications and intrusions which occur in this process.

Within the interview, 'meaning' arises at a number of levels. First, it arises at the level of verbal content. What was the question and what is the answer? Much has been written about asking the right sort of question in an interview, whether to use direct or indirect questions, the appropriate form of words, and the dangers of certain questions such as leading or multiple forms. Skilful interviewers do not seem to be constrained by rigid rules but show flexibility, constantly probing and following up interesting leads. They tend to ask: 'Tell me', 'When was that?', 'How was that?', 'What did you do?' and perhaps the most difficult question of all, 'Why?'

Second, the question of meaning arises at the level of recording the interview material. What gets lost or distorted when an interviewer distils a reply into notes or makes a decision? Third, a consideration arising especially in the research interview is: what has happened to the original meaning when a response is coded, probably into a pre-determined category, and is lumped together with others when the study is reported?

However, the verbal content of the message is only a small part of the signal. Many researchers assert that the non-verbal component of a signal is of greater importance. Argyle (1973, 1975) in particular has drawn our attention to the role of non-verbal communication factors such as:

* bodily movements: body language: gestures;
* facial expression;
* eye movements and eye contact;
* personal space: proximity.

Socially skilled performers are simultaneously transmitting signals using all these components together with verbal material whilst reacting to similar signals constituting feedback from their partners.

Utilizing and decoding this complex of information involves us in consideration of interpersonal perception, a key area in the analysis of interviewing. How we form judgements about other people is at the heart of interview decisions: the substantial literature on this topic, for example Cook (1979), suggests that the information we use includes:

* a person's actions;
* the situation in which the person is observed;
* appearance (including facial expression, physique, speech characteristics and dress style);
* non-verbal cues mentioned previously.

The powerful influence of some cues is seen most clearly in the study of stereotypes. Picking up one piece of information and building often unwarranted assumptions upon it is the classic error in judging others. Reacting to a regional accent, to hair colour, to ethnic origin or any other isolated item is all too common. Such a reaction, especially to irrelevant information, is usually dubbed the 'halo effect'. Since the judge or interviewer is striving for cognitive consistency, information is often interpreted in such a way that it fits this single judgement. Thus favourable material or even attributions will be ascribed to a liked person. Contrariwise, undue weight may be given to negative indications in the case of dislike. Clearly, interviewers must be constantly on their guard against introducing bias of this kind. Awareness of their prejudices and the sorts of errors we make in judging others will help.

It is the process component of interviewing which has received most attention in the training of interviewers. Such training commonly takes the form of general social skills training together with exercises directed at the specialization of the interviewer; for example, obtaining clinically relevant material in the hospital setting. Just how effective training may be is not easy to assess. Largely this is so because published studies of interview training tend to use different criteria, thus making comparisons difficult. The benefits to the trainee probably come from receiving informed feedback in role-playing or group tasks about their performance together with enhanced self-awareness.

Content
The point has been made that the absence of a shared common aim or the lack of a clear plan in an interview leads to many difficulties. Specifically, criticisms in terms of interview decisions tend to the view that they may leave much to be desired. It is claimed, for example, that the research literature points overwhelmingly in this direction. Without wishing to dismiss the many studies leading to this conclusion, it must be pointed out that they cover a wide range of interview outcomes made by many interviewers at different levels of experience and training with their decisions based on imprecise criteria. The message of these studies seems to be that all concerned with interviews should be aware of the shortcomings and take steps to overcome them. Apart from errors arising from factors already mentioned in describing context and process aspects at an interview, the principal source is often the lack of a clear plan for an interview; in other words, content must be tailored to the particular aim in mind, each interview requiring careful planning with preparation related to a desired outcome. By way of illustration let us consider the content of interviews within the three professional contexts of counselling, job interviews and research interviewing.

COUNSELLING: OCCUPATIONAL GUIDANCE. What is the aim of an occupational guidance procedure? At one time the approach was modelled upon the notion of talent matching: specify the job, specify the person and attempt to match

the two. On the job side of the equation, techniques of task
analysis, job description and content specification were
developed whilst evidence of congruent relevant behaviour
was sought from the interviewee. It is no coincidence that
the heyday of this approach coincided with the early boom in
psychological test production. Aptitude tests, occupational
interest guides, and tests of specific skills were all produced to aid the matching. Today, with the application of
computer-based matching procedures, the approach is enjoying
a revival. The role of the interview in this model was
largely to establish the congruence of job and applicant
profiles by comparison through discussion. From this approach evolved the contemporary developmental model, with
emphasis on career decision making as a process over time,
starting in the early years with educational counselling,
proceeding to occupational counselling and then to career
development counselling, with perhaps counselling for retirement in later years. Thus there may be many interviews
within this model each with a specific aim, the sum aimed at
the overall development of the individual. Among the sub-
goals of this process we can recognize the following:

* self-appraisal: equipping the client to achieve
  realistic self-assessment;
* self-perception: providing frames of reference,
  categories of occupationally significant behaviours;
* job perception: acquiring the skills required to assess
  the world of work in terms of job content, values, roles
  and life style;
* reality testing: matching aspirations and goals with
  opportunities within one's limitations;
* setting goals and objectives: specifying attainable
  goals and precise objectives;
* hypothesis generation: helping the client to generate
  occupational 'theories';
* interaction of the person and the job environment:
  examining the complexities of the person/work situation
  interaction;
* sharing information: providing the client with educational and occupational information, and providing the
  counsellor with perceptions of the client;
* task setting: translating immediate goals into discrete
  tasks, such as finding an address, seeking information,
  reading a pamphlet, etc.

The task of the interviewer/counsellor therefore becomes
that of achieving these goals at the appropriate time and in
a manner which meets the client's needs. Flexibility, wide
background knowledge and the ability to relate to the client
are clearly prerequisites on the part of the counsellor.
Similar goals are shared by modern staff appraisal schemes
and staff development procedures.

JOB INTERVIEWS. Being interviewed for a job, for promotion

or for annual assessment is probably the most commonly experienced form of interview. It has certainly attracted a substantial body of folk-lore, myth, jokes and hard-luck stories. That this is so is, in itself, of considerable psychological significance. The job interview comes in many varieties, not least the panel interview. Here especially the crucial importance of planning an interview is seen. The justifiable criticism of such encounters is frequently due first to poor interviewing skills on the part of the individual board members, and second to the lack of an agreed role for each.

Whilst not normally included under the heading of interviews, such behavioural observation techniques as role-playing by candidates, group discussions, problem-solving exercises and others raise the same problems previously mentioned of reliable and valid judgements about other people.

Two examples of interview plans used in job interviews will be presented here: one is a general approach commonly employed, namely, the biography; the second a well-known technique called the Seven-Point Plan.

1. The biography: the majority of job interviews employ this approach, often, however, in an undisciplined fashion, hunting and pecking at a person's history. However, a simple structure which can be readily shared consists of establishing landmarks within relevant areas; commonly times of change such as leaving school. Bearing in mind the selectivity of recall, in itself an important indicator within an interview, and that the recent past may be more accessible, one should not expect uniform coverage of a life history. This raises the problem of breadth and depth within the interview in relation to the relevance of the information. Too often an interviewer will spend time on an irrelevant area, missing the opportunity to explore a significant point in detail.

However, a plan such as that shown in figure 3 provides a secure frame of reference for interviewer and interviewee. Not least, the interviewee can be assembling information and anticipating questions; the task is not unlike talking through a curriculum vitae. A final benefit of this approach is that it enables the interviewer to check dates, spot gaps in the account and draw out the inter-relationships between

Figure 3

	Education	Interests	Home	Work
The past Landmarks The present	Dates			

events. This approach is underpinned by application forms and curricula vitae, which are customarily set out in biographical order.

2. The Seven-Point Plan: probably the best known of all assessment and interview formats, the plan was originally developed by Alec Rodger within the framework of the talent matching approach to occupational guidance. It was intended to apply to both candidates and jobs, to obtain relevant information about people and, by asking the same questions of a job, to facilitate matching.

The plan was rapidly adopted for job interviewing and has undoubtedly been highly influential in so far as it provides the unskilled interviewer with a robust, easily understood framework within which to work. Over the years a number of modifications have been suggested to the original plan. Similarly based schemes have been published, but what is essentially the original is presented here (Rodger, 1974).

1. Physical characteristics:
   Physical abilities of occupational importance.
   State of health. Vision, hearing. Appearance. Speech.
2. Attainments (and previous experience):
   Educational background, achievements. Occupational and professional training. Experience. How well has this person done? Personal achievements in any area: sports, pursuits, etc.
3. General ability:
   Especially general intelligence and cognitive skills - words, numbers, relationships.
4. Special aptitudes:
   Particularly occupationally applicable talents - scientific, mechanical, mathematical, practical, literary, artistic, social skills.
5. Interests:
   Often the core information: type of interests, how they are pursued, to what effect. Intellectual, practical, physical, social and artistic interests may be occupationally significant.
6. Personality:
   What is this person like? Especially in terms of self-perception. Social relationships, behaviour indicative of self-reliance, dependability.
7. Circumstances:
   The context of the person's life in so far as it affects his aspirations. Family circumstances, financial background, current problems.

The first six points apply particularly to the study of jobs. What physical characteristics, what attainments and so on are required for this job? It should be added that Rodger emphasized the importance of paying attention to individual likes and dislikes, to difficulties or distastes mentioned by people, and to the individual's strengths and weaknesses when applying the plan; in particular, stressing the importance of negative information in making selection decisions and the noting of danger signs.

Finally, in considering job interviews it should be noted that advice and preparation for interviewees is widely available in relation to the job interview. Social skills training and self-presentation courses are examples.

RESEARCH INTERVIEWS. The place of the interview in social research is central. Its contribution ranges from preliminary information gathering to a place as the principal research tool. Clearly it takes many forms but the main dimension along which it varies is that of being unstructured/structured, from free to semi-structured to structured. Here, the highly structured form typically found in market research and surveys is considered, the characteristics of the unstructured form being similar to counselling interviews. For the structured approach a unique feature is the use of an interview schedule: in effect, a carefully prepared script meticulously adhered to by the interviewer. A great deal of thought is put into preparing the schedule in order that question form and content, question order, response mode, use of response aids and other factors can be taken into account.

Customarily these factors are checked by conducting pilot studies. Another feature of research interviewing is the attention paid to teaching interviewers how to present a particular schedule, together with supervision of their work in the field. Finally, since it is often the case that large numbers of respondents are involved, it is usual to design the schedules with data analysis in mind: for example, the coding of responses by interviewers for data entry.

As an example of research interviewing the approach of the Government Social Survey is now described. The Social Survey began work dealing with wartime problems of the 1940s. It is now a Division of the Office of Population Censuses and Surveys carrying out a wide range of studies of social and economic interest for public departments. A detailed description of the practices and procedures it employs is to be found in the handbook for interviewers (Atkinson, 1971).

Steps in producing such surveys include:

* identifying research question: decide on form and content of survey, consider costs;
* draft proposals: content of schedule, sampling of respondents;
* pilot stage: explore degree of structure appropriate, such as free to highly. Coding of replies. Analyse pilot material;
* brief and train interviewers: careful training including practice on schedule. How to contact the public. Identifying the person to be interviewed (e.g. by age,

sex, role). Putting over the purpose of the survey; problem of refusals or lack of co-operation. Conducting the interview: defining the roles of interviewer and informant;

* timetable: prepare addresses, number of interviewees, target dates;
* carry out field survey: interviewers adhere to research officers' instructions on each question. Comprehend the purpose of each question: (i) factual information; (ii) expression of opinion; (iii) attitude measures.
Deploy response modes without distortion: open questions with free response, closed/forward choice questions with pre-coded or scaled responses. Interviewers practise use of response aids: prompt cards for scaled responses, self-completion scales, repertory grids, examples of products in market research. Interviewers pay particular attention to prompting and probing. Guard against distortion in recording data: both precoded and open response items are susceptible;
* coding: check schedules and categorize response;
* computing: produce tables, analyse data;
* conclusion: write report.

Purpose

At this stage in the discussion of our model of an interview it must be clear that so many varieties exist as to demand careful consideration of each in terms of purpose. The variety of purposes has been mentioned, and also that the approach may vary from structured to unstructured according to purpose. Thus a number of recognizable forms of interview have emerged to meet particular needs. Examples include:

* non-directive counselling, client-centred therapy;
* psychotherapeutic encounters of many kinds;
* depth interviews emphasizing motivational factors;
* group interviews involving a number of respondents in a discussion group type format;
* psychological testing, especially individual tests such as WAIS (Wechsler Adult Intelligence Scale);
* problem-solving interviews such as individual role-playing for a variety of purposes.

Consequences

Accepting the purposive nature of the interview implies that outcomes are important for all concerned and that their nature depends on the situation, and not least how the situation is perceived. For the interviewer, this will involve achieving the particular aims which have been identified together with maintenance of professional competence; for example, in the research interview maintaining the validity, reliability and precision of data with errors eliminated as far as possible.

For the interviewee or respondent one might ask: what do they get out of the experience? All too often what might be called the public relations aspect of interviewing is ignored. Symptoms of this include fears on the part of correspondents regarding the confidentiality of data, or that in some way they are being threatened. Such considerations appear to bring us full circle, for if attention is paid to the initiation stage of the proceedings by way of setting the scene such alarms can be reduced. Nevertheless, the sometimes necessary use of subterfuge in research needs to be handled with great care, a minimum requirement being the provision of an adequate explanation after the event or an account of the research.

References

Argyle, M. (1973)
Social Interaction. London: Tavistock.
Argyle, M. (1975)
Bodily Communication. London: Methuen.
Atkinson, J. (1971)
A Handbook for Interviewers (2nd edn). London: HMSO.
Bartlett, F.C. (1932)
Remembering. Cambridge: Cambridge University Press.
Cook, M. (1979)
Perceiving Others. London: Methuen.
Orne, M.T. (1962)
On the social psychology of the psychology experiment. American Psychologist, 17, 776-783.
Rodger, A. (1974)
Seven Point Plan. London: NFER.
Rosenthal, R. and Rosnow, R.L. (1969)
The volunteer subject. In R. Rosenthal and R.L. Rosnow (eds), Artifact in Behavioral Research. New York: Academic Press.

Questions

1. 'The interview is a wide-band procedure with low fidelity'. Discuss.
2. Assess the contribution of the study of social skills to the improvement of job selection interviewing.
3. 'Interviewing is the most commonly used selection tool'. Why do you think this is and what else are its strengths and weaknesses?
4. What future do you see for the interview?
5. Discuss the significance of role expectations for the conduct of an interview.
6. Write an account of the function of non-verbal communication in the interview.
7. Critically assess the form of an interview in a counselling situation with which you are familiar.
8. What are the advantages and disadvantages of using a scheme such as the Seven Point Plan for job interviewing?
9. Identify common sources of error in research interviewing. How might these be eliminated?

10. Choose a particular type of interview and design an appropriate interviewer training course.

Annotated reading

Anstey, E. (1976) An Introduction to Selection Interviewing London: HMSO.
Originally prepared for staff training in the Civil Service, this practical guide is useful for the advice it gives on general preparation for selection interviewing as well as the conduct of interviews.

Bingham, W.V. and Moore, B.V. (1959) How to Interview (4th edn). New York: Harper & Row.
A classic work. An early attempt to offer general guidance for those engaged in selection, survey interviews and counselling. Rather general in its approach.

Cannel, C.F. and Kahn, R.L. (1968) Interviewing. In G. Lindzey and E. Aronson (eds), The Handbook of Social Psychology, Volume II: Research methods (2nd edn). London Addison-Wesley.
A systematic account of the research interview. Tends towards a theoretical presentation; for example in its discussion of problems of reliability and validity and measurement. Includes discussion of interview technique, question form and the training of interviewers.

Cross, C.P. (1974) Interviewing and Communication in Social Work. London: Routledge & Kegan Paul.
A useful guide to the 'helping' interview. Represents the movement towards enhancing social skills of all involved in such encounters.

Sidney, E. and Brown, M. (1973) The skills of Interviewing. London: Tavistock.
Aimed at managers, especially personnel staff. A generally acclaimed book, based on the extensive experience of the authors, it offers a very practical guide to the selection interview.

Sidney, E., Brown, M. and Argyle, M. (1973) Skills with People. London: Hutchinson.
A guide for managers. Concerns itself with a wide range of topics: communication in general, social skills, interviews, meetings and committees, interpersonal skills and training in social skills.

Ungerson, B. (ed.) (1975) Recruitment Handbook (2nd edn). London: Gower Press.
Very useful guide to the context of job interviewing, preparing job specifications, advertising, references; all the supporting activities of selection are covered.

Exercises are suggested for each component of the interview model (figure 1).

Initiation

As an INTERVIEWER: planning

1. Imagine that you were about to carry out one of each of the three examples of interview used in the chapter. Draft a plan for each interview.

* occupational counselling for a client;
* interviewing an applicant for your job;
* a small survey. Contemporary social and economic conditions provide many topics. For example, a proposed local radio service.

2. Job or employment interviewing provides a basis for training your client in useful skills; there are many exercises that you can develop yourself. To start you off here are some suggestions:

* write a job description;
* analyse job advertisements in a local or national newspaper;
* draft an advertisement for a job;
* design a job application form;
* design a request for a reference;
* design an interview report form.

As an INTERVIEWEE: how to be interviewed

* produce a biographical sketch map of yourself using the plan suggested in the chapter. Fill in the dates; note the landmarks in your history. What were their consequences?
* produce a curriculum vitae for yourself: it could be useful!
* find an advertised job which interests you. Try to find out as much as possible about the firm, or organization, the job itself, career prospects, entry requirements.
* using the Seven-Point Plan as a basis assess yourself by listing information on each point which you think is occupationally significant. What does this account of yourself tell you?
* working with a partner practice job interviewing.

Conduct

CONTEXT: it is often said that the 'hidden interview' is more significant than that which is open; that is to say, we choose to conceal things about ourselves from others, and possibly from ourselves. In a nutshell, we avoid saying what we really mean. Try filling in the following table with topics for each context and compare the open and hidden situations.

Contexts	Open (readily volunteered)	Hidden (tend to be concealed)
Doctor's surgery		
Police station		
Chatting in a pub		
Talking to a market researcher in your own home		
Marriage Guidance Clinic		
Client's home		

Play the Sherlock Holmes game. Observing a stranger in the street, in a café or wherever, try to decide 'who' they are. What is their work, what are their interests, what family background, what are their attitudes to X, Y and Z and so on? Consider the evidence on which you are basing your impression; what stereotypes are involved? This is a potentially frustrating game if you cannot check on your impressions!

PROCESS: a wide range of exercises can be developed for yourself covering the process of interviewing, and much depends on the resources available to you. Some exercises require no material resources, others video- or audio-recording facilities. For example:

*   Role-playing: from ad hoc exercises to prepared play-lets. It is important to make the situation realistic and locate it within the experience of the participants. It should not become mere entertainment. Like all the other exercises it requires careful analysis afterwards for maximum benefit.
*   Simulations: prepared training situations.
*   Case studies: require a great deal of careful preparation of relevant material.
*   Recording: audiotape-recording still offers an opportunity to analyse part of the process. Video-recording is now widely used for interviewer training providing aspects of the situation not hitherto available to the trainee. However, it is important to consider what limitations these recording techniques bring with them. For example, the selection of certain shots, use of camera angles and editing consequences.

A number of simple games can be used to examine aspects of the communication model outlined. In particular, seeing what effects restrictions placed on components of the system might have.

1.   Restricted communication

Game 1 - The telephone game
In pairs, sit back to back and hold a 'telephone' type
conversation. What is the effect on verbal context? Is there
a reduction of non-verbal components, or not?

Game 2 - The numbers game
In pairs, each person transmits a message using numbers only
as the 'words' - '15-3-7' etc. What are the effects on verbal inflection; bodily movements, gestures? Was the message
received correctly? Are there encoding and decoding
problems?

Game 3 - The miming game
In pairs, transmit a message each in mime. Look for ges-
ures, grimaces, stereotypes. How is the message coded?

2.   Input-output comparisons
Game 1 - The whispering game
Pass a message around of group by each person whispering to
the next. Analyse distortions.

Game 2 - Listening. We tend to take listening for granted.
In fact, we hear parts of utterances, start to reply, interrupt, make reinforcing noises and so on. Try listening.

Although observation of other people is part of our everyday
lives, we can profit from paying systematic attention to the
natural behaviour of people around us (person perception or
man-watching). For example:

*   elements of non-verbal communications;
*   people talking in pairs or larger groups;
*   public interaction in various situations;
*   portrayal of roles in films, on television and in
    literature;
*   television interviews.

CONTENT: there is a good deal of overlap, as far as the
exercises are concerned, with the 'initiation' of the model
and the suggestions made there can equally well be applied
here. In addition, there are a number applicable to counselling and job interview situations. For example:

1. Who am I?
Either write an autobiography or answer that question a
number of times, say ten. Try to rank order your answers in
terms of salience. Which answers would you wish to keep?
Which discard?

2. Self-perception
Try interviewing yourself. Try listing all the adjectives
you can think of which describe you: ask somebody who knows
you to discuss them. Try constructing a self-perception

scale for yourself by taking pairs of adjectives such as happy-sad and placing yourself on a five-point scale with these attributes as the extremes. What is your profile on this scale?

Purpose
Consult the literature for information on the different forms of interview mentioned.

Consequences
Attempt the exercise of writing a precise specification of the outcome you would wish for different sorts of interview. For example, in an assessment (intake) interview with the parents of a difficult child what are the different needs of interviewer and interviewee? What are their perceptions of the possible outcomes? Finally, what criteria should be used when judging the value of the encounter for each party?

17

Communicating through the media
Dennis Howitt

It is easy to blame the mass media for much of what we
consider undesirable in society. If we believe that education standards are declining we blame television for distracting our children from their schoolwork. The mass media
are blamed for making people lazy, greedy, violent and sexy.
However, claims about the effects of the mass media tend
to overemphasize their true impact. This does not mean that
the media have no role to play in persuading people, in
disseminating information, and bringing about social change.
But it does mean that we have carefully to separate myth
from reality, fact from fiction. This chapter illustrates
the usefulness of the mass media for professional people. We
also outline some of the things that need to be taken into
account when trying to understand the effects of the mass
media.

Does advertising really work?

One argument about the mass media has certain attractions.
It is claimed that industry and commerce would not pay out
large sums to advertise products in the mass media unless
this increased sales. Why pay enormous bills for full colour
spreads in magazines, 60-second commercials on television
and the like, if they do not work? There is probably a lot
of truth in this. But does it follow that anyone can be sold
anything through clever advertising? If it does then it is
difficult to explain the failure of many heavily advertised
products to sell well. Most advertising acts through inform-
ing the public about products that satisfy an existing need,
so advertising rarely creates a need in the first place. In
any case, in mass production industries a successful advertising campaign may need to produce only a relatively small
increase in sales to be financially worth while. Also, we
should not forget that an advertising campaign in the mass
media is often just one part of a much larger marketing
campaign. The advertiser may also be offering price reductions in stores, providing free gifts, giving incentives to
retailers and salesmen, having store displays, or using any
of a multitude of other selling devices. In other words, the
advertising campaign may be mistakenly credited for what is
essentially a successful marketing campaign in general. Surprisingly, very little research is available on the success

of advertising. This is probably because research is expensive and its findings potentially embarrassing to those whose business it is to plan advertising campaigns. Indeed, most of the more satisfactory evidence we have about the effectiveness of advertising comes from the study of public service topics such as road safety and health campaigns.

Advertising and welfare: an illustrative case

Poverty may seem poles apart from the affluence that most commercial advertising feeds on, but poverty research provides us with a good example of the severe limitations of advertising and the mass media. Welfare benefits which have to be applied for (rather than those which are given automatically) tend not to be taken up by all those who are eligible. Many people who need benefits simply do not claim them. Non-take-up rates vary according to the benefit in question. It is estimated, for example, that the take-up of free school meals by those eligible is roughly 80 per cent of the maximum and that for rent rebates the figure is about 70-75 per cent. The alleviation of poverty is desirable in itself but also for the consequences for health, education, and even industry which follow from it. So the issue does not merely have implications for the social services, but also for the medical profession, teachers, and many others.

Members of the Child Poverty Action Group (Meacher, 1971) asked the Department of the Environment to help answer the question of how much the take-up of a means-tested benefit could be increased by an advertising campaign. The object of the advertising campaign was to encourage eligible people to take up rate rebates. The campaign itself consisted of leaflets distributed through letter boxes, advertisements placed weekly in three local newspapers, some posters on hoardings, and some unplanned television publicity. The theme stressed was that if you pay rent, you probably pay rates and you could be entitled to a rate rebate.

The research design employed two groups of individuals: those from particularly low-income areas, and a more general control group from the same London borough. People were interviewed both before and after the advertising campaign. Borough records could be checked to see whether individuals actually took up their rate rebates. Overall for the low-income area survey, 12 per cent of eligible persons were claiming rate rebates before the campaign, a figure which increased to 19 per cent afterwards. This is hardly a major change and, even if we assume that all the increase in take-up was due to the advertising campaign, it is little more than a 50 per cent increase over a very low baseline. Looking at the data more closely it becomes apparent that pensioners before the campaign had a take-up rate of 15 per cent which increased to 23 per cent, whereas no low-income family claimed either before or after the campaign. So effects of advertising depended on the poverty group in question.

The advertising campaign was not a total failure and was in some ways a success. Naturally one of the aims of the campaign was to inform people of the availability of rate rebates. Table 1 shows the data obtained in the low-income area.

Table 1

Rate rebates claimed before and after advertising campaign

	Before campaign	After campaign
Percentage claiming rebate	12	19
Percentage unaware of rebate	82	39
Percentage aware of but not claiming rebate	6	42

Obviously the advertising campaign increased awareness of rate rebates substantially but did not effectively motivate people to actually claim money. Also the advertising campaign still left 39 per cent of the sample ignorant of their rights.

Other data from the study showed that the advertising campaign was more effective at reaching people who did not need it than those who did need it. Fifty-eight per cent of people who had been claiming rebates received the leaflets but only 23 per cent of those who did not claim received the leaflets. Similarly, 62 per cent of people who had been claiming rebates saw at least one of the newspaper advertisements on rebates whereas only 35 per cent of non-claimants did. That is to say, many non-claimants were not exposed to vital information. So one reason why the advertising campaign was in some ways unsuccessful was because of differential exposure to the advertisement. But this cannot explain all of the findings because many who became aware of their rights as a result of the advertising campaign still did not claim. How can this be explained?

One important reason was that many of the eligible non-claimants had become confused. Although the advertising campaign had made them aware of the rebates they thought they were ineligible. This left about 40 per cent of the aware individuals who realized that the rebates were relevant to themselves but still did not claim. How do we explain this? Several possibilities became clear from the research. Some did not apply because the benefit to themselves would be very small (for example, if they paid very little rent), some were put off by their inability to cope with a complex claims procedure, some were put off by the failure of a previous claim, some were afraid of their landlord or of officials, and others were proud of their independence from the welfare state and feared the stigma which they thought was associated with making a claim.

Whatever the reason for non-take-up, it is clear that the power of advertising is limited. While the advertising campaign worked well in this case as a publicity exercise (despite problems of not reaching those most in need), it was a relative failure at motivating the target audience into doing what was required. No one would argue that these poor did not need the money, but for one reason or another they failed to claim it. Fear of embarrassment and stigma was stronger for these people than economic motives. Remember that most advertising is designed to make you pay for something. Rebates and other benefits are an addition to one's resources, yet people failed to claim.

Other effects of the media

But it is possible that the mass media themselves might contribute to the failure to take-up welfare benefits. Golding and Middleton (1978) have argued that anti-claimant stories like those headed 'Parasites - The scrounging Kinches cost you £500', 'Big new war on dole cheats', 'Pay code breached by welfare rises', and the like, simply reinforce or even create an atmosphere in which those receiving welfare benefits are seen as idle, feckless scroungers. Evidence suggests that the coverage by the press, radio and television of welfare and social security news is largely about abuse of social security. Thirty-one per cent of social security benefit stories related tales of abuse and as many as 13 per cent involved legal proceedings. The image put over by the 'scroungerphobia' of the news media perhaps contributes to the numbers not claiming much-needed benefits by amplifying the feeling that to do so would be to risk social stigma.

While on the theme of advertising and social problems we should make a note of the criticism that advertisements often 'sell' more than the product they intend to sell. The emphasis on a rich luxuriant life style in some advertisements might encourage people to become more and more consumption orientated to the exclusion of other important aspects of life. A similar, but not identical, argument has been made about the advertising of proprietary drugs on television. It claims that those advertisements which encourage the use of proprietary drugs also encourage the use of illicit drugs such a marijuana. The following quotation from an American committee which examined drug advertising states the case strongly:

> The message ... is clear and shocking: certain kinds of advertising stand accused of seducing the young to drug dependency and creating vulnerability to drug abuse ... the drug culture finds its fullest flowering in the portrait of American society which can be pieced together out of hundreds of thousands of advertisements and commercials. It is advertising which mounts so graphically the message that pills turn rain into sunshine, gloom into joy, depression into euphoria; solve problems, dispel doubt.

Although controls on advertising are much tighter in some countries than in the USA there is no escaping the general argument. Milavsky, Pekowsky, and Stipp (1975-76) studied this very problem. A good measure of exposure to television drug advertising was related to the actual use of both legal and illicit drugs by teenage boys. The proprietary drugs included not merely simple ones like aspirin but also ones designed to act psychologically by altering mood. There was a slight tendency for boys who saw the most drug advertising on television to be those who used such drugs. This could be interpreted to mean that exposure to drug advertisements encourages the use of drugs. Some caution has to be applied in studies such as this since it is possible that boys who already take drugs watch such advertising because they are more interested in drugs, and not the other way around. The evidence is at least suggestive of the effectiveness of advertising to sell proprietary drugs. There was no evidence in this case that the use of illicit drugs was influenced by watching advertisements for legal proprietary drugs.

The lessons illustrated by the above case studies

We have already discussed an aspect of advertising and social problems concerned with the non-take-up of rate rebates. However, professions other than social workers have similar needs to communicate to large sections of the general public. The aims of much preventive medicine cannot be achieved solely by dealing with the unhealthy, who have regular contact with the medical profession. Those who are healthy and who do not go to doctors may also benefit from health education. The physiotherapist may likewise feel that there is a lot of information that the general public might benefit from if they had it. Educationists might wish to inform parents via the media of modern ideas about education. Some aspects of the work of many professions might be improved or aided by the mass media. The lessons of the above case studies are important in understanding the strengths and limitations of the mass media.

One lesson to be learnt before going any further is that the effects of the mass media are rarely as simple or direct as we might assume. For example, studies of the effects of communications have fallen into four main categories:

* studies of the characteristics of the source of the communication;
* studies of the characteristics of the channel of communication (e.g. person to person, radio, television, etc.);
* studies of the content of communication;
* studies of the target of the communication.

Although it is possible to illustrate the roles of each of the members of this quartet (source, channel, content and target), it is very difficult to make broad generalizations about any of them. For example, certain sources of communication are seen as much more credible than others. Some

might see the Trades Union Congress as a more trustworthy
source of information than the Confederation of British
Industries. Research has shown that initially we tend to
accept the message of a high credibility source but that,
over time, the lower credibility source's message may become
more accepted largely because we forget the source of the
message and merely retain its contents. This is called the
'sleeper' effect, since it lies dormant for a while until
the source is forgotten. An example of this is that initially when we hear immigration figures proffered by a neo-
Nazi organization we reject them as being worthless because
of the nature of their source. A few months later we may
recall the figures but fail to remember their source. Possibly we will be influenced in our thinking by those immigration statistics now we have forgotten their origins. The
channel of communication is known to be important in some
ways as well. For example, recent studies have suggested
that a message transmitted via television is more likely to
be believed by the public in general than messages transmitted via other mass media. The content of communications
has been studied in many ways. For example, one line of
research over the years has been on the effects of fear-
arousing appeals. People might be persuaded about things
more readily if the frightening consequences of their actions were spelt out. If you wish to stop promiscuity, the
argument goes, then the consequences of venereal disease
and the problems of single-parent families must be shown
as graphically as possible. The earliest approach on this
tended to suggest that, contrary to expectations, fear-
arousing appeals were counter-productive and were inferior
to more neutral appeals as means of producing change.
However, it has not been a very stable finding and other
research has contradicted this. Finally, the target of the
communication is an important variable when we try to assess
the effectiveness of communications. There is some evidence
of a slight but general tendency for certain individuals to
be more easily persuaded than others no matter what the
issues. However, we do not understand what makes people
suggestible, and easily recognizable specific factors such
as sex and intelligence do not seem to contribute anything
to general persuasibility. A feature common to nearly all
the above examples is that it is very difficult to make any
sort of simple generalization about the effects of communications; precise predictions are not possible. So we should
not assume that because we try to change people using the
mass media we will necessarily succeed. But we can still
point to common features of the communication process. Our
example of trying to persuade the poor to take up rate rebates gives us strong clues about general principles under
the mass media and persuasion. Some of these are examined
below.

Common features of the communication process

Attitudes and opinions are anchored in the individual's social environment

We saw in the rent rebate study that a proportion of those eligible for rate rebates did not claim because they were afraid of the stigma involved. The stigma is essentially that the individual is not living up to the standards of self-reliance and pride held by other members of the community which the individual relates to and respects. The psychological as well as social costs of applying for rebates outweighed the cash benefits. It has been frequently found in psychological research that an individual's most important attitudes and opinions are firmly embedded in a web of psychological and social needs. So changes in attitudes and opinions usually require a radical change in that web of psychological and social needs. People do not have attitudes and opinions for no reason at all. They tend to be in some way functional to them, to fulfil some purpose. These purposes can vary greatly, but clearly it helps our relationships if we share the same attitudes and opinions as our family and friends. It would be very difficult for a member of a religious group to retain ties with friends in the church if the member suddenly loses faith.

Newcomb (1957) showed the social basis of attitude change quite dramatically in one of his studies. Bennington was a women's college in which the teaching faculty was markedly more liberal than the girls' families, which were mainly wealthy and conservative. The girls entering this college entered an environment which was ideologically the opposite of their home background. Over a period of many years, Newcomb charted the progress of this group of girls and tried to isolate the factors which led to the adoption of the attitudes and values of the liberal college rather than retaining the conservative home values. The women who became most integrated and active in the college community were the ones who changed their attitudes in line with the atmosphere of the college. Those who did not change tended to retain strong ties with home and others with more conservative attitudes and values. These changes persisted over a lengthy period: the girls were studied 25 years later and the liberal attitudes and values were particularly stable amongst those who married husbands with attitudes in line with those of the college.

It may be, of course, that the psychological and social needs of individuals may predispose them to accept what the mass media say. For example, some might be willing to accept the media's view of the causes of strikes simply because the media support their own political position on industrial relations.

Conclusion 1

THE PERSUASIVE EFFECTS OF THE MASS MEDIA ARE REDUCED AND ENHANCED BY THE PSYCHOLOGICAL AND SOCIAL CIRCUMSTANCES OF THE INDIVIDUAL.

The mass media do not always speak with one voice
Although the professional person may be very clear what
message he wishes to get across to the audience, others wi
access to the media may have different purposes. In our
welfare case study, the message to collect benefits was in
contrast with the media's 'view' that people on welfare are
scroungers. Similar instances occur very frequently. For
example, what is the point of broadcasting propaganda
against drinking and driving if the media at the same time
allow advertising which suggests very strongly that drinking
is fun and socially desirable? What is the point of Health
Education Council buying advertising time to preach a mess·
age against overweight if the food industry pushes high cal-
orie, low nutrition foods? Quite clearly, in a society where
the mass media are relatively free, competing messages are
common. One implication, of course, is that to some exten·
the conflicting messages will cancel each other out. Evidence suggests that election campaigns may be ineffective
means of changing voting behaviour. Despite the huge amou·
of time and resources allotted to election campaigns by all
sides, it has been shown (Butler and Stokes, 1969) that onl·
a very small percentage of people actually change their
voting behaviour from one election to the next. The figure
can be as low as two or three per cent.

Conclusion 2

THE PERSUASIVE EFFECTS OF THE MEDIA MAY BE RED·
BY COMPETING MESSAGES WHICH SAY RATHER DIFFER·
THINGS.

The audience may not interpret the message as intended
In our case study we saw that some individuals saw the
advertisements about rate rebates but misunderstood the
message and thought that rate rebates did not apply to then·
This clearly shows that a message may be reinterpreted by
the audience. In other words, the mass media do not alway·
communicate their intended message effectively. A graphic
example comes from a classic study of prejudice by Cooper
and Jahoda (1947). Anti-racist cartoons were shown to know·
bigots. The cartoons were supposed to preach an anti-
prejudice message in a humorous manner. But anti-semites
largely interpreted the message of the cartoons to be anti-
Jewish, not anti-bigotry. Another example of how a messag·
can become distorted comes from an American television pr·
gramme where a particularly violent incident was intention-
ally softened by shielding the action behind filing cabinets
so that the violence was implied, not seen. However, the
audience assumed that the victim was being raped rather th·
physically assaulted.

Conclusion 3

THE IMPACT OF THE MASS MEDIA DEPENDS IN PART ON
THE WAY THE AUDIENCE PERCEIVES THE MESSAGE.

The mass media do not always reach the right people
We saw in our case study how the people who needed to kno·

most about rate rebates were less likely to be aware of the advertising than those already receiving the benefits.

People do not have to watch television or read the newspapers: they do not watch every programme or read every page, and there is no guarantee that the audience for any message is the audience one requires. In the advertising industry this problem is partly overcome by careful research into what types of people watch what, read what, and buy what. It is thereby possible to maximize the size of the desired audience for any advertisement. This is not so simple with non-commercial applications of the mass media. The phrase 'selective exposure' indicates that exposure to the mass media is much more of a motivated process than might be imagined. For example, there is evidence that party political broadcasts are seen more by supporters of that party than by those of the other political parties. Similarly, it is known that the readers of right-wing newspapers are right-wing themselves. There is also, of course, 'unselective' exposure. One likes to think of the less popular programmes - those with small audiences - as reaching a small, select, interested but specialized audience, and the very popular programmes - those reaching massive audiences - as reaching the unselective, undiscriminating, heavy viewer. But this is not at all the case. The most popular programmes are those with the most selective viewers since it is necessary for a good many individuals to deliberately put the programme on in order to have a big viewing figure. The minority programmes tend to be seen by the people who do not switch the set off: the undiscriminating audience. No communication can be effective if it fails to reach its selected audience.

Conclusion 4

THE EFFECTIVENESS OF THE MASS MEDIA TO PERSUADE PEOPLE MAY BE LIMITED BY THE FAILURE TO REACH THE TARGET AUDIENCE.

Information and motivaton are not the same

Since many people in our case study who knew about rate rebates did not claim them it is obvious that having information about something is not necessarily sufficient to motivate the individual to act in accordance with that knowledge. This is less trite than it at first sight appears and is perennially overlooked by those who comment on the harm done by, and the power of, the mass media. But we can all think of knowledge we have which we have not used in any way. For example, most of us have a very good idea how to cause violent injury to others, but by and large this knowledge is not used.

Conclusion 5

IN GENERAL, KNOWLEDGE GAINED FROM PERSUASIVE COMMUNICATIONS IN ITSELF DOES NOT MOTIVATE BEHAVIOUR.

General conclusion

It should be clear from our analysis so far that, in order to understand the effects of any communication, the psycho logy and the social environment of the target of the commu nication, the message, the competing messages, and the us of the mass media by the individual all have to be taken into account. A very misleading impression of the effects o the mass media will be formed from studying the apparent contents of the communication alone.

The mass media and the professions

Our discussion so far has emphasized just one function that the mass media can perform for the members of a professio That is, we have discussed the use of the mass media to contact clients en masse to persuade them to adopt some particular form of behaviour. But this is only one aspect of the use of the mass media as a tool by professions. There are at least two other important ones, explained below.

Disseminating information through the profession

Professions have a responsibility to keep their members abreast of the news and latest developments in their field. Mass media may help here.

Professions increasingly need to consider their public image and public relations

Some professions, for example, tend to be treated rather unfavourably by the press. For instance, teachers and socia workers tend to be dealt with less kindly than, say, doctors and nurses. The legal profession may seem to some to need all the favourable publicity it can get, as do managers and trade unionists. Some professions may have no public image at all.

Both these aspects of the professional's need for the mass media illustrate further general principles about the mass media. Let us look at communications about news and innovations in a profession first.

The flow of communications

It is far too simple to assume that information flows directly from the mass media to individuals. Although this does happen it is merely one of the many possibilities. This simple process is called the one-step flow of communication to indicate there is just one stage in the process: the communication is broadcast and operates directly on the individual. The two-step flow of communication refers to a more complex situation. Here the mass media operate on some individuals who then influence others who had not been influenced by the media directly. These intermediaries are called 'opinion leaders' for the obvious reason that they try out new ideas before others and lead others to try these ideas out. Of course, we may have much more complicated communication networks than this with multi-step flows of communication, but the two-step flow reveals the rudiments of the process clearly. Furthermore, it is perfectly possible that the one-step, two-step, and multi-step processes co-exist at the same time. For example, an individual may be partially influenced directly by the mass media but also further influenced by an opinion leader.

Opinion leaders in professional groups are therefore early adopters of new ideas (techniques, procedures, products, etc.). It has been shown that early adopters differ in many respects from later adopters of an innovation in a profession. These differences will differ from one profession to another and from one innovation to another. A good example of this is that the early adopters of a new drug in the medical profession read more professional journals than later adopters. However, it is notable that journals and other media of communications seem to be secondary to the salesman in disseminating information about new drugs. Furthermore, there is an important distinction between the sources of information which provide knowledge about a new drug and those which are the most influential in persuading an individual to prescribe it. One study found that salesmen were credited as being the original source of knowledge by 57 per cent of doctors. Colleagues were identified as a source of knowledge by only 7 per cent of doctors. When asked about influential sources leading to adoption of drugs, the doctors nominated salesmen only 38 per cent of the time, but colleagues were nominated by 20 per cent of doctors. Similarly, whereas only 7 per cent of doctors credited journal articles with being the original source of knowledge about a drug, 23 per cent of them credited journal articles as the most influential source of information. It is interesting to note that early adopters of the new drug tend to be very cautious in its use whereas the later adopters, since they can build on the experience of others, prescribe much more readily. Clearly the early adopters were not just gullible and the late adopters slow since the process of adoption seems to be rather rational. Early adopters were cautious because they had less information with which to work.

The study of communication networks within professions can help to show how a profession changes over time. It can be valuable in understanding how individuals come to accept new ideas.

The image of the profession

We should not forget that so far, although we have dissected the audience of the mass media fairly thoroughly, we have taken the mass media as a given. But of course the mass media organization is a worth-while subject of study in itself. It is the mass media organizations which decide what should be broadcast (within limits set by government), what is news and what is not, who should get access to the media and who should not, and who should comment on current affairs and who should not. In other words, the mass media organization constructs the messages to be broadcast. Now it is no matter whether we are speaking of the largest television company in the world or the producers of the smalles professional journal; the principle remains the same.

If we take the example of articles in professional journals, it is absolutely clear that those responsible for the preparation and publication of a journal have an influence on what is actually published. Editors may decide that an article is not relevant to their journal; they may send it to referees who decide that the article is not good enough for publication since it is based on inadequate research or argument; the production manager may be unable to find space for its publication, and so forth. The individuals who make decisions as to whether or not the article is published are termed gatekeepers, since they may open or keep closed the 'gates' which lead to publication. Furthermore, the content of the media may be influenced by wheth or not information has been actively sought by, say, the editor or whether members of the profession choose to bring information to the attention of the journal.

This last point brings us to public relations. It is too easy to assume that the mass media actively seek all the news and information they disseminate. This is, of course, partly true but the mass media also rely on information being offered to them. Set-piece occasions such as conferences provide ideal circumstances for the collection of news. Thus more is reported in the press about psychology at the time of the psychologists' annual conference than at any other time. News sometimes corresponds to the common view of unexpected events monitored and published by the media, but much of it consists of events which the news media plan to cover weeks in advance.

In general a profession, if it wishes to present a certain image of itself, needs actively to seek publicity outlets in the mass media. The need to use the press in this way will vary from profession to profession. However, if the following comments by the Glasgow Media Group (1976) are correct then many of the professions associated with industry would seem to be faced with a particular serious problem of correcting the image of industry in the mass media:

> the picture of society in general and industrial society in particular, that television news constructs ... at its most damaging includes ... the laying of blame for society's industrial and economic problems at the door of the workforce. This is done in the face of contradictory evidence which, when it appears, is either ignored, smothered, or at worst, is treated as if it supports the inferential frameworks utilised by the producers of news.

Whether or not such tendencies in the news media will actually influence the audience is arguable. But this is to take us back in full circle to the effects of the mass media.

nclusion

The main points to consider when studying the effects of mass communications are:

*   CLIENTS: (i) how are attitudes and opinions anchored in the individual's social environment? (ii) What are the competing voices in the mass media issuing different messages? (iii) How does the audience interpret the persuasive message? (iv) Is the right audience being reached by the message? (v) Is the information motivating?
*   OTHER PROFESSIONALS: careful study of the communication network of a profession may serve as an aid to understanding and promoting change in a profession.
*   IMAGE OF THE PROFESSION: professions may care to enhance their public image by careful use of the mass media.

ferences

Butler, D. and Stokes, D. (1969)
Political Change in Britain. London: Macmillan.
Cooper, E. and Jahoda, M. (1947)
The Evasion of Propoganda. Journal of Psychology, 23, 15-25 .
Glasgow Media Group (1976)
Bad News. London: Routledge & Kegan Paul.
Golding, P. and Middleton, S. (1978)
Welfare abuse and the media. New Society, 46, 195-197.
Meacher, M. (1971)
Rent Rebates. London: Child Poverty Action Group.
Milavsky, J., Pekowsky, B. and Stipp, H. (1975-76)
TV drug advertising and proprietary and illicit drug use among teenage boys. Public Opinion Quarterly, 39, 457-481.
Newcomb, T. (1957)
Personality and Social Change: Attitude formation in a student community. New York: Holt, Rinehart & Winston.

uestions

1. What are some of the factors which help determine whether the mass media are effective at changing people?
2. To what extent is mass communication a social process?
3. What is the potential of the mass media for use by your profession (or from a profession of your choice)?
4. Draw a diagram to illustrate the flow of communications in your profession. Discuss this and ways in which the speed and quality of communications could be improved.
5. Describe the ways in which the mass media portray your profession or any group to which you belong. Do you think that it is possible to improve this portrayal?
6. Discuss the way in which the content of the mass media conflict with the aims of your profession or with your personal beliefs.
7. Describe the main things you would take into account if

you were planning an advertising campaign relevant to your profession.

8. What do we mean by the following: (i) opinion leaders; (ii) two-step flow of communication; (iii) selective perception and selective exposure; (iv) sleeper effect.
9. To what extent do individuals differ in their potential to be influenced by the mass media?
10. Drawing on illustrative examples, outline some of the different ways in which the mass media influence people.

Annotated reading

Brown, R. (ed.) (1976) Children and Television. London: Collier Macmillan.
> A book of readings which presents an overview of theory and research into mass communications. Most contributions are British or European.

Howitt, D. and Cumberbatch, G. (1975) Mass Media Violence and Society. London: Elek Science.
> This is the most detailed book devoted to the television violence issue. The authors present a thoroughgoing account of the mass media in society and the difficulties of research in this area.

Liebert, R.M., Neale, J.M., and Davidson, E.S. (1973) The Early Window. New York: Pergamon.
> An account of American research on the effects of television on young people. Contains content analysis data, material on advertising, educational television and control of the mass media as well as violence research.

Noble, G. (1975) Children in front of the Small Screen. London: Constable.
> A very psychological approach to television research. Stresses psychological processes and mechanisms much more than most texts. Goes into the production side of the television.

Whale, J. (1977) The Politics of the Media. Glasgow: Fontana.
> This is not about psychology at all in a formal sense. It is an account of some of the economic and political pressures controlling the mass media. The material is relevant to several parts of the chapter.

Finally, students might like to read more about the psychology of attitude change. Most introductory text books in psychology contain relevant material but the following is short and easily obtainable:

Reich, B. and Adcock, C. (1976) Values, Attitudes and Behaviour Change. London: Methuen.

1. Content analysis of mass communications

A content analysis is basically a record of the frequency
of occurrence of certain types of events (e.g. trade union
news, violence) in the mass media. One merely scans the
media for instances of the occurrence of certain types of
material. Carry out a content analysis of a mass medium to
test one of the following suggestions: newspaper or magazine
advertisements contain sexist images; the news on television
consists of very few unexpected events (i.e. tends to include an overwhelming proportion of planned happenings);
that violence is more common in early evening programmes
(when children are watching) than in late evening programmes; or that the mass media give a distorted picture
of the nature of work in Britain.

There are a number of decisions that you need to make.
To some extent these decisions may be arbitrary and
dependent upon practicalities, but nevertheless they are
important.

* Define the areas of content you are interested in. For
  example, violence might be defined as the intention to
  hurt or harm, sexism might be defined as images which
  hint that women should be primarily housewives and
  mothers, women are not so competent as men, or that
  women are important mainly for their bodies. The definition used will need to come out of discussion in
  class.
* Define the mass media to be sampled. There is so much
  mass communication that it is unlikely that a small
  project could cope with much other that a single medium
  of mass communication (e.g. either television or the
  newspapers).
* Define the time period to be sampled. This will probably
  be the current week's output since archival material is
  not likely to be available, and much more than a week's
  output is difficult to handle physically.
* Define what is to be sampled. Are we going to analyse
  every newspaper or just a selection of them, are we
  going to analyse every television programme or just
  those broadcast at certain times, etc.?
* Decide how the information is to be recorded. Devise a
  form to be used by the content analyst.

The complexity of a content analysis can vary enormously
so it is necessary to pitch the work at a level which is
within your capacity. The simplest way of carrying out a
content analysis is simply to search for examples of a particular type of content. For example, you could search the
daily newspapers for a week in order to pick out examples
of advertisements which are sexist in nature. An added complexity would be to ask whether there are more sexist advertisements in tabloid papers than in the so-called 'quality
newspapers'. At a much higher level of complexity one could,

for example, videotape all the programmes broadcast on television during the period 6 p.m. to 10 p.m. for a week. The tapes could then be analysed for, say, religious content. The complexity of the analysis could vary. The analysis may include a record of the type of programme a particular type of content appeared in, the time period in which it was broadcast, etc. Furthermore, it is possible to use more than one individual to make judgements independently about the contents of a particular programme, for example, so that some estimate of the reliability of raters may be made.

2. When do attitudes change in real life?

Much mass communications research on attitude change takes the form of laboratory experiments in which viewers are separated from their real-life social ties. This tends to encourage attitudes to be changed. Carry out a survey to find out the conditions under which people have changed their attitudes and whether the mass media have had an influence.

Design a short questionnaire to elicit from your respondents examples that they could remember of when they had changed their attitudes about significant things (politics, race, religion, etc.). For each of the examples they describe to you find out:

*   whether there had been any changes in their style of life at the time their attitudes changed (e.g. they went to college, found a new job, etc.);
*   the factors that influenced them (e.g. did the mass media have a role to play)?

Try to draw conclusions about the circumstances in which attitudes change in real life and the relative contribution of the mass media to these changes.

The purpose of this project is quite simply to encourage you to think of attitudes as being rather more stable than is often thought and embedded firmly in your social network. Probably you will discover that many respondents find it very difficult to think of examples where they had changed their minds; but this is significant in itself. Furthermore, it will probably be noticed that such changes are associated with significant changes in life style or with other upheavals in one's life, the reasons for this being that such changes are related to changes in social influences.

3. Produce a video programme or newspaper article

In the mass media chapter the results of various pieces of research into the effects of the mass media are described. Using whatever principles you can gather from these, produce a videotape or newspaper article which is designed to be persuasive. Naturally this involves your deciding what sort of persuasive communication you are to make (e.g. safety, health, politics, etc.). Try to design your actual programme or article in such a way that the viewer or reader is both entertained and informed.

Try out an audience evaluation of the programme or article. This can be as simple or complex as you like. The simplest way of doing it is probably to show it to a selection of people and to discuss with them their impressions of it. However, if it is so desired, you could write a special questionnaire which asks the audience specific questions about the material they have read or seen.

4. Investigate an individual's media consumption patterns and relate these to that individual's personality and life style

It is often suggested that what people do with the mass media is more important than what the mass media do to people. By this is meant that people use the mass media to obtain information, as a substitute for real social interaction, and as a reflection of their own style of life. Investigate an individual's mass media consumption patterns from the point of view of uses and gratifications researchers.

This will involve several things:

* a record of the individual's mass media usage will need to be made. This includes programmes watched, newspapers, magazines, and radio;
* a biographical account of the individual: family background, education, work, hobbies, etc.;
* a personal account from the individual of media exposure and usage, and what satisfactions are gained.

Naturally it is necessary to hypothesize about the relationships between the individual and actual media consumption. For example, are the newspapers read typical of someone in that individual's social class? Finally, it is necessary to ask yourself the question of whether you can explain the individual's media consumption patterns sufficiently well using this uses and gratifications approach.

Uses and gratifications of the mass media is an appealing and common-sense approach to the study of the mass media. It is also something which could be readily approached by most readers as a small project. The big difficulty emerges not so much in the collection of information but in the way in which it is possible to relate media usage to life style. In some instances this will be fairly obvious such as in the case of the type of newspaper read where there are, for example, distinct social class markets. However, in other instances such as very popular television programmes, the links may be difficult to forge. The main reason for this is that in order for a television programme to have an audience of around 15 million it has to appeal to a very wide cross-section of the population. Nevertheless, with intelligent examination, it should be possible to find examples within anyone's media consumption which seem to fit in well with the life style or personality. Do not forget that not viewing is as much a viewing pattern as viewing for seven hours a day.

18

Bargaining and negotiation
Ian E. Morley

According to Adam Smith, 'Man is an animal that makes bargains - no dog exchanges bones with another.' More generally, people exchange ideas. They negotiate, or confer in an attempt to define or redefine the terms of their relationships.

We believe that psychologists can contribute to our understanding of the ways negotiators prepare for bargaining and negotiate their case. In particular, we argue that:

* to understand the process of negotiation we need to combine 'models of negotiation' with 'models of man';
* planning and process may be regarded as the intra-group and inter-group aspects of a task which engage the 'core' processes of information interpretation, influence and decision-making;
* structure in the process of negotiation is determined by the working out of the core processes which are involved;
* attempts to influence the other depend upon the ways in which negotiators resolve 'dilemmas' built into the negotiation task;
* an understanding of the effects of uncertainty, complexity and stress is central to the psychology of bargaining and negotiation;
* negotiation is a skill. More precisely, 'the skilful negotiator is one who understands the risks and opportunities associated with his work; knows what resources he can bring to bear, and is able to protect or pursue the values and interests seen at stake' (Morley, 1981).

Recent work on the psychology of conflict, commitment and choice is considered in some detail. Following Janis and Mann (1977), we emphasize:

Man's vulnerability to gross errors in arriving at a decision through superficial search and biased information processing ... we see man not as a cold fish but as a warm-blooded mammal, not as a rational calculator always ready to work out the best solution but as a reluctant decision-maker - beset by conflicts, doubts, and worry, struggling with incongruous longings, antipathies and loyalties, and seeking relief by procrastinating, rationalizing or denying responsibility for his own choices (Janis and Mann, 1977).

We discuss psychology's view of 'rational man' and present evidence that 'skilled' negotiators bargain in ways which help others to manage the uncertainties and complexities of the negotiation task.

ersons, parties and
odels of negotiation

Model 1: Negotiation as a game of strategy

Negotiation is sometimes regarded as a game of strategy, analogous to games such as poker or chess. Furthermore, like chess, it is sometimes compared to an exercise in war in which moves are visible to each of the sides. It is, however, probably a mistake to think of negotiation in this latter way. Therefore, rather than study poker or chess, psychologists have utilized abstract games of a kind which are thought to reveal the logical structure of certain of the bargaining problems negotiators face. Research suggests that those who show dissimilar behaviour in one game may appear almost indistinguishably alike in another. What is important is the reward structure of the game, the way that structure is displayed, and the social meaning participants read into the game.

The process of negotiation is analysed in terms of a sequence of behavioural dilemmas inherent in the nature of the task: for example, shall I stand firm or risk signalling flexibility? Negotiators make choices guided by expectations about the others' response. Outcomes depend upon the accuracy of their diagnoses and the skill with which they construct appropriate moves.

Model 2: Negotiation as struggle

'Pressure bargaining' or 'dispute settlement' models preserve the flavour of strategic thinking by emphasizing 'concealment' and 'competitive' strategies (Winham, 1977a). They recognize the truth in the common-sense view that negotiators only modify their positions when they have fought to the limit. Negotiation is seen as a struggle in which negotiators move stepwise toward an agreement which will be acceptable to both. It is a struggle which in itself validates the final terms, demonstrating that participants have done the best they can.

Model 3: Negotiation as collaboration

Common sense would suggest that in some cases negotiators are more willing to work towards agreement than in others. Negotiation may, therefore, be viewed in terms of a 'collaborative model' in which parties make sacrifices, rather than concessions, in the pursuit of some overriding goal. For example, Strauss' description of the negotiations to achieve economic union between Belgium, the Netherlands, and Luxembourg shows the parties 'kept major focus on the shared benefits of economic union' (Strauss, 1978). Elements of threat and manipulation were still there but negotiators did not, in general, openly exploit asymmetries in the balance of power. In Winham's terms, strategy was more a matter of forestalling the consideration of certain unattractive solutions than a matter of extracting change of position from an adversary (Winham, 1977a).

Model 4: The 'two-track' or 'boundary role' model

Frequently, negotiators belong to, and work for, organizations. They negotiate rules or interpret the manner in which they are to be applied. The attitude they adopt is determined by internal negotiations which place various kinds of restriction on their autonomy at the negotiation table. In some cases the restriction applies to 'latitude of decision'. In others it comes from uncertainty about the policy the organization wishes to pursue. Negotiators therefore monitor their constituents (where should we be?) as well as their opponents (where are they?) (Druckman, 1977). The process of negotiation may be charted by mapping the extent to which they are responsive to the one or the other. Following Druckman, we call this the 'two-track' or 'boundary role' model of negotiation.

Model 5: Negotiation as interpersonal and interparty exchange

The work of Douglas (1962) may be used to elaborate the nature of the two tracks which follow from negotiators' boundary roles. Let us say, rather, that negotiators operate at two levels; that it is possible to distinguish interpersonal and interparty forces which act on the members of negotiation groups. Party forces operate insofar as negotiators are representatives of groups. Personal forces derive from relationships built up at the bargaining table. The former (party) relationship is the superordinate (or dominant) one; the main struggle. The latter (personal) relationship is the subordinate (or diplomatic) one, which 'tidies up the battle'. The relative emphasis upon the one or the other changes as negotiation proceeds.

Studies of bargaining relationships have recently come to the fore in industrial relations research. 'Strong' relationships have important cognitive, affective, and motivational elements. They allow negotiators to exchange information freely, indicating (say) the likely reaction of one organization to proposals from the other. They are affectively positive in terms of trust, respect, liking, and so on. They are 'co-operative', rather than 'individualistic' or 'competitive'.

A systems view of industrial negotiations

Each of the models we have outlined draws our attention to certain aspects of the process of negotiation. What is not yet clear is how descriptions of process are to be linked to descriptions of the environment of which the negotiation forms a part. A 'systems model', adapted from Allen, is shown in figure 1.

Conflict begins when some change in existing circumstances, sometimes inadvertent, sometimes deliberate, creates a situation in which one party feels it must confront another. That is, conflict starts with some input from the environment.

The 'working core' of the model is the transformation element, the process of negotiation. Input is coded, summarized and sorted and a decision made to act. The activity is activity of information search and influence. The 'core processes' of the model are the processes of information interpretation (including the search for information), influence, and decision making.

The control element contains policies, decision rules, and goals. In negotiation, policies and decision rules (themselves the product of social action) operate upon the process of intra-organizational bargaining to produce a more detailed specification of goals. Controls are also imposed by various background factors and negotiating conditions.

The memory element contains the data storage facilities of the management and union organizations.

The output element contains the product of the negotiation including effects on the attitudes of the negotiators, and members of the domestic groups (constituencies) which they represent.

Finally, the model contains a loop for feedback of effects, emphasizing once again the importance of continuity in the relationships between the sides. The loop also reminds us that negotiations are part of a more general process in which practitioners learn about the methods and expectations of the other side. Allen's model underlines the importance for practitioners of working out what their opponents are trying to do.

First, negotiation is described as a transformation element. That is, input requires interpretation (diagnosis) as well as action (treatment). It is all too easy to think of negotiation in terms of strategy, tactics, and struggle without considering why the struggle is perceived in this or that kind of way. The systems model reminds us that negotiators are operating in an uncertain, threatening environment in which they use their mental resources to make sense of what is going on.

Second, the language of control suggests that negotiators operate within a system of constraints. To understand an opponent's behaviour it may be necessary to identify the constraints, perceived from the point of view of that opponent. Strong bargaining relationships help negotiators do this kind of job.

Differences in issue emphasis

The control element
Bonham (1971) set up a laboratory simulation of some of the

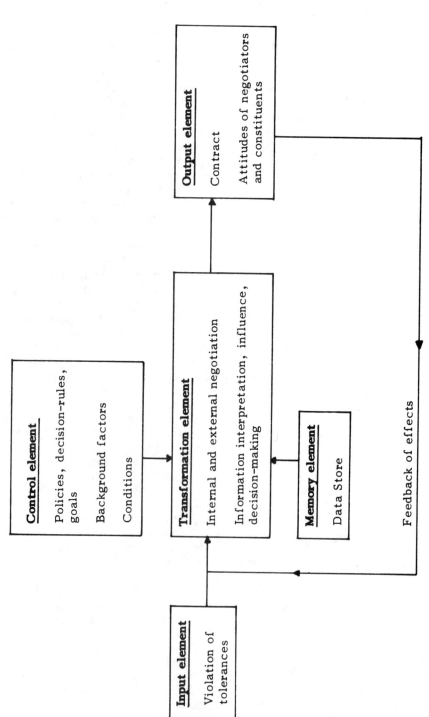

Figure 1

A 'systems model'
From Allen, 1971.

disarmament negotiations which took place between 1946 and
1961. Differences in issue emphasis (priority to arms reduction versus priority to problems of inspection) led to
two rather different patterns of behaviour. Either participants exchanged fewer messages and tried to 'avoid the
problem'; or they increased their activity, partly to make
more attacks on the motives of the others. All in all,
Bonham felt it legitimate to conclude that differences in
the relative saliency of the issues produce misunderstanding, negative attitudes, hostile interaction, fewer concessions and a lower probability of eventual agreement
(Bonham, 1971).

Problems of social judgement
Typically, negotiators balance gains on one issue against
losses on another. 'Cognitive conflict' arises when negotiators trade off values in different ways. Balke, Hammond
and Meyer (1973) asked practitioners to 're-enact' negotiations, rating the acceptability of different kinds of agreement. the results obtained from this study and others show
that 'inconsistency' in judgement is a major source of conflict in negotiation between groups. To quote Brehmer and
Hammond (1977):

> the inability to describe judgement policies accurately
> and completely is one of the major reasons why cognitive
> conflict between persons is so hard to resolve and
> successful negotiation is so elusive. For while the
> student of human judgement will realize that the des-
> criptions of judgement policies produced by introspec-
> tion are likely to be inaccurate and incomplete because
> of human INABILITY to be otherwise, the lay person will
> attribute inconsistencies, inaccuracies, and incom-
> pleteness to an INTENTION TO BE DEVIOUS; current
> folklore suggests that it is naive to do otherwise.
> Failure to acknowledge the limitations of human
> judgement results in the attribution of evil intent to
> the other person.

Background factors
Negotiators define their representative task in different
ways, depending on control factors which, in a sense, 'link'
them to their constituency groups. Broadly speaking, the
greater the 'pressure' on representatives the greater their
concern explicitly to demonstrate their commitment to group
positions, and to 'confirm and validate' the final settlement by their behaviour at the negotiation table. Thus negotiation takes longer when representatives face post-
negotiation evaluation by members of a cohesive group.

Psychologists also investigated the ways in which a
constituency looks at its spokesman. For example, Klimoski
and Breaugh (1977) have argued that, in some cases, 'performance doesn't count'. In their study the 'behaviour of
outsiders was censured and their agreements rejected',

despite a level of performance comparable to representatives who came from inside the group.

It is not just that negotiation takes longer in certain circumstances than others. Settlements may exhibit greater variability, reflecting unilateral domination by one of the sides, depending (say) upon perceptions of the 'win-lose' character of the conflict, or its links with more ideological disputes.

Conditions of negotiation

To conclude our discussion of the control element, let us say a little about some of the conditions which may be important. We have two lines of research in mind.

The first is geared to Douglas' model of negotiation. It has investigated the proposition that formal systems of communication (which restrict the cues one person can transmit to another) affect the balance between interpersonal and interparty forces. Evidence has been obtained to show that negotiators given the stronger case drive harder bargains when formal rather than informal systems of communication are used (Morley and Stephenson, 1977).

The second line of research deals with some of the effects of 'situational complexity'. Put simply, negotiations become complex:

> when there are a lot of 'things' to be kept in mind, either issues being debated or positions taken by different parties, or implications that the negotiation might have for the environment. Complexity is created also under conditions of uncertainty, when information that is needed is difficult or costly to obtain or is simply unavailable (Winham, 1977b).

Following Winham we refer to the 'size' of the negotiation situation when there are lots of things to be kept in mind. We use the term uncertainty when information is difficult to obtain or is ambiguous once it is obtained. As the size the negotiation situation is increased, negotiators may not have time to study important documents and work out what is going on. More generally, increasing the size of negotiation may lead to uncertainty about value judgements of one's own. Parties are less likely to agree on the nature of concessions, or even that concessions have been made. The more complex the negotiation (particularly if it is multilateral rather than bilateral), the harder it will be to establish that a breakthrough has been made. Uncertainty will increase. It will be harder to estimate what opponents are likely to accept. Note that the negotiators questioned by Balke et al (1973) were confident they understood their counterpart's policies, a belief based on years of association and negotiation. Yet they were wrong.

The transformation element

In Allen's framework the transformation element contains the process of negotiation, both internal (within parties) and external (between parties). It also contains the processes of conciliation, mediation, or arbitration. We are not sure what Allen intended but, except for arbitration, psychologists have emphasized the similarities between what might seem like disparate elements in the process of transformation.

Here we want to emphasize that preparation and process are linked by virtue of the fact that they are intra-group and inter-group phases of a complex task. The output of one is input to the other which provides input in its turn: and so on. Both involve the core processes of information interpretation, influence, and decision making. We are not sure that the internal process can 'be explained in precisely the same terms as the external process' (Anthony, 1977) but we do think that the similarities are more important than the differences.

1. THE PROCESS OF INTERNAL ADJUSTMENT. By and large the process of internal adjustment has been taken for granted, rather than studied in detail. So far as laboratory research is concerned there have been studies of the effects of role reversal; preparation in strategy versus study groups; the effects of linking conflicts to more basic values (system maintenance versus system change); and the effects of preparation for negotiation in a group.

Much the most important research, however, has been conducted by Rackham and Carlisle (1978b), who compared the planning techniques used by 'effective' and 'average' negotiators. By 'effective', Rackham and Carlisle meant a negotiator (i) rated as such by both sides, union and management, supplier and purchaser; (ii) with a good 'track record' in terms of reaching agreements; and (iii) able to reach agreements which 'stick'. 'Average' negotiators were those who failed with respect to (i) or (ii) or (iii), or negotiators for whom no criterion data were available.

Briefly, the 'effective' negotiators considered a wider range of 'options for action' than 'average' negotiators, and were more likely to identify a range of possible outcomes than think in terms of fixed objectives. In short, they recognized that what can be achieved is partly a function of what is available. An 'effective' plan is a plan which survives contact with the opposition and does not require a 'mental change of gear' when they fail to react as they should. It is, for example, a mistake to rely on verbalizations such as, 'First I'll bring up A, then B, then C, then D'. Effective negotiators used plans which were independent of sequence: 'issue planning' rather than 'sequence planning', as Rackham and Carlisle say.

2. THE PROCESS OF EXTERNAL ADJUSTMENT: STAGES IN NEGOTIATION. Research by Douglas implies that, to be successful, negotiators must separate in time the interpersonal and inter-party demands of their task. Apparently,

negotiations which end in agreement go through stages, so
that: 'changes in overt behavior come as spurts, often
rather abrupt ones, following periods of prolonged circular
activity which appear to accomplish remarkably little in a
forward direction' (Douglas, 1962). Indeed, Douglas goes so
far as to say that, during the first stage of negotiation,
it is precisely 'to the extent that the contenders can
intrench their seeming disparity' that they 'enhance their
chances for a good and stable settlement in the end'
(Douglas, 1957). That is, in some sense, not to disagree
means not to solve the problem.

Initially (stage I) the negotiators observed by Douglas
showed 'prodigious zeal' for discrediting their opponents.
Speeches were exceptionally long and emphasized the representative role participants had to play. Apparently the
activity functioned to provide 'a thorough and exhaustive
determination of the range within which the parties will
have to do business' (Douglas, 1957). Presumably this helped
participants to avoid positions which were non-starters. It
may also have forced negotiators to look beyond the easy,
obvious solutions. Subsequently (stage II) negotiators
subordinated their representative roles whilst engaging in
unofficial behaviours designed to reconnoitre the bargaining
range and give a more precise idea of the settlements which
might be obtained. Finally (stage III) negotiators returned
to an emphasis upon their representative roles, as they
moved to commit their parties to an agreement and 'preci-
pitate a decision-making crisis'.

Stages I and II allow negotiators to assess the
'strength of position' of the parties (Morley and
Stephenson, 1977). Initially,

> the parties are either uncertain or mistaken about
> relative bargaining power, primarily because they cannot
> know the value of each other's interests at stake and
> how firm the other ultimately will be. Toward the end of
> the confrontation stage, the parties develop fairly
> clear, if not correct, pictures of mutual resolve and
> hence relative bargaining power, and then a process of
> resolution occurs - either compromise or one-sided
> capitulation depending on the revealed power relations.
> Process is therefore practically inseparable from power
> since it is through process that the true power rela-
> tions become manifest in the parties' values and
> perceptions (Snyder and Diesing, 1977).

If the first stage of negotiation allows negotiators to 'get
on the record a turgid edition of what they wish to say
about themselves and their positions', the second allows the
argument to get truly under way. It allows the bargaining
relationship between the negotiators to come to the fore.

In this respect it is interesting to note that 'the
systems of argument employed tend to differ between stewar
who have a strong bargaining relationship and those who do

not' (Batstone, Boraston and Frenkel, 1977). When stewards enjoyed a strong bargaining relationship with an opponent they were more likely (i) to emphasize their 'leader' role within the workforce; (ii) stress 'the men are on my back' rather than 'the men have instructed me'; (iii) demonstrate their understanding of management politics; and (iv) attempt to work out how particular goals could be achieved.

Accordingly, there is an important sense in which stage II can be regarded as a 'problem-solving' stage, but it is problem-solving with an irreducibly political component. The behaviour followed by the negotiators follows from and functions to develop or maintain the bargaining relationship between the negotiators 'at the table'.

3. THE PROCESS OF EXTERNAL ADJUSTMENT: BID AND COUNTERBID: social scientists have assumed (frequently) that negotiation involves little more than a process of bid and counterbid. Douglas' analysis does not necessarily diminish the importance of bid and counterbid but makes it clear that any concession-convergence process is likely to occur late in the day, once the participants have established an 'exchange rate' determining what sized concession from A is equivalent to what sized concession from B.

Magenau and Pruitt (1979) take the view that current levels of demand, are to be understood in terms of nego-tiators' levels of aspiration (LOA) and the minimum neces-sary share (MNS). Thus, if negotiator A is asking for an increase of 25 per cent as part of a strategy designed to secure 15 per cent, his LOA is defined by the value (to him) of achieving a settlement at 15 per cent. A's MNS, if he has one, is defined by 'the smallest level of value acceptable in the foreseeable future' or the 'level below which he would rather break off negotiation than reach agreement' (Magenau and Pruitt, 1979).

What is important is the suggestion that the nature of the concession-convergence process depends upon the presence or absence of a solution that is above the negotiators' minimum necessary shares (i.e. can be sold to domestic organizations), is perceptually prominent (to emphasize this really is the end), and is supported by one or more moral rules.

Given such a solution it seems that negotiators are inclined to match the other's offers. That is, 'the more he demands initially, the more they will demand ... The more rapidly he concedes, the faster are their concessions' (Magenau and Pruitt, 1979). Otherwise, a mismatch occurs. That is, 'If he makes a large initial demand, they make a small one ... If he makes a large concession they make small ones' (Magenau and Pruitt, 1979). Almost certainly, a detailed analysis has to be more complicated than this to take account of deadlines, time cost, and so on, but enough has been said to indicate some of the moves which might be made.

Walton and McKersie's behavioural theory

Walton and McKersie in 'A Behavioral Theory of Labor Negotiations' (1965) have provided the 'classic' statement of certain psychological aspects of the process of collective bargaining. Labour negotiations are treated as one example of the more general class of 'social negotiations' which occur whenever 'two or more complex social units ... are attempting to define or re-define the terms of their inter-dependence' (Walton and McKersie, 1965). More precisely, their theory contains five main elements.

The elements of the theory

First, Walton and McKersie identify four 'sub-processes' which serve different goals and operate according to different internal dynamics: distributive bargaining, in which negotiators settle the issues which divide them; integrative bargaining, in which they work through problem areas of joint concern; attitudinal structuring, by which they modify or maintain the bargaining relationships they have built up; and intra-organizational bargaining, the process of internal adjustment in which negotiators influence, and respond to, the demands of the domestic organizations they represent.

Second, there is a theory of individual choice behaviour in distributive bargaining, namely maximization of 'subjectively expected utility' or SEU. Third, there is a theory of individual choice behaviour in integrative bargaining, namely 'utility matching'. Fourth, there is a discussion of the tactical possibilities that negotiators can exploit, with tactics classified according to the 'internal logic' of the sub-processes they are designed to serve. Fifth, there is a discussion of the ways in which the 'sub-processes' place conflicting demands upon the participants. For example, Walton and McKersie argue that: 'the techniques for fostering the integrative process are generally the reverse of the techniques for implementing the distributive process' (Walton and McKersie, 1965).

Distributive and integrative bargaining

What is immediately apparent is the contrast between distributive and integrative bargaining which Walton and McKersie's theory contains. However, the nature of this distinction is not at all clear. Anthony (1977) has developed the point in the following way:

> Bargaining implies a difference in interests and objectives. Collective bargaining is concerned to reach accommodations, often of a temporary nature, between different interests and expectations. In this sense collective bargaining is almost always what Walton and McKersie define merely as a subprocess; it is always distributive bargaining in which the parties are negotiating over the distribution of scarce resources, money, status, or power.

From this point of view 'integrative bargaining' is simply

distributive bargaining in which participants adopt a collaborative rather than a competitive approach to the problems of distribution which are involved.

Research on integrative bargaining

Before moving on to the other aspects of Walton and McKersie's theory it is, perhaps, worth considering the kind of research psychologists have conducted under the heading of 'integrative' bargaining. To do so, we should note that some laboratory tasks, often those which simulate negotiation between buyer and seller, allow one negotiator to increase the profit obtained by the other at little or no personal cost. In other words, one negotiator (say A) may be able to maintain a given level of profit whilst maximizing the joint gain (A's profit plus B's profit). Some writers use the term 'integrative' to refer to distributive bargaining which is efficient in this kind of way.

One line of research shows that under some circumstances joint profit is maximized provided only that 'one individual behaves systematically and that the other one terminates the process by accepting the highest offer available to him' (Kelley and Schenitzki, 1972). A second shows that 'a period of conflict is often necessary before people look beyond the easy obvious options in search of those that provide more joint profit' (Pruitt and Lewis, 1975). The conflict which was productive was, however, conflict guided by a co-operative rather than a competitive 'mode of thought'.

The sub-processes of attitudinal structuring and intra-organizational bargaining

Attitudinal structuring and intra-organizational bargaining may be described as 'sub-processes' in ways distributive bargaining and integrative bargaining may not. Nevertheless, their status is not entirely clear. Anthony (1977) has argued that attitudinal structuring is best regarded as identifying tactics which may be selected as part of an overall co-operative or collaborative approach. He has added that 'There is a further confusion over the sub-process "intra-organizational" bargaining because this represents neither strategic nor tactical concerns but rather an environmental characteristic of the total field within which bargaining takes place' (Anthony, 1977).

Evaluation

Despite this, 'A Behavioral Theory of Labor Negotiations' remains a valuable work. First, the discussion of strategy and tactics is extremely thorough. Second, the discussion of attitudinal structuring reminds us that negotiation skill is not just a matter of learning which tactical opportunities are available. Rather, the bargaining process is 'constrained' by continuities in the relationships between the persons and parties involved: tactics must be seen to follow naturally from that process as it 'unfolds'. Third, Walton and McKersie have demonstrated the multiplicity of outputs from the process of collective bargaining: obtaining favourable agreements, avoiding disasters, maintaining good-will, improving bargaining relationships, educating consti-tuents and the like. To the extent that negotiators seek different outputs, and establish different objectives, we may say that their choice of strategy is 'constrained' in various ways. Finally, Walton and McKersie have demonstrat the importance of a theory of individual decision-making, or choice, one of the 'core' processes which we now consider in rather more detail.

Information interpretation, influence and decision making

Walton and McKersie predicated their account of distributive bargaining upon a prescriptive theory which says that the rational thing for negotiators to do is to choose that outcome which maximizes subjectively expected utility (SEU What is important here is that SEU theory is one example of a more general class of theories which define rational be-haviour in 'analytic' terms (Steinbruner, 1974). 'Analytic' decision makers recognize that different policies lead to different benefits and carry different costs. As information comes in, they are able to spell out the implications of different choices in more and more detail. The 'optimal' choice is identified by comparing, however roughly, the costs and benefits attached to each option, explicitly identifying the trade-off relationships which are involved. The decision-makers confront the uncertainties in their environment and do their best to work out the most sensible policy, all things considered.

There are good reasons, however, to suppose that, in many cases, people have neither the time, the energy, nor the ability to carry out the mental operations required by analytic theories of choice. As negotiations become more complex settlements may be accumulated 'from the bottom u rather than conceptualized in advance. Thus, negotiators SATISFICE rather than maximize; they control uncertainty by looking for a settlement which is 'good enough' in terms of a few key variables such as domestic support, precedent, and so on. The risk is, of course, that they will fail to appreciate important implications of the agreements which are reached.

A negotiator is likely to use different strategies, at different times and in different circumstances (Janis and Mann, 1977). Broadly speaking, the more complex the nego-tiation the lower the probability that negotiators will proceed according to the analytic paradigm which has been outlined. However, the more general point is that to under-stand the process of negotiation it is important to ask whether, and if so how, negotiators cope with the infor-mation processing demands of their task.

Essentially, given input ('violation of tolerances'), negotiators must first define the nature of the 'challenge' and work out what is going on. Second, they must decide wh they will try to do; consider means to achieve those ends; take note of likely reactions from the other side; and decide on a strategy for 'sorting things out'. Third, they must revise their policies in the light of information obtained once bargaining is under way.

Information interpretation and rationality in negotiation

Negotiation is one example of decision making under uncertainty, not least because values, interests, and power relations have to be worked out as arguments are presented and moves are made. Negotiators cannot escape questions about the validity of information presented by the other side. Negotiation as a process includes negotiators' attempts to impose order and certainty, and work out what is going on. However, there is a sense in which negotiators may exercise too much ingenuity in sorting what is essential from what is not.

The interpretation of input, 'violations of tolerances', requires an assessment of the intentions of the other side. People look for some kind of 'master script' which defines in ordinary language the threats and opportunities which they are likely to face (Morley, 1981).

Initially, it is inevitable that messages will be interpreted in the light of scripts formulated at a very high level of generality, in terms of 'images' of the other. However, following Snyder and Diesing (1977) we may then distinguish two kinds of development. 'Rational' bargainers are those who learn from the process of negotiation so that their images of the others are corrected or updated by what happens 'at the table'. More precisely, 'rational' bargainers sharpen their images of the others, differentiating general knowledge of the opponents' aims from what is implied by their behaviour at the time.

In contrast, 'irrational' bargainers are those whose perceptions, from first to last, are dominated by the general characteristics of their images of the others. In some cases of 'endemic conflict' the image of the other appears more like the image of an 'enemy' and it is, perhaps, appropriate to say 'the bargainer "knows" what is going on and is not going to be fooled by any new information' (Snyder and Diesing, 1977).

'Irrational' bargainers are 'irrational' in two kinds of way. They hold a rigid system of beliefs, retain and defend images and policies even when, to outsiders, they are clearly 'out of date'. Furthermore, their beliefs are organized so that all considerations point to the same strategic choice. This policy is seen as superior to others in all important respects. Jervis (1976) argues that this is a kind of 'overkill' in which the belief system minimizes the conflict between different kinds of constraint. It is 'irrational' because we can be fairly sure that the world is not so benign; negotiation is complex because it requires one kind of constraint to be balanced, or traded-off, against another.

It is in recognition of this that Drucker (1970) describes 'The Effective Executive' as one who understands 'the need for organized disagreement'.

> Decisions of the kind the executive has to make are made
> well only if based on the clash of conflicting views,
> the dialogue between different points of view, the
> choice between different judgments. The first rule in
> decision-making is that one does not make a decision
> unless there is disagreement (Drucker, 1970).

The 'rational' bargainer described by Snyder and Diesing is
rather like the 'effective executive' described by Drucker.
Each begins with tentative judgements and initiates an
active search for new information. The search is designed to
root out ideas which are plausible, but false or incomplete.
It is designed to test hypotheses so that conclusions follow
from, rather than precede, the 'facts' which are obtained.
Each attempts to understand the problem from the perspective
of the other side, and makes moves designed to reduce
ambiguity, clarify communications, and slow negotiation down
(Rackham and Carlisle, 1978a; Morley, 1981).

Three aspects of this treatment deserve further comment.
First, the search for information involves elements such as
diagnosing the basic cause of a given demand; looking for
alternative means to achieve the same ends; determining
which aspects of the other's position are flexible, and by
how much; and so on. If negotiators are to do these jobs
they must attempt a realistic assessment of the bargaining
power they have relative to their opponents. That is to say,
they must make estimates of the kind: how do the costs to
the others of rejecting my proposals compare with their
costs if they accept my proposal?

Second, rational bargainers concentrate their efforts in
attempts to work out the strategies of the others, since to
ask, 'Is my strategy working?', is to invite wishful thinking of one kind or another (Snyder and Diesing, 1977).
Furthermore, although Snyder and Diesing do not make this
explicit, we are tempted to extend the analogy with the
effective executive and argue that rational bargainers ask,
'What does this fellow have to see if his position were,
after all, tenable, rational, intelligent?' (Drucker, 1970).

Third, rational bargainers appreciate that signals clear
to them may be interpreted differently by others. Accordingly, a rational bargainer

> builds redundancy into his ... messages ... He does not
> assume that the opponent 'must know' what he is doing,
> but rather assumes the situation is pretty confused.
> Consequently he tries to send a message several dif-
> ferent ways, always through a different channel, and
> keeps repeating the same theme. The purpose is to break
> through the resistance set up by the opponent's mistaken
> expectations and also to give him time to test, retest,
> and adjust his expectations (Snyder and Diesing, 1977).

The reader should note that this is not just a theoretical
analysis. Snyder and Diesing's account is derived from the

empirical study of documents describing crisis bargaining between nations. It is consistent with other work.

For example, the 'effective' negotiators studied by Rackham and Carlisle (1978a) tended to label messages as questions, suggestions, warnings (rather than threats) and so on; they were less likely to respond immediately to proposals with counter-proposals of their own, possibly because they recognized the proposal might not be perceived as a proposal at all (but as 'blocking' or 'disagreement'); they made frequent attempts to summarize positions and test the other's understanding of what was going on; they organized disagreement so that ambiguities were cleared up and each gained an understanding of how the other would proceed; and they showed a proper respect for difficulties likely to arise when agreements were put into effect.

Power and influence

Psychologists have taken the view that power is to be analysed in terms of potential for influence: that there is a kind of 'negotiation power' deriving from the personal resources of the negotiators, from 'facility and shrewdness in the execution of negotiation tactics' (Stevens, 1963).

From one point of view the power derives from negotiators' ability to choose an appropriate strategy, meaning a set of tactics ordered in a certain kind of way. Here we argue that the selection and sequencing depends on the way negotiators view certain 'behavioural dilemmas' inherent in their task. Some of the dilemmas are linked to questions of information interpretation which have already been raised. For example, should an issue be treated on its merits or as a symptom of a more basic conflict which happens to have been expressed in this particular way? Does this clause have to be spelled out in detail? Or will the other keep the spirit of the agreement in areas not explicitly put into words?

Other dilemmas follow from a negotiator's concern to protect his reputation for resolve. Consider the question, 'Shall I make a concession or not?' According to Pruitt (1971), negotiators face costs whichever decision they make. To stand firm may be to nail my colours to a position I cannot possibly maintain, or make it look as if I am not trying to reach an agreement at all. But to move too early may give my opponents the expectation that more will follow if they persist. Some ways of dealing with the dilemma are outlined in Morley (1981).

Strategies are, of course, designed to influence others' behaviour. Consequently, it is important to realize that negotiation is not the same as other forms of debate. 'Effective' negotiators tend 'to advance single reasons insistently' rather than provide mutually supporting reasons to back up proposals they have made. Apparently, a negotiating position is only as credible as the weakest argument in the chain, but to influence others it is necessary to know what counts as a strong argument from their point of view.

Negotiation as decision making

In one sense negotiators continually face a threefold choice: to accept the offer on the table, to continue in the hope of negotiating better terms, or to break off negotiation, for the time being at any rate. However, it is perhaps more useful, analytically, to identify major choice points in terms of the decision whether to negotiate or not; the decision to pursue these objectives rather than those; the choice of this strategy rather than that; the decision to stay with this strategy rather than that; and, finally, the decision whether or not to accept the 'final' offer which has been made.

Decisional conflicts as sources of stress

The negotiators studied by Douglas were not only experience but had a good deal of third-party help. Douglas described one mediator as 'a perceptualizer of each to the other',

> and in the course of fashioning ready-made perceptions about each for the other, he appended his own embellishments in such a manner as, not to deceive, but to highlight, intensify, or otherwise single out certain elements for special attention ... Such tactics would unquestionably influence a party's estimate of the status of the conflict (Douglas, 1962).

Without such help it is not too difficult to believe that the concession dilemma identified by Pruitt may have deepened to the point where negotiators felt whatever they did was likely to be wrong. Under such circumstances, particularly when issues are complex, or there is a feeling that the environment cannot be controlled at all, negotiators may 'short circuit' the activities of information interpretation and information search, ignoring authentic warnings that things are going wrong.

Essentially, we propose to treat the concession dilemma as one example of a 'decisional conflict' in which there are 'simultaneous opposing tendencies within the individual to accept and reject a given course of action' (Janis and Mann, 1977). According to Janis and Mann, decisional conflicts produce intense stress when individuals face a 'crisis situation' in which each course of action carries serious risks and they see little hope of obtaining new information to reduce some of the uncertainty.

They argue, further, that the individual seeks forms of 'defensive avoidance' which enable him 'to escape from worrying about the decision by not exposing himself to cues that evoke awareness of anticipated losses' (Janis and Mann, 1977). If the decision can be postponed or delayed the individual will procrastinate; if the deadline is tight the individual will try to shift the responsibility to someone else, or 'bolster' the decision in various ways, warding off stress 'by selective attention and distorted information processing' (Janis and Mann, 1977).

Finally, Janis and Mann argue that their analysis applies not only to individuals but also to groups, to teams. In their view, being in a group amplifies the tendency of individuals to avoid raising controversial issues or confront difficulties head on. Apparently, group members are motivated (i) to shift responsibility, by seeking out the policy alternative favoured by the leader, or the most esteemed person, and (ii) to pool their resources collectively to bolster (rationalize) the choice the individual would like to make.

Janis and Mann refer to this collective tendency as 'groupthink' and argue that it is fostered when members belong to a cohesive group, 'insulated' from others in the organization; when leaders direct attention to the policy they would prefer; and when the group lacks systematic procedures for information appraisal and search. They argue, also, that the way to reduce tendencies towards groupthink is not to change the composition of the group. Rather, it is to ensure that the group devotes its energies to the right kinds of task.

Essentially, Janis and Mann have extended work on emergency decision making to cover all cases of decision making in which participants are concerned or anxious about the possibility that they may not attain the objectives which they seek. Details of the analysis are still being worked out, but one thing is clear; not to disagree, not to express 'organized dissent', means not to solve the problem. Dissent, properly conducted, is essential to clarify one's own position, and the position of the other side.

eferences

Allen, A.D. Jr (1971)
A systems view of labor negotiations. Personnel Journal, 50, 103-114.

Anthony, P.D. (1977)
The Conduct of Industrial Relations. London: Institute of Personnel Management.

Balke, W.M., Hammond, K.R. and Meyer, G.D. (1973)
An alternative approach to labor-management relations. Administrative Science Quarterly, 18, 311-327.

Batstone, E., Boraston, I. and Frenkel, S. (1977)
Shop Stewards in Action: The organization of workplace conflict and accommodation. Oxford: Blackwell.

Bonham, M.G. (1971)
Simulating international disarmament negotiations. Journal of Conflict Resolution, 15, 299-315.

Brehmer, B. and Hammond, K.R. (1977)
Cognitive factors in interpersonal conflict. In D. Druckman (ed.), Negotiations: Social psychological perspectives. Beverly Hills: Sage.

Douglas, A. (1957)
The peaceful settlement of industrial and inter-group disputes. Journal of Conflict Resolution, 1, 69-81.

Douglas, A. (1962)
Industrial Peacemaking. New York: Columbia University Press.

Drucker, P.F. (1970)
The Effective Executive. London: Pan Business Management.

Druckman, D. (1977)
Boundary role conflict: negotiation as dual responsiveness. In I.W. Zartman (ed.), The Negotiation Process: Theories and applications. Beverly Hills: Sage.

Janis, I.L. and Mann, L. (1977)
Decision Making: A psychological analysis of conflict, choice and commitment. London: Collier Macmillan.

Jervis, R. (1976)
Perception and Misperception in International Politics. Princeton, NJ: Princeton University Press.

Kelley, H.H. and Schenitzki, D.P. (1972)
Bargaining. In C.G. McClintock (ed.), Experimental Social Psychology. New York: Holt, Rinehart & Winston

Klimoski, R.J. and Breaugh, J.A. (1977)
When performance doesn't count: a constituency looks at its spokesman. Organizational Behavior and Human Performance, 20, 301-311.

Magenau, J.A. and Pruitt, D.G. (1979)
The social psychology of bargaining: a theoretical synthesis 1. In G.M. Stephenson and C.J. Brotherton (eds), Industrial Relations: A social psychological approach. Chichester: Wiley.

Morley, I.E. (1981)
Negotiation and bargaining. In M. Argyle (ed.), Handbook of Social Skills, Volume 2. London: Methuen.

Morley, I.E. and Stephenson, G.M. (1977)
The Social Psychology of Bargaining. London: George Allen & Unwin.

Pruitt, D.G. (1971)
Indirect communication and the search for agreement in negotiation. Journal of Applied Social Psychology, 1, 205-239.

Pruitt, D.G. and Lewis, S.A. (1975)
Development of integrative solutions in bi-lateral negotiation. Journal of Personality and Social Psychology, 31, 621-633.

Rackham, N. and Carlisle, J. (1978a)
The effective negotiator - Part 1: the behaviour of successful negotiators. Journal of European Industrial Training, 2, 6-11.

Rackham, N. and Carlisle, J. (1978b)
The effective negotiator - Part 2: planning for negotiations. Journal of European Industrial Training, 2, 2-5.

Snyder, G.H. and Diesing, P. (1977)
Conflict Among Nations: Bargaining decision making and system structure in international crises. Princeton, NJ: Princeton University Press.

Steinbruner, J.D. (1974)
The Cybernetic Theory of Decision. Princeton, NJ: Princeton University Press.
Stevens, C.M. (1963)
Strategy and Collective Bargaining Negotiation. New York: McGraw-Hill.
Strauss, G. (1978)
Negotiations: Varieties, contexts, processes, and social order. London: Jossey-Bass.
Walton, R.E. and McKersie, R.B. (1965)
A Behavioral Theory of Labor Negotiations: An analysis of a social interaction system. New York: McGraw-Hill.
Winham, G.R. (1977a)
Negotiation as a management process. World Politics, 30, 97–114.
Winham, G.R. (1977b)
Complexity in international negotiation. In D. Druckman (ed.), Negotiations: Social psychological perspectives. Beverly Hills: Sage.

Questions

1. Write an essay on negotiation, considered as a skill.
2. Outline the Janis and Mann model of decisional conflict and evaluate its significance for the study of negotiation.
3. Outline and discuss Douglas' model of successful negotation.
4. Why are negotiations sometimes more difficult than they need to be?
5. 'The basic operation of interests which exists within negotiation is mediated by personal relationships which facilitate the constructive resolution of problems'. Discuss.
6. What do effective negotiators do?
7. Discuss the link between bargaining power and bargaining process.
8. Evaluate the Walton and McKersie 'behavioural theory'.
9. Outline and discuss the distinction between rational and irrational kinds of bargaining.
10. Outline and discuss some of the 'behavioural dilemmas' inherent in the negotiation task.

Annotated reading

Atkinson, G.M. (1975) The Effective Negotiator. London: Quest.
   One of the best of the 'how to do it' books, including a number of extremely interesting suggestions designed to help negotiators set objectives based firmly on the realities of the power position between the sides.

Druckman, D. (ed.) (1977) Negotiations: Social psychological perspectives. Beverly Hills: Sage.
   Contains 13 chapters illustrating the kinds of problems psychologists take to be important in the study of negotiation. Some of the chapters are technical and

require a background in psychology. Others may be read without detailed preparation.

Lockhart, C. (1979) Bargaining in International Conflicts. New York: Columbia University Press.
    A clear and well-written statement of the processes of information interpretation, influence and decision-making as they occur in negotiation groups.

Miron, M.S. and Goldstein, A.P. (1979) Hostage. Oxford: Pergamon Press.
    An extremely interesting account of the skills involved in 'hostage negotiations'. In many respects the book is a manual to be used in training the police.

Morley, I.E. (1980) Negotiation and Bargaining. In M. Argy (ed.), Handbook of Social Skills, Volume 2. London: Methuen.
    Provides an account of negotiation skill. Discusses some of the psychological factors which promote success in negotiation. Readers may be interested in some of the other social skills outlined in Argyle's book.

Morley, I.E. and Stephenson, G.M. (1977) The Social Psychology of Bargaining. London: George Allen & Unwin.
    Provides a detailed review of laboratory research and a report of a programme of research designed to investigate Douglas' ideas. Includes transcripts of actual cases.

Stephenson, G.M. (1978) Negotiation and collective bargaining. In P.B. Warr (ed.), Psychology at Work (2nd edn). Harmondsworth: Penguin.
    A concise account which places negotiation for agreement in the context of a more general treatment of relations between groups.

Stephenson, G.M. and Brotherton, C.J. (eds) (1979) Industrial Relations: A social psychological approach. Chichester: Wiley.
    A collection of 16 chapters reviewing the contribution of psychology to various aspects of industrial relations.

Exercises

1. Tracking an industrial dispute

The purpose of this project is to construct a diary of an industrial dispute. Typically such disputes receive a good deal of coverage in the press and on radio and television newscasts, so you will have plenty of raw data to handle. You will need to invest in a number of daily newspapers and be able to tape-record off-the-cuff comments made by the participants when talking to news reporters. By 'participants' we mean not only the principal negotiators but individual workers, politicians, etc., who choose to become involved. You should acquire a scrapbook with material covering the duration of the dispute. The analysis you conduct will be influenced by the different models of bargaining discussed by Morley. For example, you can establish a number of points: whether the two sides state their case clearly at the outset, the extent to which negotiators refer to their constituents (i.e. those whom they represent), the degree of emotion inserted into statements, indications of a willingness to shift position, the nature of comments made when the dispute is over. Was it possible to infer at the outset what the final outcome would be and why? Is it clear why the issue over which the dispute arose needed to become a dispute in the first place? Are the statements made by particular individuals consistent over time? If you have access to various newspapers, analyse the views expressed in reports of the dispute. Do the newspapers maintain a constant and unchanging view or does the view alter as new information arises and the arguments put by one party or another become clarified? Try to construct a flow chart which describes the course of the dispute. Try also to describe the thoughts and intentions of the participants when they enter negotiation at the various stages of the dispute.

2. Reconstructing an industrial dispute or wage bargaining encounter

If you have completed Exercise 1, you might wish to follow it up by reconstructing the parts of the principal participants and simulating their first and final meetings; that is, moving from early presentation of the case of both sides to the final meeting at which some agreement is reached. As well as the principal participants you will need to have two groups of constituents. Among the consituents you will need a variety of viewpoints; some members will seek confrontation, others compromise or even compliance. Therefore, before entering into negotiation with the other side, each representative will need to reach an agreement within the group represented as to the range of possible courses of action. To increase the authenticity of the exercise, it would be sensible for the various groups to meet out of earshot of each other, so that there will be genuine ignorance of the other party's views. If you wish to create your own exercise rather than simulate a real dispute which you have studied, this should not prove too difficult: for example, the encounter will be focussed on the annual salary negotiation between a group of public service workers (say, teachers or nurses) and the local government employers. Let us suppose that central government has set cash limits upon all expenditure in the public services for the coming year. However, the level of inflation exceeds the stated level of pay awards which the government favours. The group in question is a large group which has slipped behind in the 'wages league' over the last three years. It is very important, if this exercise is to work, that all participants prepare a very careful brief for all their meetings, and that they

confer with the groups which they represent. If enough
people are willing to participate, some could take the role
of observers, watching the discussions which take place
among all the groups. When the exercise is over, the observers could lead a discussion involving all the participants
during which people would be encouraged to say what they
observed and how they felt at particular points in the
exercise. After the discussion session, go back to Morley's
text to see which model of bargaining best fits your own
simulation.

3. Decision making at the village council

Set up a committee of six people, one of whom will be the
chairperson. The remaining five represent different interest
groups within the village. A benefactor has just bequeathed
the sum of £5,000 to the village to be spent 'as a memorial
to the benefactor and in a manner which will be of lasting
value to the inhabitants of the village'. Five proposals
have been put forward and the purpose of the meeting is to
make a decision about spending the money. Because of the
terms of the benefactor's Will the project which is favoured
must be put into immediate effect, to ensure that the money
is spent within the specified time. Otherwise the money will
be donated to the local dog pound for the care of stray
dogs. The five proposals are as follows.

* A BUS SHELTER. The bus which departs hourly for the
  local town, leaves from the village square, which in wet
  weather becomes very windy and in hot weather becomes
  unbearably exposed. Many different groups use the bus as
  the local town is the principal place of employment for
  people in the village, and has a major shopping centre
  and the local high school. The estimated cost for a bus
  shelter is £4,000.

* REPAIRS TO THE PARISH CHURCH ROOF. The parish
  has a medieval church, which has featured in several
  architectural histories of England. The church is well
  attended for services and runs a lively Sunday school.
  The vicar has just discovered that there is a patch of
  dry rot in the church roof. The total cost of repairs
  will exceed £20,000. However, those who support this
  proposal believe that the £5,000 available will attract
  further funds and will form the basis of an appeal.
  Certainly, it would enable the work to be started.

* ALTERING THE OLD CRICKET PAVILION FOR THE
  SCOUT GROUP. The village is rather proud of its scout-
  ing group, which was formed in the early days of Baden-
  Powell. Last year the Scout Hall, a wooden building at
  the edge of the village, was struck by lightning and
  was burnt to the ground before the fire engine arrived.
  There are many young people in the village and some
  people think the scout group increases solidarity and
  helps to ensure that young people respect the village
  and will remain there when they become adults and set

up their own families, rather than move to the local town. It would cost too much money to build a new hall. However, it has been suggested that for £3,000 the old cricket pavilion could be modified. The pavilion has no toilets or electricity supply and the roof leaks.

* TOYS FOR THE PLAYGROUP. A new housing estate has been built on the outskirts of the village and there are a number of children of pre-school age. The mothers of the children have organized a playgroup which some 30 children attend at any one session. However, the playgroup has no funds, is run by volunteer workers, and is short of educational toys, climbing frames and other equipment. The group was set up last summer in the Church Hall before it was realized that the hall would be much too cold for the children in the autumn and winter. Therefore, apart from the equipment needed, the electricity supply to the hall has to be modernized and there will have to be at least two large heaters installed to make the hall comfortable. The playgroup organizer was horrified to discover, when she had completed her arithmetic, that the total bill would come to £2,000. There is no possibility of the mothers raising the cash.

* A WAR MEMORIAL. Members of the village have fought and died for their country in two world wars. However, there is no suitable memorial to the dead and Major Blimp, who could almost be described as the village squire, is rather keen that the village should pay tribute to its past. He also thinks that the young people in the village do not appreciate the ravages of war or the sacrifices which people of his generation made. He believes that the erection of the memorial will create a focal point in the village square and remind everyone of greater things. The cost of the memorial (a large stone construction) will be £10,000, and Major Blimp is so keen that the memorial should be built that he is willing to pay for half the cost if a further £5,000 can be found.

Each person should prepare a case and, if necessary, refer back to their constituent group whose interests they will represent at the meeting. The chairperson should begin the meeting by pointing out that the Committee has a very hard job to do, particularly since a decision must be reached that day: every member of the Committee will have strong views and the chairperson expresses the hope that they will all allow each other to present their case in turn. Whatever the decision some people must be disappointed. The cost for failing to make a decision will be the loss of the £5,000 to the dog pound in the local town.

Observers should monitor the committee meeting, making a diary of all events; that is, who speaks when and for how long, the nature of the arguments, the appeals to common interests, suggestions for compromise and so on. If the

Committee comes to a conclusion, are the observers able to explain how it was reached? At the end of the exercise, ask each participant how they felt at different points in the Committee's proceedings.

19

Organizational behaviour
R. Payne

Organizational behaviour is concerned with refining our
knowledge about the behaviour of individuals and groups in
organizations and their role in the growth, development and
decline of organizations. These various outcomes are also
determined by the financial, political and technological
environment in which the organization functions, so
researchers in 'organizational behaviour' also study these
organization-environment relations and their impact on the
behaviour of individuals and groups. It is a multi-
disciplinary enterprise involving economics, politics,
engineering, management science, systems theory, industrial
relations, sociology and psychology.

<table>
<tr><td>What are organizations like?</td><td>As with men an organization is:</td></tr>
</table>

    Like all other organizations
    Like some other organizations
    Like no other organizations.

In any professional work role one will encounter a unique
organization, like no other organization. In this chapter we
will deal with the ways in which organizations are the same
as each other and the ways in which groups of organizations
are similar to each other, but different from other types of
organizations. Apart from its intrinsic interest such information will enable you to appreciate the ways in which your
own organization is unique, and also help you understand
something about why it is the way it is.
    We are concerned with work organizations so part of our
definition must be that an organization exists in order to
get work done. They differ in the way they achieve this and
two of the major reasons for the differences are (i) the way
the organization divides its work into different tasks and
(ii) how it co-ordinates those tasks. Most organizations
contain several or many people but according to the present
definition an organization could consist of only one person. Two different silversmiths may divide the different
parts of their work in different ways and co-ordinate the
tasks differently. One of them might choose to design and
make one complete article at a time. The other might make

bowls one week, handles the next week, assemble them the next week and then polish and finish them.

They represent two different organizational structures. Similarly, seven people may work together and agree that each is capable of doing all the tasks that are required to get the work done and the co-ordination of these tasks will be left to the whim of the individuals on a day-to-day basis. Another seven people might have six people each doing different tasks with one person left to co-ordinate the work they do. One thing that is well proven is that once the work of the organization requires more than just a handful of people there is a strong preference for dividing work into different tasks and giving some people (managers) responsibility for supervising and co-ordinating them.

Mintzberg (1979) describes five main ways in which organizations achieve co-ordination amongst people doing different tasks. They are:

* mutual adjustment which relies on informal, day-to-day, communication and agreements. Small companies of professionals operate in this way, such as architects, consulting engineers or small builders;

* direct supervision where one person takes the responsibility for ensuring that other people satisfactorily complete the tasks they have been allocated. The typical factory with its hierarchy of charge hands, supervisors and managers exemplifies this type of co-ordination;

* standardization of work processes refers to the situation where work has been carefully designed from the outset so that the system or technology determines what work gets done. As they say in the car industry, 'The track is the boss'. That is, the operator's work is so organized that he can only screw nuts on wheels, or only place the front seat in the car, or only spray the right side, etc.;

* standardization of work outputs achieves co-ordination by specifying the nature and quality of the completed task. The salesman must take X orders, the craftsman make so many articles. How they do it is not specified, but what they must achieve is;

* standardization of skills is what has produced professions. Doctors, lawyers, teachers and engineers are replaceable parts. In theory anyone with the correct training can be substituted for any other without creating major difficulties of co-ordination. This substitutability is captured in the colloquialism, 'He's a real pro!'

Mintzberg proposes that the major functional parts of more complex organizations can be divided into five broad categories. At the top of the organization there are people whose main role is to determine the goals and policies of the company. These occupy the 'strategic apex'. Below them are the managers and supervisors who have the responsibility of ensuring that policies and procedures are followed: 'the middle line'. They manage the people who work most directly on the outputs or services of the organization and these Mintzberg describes as the 'operating core'. To the right and left of the middle line, and subordinate to the strategic apex, there are people supporting the main workflow of the organization. There are those in the 'technostructure' whose job is to assist the middle line and the operating core by analysing problems and providing solutions and systems for monitoring and implementing them. They include professional workers such as work study analysts, planning and systems analysts, accountants and personnel analysts. The latter assist this analysing and control process by standardizing skills and rewards. The 'support staff' are not directly connected to the main workflow of the organization but they provide services enabling the rest of the organization to function. They include staff handling the payroll, mailroom, cafeteria, reception, legal advice and research and development. In large organizations any one of these departments may be large enough to have the same five-fold structure so that one gets organizations within organizations.

This very general model is most easily recognized in production organizations but it can also describe the structure of schools, universities or hospitals. In a hospital, however, professionals are the operating core: the doctors, nurses, physiotherapists, occupational therapists and radiologists who provide the treatment and care. Other professionals, such as planners and trainers, are in the technostructure and basic research scientists or laboratory staff will be in the support staff. Thus professionals serve different functions within the same organization. Figure 1 presents a conventional tree diagram of a secondary school structure with Mintzberg's concepts overlaid. Note the small technostructure which is provided mainly by the local authority and the inspectorate. They are, strictly speaking, outside the school and this is indicated by a dotted line.

Building on these two sets of concepts and reviewing a large body of literature Mintzberg concludes there are five basic types of organizations. They are theoretical abstractions but some organizations approximate to the pure types and many larger organizations are hybrids of the types or contain examples of more than one pure type within them. Mintzberg continues his fascination with the number five by offering a pentagon model of the pure types. A simplified version appears in figure 2.

The different forms of co-ordination pull the organization towards different structures. The strategic apex pulls the organization structure upwards to centralized decision making and direct supervision. The name for this type is 'simple structure' and some of the organizations that frequently take this form are newer, smaller, autocratic organizations. The technostructure's function is to

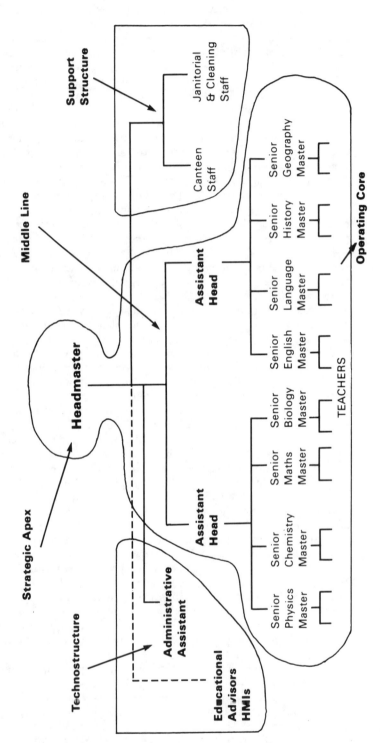

HMIs = Her Majesty's Inspectorates

Figure 1

A tree diagram of a school with Mintzberg's elements of structure superimposed

Figure 2

Mintzberg's pentagon
From H. Mintzberg (1979). 'The Structure of Organizations:
A synthesis of research'. Reprinted by permission of
Prentice-Hall Inc., Englewood Cliffs, New Jersey.

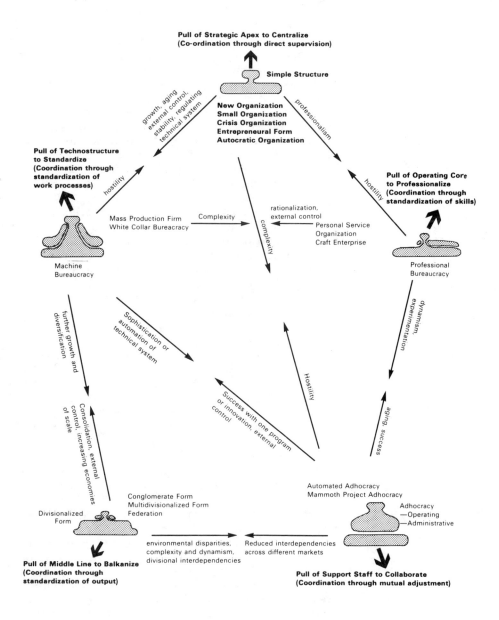

standardize and control the work processes so it pulls in that direction. Mintzberg mixes two metaphors to describe the resulting structure as a 'machine bureaucracy'. The bureaucratic element in the metaphor conveys the written procedures and documents designed to prescribe and control the system, and the machine element conveys the rationality, predictability and reliability of the design that has gone into it. A car or television assembly line plant are good examples.

The third pull is that exercised by professionals. They wish to exercise the skills their training has provided and argue the case for the quality of what they do within the discretion of their professionalism. This striving for autonomy is reflected in the small technostructure that these 'professional bureaucracies' have (see figure 1 for the school example). Note they are still bureaucratic. Despite their professionalism, organizational size leads to greater complexity which requires records to be kept, minutes taken, standard procedures followed, and professional standards maintained. Hospitals, universities and craft organizations tend towards this form because the services they supply need people with complex skills and professional training. Since they employ so many professionals it is not surprising that their needs and values influence the way the organization functions.

The fourth group to bid for influence in the design of the organization is the middle management. They too wish to be regarded as professionals and have the responsibility for their production/workflow units. They achieve this autonomy only by agreeing to conform to set standards in the production of the output or service: that is, standardization of outputs. The strategic apex co-ordinates the different units and supplies financial and technical resources, but each unit acquires reasonable autonomy to create the 'divisionalized structure'. This is common in conglomerates such as Imperial Chemical Industries which has separate divisions dealing with organic chemicals, agriculture, fibres and plastics. Within each autonomous division, of course, one may find a different structure: the 'machine bureaucracy' is prevalent, but if a separate research division exists it may be a 'professional bureaucracy' or 'adhocracy'.

The support staff represent the final force. Their preference is to co-ordinate by mutual adjustment and they are frequently supported in this by the 'operating core'. This would be the case in the Research Division just mentioned since the operating core would be scientists who are imbued with values of freedom and innovation. This produces a structure which Mintzberg calls 'adhocracy'. The title attempts to convey the fact that there are limited formal structures and that action and responsibility are defined by the current problem rather than past precedents or personal prestige. Large research and development projects sometimes take this form, as do smaller groups of professionals, such as advertising organizations. It can also serve the needs of the automated factory. Since automation itself controls and

monitors the workflow process, the executives and their
technical staff can concentrate on designing new products
and the processes to market, produce and distribute them.

Mintzberg's thesis is that all organizations experience
these five forces and that in a search for harmony one of
the forces becomes dominant at any particular point in the
organization's history. The dominant force pulls towards one
of the five configurations. As circumstances change, however, the dominant forces change.

The arrows in figure 2 indicate the main forces acting
on each type trying to move it towards another type. The
results of these forces are the myriad of organizational
forms we actually find in the world.

In summary, the very essence of organization is the co-
ordination of activities. There appear to be a limited
number of ways in which co-ordination is achievable. They
are co-ordination by mutual adjustment, direct supervision,
standardization of work procedures, standardization of work
outputs and standardization of inputs or skills. If any of
these forms of co-ordination dominate in an organization
they tend to lead to a structure of a particular type. Thus
co-ordination by mutual adjustment tends to produce an
'adhocracy'. Direct supervision leads to 'simple structure',
while standardization of work processes tends to produce
the pure 'machine bureaucracy'. The 'divisionalized structure' arises from a desire to co-ordinate by standardizing
the quantity and quality of work outputs, whilst standardizing inputs (skills) results in a 'professional bureaucracy'. These are 'pure' types and most organizations
contain elements of more than one. We now consider some
of the factors that produce these hybrids.

Why are organizations the way they are?

Organizations are as they are because people choose, with
more or less awareness, to make them that way. It is only
too easy to start talking as if organizations make choices,
but it is the men and women in them who determine their
nature. This is not to say these decision makers are totally
unconstrained. The fundamental purpose of the organization
sets contraints, though organizations doing the same things
may organize very differently to do them. A basic distinction is whether the organization manufactures things or provides a service. The latter could include providing treatment, providing education, selling goods or doing research.
One reason that this is such a basic choice is that the
decision to manufacture almost certainly involves the use of
energy, tools and technology to a much greater degree than
is likely in providing a service. This area of organizational theory has become known as the 'technological imperative' implying that certain forms of technology force
certain kinds of organizational structure (see Woodward,
1965).

Quite a lot of empirical research has been done on this
subject. Woodward's work (1965) has had a lasting impact.
She developed a way of classifying different kinds of

production or workflow technology. Note that this concept applies to the way products are manufactured, not the natur of the product itself. Woodward constructed a scale of production technology which can be described as ranging along a dimension from simple to complex, or more accurately as smoothness of production. The least smooth form she called unit production. This is where things are produced one at a time. A craftsman producing hand-made furniture would com into this category, but so would an organization producing ships, railway engines or large, complex computers. Each item is assembled as an individual product. Further along this production technology dimension one moves into mass production which can be sub-divided into small batch production such as might characterize a toy manufacturer, and large-batch production which occurs in the motor industry. The most complex and integral form of production technolog; is in continuous-flow or process production where the product never, or rarely, ceases to be produced. Oil refineries and certain parts of the chemicals industry are good examples.

Table 1 contains an example of the relationship between production technology and a aspect of organizational structure. The table contains information about three different size-bands of companies and the average number of people p supervisor in each size band for each of the three production technologies.

Table 1

Number of operators per supervisor classified according to production technology and organization size
From Woodward, 1965; reprinted with the permission of Oxfo University Press.

	Size of organization		
Production technology	400–500	850–1000	3000–4000
Unit	1:22	1:35	1:26
Mass	1:14	1:14	1:18
Process	1:8	1:8	1:8

In organizations employing unit production technology, the medium-sized organizations (850–1000 employees) tend to hav more employees per supervisor. Regardless of size, unit production employs fewer supervisors than the other two forms of production technology. This is largely because the operating core consists of skilled workers whose training controls the quality of the output: the building of ships or

railway engines is a relevant example. Mass production technologies are designed to use relatively unskilled labour and
therefore they have to be more closely supervised. Process
production employs the most supervisors because the technology is complex and mistakes can be very costly, so the
whole process is very closely monitored. Toxic chemicals and
float glass manufacturing illustrate such processes. In mass
production and process production technologies size appears
not to affect the number of supervisors employed. This
latter conclusion from Woodward's data is perhaps the most
tenuous (see Hickson, Pugh and Pheysey, 1969).

There is some controversy in the literature as to
whether organizational size or production technology is the
more important determinant of organizational structure. A
large body of work carried out by researchers from the
university of Aston in Birmingham (Pugh and Hickson, 1976;
Pugh and Hinings, 1976) showed organizational size to be a
much stronger predictor of degree of bureaucratization. By
bureaucratization they meant that the organization had
divided its work into specialist roles (high division of
labour) and that co-ordination was achieved by a hierarchical system supported by standardization of procedures which
were formalized into written documents and records. In
Mintzberg's terms it was a 'machine bureaucracy'. Organizational size was correlated with bureaucratization 0.69,
whilst production technology correlated only about 0.30. The
Aston workers did qualify their findings by showing that
technology had a greater impact on the structure at the
bottom of the organization (the operating core). In medium-
sized mass production organizations the operating core would
have more precisely defined jobs and duties than would
operators in a medium-sized unit production technology.
However, the roles and role definitions relating to managers
in the two organizations would be very similar.

Summarizing briefly, both the decision to employ a
particular mode of production and the decision to grow
bigger begin to put important constraints on how the organization should structure/organize itself if it is to succeed.
One of Woodward's findings was that organizations which had
deviant structures for the technology they used tended to be
the least successful. Other factors influence the design of
the organization, however. Some are external to the system
and some are internal.

External influences on structure
The external ones include the market/clients the organization is trying to serve; the knowledge/technical change that
is occurring in the world; the economic situation resulting
from changes in the availability of resources such as raw
materials and finance; and the political changes resulting
from government legislation. Space prevents a separate discussion of these but together they may be construed as factors which create environmental uncertainty or turbulence
(Metcalfe and McQuillan, 1977). To cope successfully with

such turbulence requires different structures from those
required to survive and develop in a stable and benign environment. One strategy large corporations adopt is to buy
out the suppliers or competitors who may be causing uncertainty. This diversification also increases the complexity
of the organization so that the divisionalized structure
tends to emerge. One of the general principles for dealing
with environmental complexity is the 'Law of Requisite
Variety' (Ashby, 1956). This states that the variety/
complexity inside a system must be sufficient to match the
variety/complexity of the environment outside the system.
Thus the diversification strategy not only reduces uncertainty but increases intra-organizational variety which also
aids in coping with turbulence. Less rich organizations cope
by relying much more on their own flexibility and ability to
respond to the uncertainty with new strategies and behaviour. One way they achieve this flexibility and responsiveness is by employing a variety of professional, technical
and scientific people, each of whom participates intimately
in the decision taken within the company. Such organizations
have few rules and regulations. This internal diversity,
however, creates problems of communication and integration.
To achieve co-ordination and integration special groups are
sometimes formed to ensure that the necessary communication
takes place. These liaison roles (Lawrence and Lorsch, 1967;
Chandler and Sayles, 1971) come to demand special skills and
qualities of their own.

A structure specially designed to facilitate co-
ordination in such situations is the 'matrix structure'.
This structure was developed and extensively used by NASA
to complete the US lunar programme. Problems of this scale
do not come neatly packaged by function or department, so
'project groups' were formed which combined specialists from
different functions (e.g. engineering, human factors,
physics, finance). The structure is decribed as a matrix
because the groups were formed by project and held responsible to the project leader (see figure 3), but each
member was also responsible to the head of a functional
department. It is this dual membership which provides the
expert back-up of the function combined with the good
communication and involvement of belonging to a project
team. These two responses, the liaison group and the matrix
structure, are variations of the Mintzberg 'adhocracy'. The
existence of these two structures implies that co-ordination
by mutual adjustment sometimes needs some structural suppo
if it is to succeed in complex environments.

Internal influences on structure
If we turn to Mintzberg's pentagon in figure 2 we can see
some of the forces within the organization which may influence its structure. These consist of the tensions between
the major groups in the organization: the top managers
and/or owners, the professionals in the technostructure and
the support structure, and the middle and lower parts of the

Figure 3

The matrix structure

		Functional departments			
		Engineering Head + 7 subs*	Physics Head + 5 subs	Finance Head + 2 subs	Maths Head + 4 subs
	A. leader + 4 members	2		1	1
Project Groups	B. leader + 8 members	2	3	1	2
	C. leader + 8 members	1	3	1	3
	D. leader + 6 members	4	1	1	

A member of a functional department may be a member of more than one project group.

workflow, the middle line and the operating core (figure 1). Those in the strategic apex want to maintain as much control as they can, but the technocrats, the middle managers and the professionals in the support structure, fight to increase their autonomy and influence. The technocrats wish to consolidate and automate the successes of the creative research staff, but the latter prefer to continue creating new products and processes. The operating core strive to professionalize their skills and provide better products/services to their clients, but the technocrats wish to rationalize and improve what already exists. As Mintzberg says, at any one time there may be harmony amongst these forces, but if the external environment changes then the internal environment must respond to it or the organization as a whole will fail. The internal tensions arise again and a new stability emerges through death, amputation, amalgamation or reconciliation.

Professionals can now see how they may be caught in any of these cross-fires. Accountants, for example, can find themselves attached to the apex, the technostructure, the operating core or the middle line. In a hospital the nurses may be in the technostructure, the middle line, the operating core or the support staff. Doctors are trained to diagnose and treat illnesses, teachers to instruct and educate and each progresses in their profession on the basis of their ability in these specific skills. Eventually, however, they become managers, administrators and policy makers with little formal training in these skills. No wonder hierarchical organizations have been accused of promoting people to the point where they reach their level of incompetence (Peter, 1969). This only goes to emphasize the flexibility required of professionals in complex organizations, for the roles they create extend far beyond those for which the professional was originally trained. Indeed, roles provide the link between the broad abstractions so far discussed and the actual behaviour of people at work.

Roles in organizations

The term structure refers to the pattern of offices or positions existing in an organization, and to the nature of the behaviour required of the people filling each of the offices. It is this dramaturgical aspect of structure, the definition of the parts to be played, that leads to the use of role as the central concept. In their work on organizational structure the Aston group (Pugh and Hickson, 1976) relied heavily on the concept in constructing their major measures, 'role specialization' and 'role formalization', and it is important in other concepts such as 'standardization of procedures' (for roles) and 'configuration' (distribution of roles). A major research project which utilized the concept contains some useful definitions and distinctions (Kahn, Wolfe, Quinn, Snoek and Rosenthal, 1964) and these are outlined below.

ROLE: the activities and patterns of behaviour that should be performed by the occupant of an office: for example, the nurse must administer drugs and follow the correct procedures in doing so.

ROLE-SET: all other office holders who interact with another office holder, the latter being designated the focal role. Figure 4 illustrates the role-set of a senior occupational therapist in a psychiatric day hospital.

ROLE EXPECTATIONS: the attitudes and beliefs that members of a social system have about what the occupant of any office ought to do; for example, as well as doing their job, teachers are expected to be honest, moral, dedicated to children.

SENT ROLE: the expectations sent to individual office holders by other members of the role-set; for example, a head of a department presses a scientist for more research, whilst colleagues expect that scientist to be a creative theoretician.

RECEIVED ROLE: the role as understood by individual occupants based on the expectations sent to them by their role-set; for example, the above-mentioned scientist interprets the message to mean, 'publish as much as you can'.

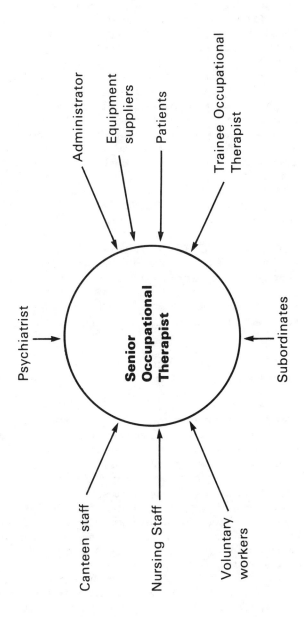

Figure 4

The role-set of a senior occupational therapist in a psychiatric day hospital

There may well be a difference between the sent role and the received role. This may be partly due to inadequate information/communication, but will also occur because the receiver, consciously or unconsciously, wishes to see the world in a way which is found comfortable and acceptable. Cognitive dissonance and perceptual defence are terms used to describe these distorting processes. The disparity may also occur because the role is not clearly specified: small, expanding organizations have often not stopped to clarify who does what and have never written role specifications. Large organizations are sometimes called bureaucracies because they do write rules and specifications for jobs and they are kept in a 'bureau'. The written word is being used here to delineate the role. We can see from the role-set in figure 4, however, that the senior occupational therapist is at the focus of a disparate set of expectations. Even if all expectations are transmitted accurately (low role ambiguity) they are likely to be in conflict. The psychiatrist may want more group work, but the nurses and trainees more individual treatment. Kahn et al defined a number of types of role conflict.

INTER-SENDER CONFLICT: the expectations of two or more role senders are incompatible.

INTER-ROLE CONFLICT: two or more of the roles we occupy are in conflict; for example, manager and trade union representative; worker and father.

INTRA-SENDER CONFLICT: the same role sender has conflicting expectations; for example, increase output and improve quality.

ROLE OVERLOAD: simply means being unable to meet the legitimate expectations of role-senders.

The fact is, of course, that role-senders also develop illegitimate expectations. This is partly because individuals in organizations are not only concerned with meeting the organization's needs; many are more concerned with meeting their own needs. Ambitious managers may develop all sorts of illegitimate ways round the rules to improve the performance of a department so that they get promotion and leave the clearing up to somebody else! On the other hand, we (as the general public) know from bitter personal experience that 'working to rule', the organization's carefully thought out, written down, legalized prescriptions, means inefficiency and frustrations for all. That is, some bending of the rules is actually highly functional for the organization. The universality of this slip between what is and what is supposed to be has been recognized by the concept of 'the informal organization'. The concept of role enables us to see how and why the slippage occurs. More generally the concepts relating to role enable the occupants of an office to analyse why their roles are the way they are, and why they are not what they expected!

he informal ganization

In work organizations role-sets do not occur randomly. They arise from the tasks to be done. In figure 4 we depict one based on the senior occupational therapist. If we were to search for others in the hospital setting we would find them centred on the surgeon's 'firm', on the portering staff, on the accident department, on the administrative office, on the junior doctors and so on. Within each of these role-sets there would be frequent face-to-face interaction and high levels of communication. Relationships between them, however, would be much less clear-cut. In the current jargon whereas within a role-set it would be a 'tightly-coupled' system. It is also obvious that members of one role-set are often members of another. The surgeon's 'firm' will contain some of the junior doctors. The surgeon will be on committees guiding policy-making which will also contain members of the administration. These formally required interactions open up informal communication channels. It is much quicker, and perhaps more revealing, to make a direct informal approach to another department than to work through the formal channels where the information has to go up, along, back, along and then down. It is faster, and perhaps more satisfying, to take the organizational hypotenuse than the organizational right angle. The fact that many people in organizations do prefer them is confirmed by studies of how managers spend their time. About 45 per cent of their time in communication is spent communicating outside the formal chain of authority.

These informal 'grapevines' appear everywhere and are very vigorous. Caplow (1966) studied rumours in wartime conditions and found they travelled surprisingly quickly and were often surprisingly accurate. Davis (1953) studied an organization of 600 people and traced the pattern of various decisions. For one letter from a customer he found that 68 per cent of the executives received the information but only three out of the 14 communications passed through the formal chain of command. Getting things done at all, and certainly getting them done quickly, depends heavily on knowing and understanding the nature of the informal organization. It seems impossible to regulate the behaviour of human beings by fiat and authority alone. Professional, ideological and social interests cross the formally defined boundaries and these reciprocal relationships very quickly begin to twine themselves around the organization's neatly designed trunk and branches. As with vines they provide extra support and bear rich fruits but they sometimes need pruning, or replanting. And if they are accidentally uprooted they can leave the ground exposed, as it may be if a consultant recommends and installs a different, perhaps more clearly prescribed structure, but one which breaks up established relationships. An organization risks relying too heavily on the informal system which is why formalization and bureau-cratization are utilized in the first place, but there is danger in trying to eliminate it altogether. Farris (1979) contrasts the formal with the informal as in table 2 and it shows clearly how the informal relies heavily on expecta-tions rather than rules. He quotes several examples of how the formal organization, or at least the managers repre-senting it, can make use of the informal organization to better achieve its purposes; for example, they place new-comers with people at crucial cross-over points in the informal network in order to teach them quickly how the system really works. Effective organizations then allow the formal and informal to work symbiotically: to sustain and support each other. Less effective ones fight a battle for the dominance of one over the other. We can see from Farris' table that the informal is, in fact, very similar to the co-ordination principle of mutual adjustment. As Mintzberg's model indicated, all organizations face the problem of resolving the tensions between the five co-ordinating mechanisms. From the universality of the informal organization it seems that adhocracy is never completely defeated.

Table 2

Some contrasts between formal and informal organizations
From Farris (1979): reprinted with permission.

Element	Organization	
	Formal	Informal
Salient goals	Organization's	Individual's
Structural units	Offices/positions	Individual roles
Basis for communication	Offices formally related	Proximity: physical, professional, task social, formal
Basis for power	Legitimate authority	Capacity to satisfy individuals' needs (often through expert or referent power)
Control mechanisms	Rules	Norms (expectations)
Type of hierarchy	Vertical	Lateral

This incipient victory of adhocracy has an influence on managerial behaviour as we see in the next section.

The difference between what is specified in a job (role) description and what actually happens can also be illustrated by the study of how managers actually spend their time. The classical description of management is that it involves planning, organizing, co-ordinating and finally controlling systems and people in order to achieve the goals outlined in the plans. A relatively small number of researchers have actually studied what managers do and one of the most influential of these pieces of research has again been done by Mintzberg (1973). In 1975 Mintzberg compared folk-lore to fact. The first element of folk-lore he discussed was that the manager is a reflective, systematic planner.

His own intensive study of five chief executives showed that only one out of 368 verbal contacts was unrelated to a specific issue and could be called general planning. A diary study of 160 British top and middle managers found they worked for a half-hour or more without interruption only once every two days (Stewart, 1967). Mintzberg concludes that not only is a manager's work characterized by brevity, variety and discontinuity but that they actually prefer action to reflection. Plans, if they exist, are formulated and re-formulated in the executive's head; they are not written down and rationally elaborated.

On the other hand, our folk-lore of the modern super-hero is that the effective executive has no regular duties to perform. He sits on the Olympian heights, waiting the calls of us lesser mortals. The facts show that he is down in the valley dealing with the unexpected directly, encouraging the peasants, negotiating with neighbours, and even mending the fences.

Executives spend much time meeting important customers, carrying out regular tours round their organizations, and officiating at rituals and ceremonies. Much of their time is spent scanning the environment for information which can then be passed to their subordinates. This is not 'hard', easily-available information but 'soft', given in confidence or as a favour, but which becomes available only as a result of maintaining regular contact: informal contacts!

A third piece of conventional wisdom is that senior managers need aggregated information which a formal management information system best provides. Computers have encouraged this view as they seemed to be able to make such information up-to-date and easily available. The evidence suggests that managers do not use the information even if it is there. They strongly prefer to rely on meetings and telephone calls. Burns (1954) found managers spent 80 per cent of their time in verbal communication, and Mintzberg 78 per cent. The latter's five managers produced only 25 pieces of mail during the 25 days he investigated them. Only 13 per cent of the mail they received was of specific and immedia use. Managers appear to operate this way because they are future orientated and their active scanning for hints and gossip is felt to be more useful than detailed understanding of the past. Such behaviour puts a heavy premium on their personal ability to store and sort information. It also makes it difficult for them to transfer their personal images and maps to others in the company.

A related piece of folk-lore is that management is a science and a profession. It is true that the technostructure in large organizations uses mathematical modelling and sophisticated planning and control techniques, but these have little influence on senior managers or even on the managers of the specialists running such facilities. All are still reliant on their intuition and judgement. This is because they manage (i) people and (ii) very complex situations: imagine the problems facing the head of a department of management services in a regional hospital authority who manages 70 professional staff ranging from computer specialists, through work study to behavioural science change agents. That it is correct to give people problems priority over situational problems is reflected in Mintzberg's conclusions about the different roles a manager must perform. These appear diagramatically in figure 5.

Figure 5

The ten roles of the manager
Reprinted by permission of the Harvard Business Review. Exhibit from, 'The Manager's Job: Folklore and fact', by Mintzberg (July-August, 1975). Copyright 1975 by the President and Fellows of Harvard College; all rights reserved.

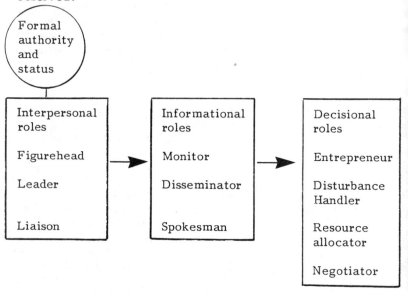

The titles of the ten roles are precise enough not to require further elaboration. The arrows indicate that the organization gives the manager the authority and status to perform the interpersonal roles, that this requirement leads to the performance of the informational roles and that this forces involvement in the decisional roles.

The effective managers are the ones who carry out all ten roles but who do so by finding ways to:

* gain control over their time: they tend to be bombarded by others so they must find ways of using these obliga-tions to others to suit their own ends. Their only other hope is that people do things for them because of per-sonal commitment. In hierarchical and competitive situ-ations this highly desirable state is often lacking. They may have to be political and devious to achieve their goals;
* some of the time thus gained must be used to determine which issues are really important in the overall picture. This ability has been called the 'helicopter capacity';
* to use the rest of their saved time to ensure that they regularly and systematically share with colleagues and subordinates their privileged information and how it fits into the images and plans that are guiding their actions.

With this amount of preparation managers have a good chance of sneaking through the interpersonal barrage that makes up their weekly war. This applies to managers and supervisors at all points in the organization: low, middle or high, in the technostructure or the support structure. For these different positions the task changes in quantity rather than quality, and in the severity of the consequences which result from failure.

Managers are, of course, professionals in their own right, but specialist professionals in organizations may face distinctive difficulties, and in the final section we consider what these may be.

rofessional roles in rganizations

We saw earlier that professionals can be located in all parts of the organization's structure and that this would demand different responses from them. A general model for examining the nature of these tensions has been proposed by Gowler and Legge (1980). They use it to derive a table showing the methods that different professional groups use to deal with the varying demands made upon them. This table (3) appears below with the addition of trade union offi-cial. Apart from revealing the variety of professional relationships, it shows how professionals need to change roles within their organization. The scientist who manages research becomes a professional manager. The trade union official also becomes a manager of his staff. The values and

Table 3

The Variety of Professional Roles
From Gowler and Legge (1980): reprinted by permission of
John Wiley & Sons.

Provider	Values/Beliefs	Core method	Outcomes	User
Scientist	Cognitive/ technical	Experimental	Prediction	Other scientists
Doctor	Therapeutic	Diagnostic	Prescription	Patient
Lawyer	Judicial	Negotiated adjudication	Proscription	Client
Administrator	Bureaucratic	Organization	Regulation	Employees
Manager	Entrepreneurial	Pragmatic	Transaction	Customers
Trades union official	Welfare and protection	Negotiation	Agreements	Membership

methods of these different professions are rarely in
sympathy.

The stresses in professional roles are further elaborated by Gowler and Legge with the model in figure 6. This
model describes 'The cruciform effect' to emphasize the
competing tensions inherent in professional roles. The
tensions can only be resolved by the choices of the professionals themselves. As figure 6 shows, professionals are
expected to provide a service to their clients based on the
expertise derived from their training. Professionals as
'worthy' people, however, are expected to demonstrate
goodness, kindness and other altruistic behaviour. But this
is not clearly defined and takes them outside their expertise. Similarly, they are pulled in opposing directions by
demands to provide a reliable and comprehensive service
requiring the application of standard methods and procedures, and yet as good professionals to be either using or
actually creating the latest innovation. In these authors'
words, 'The professional is trapped between morality and
expediency as he attempts to match the absolutism which
vindicates professional authority with the relativism which
vindicates professional practice'. How these tensions will
appear in specific roles and in specific organizations it is
not possible to predict. You will have to fill in the boxes
for yourself, but the models will help to identify the
general nature of the issues you are likely to face. The
cruciform effect has a visual similarity to a role-set, of
course, and the model would be helpful too in putting bones
on this ubiquitous skeleton.

Figure 6

The cruciform effect in professional roles

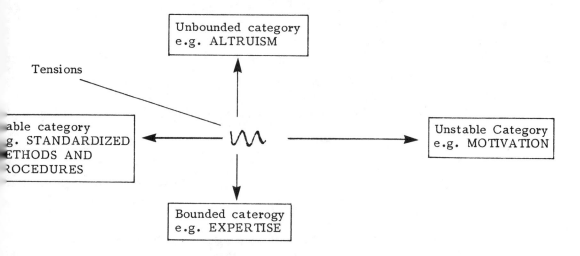

Tensions

Indeed, the whole chapter is a series of skeletons, but they do constitute an introduction to the anatomy and physiology of organizations.

erences

Ashby, W. (1956)
An Introduction to Cybernetics. London: Chapman & Hall.

Burns, T. (1954)
The directions of activity and communication in a departmental and executive group. Human Relationships, 7, 73-97.

Caplow, T. (1966)
Rumours in War. In A.H. Rubenstein and C.J. Haberstroth (eds), Some Theories of Organization. Homewood, Ill.: Irwin-Dorsey.

Chandler, M.K. and Sayles, L.R. (1971)
Managing Large Systems. New York: Harper & Row.

Davis, K. (1953)
Management communication and the grapevine. Harvard Business Review, Sept.-Oct., 43-49.

Farris, G.F. (1979)
The informal organization in strategic decision-making. International Studies of Management and Organization, 9, No. 4, 131-152.

Gowler, D. and Legge, K. (1980)
Evaluative practices as stressors in occupational settings. In C.L. Cooper, and R. Payne (eds), Current Concerns in Occupational Stress. Chichester: Wiley.

Hickson, D.J., Pugh, D.S. and Pheysey, D.C. (1969)
Operations technology and organization structure: an empirical reappraisal. Administrative Science Quarterly, 378-397.

Kahn, R.L., Wolfe, D.M., Quinn R.P., Snoek, J.D. and Rosenthal, R. A. (1964)
Organizational Stress. New York: Wiley.
Lawrence, P.R. and Lorsch, J.W. (1967)
Organization and Environment. Boston: Harvard Business School.
Metcalfe, L. and McQuillan, W. (1977)
Managing turbulence. In P.C. Nystrom and W.H. Starbu (eds), Prescriptive Models of Organization. Amsterdam: North-Holland.
Mintzberg, H. (1973)
The Nature of Managerial Work. New York: Harper & R
Mintzberg, H. (1975)
The manager's job: folklore and fact. Harvard Business Review, July-August, 49-61.
Mintzberg, H. (1979)
The Structuring of Organizations. Englewood Cliffs, NJ: Prentice-Hall.
Peter, L.F. (1969)
The Peter Principle. New York: William Morrow.
Pugh, D.S. and Hickson, D.J. (eds) (1976)
Organizational Structure in its Context. Farnham: Saxon House/Teakfield Press.
Pugh, D.S. and Hinings, C.R. (1976)
Organization Structure Extensions and Replications. Farnborough, Hants.: Saxon House.
Stewart, R. (1967)
Managers and Their Jobs. London: Macmillan.
Woodward, J. (1965)
Industrial Organization: Theory and practice. Oxford: Oxford University Press.

Questions

1. Describe the different ways by which organizations attempt to achieve co-ordination. Give examples of each.
2. What is a matrix organization? When is it likely to be used?
3. What type of organizational structure(s) would you expect to find in (i) a medium-sized general hospital; (ii) a department store?
4. Illustrate your understanding of the concepts related to role-set by analysing the role of student (or any suitable variation of that).
5. Compare and contrast the formal versus the informal organization. Provide examples from an organization of which you are a member.
6. Why do informal organizations develop?
7. What is the cruciform effect? How might it apply to the job of social worker (or any suitable variant)?
8. Compare and contrast stereotypes about managerial roles with what managers actually do.
9. Why might the training of professional workers fail to truly prepare them for a career in a large organization?

10. Which of the main types of organizational structure most appeals to you? Why?

Annotated reading

Child, J. (1977) Organization: A guide to problems and practice (paperback). New York: Harper & Row.
  A readable and informed account of the meaning of organizational structure. It discusses the choices managers have when faced with designing an organization around the issues of shaping the jobs/roles people do, having tall or flat chains of command, grouping activities by function, product or some mixture, mechanisms for integrating the divisions so created, and how to control the humans working in the system. Child also discusses how to change organizations and the future forms they may need/choose to adopt.

Handy, C. (1976) Understanding Organizations. Harmondsworth: Penguin.
  This is an extremely well written and lively book, rich with pertinent examples. The first part introduces basic concepts for understanding organizations: motivation, roles, leadership, power and influence, group processes, structure and politics. The second part applies the concepts to problems such as how to design organizations, how to develop and change them and the working of the various aspects of organizations as systems (budgets, communications, computers, bargaining). The last chapter describes what it is like to be a manager and the dilemmas faced. The book has a very useful third section which is a guide to further study for each of the 12 chapters.

Mintzberg's ideas are only available in his recent book (1979) The Structuring of Organizations. Englewood Cliffs, NJ: Prentice-Hall.
  This is a detailed review and synthesis of a mass of literature on organizations, but the first chapter describes the five co-ordinating mechanisms and the last describes the five types of structures and the pentagon model.

Warr, P.B. (ed) (1978) Psychology at Work (2nd edn). Harmondsworth: Penguin.
  This book contains 16 chapters, each written by different authors. It is moderately technical in places, but much of it is quite understandable to the non-psychologist. The chapters cover the following topics: hours of work and the 24-hour cycle, workload and skilled performance, training, the design of machines and systems that optimize human performance, accidents, computers and decision making, selection, interviewing, negotiation and collective bargaining, leadership, attitudes and motives, job redesign and employee

participation, work stress, counselling in work settings, how to change organizations and organizational systems as psychological environments.

Exercises

1. Interviewing a professional worker

The aim of this interview is to explore the individual's roles within the organization within which he works, and to see how he is affected by aspects of the organization. You should relate the theories and concepts discussed in this chapter to a real-life organization. Remember that a research interview must be prepared very carefully. You should consult the material on interviewing in this book. The issues which need to be explored will include the following:

* the history and development of the organization in question;
* whether it has undergone changes in structure and, if so why;
* the type of organization it now is;
* in which part of the organization your interviewee is employed;
* which are the dominant adjustment mechanisms used in the organization;
* whether vertical and/or horizontal conflicts arise;
* how tensions are resolved;
* what attracts your interviewee to working in the organization and what keeps the interviewee at the job;
* how your interviewee's efforts are rewarded and what types of reinforcement are used in the organization;
* whether your interviewee has ever considered resigning;
* whether your interviewee believes that there are good or bad leaders in the organization;
* whether your interviewee believes in the idea of an 'ideal leader', and how leaders within the organization match up to the ideal;
* how people are trained to enter the profession.

In analysing the results of your interview the following concepts should be borne in mind: Mintzberg's pentagon; role and role-set; the cruciform effect; types of reinforcement and the various learning theories; modelling; motivation.

2. Study of formal and informal organizations

Observe a few organizations (both formal and informal) to examine their structure (both horizontal and vertical) and the roles that group members play. On the basis of what you have read in the chapter prepare a means of tabulating your observations. Ensure that you sample a variety of organizations. You yourself belong to a family and perhaps a religious group and various clubs; it is possible to attend a Magistrates Court, a meeting of the town or county council or an outpatients' clinic at a local hospital. Where possible extend the study to include interviews with members of the organizations concerned. Having obtained the data, set up a matrix to compare and contrast the organizations sampled. Try to identify those characteristics which make organizations efficient in achieving their goals. Does an organization have to be 'formal' to be efficient; will criteria of 'efficiency' vary for different groups? If you detect evidence of dysfunction what suggestions would you make for improving the organization?

Part five

Special Problems and their Treatments

20

Pain
Colette Ray

Pain may be defined as an unpleasant sensation which is
focussed upon the body, and is often but not always
associated with tissue damage. While it may be generally
true that physical injury produces pain and that pain occurs
as a result of injury, this is by no means always the case.
There are many syndromes for which a somatic explanation
is not easily available, and the source of the disorder can
be attributed either to an abnormality in the way in which
normal sensory inputs are processed or to psychological
factors. Similarly, people may meet with injury but fail to
experience pain as a consequence. This will sometimes happen
if the damage occurs suddenly in a compelling situation,
such as in battle or on the sportsfield, where attention and
emotions are directed elsewhere. It is difficult, therefore,
to determine in a priori terms when pain should and should
not be experienced, and we must rely primarily upon the
individual's own self-report to indicate whether it is present or absent and the intensity of his feelings. Given a
similar degree of pain, however, any two people will react
to this in different ways. They may vary in their evaluation
of the symptom's significance; in their emotional reactions
and expression of these; in the extent to which they complain verbally about the pain and the kinds of remedies they
seek; and in the effect that the pain has upon their family,
occupational and social activities. Such reactions to symptoms are distinct from the symptoms themselves and are
generally referred to as 'illness behaviour' (Mechanic and
Volkart, 1960). A number of factors will influence these
behaviours, including the individual's personality and
cultural background and the rewards and expectations
associated with pain.

Personality and culture

It has been widely argued that pain will in some cases have
a psychodynamic significance: that is, a psychological
meaning and function. Freud regarded it as a common con-
version syndrome, representing the transformation of a repressed drive into physical symptoms; the pain need not be
created to achieve this end, but may be selected from a
background of 'possible' pain as that which best fulfils a
specific symbolic function. A state of emotional disturbance

393

can also influence pain in a less specific way, if the person fails to recognize the true nature of the disturbance and seeks instead an explanation in terms of everyday physical symptoms which might otherwise be ignored. An individu who is generally over-preoccupied with physical concerns would be most likely to misattribute psychological distress to somatic symptoms in this manner. Engel (1959) has suggested that there is a 'pain prone personality', characterized by feelings of guilt which can be in part relieved by pain; other relevant characteristics he lists are a family history of violence and punishment, a personal history of suffering and defeat, a state of anger and hostility which is turned inwards rather than outwards and conflict over sexual impulses. The immediate 'trigger' for pain in the case of such a personality may be the loss of someone valued, and several writers have seen physical pain as a symbol of real or imagined loss.

People show consistency in their response to pain over time, while there are distinct differences between people. Generally speaking, women are more responsive than men, and the young more than the old. The relationship between pain responses and personality traits has been extensively studied, particularly with respect to neuroticism and extraversion. There is some tendency for the former to be related to pain proneness, but many inconsistent findings have been obtained both in the laboratory and in natural settings. Extraverts under some conditions tolerate pain better than introverts, but may in some situations report more pain because of a greater readiness to brave the possibility of social disapproval. Many studies have looked at pain in psychiatric patients, and at the personality profiles of pain patients compared with those of control samples. A relatively high incidence of pain is found in psychiatric groups and pain patients have a more 'neurotic' profile than control groups (see Sternbach, 1974). It is, however, unclear to what extent personality disturbance predisposes to pain and to what extent the experience of pain causes emotional difficulties. The relative importance of these two different effects will depend upon whether the context is that of psychiatric patients who experience pain, or pain patients without a psychiatric history; in the former case maladjustment is likely to give rise to physical pain rather than the reverse, while in the latter emotional difficulties will generally be a consequence, rather than a cause, of pain.

Responses to pain differ not only between individuals and groups within a society, but also between cultures. All groups develop norms or expectations of how one should perceive and react to any particular situation, and individuals will adopt these to the extent that they are part of or identify with the group. Some norms are prescriptive: that is, there is a certain pressure upon the individual to conform with expectations in this respect, and deviation will meet with disapproval. An example of such a norm relevant to pain behaviour would be the expectation that one should not evade one's obligations by faking or 'malingering'. Descriptive norms, in contrast, do not imply an obligation to conform, but merely describe the behaviour which is characteristic or typical of the group. Cultural stereotypes suggest the existence of differences between nationalities in their expression of pain, and there is empirical evidence for such differences. Zborowski (1969) studied a group of American male patients and compared reactions for those of Jewish, Irish, Italian and Old American descent. Both Old Americans and Irish Americans were inhibited in the expression of pain, while the Italians and Jewish patients were more reactive. These latter groups both sought to draw attention to their pain by this expressive behaviour, but their underlying aims were different. The Italians were primarily concerned with obtaining relief from pain, while for the Jewish patients the primary concern was to discover the cause of the symptom. These cultural differences appear quite reliable, since Zborowski's findings were supported by those of a study in which the responses of similar groups were compared, but in a very different laboratory setting (Sternbach and Tursky, 1965).

Rewards and expectations

Learning theorists make a distinction between a respondent behaviour which is closely linked with the occurrence of a particular stimulus or situation and does not require any other support for its establishment or maintenance, and an operant behaviour which is not directly elicited by the stimulus but can become associated with it given appropriate conditions of reinforcement. Reinforcement is defined as any event which strengthens a behaviour; rewards will generally operate as reinforcers, as will the termination of an aversive stimulus, while punishment generally weakens behaviour. This kind of analysis may be applied to pain behaviour (Fordyce, Fowler, Lehmann and de Lateur, 1968). We can assume that certain responses to pain, withdrawal or crying for example, will be directly elicited by the experience, whilst others may be prompted by the experience but depend effectively upon the outcomes which they produce. An individual may thus adopt and maintain a number of pain behaviours because they bring rewards such as sympathy and nurturance, and enable him to avoid activities or obligations which he finds unpleasant.

Behaviour will not only be influenced by the rewards associated with different kinds of response, but also by an awareness of how other people react in a similar situation. The experience of pain may involve considerable uncertainty, and when faced with uncertainty people often look to others as guides to determine both how the experience should be interpreted and the norms governing behaviour in that situation. This process has been described as one of 'social comparison' (Festinger, 1954). We compare our own interpretations and reactions with those of others to decide whether or not they are valid or appropriate in the circumstances, and may seek a lead from another before making our own interpretation and response. Thus the presence of a calm individual to act as a model may reduce the response to a painful stimulus, and the presence of one who appears distressed may intensify the response. Such effects have been demonstrated in the laboratory, in studies where the experimenter recruits a confederate who supposedly undergoes electric shocks similar to those to which the subject is indeed exposed, and instructs him to react to these with or without expression of pain and distress. Both 'tolerant' and 'intolerant' models in such studies can change subjects' reports of the intensity of the pain they experience and their willingness to tolerate shocks of various intensities. Similar effects can be observed in clinical settings; patients with problems or treatments in common will observe each other, develop expectations about pain intensity and the course of recovery, and learn the norms of pain expression within that group. Modelling processes will occur within the family but over a longer period of time. Children's reactions to pain will be influenced by their observations of their parents' behaviour, and the child whose parents focus upon his or their own pain symptoms and react strongly to these may come to react in the same way. This effect would initially operate with respect to specific situations but could then generalize to pain behaviour in general.

Theory and research

Early theories regarded pain as arising from the relatively direct transmission of signals from 'nociceptors' to pain centres in the brain, and the receptors, pathways and centres involved were thought to be specific to pain. The assumption of specificity does not, however, seem justified, and this simple model cannot account for many common pain phenomena, including the known effects of psychological factors such as experience, motivation, attention and emotionality. A recent theory which has attracted much interest is the gate-control theory (see Melzack, 1973). The gate referred to is a hypothetical mechanism at the level of the spinal cord, which is assumed to modulate signals from the periphery before they are centrally processed. It is suggested that this mechanism is situated in the substantia gelatinosa and has its effect by inhibiting or facilitating the transmission of signals from the dorsal horns to the adrenolateral pathways of the spinal cord. Activity in peripheral fibres will not only influence the transmission of pain signals directly but also affects the operation of the gate, as can central brain processes. Three distinct psychological dimensions of the pain experience have been related to these neurophysiological concepts. These are the sensory-discriminative, the motivational-affective and the cognitive-evaluative dimensions respectively. The first is associated with the rapidly conducting spinal systems projecting to the thalamus, the second with reticular and limbic structures, and the third with neocortical processes.

The model is a complex and dynamic one, and can hence explain many diverse phenomena.

Some areas of research focus upon physiological aspects of pain, while others are more directly concerned with identifying those factors which can modify the experience. These investigations are carried out both in laboratory and in clinical settings. Experimental laboratory studies may be criticized on the grounds that the kinds of pain that can be induced and the conditions in which it is experienced are rather different from those that apply under natural conditions. They do, however, allow the researcher to control and monitor carefully the variables under study. Various methods of inducing pain have been developed for this purpose. These include application of heat or pressure; administration of electric shocks; the cold pressor test for which the subject has to immerse his hand in ice-cold water; and the sub-maximal tourniquet technique which produces ischaemic pain. Using such methods experimenters can study the effects of various manipulations upon pain measures such as the threshold, or the point at which the subject first reports pain, and tolerance level or the point at which he requests that the painful stimulus be terminated. Threshold and tolerance levels are not appropriate for use in the context of naturally occurring pain, and measures in clinical situations are primarily concerned with the assessment of subjective intensity. Estimates of this may be obtained by asking the patient to rate the symptom on a scale which is gradated by numbers or by verbal descriptions representing different levels of pain from mild to severe. The experience of pain does, however, vary in quality as well as in degree. Melzack and Torgerson (1971) have thus developed a questionnaire which enables patients to describe their symptoms in terms of a wide range of adjectives such as sharp, tugging, aching, piercing, nagging and so on. These descriptions can be related to the three dimensions of pain described earlier.

Somatic therapies

The chemical agents used in the treatment of pain are numerous and varied in their nature. They include, first, narcotic drugs such as opium, morphine and their derivatives; these act centrally and produce both pain relief and a state of tranquillity. There is, however, a risk of establishing a dependency and this obviously places constraints on the way in which they may be employed. A second category comprises the psychotropic drugs or minor tranquillizers and anti-depressants; these are directed at the reduction of emotional distress rather than the pain experience per se. Third, there are agents which act peripherally and not centrally; examples are the salicyclates and analine derivatives, including aspirin and phenacetin. These have anti-pyretic and anti-inflammatory properties which can reduce pain, although not as effectively as the narcotic agents. They can have physical side effects if taken in large quantities or over long periods of time. Recent developments in the study of the brain's chemistry may provide new directions in the psychopharmacological treatment of pain. Opiate-binding sites have been discovered in the dorsal horns and in the central nervous system, and there is much interest currently in substances such as encephalin and the endorphins which are naturally occurring morphine-like peptides. It seems that morphine and similar substances may produce their effects by mimicking the action of these endogenous peptides. However, we are still far from fully understanding the properties of these compounds and the way in which they interact with the complex anatomical structures involved in the transmission of pain.

In many cases chemical therapies provide insufficient relief, or cannot be used in the quantities required for adequate relief because of their side effects, and other forms of physical treatment may then be demanded. Surgical procedures designed to interrupt the nervous system's transmission of pain signals have been carried out at many different sites from the periphery to the centre, but the general effectiveness of such procedures is disappointing. There have been some encouraging results, but in many cases where relief is obtained it may only be temporary. This outcome, in the context of the irreversibility of the procedures employed, has focussed attention on less drastic forms of treatment. One of these is to 'block' sensory input by injecting alcohol or a local anaesthetic agent such as procaine into the nerve root. Another is to increase this input by peripheral stimulation. This practice is conceptually similar to the 'counter-irritation techniques' that have been commonly used throughout history. These have included hot fomentations, vigorous massage, and the raising of blisters and dry cupping. For the latter a cupping glass, with the air partly withdrawn from it by means of an air pump or flame, was drawn across the skin, thus raising a painful red weal. Both nerve blocks and peripheral stimulation can be very effective in the treatment of appropriate syndromes. Not only may they have an immediate effect through restoring normal sensory inputs, but they can disrupt abnormal patterns of central nervous system activity and thus permanently affect the way in which pain is processed.

A method that may comprise important psychological as well as physical factors is acupuncture. This has only recently been applied to the control of pain and is most often used in the context of surgery. The procedure involves inserting needles into one or several skin areas, and these needles are then stimulated either manually or electrically. The successes claimed may be in part attributable to effects associated with peripheral stimulation, but Chaves and Barber (1974) have proposed a number of psychological bases for its apparent efficacy. These include the fact that a low level of anxiety is looked for in those selected for treatment by this method; the expectation among these patients that the experience will be pain free; a thorough preparation before surgery with a strong suggestion of pain relief, and exposure to models who have successfully undergone the experience; and the distractions associated with the general procedure which should draw attention away from the operation itself. These authors also suggest that the pain of surgery may be generally exaggerated, and point out that acupuncture is not generally used in isolation but in combination with sedatives and analgesics. The apparent success of acupuncture may then depend upon the existence of such physical and psychological supports, but as yet the relative contribution of these factors and of any direct somatic effects of the technique is unknown.

Psychological approaches to therapy

We cannot have direct access to another's experience and must make inferences about this on the basis of overt behaviours, such as motor activity, autonomic reactions, verbal descriptions, and so forth. Some psychologists argue from this that any distinction between experience and behaviour will be unproductive, and that the psychological analysis of pain and treatments for its relief should be directed at the behavioural level (Fordyce, Fowler, Lehmann, de Lateur, Sand and Trieschmann, 1973). With respect to therapy, typical goals would then be the reduction of help-seeking and dependent behaviour, a decrease in the medications taken, and an increase in physical and social activity. The therapist would first identify those behaviours thought to be undesirable within this framework, and would then seek the co-operation of the individual's family and friends in withdrawing the presumably rewarding conditions which serve to maintain these. For example, they might be advised to meet unreasonable requests for assistance with disapproval and reluctance, and to respond to legitimate demands or complaints helpfully but without the accompanying expressions of sympathy and concern which serve to reinforce these. At the same time, alternative desirable behaviours would be met with attention, approval and encouragement. This approach is most obviously appropriate where changes have occurred as a response to suffering, and have been maintained in spite of the removal of the pain source because they are found to fulfil other needs. It may also help in cases where the underlying condition cannot be alleviated, in this context by motivating the individual to lead as normal a life as possible in the circumstances, and to avoid the temptation of making a 'career of suffering'. A behavioural approach may not alter the intensity of the pain experienced, and pain may even intensify during therapy as physical activity increases. Nevertheless, a change at this level can have a positive impact on emotional adjustment and can improve the general quality of life for both the individual and his family.

Other psychological therapies attempt to modify the underlying experience of pain rather than the behaviours associated with this. One such approach is to provide training in the use of cognitive strategies which either direct attention away from pain or restructure the experience so that it is no longer distressing. The sufferer may be instructed to counter the pain when it occurs by attending to distractions in the environment rather than to his sensations, or by constructing fantasies and concentrating on thoughts which are incompatible with these. He may, alternatively, be advised to acknowledge the painful sensations but to reinterpret them in imagination as something less worrying or take a 'clinical' attitude which distances him emotionally. There have been many attempts to study the effectiveness of these strategies in laboratory experiments, but with suprisingly inconsistent results. One reason for the failure of some studies to demonstrate a positive effect may be the difficulty of ensuring that subjects follow the instructions faithfully. Those in the experimental group will sometimes reject the strategy suggested to them and substitute their own, while the control group may spontaneously employ strategies even though not instructed to do so (Scott, 1978). The very nature of the problem suggests that cognitive strategies in general play an important role in coping with pain, but it presents considerable methodological difficulties in establishing the effectiveness of a given strategy, either in absolute terms or in comparison with another strategy.

A third clearly psychological approach to pain therapy is that of hypnosis. Here the aim is to manipulate the experience directly by means of suggestion. There has been much discussion about the nature of hypnosis. Some have thought of it as a special state of consciousness or trance which is distinct from other experiences, but others have argued that it is an example of complete or almost complete absorption in a particular role and conformity with the expectations associated with this (Sarbin and Anderson, 1964). The subject has faith in the hypnotist's power to influence him, and is prepared to accept such influence to the extent that not only his outward behaviour but also his subjective experience will be modified. Hypnotic suggestion has been used for pain relief in surgery, dentistry, terminal care and obstetrics (Hilgard and Hilgard, 1975). Verbal reports of pain are affected by hypnosis, but involuntary physiological responses such as heart rate or galvanic skin responses are not generally affected. This indicates that there is still some sense in which the pain is present, and it has been suggested that the absence of the subjective experience of pain under hypnosis is a form of dissociation, with pain being processed at a preconscious, but not at a conscious, level. In one study subjects were trained to make two reports of pain simultaneously, one using a key press and another by verbal description, and the results supported the dissociation hypothesis. The key press response indicated more pain than the verbal report, although less pain than that reported verbally under comparable conditions but in a normal 'waking' state.

Hypnosis is not itself a means of preventing or alleviating pain, but a method for increasing the potency of the suggestion of analgesia made to the subject while in this state. Suggestion can have a powerful effect outside the context of hypnosis merely by creating the expectation of pain relief, and this is the basis of the well-known placebo effect. A placebo drug is a neutral substance which has a positive influence because of the expectations created by the context in which it is administered, and all treatments can be assumed to have some placebo element given that the subject is aware of their intended purpose. Substances which are known to be pharmacologically inert are thus used for comparison purposes in drug trials, rather than no treatment, in order to control for the anticipation of relief and provide a true baseline for evaluating the active and specific influence of the drug on trial. It is estimated that placebo treatments can alleviate surgical pain in about one-third of patients; laboratory studies produce lower estimates, but a significant proportion of subjects are still found to benefit. The effectiveness of a placebo will vary with the situation in which it is administered and with the status and manner of the person who administers it, since effectiveness will depend on expectations and the latter will be influenced by these factors. It will vary also with the individual to whom it is administered, and people can be grouped as either 'reactors' or 'nonreactors'; the former are not only more responsive to placebos, but are less differentially responsive to active drugs. While from a methodological viewpoint placebo effects may often be regarded as 'mock' effects for which controls must be introduced, from an applied perspective it is evident that the patient's expectations can be construed as powerful and legitimate agents of change. Their general influence will be added to that produced by the specific nature of any physical or psychological manipulation which is, with the patient's awareness, diverted at the treatment of pain, and can significantly enhance the therapeutic impact of these.

Psychological preparation for pain

The occurrence of pain may sometimes be anticipated before the event: for example, if a patient is scheduled for an unpleasant medical examination. Many of the treatments referred to earlier may be used as a form of preparation for a painful experience as distinct from an agent for relief once pain has occurred, but particular attention has recently been given to psychological preparation with an emphasis on those forms which enhance 'cognitive control'. These involve the provision of information which enables the individual to predict accurately what will happen in the situation and the nature of his experience, and instructions in strategies which may be employed to maximize the chances of successful coping. A number of laboratory studies have investigated the effect of the former, 'informational control', and have found that the stressfulness of electric shock and similarly noxious stimuli is reduced if subjects are made aware in advance of the timing and intensity of these and the fact that there is no danger of actual injury. The potential of the second kind of manipulation, 'strategic control', is demonstrated by the work of Turk (1978) who has developed a procedure for enhancing subjects' ability to control their response to painful stimuli, hence increasing their resistance to stress and tolerance for pain. The training procedure is quite complex. First, the subjects are given general instruction in the nature of pain; it is not considered essential that the explanation should be theoretically valid, but merely that it should provide a framework within which the experience may be conceptualized and the recommendations for coping presented. In the second stage of the procedure the subjects are trained to relax physically and mentally, and are provided with a selection of varied cognitive strategies with which to confront and control the pain. These strategies are similar to those described earlier, comprising methods both for redirecting attention and reinterpreting the experience. In this context, however, they are presented as a 'package' from which the subjects will select those suited to their personal needs. At this stage they will also be asked to generate feedback statements that can later be used to foster a feeling of control while in the painful situation and provide self-reinforcement. The final stage is that of rehearsal, where the subjects imagine the painful situation and their reactions, and subsequently play the role of a teacher instructing someone else in the procedure. This training has been found to increase pain endurance considerably in a cold pressor task. Subjects were able to extend the time during which they kept their hand in ice-cold water by 75 per cent, from before to after training, and this compared with a 10 per cent improvement for a 'placebo' group who had been given attention and encouragement but no instruction in specific cognitive techniques. The experimental group also showed a significant decrease in pain ratings.

It might be argued that many of the laboratory studies that have investigated informational control have involved highly structured and artificial tasks, and that the results might not be applicable to patients' experiences in clinical settings. It might also be pointed out that the cognitive training described above is highly complex; it has several components and stages and is orientated towards the particular personality and needs of each individual. It thus requires some investment of time and effort on the part of both the trainer and trainee, and such elaborate procedures might not be practicable in most naturally occurring situations. Similar, positive effects of preparation have, however, been found both under hospital conditions and in laboratory studies which have simulated these closely in terms of the nature of the painful procedures employed and the complexity of the preparation attempted.

Some of the most influential studies carried out in this area have been those conducted by Johnson and her colleague

(Johnson, 1975). In one of the first of these, male subjects
were exposed to ischaemic pain in the laboratory and were
either told what physical sensations they might expect as a
result of the procedure, or the procedure itself was described without elaborating the sensations associated with
it. It was found that the former preparation reduced distress, but the latter was ineffective in comparison with
a control group. The intensity of the sensations experienced
by the two information groups was the same, and the results
could not be accounted for by group differences in either
the degree of attention paid to these sensations or the
anticipation of possible harm. It seemed, then, that this
effect must have been due to the expectations held by subjects about what they were to experience, with more accurate
expectations being associated with lower levels of distress.
Further studies have used patients undergoing a variety of
stressful medical examinations or treatments, including
gastroendoscopy, cast removal and gynaecological examination. These too point to the conclusion that providing
information about what to expect reduces stress and un-
pleasantness, especially if this focusses upon what the
subject will experience rather than the objective nature of
the procedure.

The effects of psychological preparation have also been
extensively studied within the context of surgery. This will
be a stressful experience for most patients, and the anticipation and experience of pain will contribute to this distress. The kinds of preparation attempted in these studies
have varied quite widely. Most have taken a broad approach,
providing information about procedures and sensations,
offering reassurance and emotional support and advising on
how to cope with physical discomfort and difficulty. The
effects of these interventions are consistently positive,
with both reductions in subjective distress and improvement
in post-operative measures of recovery. Two such studies
which have focussed on pain are those of Egbert, Battit,
Welch and Bartlett (1964) and Hayward (1975). Wherever preparation comprises a number of different components it is
difficult to determine which of these are responsible or
necessary for the effectiveness of the whole. Some research
has thus attempted to isolate and compare different kinds of
preparation. It seems, for example, that providing instructions on how to cope with physical difficulties is not in
itself very helpful, but is beneficial when presented
against a background of accurate expectations (Johnson,
Rice, Fuller and Endress, 1978). Only one study has attempted any detailed training in cognitive strategies and looked
systematically at the impact of this training. Langer, Janis
and Wolfer (1975) encouraged the development of coping
devices, such as the reappraisal of threatening events,
reassuring self-talk and selective attention, and showed a
significant and independent effect of this instruction.

There is, then, evidence from a number of studies that
the distress associated with an unpleasant procedure can be

reduced by making the individual aware of what this involves from his point of view. It is, however, important to recognize that such information can only be expected to have a beneficial effect if it is presented in a reassuring way: creating an expectation of pain, whether accurate or not, can of course alarm the patient and counteract any positive effects of informational control. Instructions or training which help the individual to cope with physical or psychological stresses also have a role in the preparation for pain, and will enhance the effects of accurate expectations.

Final comments

The experience of pain depends upon a complex signalling system whose functions are determined by neurophysiological and biochemical influences which are not yet understood but are acted upon by physical and psychological factors of which we have some knowledge. These influences are many and varied, and provide a relatively broad scope for treatment. Some cases may call for one form of therapy rather than another, but for many a combination of physical and psychological approaches will present the most productive strategy.

A number of writers have called attention to the importance of the doctor-patient relationship in the treatment of pain. Szasz (1968) and Sternbach (1974) have pointed to motives which can cause the patient to resist abandoning his symptoms, and show how the physician may play a complementary role which facilitates these efforts: the patient who wishes to maintain his invalid status will have this claim effectively legitimized by the doctor who continues to treat him as though he were ill. Another common theme of doctor-patient interaction is an attempt by the patient to place responsibility for the outcome of treatment on the physician's shoulders, with the latter accepting this responsibility because of an eagerness to help and a reluctance to admit to the limitations of his professional skill. Such attitudes have been criticized as maladaptive. It has been argued that doctors should discourage passivity and helplessness, and cultivate a co-operative and problem-orientated relationship in which the patient takes an active role. This will involve confronting any undesirable attitudes he holds towards the pain, and emphasizing that the outcome of treatment will be determined as much by his own efforts as by what can be done for him. Sympathy and reassurance can reinforce pain behaviour and can foster a dependency which discourages self-help and the development of strategies for coping.

On the other hand, the total care of the pain patient should be concerned not only with the relief of pain but also with the psychological stress to which this suffering can give rise. The danger of emotionally isolating the patient is as real as that of over-protecting him. The attitude of family, friends and even professional helpers may be complex and emotionally charged, reflecting both an altruistic concern for the victim's welfare and personal fears and conflicts associated with suffering. The distress of the person in pain will in itself be distressing, particularly where it seems that there is little hope of providing immediate relief, and this can prompt either physical withdrawal or psychological distancing to prevent or defend against emotional upset. Moreover, pain is greatly feared, both for its own sake and because of its association with illness, injury and death, and contact with suffering can elicit anxiety about one's own vulnerability in this respect. This, too, can lead to avoidance or a reluctance to become practically and emotionally involved. Finally, while suffering is often unmerited, the recognition of this is disquieting, since it reminds us of the injustice of the world and our powerlessness in the face of events. Experimental studies have found that blameless victims are sometimes perceived as responsible for their fate, or are derogated so that this fate appears to be less unjust. We can predict from these studies that feelings towards the pain victim in real life might sometimes have a hostile element, and bear the implication that he is in some way to blame for his situation whether or not this is the case.

Few would dispute the importance of emotional support in alleviating immediate distress, and the availability of social support is a key factor in protecting an individual under stress from long-term maladjustment. It is therefore important to adopt a balanced approach in the care and management of the person in pain, helping him to help himself while at the same time providing the sympathy and reassurance to reduce anxiety and prevent despair.

References

Chaves, J.F. and Barber, T.X. (1974)
Acupuncture analgesia: a six-factor theory.
Psychoenergetic Systems, 1, 11-21.

Egbert, L.D., Battit, G.E., Welch, C.E. and Bartlett, M.K. (1964)
Reduction of post-operative pain by encouragement and instruction of patients. New England Journal of Medicine, 270, 825-827.

Engel, G.L. (1959)
'Psychogenic pain' and the pain prone patient. American Journal of Medicine, 26, 899-918.

Festinger, L.A. (1954)
Theory of social comparison processes. Human Relations, 7, 117-140.

Fordyce, W.E., Fowler, R.S. Jr, Lehmann, J.F. and de Lateur, B.J. (1968)
Some implications of learning in problems of chronic pain. Journal of Chronic Diseases, 21, 179-190.

Fordyce, W.E., Fowler, R.S. Jr, Lehmann, J.F., de Lateur, B.J., Sand, P.L. and Trieschmann, R.B. (1973)
Operant conditioning in the treatment of chronic pain. Archives of Physical Medicine and Rehabilitation, 54, 399-408.

Hayward, J.C. (1975)
Information: A prescription against pain. London: Royal College of Nursing.

Hilgard, E.L. and Hilgard, J.R. (1975)
Hypnosis in the Relief of Pain. Los Altos: Kaufmann.

Johnson, J.E. (1975)
Stress reduction through sensation information. In I. G. Sarason and C.D. Spielberger (eds), Stress and Anxiety: Volume II. Washington, DC: Hemisphere.

Johnson, J.E., Rice, V.H., Fuller, S.S. and Endress, M.P. (1978)
Sensory information, instruction in a coping strategy, and recovery from surgery. Research in Nursing and Health, 1, 4-17.

Langer, E.L., Janis, I.J. and Wolfer, J.A. (1975)
Reduction of psychological stress in surgical patients. Journal of Experimental Social Psychology, 11, 155-165.

Mechanic, D. and Volkart, E.H. (1960)
Illness behavior and medical diagnosis. Journal of Health and Human Behavior, 1, 86-94.

Melzack, R. (1973)
The Puzzle of Pain. Harmondsworth: Penguin.

Melzack, R. and Torgerson, W.S. (1971)
On the language of pain. Anaesthesiology, 34, 50-59.

Sarbin, T.R. and Anderson, M.L. (1964)
Role-theoretical analysis of hypnotic behavior. In J. Gordon (ed.), Handbook of Hypnosis. New York: Macmillan.

Scott, D.S. (1978)
Experimenter-suggested cognitions and pain control: problem of spontaneous strategies. Psychological Reports, 43, 156-158.

Sternbach, R.A. (1974)
Pain Patients: Traits and treatment. New York: Academi Press.

Sternbach, R.A. and Tursky, B. (1965)
Ethnic differences among housewives in psychophysical and skin potential responses to electric shock. Psychophysiology, 1, 241-246.

Szasz, T.S. (1968)
The psychology of persistent pain: a portrait of l'homme douloureux. In A. Soulairac, J. Cahn and J. Charpentier (eds), Pain. New York: Academic Press.

Turk, D.C. (1978)
Application of coping-skills training to the treatment of pain. In I.G. Sarason and C.D. Spielberger (eds), Stress and Anxiety: Volume V. Washington, DC: Hemisphere.

Zborowski, M. (1969)
People in Pain. San Francisco: Jossey-Bass.

Questions

1. What cues might we use in determining whether a person is in pain and the degree of pain experienced?

2. Describe the range of chemical and physical therapies available for the treatment of pain.
3. Can pain be treated using psychological methods alone?
4. Write a short essay on the use of hypnosis and acupuncture in the treatment of pain.
5. What is a placebo effect? What role can it play in the treatment of pain?
6. How do factors such as personality and culture influence pain behaviour, and in what sense can it be said that pain is 'learnt'?
7. What criteria might be employed in selecting one form of pain treatment rather than another?
8. What psychological preparation would you recommend for an adult who has to undergo an unpleasant medical examination or treatment?
9. What psychological preparation would you recommend for a child who has to undergo an unpleasant medical examination or treatment?
10. Discuss the possible disadvantages of being either too 'soft' or too 'hard' in one's attitude toward the pain patient.

Annotated reading

McCaffery, M. (1972) Nursing Management of the Patient with Pain. Philadelphia: Lippincott.

Fagerhaugh, S. and Strauss, A. (1977) Pain Management: Staff-patient interaction. Reading, Mass.: Addison-Wesley.

Hayward, J.C. (1975) Information: A prescription against pain. Royal College of Nursing.
  These three books focus on applied aspects of pain, relating theoretical knowledge to problems of patient care. The text by J. C. Hayward describes a study concerned with the psychological preparation of surgical patients.

Melzack, R. (1973) The Puzzle of Pain. Harmondsworth: Penguin.

Sternbach, R.A. (1974) Pain Patients: Traits and treatment. New York: Academic Press.
  Both of these books provide a broad introduction to physiological, psychological and social aspects of pain and its treatment.

Weisenberg, M. and Tursky, B. (eds) (1976) Pain: New perspectives in therapy and research. London: Plenum.

Sternbach, R.A. (ed.) (1976) The Psychology of Pain. New York: Raven.
  These are collections of papers, recommended for students who wish to consider issues and controversies within the area in greater detail than that provided by the introductory texts.

Exercises

1. Visits to the dentist

Talk with a number of people about their experiences of going to the dentist for treatment. What cognitive strategies, if any, do they use for reducing either their anxiety or pain in this situation? What is their reaction to the waiting room, the clerical and nursing staff, and the dentist him- or herself? Experiences other than a visit to the dentist might be used, but the experience must be one to which the subjects have been quite frequently exposed. You could either interview friends and acquaintances informally, or construct a short questionnaire to elicit information in a more structured form. The questionnaire should cover details of the respondent's background (sex, age, occupation, etc.), frequency and nature of visits to the dentist, anxiety experienced before and during treatment, and use of specified types of cognitive strategy.

2. What makes a pain painful?

Think of three occasions on which you have experienced pain where the pain has been different in kind but roughly equivalent in intensity. Taking two of these three occasions at a time, list the differences in (i) the quality of the pain sensation and (ii) your feelings associated with the pain and the situation in which it was experienced. Can you account for (i) in terms of (ii)? The purpose of this exercise is to prompt you to explore the nature of your own pain experiences, and to think of emotional and situational parameters which might influence them.

3. Attitudes towards medication

Conduct an informal survey among your friends and acquaintances to determine the extent of their use of non-prescribed medications for pain and the circumstances in which they use these. Again, the method used could be an informal and unstructured interview, or a short questionnaire constructed to elicit the information required. The data, however obtained, can then be used to consider the reasons for differences between people in the medication they use. You can follow this up by exploring attitudes to prescribed medication and the influence of such attitudes on patient compliance.

4. Keeping a pain diary

Keep a diary for a week, documenting all the occasions on which you experience any pain whatsoever. Note the nature and source of the pain, its intensity (on a scale from 1 to 5 where 1 = mild and 5 = severe), and the effects of the pain on your behaviour. As in exercise 2, the purpose is to make you more aware of your own pain experience. Here the pain will probably be of a relatively 'trivial' form, and the focus is on its behavioural impact. This is an exercise which you can carry out on your own; but if a friend does it as well, you could compare the number ratings each of you has given for similar discrepancies in experience as opposed to individualistic interpretations and use of the scale.

5. Coping strategies

Talk with people who suffer regularly from a particular pain, such as headache or dysmennorhoea. How do they cope with the pain when it occurs, and to what extent do their strategies seem adaptive or maladaptive to you? If you have friends who carry out the exercise as well, you can complete a list of the different coping strategies people use. Given each of the individuals who are interviewed, how adaptive are the strategies in relation to their needs? Can a strategy be adaptive for one person and maladaptive for another? Why might this be? How are people's coping strategies influenced by the responses around them?

6. Benefits and costs of being ill

Interview people with a view to finding out how they perceive illness and aspects of being ill. How are symptoms identified? How are decisions made to visit a general practitioner? What is the attitude of their doctor? What are the costs and benefits of being confined to bed? (Loss of earnings may be a financial cost, but consider the gaining of attention, and gifts, and the release from responsibilities.) Could there be advantages in being ill, and might these motivate an individual to experience pain in a particular way?

21

Psychopathology
D. A. Shapiro

'Psychopathology', literally defined, is the study of disease of the mind. Our society entrusts most of the care of individuals whose behaviour and experience are problematic or distressing to medical specialists (psychiatrists). Being medically trained, psychiatrists see their work as requiring diagnosis and treatment of 'patients'. Psychologists, on the other hand, have sought alternative means of understanding abnormal behaviour, and the aim of this chapter is to outline the progress that has been made in this direction.

The varieties of psychopathology

A good way to appreciate the great variety of problems we are concerned with is to examine the system of classification used by psychiatrists, summarized in table 1. Reader requiring more detailed descriptions of these should consult a psychiatric textbook. In the NEUROSES, the personality and perception of reality are fundamentally intact, although emotional disturbances of one kind or another, usually involving anxiety or its presumed effects, can make life very difficult for the individual. The PSYCHOSES, on the other hand, are characterized by gross impairments in perception, memory, thinking and language functions, and the individual is fundamentally disorganized, rather than merely emotionally disturbed. However, there is no clear-cut brain disease, and so the disorder cannot be explained in purely biomedical terms. The layman's conception of 'madness' is based on the symptoms of schizophrenia, including delusions (unshakeable, false beliefs), hallucinations (such as hearing 'voices') and thought disorder (manifested in 'garbled' speech). The third category of table 1, personality disorders, comprises deeply ingrained, motivational and social maladjustments. Table 1 also includes organic syndromes, which are behaviour disorders associated with identified brain disease. Not included in the table are the important group of psychosomatic illnesses. These are characterized by physical symptoms whose origins are in part psychological (emotional). They include asthma, high blood pressure, gastric and duodenal ulcers. More generally, psychological stress is increasingly implicated in many physical illnesses.

Table 1

Major category	Neuroses (milder disturbances)				
Causative syndromes	Anxiety state	Obsessive-compulsive disorders	Phobias	Conversion reactions	Neurotic depression
Characteristic symptoms	Palpitation, tires easily, breathlessness, nervousness anxiety	Intrusive thoughts, urges to acts or rituals	Irrational fears of specific objects or situations	Physical symptoms, lacking organic cause	Hopelessness dejection

Major category	Psychoses (severe non-organic disturbances		Personality disorders (antisocial disturbances)		Organic syndromes	
Causative syndromes	Affective disorders	Schizophrenia	Psychopathic personality	Alcoholism and drug dependence	Epilepsy	Severe mental handicap
Characteristic symptoms	Disturbances of mood, energy and activity patterns	Reality distortion, social withdrawal, disorganization of thought, perception and emotion	Lack of conscience	Physical or psychological dependence	Increased susceptibility to convulsions	Extremely low intelligence, social impairments

The medical model of psychopathology

Before describing psychological approaches to behaviour disorder, it is necessary to examine critically the predominant medical approach. This makes three major assumptions, which are considered in turn.

The diagnostic system
The first assumption of the medical model is that the various kinds of abnormal behaviour can be classified, by diagnosis, into syndromes, or constellations of symptoms regularly occurring together. This diagnostic system has already been summarized in table 1. It has a number of disadvantages. First, some disorders appear to cut across

the boundaries of the system. Thus an individual whose severe anxiety is associated with fears of delusional intensity may defy classification as 'neurotic' or 'psychotic'. Second, scientific studies of the ability of psychiatrists to agree on the diagnosis of individuals have suggested that the process is rather unreliable, with agreement ranging from about 50 per cent to 80 per cent depending upon the circumstances (Beck, Ward, Mendelson, Mock and Erlbaugh, 1962). Third, research also suggests that the diagnosis given to an individual may bear little relationship to the symptoms the individual has (Zigler and Philips, 1961). Fourth, the diagnosis of psychiatric disorder is much more subjective and reflective of cultural attitudes than is the diagnosis of physical illness; one culture's schizophrenic might be another's shaman; similar acts of violence might be deemed heroic in battle but psychopathic in peacetime. Careful comparisons of American and British psychiatrists have shown that the two groups use different diagnostic criteria and hence classify patients differently.

Despite these limitations, the psychiatric classification persists. This is largely because no better descriptive system has been developed, whilst improvements have been obtained in the usefulness of the system by refining it in the light of earlier criticisms. For example, agreement between psychiatrists has been improved by standardization of the questions asked in diagnostic interviews and the use of standard decision-rules for assigning diagnoses to constellations of symptoms. But it is still necessary to bear in mind that the diagnostic system is not infallible and the 'labels' it gives individuals should not be uncritically accepted.

Physiological basis of psychopathology

The second assumption of the medical model is that the symptoms reflect an underlying disease process, physiological in nature like those involved in all illnesses, causing the symptoms. Three kinds of evidence are offered in support of this. First, the influence of hereditary factors has been assessed by examining the rates of disorder among the relatives of sufferers. To the extent that a disorder is heritable, its origins are considered biological in nature. For example, comparison between the dizygotic (non-identical) and monozygotic (identical) twins of sufferers suggests that there is some hereditary involvement in schizophrenia, anxiety-related disorders, depression and antisocial disorders, with the evidence strongest in the case of schizophrenia (Gottesman and Shields, 1973). Studies of children adopted at birth also suggest that the offspring of schizophrenic parents are more liable to suffer from schizophrenia than other adopted children, despite having no contact with the biological parent. On the other hand, the evidence also shows that hereditary factors alone cannot fully account for schizophrenia or any other psychological disorder. Even among the identical twins of schizophrenics, many do not develop the disorder. Both hereditary and environmental influences are important.

The second line of evidence for a 'disease' basis of psychopathology concerns the biochemistry of the brain. This is a vastly complex subject, and one whose present methods of investigation are almost certainly too crude to give other than an approximate picture of what is going on. Over the years, a succession of biochemical factors have been suggested as causes for different forms of psychopathology. Unfortunately, the evidence is not conclusive, as biochemical factors found in sufferers may be consequences rather than causes. Hospital diets, activity patterns or characteristic emotional responses may influence the brain biochemistry of disordered individuals.

Despite these problems, there are some promising lines of biochemical research. For example, it has been suggested that schizophrenia may be caused by excess activity of dopamine, one of the neurotransmitters (substances with which neurons stimulate one another: see Snyder, Banerjee, Yamamura and Greenberg, 1974). This suggestion is supported by the similarity in molecular structure between dopamine and the phenothiazine drugs which are used to alleviate schizophrenia, suggesting that these drugs block the reception of dopamine by taking its place at receptors which normally receive it. These drugs also cause side effects resembling the symptoms of Parkinson's disease, which is associated with dopamine deficiency. Although this and other evidence support the dopamine theory of schizophrenia, some research has failed to support it, and so the theory has yet to be universally accepted. In sum, biochemical evidence is suggestive, and consistent with presumed physiological origins of psychopathology, but it is not conclusive, nor can such evidence make a psychological explanation redundant. It is best seen as an important part of our understanding of psychopathology, whose causal significance varies from one disorder to another.

The third line of evidence for the physiological basis of psychopathology concerns disorders with clear organic causes. Disease or damage to the brain can result in severe disturbance of behaviour. A classic example of this is 'general paresis of the insane', whose widespread physical and mental impairments were discovered in the last century to be due to the syphilis spirochete. This discovery encouraged medical scientists to seek clear-cut organic causes for other psychological abnormalities. A large number of organic brain syndromes have been established, in which widespread cognitive and emotional deficits are associated with damage to the brain by disease, infection, or injury. Epilepsy, in which the individual is unusually susceptible to seizures or convulsions, is associated with abnormal patterns of brain activity measured by the electroencephalogram (EEG) even between seizures. Many individuals with severe mental handicap (cf. Clarke and Clarke, 1974), who attain very low scores on tests of general intelligence and show minimal adaptation to social requirements and expectations, suffer from clear-cut organic pathology, often accompanied by severe physical abnormalities.

On the other hand, all of these disorders are affected by the person's individuality, experience and environment. For example, similar brain injuries result in very different symptoms in different individuals. Those suffering from epileptic seizures can make use of their past experience to avoid circumstances (including diet and environmental stimuli) which tend to trigger their convulsions. Most mentally handicapped people do not have clearly identifiable organic illnesses. Even among those who do, the environment can make a big difference to the person's ability to learn the skills of everyday living. Psychologists have found that special training can help mentally handicapped people who might otherwise appear incapable of learning.

Medical treatment of psychopathology

The third assumption of the medical model concerns how psychopathology should be managed. Physical treatments are offered in hospitals and clinics to persons designated 'patients'. It is beyond our present scope to describe the extensive evidence supporting the effectiveness of drugs and electro-convulsive therapy (ECT), the major physical treatments currently employed. However, there are several reaso: why psychologists are often inclined to question the support this evidence gives to the medical model. First, individuals differ in their responsiveness to physical treatments, and nobody really understands why some individuals are not helped. Second, the fact that abnormal behaviour can be controlled by physical means does not prove that its origins are physical. Third, the physical treatments often lack a convincing scientific rationale to explain their effects.

The medical model: conclusions

In sum, the medical model gains some support from the evidence, but is sufficiently defective and incomplete to warrant the development of alternative and complementary approaches. Although the diagnostic system is of some value, it must be used with caution. Although hereditary influences, biochemical abnormalities and organic pathology have a part to play in our understanding of psychopathology, they cannot explain its origins without reference to environmental and psychological factors. The apparent efficacy of physical treatment does not establish the physical origins of what they treat. The remainder of this chapter is concerned with five alternative approaches developed by psychologists and social scientists, and assesses their contribution with respect to some of the most important kinds of psychopathology. The evidence presented is, of necessity, very selective, and a full appreciation of these approaches can only follow more extensive study. It should also be borne in mind that the present emphasis on origins of disorder entails a relative neglect of research on treatment.

The statistical model identifies individuals whose behaviour or reported experience is sufficiently unusual to warrant attention on that basis alone. Abnormal individuals are those who greatly differ from the average with respect to some attribute (such as intelligence or amount of subjective anxiety experienced). For example, according to Eysenck (1970), people who score highly on dimensions known as 'neuroticism' (very readily roused to emotion) and 'introversion' (quick in learning conditioned responses and associations) are likely to show what the psychiatrist calls 'anxiety neurosis'. Although this approach is commendably objective, it is not very helpful alone. Not all unusual behaviour is regarded as pathological. Exceptionally gifted people are an obvious case in point. Some statistically abnormal behaviours are obviously more relevant to psychopathology than are others, and we need more than a statistical theory to tell us which to consider, and why. But the model is of value for its suggestion that 'normal' and 'abnormal' behaviour may differ only in degree, in contrast to the medical model's implication of a sharp division between them.

The psychodynamic model is very difficult to summarize, based as it is on theories developed early in the century by Freud, and revised and elaborated by him and subsequent workers within a broad tradition (Ellenberger, 1970). Like the medical model, it seeks an underlying cause for psychopathology, but this is a psychological cause, namely, unconscious conflicts arising from childhood experiences. Freudians have developed a general theory of personality from their study of psychopathology. Freud viewed the personality as comprising the conscious ego, the unconscious id (source of primitive impulses) and partly conscious, partly unconscious super-ego (conscience). The ego is held to protect itself from threat by several defence mechanisms. These are a commonplace feature of everyone's adjustment, but are used in an exaggerated or excessively rigid manner by neurotic individuals, and are overstretched to the point of collapse in the case of psychotic individuals.

For example, neurotic anxiety is learnt by a child punished for being impulsive, whereupon the conflict between wanting something and fearing the consequences of that desire is driven from consciousness (this is an example of the defence mechanism known as repression). According to this theory, pervasive anxiety is due to fear of the person's ever-present id impulses, and phobic objects, such as insects or animals, are seen as symbolic representations of objects of the repressed id impulses. Dynamic theory views depression as a reaction to loss in individuals who are excessively dependent upon other people for the maintenance of self-esteem. The loss may be actual (as in bereavement) or symbolic (as in the misinterpretation of a rejection as a total loss of love). The depressed person expresses a child-like need for approval and affection to restore self-esteem. In psychotic disorders such as schizophrenia, the collapse of the defence mechanisms leads to th predominance of primitive 'primary process' thinking.

Despite its considerable impact upon the ways in which we understand human motivation and psychopathology, psych dynamic theory has remained controversial. Most of the evidence in its favour comes from clinical case material, as recounted by practising psychoanalysts, whose work is based on the belief that unconscious conflicts must be brought to the surface for the patient to recover from the symptoms they have engendered. Whilst this method often yields compelling material which is difficult to explain in other terms (Malan, 1979), it is open to criticism as insufficiently objective to yield scientific evidence. It is all too easy for the psychoanalyst unwittingly to influence material produced by the patient, and the essential distinction between observations and the investigator's interpretations of them is difficult to sustain in the psychoanalytic consulting-room. The abstract and complex formulations of psychodynamic theory are difficult to prove or disprove by the clear-cut scientific methods favoured by psychologists, and the patients studied, whether in Freud's Vienna or present-day London or New York, are somewhat unrepresentative.

There is some scientific evidence which is broadly consistent with psychodynamic theory; for example, the defects in thinking found in schizophrenia are compatible with the dynamic concept of ego impairment, and loss event of the kind implicated by dynamic theory are associated with the onset of depression. Although psychologists hostile to dynamic theory can explain these findings in other terms, there is little doubt that the theory has been fruitful, contributing to psychology such essential concepts as unconscious conflict and defence mechanism.

The learning model

The learning model views psychopathology as arising from faulty learning in early life, and conceptualizes this process in terms of principles of learning drawn from laboratory studies of animals and humans. The most basic principles are those of Pavlovian or 'classical' conditioning (in which two stimuli are presented together until the response to one stimulus is also evoked by the other), and 'operant' conditioning (whereby behaviour with favourable consequences becomes more frequent). According to proponents of the learning model, the symptoms of psychopathology are nothing more than faulty habits acquired through these two types of learning. The 'underlying pathology' posited by the medical and psychodynamic models is dismissed as unfounded myth.

For example, it is suggested that phobias are acquired by a two-stage learning process; first, fear is aroused in response to a previously neutral stimulus when this stimulus occurs in conjunction with an unpleasant stimulus; then the person learns to avoid the situation evoking the fear, because behaviour taking the person away from the situation is rewarded by a reduction in fear. Another learning theory is that schizophrenic patients receive more attention and other rewards from other people, such as hospital staff, when they behave in 'crazy' ways, thereby increasing the frequency of this behaviour. Again, depressed people are seen as failing to exercise sufficient skill and effort to 'earn' rewards from situations and from other people; a vicious circle develops and activity reduces still further in the absence of such rewards.

In general, the learning model provides a powerful set of principles governing the acquisition of problem behaviour. But it has severe limitations. For example, the fact that fears and phobias can be established by processes of conditioning in the laboratory does not prove that this is how they come about naturally. The theory cannot readily explain how people acquire behaviours which lead to such distress (it is hardly 'rewarding' to suffer the agonies of depression or anxiety, and learning theorists acknowledge their difficulty over this fact by referring to it as the 'neurotic paradox'). Recently, learning theorists have examined the important process of imitative learning or modelling, whereby the behaviour of observers is influenced by another's actions and their consequences. Fear and aggression can be aroused in this way, with obvious implications for the transmission of psychopathology from one person (such as a parent) to another. But human thinking is considered by many psychologists too complex to be understood in terms of these relatively simple learning theories. Hence the development of the cognitive approach, to which we now turn.

The cognitive model

The cognitive model focusses upon thinking processes and their possible dysfunctions. 'Neurotic' problems are seen as due to relatively minor errors in reasoning processes, whilst 'psychotic' disorders are held to reflect profound disturbances in cognitive function and organization.

For example, it is well known that depressed people hold negative attitudes towards themselves, their experiences and their future. According to cognitive theory, these attitudes give rise to the feelings of depression (Beck, 1967). Although an episode of depression may be triggered by external events, it is the person's perception of the event which makes it set off depressed feelings. Experiments in which negative beliefs about the self are induced in non-depressed subjects have shown that a depressed mood does indeed follow. But whether similar processes account for the more severe and lasting depressive feelings of clinical patients is another matter, although the promising results of 'cognitive therapy', in which the attitudes of depressed patients are modified directly, may be taken as indirect evidence for the theory.

Cognitive theory also embraces people's beliefs about the causation of events (known as attributions). For example, it has been suggested that the attributions one make concerning unpleasant experiences will determine the impact of those experiences upon one's subsequent beliefs about oneself; thus, if a woman is rejected by a man, this is muc more damaging to her self-esteem if she believes that the main cause of the event is her own inadequacy, than if she attributes the event to the man's own passing mood. An attributional approach suggests that failure experiences are most damaging if individuals attribute them to wide-ranging and enduring factors within themselves. Consistent with this, depressed people have been found to attribute bad outcomes to wide-ranging and enduring factors within themselves, whilst they attribute good outcomes to changeable factors outside their control.

Psychologists have devoted considerable efforts to precise descriptions of the cognitive deficits of schizophrenic patients through controlled laboratory experiments. For example, schizophrenics have difficulty performing tasks requiring selective attention to relevant information and the exclusion from attention of irrelevant information. Schizophrenics are highly distractable. This may help to explain how irrelevant features of a situation acquire disproportionate importance and become interpreted as part of their delusional systems of false beliefs, or how speech is disorganized by the shifting of attention to irrelevant thoughts and mental images which other people manage to ignore.

The cognitive approach is of great interest because it combines the systematic and objective methods of experimental psychology with a thoroughgoing interest in an important aspect of human mentality. It is a very active 'growth area' of current research, and shows considerable promise. It is perhaps too soon to evaluate many of its specific theories, however, and it does carry the risk of neglecting other aspects of human behaviour.

The socio-cultural model

The final model to be considered attributes psychopathology to social and cultural factors. It focusses upon malfunctioning of the social or cultural group rather than of an individual within that group.

In terms of the socio-cultural model schizophrenia, for example, has been considered both in relation to the quality of family life and to larger socio-economic forces. Within the family, behaviour labelled schizophrenic is seen as a response to self-contradictory emotional demands ('double binds') from other family members, notably parents, to whic no sane response is possible. Although graphic accounts have been offered of such patterns in the family life of schizophrenic patients, there is no evidence that these are peculiar to such families. If anything, the research evidence suggests that abnormalities of communication within the families of schizophrenics arise in response to the behaviour of the patient, rather than causing the disorder. Looking beyond the family, the higher incidence of schizophrenia amongst the lowest socio-economic class, especially in inner city areas, is attributed to the multiple deprivations suffered by this group. Episodes of schizophrenia are triggered by stressful life events, some of which are more common, or less offset by social and material supports, amongst lower-class people. On the other hand, cause and effect could be the other way round, with persons developing schizophrenia 'drifting' into poverty-ridden areas of the city. Indeed, schizophrenic patients tend to achieve a lower socio-economic status than did their parents.

The socio-cultural approach is of undoubted value as a critical challenge to orthodox views, and has generated useful research into social and cultural factors in psychopathology. Its proponents have also made valuable contributions by bringing a greater humanistic respect for the personal predicament of troubled individuals, and to the development of 'therapeutic communities' and family therapy as alternatives to individually-centred treatments. However, many of its propositions concerning cause-effect relationships have not stood the test of empirical research.

The psychology of illness

It is well known that certain physical illnesses are related to psychological factors. These 'psychosomatic disorders' include ulcerative colitis, bronchial asthma and hypertension. It is not so widely appreciated, however, that psychological factors may be involved in any physical illness. This is because the physiological changes associated with stress (for instance, the release of the 'stress hormones' such as adrenalin) can suppress immune responses and so increase the individual's susceptibility to many diseases, ranging from the common cold to cancer (Rogers, Dubey and Reich, 1979). Many aspects of a person's life have been implicated in ill-health, presumably because of their effects on such physiological mechanisms. These include physical stresses such as noise, highly demanding and/or repetitive jobs (whether physical or mental), catastrophic life events (such as accidents, illness or bereavement) and major emotional difficulties (such as marital discord).

However, for physical illness as for psychopathology, the cause-effect relationship is not simple. Some individuals are more constitutionally stress-prone than others, it appears. Some people live in congenial and supportive surroundings, enabling them to withstand pressures which might otherwise lead to illness. Most of the events implicated in psychological distress and ill-health are in part the results of the individual's own state and behaviour. For example, marital conflict may reflect prior strains felt by the individuals involved. Furthermore, the impact of a stressful event or circumstance depends on the individual's appraisal of it. For example, noise is less distressing if we know we can silence it should it become unbearable. Thus consideration of psychological factors in ill-health demonstrates clearly the interaction between features of individuals and of their surroundings. For physical illness as for psychopathology, we must realize that there are many interacting causes rather than imagine that any one factor is alone responsible for the problem at issue.

Conclusions

Each of the approaches surveyed has contributed to our understanding of psychopathology. The evidence presented for each can only illustrate the massive amounts of research which have been carried out. Nonetheless, several clear themes emerge which have profound implications for our present and future knowledge of psychopathology.

First, the system of classification is inadequate, and research shows that different people within the same broad diagnostic group (such as schizophrenia) behave very differently; it therefore follows that different causes may be found for the difficulties experienced by these sub-groups of people.

Second, the different approaches could profitably be integrated rather more than they have been in the past. For example, elements of the medical, statistical, socio-cultural and cognitive approaches have been combined in recent work on schizophrenia, in which the vulnerability of an individual to the disorder is seen as reflecting both heredity and environment; this vulnerability determines whether or not a person experiences schizophrenia when faced with stresses which are too much to cope with (Zubin and Spring, 1977). The fact that psychopathology generally has multiple causes lends particular urgency to the need to construct broad theories incorporating the facts which were hitherto regarded as supporting one or another of the competing approaches.

Third, the different approaches have more in common than is often acknowledged. In relation to schizophrenia, for example, the breakdown of ego functioning described by psychodynamic theory resembles the inability to process information identified by cognitive theory.

Fourth, the limitations of existing models have encouraged the growth of alternative approaches. For example, the 'transactional' approach emphasizes the importance of the individual's active part in bringing about apparently external stressful events and pressures (Cox, 1978). This approach views the individual as neither a passive victim of circumstances, nor as irrevocably programmed from birth to respond in a particular way. Person and environment are seen as in continuous interaction, so that one-way cause-effect analysis is inappropriate. For example, harassed executives and mothers of small children bring some of the stress they suffer upon themselves as they respond sharply to colleagues or children and thus contribute to a climate of irritation or conflict. Research using this approach has only recently begun, but it holds considerable hope for the future.

Finally, what can this psychological study of psychopathology offer the professional? There are as yet no certain answers to such simple questions as 'What causes schizophrenia?' or 'Why does Mrs Jones stay indoors all the time?' If and when such answers become available, they will not be simple. They will involve many interacting factors. Meanwhile, the psychological approach teaches us a healthy respect for the complexity of the human predicament, and is a valuable corrective to any tendency to offer simplistic or unsympathetic explanations of human distress. Furthermore, professionals will often find it illuminating to apply some of the approaches outlined here to help understand distressed individuals they encounter in their daily work.

References

Beck, A.T. (1967)
Depression: Clinical, experimental and theoretical aspects. New York: Harper & Row.

Beck, A.T., Ward, C.H., Mendleson, M., Mock, J.E. and Erlbaugh, J. (1962)
Reliability of psychiatric diagnosis II: a study of consistency of clinical judgments and ratings. American Journal of Psychiatry, 119, 351-357.

Clarke, A.M. and Clarke, A.D.B. (1974)
Mental Deficiency: The changing outlook (3rd edn). London: Methuen.

Cox, T. (1978)
Stress. London: Macmillan.

Ellenberger, H.F. (1970)
The Discovery of the Unconscious. London: Allen Lane/ Penguin.

Eysenck, H.J. (1970)
The Structure of Human Personality. London: Methuen.

Gottesman, I.I. and Shields, J. (1973)
Genetic theorising and schizophrenia. British Journal of Psychiatry, 122, 15-30.

Malan, D.H. (1979)
Individual Psychotherapy and the Science of Psychodynamics. London: Tavistock.

Rogers, M.P., Dubey, D. and Reich, P. (1979)
The influence of the psyche and the brain on immunity and disease susceptibility: a critical review. Psychosomatic Medicine, 41, 147-164.

Snyder, S.H., Banerjee, S.P., Yamamura, H.I. and Greenberg, D. (1974)
Drugs, neurotransmitters and schizophrenia. Science, 184, 1243-1253.

Zigler, E. and Philips, L. (1961)
Psychiatric diagnosis and symptomalogy. Journal of Abnormal and Social Psychology, 63, 69-75.

Zubin, J. and Spring, B. (1977)
Vulnerability - a new view of schizophrenia. Journal of Abnormal Psychology, 86, 103-126.

Questions

1. What problems are raised by the diagnostic system used by psychiatrists? Can it be improved?
2. What can the study of twins tell us about psychopathology?
3. Outline the evidence for a biochemical basis for schizophrenia.
4. How useful is the medical model of psychopathology? Do it have any disadvantages?
5. Outline the statistical approach to psychopathology, indicating its value and limitations.
6. What is wrong with psychoanalysis as a scientific method of investigating psychopathology?
7. Is psychopathology simply behaviour which has been learnt because it produces rewards?
8. Which of the models of psychopathology do you prefer? Give your reasons.
9. How can psychological factors affect susceptibility to physical illness?
10. Which forms of psychopathology would be particularly disabling to a person employed in your profession, and why?

Annotated reading

Bannister, D. and Fransella, F. (1980) Inquiring Man (2nd edn). Harmondsworth: Penguin.
> A persuasive account of George Kelly's personal construct approach to psychology and psychopathology, written by two of its leading exponents.

Davison, G.C. and Neale, J.M. (1977) Abnormal Psychology: An experimental clinical approach (2nd edn). New York: Wiley.
> The chapter can provide no more than an introduction to psychopathology. This is the best of the textbooks available: it is readable, comprehensive and, in general, accurate. It is useful in teaching, and has been drawn upon extensively for drafting the chapter. If you want to follow up any aspect of the chapter in more detail, look up the topic in the Index of this book.

Hilgard, E.R., Atkinson, R.L. and Atkinson, R.C. (1979) Introduction to Psychology (7th edn). New York: Harcourt Brace Jovanovich (chapters 14, 15 and 16).
> Intermediate in length between the present chapter and the Davison and Neale book, this group of chapters gives a good general account. Chapter 14 reviews conflict and stress in terms of both experimental and psychoanalytic work; chapter 15 gives a good outline of much of the ground covered in this chapter; and chapter 16 discusses methods of treatment.

Inechen, B. (1979) Mental Illness. London: Longman.
This reviews the field from a sociological viewpoint,
and covers a good deal of research on social factors in
psychopathology.

Seligman, M.E.P. (1975) Helplessness: On depression,
development and death. New York: Freeman.
Seligman presents his theory of learnt helplessness in
a very stimulating and engaging book. Although the
theory was based on laboratory studies with animals,
Seligman has injected a great deal of 'human interest'
into this account. Students who are especially
interested in the theory of depression should note,
however, that Seligman's ideas have moved on since the
book was written to incorporate attributional concepts.

Spielberger, C. (1979) Understanding Stress and Anxiety.
New York: Harper & Row.
A very readable and well-illustrated introduction to
experimental and clinical work on stress and anxiety,
recommended for the student wishing to look further into
these aspects.

Stafford-Clark, D. and Smith, A.C. (1979) Psychiatry for
Students (5th edn). London: Allen & Unwin.
The present chapter does not attempt to do full justice
to psychiatry. This is the most readable of the general
textbooks on psychiatry, written for students rather
than practitioners. It is a good source for more details of psychiatric symptoms, disorders and treatments.

Exercises

An important caution for the reader
Many of the projects in this book involve obtaining information from individuals. People have a right to protect personal information, and as we, as Editors, have emphasized
in our Preface to the book, such a right must be treated
as sacrosanct by the psychologist. The projects which follow
involve a great deal of self-revelation and discovery. Because they are personal they can arouse anxiety, therefore
they should only be attempted on a voluntary basis. If you
have a friend with whom you can share some aspects of the
exercises then you will benefit from a sharing of experience. Again, however, we must emphasize that there is no
self-evident right which allows a person access to another
person's thoughts and feelings. This principle must be borne
in mind so that people can stop participating at any time
they choose and should not feel subject to group pressure.

1. Visits to a psychiatric hospital
There is no substitute for the direct experience of meeting
psychiatric patients or seeing videotapes of them talking
about their problems. If you are a member of a profession,
you may have trained colleagues working in psychiatric settings who should be able to arrange visits for you. You may

423

be a member of a voluntary organization which visits psychiatric patients on a regular basis. Failing that, you could
approach clinical psychologists working in the local NHS
District Psychology Department (usually based at a large
psychiatric hospital or in a District General Hospital) or
University Department of Psychology or Psychiatry. Clinical
psychologists, like all professionals, are busy and their
time is scarce; but they are often especially interested in
interdisciplinary collaboration over training, and so may be
able to help you. If you are at school or college a member
of staff should be able to make arrangements for a visit.

You should find out about both chronic (long-stay) and
acute (short-stay) patients, as well as the large numbers of
people who attend for out-patient appointments, and come a
day-patients whilst living at home. Many psychiatrists and
psychologists prefer to show videotapes rather than have
groups of students visiting their patients, both for ethical
and practical reasons.

It is worth while to make a point of meeting members
several different professions (such as psychiatrists, nurses, social workers, psychologists, occupational therapists)
and learning about their different approaches and skills.

If sufficient time is available to students and the
staff arranging the visit, a programme of several visits is
very worth while. You should seek the advice of the staff
arranging your visit in arranging a programme.

To derive the greatest benefit from your visit, you
should take notes during and/or after visiting, and write an
account of what you have seen and your impressions of it.
Preferably, this will be more than just a 'First I saw this,
then I saw that' catalogue. Students should formulate
objectives and focus on these. What is feasible will depend
on the facilities available to you. Possibilities include:

* an imaginative reconstruction of the experience of a
  patient you have seen, perhaps including an account of
  the circumstances leading to hospital admission;
* a comparison of the objectives, methods and assumptions
  of two or more of the helping professions encountered
  during your visit;
* an application of one or more of the 'models of psychopathology' to one or more individuals you have encountered. Try and ask yourself if the model 'fits' what you
  know of the person. Does the model help you understand
  the person any better?;
* examination of interactions between staff and patients,
  with special reference to the likely effects upon
  patients of the way staff respond to them.

Other chapters in this book supply psychological concepts to
help you with this exercise. Especially relevant are the
chapters on social skills and interpersonal behaviour,
interviewing, changing behaviour and counselling and
helping.

2. Positive and negative self-statements

According to the cognitive theory of depression, our moods
are affected by the kinds of beliefs we hold about ourselves, the world, and the future. You can obtain an idea of
how pervasive such statements are by keeping a record of
thoughts that occur to you about yourself as you go about
your daily life. Whenever convenient, write down any self-
statements that have crossed your mind during the day, and
then rate your mood at the time (or as you think about it
now, if you cannot recall the mood) on a scale from 0 to 10
(0 = very unhappy; 10 = very happy). You will probably find
that negative statements are associated with relatively
unhappy stress and positive ones with happy states. We must
emphasize that this exercise does not serve to tell whether
you are clinically depressed, but only to demonstrate how,
in all of us, mood varies alongside our beliefs about
ourselves.

You can also try collecting self-statements made by
other people, either in conversation with yourself or overheard in public places, and so on. Although statements made
to others are of course very different from one's private
thoughts (and you could make another exercise out of considering what kinds of differences there are between private
and public self-statements), you will learn a lot from the
great variety of self-statements you hear. They are often a
clue to the person's mood state, even if the person is not
altogether aware of it.

3. The repertory grid

To help understand how individuals feel about themselves and
some of the important people in their lives, psychologists
have developed the repertory grid. The theoretical underpinnings of this technique are discussed in the chapter by
Don Bannister. You can see how the repertory grid works by
following the simple three-stage instructions given here.

STEP 1: define the 'constructs' you use in thinking about
people. Our grid is concerned with ten people, most of whom
are real, although one is imaginary. They are numbered and
you should write down the name of each person.

1. Your father (or nearest equivalent if you did not grow
    up with him).
2. Your mother (or nearest equivalent if you did not grow
    up with her).
3. A male close friend or intimate (think of one actual
    person).
4. A female close friend or intimate (think of an actual
    person).
5. A male you dislike (an actual person).
6. A female you dislike (an actual person).
7. Yourself.
8. Yourself as you would like to be (your imaginary 'ideal'
    self).

9. A fellow student who appears very successful as a student (an actual person).
10. Someone who is very popular with other people (an actual person).

These ten people are known as the 'elements' of the grid. Now we have to devise ten 'constructs', or concepts you use to differentiate one person from another. Do this by thinking about the ten people in groups of three ('triads'). The first triad consists of elements 3, 5 and 9. For example, suppose that the person you have chosen as element 3 is called Tom, element 5 is Dick, and element 9 is Harry. Decide which two of the three are most alike, as people, and then write down a word or short phrase that describes what they have in common that makes them different (in your eyes) from the third member of the triad, and a further word or phrase (usually the 'opposite' of the first expression) which indicates how the third member is different.

For example, Tom and Dick might be 'kind' whilst Harry is 'cruel', or Tom and Harry might be 'always fooling around' whilst Dick is 'deadly serious'. The two opposite descriptions form the 'poles' of the construct, which can be 'serious'. When you have devised your own construct from your own elements 3, 5 and 9, repeat the process for the following nine triads, so that you have a list of ten constructs: 1,2,7; 1,8,10; 2,7,8; 3,4,7; 5,7,8; 6,7,10; 2,6,8; 1,5,8; 3,7,9. Make sure that each of your ten constructs is different in meaning from all the others. If you come up with a construct which is too similar to one you already have, think again about the triad.

STEP 2: draw up the grid. To prepare the grid, draw up a table with 10 rows and 10 columns. Down the side of the table, write down the constructs (both poles of each, e.g. 'cruel'-'kind'). Along the top, write the names of the people you have been using for the ten elements. To fill in the grid, consider each construct in turn, and decide which five elements are best described by the first pole (for example, cruel) and which five elements are best described by the second pole (for example, kind). Fill in the row for the construct by marking a '+' in the column for each element belonging at the second pole. It is important that there are five '+'s and five '-'s in each row. You may feel that your choices are very limited by this procedure, but you should try your best to divide your people into two equal groups on every construct.

STEP 3: analyse the grid. There are many ways in which a grid can be analysed, but we will concentrate on two simple ways of describing it. Do not read this section before you have completed the grid as this might influence the way you complete it, and make it less interesting.

* Similarity between elements. You can find out how similarly you tend to view the different people represented

in the grid. This is done by seeing how many times two people are placed at the same pole of the construct. For example, to find out how close together your father and mother are on the grid, you can scan the first two columns and score '1' for every construct, which is as different as they could be on this kind of grid) to 10 (meaning that they are seen similarly on every construct, which is as similar as is possible on this grid). Certain parts may be of particular interest, such as elements 7 and 8 (self and 'ideal self') whose similarity is a measure of the extent to which you feel you live up to your ideals. You could also consider the extent to which you see your intimates (elements 4 and 5) as resembling your parents (elements 1 and 2).

* Similarity between constructs. In a similar fashion, you can take a pair of constructs, and see how many of the ten elements are rated similarly on the two documents, scoring a '1' for every element which you gave the same score (a '+' or a '-') on the two constructs. This shows how similarly you tend to use the two constructs to describe people. Most people find the greatest similarity between constructs with a strongly evaluative ('good-bad') flavour to them.

These measures of similarity illustrate the kinds of information obtainable from a grid. Psychologists who use grids believe that they yield more information than simply asking the person direct questions such as 'How satisfied are you with yourself?' or 'Is your lover more like your father or your mother?' Although this grid cannot be used to diagnose psychopathology or as a basis for saying whether someone is in any sense 'abnormal', it can suggest insights into the way the person feels about other people, and this is often useful information for the psychologist trying to understand an individual's predicament.

A group of students could usefully pool the results from all their individual grids. Although every grid is unique to the individual, describing ten people in that person's life in terms which are especially meaningful to that individual, comparisons can be made in certain respects. You could collate, for example, the element similarity measures described above for the whole class. If you do this, it is important to respect the individual's wishes concerning the confidentiality of data; it may be best to collect the results in such a way as to ensure anonymity.

This exercise is but one way of using the repertory grid. For further information about the theory and uses of this and other variants of the repertory grid method see the annotated readings associated with the chapter by Don Bannister.

22

Counselling and helping
Barrie Hopson

Counselling today

From a situation in the mid-1960s when 'counselling' was seen by many in education as a transatlantic transplant which hopefully would never 'take', we have today reached the position of being on board a band-wagon; 'counsellors' are everywhere: beauty counsellors, tax counsellors, investment counsellors, even carpet counsellors. There are 'counsellors' in schools, industry, hospitals, the social services. There is marriage counselling, divorce counselling, parent counselling, bereavement counselling, abortion counselling, retirement counselling, redundancy counselling, career counselling, psychosexual counselling, pastoral counselling, student counselling and even disciplinary counselling! Whatever the original purpose for coining the word 'counselling', the coinage has by now certainly been debased. One of the unfortunate consequences of the debasing has been that the word has become mysterious; we cannot always be sure just what 'counselling' involves. One of the results of the mystification of language is that we rely on others to tell us what it is: that is, we assume that we, the uninitiated, cannot know and understand what it is really about. That can be a first step to denying ourselves skills and knowledge we already possess or that we may have the potential to acquire.

It is vital that we 'de-mystify' counselling, and to do that we must look at the concept within the broader context of ways in which people help other people, and we must analyse it in relation to objectives. 'Counselling' is often subscribed to as being 'a good thing', but we must ask the question, 'good for what?'

Ways of helping

'Counselling' is only one form of helping. It is decidedly not the answer to all human difficulties, though it can be extremely productive and significant for some people, sometimes. Counselling is one way of working to help people overcome problems, clarify or achieve personal goals. We can distinguish between six types of helping strategies (Scally and Hopson, 1979).

* Giving advice: offering somebody your opinion of what would be the best course of action based on your view of their situation.

* Giving information: giving a person the information he needs in a particular situation (e.g. about legal rights, the whereabouts of particular agencies, etc.). Lacking information can make one powerless; providing it can be enormously helpful.
* Direct action: doing something on behalf of somebody else or acting to provide for another's immediate needs; for example, providing a meal, lending money, stopping a fight, intervening in a crisis.
* Teaching: helping someone to acquire knowledge and skills; passing on facts and skills which improve somebody's situation.
* Systems change: working to influence and improve systems which are causing difficulty for people; that is, working on organizational development rather than with individuals.
* Counselling: helping someone to explore a problem, clarify conflicting issues and discover alternative ways of dealing with it, so that they can decide what to do about it; that is, helping people to help themselves.

There is no ranking intended in this list. What we do say is that these strategies make up a helper's 'tool-bag'. Each one is a 'piece of equipment' which may be useful in particular helping contexts. What a helper is doing is to choose from available resources whichever approach best fits the situation at the time.

There are some interesting similarities and differences between the strategies. Giving advice, information, direct action, teaching and possibly systems change recognize that the best answers, outcomes, or solutions rely on the expertise of the helper. The 'expert' offers what is felt to be most useful to the one seeking help. Counselling, on the other hand, emphasizes that the person with the difficulty is the one with the resources needed to deal with it. The counsellor provides the relationship which enables the clients to search for their own answers. The 'expert' does not hand out solutions. This does not deny the special skills of the helper, but does imply that having 'expertise' does not make a person an 'expert'. We all have expertise. In counselling, the counsellor is using personal expertise to help to get the clients in touch with their own expertise. Counselling is the only helping strategy which makes no assumption that the person's needs are known.

Teaching, systems change, and counselling are only likely to be effective if the 'helper' has relationship-making skills. Giving advice, information and direct action are likely to be more effective if he has them. Systems change is different in that it emphasizes work with groups, structures, rules and organizations.

The counsellor possibly uses most of the other strategies at some time or other, when they seem more appropriate than counselling. The other strategies would have an element of counselling in them if the 'helper' had the necessary skills. For example, a new student having difficulties making friends at school could lead to a counsellor, in addition to using counselling skills, teaching some relationship-building skills to the student, getting the staff to look at induction provision, making some suggestions to the student, or even taking the student to a lunchtime discotheque in the school club.

Who are the helpers?

Strictly speaking we are all potential helpers and people to be helped, but in this context it may be useful to distinguish between three groups.

Professional helpers
These are people whose full-time occupation is geared towards helping others in a variety of ways. They have usually, but not always, received specialist training. Social workers, doctors, teachers, school counsellors, nurses, careers officers and health visitors are a few examples. They define their own function in terms of one or more of the helping strategies.

Paraprofessional helpers
These people have a clearly defined helping role but it does not constitute the major part of their job specification or represent the dominant part of their lives, such as marriage guidance counsellors, priests, part-time youth workers, personnel officers and some managers. Probably they have received some short in-service training, often on-the-job.

Helpers in general
People who may not have any specially defined helping role but who, because of their occupational or social position or because of their own commitment, find themselves in situations where they can offer help to others, such as shop stewards, school caretakers, undertakers, social security clerks or solicitors. This group is unlikely to have received special training in helping skills. In addition to these groupings there are a variety of unstructured settings within which helping occurs: the family, friendships, and in the community (Brammer, 1973).

What makes people good helpers?

In some ways it is easier to begin with the qualities that quite clearly do not make for good helping. Loughary and Ripley (1979) people their helpers' rogue's gallery with four types of would-be helpers:

* the 'You think you've got a problem! Let me tell you about mine!' type;
* the 'Let me tell you what to do' type;
* the 'I understand because I once had the same problem myself' person;
* the 'I'll take charge and deal with it' type.

The first three approaches have been clearly identified as

being counter-productive (Carkhuff and Berenson, 1976) while the fourth one certainly deals with people's problems but prevents them ever learning skills or concepts to enable them to work through the problem on their own the next time it occurs. The only possible appropriate place for this person is in a crisis intervention. However, even this intervention would need to be followed up with additional counselling help if the needy person were to avoid such crises.

Rogers (1958) came out with clearly testable hypotheses of what constitutes effective helping. He said that helpers must be open and that they should be able to demonstrate the following qualities:

* unconditioned positive regard: acceptance of clients as worth while regardless of who they are or what they say or do;
* congruence: helpers should use their feelings, their verbal and non-verbal behaviour should be open to clients and be consistent;
* genuineness: they should be honest, sincere and without façades;
* empathic: they should be able to let clients know that they understand their frame of reference and can see the world as the client sees it, whilst remaining separate from it.

These qualities must be not only possessed but conveyed: that is, the client must experience them.

Truax and Carkhuff (1967) put these hypotheses to the test and found considerable empirical support for what they identified as the 'core facilitative conditions' of effective helping relationships - empathy, respect and positive regard, genuineness, and concreteness - the ability to be specific and immediate to client statements. They differed from Rogers in that whereas he claimed that the facilitative conditions were necessary and sufficient, they only claimed that they were necessary. Carkhuff has gone on to try to demonstrate (Carkhuff and Berenson, 1976) that they are clearly not sufficient, and that the helper needs to be skilled in teaching a variety of life and coping skills to clients. The other important finding from Truax and Carkhuff was that helpers who do not possess those qualities are not merely ineffective, for they can contribute to people becoming worse than they were prior to helping.

The evidence tends to suggest that the quality of the interpersonal relationship between helper and client is more important than any specific philosophy of helping adhered to by the helper. This has been demonstrated to be the case in counselling, psychotherapy and also teaching (Aspy and Roebuck, 1977). A recent review of the many research studies on this topic would suggest, as one might expect, that things are not quite that simple (Parloff, Waskow, and Wolfe, 1978), but after a reappraisal of the early work of Truax and Carkhuff and a large number of more recent

studies, the authors conclude that a relationship between
empathy, respect and genuineness with helper effectiveness
has been established. They also shed light on a number of
other factors which have been discussed periodically as
being essential for effective therapists (their focus was
therapy, not helping):

* personal psychotherapy has not been demonstrated to be
  a prerequisite for an effective therapist;
* sex and race are not related to effectiveness;
* the value of therapist experience is highly
  questionable; that is, someone is not necessarily a
  better therapist because of greater experience;
* therapists with emotional problems of their own are
  likely to be less effective;
* there is some support for the suggestion that helpers
  are more effective when working with clients who hold
  values similar to their own.

What they do point out is the importance of the match
between helper and client. No one is an effective helper
with everyone, although we as yet know little as to how to
match helpers with clients to gain the greatest benefits.

**Helping and human
relationships**

Carl Rogers states very clearly that psychotherapy is not a
'special kind of relationship, different in kind from all
others which occur in everyday life' (1957). A similar
approach has been taken by those theorists looking at the
broader concept of helping. Brammer (1973) states that
'helping relationships have much in common with friendships,
family interactions, and pastoral contacts. They are all
aimed at fulfilling basic human needs, and when reduced to
their basic components, look much alike'. This is the approach of Egan (1975) in his training programmes for effective interpersonal relating, of Carkhuff and Berenson (1976)
who talk of counselling as 'a way of life', of Illich, Zola,
McKnight, Kaplan and Sharken (1977) who are concerned with
the de-skilling of the population by increasing armies of
specialists, and of Scally and Hopson (1979) who emphasize
that counselling 'is merely a set of beliefs, values and
behaviours to be found in the community at large'. Considerable stress is placed later in this chapter on the trend
towards demystifying helping and counselling.

Models of helping
Any person attempting to help another must have some model
in mind, however ill-formed, of the process which is about
to be undertaken. There will be goals, however hazy, ranging
from helping the person to feel better through to helping
the person to work through an issue independently. It is
essential for helpers to become more aware of the value-
roots of their behaviours and the ideological underpinning
of their proffered support.

> The helper builds his theory through three overlapping stages. First he reflects on his own experience. He becomes aware of his values, needs, communication style, and their impact on others. He reads widely on the experience of other practitioners who have tried to make sense out of their observations by writing down their ideas into a systematic theory ... Finally the helper forges the first two items together into a unique theory of his own (Brammer, 1973).

Fortunately, in recent years a number of theorists and researchers have begun to define models of helping. This can only assist all helpers to define their own internal models which will then enable them in turn to evaluate their personal, philosophical and empirical bases.

CARKHUFF AND ASSOCIATES: Carkhuff took Rogers' ideas on psychotherapy and expanded on them to helping in general. He has a three-stage model through which the client is helped to (i) explore, (ii) understand and (iii) act. He defines the skills needed by the helper at each stage of the process (Carkhuff, 1974), and has also developed a system for selecting and training prospective helpers to do this. Since the skills he outlines are basically the same skills which anyone needs to live effectively, he suggests that the best way of helping people is to teach them directly and systematically in life, work, learning and relationship-building skills. He states clearly that 'the essential task of helping is to bridge the gap between the helpee's skills level and the helper's skills level' (Carkhuff and Berenson, 1976). For Carkhuff, helping equals teaching, but teaching people the skills to ensure that they can take more control over their own lives.

BRAMMER (1973) has produced an integrated, eclectic developmental model similar to Carkhuff's. He has expanded Carkhuff's three stages into the eight stages of entry, classification, structure, relationship, exploration, con-solidation, planning and termination. He has also identified seven clusters of skills to promote 'understanding of self and others'. His list of 46 specific skills is somewhat daunting to a beginner but a rich source of stimulation for the more experienced helper.

IVEY (1971) AND ASSOCIATES have developed a highly systematic model for training helpers under the label 'microcounselling'. Each skill is broken up into its constituent parts and taught via closed-circuit television, modelling and practice.

HACKNEY AND NYE (1973) have described a helping model which they call a 'discrimination' model. It is goal-centred and action-centred and it stresses skills training.

KAGAN, KRATHWOHL (1967) AND ASSOCIATES have also developed a microskills approach to counsellor training which is widely used in the USA. It is called Interpersonal Process Recall which involves an enquiry session in which helper and client explore the experience they have had together in the presence of a mediator.

EGAN (1975) has developed perhaps the next most influential model of helping in the USA after Carkhuff's and,
indeed, has been highly influenced by Carkhuff's work. The
model begins with a pre-helping phase involving attending
skills, to be followed by Stage I: responding and self-
exploration; Stage II: integrative understanding and dynamic
self-understanding; and Stage III: facilitating action and
acting. The first goal labelled at each stage is the
helper's goal and the second goal is that of the client.

LOUGHARY AND RIPLEY (1979) approach helping from
a different viewpoint, which, unlike the previous theorists,
is not simply on the continuum beginning with Rogers and
Carkhuff. They have used a demystifying approach aimed
at the general population with no training other than what
can be gleaned from their book. Their model is shown in
figure 1.

Figure 1

Model of helping
From Loughary and Ripley (1979)

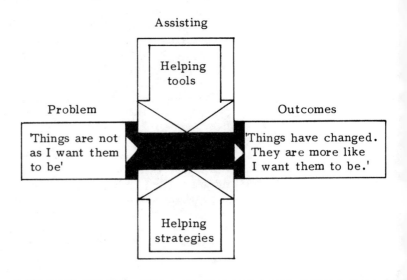

The helping tools include information, ideas, and skills
(such as listening and reflecting dealings). The strategies
are the plans for using the tools and the first step is
always translating the problem into desired outcomes. Their
four positive outcomes of helping are: changes in feeling
states, increased understanding, decisions, and implementing
decisions. Their approach does move away from the
counselling-dominated approach of the other models.

HOPSON AND SCALLY: we reproduce our own model in
some detail here, partly because it is the model we know
best and it has worked very effectively for us and for the
3,000 teachers and youth workers who have been through our

counselling skills training courses (Scally and Hopson, 1979), but also because it attempts to look at all the aspects of helping defined at the beginning of this chapter.

Figure 2 outlines three goal areas for helpers, central to their own personal development. It also defines specific helping outcomes. Helpers can only help people to the levels of their own skills and awareness (Aspy and Roebuck, 1977). They need to clarify their own social, economic and cultural values and need to be able to recognize and separate their own needs and problems from those of their clients. Helpers see in others reflections of themselves. To know oneself is to ensure a clarity of distinction between images: to know where one stops and the other begins. We become less helpful as the images blur. To ensure that does not happen, we need constantly to monitor our own development. Self-awareness is not a stage to be reached and then it is over. It is a process which can never stop because we are always changing. By monitoring these changes we simultaneously retain some control of their direction.

From a greater awareness of who we are, our strengths, hindrances, values, needs and prejudices, we can be clearer about skills we wish to develop. The broader the range of skills we acquire, the larger the population group that we can help.

As helpers involved in the act of helping we learn through the process of praxis. We reflect and we act. As we interact with others, we in turn are affected by them and are in some way different from before the interaction. As we attempt to help individuals and influence systems we will learn, change, and develop from the process of interaction, just as those individuals and systems will be affected by us.

Having access to support should be a central concern for anyone regularly involved in helping. Helpers so often are not as skilled as they might be at saying 'no' and looking after themselves.

We would maintain that the ultimate goals of helping are to enable people to become self-empowered and to make systems healthier places in which to live, work and play.

Self-empowerment

There are five dimensions of self-empowerment (Hopson and Scally, 1980a).

* Awareness: without an awareness of ourselves and others we are subject to the slings and arrows of our upbringing, daily events, social changes and crises. Without awareness we can only react, like the pinball in the machine that bounces from one thing to another without having ever provided the energy for its own passage.
* Goals: given awareness we have the potential for taking charge of ourselves and our lives. We take charge by exploring our values, developing commitments, and by

Figure 2

Goals of helping

GOALS OF HELPING

SELF-EMPOWERED INDIVIDUALS	PERSONAL DEVELOPMENT OF THE HELPER	HEALTHY SYSTEMS (MICRO, MACRO)	SPECIFIC OUTCOMES

SELF-EMPOWERED
INDIVIDUALS

|

Possessing
awareness
/ | \
self others the world

GOALS

commitments outcomes
|
VALUES

SKILLS
(see figure 3)

INFORMATION
/ | \
self others the world

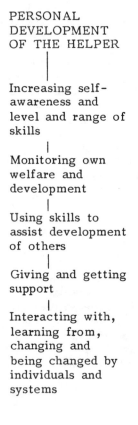

PERSONAL
DEVELOPMENT
OF THE HELPER
|
Increasing self-
awareness and
level and range of
skills
|
Monitoring own
welfare and
development
|
Using skills to
assist development
of others
|
Giving and getting
support
|
Interacting with,
learning from,
changing and
being changed by
individuals and
systems

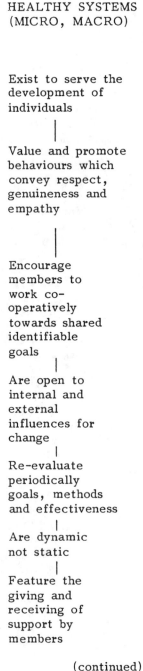

HEALTHY SYSTEMS
(MICRO, MACRO)

Exist to serve the
development of
individuals
|
Value and promote
behaviours which
convey respect,
genuineness and
empathy
|
Encourage
members to
work co-
operatively
towards shared
identifiable
goals
|
Are open to
internal and
external
influences for
change
|
Re-evaluate
periodically
goals, methods
and effectiveness
|
Are dynamic
not static
|
Feature the
giving and
receiving of
support by
members

SPECIFIC
OUTCOMES

Increase
understanding
|
Changes in
feeling states
(discharge or
exploration)
|
Able to make
a decision
|
Able to
implement
a decision
|
Confirms a
decision
|
Gets support
|
Adjusts to a
situation
which is not
going to
change
|
Examines
alternatives
|
Receives
direct
action/
practical
help
|
Increases
skills,
develops
new ones

(continued)

436

Focus on
individual's
strengths
|
And builds on
them
|
Use problem
solving strate-
gies rather than
scapegoating,
blaming or focus-
sing on faults
|
Use methods which
are consistent
with goals
|
Encourage power-
sharing and enable
individuals to
pursue their own
direction as a
contribution to
shared goals
|
Monitor their own
performance in a
continuing cycle of
reflection/action
|
Allow people
access to those
whose decisions
have a bearing
on their lives
|
Have effective
and sensitive
lines of
communication
|
Explore differ-
ences openly and
use compromise,
negotiation and
contracting to
achieve a maxi-
mum of win/win
outcomes for all
|
Are always open
to alternatives

Receives
information
|
Reflects on
acts

specifying goals with outcomes. We learn to live by the question: 'what do I want now?' We reflect and then act.

* Values: we subscribe to the definition of values put forward by Raths, Harmin and Simon (1964): a value is a belief which has been chosen freely from alternatives after weighing the consequences of each alternative; it is prized and cherished, shared publicly and acted upon repeatedly and consistently. The self-empowered person, by our definition, has values which include recognizing the worth of self and others, of being proactive, working for healthy systems, at home, in employment, in the community and at leisure; helping other people to become more self-empowered.

* Life skills: values are good as far as they go, but it is only by developing skills that we can translate them into action. We may believe that we are responsible for our own destiny, but we require the skills to achieve what we wish for ourselves. In a school setting, for example, we require the skills of goal setting and action-planning, time management, reading, writing and numeracy, study skills, problem-solving skills and how to work in groups. Figure 3 reproduces the list of life skills that we have identified at the Counselling and Career Development Unit (Hopson and Scally, 1980b) as being crucial to personal survival and growth.

* Information: information is the raw material for awareness of self and the surrounding world. It is the fuel for shaping our goals. Information equals power. Without it we are helpless, which is of course why so many people and systems attempt to keep information to themselves. We must realize that information is essential (a concept), that we need to know how to get appropriate information, and from where (a skill).

Healthy systems

Too often counsellors and other helpers have pretended to be value free. Most people now recognize that fiction. Not only is it impossible but it can be dangerous. If we honestly believe that we are capable of being value free, we halt the search for the ways in which our value systems are influencing our behaviour with our clients. If we are encouraging our clients to develop goals, how can we pretend that we do not have them too? Expressing these goals can be the beginning of a contract to work with a client for, like it or not, we each have a concept, however shadowy, for the full functioning healthy person to which our actions and helping are directed.

As with clients, so too with systems. If we are working towards helping people to become 'better', in whatever way we choose to define that, let us be clear about what changes we are working towards in the systems we try to influence. Figure 2 lists our characteristics of healthy systems. Each of us has our own criteria so let us discover them and bring them into the open. Owning our values is one way of demonstrating our genuineness.

ℊure 3

eskills: taking charge of yourself and your life

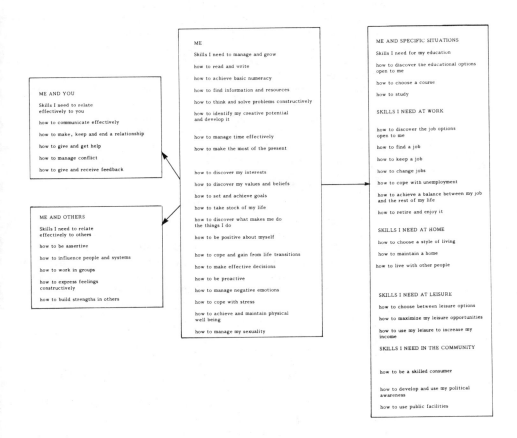

ME

Skills I need to manage and grow

how to read and write

how to achieve basic numeracy

how to find information and resources

how to think and solve problems constructively

how to identify my creative potential and develop it

how to manage time effectively

how to make the most of the present

how to discover my interests

how to discover my values and beliefs

how to set and achieve goals

how to take stock of my life

how to discover what makes me do the things I do

how to be positive about myself

how to cope and gain from life transitions

how to make effective decisions

how to be proactive

how to manage negative emotions

how to cope with stress

how to achieve and maintain physical well being

how to manage my sexuality

ME AND YOU

Skills I need to relate effectively to you

how to communicate effectively

how to make, keep and end a relationship

how to give and get help

how to manage conflict

how to give and receive feedback

ME AND OTHERS

Skills I need to relate effectively to others

how to be assertive

how to influence people and systems

how to work in groups

how to express feelings constructively

how to build strengths in others

ME AND SPECIFIC SITUATIONS

Skills I need for my education

how to discover the educational options open to me

how to choose a course

how to study

SKILLS I NEED AT WORK

how to discover the job options open to me

how to find a job

how to keep a job

how to change jobs

how to cope with unemployment

how to achieve a balance between my job and the rest of my life

how to retire and enjoy it

SKILLS I NEED AT HOME

how to choose a style of living

how to maintain a home

how to live with other people

SKILLS I NEED AT LEISURE

how to choose between leisure options

how to maximize my leisure opportunities

how to use my leisure to increase my income

SKILLS I NEED IN THE COMMUNITY

how to be a skilled consumer

how to develop and use my political awareness

how to use public facilities

What is counselling?

Having identified six common ways of helping people, counselling will now be focussed on more intensively, which immediately gets us into the quagmire of definition.

Anyone reviewing the literature to define counselling will quickly suffer from data-overload. Books, articles, even manifestoes, have been written on the question.

In training courses run from the Counselling and Career Development Unit we tend to opt for the parsimonious definition of 'helping people explore problems so that they can decide what to do about them'.

The demystification of counselling

There is nothing inherently mysterious about counselling. It is merely a set of beliefs, values and behaviours to be found in the community at large. The beliefs include one that says individuals benefit and grow from a particular form of relationship and contact. The values recognize the worth and the significance of each individual and regard personal autonomy and self-direction as desirable. The behaviours cover a combination of listening, conveying warmth, asking open questions, encouraging specificity, concreteness and focussing, balancing support and confrontation, and offering strategies which help to clarify objectives and identify action plans. This terminology is more complex than the process needs to be. The words describe what is essentially a 'non-mystical' way in which some people are able to help other people to help themselves (see figure 4).

Training courses can sometimes encourage the mystification. They talk of 'counselling skills' and may, by implication, suggest that such skills are somehow separate from other human activities, are to be conferred upon those who attend courses, and are probably innovatory. In fact, what 'counselling' has done is to crystallize what we know about how warm, trusting relationships develop between people. It recognizes that:

* relationships develop if one has and conveys respect for another, if one is genuine oneself, if one attempts to see things from the other's point of view (empathizes), and if one endeavours not to pass judgement. Those who operate in this way we describe as having 'relationship-building skills';
* if the relationship is established, an individual will be prepared to talk through and explore thoughts and feelings. What one can do and say which helps that to happen we classify as exploring and clarifying skills (see figure 4);
* through this process individuals become clear about difficulties or uncertainties, and can explore options and alternatives, in terms of what they might do to change what they are not happy about;
* given support, individuals are likely to be prepared to, and are capable of, dealing with difficulties or problems they may face more effectively. They can be helped by somebody who can offer objective setting and action planning skills.

Counselling skills are what people use to help people to help themselves. They are not skills that are exclusive to one group or one activity. It is clear that the behaviours, which we bundle together and identify as skills, are liberally scattered about us in the community. Counselling ideology identifies which behaviours are consistent with its values and its goals, and teaches these as one category of helping skills.

ie counselling process

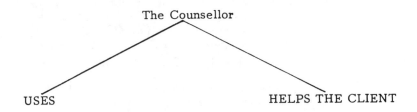

The Counsellor

USES   HELPS THE CLIENT

RELATIONSHIP BUILDING SKILLS	respect genuineness empathy	to feel valued, understood and prepared to trust the counsellor
EXPLORING AND CLARIFYING SKILLS	contracting open questions summarizing focussing reflecting immediacy clarifying concreteness confronting	to talk and explore to understand more about how he feels and why to consider options and examine alternatives to choose an alternative
	objective setting action planning problem-solving strategies	to develop clear objectives to form specific action plans to do, with support, what needs to be done

COUNSELLING IS HELPING PEOPLE TO HELP THEMSELVES

What may happen, unfortunately, is that the promotion of counselling as a separate training responsibility can increase the mystification. An outcome can be that instead of simply now being people who, compared to the majority, are extra-sensitive listeners, are particularly good at making relationships, and are more effective at helping others to solve problems, they have become 'counsellors' and licensed to help. A licence becomes a danger if:

*   those who have it see themselves as qualitatively different from the rest of the population;
*   it symbolizes to the non-licensed that they are incapable, or inferior, or calls into question valuable work they may be doing, but are 'unqualified' to do.

It is important to recognize that labelling people can have unfortunate side effects. Let us remember that whatever th nomenclature - counsellor, client or whatever - at a particular time or place, they are just people. All, at some time or other, will be able to give help, at other times will need to seek or receive help. Some are naturally better fitted to help others; some by training can improve their helping skills. All, through increased awareness and skill development, can become more effective helpers than they are now.

Counselling is not only practised by counsellors. It is a widespread activity in the community and appears in several guises. Its constituent skills are described variously as 'talking it over', 'having a friendly chat', 'being a good friend' or simply 'sharing' with somebody. These processes almost certainly include some or all of the skills summarized in figure 4. Often, of course, there are notable exceptions: for instance, we do not listen well; we cannot resist giving our advice, or trying to solve problems for our friends; we find it difficult to drop our façades and roles. Counselling skills training can help reduce our unhelpful behaviours and begin to develop these skills in ourselves, making us more effective counsellors, as well as simply being a good friend. In almost any work involving contact with other people, we would estimate there is a potential counselling component. There is a need for the particular interpersonal skills categorized here as coun-selling skills to be understood and used by people at large, but particularly by all people who have the welfare of others as part of their occupational roles. Specialist 'counsellors' have an important part to play, but it is not to replace the valuable work that is done by many who would not claim the title. Having said that, people sometimes think they are counselling, but in fact are doing things very far removed: disciplining, persuading people to conform to a system, and so on.

Types of counselling

Developmental versus crisis counselling
Counselling can operate either as a response to a situation

or as a stimulus to help a client develop and grow. In the past, counselling has often been concerned with helping someone with a problem during or after the onset of a crisis point: a widow unable to cope with her grief, the boy leaving school desperate because he has no idea what job to choose, the pregnant woman with no wish to be pregnant. This is a legitimate function of counselling, but if this is all that counselling is, it can only ever be concerned with making the best of the situation in which one finds oneself. How much more ambitious to help people anticipate future problems, to educate them to recognize the cues of oncoming crisis, and to provide them with skills to take charge of it at the outset instead of running behind in an attempt to catch up! This is counselling as a stimulus to growth: developmental as opposed to crisis counselling. All successful counselling entails growth, but the distinction between the two approaches is that the crisis approach generates growth under pressure, and since this is often limited only to the presenting problem, the client's behavioural and conceptual repertoire may remain little affected by the experience. There will always be a need for crisis counselling in a wide variety of settings, but the exciting prospect of developmental counselling for growth and change has only recently begun to be tackled.

Individual counselling
As counselling was rooted in psychotherapy it is hardly surprising that the primary focus has been on the one-to-one relationship. There are a number of essential elements in the process. Clients are to be helped to reach decisions by themselves. This is achieved by establishing a relationship of trust whereby individual clients feel that the counsellor cares about them, is able to empathize with their problems, and is authentic and genuine in relating to them. Counsellors will enter the relationship as persons in their own right, disclosing relevant information about themselves as appropriate, reacting honestly to clients' statements and questions, but at no time imposing their own opinions on the clients. Their task is to facilitate the clients' own abilities and strengths in such a way that clients experience the satisfaction of having defined and solved their problems for themselves. If a client lacks information on special issues, is incapable of generating alternative strategies, or cannot make decisions in a programmatic way, then the counsellor has a function as an educator whose skills are offered to the client. In this way the client is never manipulated. The counsellor is negotiating a contract to use some skills which are possessed by the counsellor, and which can be passed on to the client if the client wishes to make use of them.

Individual counselling has the advantages over group counselling of providing a safer setting for some people to lower their defences, of developing a strong and trusting relationship with the counsellor, and of allowing the client maximum personal contact with the counsellor.

Group counselling

Group counselling involves one or more counsellors operating
with a number of clients in a group session. The group size
varies from four to sixteen, with eight to ten being the
most usual number. The basic objectives of group and individual counselling are similar. Both seek to help the
clients achieve self-direction, integration, self-
responsibility, self-acceptance, and an understanding of
their motivations and patterns of behaviour. In both cases
the counsellor needs the skills and attitudes outlined
earlier, and both require a confidential relationship. There
are, however, some important differences (Hopson, 1977).

*   The group counsellor needs an understanding of group
     dynamics: communication, decision making, role-playing,
     sources of power, and perceptual processes in groups.
*   The group situation can provide immediate opportunities
     to try out ways of relating to individuals, and is an
     excellent way of providing the experience of intimacy
     with others. The physical proximity of the clients to
     one another can be emotionally satisfying and suppor-
     tive. Clients give a first-hand opportunity to test
     others' perception of themselves.
*   Clients not only receive help themselves; they also help
     other clients. In this way helping skills are generated
     by a larger group of people than is possible in
     individual counselling.
*   Clients often discover that other people have similar
     problems, which can at the least be comforting.
*   Clients learn to make effective use of other people, not
     just professionals, as helping agents. They can set up a
     mutual support group which is less demanding on the
     counsellor and likely to be a boost to their self-esteem
     when they discover they can manage to an increasing
     extent on their own.

There are many different kinds of group counselling. Some
careers services in higher education offer counsellor-led
groups as groundwork preparation for career choices; these
small groups give older adolescents an opportunity to
discuss the inter-relations between their conscious values
and preferred life styles and their crystallizing sense of
identity. Other groups are provided in schools where young
people can discuss with each other and an adult counsellor
those relationships with parents and friends which are so
important in adolescence. Training groups are held for
teaching decision-making skills and assertive skills. There
are also groups in which experiences are pooled and mutual
help given for the married, for parents, for those bringing
up families alone and for those who share a special problem
such as having a handicapped child. All these types of
groups are usually led by someone who has had training and
experience in facilitating them. The word 'facilitating' is
used advisedly, for the leader's job is not to conduct a
seminar or tutorial, but to establish an atmosphere in which

members of the group can explore the feelings around a particular stage of development or condition or critical choice.

Another type of group is not so specifically focussed on an area of common concern but is set up as a sort of laboratory to learn about the underlying dynamics of how people in groups function, whatever the group's focus and purpose may be. These are often referred to as sensitivity training groups (e.g. Cooper and Mangham, 1971; Smith, 1975). Yet a third category of group has more therapeutic goals, being intended to be successive or complementary to, or sometimes in place of, individual psychotherapy. This type of group will not usually have a place in work settings, whereas the other two do have useful applications there. Obvious uses for this type of group occur in induction procedures, in preparation for retirement, in relation to job change arising from promotion, or in relation to redundancy. The second type of group is employed in training for supervisory or management posts, though one hears less about their use in trade unions.

Schools of counselling
Differences in theories of personality, learning and perception are reflected in counselling theory. It is useful to distinguish between five major schools.

1. Psychoanalytic approaches were historically the first. Psychoanalysis is a personality theory, a philosophical system, and a method of psychotherapy. Concentrating on the past history of a patient, understanding the internal dynamics of the psyche, and the relationship between the client and the therapist are all key concerns for psycho-analysis. Key figures include Freud, Jung, Adler, Sullivan, Horney, Fromm and Erikson.

2. Client-centred approaches are based upon the work of Rogers, originally as a non-directive therapy developed as a reaction against psychoanalysis. Founded on a subjective view of human experiencing, it places more faith in and gives more responsibility to the client in problem-solving. The techniques of client-centred counselling have become the basis for most counselling skills training, following the empirical evaluations by Truax and Carkhuff (1967).

3. Behavioural approaches arise from attempts to apply the principles of learning to the resolution of specific behavioural disorders. Results are subject to continual experimentation and refinement. Key figures include Wolpe, Eysenck, Lazarus and Krumboltz.

4. Cognitive approaches include 'rational-emotive therapy' (Ellis), 'transactional analysis' (Berne) and 'reality therapy' (Glasser), along with Meichenbaum's work on cognitive rehearsal and inoculation. All have in common the belief that people's problems are created by how they

conceptualize their worlds: change the concepts and feelings will change too.

5. Affective approaches include 'Gestalt therapy' (Perls), 'primal therapy' (Janov), 're-evaluation counselling' (Jackins), and 'bioenergetics' (Lowen). These have in comm the belief that pain and distress accumulate and have to be discharged in some way before the person can become whole think clearly again.

There are many other approaches and orientations. The existential-humanistic school is exemplified by May, Maslow Frankl and Jourard. Encounter approaches have been develop by Schutz, Bindrim and Ichazo, 'psychosynthesis' by Assagioli, 'morita therapy' by Morita, and 'eclectic psychotherapy' by Thorne. In the United Kingdom the biggest influence on counsellor training has been from the client-centred school. Behavioural approaches are becoming more common and, to a lesser extent, so are transactional analysis, Gestalt therapy and re-evaluation counselling.

Where does counselling take place?

Until recently counselling was assumed to take place in the confines of a counsellor's office. This is changing rapidly. It is now increasingly accepted that effective counselling, as defined in this chapter, can take place on the shop floor, in the school corridor, even on a bus. The process is not made any easier by difficult surroundings, but when people need help, the helpers are not always in a position to choose from where they would like to administer it. Initial contacts are often made in these kinds of environment, and more intensive counselling can always be schedule for a later date in a more amenable setting.

What are the goals of counselling?

Counselling is a process through which a person attains a higher stage of personal competence. It is always about change. Katz (1969) has said that counselling is concerned not with helping people to make wise decisions but with helping them to make decisions wisely. It has as its goal self-empowerment: that is, the individual's ability to move through the following stages.

* 'I am not happy with things at the moment'
* 'What I would prefer is ...'
* 'What I need to do to achieve that is ...'
* 'I have changed what I can, and have come to terms, for the moment, with what I cannot achieve'.

Counselling has as an ultimate goal the eventual redundancy of the helper, and the activity should discourage dependency and subjection. It promotes situations in which the person's views and feelings are heard, respected and not judged. It builds personal strength, confidence and invites initiative and growth. It develops the individual and encourages control of self and situations. Counselling obviously works for the formation of more capable and effective individuals, through working with people singly or in groups.

In its goals it stands alongside other approaches concerned with personal and human development. All can see how desirable would be the stage when more competent, 'healthier' individuals would live more positively and more humanly. Counselling may share its goals in terms of what it wants for individuals; where it does differ from other approaches is in its method of achieving that. It concentrates on the individual - alone or in a group - and on one form of helping. Some other approaches would work for the same goals but would advocate different methods of achieving them. It is important to explore the inter-relatedness of counselling and other forms of helping as a way of asking, 'If we are clear about what we want for people, are we being as effective as we could be in achieving it?'

ounselling outcomes

This chapter has defined the ultimate outcome of counselling as 'helping people to help themselves'. A natural question to follow might be, 'to help themselves to do what?' There follows a list of counselling outcomes most frequently asked for by clients:

* increased understanding of oneself or a situation;
* achieving a change in the way one is feeling;
* being able to make a decision;
* confirming a decision;
* getting support for a decision;
* being able to change a situation;
* adjusting to a situation that is not going to change;
* the discharge of feelings;
* examining options and choosing one (Scally and Hopson, 1979).

Clients sometimes want other outcomes which are not those of counselling but stem from one or more of the other forms of helping: information, new skills, or practical help.

All of these outcomes have in common the concept of change. All counselling is about change. Given any issue or problem a person always has four possible strategies to deal with it:

* change the situation;
* change oneself to adapt to the situation;
* exit from it;
* develop ways of living with it.

s counselling the best vay of helping people?

In the quest for more autonomous, more self-competent, self-sufficient individuals the helper is faced with the question 'If that is my goal, am I working in the most effective way

towards achieving it?' As much as one believes in the poten
tial of counselling, there are times when one must ask
whether spending time with individuals is the best
investment of one's helping time and effort.

Many counsellors say that time spent in this way is
incredibly valuable; it emphasizes the importance of each
individual, and hence they justify time given to one-to-one
counselling. At the other end of the spectrum there are
those who charge 'counsellors' with:

* being concerned solely with 'casualties', people in
  crisis and in difficulty, and not getting involved with
  organizational questions;
* allowing systems, organizations and structures to
  continue to operate 'unhealthily', by 'treating' these
  'casualties' so effectively.

To reject these charges out-of-hand would be to fail to
recognize the elements of truth they contain. One respects
tremendously the importance that counselling places on the
individual, and this is not an attempt to challenge that.
What it may be relevant to establish is that counselling
should not be seen as a substitute for 'healthy' systems,
which operate in ways which respect individuality, where
relationships are genuine and positive, where communication
is open and problem-solving and participation are worked at
(see figure 2). 'Healthy' systems can be as important to the
welfare of the individual as can one-to-one counselling. It
is unfortunate therefore that 'administrators' can see personal welfare as being the province of 'counselling types',
and the latter are sometimes reluctant to 'contaminate'
their work by getting involved in administrational or
organizational matters. These attitudes can be very detrimental to all involved systems. The viewpoint presented here
is that part of a helper's repertoire of skills in the 'tool-
bag' alongside counselling skills should be willingness, and
the ability, to work for systems change. Some counsellors
obviously do this already in more spontaneous ways; for
example, if one finds oneself counselling truants, it may
become apparent that some absconding is invited by timetable anomalies (French for remedial groups on Friday
afternoons?). The dilemma here is whether one spends
time with a series of individual truants or persuades the
designers of timetables to establish a more aware approach.

One realizes sometimes also that one may, in counselling, be using one's skills in such a way that individuals
accept outcomes which possibly should not be accepted. For
example, unemployment specialists in careers services sometimes see themselves as being used by 'the system' to help
black youths come to terms with being disadvantaged. Such
specialists ask whether this is their role or whether they
should in fact be involved politically and actively in
working for social and economic change.

Resistance to the idea of becoming more involved in
'systems' and 'power structures' may not simply be based

upon a reluctance to take on extra, unattractive work. Some will genuinely feel that this approach is 'political' and therefore somehow tainted and dubious. It is interesting that in the USA during the last five years there has been a significant shift in opinion towards counsellors becoming more ready to accept the need to be involved in influencing systems:

> Their work brings them face to face with the victim of poverty; or racism, sexism, and stigmatization; of political, economic and social systems that allow individuals to feel powerless and helpless; of governing structures that cut off communication and deny the need for responsiveness; of social norms that stifle individuality; of communities that let their members live in isolation from one another. In the face of these realities human service workers have no choice but to blame those victims or to see ways to change the environment (Lewis and Lewis, 1977).

In this country, perhaps a deeper analysis is needed of the 'contexts' in which we work as helpers.

Can counselling be political?

It is very interesting that in his recent book, Carl Rogers (Rogers, 1978) reviewing his own present position vis-à-vis counselling, indicates the revolutionary impact of much of his work as perceived by him in retrospect. Perhaps identifiable as the 'arch-individualist', Rogers signals now that he had not seen the full social impact of the values and the methodology he pioneered. He writes eloquently of his realization that much of his life and work has in fact been political, though previously he had not seen it in those terms. Counselling invites self-empowerment; it invites the individual to become aware and to take more control; it asks 'How would you like things to be?' and 'How will you make them like that?' That process is a very powerful one and has consequences that are likely to involve changing 'status quos'. Clearly processes that are about change, power, and control are 'political' (although not necessarily party political).

From this viewpoint counsellors are involved in politics already. As much as one may like there to be, there can really be no neutral ground. Opting out or not working for change is by definition maintaining the status quo. If the 'status quo' means an organization, systems or relationships which are insensitive, uncaring, manipulative, unjust, divisive, autocratic, or function in any way which damages the potential of the people who are part of them, then one cannot really turn one's back on the task of working for change. 'One is either part of the solution or part of the problem!' We have argued (Scally and Hopson, 1979) that counsellors have much to offer by balancing their one-to-one work with more direct and more skilled involvement in making systems more positive, growthful places in which to live and work.

To counsel or to teach?

Counselling is a process through which a person attains a higher level of personal competence. Recently, attacks have been made on the counselling approach by such widely differing adversaries as Illich (1973) and Carkhuff (Carkhuff and Berenson, 1976). They, and others, question what effect the existence of counsellors and therapists has had on human development as a whole. They maintain that, how benevolent the counselling relationship is felt to be by those involved, there are forces at work overall which are suspect. They suggest:

* that helpers largely answer their own needs, and consciously or unconsciously perpetuate dependency or inadequacy in clients;
* helping can be 'disabling' rather than 'enabling' because it often encourages dependency.

For counsellors to begin to answer such charges requires a self-analysis of their own objectives, methods and motives. They could begin by asking:

* how much of their counselling is done at the 'crisis' or 'problem' stage in their clients' lives?
* how much investment are they putting into 'prevention' rather than 'cure'?

To help somebody in crisis is an obvious task. It is, however, only one counselling option. If 'prevention' is better than 'cure' then maybe that is where the emphasis ought to be. Perhaps never before has there been more reason for individuals to feel 'in crisis'. Toffler (1970) has identified some likely personal and social consequences of living at a time of incredibly rapid change. Many, like Stonier (1979), are forecasting unparallelled technological developments over the next 30 years which will change our lives, especially our work patterns, dramatically. There are so many complex forces at work that it is not surprising that many people are feeling more anxious, unsure, pessimistic, unable to cope, depersonalized, and helpless. Helpers are at risk as much as any, but are likely to be faced with ever-increasing demands on their time and skills. Again, this requires a reassessment of approaches and priorities, which could suggest a greater concentration on the development of personal competence in our systems. We need to develop more 'skilled' (which is not the same as 'informed') individuals and thereby avert more personal difficulties and crisis. One view is that this, the developmental, educational, teaching approach, needs to involve more of those who now spend much time in one-to-one counselling; not to replace that work but to give balance to it.

Personal competence and self-empowerment, which are the 'goals' of counselling, can be understood in many ways. A recent movement has been to see competence as being achievable through skill development. 'Life skills' are becoming as large a band-wagon as counselling has become.

We are producing a series of Lifeskills Teaching Programmes (Hopson and Scally, 1980b) which cover a range of more generic personal skills: for example, 'How to be assertive rather than aggressive', 'How to make, maintain and end relationships', 'How to manage time effectively', 'How to be positive about oneself', 'How to make effective transitions', etc. (figure 3). The programmes attempt to break down the generalization of 'competence' into 'learnable' units, with the overall invitation that, by acquiring these skills, one can 'take charge of oneself and one's life'. We have the advantage, working in a training unit, of being able to work directly with teachers and youth workers on the skills this way. Aspy and Roebuck (1977) have identified that the most effective teachers are those who have, and demonstrate, a high respect for others, who are genuine, and display a high degree of empathy with their students. Many professional counsellors therefore should have the basic qualities required in teaching, and could make appreciable contributions by being involved in programmes in the community which encourage 'coping' and 'growth' skills. More personally skilled individuals could reduce the dependence, inadequacy and crises which are individually and collectively wasteful, and take up so much counselling time.

Towards a 'complete helper'

The argument here is for the development of more complete helpers, more 'all-rounders', with a range of skills and 'tool-bags' full of more varied helping equipment. It is possible to work to increase the level of skill in each particular helping technique and go for 'broader' rather than 'higher' skill development. This diagram (figure 5) could map out for individual helpers how they may want to plan their own development.

On a graph such as this an effective teacher may be placed typically along the line marked 'x'. A full-time counsellor working in a school or workplace may typically be indicated by the line marked 'o'. An organization-change consultant may typically be somewhere along the dotted line.

How much one wants to be involved in helping, at whatever level and in whatever form, obviously depends upon many factors. How much one sees helping as part of the roles one fills; how much helping is part of the job one does; how much one wants to be involved as a part-time activity; how much helping is consistent with one's values, politics and personality; all will have a bearing on where an individual may wish to be placed on the graph. One person may decide to specialize in a particular approach and develop sophisticated skills in that field. Another may go for a broader approach by developing skills from across the range. Yet another may at particular times develop new specialisms as a response to particular situations or as part of a personal career development.

Figure 5

Helpers' skills levels and possible approaches to increasing them
(What skills do I have and in which directions can I develop?)

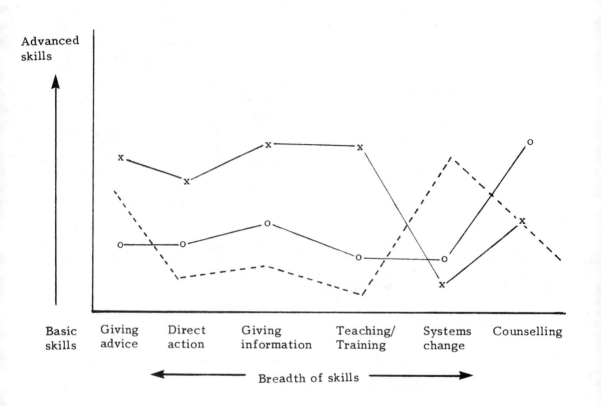

What is advocated here is that basic helping skills can be regarded as essential life skills. These skills can be made available to, and developed very fully in, professional helpers and in those for whom helping is part of their job specification in the workshop, in hospitals, in the social service agencies or in education. They can also be taught to young people in schools and at work.

Counselling in the UK

It is interesting that 'counselling' was a term rarely used in Britain until the mid-1960s. According to Vaughan's analysis (1976), three factors gradually tended to focus more attention on this area. One was the emergence throughout this century of a wider band of 'helping' professions, such as the Youth Employment Service, the social work services, and psychotherapy, as well as other 'caring' organizations, such as marriage guidance, and more recently such bodies as the Samaritans and Help the Aged. A second was the development of empirical psychology and sociology, which began to offer specific techniques for the analysis of personal difficulties; and a third was the rapid spread from about the mid-1960s onwards of the concept of counselling as a specific profession derived almost wholly from North America, where it had undergone a long evolution throughout the century from about 1910. Thus today we have a situation comparable in some ways to that of the development of primary education in Britain before the 1870 Act. A new area of specialization seems to be emerging.

It is just because a new area of specialization is developing that people already engaged in, or about to involve themselves in, counselling need to think carefully of where and how they wish to invest their time and resources. Counselling clearly is an important way of helping people, but it is not the only way.

References

Aspy, D.N. and Roebuck, F.N. (1977)
Kids Don't Learn from People They Don't Like. Amherst, Mass.: Human Resource Development Press.

Brammer, L.M. (1973)
The Helping Relationship. Englewood Cliffs, NJ: Prentice-Hall.

Carkhuff, R.R. (1974)
The Art of Helping. Amherst, Mass.: Human Resource Development Press.

Carkhuff, R.R. and Berenson, B.G. (1976)
Teaching As Treatment. Amherst, Mass.: Human Resource Development Press.

Cooper, C.L. and Mangham, I.L. (eds) (1971)
T-Groups: A survey of research. Chichester: Wiley.

Egan, G. (1975)
The Skilled Helper. Monterey, Ca: Brooks/Cole.

Hackney, H.L. and Nye, S. (1973)
Counseling Strategies and Objectives. Englewood Cliffs, NJ: Prentice-Hall.

Hopson, B. (1977)
Techniques and methods of counselling. In A.G. Watts (ed.), Counselling at Work. London: Bedford Square Press.

Hopson, B. and Scally, M. (1980a)
Lifeskills Teaching: Education for self-empowerment. Maidenhead: McGraw-Hill.

Hopson, B. and Scally, M. (1980b)
Lifeskills Teaching Programmes No. 1. Leeds: Lifeskills Associates.

Illich, I. (1973)
Tools of Conviviality. London: Calder & Boyars.

Illich, I., Zola, I.K., McKnight, J., Kaplan, J. and Sharken, H. (1977)
The Disabling Professions. London: Marion Boyars.

Ivey, A.E. (1971)
Microcounseling: Innovations in interviewing training. Springfield, Ill.: Thomas.

Kagan, N., Krathwohl, D.R. et al (1967)
Studies in Human Interaction: Interpersonal process recall stimulated by videotape. East Lansing, Mich.: Educational Publication Services, College of Education, Michigan State University.

Katz, M.R. (1969)
Can computers make guidance decisions for students? College Board Review, New York, No. 72.

Lewis, J. and Lewis, M. (1977)
Community Counseling: A human services approach. New York: Wiley.

Loughary, J.W. and Ripley, T.M. (1979)
Helping Others Help Themselves. New York: McGraw-Hill

Parloff, M.B., Waskow, I.E. and Wolfe, B. (1978)
Research on therapist variables in relation to process and outcome. In S.L. Garfield and A.E. Bergin (eds), Handbook of Psychotherapy and Behavior Change: An empirical analysis (2nd edn). New York: Wiley.

Raths, L., Harmin, M. and Simon, S. (1964)
Values and Teaching. Columbus, Ohio: Merrill.

Rogers, C.R. (1957)
The necessary and sufficient conditions of therapeutic personality change. Journal of Consulting Psychology, 21, 95-103.

Rogers, C.R. (1958)
The characteristics of a helping relationship. Personnel and Guidance Journal, 37, 6-16.

Rogers, C.R. (1978)
Carl Rogers on Personal Power. London: Constable.

Scally, M. and Hopson, B. (1979)
A Model of Helping and Counselling: Indications for training. Leeds: Counselling and Careers Development Unit, Leeds University.

Smith, P.B. (1975)
Controlled studies of the outcome of sensitivity training. Psychological Bulletin, 82, 597-622.

Stonier, T. (1979)
On the Future of Employment. N.U.T. guide to careers work. London: National Union of Teachers.

Toffler, A. (1970)
Future Shock. London: Bodley Head.

Truax, C.B. and Carkhuff, R.R. (1967)
Toward Effective Counselling and Psychotherapy: Training and practice. Chicago, Ill.: Aldine.

Vaughan, T. (ed.) (1976)
Concepts of Counselling. London: Bedford Square Press.

1. Distinguish counselling from other forms of helping.
2. How can counselling and helping be 'demystified'?
3. How large a part do you think counselling does and should play in your work?
4. Distinguish between counselling and counselling skills.
5. Who are 'the helpers'?
6. What makes people effective helpers?
7. Compare and contrast two different models of helping.
8. What in your opinion are the legitimate goals of helping and why?
9. How useful a concept is 'self-empowerment' in the context of helping?
10. What are the advantages and disadvantages of individual and group counselling techniques?

Annotated reading

Corey, G. (1977) Theory and Practice of Counseling and Psychotherapy. Monterey, Ca: Brooks/Cole.
    This contains an excellent review of all the schools of counselling described in the chapter. There is an accompanying workbook designed for students and tutor which gives self-inventories to aid students in identifying their own attitudes and beliefs, overviews of each major theory of counselling, questions for discussion and evaluation, case studies, exercises designed to sharpen specific counselling skills, out-of-class projects, group exercises, examples of client problems, an overview comparision of all models, ethical issues and problems to consider, and issues basic to the therapist's personal development.

Corsini, R. (ed.) (1977) Current Psychotherapies (2nd edn). Itasca, Ill.: Peacock Publications.
    An excellent introduction to the main schools of psychotherapy by leading practitioners who have been bullied to stick to the same format. Covers psychoanalysis, Adlerian, client-centred, analytical, rational-emotive therapy, transactional analysis, Gestalt, behavioural, reality, encounter, experiential and eclectic. Contributors include Carl Rogers, Albert Ellis, William Glasser, Alan Goldstein, Will Schutz and Rudolf Dreikurs.

Egan, G. (1975) The Skilled Helper. Monterey, Ca: Brooks/Cole.
    This text is now widely used in counselling skills training throughout the USA. It aims to teach the skills of attending, responding, stimulating and helping the client to act. It emphasizes the importance of teaching the same skills to clients as to counsellors. There is an accompanying training manual packed with group

exercises for the tutor to use to teach the skills in
Egan's model.

Vaughan, T.D. (ed.) (1975) Concepts of Counselling. British
Association for Counselling, London: Bedford Square Press.
A guide to the plethora of definitions of counselling.
Uneven, illuminating, with some useful descriptions of
developments in the UK.

Exercises

1. Facilitating skills

One of the characteristics of the counsellor as described by
Hopson is that of facilitating. That means enabling others
to talk freely about themselves. Think of someone you know
who is a 'good listener'. Observe that person interacting
with others. Before doing so make sure you have read the
chapter by Argyle on social behaviour. Is there anything
characteristic about the behaviour of your good listener?
Do these characteristics affect the ways in which other
people talk to them? Do you think you could use your observations as a guide for altering your own behaviour when
interacting with others, or even for setting up a 'listening
skills' course? Now think of someone you know whom you think
is a 'poor listener'. Repeat the exercise to determine
whether your poor listener has special characteristics which
contrast with those of the good listener.

2. People you would like to talk to

Imagine that something unpleasant has happened to you or
that you have done something of which you are ashamed.
Whatever it is causes you great anxiety and you feel a need
to get things off your chest. Make a list of people you know
and rank them for 'The person I could talk to best/second
best' and so on. Having ranked them, try to put your reasons
for ranking individuals high or low on the list. How much do
your comments reflect your views of yourself as well as of
the other person? Are there people who are low on your list
but might feature highly on the list of someone else you
know?

3. Problems with studying

This is a role-play exercise. The client is a student who is
having difficulty in reading, completing homework assignments, paying attention in classes or lectures, and meeting
deadlines. Since you are unlikely to be a total paragon of
virtue, there have probably been occasions when your own
work habits were not the most desirable, so you should be
able to manage this role. The counsellor provides a service
for students with this set of difficulties. The person
playing the counsellor role should read Hopson's chapter
carefully before preparing for the interview. It can be
useful for the client to prepare a briefing card. This may
take the following form.

You are 18 years of age. This is your final year at
school and you have some important examinations in two
months' time. There has been difficulty at home recently
because your younger brother has been staying out very
late at night, contrary to your parents' wishes. This
has caused a number of arguments and you have been drawn
in. Also, you have broken up with your girl/boyfriend
recently and you feel lonely as a result. You should
have handed in three essays by the end of last week, but
you find you cannot get down to work. As soon as you
open a book, your mind wanders and you start having
distracting thoughts. Things get worse and worse because
failing to get your work done makes you anxious. You
therefore start avoiding trying to work in order to
avoid feeling anxious. Things have entered a vicious
circle and you have decided you must go and see the
school counsellor. Your examinations are very important
to you because if you do well you will go to university,
which is something you have wanted to do for several
years.

If you have a third person who wishes to participate in
this exercise they can monitor the role-play and make notes
about the client and the counsellor to enable discussion
afterwards. Also, of course, you can change roles to see
what it is like to be the other person.

DE-ROLING. It is normal practice after a role-playing
exercise for the participants to 'de-role' themselves. This
involves making a clear statement saying who they are, why
they are present and that they are no longer the person they
have portrayed.

23

Institutional climates
Jim Orford

A person's behaviour is influenced by the surrounding
environment, as well as by attributes which the person
brings to that environment, such as personality, abilities
and attitudes; behaviour is a function of person and
environment. Many people either live or work in institutions
of one kind or another. For such people, the institution
constitutes an important part of their environment. For some
people it constitutes almost their total environment. Those
who work in an institutional setting cannot fail to notice
how the institution influences its members, either for good
or ill. Many will have felt frustrated by the values which
the institution seems to embody, or by the practices which
are prevalent within it, feeling that members could be
helped more if things were otherwise, or even that members
are being harmed by the institution. The great importance of
these matters has begun to be recognized in psychology and
there is a growing psychological literature on the organization of institutions and how to change them. The study of
institutions holds wider lessons for social psychology too.
An institution is a social psychological laboratory. The
experiments which take place there are naturally occurring
experiments in the psychology of social interaction, social
roles, intergroup attitudes, conflict and cohesiveness. The
study of institutions is of vital significance for both
theoretical and applied psychology.
Much of the literature on the subject concerns health
care or social service institutions such as mental hospitals
and hostels or homes for children, the elderly, or the
disabled. Although many of the examples upon which this
chapter draws are taken from such institutions, the chapter
attempts to build up a general picture of institutional life
which is equally as relevant, for example, to educational
institutions such as schools and colleges, and to penal institutions such as prisons and detention centres. These different institutions have a great deal in common. Each is a
collection of people, gathered together in a special building or group of buildings. These people are not normally
linked by family ties, but are there because of the special
'needs' (for education, care, treatment, rehabilitation, or
punishment) of inmates, users, or 'clients' (pupils, members, patients, residents). It is the responsibility of

another group of people, the staff, to provide for the clients' needs. This they are in a position to do on account of their special training, skills, or occupation (as teacher, prison officer, warden, doctor or nurse). Usually the institution has been set up by, and is part of, a larger organization which is responsible for managing the institution. Penal institutions in Britain are governed by the complex machinery of the Home Office; hospitals by the Department of Health and its network of Regional, Area and District Authorities, each with a complex system of members, officers and management teams; local authority schools and homes by committees and sub-committees of elected and co-opted representatives, the Authority's officers and the institution's committee of governors or managers; and institutions run by voluntary bodies by their trustees and management committees. Institutions are almost always influenced by people, often a large number of them, who have control over the institution but who are not involved in day-to-day work with the institution's clients. It is more than purely academic to consider some of these defining features of human service institutions. They immediately suggest ways in which an institution differs from a person's own home, and hence they indicate where some problems with institutions are to be expected. The small family home provides the clearest contrast to the large residential institution. People are not gathered together in the former on account of their special needs or their special qualifications, there is no demarcation between staff and clients, and the influence of outside organizations is minimal. It is no wonder that a great deal of thought and effort has been devoted to the goal of making institutions as normal and home-like as possible. Many other comparisons and contrasts between organizations and groups could be made, and there is no absolute definition of an institution.

eal types: the total stitution and the erapeutic community

It is important to be clear what is meant by a 'total institution' and by the term 'therapeutic community'. They are important ideas which have had much influence but as terms they are liable to be used loosely, and hence may obscure rather than reveal the true facts about institutional climates. In a much-read and often-quoted collection of essays, Goffman (1961) noted that it is normal in modern society for people to conduct different aspects of their life, for example sleeping, playing and working, in different places, with different people, and under different authorities. Total institutions, in contrast, are places where these barriers between different spheres of life are broken down. All aspects of life are conducted in the same place and, most importantly, under the same single authority. It is quite likely that activities are tightly scheduled by those in authority in accordance with an overall plan. He noted that many penal and caring institutions were total institutions in this sense. So were a number of places, with which this chapter is less concerned, such as army barracks, ships and monasteries. On the other hand, certain places with which we are concerned, such as day schools and day hospitals or centres, would not qualify as total institutions.

It is also important to recognize the variety of climates which exist even within total institutions. Tizard, Sinclair and Clarke (1975) point out the danger of generalizing from studies of single institutions, such as Goffman's study of an American mental hospital. Used loosely, the expression 'total institution' can give rise to a misleading stereotype. There is now ample evidence, some of which is considered later in this chapter, that institutions vary greatly, and furthermore that individual institutions can be changed.

Nevertheless, the harm that institutions may do has increasingly been recognized. Barton (1959) has gone so far as to say that the symptoms of institutionalization are so well marked that they constitute a disease entity which he called 'institutional neurosis'. He has written:

> Institutional Neurosis is a disease characterized by apathy, lack of initiative, loss of interest ..., submissiveness, and sometimes no expression of feelings of resentment at harsh and unfair orders. There is also lack of interest in the future ..., a deterioration in personal habits ..., a loss of individuality, and a resigned acceptance that things will go on as they are.

The concept of the 'therapeutic community' is an important one because it represents one type of ideal contrasting markedly with the most inhumane or least therapeutic institutional climates. The model therapeutic community was the Henderson Unit at the Belmont Hospital in Surrey. The unit described by Maxwell Jones (1952) and studied by Rapoport (1960), was principally aimed at helping young adult psychiatric patients, many of whom had problems of repeated antisocial conduct and who were difficult to accommodate elsewhere. Amongst the ideals of the therapeutic community are an emphasis on active rehabilitation as opposed to custodialism; democratization, namely that decision making about the unit's affairs should be shared amongst staff and patients alike; permissiveness, that is, that distressing or deviant behaviour should be tolerated rather than repressed in the interests of institutional conformity; communalism, that is, that the climate should be informal without the development of highly specialized roles, and that relationships should be close but never exclusive; and reality confrontation, that is, that patients should be continually given interpretations of their behaviour as other members of the unit see it. It is important to appreciate that the Henderson model is a very specific one. Structurally it was a total institution and although its climate was undoubtedly in contrast to that of many large impersonal institutions, in some ways it was rather formal, with a detailed programme of therapeutic and administrative groups, work assignments and other activities. Units are often self-styled 'therapeutic communities', but they are rarely aiming to recreate the type of therapeutic community unit described by Jones and Rapoport.

ructural features of stitutions

There are many separate features of institutions which contribute to climate and a number of these are considered in turn.

Size

There is considerable evidence that people prefer, and are more active socially in, small units of organization. One explanation for these findings is based on the idea of 'manning'. Where there are relatively few patients, pupils or residents, there are relatively many tasks and activities for them to undertake. There is much scope for involvement in activity; the setting may be said to be relatively under-manned. In contrast, settings with relatively many individuals may be over-manned, with relatively less opportunity for involvement for all.

This is perhaps why efforts are often made to break up an institution into smaller, more manageable, groups such as classes, houses or year groups in schools, and wards and small units within hospitals. Unfortunately, the overall institution may continue to exercise a strong influence on the smaller units that comprise it. One recent study (reported in Canter and Canter, 1979) found that staff working in institutions for handicapped children adopted more institution-orientated as opposed to child-orientated practices in looking after the children when their unit was part of a larger overall institution. The size of the unit itself was unimportant. Individual units within institutions are rarely fully autonomous but continue to be dependent on the larger institution in many ways. This notion of auto-nomy is an important one to which this chapter returns.

Location

Location is of both symbolic and concrete significance. The isolated mental hospital symbolizes community attitudes to the mentally ill, for example. Other features of institutions may symbolize a similar relationship between institution and community. Prisons are often located in cities but their isolation is ensured by their high walls and impenetrable, fortress-like entrances; they are in the community, but not of it. It is important to consider what factors are operating to promote closeness of contact between an institution and its local community, and what factors are operating to inhibit it. It is interesting to speculate, for example, on whether a prominent sign announcing that a house is a home for the elderly eases visiting by members of the community or makes it more difficult? Certainly many small residential caring units such as hostels and halfway houses pride themselves on carrying no such institutional signboard.

Ease of access to community facilities may be crucial for those who must remain in an institution for a long time. A lack of interest in, or desire to return to, life outside are considered by Barton and others to be amongst the main features of institutionalization, and he lists loss of contact with the outside world, loss of personal friends, and loss of prospects outside as three of its main causes.

The issue of location illustrates an important point about the psychology of social organizations. The point is that no single variable is independent of others, and consequently it is almost impossible to impute causal significance to single features of institutions. In this case, it is very unlikely that the location of an institution is independent of the philosophy or ideology under which it operates, or the attitudes of staff who work in it. A rehabilitation philosophy is likely to be associated with close community contacts, either because the institution was located close to the community in the first place, or because means had been found to overcome an unsatisfactory location.

Internal design

Large rooms with high ceilings, glossy interior wall paint in drab colours, no change of decor from one area to another, lack of personalization by the use of pictures, photographs and ornaments, lack of privacy, even sometimes extending to a bathroom and toilet, absence of individualized sleeping accommodation, few personal possessions or places to keep them, and generally an absence of opportunity to express individuality; these are amongst the internal design features of an institution which contribute to an institutional as opposed to homely atmosphere.

Once again, however, it is important to avoid over-simple ideas of cause and effect. Two examples from Canter and Canter's book (1979) on the influence of design in institutions illustrate this point. One example concerns the first several years' operation of a purpose-built unit for disturbed children. A number of features, such as outside play facilities, were designed by the architect with the express purpose of reducing institutional climate. Others, such as doors for bedrooms, were strongly advocated by the director and were eventually installed. Observation of the day-to-day life of the unit, however, led to the view that the overwhelming ideology of the unit, which placed emphasis on the children's disturbance and on the need for staff control and surveillance, undermined the use of these design features. Play facilities were rarely spontaneously used, bedroom doors were hardly ever closed, and rooms which were designed for personal use were used as seclusion rooms for punishment. The second example concerns a purpose-built forensic unit where it was possible to show, by a process of behaviour mapping (a procedure whereby a map of who does what and where is produced by observing samples of behaviour in different places at different times), the use to which different spaces were put and the meanings that became attached to them. Certain areas were clearly designated as staff offices, and others as patient lounges. As a result, segregation of staff and patients was the rule rather than the exception.

One small-scale feature of physical layout which is relatively easily manipulated is that of seating arrangement. The terms 'sociopetal' (meaning encouraging interpersonal relationships) and 'sociofugal' (discouraging relationships) have been used to describe possible seating arrangements in institutions. Seats in the lounge areas of old people's homes and other institutions are often arranged around the edge of the room or in some other sociofugal pattern, such as in rows facing a television set. Sociopetal patterns, on the other hand, have been found to lead to more interaction, more multi-person interaction, and more personal conversations. Once again, it is important to appreciate other, more human, aspects of the environment. It is often found, when attempts have been made to rearrange furniture in a more sociopetal fashion, that there is a tendency for the seating to revert to its former arrangement. It is as if the institution has a will of its own and is in some way resistant to change. Exploring how this reversion to type comes about, and making a diagnosis of what is to blame, may provide vital insights into the nature of the institution.

It is worth speculating on the function which may be served by furniture arrangement in different types of institution. For example, why is the seating arrangement of pupils in a primary school often very different from, and usually more sociopetal in design than, that to be found in a secondary school? Is this difference accidental, or does it say something about the expected relationship between teacher and pupils, and perhaps thereby about the whole underlying philosophy of education?

Rules, regulations and routines

Studies of institutional practices

Considerable progress has been made in describing the variety which exists within health and social care residential institutions. Similar variety exists within educational establishments, and within penal settings.

Studies have compared hostels and hospitals for mentally handicapped children, and have found the latter to be much more institutional in their handling of the children: routine is more rigid, children are more likely to be treated en bloc, treatment is less personalized, and social distance between staff and children is greater. Wide variation is found in the degree of 'ward restrictiveness' in adult mental hospitals. Similar variation exists in halfway houses for ex-psychiatric patients. On average, hostels are less institutional than mental hospitals, the former having between one-half and two-thirds the number of 'restrictive practices' found in the average hospital ward in one study. However, considerable variation is found in both types of facility and there is an overlap between them. Some of the hostels, whilst being small in size, and designed to provide a link between the large institution and the community, nevertheless retain a number of institutional practices. In one instance a hostel had more institutional practices than the hospital rehabilitation ward from which most of its residents came.

A key idea linking these studies is that of clients' decision making freedom. Table 1 provides an indication of some of the major areas of decision making considered in such studies. The list could be expanded greatly to include a large range of day-to-day activities over which most people are able to exercise personal choice. Whether an institution allows this exercise of choice to continue for its clients or whether these decision-making freedoms are curtailed is crucial in determining whether an institution creates a therapeutic climate or institutionalization.

Table 1

A range of decisions which may be allowed or restricted in institutions and which are illustrative of those considered in studies of institutional practices

What time to get up and go to bed
What to wear
What to eat for breakfast and other meals
Planning future meals
Whether to make a drink or snack
Whether to visit the local shops
Whether to go to work
Whether to go to the pictures
How to spend own money
When to have a bath
When to have a haircut
Whether to have medicine
Deciding arrangement of own room
Deciding decoration of own room
Whether to smoke
Whether to play the radio or TV
When to invite friends in
Whether to have a sexual relationship with a friend
Planning decoration or repair of the place
Deciding how to care for or control other members
Deciding policy

Staff autonomy
Reference has already been made, when considering the size of an institution, to the importance of a unit's autonomy

within the larger institution. Decision-making freedom may be limited not only for clients but also for those staff who have the closest dealings with them. The advantages of the informality which can occur in a truly independent small unit are illustrated by an incident which occurred at Woodley House, an American halfway house for the mentally ill. It concerned a dispute between pro- and anti-television factions in the house. The former decided to convert part of the basement of the house for their use, leaving the living room to the others. A staff member took them in her car to buy paint and other materials and later the same day the newly-decorated television room was in use. Such an incident could not easily occur in that way in a larger and more formal institution. There are a number of reasons for this, one being that the staff member at Woodley House was not limited to a prescribed professional role, and there were no other members of staff upon whose role territory she was trespassing.

It is this variable of staff autonomy which Tizard et al (1975) considered to be one of the strongest influences upon the quality of staff-client interaction in an institutional setting. The firmest evidence for this hypothesis is contained in a chapter of their book written by Barbara Tizard. It concerns residential nurseries run by voluntary societies. She observed 13 such units, all of which had been modernized in recent years to provide 'family group' care. Mixed-age groups of six children each had their own suite of rooms and their own nurse and assistant nurse to care for them. Despite this effort at 'de-institutionalizing', marked differences existed in the degree to which nurses were truly independent agents. Nurseries were divided by the research team into three classes on the basis of the amount of unit autonomy. The first group, it was felt, was in effect run centrally by the matron:

> Decisions were made on an entirely routine basis or else referred to the matron. Each day was strictly time-tabled, the matron would make frequent inspections of each group, and freedom of the nurse and child was very limited. The children were moved through the day 'en bloc' ... The nurse had little more autonomy than the children, e.g. she would have to ask permission to take the children for a walk or to turn on the television set. As in hospital each grade of staff wore a special uniform, and had separate living quarters, and the nurse's behaviour when off duty was governed by quite strict rules.

At the other extreme was a group of nurseries which more closely approximated a normal family setting:

> The staff were responsible for shopping, cooking, making excursions with the children and arranging their own day. The children could move freely about the house and garden and the staff rarely referred a decision to the

matron. The nurse-in-charge did not wear uniform, and her off-duty time was not subject to rules. Her role, in fact, approximated more closely to that of a foster-mother. Since she could plan her own day and was not under constant surveillance she could treat the children more flexibly.

A third group of nurseries was intermediate in terms of independence. As predicted, the more autonomous staff were observed to spend more time talking to children, and more time playing, reading and giving information to them. Furthermore, children in units with more autonomous staff had higher scores on a test of verbal comprehension. The difficulty of teasing out what is important in complex social situations, such as those that exist in institutions, is illustrated by Barbara Tizard's findings. Autonomy was correlated with having a relatively favourable staff-to-child ratio and hence we cannot be certain that autonomy is the crucial variable.

Nevertheless, an effect of staff hierarchy was noticed which could explain the apparent importance of autonomy. When two staff were present at once, one was always 'in charge'. This had an inhibiting effect on a nurse's behaviour towards children: she would function in a 'notably restricted way, talking much less and using less "informative talk" than the nurse in charge'. This might explain differences between autonomous and less independent units, as staff in the latter type of unit would be much more likely to feel that someone else was in charge whether that person was present or not.

Flexible use of space, time and objects
Inflexible routine is one of the major charges brought against the institution by such writers as Barton and Goffman. Institutional life can be 'normalized' as much as possible by allowing flexible use of different areas of buildings and grounds, by varying time schedules, and by allowing flexible use of objects such as kitchen and laundry equipment, televisions, radios and record players. Residential institutions usually deprive adult inmates of the opportunity to take part in 'complete activity cycles'. Instead of taking part in a complete cycle of shopping for food, preparing it, eating, clearing away and washing up after it, residents may simply be required to eat what others have purchased and prepared, rather like guests in a hotel.

Staff attitudes and behaviour

Ideology
The influence of an institution's ideology or philosophy is pervasive, although its significance can be missed altogether by those taken up in the day-to-day activities of the place. Many examples could be given. The philosophy of a progressive school such as Summerhill, with its emphasis

on personal development, is distinct from that of a regular
secondary school with its emphasis on academic learning. The
rehabilitation philosophy of Grendon Underwood prison is
distinct from that of most closed penal establishments with
their emphasis on custody. Many institutions have mixed and
competing ideologies. These frequently give rise to conflict
within the institution, the different ideologies often being
represented by different cadres of staff. For example,
educational and child care philosophies compete within
institutions for handicapped children, as do educational and
disciplinary philosophies within institutions for young
delinquents. Important shifts may take place gradually over
time. For example, a general shift from a custodial philosophy to a more therapeutic ideology has occurred in mental
hospitals over the last several decades. Quite recently some
of those working in British prisons have detected a move in
the opposite direction in response to the call for tighter
security.

Words such as 'open' to describe penal institutions,
'progressive' to describe educational facilities, and
expressions such as 'therapeutic community' to describe an
institution for residential care, all serve as public
announcements of ideology and intended behaviour. However,
it has already been noted that terms such as 'therapeutic
community' are frequently used loosely, and sufficient is
known about the absence of a strong correlation between
attitudes and behaviour to make us doubtful that ideal
philosophies will always be perfectly borne out in
practice.

Staff attitudes

Nevertheless, no one who has worked in an institution for
very long can have failed to notice what appear to be
marked individual differences in staff attitudes. In the
mental hospital setting questionnaires have been devised to
detect staff attitudes of 'custodialism' or 'tradition-
alism'. The matter is by no means simple, however, and
attitudes vary along a number of dimensions. For example,
one study distinguished between 'restrictive control' and
'protective benevolence'. Staff high on restrictive control
tended to be described as 'impatient with others' mistakes'
and 'hardboiled and critical', and not 'sensitive and
understanding' and 'open and honest with me'. Those high on
protective benevolence, on the other hand, were described
as 'stays by himself' and 'reserved and cool', and not 'lets
patients get to know him' and 'talks about a variety of
things'. Staff members high on this attitude scale expressed
attitudes that appeared to suggest kindliness towards
patients and yet they appear to have been seen by the latter
as basically aloof, distant and non-interacting.

A study of hostels for boys on probation also illustrates the complexity of the matter. This study examined the
relationship between failure rate, based on the percentage
of residents leaving as a result of absconding or being re-

convicted, and the attitudes of 16 different wardens. Two components of attitude were identified, each positively associated with success: strictness as opposed to permissiveness; and emotional closeness, which included warmth and willingness to discuss residents' problems with them, versus emotional distance. However, the two components, each separately associated with success, were negatively associated with one another. Hence wardens who displayed more warmth and willingness to discuss problems were also likely to be over-permissive, whilst those who were relatively strict tended to be lacking in emotional closeness. The ideal combination of warmth and firmness was a combination relatively rarely encountered.

Individual staff attitudes can partly be explained in terms of individual differences in general attitudes or personality: members of staff who are more generally authoritarian in personality tend to hold more custodial attitudes. This alone, however, cannot explain differences that are found between different institutions. Although the correspondence is far from complete, it has been found to be the case that where the prevailing policy is custodial, staff subscribe to a custodial view and tend to be generally authoritarian in personality. This raises the fascinating question of how such relative uniformity comes about. It can be presumed that the same three main processes are at work as those that operate to produce consensus and similarity of attitude in any social group or organization. The three processes are (i) selection-in, (ii) selection-out, and (iii) attitude change. Selection of new staff will most likely operate in a way that increases uniformity of attitude, both because certain people are more attracted than others by the prospect of working in a particular institution, and also because certain potential staff members are thought more suitable by those responsible for the selection (selection-in). Staff remain in one place for a variable length of time, and the institution may retain for longer periods those members whose attitudes are in conformity with the prevailing ideology (selection-out).

As social psychological experiments on conformity show so clearly, it is difficult to maintain a non-conformist position in the face of combined opinion, and the third process - attitude change - is likely to be a strong factor.

Staff behaviour and staff-client social distance
Although research leads us to expect none too close a correspondence between attitudes and behaviour, a number of studies in institutions suggest that philosophy and attitudes can be conveyed to residents via staff behaviour. Studies of units for handicapped children, for autistic children, and for the adult mentally ill, suggest that staff behaviour towards clients is more personal, warmer and less rejecting or critical when management practices are more client-orientated and less institution-orientated. Large

differences have also been detected in the amount of time which staff members in charge of hostel units spend in face-to-face contact with their residents. Sharing space and activities together, and spending relatively more time in contact with one another, may be the most important factors in reducing social distance.

Social distance between staff and clients was an important concept in Goffman's and Barton's analyses of institutions. Avoidance, or reduced time in contact, is a fairly universal indication of lack of affection and often of prejudiced and stereotyped attitudes. There are numerous means of preserving social distance including designation of separate spaces, such as staff offices. A clearly designated staff office makes staff and client separation easier, but such a space may be used in a variety of different ways. The door may be kept open, or closed, or even locked with a key only available to staff.

Controversy often surrounds the wearing of staff uniform in institutions. There are arguments for and against, but inevitably the uniform creates or reinforces a distinction and may therefore increase social distance. A movement away from the traditional institutional organization is very frequently accompanied by the abandonment of uniforms where these previously existed. The use of names and titles in addressing different members of a community is another indication of the presence or absence of social distance. Forms of address are known to be good signs of both solidarity and status within social groups. The reciprocal use of first names is a sign of relative intimacy, and the reciprocal use of titles (Mr, Mrs, etc.) a sign of distance. Non-reciprocal forms of address, on the other hand, are indications of a status difference, with the person of higher status almost always using the more familiar form of address (say a first name or nickname) in addressing the person of lower status, and the latter using title and surname towards the former, or even a form of address which clearly indicates the former's superior status (sir, boss, etc.). If forms of address change as people get to know one another better, it is usually the person of higher status who initiates the use of familiar forms of address first.

Hence an examination of a particular institution in terms of designated spaces for staff and others, uniforms and other visual indications of role or rank, and of forms of address, can give useful clues to status divisions and social distance within the institution. However, it is of the utmost importance to keep in mind that social distance, like all of the social psychological features of institutions considered here, is a highly complex matter. It has been suggested, for example, that there are at least two distinct forms of social distance, namely status distance and personal distance. If these aspects of social distance are relatively independent, as has been suggested, it follows that status distance need not necessarily preclude the formation of a personally close relationship.

Institutions as complex systems

The client contribution

Staff may be crucial determinants of climate, particularly senior staff, but so too are the institution's users or clients. The climate in an institution is the product of a bewildering complexity of factors which interact in ways that are far from straightforward. No simple theory which attempts to explain what goes on inside an institution in terms of physical design alone, of the attitudes of senior staff alone, or of management practices alone, can do justice to them. It would be as faulty to ignore the personalities, abilities and disabilities of the users as it would be to ignore the philosophy of the institution or the design of its buildings. This point is forcefully brought home in Miller and Gwynne's (1972) account of homes catering for people with irreversible and severe physical handicaps where the most likely termination of residence is death. They contrasted two ideologies which they believed existed in such institutions: the 'warehousing' philosophy, with its emphasis upon physical care and the dependence of residents; and the 'horticultural' philosophy, with its emphasis on the cultivation of residents' interests and abilities. They stress that each has dangers - the one of dependence and institutionalization, the other of unrealistic expectations being set - and that each is a response to the serious nature of the residents' handicaps.

There are a number of studies of social behaviour on the wards of mental hospitals which prove the point that social climate depends upon the mix of patients who are residing there. A clear instance was provided by Fairweather's (1964) study which is described more fully below. Introducing changes of a progressive nature on a hospital ward increased the level of social interaction generally but significant differences between different patient groups still persisted, with non-psychotic patients interacting most, acute psychotic patients an intermediate amount, and chronic psychotic patients the least. The mix of clients is especially crucial where group influence is considered to be one of the principal media of change (whether the change desired be educational, therapeutic or rehabilitative). Even in the relatively permissive climate of the Henderson therapeutic community, those with particularly socially disruptive personalities cannot be tolerated and, if accidentally admitted, may have to be discharged.

Under circumstances where group influence operates, it is particularly important that the client group exerts its main influence in a manner consistent with the overriding philosophy espoused by staff. This is always in danger of going wrong in secondary schools where the 'adolescent sub-culture' may exert a countervailing force, and in prisons where the 'inmate code' has to be contended with. In Canadian schools and centres for juvenile delinquents a procedure known as the 'Measurement of Treatment Potential' (MTP) has been in use to assess this aspect of climate. Where clients choose as liked fellow clients the same members as those whose behaviour is approved of by staff, then treatment potential is considered to be high. When there is a mismatch between residents' and staff choices, treatment potential is said to be low.

Climate

Many factors contributing to climate have been considered in this chapter and there are many others which it has not been possible to consider. Repeatedly emphasized has been the complex way in which these factors interact to influence the climate of an institutional unit. 'Climate', a word used here to cover any perceptions of, or feelings about, the institution held by those who use it, work in it or observe it, is not the same thing as success, effectiveness, or productivity. However, the latter are notoriously difficult to define, let alone measure, whereas people's perceptions of atmosphere can be collected and their relationships with features of the institution analysed. A massive programme of research along these lines has been conducted by Moos (1974). He has devised a series of questionnaires to tap the perceptions of members of various types of institutions and organizations. The most thoroughly tested of these scales is the Ward Atmosphere Scale (WAS), which assesses perceptions along the ten dimensions shown in table 2. This list was based upon earlier research by others as well as a great deal of preliminary work of Moos' own. He claims that dimensions 1-3 (the relationship dimensions) and 8-10 (the system maintenance and system change dimensions) are equally relevant across a wide range of institutions including schools, universities, hospitals and penal institutions. Dimensions 4-7 (the personal development dimensions), on the other hand, need modification depending upon the setting.

Amongst the many findings from research based upon the WAS and similar scales are the following. First, when staff and patient perceptions are compared in hospital treatment settings, average staff scores are regularly found to be higher on all dimensions except Order and Organization (no difference between staff and patients), and Staff Control (patients scoring higher than staff). Second, when scores are correlated with size of unit and with staff-to-patient ratio, it has been found that Support and Spontaneity are both lower and Staff Control is higher where patient numbers are greater and staff-to-patient ratios are poorer (MTP has also been found to correlate with smallness of size and favourability of staff to pupil ratios). Third, where patients have greater 'adult status' (access to bedrooms, television, unrestricted smoking, less institutional admission procedure, etc.), Spontaneity, Autonomy, Personal Problem Orientation, and Anger and Aggression are all higher and Staff Control is lower. Fourth, all scales correlate positively with ratings of general satisfaction with the ward and with ratings of liking for staff, with the exception of Staff Control which correlates negatively with both.

Table 2

The 10 dimensions measured by Moos' Ward Atmosphere Scale

RELATIONSHIP DIMENSIONS

1. Involvement measures how active and energetic patients are in the day-to-day social functioning of the ward. Attitudes such as pride in the ward, feelings of group spirit, and general enthusiasm are also assessed.

2. Support measures how helpful and supportive patients are towards other patients, how well the staff understand patient needs and are willing to help and encourage patients, and how encouraging and considerate doctors are towards patients.

3. Spontaneity measures the extent to which the environment encourages patients to act openly and to express freely their feelings towards other patients and staff.

PERSONAL DEVELOPMENT DIMENSIONS

4. Autonomy assesses how self-sufficient and independent patients are encouraged to be in their personal affairs and in their relationships with staff, and how much responsibility and self-direction patients are encouraged to exercise.

5. Practical Orientation assesses the extent to which the patient's environment orients him towards preparing himself for release from the hospital and for the future.

6. Personal Problem Orientation measures the extent to which patients are encouraged to be concerned with their feelings and problems and to seek to understand them through openly talking to other patients and staff about themselves and their past.

7. Anger and Aggression measures the extent to which a patient is allowed and encouraged to argue with patients and staff, and to become openly angry.

SYSTEM MAINTENANCE AND SYSTEM CHANGE DIMENSIONS

8. Order and Organization measures the importance of order on the ward; also measures organization in terms of patients (do they follow a regular schedule and do they have carefully planned activities?) and staff (do they keep appointments and do they help patients follow schedules?)

9. Programme Clarity measures the extent to which the patient knows what to expect in the day-to-day routine of the ward and how explicit the ward rules and procedures are.

10. Staff Control measures the necessity for the staff to restrict patients: that is, the strictness of rules, schedules and regulations, and measures taken to keep patients under effective control.

Changing institutions   A knowledge of the factors discussed in this chapter should enable those involved in policy, planning and management to generate ideas for constructive change, and those in relatively junior positions to try and bring about change in their practice within the prevailing limits of autonomy. However, major changes may require innovations or interventions from outside and it is these that are now discussed in the remainder of this chapter.

Innovative programmes

One of the best documented programmes of institutional change in the mental health care system is the work reported in a series of publications by Fairweather and his colleagues. The first report (Fairweather, 1964) described dramatic differences in patient social behaviour between an experimental 'small group' ward and a physically identical 'traditional' ward in a mental hospital. In the traditional ward, staff members made final decisions on all important matters. By contrast, on the small group ward it was the responsibility of a group of patients to orient new fellow patients to the ward, to carry out work assignments, to assess patient progress, and to recommend privileges and even final discharge. The total experiment lasted for six months, and staff switched wards halfway through. Social activity was at a much higher level on the small group ward, and the climate in the daily ward meeting was quite different with more silence and staff control on the traditional ward, and more lively discussion, less staff talk, and many more patient remarks directed towards fellow patients on the small group ward. Nursing and other staff evaluated their experience on the small group ward more highly, and patients spent significantly fewer days in hospital.

In a further report, Fairweather, Sanders, Cressler and Maynard (1969) compared the community adjustment of ex-patients who moved together as a group from a small group ward in the hospital to a small hostel unit in the community (the 'lodge'), and others who moved out of the hospital in the normal way. The results were quite dramatic, with the lodge group surviving much better in the community in terms of the prevention of re-admission to hospital, the amount of time in work (much of which was organized by the ex-patient group as a consortium), and residents' morale and self-esteem. This is a particularly good example of the setting-up from scratch of a new small institution designed to avoid many of the most disagreeable features of large institutions.

Changes in the philosophies and modes of practice in institutions mostly take place over a period of years as a result of the slow diffusion of new ideas. A third report by Fairweather, Sanders and Tornatsky (1974) was concerned with this process. Having established the value of the lodge programme, they set out to sell the idea to mental hospitals throughout the USA. They were concerned to know the influence of a number of variables upon the diffusion process, and consequently adopted a rigorous experimental approach. First, they varied the degree of effort required on the part of the hospital contacted in order to accept the initial approach offered. Of 255 hospitals contacted, one-third were merely offered a brochure describing the lodge programme per cent accepted but only 5 per cent finally adopted the lodge programme), one-third were offered a two-hour work about the programme (80 per cent accepted and 12 per cer finally adopted), and one-third were offered help with setting up a demonstration small group ward in the hospital fo a minimum of 90 days (only 25 per cent accepted but 11 p cent finally adopted the lodge). A second variable was the position in the hospital hierarchy of the person contacted with the initial approach offer. One-fifth of initial contacts were made to hospital superintendents and one-fifth t each of the four professions, psychiatry, psychology, socia work and nursing. This variable turned out to be relatively unimportant: contacts were just as likely to result in the adoption of the lodge programme when they were made to people in nursing as to superintendents or those in psychiatry.

Much more important than the status of the person wh initiates an idea is, according to Fairweather et al, a high level of involvement across disciplines, professions, and social status levels within the institution. When change did occur there was most likely to exist a multi-disciplinary group which spearheaded the change, led by a person who continuously pushed for change and attempted to keep the group organized and its morale high. The disciplinary group to which this person belonged was of little importance. Nor was change related to financial resources. The need for perseverance is stressed. The need to keep pushing for change despite 'meetings that came to naught, letters that stimulated nothing, telephone calls unreturned, and promise unkept' is a necessary ingredient of institutional change.

Action research
Fairweather's studies concerned the setting-up of new facilities or units. If, on the other hand, constructive change is to be brought about in existing institutions and their units, the total climate of the institution, and particularly the autonomy of the individual staff members, are limiting factors. A number of schemes have been described for providing helpful intervention from outside in the form of a person or team who act as catalysts or chang agents. Several of these involve the process known as Actio Research. For example, Towell and Harries (1979) have des cribed a number of changes brought about at Fulbourne psychiatric hospital in Cambridgeshire with the help of a specially appointed 'social research adviser'.

The process begins when the interventionist(s) is invited to a particular unit to advise or help. It is stressed that the initiative should come from the unit and not from the interventionist, although it is clearly necessary for the latter to advertise the service being offered, and Moos (1974), for example, has argued that feeding back research data on social climate can itself initiate a change process. After the initial approach there follows a period during

which the action researcher gets to know the unit, usually
by interviewing as many members as possible individually, by
attending unit meetings, and by spending time in the unit
observing. Then follow the stages which give 'action
research' its name. With the help of the action researcher,
members of the unit (usually the staff group collectively)
decide upon a piece of research which can be quickly mounted
and carried through and which is relevant to the matter in
hand. The results of this research are then used to help
decide what changes are necessary. The action researcher
remains involved during these phases and subsequently as
attempts are made to implement changes and to make them
permanent.

For example, one of the Fulbourne projects concerned a
long-stay ward which had adopted an 'open door', no-staff-
uniforms policy and which was designated as suitable for
trainee nurses to gain 'rehabilitation experience'. The
staff, however, felt 'forgotten' at the back of the hospital, felt that scope for patient improvement was not often
realized, and that they were unable to provide the rehabilitation experience intended. The social research adviser
helped the staff devise a simple interview schedule which
focussed on such matters as how patients passed their time,
friendships among patients, and feelings patients had about
staff and their work. Each member of staff was responsible
for carrying out certain interviews and for writing them up
and presenting them to the group. All reports were read by
all members of staff and discussed at a special meeting.
The group reached a consensus that patients were insular,
took little initiative, expected to be led by staff, had no
idea of 'self-help', saw little treatment function for the
nurses, saw little purposeful nurse-patient interaction,
and had only negative feelings, if any, towards fellow
patients.

Although there were no immediate or dramatic changes,
a slow development over a period of 18 months was reported
in the direction of a much increased 'counselling approach
to care'. The research interview was incorporated into
routine care. This itself involved the setting-up of a
special contact between individual nurse and individual
patient, a factor which is mentioned in other projects
described by Towell and Harries and by many other writers
who have described constructive changes in institutions. At
first the social research adviser took a leading role in
groups in helping to understand the material gathered in
interviews. This role was later taken over by the ward
doctor and later still by a senior member of the nursing staf
At this point the social research adviser withdrew. Later on
patients read back interview reports and there were many
other signs of reduced staff and patient distance. Over the
three-year period during which these changes came about, the
number of patients resettled outside the hospital increased
from two in the first year to eight in the second and eleven
in the third.

It is stressed by those who have described 'action research' and schemes like it, such as 'administrative consultation' and the type of social systems change facilitated by a consultant described by Maxwell Jones (1976), that staff of a unit must be fully involved and identified with any change that is attempted. It is relatively easy to bring about acceptance of change on an attitudinal level, largely through talking, but to produce a behavioural commitment to change is something else. Those who have writ of the 'action research' process talk of the importance of 'ownership' of the research activity. The aim is to get the unit's members fully involved and to make them feel the research is theirs.

Resistance to change

We should expect such complex social systems, whose mode of operation must have been arrived at because it serves certain needs or produces certain pay-offs for those involved, to be resistant to change. Particularly should we expect it to be resistant to change when this threatens to involve change in status and role relationships. Unfortunately, it is just such changes for which we so frequently search. The themes of decision-making autonomy and social power have been constant ones throughout this chapter; the lie at the heart of what is wrong with many of the worst institutions. Maxwell Jones (1976) believes it is almost always the required task of the social systems facilitator to 'flatten' the authority hierarchy, and to support lower status members in taking the risks involved in expressing their feelings and opinions, whilst at the same time supporting higher status members in the belief that they can change in the direction of relinquishing some of their authority.

As in most earlier sections of this chapter, examples o attempts to change institutions or parts of institutions have been taken from the mental health field. Nevertheless the processes and problems involved can be recognized by those whose main concern is with other types of institution such as the, educational and penal. In particular, those who have in any way, large or small, attempted to change such institutions can recognize the problem of resistance to change. Nothing illustrates better the need to add to our understanding of how institutions work. In the process of finding out more on this topic we learn more of Man in a social context, which is part of the central core of the study of psychology.

References

Barton, R. (1959; 3rd edn, 1976)
    Institutional Neurosis. Bristol: Wright.
Canter, D. and Canter, S. (eds) (1979)
    Designing for Therapeutic Environments: A review of research. Chichester: Wiley.

Fairweather, G.W. (ed.) (1964)
Social Psychology in Treating Mental Illness. New York:
Wiley.

Fairweather, G.W., Sanders, D.H., Cressler, D.L. and Maynard, H. (1969)
Community Life for the Mentally Ill: An alternative to
institutional care. Chicago, Ill.: Aldine.

Fairweather, G.W., Sanders, D.H. and Tornatsky, L.G. (1974)
Creating Change in Mental Health Organizations. New
York: Pergamon.

Goffman, E. (1961)
Asylums: Essays on the social situation of mental
patients and other inmates. New York: Anchor Books,
Doubleday.

Jones, Maxwell (1952)
Social Psychiatry: A study of therapeutic communities.
London: Tavistock. (Published as The Therapeutic
Community, New York: Basic Books: 1953.)

Jones, Maxwell (1976)
Maturation of the Therapeutic Community: An organic
approach to health and mental health. New York: Human
Sciences Press.

Miller, E.J. and Gwynne, G.V. (1972)
In Life Apart: A pilot study of residential institutions
for the physically handicapped and the young chronic
sick. London: Tavistock.

Moos, R.H. (1974)
Evaluating Treatment Environments: A social ecological
approach. New York: Wiley.

Rapoport, R.M. (1960)
Community as Doctor: New perspectives on a therapeutic
community. London: Tavistock.

Tizard, J., Sinclair, I. and Clarke, R.V.G. (eds) (1975)
Varieties of Residential Experience. London: Routledge &
Kegan Paul.

Towell, D. and Harries, C. (1979)
Innovations in Patient Care. London: Croom Helm.

uestions

1. Give two different definitions of 'institution' and give
   examples of places which fit both definitions, which fit
   one but not the other, and which fit neither.
2. What do you understand by the term 'total institution'?
   Why is it thought that they may do harm?
3. What principles are embodied in a proper Therapeutic
   Community? Is it possible in your view to say when these
   have been achieved, and when not?
4. What structural features contribute to the climate of an
   institution, and why?
5. How can the internal design of an institutional unit be
   changed to bring about change in the behaviour of those
   who live or work in it?

6. Discuss the proposition that the most important thing t change in an institution is staff attitudes.
7. Are staff more important than the users or residents in determining the climate of an institution, and in what ways might social distance between staff and residents of an institution be detected?
8. What formal and informal methods would you use to ass the climate or atmosphere of an institution?
9. What important principles should be kept in mind when trying to change an institution in some way?
10. The only sensible thing to do with institutions is to abolish them altogether. Discuss.

Annotated reading

Barton, R. (1959; 3rd edn, 1976) Institutional Neurosis. Bristol: Wright.
> This is now a classic book, describing institutionaliza-tion as a state analogous to a disease. It is written from a medical perspective but is brief, easy to read, describes the effects of institutionalization within a hospital setting, and forcefully makes the point that the state can arise in any institutional setting.

Fairweather, G.W., Sanders, D.H., Cressler, D.L. and Maynard, H. (1969) Community Life for the Mentally Ill: A alternative to institutional care. Chicago: Aldine.
> The main part of this book describes the story of a group of mental hospital patients who left the hospital together and set up home in a 'lodge', living and working productively together. Elsewhere in the book research findings are reported. Those who enjoy reading about research findings may also wish to read Fairweather, G. W. (ed.) (1964), 'Social Psychology in Treating Mental Illness', New York: Wiley.

Goffman, E. (1961) Asylums: Essays on the social situation of mental patients and other inmates. New York: Anchor Books, Doubleday.
> Another classic volume, in which a sociologist describes the events and processes he saw in a large American mental hospital. The book is full of telling socio-logical insights, but it is important when reading 'Asylums' to have in one's mind the knowledge that not all institutions, not even all mental hospitals, are alike and that there are important differences amongst them.

Jones, Maxwell (1952) Social Psychiatry: A study of therapeutic communities. London: Tavistock. (Published as 'The Therapeutic Community', New York: Basic Books, 1953.
> Again a classic book. The original description of the concept of the Therapeutic Community. Revolutionary in its time and still very well worth reading to understand the basic ideas behind the concept.

King, R.D., Raynes, N.V. and Tizard, J. (1971) Patterns
of Residential Care: Sociological studies in institutions
for handicapped children. London: Routledge & Kegan Paul.
   This book is detailed and has quite a high research
   content. It is especially useful for the definitions and
   criteria for assessing institutional practices Because
   of this it has been an influential book upon which later
   research has been based.

King's Fund (undated). Living in Hospital: The social needs
of people in long-term care. London: Research Publications
Limited.
   This is an easy to digest pamphlet designed to be read
   by people who work in institutions. It poses a number of
   very detailed questions which readers should ask themselves about the environments created in their own
   institutions for those who reside there.

Miller, E.J. and Gwynne, G.V. (1972) A Life Apart: A pilot
study of residential institutions for the physically handicapped and the young chronic sick. London: Tavistock.
   This is an account of a study of several homes and
   hospital units for a very disadvantaged group, most of
   whom would never leave the institutions in which they
   were resident. It describes several places in considerable detail and in the course of so doing raises many
   of the issues with which the present chapter on
   institutional climates is concerned.

Otto, S. and Orford, J. (1978) Not Quite Like Home: Small
hostels for alcoholics and others. Chichester: Wiley.
   This book is in two parts. The first reviews work on
   institutions and on small hostels for the mentally ill,
   offenders, and people with drinking problems in
   particular. The second part describes in detail a
   research study of two particular hostels for problem
   drinkers. It covers a great deal of important ground but
   is probably not so easy to read as some of the other
   books suggested.

Rutter, M., Maughan, B., Mortimore, P. and Ouston, J.
(1979) Fifteen Thousand Hours: Secondary schools and their
effects on children. London: Open Books.
   Here is a recent account of a detailed research project
   concerning the organization of a number of London
   secondary schools and their effect on the pupils'
   achievement and behaviour. The research is detailed and
   painstaking and the book is probably not easy to read,
   but for those who find statistics heavy going it
   contains some valuable passages about differences in
   school organization.

Tizard, J., Sinclair, I. and Clarke, R.V.G. (eds) (1975)
Varieties of Residential Experience. London: Routledge &
Kegan Paul.

This book is an important collection of chapters written by different authors describing a variety of studies of residential institutions of one kind or another, mostly for children or adolescents. Particularly important are the first chapter in which the editors criticize the simplicity of Goffman's approach in 'Asylums', and the chapter by Barbara Tizard in which she shows how residential nurseries can be run in very different ways.

Towell, D. and Harries, C. (1979) Innovations in Patient Care. London: Croom Helm.

These authors describe how changes were brought about in the running of a mental hospital. Particularly inspiring is chapter 2 which describes how significant change was brought about in an acute psychiatric ward and on a long-stay ward.

Walter, J.A. (1978) Sent Away: A study of young offenders in care. Farnborough, Hants.: Teakfield.

Walter's book describes his detailed observations and results of interviews at one Scottish List D school (the equivalent of the English Community Home or, as it used to be called, Approved School). It is a racy, easy to read account, concentrating particularly on the overall ideology or philosophy of the school and its effect upon staff and boys.

Exercises

A study of institutional life

Think of institutions, preferably three in number (for example, an old people's home, or children's long-stay home or a family therapy centre) in which you have worked (or are working now) as a member of 'staff'; and at least one in which you have been (or are now) in the role of 'client'. As wide a spread of 'purposes' as possible should be represented; for example, one might be 'therapeutic' and one educational. The questions below are about the nominated institutions. In all cases they should be answered in relation to more than one institution; you should then be in a position to be able to compare institutions in the parameters concerned. You should note that many of the questions demand quite detailed knowledge; therefore you need more than a superficial knowledge, which in turn requires some extended contact with the institution. Casual sampling is unlikely to give sufficient information. However, you are likely to have belonged to several institutions (for example, your schools and your present college) and you may have worked in a voluntary capacity in a local institution.

* Who are the 'users' or 'clients'?
* Who are the 'staff' who provide for the users' needs?
* What would you say is the main purpose of the institution?
* Are there any other categories of important people other

than those you have listed as users and staff? How do they fit into the organization?

* Who influences the institution without actually working in it from day to day? How important is their influence, and why?

* Are any of your institutions 'total' in Goffman's sense? Do any of them involve blurring of boundaries between spheres of life yet not amounting to a total institution?

* From your own experience, do you recognize 'institutionalization' as possible in your institution? Can you add to the list of 'symptoms' of institutionalization which Barton gives? Do you think it is possible for something like institutionalization to occur in institutions that are non-residential (that is, institutions where clients do not sleep)? If so, how is institutionalization different in residential and non-residential institutions?

* Do you think that your institution should embody any or all of the five therapeutic community ideals? Do others in your institution think the institution should embody these ideals? Do you think that your institution does in practice embody these ideals? Are there discrepancies between your answers to these three questions? Where do the discrepancies lie and can you begin to account for them?

* How large is your institution? If it contains more than 10-12 members, how is it broken up into smaller sub-units, if at all? How independent of the rest of the organization is your sub-unit? Are members in different sub-units for different purposes? In what way is your sub-unit dependent on the whole institution (list as many ways as you can)?

* List as many roles and tasks in which you are involved in the institution as you can. For each role or task list the other members (titles will do) to whom you have to relate in order to perform that role or task adequately.

* How is your institution advertised at its entrance, if at all? Is it located within its local community? Are its members also members of the immediate local community? If not, how is this so? Who visits your institution from the local community? Is visiting in your view made easy or difficult? Are there regulations about visiting? Are visitors made welcome, and are facilities provided for them?

* Is the interior decor of your institution homely? In what way is it not?

* Comment on the degree of privacy available for members in the institution. Is there room for personal possessions? What are the sleeping, bathing and toileting arrangements?

* How is food provided in the institution, if at all? How many members are involved in the cycle of activities which includes the preparation, eating and clearing up after eating food? How many stages involve users/clients

of the institution, and how many staff?
* Who uses which areas, rooms, and facilities in the
  institution? Who cannot use which areas, rooms and
  facilities? In which areas of the institution do you
  personally feel most comfortable, and in which least
  comfortable? In which do you feel at home, and not at
  home? Are you excluded from any, and why?
* Draw a plan of the seating arrangements in two different
  rooms or areas within the institution where members
  spend quite a lot of time. Are the arrangements you have
  drawn generally sociopetal or sociofugal? Why are they
  like that? Who put them that way? Have they ever been
  arranged differently, and what happened when they were
* Can you name examples of institutionally-orientated
  practices which occur in your institution? These may
  fall under one of the four headings of rigid routine, en
  bloc treatment, treatment which is not personalized and
  social distance between staff and clients. You may be
  able to think of practices which do not fall within
  these areas, however. In each case, can you think of
  ways in which the practice could be changed?
* Consider the range of decisions listed in table 1.
  Choose any two or three from the list. Who decides on
  these issues? Can users/clients decide freely for themselves, or do they decide jointly with staff; can staff
  who are in closest touch with the users/clients decide,
  or are decisions made partly or wholly by more senior
  members of staff or a higher authority?
* How is selection/input of new members (users, staff and
  others) handled in the institution? Do users have any
  say at all, and if so how much? Do staff who are in
  closest touch with users have any say, and if so how
  much? Who does decide on selection? Next time a new
  member (user, staff or other) is selected or admitted as
  a member to the institution, observe the process closely
  and/or ask questions about it until you feel you could
  write a full account of the complete process of re-
  cruiting a new member.
* Prepare a short questionnaire concerning attitudes
  towards users/clients (alternatively a sub-group of
  users, or members of staff, or others, might be the
  object of the questionnaire). Do this by recording
  statements which you make yourself, which you overhear
  other people making, or which are written down in any
  documents which the institution produces for internal or
  outside use. Discard those that are not clear and type
  the remainder on the left-hand side of the page. On the
  right-hand side draw columns headed at the top: strongly
  agree; not sure; disagree; strongly disagree. Make sure
  that the instructions of questionnaire are quite clear
  and unambiguous. Administer the questionnaire to yourself and a small sample of other people within the institution. Examine the results collectively with those
  who have helped by filling in the questionnaire. What
  difficulties in people's attitudes do you detect?

* How much time do you spend each day or each week with members of different groups within the institution? If you are not certain, keep a diary for a week. Are there categories of people you spend no time with, or very little time with? Are there others you spend disproportionally much time with? Why is this?

* Do any members of your institution wear uniforms, or insignia of any kind? What purposes do you think these serve? Are their uses debated or are they controversial? Collect a range of opinions on the use of uniforms or insignia if any exist.

* How do people address one another within your institution? Are first names, surnames or titles used? Is one method of address used universally throughout the institution, or are there different patterns depending upon the people concerned or their roles? Do you personally use a similar mode of address with everyone, including all staff and users of the institution? If there is any variation, why is this? Has your method of addressing, or being addressed by, anyone in the institution changed recently, and if so why? Would you like your present mode of address to or from anyone in the in the institution to change in the future? What do you anticipate would happen if you tried changing it now? If you think it is possible, try changing it and record what happens.

* How would you describe the climate or atmosphere in your institution? List as many adjectives or phrases as you can to describe the 'feel' of the institution as it is at present or when you last knew it. Has the atmosphere changed over time? If so, can you describe the change, contrasting the climate at dfferent times? Can you begin to account for the difference?

* Observe at least one type of meeting which takes place within the institution. Who sits where? Who is included in the meeting, and who excluded? Who leads or chairs the meeting ? Who talks a lot and who a little? To whom are remarks mainly addressed? What is discussed, and what if anything would you say is not discussed but should be, or else is discussed elsewhere? What would you say is the climate of the meeting (use as many adjectives or phrases as you can to describe the 'feel' of the meeting)? What sort of things, if any, do you think members of relatively lower status in the organization are able to say in such meetings and which things do they not feel able to say?

* Describe in general terms a recent conflict within the institution. How did the issue arise, and how did events develop? Did people take sides? Was the matter well resolved or badly? Would you say anyone was scapegoated?

* How does change come about in the institution? Who or what is that catalyst for change?

* Does information or data already exist in some form in the institution which could be made more use of for purposes of discussion and to suggest change?

24

Dying and bereavement
A. T. Carr

Demographic trends

If you had been born at the beginning of this century, your life expectancy at birth would have been 44 years if you were male or 48 years if you were female. If you were born today, your initial life expectancy would be 70 years or 76 years respectively. These figures reflect an ageing of the population that has occurred in all western industrial societies over the past 80 years. Although we all will die, most of us will do so at a relatively advanced age. Although we all will be bereaved, most of us will not suffer this until we are young adults or until we are in our middle years.

The fatal conditions of the present day, once hidden by the mass diseases, are those associated with longevity. In 1978, almost 590,000 people died in England and Wales and 85 per cent of these deaths were attributable to only three categories of illness: diseases of the circulatory system (heart and blood circulation), neoplasms (cancer) and diseases of the respiratory system (OPCS, 1979). Also, more than two people in every three now die in institutions of one form or another.

In the absence of any radical changes of events, the vast majority of us will die aged 65 years or over, in an institution of some sort and as a result of a disease of our circulatory system, or respiratory system, or of cancer. This underlines an important feature of dying and death at the present time: they have become unfamiliar events that take place in unfamiliar surroundings, watched over by unfamiliar people. We all know that we will die and that we may be bereaved, yet we have very little relevant experience upon which to develop our construing or anticipation of these events and states.

Telling

The majority of fatally ill people realize, at some point, that they will not recover, even if they have not been informed of the nature of their illness. However, it would appear that only about half of all fatally ill people appreciate their condition before significant changes in health force the conclusion 'I am dying'. This is almost certainly an under-estimate: there will be some people who know that they will not recover but who do not communicate this.

Although about one-half of terminally ill people appear to appreciate the seriousness of their illness, this awareness is usually achieved independently, informally and indirectly. No more than 15 per cent of terminally ill cancer patients are told of their prognosis either by their general practitioner or by a hospital doctor (Cartwright, Hockey and Anderson, 1973). This contrasts markedly with the experiences of their close relatives. Almost 90 per cent of the close relatives of terminally ill patients are aware that the patient's illness is terminal and most of them are informed of this by a general practitioner or by a hospital doctor. There are several implications of these data, the two most obvious being that fatally ill people and their principal carers often do not share the same information about the illness, and that doctors usually are unwilling to tell patients when they have a disease that will kill them. Perhaps the most serious consequence is that one or more of the familial participants has to cope with the demands of this most stressful period without adequate support.

It is remarkable how little emphasis is placed upon the wishes of the patient. Most people, including doctors, whether they are young or old, ill or well, say they would want to know if they had a fatal illness or that they are glad they do know. Several studies have examined this issue and the results are consistent in showing that more than 70 per cent of all the samples used say they would want to be informed if they had a terminal disease. It is clear that most people say they would want to be informed of the seriousness of their illness and most doctors say that they would want to be told; yet the majority of fatally ill patients are not told. Also, the existence of a real threat to life does not reduce the very high proportion of people who want to know if they have a fatal illness.

In general, learning that one has a fatal illness is followed by a period of disquiet, even grief, although the emotional response may be concealed from others. It is worth noting that some patients do not 'hear' or at least appear not to remember, what they have been told regarding their prognosis. Although it has been proposed that the defence mechanism of denial is a ubiquitous response to learning of a fatal prognosis (Kubler-Ross, 1969), there are other more mundane possibilities. The first is the use of terminology that may have very precise meanings for a professional but which may mean nothing, or something very different, to the patient. To inform a patient of 'malignant lymphoma' or 'secondary metastases' may not constitute communication. Even when the words that are used are understood reasonably well, they may not convey what was intended. For some individuals, the knowledge of their impending death will be extremely distressing; in such cases the person may be quite unable to accept what is plain to everybody else. They may become distraught as their bodies show increasing signs of impending death while they continue to deny that they are dying. Such extreme responses, as a terminal illness progresses, correspond to denial as elucidated by Kubler-Ross (1969). However, it would be inappropriate to regard as denial a person's failure to comprehend or to recall initial statements about prognosis. Quite apart from the communication problems mentioned above, if people have no prior suspicions that their conditions may be terminal it is probable that they will be unable to accept a fatal diagnosis. It is not that they refuse to accept such information but they are unable to accept it. It demands a radical revision of their view of the world and such a major psychological adjustment takes time. Initially, such news is not disbelieved, but on the other hand, it cannot be fitted into a person's perception of the world: it cannot be accommodated. The revised view of the world will need to be tested, amended and confirmed in the light of further information. The person will seek such information in what people say, how they behave and how his body feels. It is only when the revised view of the world 'fits', in the sense that it is not violated by new observations or new information, that the person is able fully to accommodate the 'truths' that have been offered. Individuals who have prior suspicions about the seriousness of their illnesses have already constructed, at least in part, a view of their world that includes themselves as dying individuals.

Our aim must be to maintain dignity, to alleviate suffering and to help people live as fully as possible for as long as they are able: they should be told what they are prepared to hear at a time when they are prepared to listen. The same principle might be kept in mind when dealing with relatives. There are indications that those who are told with care show improved family relationships, less tension and less desperation during their terminal illnesses than those who are not (Gerle, Lunden and Sandblow, 1960). Helping a person towards fuller awareness of, and adjustment to, a fatal prognosis is the beginning of a communication process which is itself an integral part of caring for the terminally ill.

Terminality and dying

The two words terminality and dying are being used to draw a distinction that can have important implications for the way in which fatally ill people are managed and treated. The main implication is that of regarding someone as terminally ill, but nevertheless as living and with some valuable life remaining, rather than regarding the person as dying with all the negative attitudes this provokes. Once illnesses have been diagnosed as terminal we need to regard patients as living and possibly living more intensely than the rest of us, until they clearly are dying. Terminality, then, begins when a terminal diagnosis is made but dying starts later, usually when death is much closer and when individuals are prepared to relinquish their biological life in the absence of valuable, functional life.

Sources of distress

Effective and appropriate care of the fatally ill requires
an awareness of potential sources of distress so that distress can be anticipated and thus be avoided or alleviated.
Of course, distress is not confined to the patient: effective care and support for those who are close to the patient
is merited not only on humanitarian grounds, but also
because of the exacerbation of the patient's suffering that
can result from the distress of relatives and friends. Table
1 summarizes some of the most common sources of distress
for patients and those who are close to them.

The listing contained in table 1 is by no means exhaustive, but it illustrates a number of points. First,
given some capacity for empathy on the part of the sur-
vivor(s) there is little that the terminally ill person
must endure that the survivor can avoid. This commonality
of the sources of distress argues strongly for the need to
attend to the welfare of survivors before they become
bereaved. Second, it is clear that almost all the potential
sources of distress are psychological in nature. Even some
of the physical symptoms such as incontinence or smells are
distressing because of our values and expectations. Also,
pain itself is an experience that is subject to psychological factors rather than a sensation that is elicited by
an appropriate stimulus.

Although we cannot examine in detail the physical distress of terminal illness, our discussion would be incomplete without a summary of this. Cartwright et al (1973) and
Ward (1974) identified retrospectively the physical symptoms
experienced by their samples of terminal cancer patients,
215 and 264 individuals respectively. These data are
summarized in table 2.

It is striking that the rank order of symptoms is the
same for both samples and a significant proportion of
patients in each sample experienced each of the symptoms
listed. Other common physical symptoms were breathing
difficulties, 52 per cent; coughing, 48 per cent (Ward); and
sleeplessness, 17 per cent (Cartwright et al).

Distress and coping

An examination of tables 1 and 2 points to a number of
psychological processes that predispose people to react with
depression and anxiety during a terminal illness. Current
approaches to depression emphasize the role of loss and
helplessness as aetiological factors. Loss refers to the
real or imagined loss of a valued object, role, activity,
relationship, etc. The individual relevance of the concept
of loss lies in the individual differences of our value
systems. For example, a person who highly values physical
abilities, physical appearance, etc., is likely to be more
at risk for depression as a result of physical debility,
tiredness and deterioration in appearance, than someone for
whom such attributes are low in a hierarchy of values.

Table 1

Common sources of distress

Fatally ill person (P)	Those who love P
Awareness of impending death	Awareness of impending bereavement
Anticipation of loss	Anticipation of loss
Physical sequelae of disease process, e.g. tumours, lesions, nausea, incontinence, breathlessness, unpleasant smells	Empathic concern, aversion, etc.
Frustration and help-lessness as disease progresses	Frustration and help-lessness as disease progresses
Uncertainty about the future welfare of the family	Uncertainty about the future welfare of the family
Anticipation of pain	
Empathic concern	Caring for P, night-sitting, tiredness, etc.
Changes in roles with family, friends, etc.	Changes in roles with family, friends, etc
Changes in abilities as illness progresses	Empathic concern
Changes in appearance as illness progresses	Empathic concern, aversion, etc.
Uncertainties about dying	Empathic concern
Dying	Empathic concern
	Discovery of death, directly or indirectly
	Practicalities, funeral, etc.
	Grief
	Role changes
	Reconstruction of life

Table 2

Symptoms suffered by terminal cancer patients

Symptom	Per cent in sample of Cartwright et al	Per cent in sample of Ward
Pain	87	62
Anorexia	76	61
Vomiting	54	38
Urinary incontinence	38	28
Faecal incontinence	37	20
Bedsores	24	13

Helplessness describes a state that is characterized by an awareness that one's behaviour is unrelated to the events which impinge upon oneself. When a person is subjected to aversive events whose occurrence, intensity, duration, etc., is quite independent of behaviour, a characteristic state may ensue. This state, which occurs in the majority of subjects tested, is known as learnt helplessness. There are individual differences in susceptibility to learnt helplessness, but the more aversive the events and the more frequently they are experienced as independent of behaviour the more likely it is to develop. It is a generalized state characterized by apathy, dysphoric mood, psychomotor retardation (i.e. slowness in thought and action), and feelings of hopelessness. Many clinical depressions are explained most fully in terms of the development of helplessness and there is evidence that sudden death is not an uncommon consequence of learnt helplessness in laboratory animals. There can be little doubt about the relevance and importance of helplessness to our consideration of the welfare of the terminally ill.

Let us now return to the sources of distress summarized in tables 1 and 2. It is clear that some of these are intrinsically uncontrollable, and others duplicate the procedures that are used in experimental work to induce helplessness in that they are aversive, uncontrollable and repeated: for instance, urinary incontinence and vomiting. Furthermore, many patients undergo physical investigations and treatments that they do not understand, that they find unpleasant or painful and about which they feel they have little choice other than to accept them passively. It is not surprising to find that depression is commonly encountered in the terminally ill. A significant minority of fatally ill people and their next-of-kin become moderately or severely depressed (about one in five people in each group). Those most at risk are adolescents, young parents with dependents those who have many physical symptoms and those who experience lengthy hospitalization.

The reciprocal interaction of physical and psychological processes must not be overlooked. We have already considere the depressive role of repeated, unpleasant physical symptoms. However, the interaction also proceeds in the other direction: adverse emotional states such as depression and anxiety augment pain and other physical discomforts. The essential point is that pain is not a simple response to an appropriate physical stimulus such as tissue damage: it is an experience that is compounded of the stimulation and the person's response to that stimulation. The motivational and emotional state of the person acts, as it were, to colour the sensation and to produce the experience we call pain. Without such 'colouring' and evaluation the sensation may be perceived but not experienced as painful.

It is the experience of most who work in terminal care that the relief of anxiety or depression through appropriate support, communication and practical help reduces the pain of patients and, not insignificantly, reduces the need for medication. The point is not that attention to the psychological state of the patient removes the need for relevant medication but that it reduces the dosages that may be required to bring relief. There are many obvious advantages that derive from this, not the least of which is the ability to alleviate pain without resorting to medications that render the patient confused, drowsy or comatose.

Anxiety arises when a future event is appraised as threatening. This appraisal is the evaluation of an event in terms of its harmful implications for the individual, harm being the extent to which continued physical and psychological functioning is endangered. Threat appraisal is a highly subjective process that depends upon the subjective likelihood of an event - that is, how probable the person feels the event to be - and the degree of harm that will result, this again being subjectively assessed. So terminally ill people are anxious to the extent that the events that they anticipate are both likely and harmful in their own terms: if events are not perceived as likely or harmful then they will not provoke anxiety.

Anxiety is an essentially adaptive emotion, in that it motivates us to initiate behaviours that prevent the anticipated harm being realized. To the extent that individuals accept that they are dying and are unable to reduce or eliminate the harmful consequences of this process, they are liable to remain anxious. An inspection of tables 1 and 2 reminds us that there are many potential types of harm that the fatally ill person is motivated, by anxiety, to alleviate. It is reassuring to note that the intense panic that is such a common feature of clinical anxiety states occurs rarely in terminal illness except, perhaps, in those who continue to deny the imminence of death as the end approaches and those for whom breathing is difficult. However, moderate anxiety is by no means uncommon in the terminally ill. This is not only an extra burden of suffering for the person but it also exacerbates other discomforts including pain.

There are few systematic reports of anxiety in terminal illness but from the data that do exist it is clear that moderate anxiety is experienced by between one-quarter and one-half of patients. The anxiety may be readily discerned in those people who are able to verbalize their fears, and who are given the opportunity to do so, but it may be less obvious in those who communicate less well verbally. However, the physiological and behavioural concomitants of anxiety are good indicators of the presence of unspoken fear. Often it is difficult to distinguish between physiological signs of anxiety such as gastric upset, nausea, diarrhoea, muscular pains, etc., and symptoms of the disease process or side effects of treatment. Nevertheless, the possibility that a patient might be persistently anxious should not be overlooked.

Given the subjective nature of threat appraisal, the causes of an individual's anxiety can be surprisingly idiosyncratic, but there are a few consistencies that may provide some clues. Younger adults expect to be distressed by pain and parting from the people they love, whereas the elderly fear becoming dependent and losing control of bowel and bladder functioning. Hinton (1972) reports that almost two-thirds of his patients who died aged 50 years or less were clearly anxious but this was true of only one-third of those aged 60 years and over. There is a clear and understandable trend for young parents of dependent children to be more anxious than other groups. Perhaps it is not insignificant that younger patients also tend to experience more physical discomfort during their terminal illnesses.

According to Hinton (1963), anxiety is more common in people with a lengthy terminal illness. He found more than 50 per cent of those who had been ill for more than one year to be clearly anxious, but only 20 per cent of those who had been ill for less than three months showed similar levels of anxiety. Although anxiety levels fluctuate during a patient's terminal illness, there is no general trend for anxiety to increase as the person draws closer to death. Some people become more apprehensive as their illnesses progress, but others become more calm during the last stages of their lives.

Some specific experiences of illness may be potent sources of anxiety. Prior episodes of intolerable pain can provoke great anxiety when they are recalled or when their return is anticipated. Difficulties in breathing are commonly associated with anxiety and a tendency to panic. Also, in the context of a mortal illness there are a number of sources of distress that are intrinsically uncontrollable and uncertain, such as the final process of dying, death and the nature of the world in which one's dependent survivors will be living. When anticipated harm remains and individuals perceive it as beyond their ability to influence, they become liable to the state of helplessness. If this is severe they may become depressed, as we have discussed: if less severe, then they may exhibit the resignation that has been termed 'acceptance' (Kubler-Ross, 1969). If they persist in their attempts to control and influence events that are beyond their reach they are likely to remain anxious and even to become more anxious as they approach death.

For the fatally ill child under five or six years of age, anxiety takes the form of separation anxiety, loneliness and fears of being abandoned. The young child does not appear to fear death and its implications, but fears are aroused by those aspects of illness and hospitalization which elicit fear in most ill children who require hospital treatment.

Between the ages of six and ten or eleven years, separation fears persist, but the child is increasingly prone to anxiety over painful treatments and bodily intrusions. Such fears of mutilation and physical harm are intensified in the absence of familiar, trusted adults. Some children in this age group, because of differing prior experiences or more advanced cognitive development, are also aware of the cessation of awareness and bodily functioning consequent upon death.

Although there is some dispute as to whether the child under ten years of age can be aware of impending death at a conceptual level, there is little doubt that many young children perceive that their illness is no ordinary illness. This is a frequent clinical observation and there is a good deal of evidence that it is so whether or not the diagnosis is discussed with the child (Spinetta, 1974). Of course there are many cues that may indicate to the child that something very serious and threatening is happening, quite apart from the numerous tests, treatments and visits to hospital. Most children are finely tuned to detect meaningful and subtle signs in the verbal and non-verbal behaviour of adults: the things that are not talked about, tone of voice, eye contact, posture, etc. Also, there are many cues that the child would find it hard to overlook: whispered conversations, unusually frequent and intense bodily contact, unusual generosity and freedom of choice with regard to presents and treats, and so on.

Parents and others usually begin to grieve for the fatally ill child soon after they accept the prognosis. Their ability to cope with this grief is an important determinant of their effectiveness in supporting the child. Since familiar adults and siblings are likely to be the child's greatest potential source of comfort and reassurance, it is important that time and attention is devoted to these significant others for the sake of the child's welfare. There are indications of a high incidence of psychological difficulties in family members, particularly siblings, during the terminal illness of a child. Clearly parents, who are themselves struggling with their own emotions, may have difficulty sustaining the other children in the family, let alone in providing comfort and reassurance to the one who is ill.

Adolescents and some younger children will be aware of the finality of death. Although dependent upon adults in a functional sense, they may perceive themselves as having important roles to play in the welfare of others and thus be subject to fears for the well-being of their survivors in much the same way as adults with dependents. Very young children may endure a terminal illness with striking calmness and acceptance of their lot, provided that their separation fears are allayed, but once they are past the age of six or seven years they become prone to a wide range of fears that exceed those of their 'normally ill' counterparts with severe, chronic, but non-fatal illness. Although children may be reluctant to express their fears, or may express them unclearly and indirectly, they should be anticipated in all aspects of care.

We have examined the range of potential sources of distress in terminal illness and the most common types of distress that result from these. Pain, anxiety and depression are sufficiently frequent and severe to merit attention when services are being planned and delivered. However, a majority of fatally ill people do not become severely anxious, deeply depressed or suffer from unrelieved pain. This does not minimize the awful suffering of the large minority or the pressing need for improvements in care to which this suffering testifies. It indicates only that, with whatever help they receive, most people who endure a terminal illness cope reasonably well, keeping their levels of distress within limits that are acceptable to themselves and to those who care for them.

The responses of people who are faced with impending death show sufficient uniformity to enable observers to write of stages, phases and patterns of coping (e.g. Kubler-Ross, 1969; Falek and Britton, 1974). Quite apart from doubts about the uniformity and progressive nature of stages of coping in terminal illness (e.g. Schulz and Aderman, 1974), it cannot be assumed that any particular individual needs to negotiate these stages in order to cope most effectively with impending death. The emotional responses and their dependent behaviours are indicators of the difficulties, and triumphs, experienced by people in their attempts to cope. The absence of a specific emotion does not mean that the person has omitted a necessary stage of the 'normal' coping pattern and that this omission detracts from the person's adjustment. Provided we do not equate 'typical' with 'ideal' or 'necessary', an awareness of the emotional stages or phases that are commonly encountered in terminal patients can help us to understand the problems they face, to provide the types of help and support that might be beneficial and to improve our ability to cope with the emotions that their behaviours arouse in relatives and in ourselves.

However, there are a number of general points that can be made about a stage model of terminal illness. The responses delineated, including denial, anger, bargaining, depression and acceptance (Kubler-Ross, 1969), are not specific to people who are facing death; they have been observed in many other stressful situations that involve loss and uncontrollable harm, such as bereavement, amputation and imprisonment. The generality evidenced by these observations does not confirm the progression of the stage model: it highlights the normality of disbelief, anger, sadness, etc., in the face of irretrievable and severe loss.

Often it is difficult to decide which stage or phase a person is in. Without reasonable certainty in the identification of stages, the predictive value of a stage model is severely impaired. This predictive aspect of the model is also reduced if the stages are not ubiquitous and if they are not successive. Clinical observation suggests that the emotion displayed by a person is responsive to many internal and external events. Perhaps all that can be said with any certainty is that some responses, when they occur, are likely to predominate earlier in a terminal illness, for example denial, and some are more likely to appear later, for example depression and acceptance.

We must take care not to lose sight of the individual in anticipating responses to a terminal illness. Fatally ill people bring with them their own particular views of themselves, their families, their futures, doctors, death, etc. The importance of individual differences during the terminal phase of life is well illustrated by the work of Kastenbaum and Weisman (1972). They found that their patients could be divided into two broad groups, both of which were aware of the imminence of death but which differed markedly in their behavioural styles. One group gradually withdrew from their usual activities and social contacts, remaining inactive until their final illness. The other group was characterized by involvement: patients in this group remained busily engaged in everyday activities until death occurred as an interruption in their living.

Dying

The relationship between a patient's reactions to a terminal illness and dying is not only that these are the psychological context within which the final process occurs, but also there are increasing indications that they influence the timing of death (see Achterberg and Lawlis, 1977). Whereas blood chemistries reflect on-going or current disease status, psychological factors are predictive of subsequent disease status and longevity. Poorer prognosis and shorter survival occurs in patients who, typically, show great dependence upon others, who deny the severity of their conditions, who have a history of poor social relationships and who do not have access to, or do not utilize, supportive social relationships during their illnesses. These patients tend to become more withdrawn, pessimistic and depressed as their illness progresses. Longer survival is associated with patients who maintain good personal and social relationships in the context of an existing network of such relationships. They can be assertive without hostility, asking for and receiving much medical and emotional support. They may be concerned about dying alone and seek to deter others from withdrawing from them without their needs being met. These patients also experience less pain, or at least complain less about pain and discomfort.

Dying is a process rather than an event that occurs at one point in time. This final process that constitutes the transition from life to death is usually of short duration, a matter of hours or days. For the vast majority of people it is not dramatic. Most people, both ill and well, express a desire to die peacefully or to die in their sleep. There is little doubt that this wish is fulfilled in most cases. Although there are a few people for whom pain or breath-lessness may increase near the end, most slip knowingly or unawares into the unconsciousness that continues until their dying is finished.

After a terminal illness lasting some months, most pa-tients are tired and wearied by their experiences. During their last days, apart from having their needs tended, patients may wish to be alone or to avoid news and problems of the 'outside world'. They may well become less talkative and prefer shorter visits. Communication tends to shift increasingly towards the non-verbal. In terms of interaction they may want little more than somebody to sit with them in silence, perhaps holding hands. It is clear from those who wish to talk briefly in their last hours of life that there is an experience of 'distance' from life. As Saunders (1978) so aptly puts it, 'They were not frightened nor unwilling to go, for by then they were too far away to want to come back. They were conscious of leaving weakness and exhaustion rather than life and its activities. They rarely had any pain but felt intensely weary. They wanted to say good-bye to those they loved but were not torn with longing to stay with them.'

Euthanasia

Euthanasia, meaning a gentle and easy death and the act of bringing this about, has been a source of discussion and controversy for many years. The level of current interest is evidenced by the large number of recent publications on the topic in the professional literature and the increasing support of the public for such organizations as the Volun-tary Euthanasia Society in the UK and the Euthanasia Edu-cation Council in the USA.

The public support for euthanasia is probably based upon an expectation that death will come as a result of a lengthy illness, an illness that may well be prolonged unduly by the application of current medical knowledge and techniques. It is based upon fears of the physical and psychological incompetence, dependence, indignity and pain that may result from a chronic or terminal illness. Even those professionals who oppose euthanasia on ethical, religious or practical grounds readily concede that such fears are not unjustified for many people. We have already examined the potential distress of terminal illness but, for many people, support for euthanasia is prompted by thoughts of an unwanted, useless existence where biological life is maintained artificially and against their wishes in a hospital, nursing home or geriatric ward. Sadly, such thoughts are all too often reinforced by cases that Saunders (1977) rightly describes as 'truly horrendous'. As a society we cannot escape the reality that far too many elderly people end their days in loneliness, isolation and degradation. Even when the physical care provided is good, the psychological distress can be great. The prima facie case for euthanasia appears to be strong.

The many logical, philosophical and ethical arguments relating to the legalization of voluntary euthanasia, both active and passive, have been well stated several times (e.g. Rachels, 1975; Foot, 1978), and space precludes their consideration here. However, these arguments frequently take little account of relevant practical and psychological issues. In drawing up the necessary guidelines for the legalization of voluntary euthanasia there are major problems in guarding against error and potential abuse, both by relatives and professionals. Nevertheless, many of these problems could be surmounted by the use and recognition of the Living Will. This document, as distributed by the Euthanasia Educational Council, is signed and witnessed when the person is in good health. Its aim is to avoid an existence in dependence, deterioration, indignity and hopeless pain.

Doctors spend their lives preserving the lives of others and alleviating their suffering. It can be argued that, in recent years, the pendulum has swung too far in the direction of the maintenance of life at the expense of the relief of distress, but the activities of doctors make demands upon their energies and their personal time that few other professions would tolerate. This degree of commitment is consistent with, and continually reinforces, a value system that places a very high priority upon the preservation of life and actions that serve this end. For individuals in whom such values relate closely to their self-concepts, the active termination of life may be damaging to their self-regard and to their concept of their own worth as individuals. Although there is little difference between active and passive euthanasia on moral and logical grounds, for individual doctors the difference may be vast and unbridgeable in terms of their own psychology. It would be quite unjustifiable to place such men in a position where society expected them to implement active euthanasia.

From the patient's point of view, the availability of euthanasia has a wider potential than the avoidance of further suffering. People who are given control over aversive and painful stimulation, by having the facility to terminate, reduce or avoid it in some way, are better able to cope with the experience. Even though the available control is rarely exercised, the aversive stimulation is better tolerated and provokes less distress. Provided that patients are quite sure that their lives can be terminated when they wish, and only when they wish, they are likely to cope better with the effects of their illness or condition and to be less distressed.

To allow patients to die in order to release them from hopelessness and irreducible suffering, while continuing to treat their current distress, is thoroughly compatible with the humanitarian principle of care. Whether or not one wishes to describe this as passive, voluntary euthanasia is a matter of personal choice. There are grounds for a more widespread recognition of this compatibility and for more weight to be given to the wishes of patients and their families. Of course, the same grounds demand that more effort, time and resources should be devoted to improving the quality of care that is offered. All such improvements weaken the case for regarding death as a desirable release from suffering, as a release that is needed so frequently that its use should be regularized. In the long term, and certainly in the shorter term, there are likely to be some people for whom death is the preferred option. It is a problem that will become more acute as our society continues to age and as the life-preserving techniques of medicine continue to develop.

Bereavement

Bereavement is a state characterized by loss. The main focus of interest is upon the loss occasioned by the death of a significant person but people are bereaved by other losses such as loss of role, loss of status, separation and amputation. The state of loss serves as the stimulus for the bereavement response, a response that is manifested culturally and individually. The cultural response constitutes mourning and is a pattern of behaviour that is learnt from and supported by one's immediate culture as appropriate following bereavement. Grief is the individual response and is the main area of concern for researchers and clinicians alike. In that grief typically follows a reasonably consistent course over time, ending ultimately in its resolution, it can be regarded as an individual process that occurs in response to individual loss.

The nature of grief
Although the major features of grief are known to most of us either intuitively or through personal experience, the chief findings of the many descriptive studies can be summarized broadly as follows:

* grief is a complex but stereotyped response pattern that

includes such physical and psychological 'symptoms' as withdrawal, fatigue, sleep disturbance, anxiety and loss of appetite;

* it is elicited by a rather well-defined stimulus situation, namely the real or imagined loss of a valued object or role, and it is resolved when new object relations are established;

* it is a ubiquitous phenomenon among human beings and appears in other social species, especially higher primates;

* it is an extremely stressful response both physically and psychologically, but grief-related behaviour is often antithetical to the establishment of new object relations and hence to the alleviation of the stress. For example, fatigue and withdrawal make it much more difficult for the bereaved person to develop new roles and new personal relationships in place of those lost through bereavement.

The complexity and stress of grief is readily appreciated when the number and nature of its components are considered. Hinton's (1972) description of grief adumbrates the most commonly observed characteristics: shock, denial, anxiety, depression, guilt, anger and a wide variety of somatic signs of anxiety. Other components include searching behaviour, suicidal thoughts, idealization of the lost person, panic, a heightened vulnerability to physical illness and to psychological disorders.

The nature of grief as a process is emphasized by the designation of stages by many observers and authors. Although there is a sequential character to the process it would be incorrect to anticipate an orderly progression through the stages in all people. As with the notion of stages in dying that was discussed earlier, the component responses of the various stages overlap and merge into one another. Also, there are frequent 'regressions' to earlier stages. Again, it is better to think in terms of components, some of which will predominate earlier in the process and others that will predominate later. In general, three stages or phases have been delineated and labelled according to inclination: perhaps the best descriptive labels are shock, despair and recovery.

Initially there may be a period of numbness and detachment depending, to some extent, on the unexpectedness of the news of the death. During this immediate response people may appear stoical and calm. Normal routines may be maintained especially where domestic or other factors structure the situation. Alternatively, people may appear dazed and quite unable to comprehend the reality of the news; they may be unresponsive to their environment and in need of care and support during this period. Whatever the specific initial reaction in a particular instance, it can last from a few minutes to two weeks or so, with the stoical reaction being the more likely to persist longer. The

bereaved person is less able than the terminally ill to deny
successfully the reality of the situation: sooner or later,
and in many different ways, powerful and pointed signs of
the reality of loss occur, such as the empty place at table,
the empty bed or chair, the funeral or the silent house when
friends and relatives depart. As with the news of terminal
diagnosis, people need time to assimilate and to accommodate
to a new state of the world. Whether the period of shock and
disbelief is long or short, a sense of unreality or even
disbelief is likely to return periodically for several
months.

As awareness of the loss develops people may express
anger at themselves, at staff or at God for not preventing
the death. Whether or not anger is present, the phase of
acute grieving or despair is the most painful. Lindemann
(1944), in his pioneering study of bereavement, observed the
following 'symptoms' as common to all individuals suffering
acute grief: somatic distress lasting between 20 minutes and
one hour at a time, feelings of tightness in the throat,
choking with shortness of breath, muscular weakness and
intense subjective distress described as tension or psychological pain. This specific response, which appears to be
unique to bereavement, occurs against a background of
stress, anxiety and sadness or depression, together with the
somatic concomitants of these emotions.

Behaviourally, grieving persons may be unable to maintain goal-directed activity, appearing disorganized and
unable to make plans. They may be restless, moving about in
an aimless fashion and constantly searching for something to
do. They may find themselves going, unwittingly, to the
places where the dead person might be found if still alive.
A preoccupation with the lost person creates a perceptual
set that leads to misinterpretations of ambiguous sights and
sounds as indicative of his being alive. Some grieving
people report seeing the dead person with a clarity that
goes beyond illusion and misperception. Such experiences
can occur long after the phase of acute grieving is past.
Obviously, the physical and psychological demands of this
period are heavy and it is not surprising that irritability
is common, especially when the person is eating and sleeping
poorly. Anger, frustration and resentment may be directed at
friends and neighbours irrespective of merit. Such feelings
may also be directed against the dead person for abandoning
the survivor.

The intense anguish of the despair phase can be unremit-
ting, rising to peaks of distress with thoughts of the loved
one who has died. Most bereaved people seem unable to
prevent themselves from thinking and talking about the one
who has died even though this usually exacerbates their distress. Whether this is conceptualized as 'grief-work' or as
repeated exposure leading to habituation, it appears to be
necessary to recovery from grief. A reduction in the frequency and intensity of periods of peak distress may be
the first sign that the process of recovery is beginning.

Although estimates vary, the acute despair phase of grief typically lasts for three to ten weeks.

The process of recovery from grief is a process of reconstruction. Although some aspects of the person's private and public 'self' may survive bereavement relatively unchanged, it is necessary to develop new roles, new behaviours and new relationships with others. Whatever else may or may not be changed by bereavement, the survivor must live without one important and potentially crucial personal relationship that had existed previously: the loss of this relationship is the loss of the psychological and practical advantages, and disadvantages, that it conferred. Socially, the survivor is now a widow or a widower rather than one of a married couple: he is now a boy without a father, or she is now a mother without a child, etc. Apart from the direct, personal impact of such changes, they also influence the way survivors are viewed and treated socially. The bereaved person has to develop a new private and public self that enables him to live in a changed world.

Although a reduction in the frequency and intensity of periods of extreme distress may herald the process of recovery, it cannot begin in earnest until there are periods in which the person is not overwhelmed with despair nor preoccupied with thoughts of the one who has died. Many bereaved people recall with clarity the moment when they realized that they had not been preoccupied with their loss: when, for a brief period at least, their thoughts had been directed elsewhere and their emotions had been less negative, even positive. These moments of 'spontaneous forgetting', together with improvements in sleeping and appetite, provide people with some opportunity to reconstrue and to reconstruct themselves and their futures. With less exhaustion and a lightening of mood, decisions and actions become more feasible and people can begin the active process of reviving previous relationships and activities, perhaps in a modified form, and of developing new ones. This period of active readjustment may never be complete, especially in the elderly, but it usually lasts for between six and 18 months after the phase of acute grief and despair.

Determinants of grief

Strictly speaking, it is inaccurate to talk of determinants of grief for the available data do not allow us to identify the causative factors that lead to variations in the response to bereavement. However, it makes intuitive sense to talk of determinants and is in keeping with other literature on the topic. Parkes (1972) groups the factors of potential importance according to their temporal relationship to the event of death, that is, antecedent, concurrent and subsequent determinants. Among antecedent factors, the most influential appear to be life stresses prior to bereavement, relationship with the deceased and mode of death. On the whole, an atypical grief response with associated psychological problems is more likely when bereavement occurs as one of a series of life crises, when the death is sudden, unanticipated and untimely, and when the relationship with the deceased had been one of strong attachment, reliance or ambivalence.

A number of demographic variables (concurrent) relate to the nature of grief. In particular, being young, female and married to the deceased increases the likelihood of problems arising after bereavement. Of course, these factors are not unrelated to such antecedent factors as strong attachment, reliance and untimely death. Other concurrent factors with adverse implications are susceptibility to grief, as evidenced by previous episodes of depression, an inability to express emotions, lower socio-economic status and the absence of a genuine religious faith.

The presence of religious faith might be placed more appropriately with subsequent determinants, for its role is likely to be one of supporting the bereaved person during the stressful period of grief. Also, someone with an active belief system probably will be associated with a supportive social group, and there is little doubt that a network of supportive social relationships is the most advantageous of the subsequent determinants. Other subsequent factors that have positive implications are the absence of secondary stresses during the period of grief and the development of new life opportunities at work and in interpersonal relationships, for instance. Again, these are more probable when a good network of supportive social relationships exists. It is worth recalling our earlier conclusion about the value of such relationships in a person's adjustment to impending death.

Among the wide range of factors that have implications for a person's reaction to bereavement, there is most controversy about the importance of anticipatory grief. As the term implies, this refers to grief that occurs in anticipation of an expected death, particularly the death of a child or a spouse. Overall, it can be concluded that younger widows experience more intense grief, with associated problems, than those aged 46 years or over. Sudden death exacerbates the severity of the grief response for young widows but not for the middle-aged or the elderly. For the latter two groups there appears to be a small effect in the opposite direction: that is, some symptoms of grief, especially irritability, are greater after a prolonged illness prior to death. It should be noted that the potentially beneficial effects of anticipatory grief are not confined to conjugal bereavement but also mitigate the response to other losses, such as that of a child. Also, it seems possible that there is an optimum period for the anticipation of death, perhaps up to six months, after which the lengthy duration of illness may increase stress and exhaustion and increase the likelihood of adverse reactions in subsequent grief.

Illness and death after bereavement
There are clear data that reveal an elevated mortality risk after bereavement. At all ages, bereaved persons experience

a higher risk of dying than married people of corresponding sex and age. The increase in risk is greater for bereaved males than females, and for both sexes, the increase is greater at younger ages.

The elevated risk of death is concentrated particularly in the first six months after bereavement especially for widowers, with a further rise in the second year for widows. The predominant causes of death are coronary thrombosis and other arteriosclerotic or degenerative heart diseases. Most of these causes can be seen as a result of continued stress and a lack of self-care. In general, when the data from replicated studies in the UK and the USA are taken together, the risk of dying is at least doubled for widows and widowers at all ages for a great variety of diseases.

Having briefly examined the possible psychological and physical consequences of bereavement, and having considered relevant predictive factors, it is important to remember that we are talking only of probabilities. A person may be at great risk of problems following bereavement, in the statistical sense, and yet survive the experience well. Another person with only favourable indicators may suffer badly and experience severe physical or psychological problems.

The vast majority of bereaved people, with a little help from their friends, cope well with the experience and reconstruct lives that are worth while in their own terms. There are no persuasive grounds for considering the provision of professional services for the bereaved. The most useful strategy is to maintain some form of non-intrusive follow-up after bereavement with ready access to an informal support group if this should be necessary. The bereaved need somebody who will listen when they want to talk, somebody who will not try to push them into things before they are ready: somebody who will support them emotionally and practically when appropriate and just by showing that they care. This demands an informal response rather than a professional one. However, professional care and concern should not end with the death of a patient: the newly bereaved person still has a long way to go and every effort should be made to ensure that they will have access to whatever social support may be needed.

References

Achterberg, J. and Lawlis, G.F. (1977)
Psychological factors and blood chemistries as disease outcome predictors for cancer patients. Multivariate Experimental Clinical Research, 3, 107-122.

Cartwright, A., Hockey, L. and Anderson, J.L. (1973)
Life Before Death. London: Routledge & Kegan Paul.

Falek, A. and Britton, S. (1974)
Phases in coping: the hypothesis and its implications. Social Biology, 21, 1-7.

Foot, P. (1978)
Euthanasia. In E. McMullin (ed.), Death and Decision. Boulder, Co: Westview Press.

Gerle, B., Lunden, G. and Sandblow, P. (1960)
   The patient with inoperable cancer from the psychiatric
   and social standpoints. Cancer, 13, 1206-1211.
Hinton, J.M. (1963)
   The physical and mental distress of the dying. Quarterly
   Journal of Medicine, 32, 1-21.
Hinton, J.M. (1972)
   Dying. Harmondsworth: Penguin.
Kastenbaum, R. and Weisman, A.D. (1972)
   The psychological autopsy as a research procedure in
   gerontology. In D.P. Kent, R. Kastenbaum and S.
   Sherwood (eds), Research Planning and Action for the
   Elderly. New York: Behavioral Publications.
Kubler-Ross, E. (1969)
   On Death and Dying. London: Tavistock.
Lindemann, E. (1944)
   Symptomatology and management of acute grief. American
   Journal of Psychiatry, 101, 141-148.
Office of Population Censuses and Surveys (1979)
   Mortality Statistics. London: HMSO.
Parkes, C.M. (1972)
   Bereavement. London: Tavistock.
Rachels, J. (1975)
   Active and passive euthanasia. New England Journal of
   Medicine, 292, 78-80.
Saunders, C. (1977)
   Dying they live. In H. Feifel (ed.), New Meanings of
   Death. New York: McGraw-Hill.
Saunders, C. (1978)
   Care of the dying. In V. Carver and P. Liddiard (eds),
   An Ageing Population. Sevenoaks: Hodder & Stoughton.
Schulz, R. and Aderman, D. (1974)
   Clinical research and the stages of dying. Omega, 5,
   137-143.
Spinetta, J.J. (1974)
   The dying child's awareness of death. Psychological
   Bulletin, 81, 256-260.
Ward, A.W.M. (1974)
   Telling the patient. Journal of the Royal College of
   General Practitioners, 24, 465-468.

Questions

1. How has the pattern of dying changed in the UK since the
   turn of the century? What has caused these changes and
   what are their consequences?
2. Who should be informed of a patient's fatal prognosis?
   Give reasons for your answer.
3. Summarize the most common sources of distress of the
   terminally ill and their families: what are the implications of these?
4. Why do terminally ill people become depressed and how
   large a problem is this?
5. How common is anxiety in terminal illness and why does
   it arise?

6. What psychological problems might arise for a fatally ill six-year-old child and his family? What steps could be taken to mitigate these problems?
7. Why should there be growing public support for the legalization of voluntary euthanasia and why is this not reflected in professional attitudes?
8. What is the bereavement response and what causes it?
9. What factors are important in influencing the nature of grief?
10. Construct a stereotypic, but detailed, character sketch of the person most likely to cope badly with a terminal illness: do the same for the person most likely to cope well. Justify your answer.

Annotated reading

Doyle, D. (ed.) (1979) Terminal Care. Edinburgh: Churchill-Livingstone.

This is a collection of papers arising from a multi-disciplinary conference. Accordingly, it provides useful reading for a wide range of health-care professionals including nurses, social workers and ministers of religion. In addition to examining the roles of different professions there are chapters on grief, domiciliary care and primary care.

Glover, J. (1977) Causing Death and Saving Lives. Harmondsworth: Penguin.

This is a clear and concise consideration of the ethical and practical problems associated with most aspects of taking life, from abortion to euthanasia. For those who want a brief but careful consideration of euthanasia and those who are seeking to place euthanasia in a wider context, this is a most valuable book.

Hinton, J. (1972) Dying. Harmondsworth: Penguin.
This is an eminently readable book by a psychiatrist with much practical experience of caring for the terminally ill and the dying. This experience enables Hinton to write with some authority on practical considerations and to place research findings in perspective. Relevant data are cited appropriately throughout the text and the book contains a good deal of useful information. The best sections are upon dying and the care of the dying and there is a concluding section on bereavement.

Kastenbaum, R.J. (1977) Death, Society and Human Experience. St Louis, Mo.: Mosby.

Written by a psychologist, but for a general readership, this book provides broad coverage of the psychological and social aspects of death at a level that is readily understood, without being unduly simplistic. Relevant data are cited together with many illustrative examples. A good deal of space is given to concepts of death, from childhood to old age, and there are sections on bereavement and suicide. A few exercises for students are also included.

Parkes, C.M. (1972) Bereavement. London: Tavistock.
This volume appeared in Pelican Books in 1975 and, although it is now beginning to age, it is probably the best single source of information on bereavement. The reader is taken progressively through the response to bereavement in its many manifestations and is provided with a clear account of grief, the factors that influence this and the nature of recovery. Illustrative examples and research findings are used throughout the text and the book concludes with a substantial section on helping the bereaved.

Russell, R.O. (1977) Freedom to Die. New York: Human Sciences Press.
Although the author examines arguments for and against the legalization of voluntary euthanasia, the tone of the volume is clearly in favour of this. The value of the book lies in its uncomplicated style, broad coverage and extensive appendices. In addition to examining the relevant arguments, the author traces the development of public awareness of euthanasia and attempts that have been made to promote the practice. The appendices include an example of the Living Will and various legislative proposals and bills that have been proposed in the UK and USA.

Smith, K. (1978) Helping the Bereaved. London: Duckworth.
This is a short and unpretentious book aimed at a general readership. It is valuable for its reliance on the statements of bereaved people to convey powerfully the experience of grief and the range of emotions and events that commonly occur. The examples help one more accurately to empathize with the bereaved.

Exercises

An important caution for the reader
Many of the projects in this book involve obtaining information from individuals. People have a right to protect personal information, and as we, as Editors, have emphasized in our Preface to the book, such a right must be treated as sacrosanct by the psychologist. The projects which follow involve a great deal of self-revelation and discovery. Because they are personal they can arouse anxiety. Therefore they should only be attempted on a voluntary basis. If you have a friend with whom you can share some aspects of the exercises then you will benefit from a sharing of experience. Again, however, we must emphasize that there is no self-evident right which allows a person access to another person's thoughts and feelings. This principle must be borne in mind so that people can stop participating at any time they choose and should not feel subject to group pressure.

1. Thinking and talking about death without anxiety

There appears to be a common taboo about talking about dying. Quite often our reason for not doing something is fear or anxiety; we may be afraid of failure, pain, or personal distress. The purpose of this exercise is to enable you to overcome some of your fears about dying by allowing you to set down your thoughts privately, on paper. Of cours if you do feel you can discuss your fears with a friend, and if your friend is also willing to exchange thoughts and feelings, you can share the experience.

The method to use is 'sentence completion'. We offer below some incomplete sentences. Write them on a sheet of paper leaving plenty of room for what you have to say. Onc you start writing you will find the exercise easier than you expect. You may wish to add further sentences of your own

* To me, death is like ...
* When I think of death I ...
* Being realistic, I think that I am most likely to die around the age of ... years, as a result of ...
* I have given this cause of death because ...
* When I think of my own death, I feel ...
* When I die I hope that ...
* If I were to die those I love would ...
* If everything was as it is now, except that yesterday I was told I had about six months to live, the five things I would be most concerned about are:

    1 ....

    2 ....

    3 ....

    4 ....

    5 ....

* If I had a young child who was about to die, I would ...
* The ways in which I could help a newly widowed relative are ...

2. Debating important issues

Below are four issues which have been covered in this chapter. All are controversial issues which could and will affect all of us at some time. They involve very important decisions, both about individuals and about medical, public and social policy. Each issue is presented in the form of two extreme alternatives.

You can debate the issues with yourself by writing down the arguments in favour or against each position on two halves of a sheet of paper. A more interesting exercise, and one which is likely to produce a fuller range of debate, is to argue the point systematically with a friend. Each of you can prepare a statement in favour of one view; you can then allocate five minutes to present the case. The problems can also be tackled by exchanging roles and arguing in favour of the other person's case, using their notes!

Try to complete the process by making a formal list of the arguments ranking them in importance, so that you can determine whether agreement can be reached.

Topics for debate

* Patients should be informed of fatal prognosis: relatives, not patients, should be informed of a fatal prognosis.
* Patients and/or relatives should be able to decide whether or not life-support measures should be withdrawn: decisions about the use of life-support measures should be made only by professionals.
* Specialized servic es are required to provide care for the terminally ill: with a little rearrangement, existing services are adequate to provide satisfactory care for the terminally ill.
* The physical and psychological risks of bereavement are such as to merit the provision of special services: the response to bereavement is a self-limiting process and does not merit professional concern.

3. Role-playing exercise

For the reasons given below these exercises should only be carried out under the supervision of an experienced instructor.

Role-playing exercises are a valuable aid to teaching any material that has implications for interpersonal skills. They are particularly useful when the situations in which the skills will ultimately be used are likely to elicit emotions that are disruptive of performance and when these situations are extremely unfamiliar. The immediacy and realism of role-playing exercises serves to emphasize issues that previously may have been appreciated only at an intellectual level.

Because these exercises are played in the present and in the first person, the level of emotional involvement can sometimes become quite intense. For this reason it is important that an instructor is present and that no student is coerced into participating as a role-player. Roles are assumed on a volunteer basis only and each participant must understand fully that they can terminate the exercise at any time simply by stating the wish to do so. Also, the instructor should retain the right to end the exercise at any point. Provided these basic precautions are observed it is extremely unlikely that any real difficulties will arise.

The basic method is to devise an interaction between two or more people that simulates a relevant activity and which is designed to illustrate important aspects of that

activity. Each role to be played is typed on a separate
index card and students are asked to volunteer for the exercise. Those who agree to play the roles are asked to leave
the room and to study the cards they are given: they should
not communicate with each other about their roles prior to
the exercise. When the exercise is carried out in a group it
can be worth while not to inform the other members of the
group of the roles to be played; however, it is easier initially to make the whole group aware of the roles but limit
each role-player's knowledge to their own roles only.

The following examples illustrate possible contents for
two role cards.

(Professional) You are a 32-year-old and married with two
young children. it is near the end of the
working day and you are looking forward to
going home. The patient is in his late
forties with two teenage children. He is
terminally ill with widespread carcinoma
(cancer) of the lung.

(Patient) You are 47 years of age and have two teenage
children. You know that you have cancer of
the lung and that you will not recover.
Recently, you have been feeling very low and
you have been sleeping poorly. You have been
thinking a lot about dying and you are feeling frightened. You work around to asking the
professional 'What is it like when people
die?' Subsequently, ask 'I know I am going to
die but I don't know what it will be like for
me: will there be much pain?' As the interaction continues raise further specific concerns about the development of your illness,
dying and the consequences for your family.
Don't worry too much about preparing these
later questions, formulate them as you go
along and ask them as the opportunity arises.

After the exercise has been enacted, that is, after the
participants feel they have nothing more to say, the group
can discuss verbal and non-verbal aspects of the encounter.
Group members can suggest how they might have portrayed the
roles enacted.

DE-ROLING. It is normal practice after a role-playing
exercise for the participants to 'de-role' themselves. This
involves a clear statement saying who they are, why they are
present and that they are no longer the person portrayed.

Ethical principles for research with human subjects

Psychologists are committed to increasing the understanding that people have of their own and others' behaviour in the belief that this understanding ameliorates the human condition and enhances human dignity. These ethical values must characterize not only applications of psychological knowledge but also the means of obtaining knowledge. Performing an investigation with human subjects may occasionally require an ethical decision concerning the balance between the interests of the subject and the humane or scientific value of the research.

Psychologists require an atmosphere of free enquiry and communication without misrepresentation of their knowledge and methods by others. They must match this freedom with ethical concern, competence, objectivity and the non-wasteful use of material resources and human resources. They have an obligation to prevent misuse through personal influence, public statement and professional sanction. They can and should promote the public understanding of psychological knowledge in such a way as to prevent its misuse or render misuse ineffective.

Psychologists have a general obligation to make the results of their research available to other psychologists, to related scientists, and to allied professions. No psychologist should seek to restrict the availability or publication of his or her own or colleagues' research without seeking the opinion of experienced and disinterested colleagues. Until such publication has permitted the verification of results and the evaluation of their apparent implications by the scientific community, psychologists have an obligation to resist the premature citation of results in wider discussions on policy, and especially their premature use in policy formulation. This general principle does not prevent a psychologist from undertaking explicitly confidential research on restricted topics (e.g. for commercial development or national security) where that research does not violate these principles.

The following set of ethical principles is issued by the British Psychological Society in the belief that a detailed list of prescribed and proscribed procedures would be impractical. It is the Society's belief that the degree of awareness and responsibility that follows from adherence to this general set of principles will serve to raise standards in psychological science and will safeguard the welfare of human subjects who contribute to it. While it would be appropriate to use this set of principles as an indication of the level of awareness that a psychologist should display, the psychologist's compliance with these principles can only be determined by those peers who are experienced with the problems which the principles encompass. Accordingly, the principles should not be used as a substitute for a considered judgement in which a case is examined on its merits in all aspects. The principles place reliance upon the opinion of the psychological community as an extension of the individual investigator's ability to anticipate the ethical issues raised and to assess the extent to which any consequences for the subject may be serious. The opinion of colleagues should also assist the investigator in determining whether the research is justified scientifically or pragmatically.

Scientific justification involves the assessment of both the conceptual importance of the potential results and their usefulness to mankind. Pragmatic justification involves assessing, for example, the likely effects of participants' guesses about the objectives of the research upon public attitudes to psychological enquiry in general and upon local voluntary participation in particular.

* Whenever possible the investigator should inform the subjects of the objectives, and, eventually, the results of the investigation. Where this is not possible the investigator incurs an obligation to indicate to the subject the general nature of the knowledge achieved by such research and its potential value to people, and to outline the general values accepted by psychologists as listed in the introduction to these principles. The investigator's name, status and employer or affiliation should be declared.

* In all circumstances investigators must consider the ethical implications and the psychological consequences for subjects of the research being carried out. Investigators must actively consider, by proper consultation, whether local cultural variations, special personality factors in the subjects or variations in procedure from procedures reported previously may introduce unexpected problems for the subject.

* An investigator should seek the opinion of experienced and disinterested colleagues whenever the research requires or is likely to involve: (i) deception concerning the purpose of the investigation or the subject's role in it; (ii) deception concerning the basis of subject selection; (iii) psychological or physiological stress; (iv) encroachment upon privacy. Geographical and institutional isolation of the investigating psychologist increases rather than decreases the need to seek colleagues' opinions.

* Deception of subjects, or withholding of relevant information from them, should only occur when the investigator is satisfied that the aims and objects of the
research or welfare of the subjects cannot be achieved
by other means. Where deception has been necessary,
revelation should normally follow participation as a
matter of course. Where the subject's behaviour makes it
appear that revelation could be stressful, or when to
reveal the objectives or the basis of subject selection
would be distressing, the extent and timing of such
revelation should be influenced by consideration for the
subject's psychological welfare. Where deception has
been substantial, the subject should be offered the
option of withholding his or her data, in accordance
with the principle of participation by informed consent.
* In proportion to the risks of stress or encroachment
upon privacy the investigator incurs an obligation to
emphasize to subjects at the outset their volunteer
status and their right to withdraw, irrespective of
whether or not payment or other inducement is offered,
and to describe precisely the demands of the investigation.
    Wherever a situation turns out to be more stressful
for an individual subject than anticipated by the investigator or than might be reasonably expected by the
subject from the introduction, the investigator has an
obligation to stop the investigation and consult an
experienced and disinterested colleague before proceeding.
* In proportion to the risks under (i)-(iv) and to the
personal nature of the information involved the investigator incurs an obligation to treat data as confidential and to conceal identities when reporting results.
* Studies on non-volunteers, based upon observation or
upon records (whether or not explicitly confidential)
must respect the privacy and psychological well-being
of the subjects.
* Investigators have the responsibility to maintain the
highest standards of safety in procedure, equipment and
premises.
* Where research involves infants and young children as
subjects, consent should be obtained from parents or
from those in loco parentis, according to the foregoing
principles. In the case of children of appropriate age,
the informed consent of subjects themselves should also
be obtained in advance. In research involving children
caution should be exercised when discussing results of
research with parents, teachers or others in loco parentis since evaluative statements may carry unintended
weight.
* If a subject solicits advice concerning educational,
personality or behavioural problems, extreme caution
should be exercised and if the problem is serious the
appropriate source of professional advice should be
recommended.

* It is the investigator's responsibility to ensure that research executed by associates, employees or students conforms in detail to the ethical decision taken in the light of the foregoing principles.
* A psychologist who believes that another psychologist or related investigator may be conducting research not in accordance with the foregoing principles has the obligation to encourage the inverstigator to re-evaluate the research in their light, if necessary consulting a responsible senior colleague as a source of further opinion or influence.

Index

(E refers to suggested exercises)